Anonymous

The Church of God Selection of Spiritual Songs

With Music for the Church and the Choir

Anonymous

The Church of God Selection of Spiritual Songs
With Music for the Church and the Choir

ISBN/EAN: 9783337296520

Printed in Europe, USA, Canada, Australia, Japan

Cover: Foto ©Lupo / pixelio.de

More available books at **www.hansebooks.com**

THE

CHURCH OF GOD SELECTION

OF

SPIRITUAL SONGS

WITH MUSIC

FOR THE CHURCH AND THE CHOIR.

HARRISBURGH, PA.:
BOARD OF PUBLICATION OF THE GENERAL ELDERSHIP OF THE CHURCH OF GOD.

PREFACE.

TWENTY-TWO years ago, "a book of Psalms, Hymns, and Spiritual Songs," known as The Church Hymn Book, was published by the authority of the General Eldership of the Church of God. At the time of its publication, this book was equal in every respect to any hymn book then in use, and it has proved during all this time an acceptable book for the service of song in the congregations of the Church of God. But during these years a revolution has been effected in books of sacred song, and an almost universal demand has arisen for collections having both hymns and tunes. The General Eldership recognized this want in some measure when, in 1878, it passed an action constituting the Board of Publication "a Revision Committee on The Church Hymn Book," and by adding to said Committee two members "to revise The Church Hymn Book," and granting this Committee "discretionary powers to publish a smaller edition with the music."

For reasons which seemed fully to justify its action, this Committee decided not to revise The Church Hymn Book, nor to issue "a smaller edition with the music," during the triennial period following the Eldership of 1878. But the demand among the churches for an improved hymn and tune book continued to spread and intensify, and at the General Eldership in May, 1881, it found expression in imperative action. The former Committee reported the reasons for not issuing a hymnal, and also recommended "that a Committee be appointed or elected, in connection with the Board of Publication, who shall constitute a Committee to publish a hymnal for the use of the Church at as early a day as possible." This recommendation was adopted. At a subsequent stage of the proceedings, the Board of Publication, together with the three brethren elected by the Eldership, was constituted the Hymnal Committee. The undersigned, composing said Committee, have given diligent attention to the work committed to their hands, and they are now, at this early date, offering this collection of "SPIRITUAL SONGS" to the Brotherhood of the Church of God, for use in the service of public praise.

In adopting this selection we have kept in view what we considered the real needs of the Church. A less complete and expensive book, which would have met in some degree the immediate and most urgent wants of the body, could have been published, but it might have proved very injudicious economy in the end. We therefore concluded to provide the Church with a hymn and tune book which should compare favorably with the various excellent denominational books now so extensively used; and one, too, which should contain nearly as large, and equally as varied, a collection of hymns as that found in The Church Hymn Book. The Committee feel assured that the mature and enlightened judgment of the Brotherhood will fully approve their action; and they anticipate that "SPIRITUAL SONGS" will be cordially accepted as a manual of worship helpful in the public services of the house of God, and contributing to the glory of the great Head of the Church. If the use of a hymn and tune book in the congregations of the Church of God shall anywise serve to perpetuate the good old practice of having all the people sing, an important incidental end will have been gained. Artistic singing is very desirable, but when it tends to discourage congregational singing, or leads to annoying differences of opinion, it may become the occasion of grave spiritual evils in the body of Christ. To avoid this, let all the people be heartily invited to take an unrestrained part in this feature of divine worship, led by one or more whose artistic training is qualification for so important a service.

The work assigned to the Committee is one which has occasioned much perplexity and considerable labor; but it has been conducted with increasing satisfaction and with the growing consciousness of rendering an important service to the churches. The result of the Committee's labors is now confidently commended to the Brotherhood, in the assured expectation that it will meet a want which has been widely felt, and with the fervent prayer that the blessing of Him who inhabits the praises of Israel may attend our labors and sanctify our songs.

I. FRAZER,   D. M. BARE,   J. H. REDSECKER, } *Committee.*
M. S. NEWCOMER, GEORGE SIGLER, C. H. FORNEY,

TABLE OF CONTENTS.

	HYMNS.
THE LORD'S DAY	1—60
THE HOUSE OF PRAYER	61—77
THE SACRIFICE OF PRAISE	78—111
THE CLOSE OF SERVICE	112—157
THE INSPIRED SCRIPTURES	158—175
GOD: THE ALMIGHTY FATHER	176—233
THE LORD JESUS CHRIST.	
Incarnation and Birth	234—256
Life and Character	257—272
Sufferings and Death	273—294
Resurrection and Reign	295—328
Exaltation and Offices	329—349
THE HOLY SPIRIT	350—380
THE GOSPEL OF GRACE.	
Man's Lost State	381—397
The Atonement	398—415
Invitations	416—444
Repentance unto Life	445—480
THE CHRISTIAN LIFE.	
Conflict with Sin	481—516
Courage and Cheer	517—584
Communion with Christ	585—639
Experience and Graces	640—674
Privileges of Believers	675—703
Discipline and Sorrow	704—748

	HYMNS.
THE CHURCH.	
Institutions	749—778
Benevolent Work	779—797
Sunday-School	798—806
Baptism	807—822
The Lord's Supper	823—889
Washing of Saints' Feet	830—842
Missions and Growth	890—932
DEATH AND RESURRECTION	933—972
THE GENERAL JUDGMENT	973—988
THE REST OF HEAVEN	989—1045
MISCELLANEOUS	1046—1072
CHANTS AND OCCASIONAL	1073—1086
	PAGE.
DOXOLOGIES	413—414
INDEX OF TUNES	415
METRICAL INDEX	417
INDEX OF AUTHORS	419
INDEX OF TEXTS	421
INDEX OF STANZAS	423
INDEX OF SUBJECTS	431
INDEX OF FIRST LINES	434

G

SPIRITUAL SONGS.

1   *Psalm 122.*   I. WATTS.

How PLEASED and blest was I,
To hear the people cry,
"Come, let us seek our God to-day!"
Yes, with a cheerful zeal,
We haste to Zion's hill,
And there our vows and honors pay.

2 Zion—thrice happy place—
Adorned with wondrous grace,
While walls of strength embrace thee round:
In thee our tribes appear,
To pray, and praise, and hear
The sacred gospel's joyful sound.

3 May peace attend thy gate,
And joy within thee wait,
To bless the soul of every guest:
The man who seeks thy peace,
And wishes thine increase,
A thousand blessings on him rest!

4 My tongue repeats her vows,
"Peace to this sacred house!"
For here my friends and kindred dwell;
And since my glorious God
Makes thee his blest abode,
My soul shall ever love thee well.

HENDON. 7s.　　　　　　　　　　　　　　　　　C. H. A. MALAN.

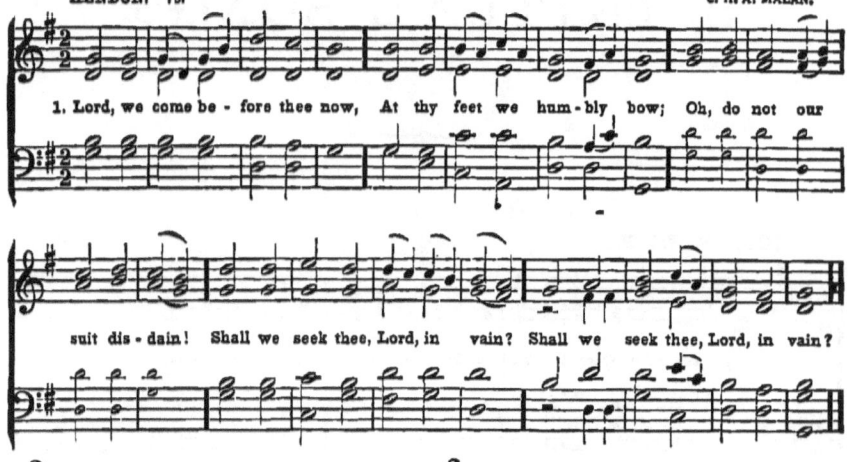

| 2 | *"Thy face we seek."* W. HAMMOND. | 3 | *Jesus intercedes.* J. MONTGOMERY. |

LORD, we come before thee now,
At thy feet we humbly bow;
Oh, do not our suit disdain!
Shall we seek thee, Lord, in vain?

2 Lord, on thee our souls depend,
In compassion now descend;
Fill our hearts with thy rich grace,
Tune our lips to sing thy praise.

3 In thine own appointed way,
Now we seek thee; here we stay;
Lord, we know not how to go,
Till a blessing thou bestow.

4 Comfort those who weep and mourn;
Let the time of joy return;
Those that are cast down lift up;
Make them strong in faith and hope.

5 Grant that all may seek and find
Thee a God supremely kind;
Heal the sick; the captive free;
Let us all rejoice in thee.

To THY temple we repair—
Lord, we love to worship there,
When within the vail we meet
Thee upon the mercy-seat.

2 While thy glorious name is sung,
Tune our lips—unloose our tongue;
Then our joyful souls shall bless
Thee, the Lord our Righteousness.

3 While to thee our prayers ascend,
Let thine ear in love attend;
Hear us, for thy Spirit pleads—
Hear, for Jesus intercedes.

4 While thy word is heard with awe,
While we tremble at thy law,
Let thy gospel's wondrous love
Every doubt and fear remove.

5 From thy house when we return,
Let our hearts within us burn;
That at evening we may say—
"We have walked with God to-day."

CHAPEL. 7s.　　　　　　　　　　　　　　　　　GERMAN CHORAL.

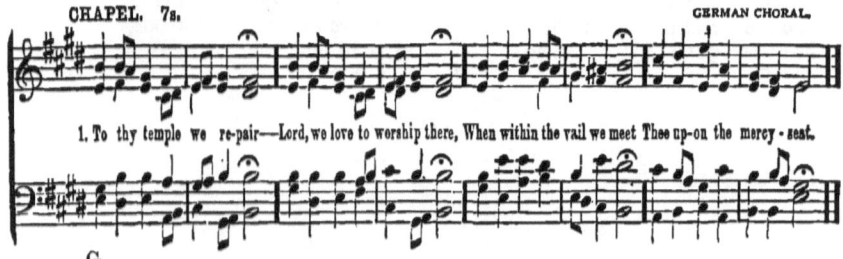

G

4   *Psalm 23.*   J. MERRICK.

To THY pastures fair and large,
Heavenly Shepherd, lead thy charge,
And my couch, with tenderest care,
'Mid the springing grass prepare.
2 When I faint with summer's heat,
Thou shalt guide my weary feet
To the streams that, still and slow,
Through the verdant meadows flow.
3 Safe the dreary vale I tread,
By the shades of death o'erspread,
With thy rod and staff supplied,
This my guard—and that my guide.
4 Constant to my latest end,
Thou my footsteps shalt attend;
And shalt bid thy hallowed dome
Yield me an eternal home.

5   *Twilight.*   S. F. SMITH.

SOFTLY fades the twilight ray
Of the holy Sabbath day;
Gently as life's setting sun,
When the Christian's course is run.
2 Peace is on the world abroad;
'Tis the holy peace of God—
Symbol of the peace within
When the spirit rests from sin.
3 Still the Spirit lingers near,
Where the evening worshiper
Seeks communion with the skies,
Pressing onward to the prize.
4 Saviour! may our Sabbaths be
Days of joy and peace in thee,
Till in heaven our souls repose,
Where the Sabbath ne'er shall close.

THE LORD'S DAY.

RAKEM. L. M. 61. I. B. WOODBURY.

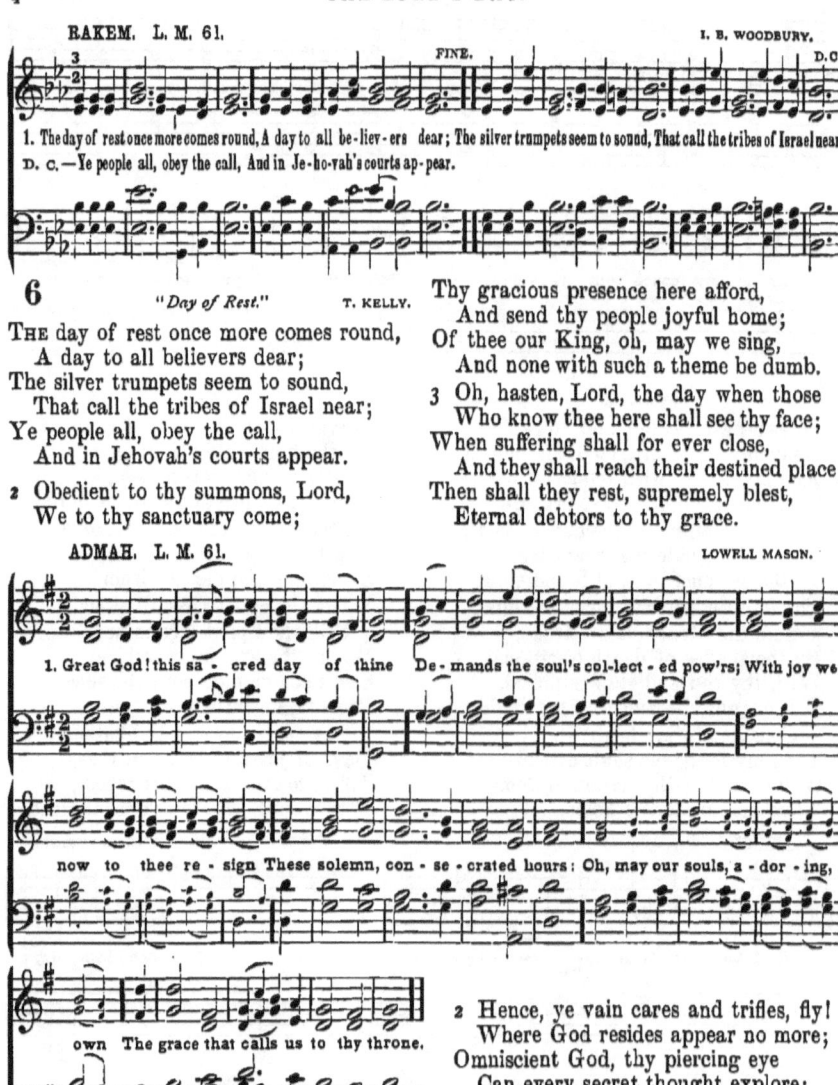

6
"Day of Rest." T. KELLY.

THE day of rest once more comes round,
 A day to all believers dear;
The silver trumpets seem to sound,
 That call the tribes of Israel near;
Ye people all, obey the call,
 And in Jehovah's courts appear.

2 Obedient to thy summons, Lord,
 We to thy sanctuary come;
Thy gracious presence here afford,
 And send thy people joyful home;
Of thee our King, oh, may we sing,
 And none with such a theme be dumb.

3 Oh, hasten, Lord, the day when those
 Who know thee here shall see thy face;
When suffering shall for ever close,
 And they shall reach their destined place;
Then shall they rest, supremely blest,
 Eternal debtors to thy grace.

7
Grace in Service. A. STEELE.

GREAT God! this sacred day of thine
 Demands the soul's collected powers;
With joy we now to thee resign
 These solemn, consecrated hours;
Oh, may our souls, adoring, own
 The grace that calls us to thy throne.

2 Hence, ye vain cares and trifles, fly!
 Where God resides appear no more;
Omniscient God, thy piercing eye
 Can every secret thought explore;
Oh, may thy grace our hearts refine,
 And fix our thoughts on things divine.

3 Thy Spirit's powerful aid impart;
 Oh, may thy word, with life divine,
Engage the ear and warm the heart;
 Then shall the day indeed be thine;
Then shall our souls, adoring, own
 The grace which calls us to thy throne.

THE LORD'S DAY.

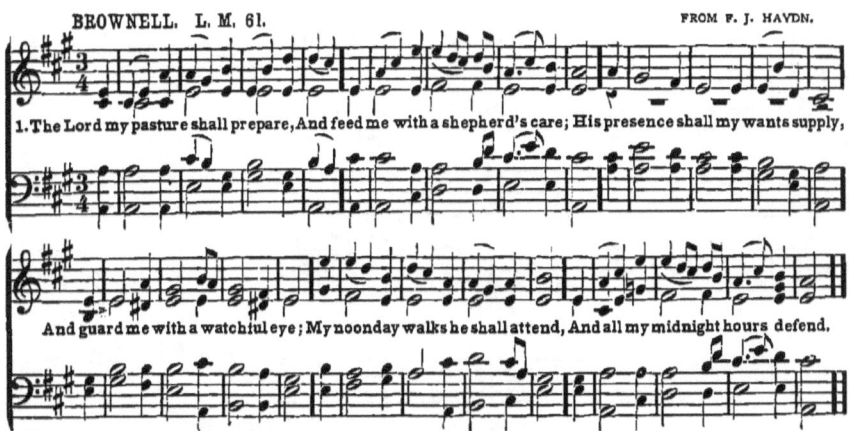

BROWNELL. L. M. 6l.   FROM F. J. HAYDN.

1. The Lord my pasture shall prepare, And feed me with a shepherd's care; His presence shall my wants supply, And guard me with a watchful eye; My noonday walks he shall attend, And all my midnight hours defend.

8   *Psalm 23.*   J. ADDISON.

The Lord my pasture shall prepare,
And feed me with a shepherd's care;
His presence shall my wants supply,
And guard me with a watchful eye;
My noonday walks he shall attend,
And all my midnight hours defend.

2 When in the sultry glebe I faint,
Or on the thirsty mountain pant,
To fertile vales, and dewy meads,
My weary, wandering steps he leads;
Where peaceful rivers, soft and slow,
Amid the verdant landscape flow.

3 Though in a bare and rugged way,
Through devious, lonely wilds I stray,
Thy presence shall my pains beguile:
The barren wilderness shall smile,
With sudden greens and herbage crowned;
And streams shall murmur all around.

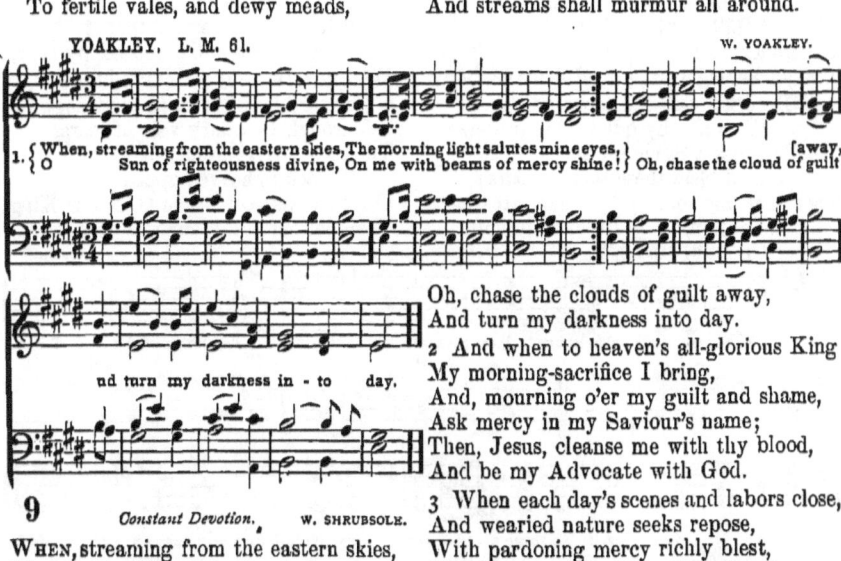

YOAKLEY. L. M. 6l.   W. YOAKLEY.

1. When, streaming from the eastern skies, The morning light salutes mine eyes, O Sun of righteousness divine, On me with beams of mercy shine! Oh, chase the cloud of guilt away, And turn my darkness in-to day.

9   *Constant Devotion.*   W. SHRUBSOLE.

When, streaming from the eastern skies,
The morning light salutes mine eyes,
O Sun of righteousness divine,
On me with beams of mercy shine!
Oh, chase the clouds of guilt away,
And turn my darkness into day.

2 And when to heaven's all-glorious King
My morning-sacrifice I bring,
And, mourning o'er my guilt and shame,
Ask mercy in my Saviour's name;
Then, Jesus, cleanse me with thy blood,
And be my Advocate with God.

3 When each day's scenes and labors close,
And wearied nature seeks repose,
With pardoning mercy richly blest,
Guard me, my Saviour, while I rest;
And, as each morning sun shall rise,
Oh, lead me onward to the skies!

THE LORD'S DAY.

LISCHER. H. M. — F. SCHNEIDER.

10 *Welcome Worship.* HAYWARD.

WELCOME, delightful morn,
  Thou day of sacred rest;
  I hail thy kind return;—
  Lord, make these moments blest:
From the low train | I soar to reach
Of mortal toys, | Immortal joys.

2 Now may the King descend,
  And fill his throne of grace;
  Thy sceptre, Lord, extend,
  While saints address thy face:
Let sinners feel | And learn to know
Thy quickening word, | And fear the Lord.

3 Descend, celestial Dove,
  With all thy quickening powers;
  Disclose a Saviour's love,
  And bless these sacred hours:
Then shall my soul | Nor Sabbaths be
New life obtain, | Enjoyed in vain.

11 *Psalm 84.* I. WATTS.

LORD of the worlds above!
  How pleasant, and how fair,
  The dwellings of thy love,
  Thine earthly temples are!
To thine abode my heart aspires,
With warm desires to see my God.

2 Oh, happy souls who pray,
  Where God appoints to hear!
  Oh, happy men who pay
  Their constant service there!
They praise thee still; and happy they,
Who love the way to Zion's hill.

3 They go from strength to strength,
  Through this dark vale of tears,
  Till each arrives at length,
  Till each in heaven appears;
Oh, glorious seat, when God, our King,
Shall thither bring our willing feet!

MILLENNIUM. H. M. — ENGLISH.

12 H.M.   *Psalm 43.*   T. DWIGHT.

Now, to thy sacred house,
　With joy I turn my feet,
Where saints, with morning-vows,
　In full assembly meet:
Thy power divine shall there be shown,
And from thy throne thy mercy shine.

2 Oh, send thy light abroad;
　Thy truth with heavenly ray
Shall lead my soul to God,
　And guide my doubtful way;
I'll hear thy word with faith sincere,
And learn to fear and praise the Lord.

3 Here reach thy bounteous hand,
　And all my sorrows heal;
Here health and strength divine,
　Oh, make my bosom feel;
Like balmy dew shall Jesus' voice
My heart rejoice, my strength renew.

4 Now in thy holy hill,
　Before thine altar, Lord!
My harp and song shall sound
　The glories of thy word:
Henceforth, to thee, O God of grace!
A hymn of praise, my life shall be.

SABBATH. 7s, 6l.   LOWELL MASON.

1. Safe-ly through anoth-er week, God has brought us on our way; Let us now a blessing seek, Wait-ing in his courts to-day: Day of all the week the best, Emblem of e-ter-nal rest, Day of all the week the best, Emblem of e-ter-nal rest.

13   *Sabbath morning.*   J. NEWTON.

SAFELY through another week,
　God has brought us on our way;
Let us now a blessing seek,
　Waiting in his courts to-day:
Day of all the week the best,
Emblem of eternal rest.

2 While we seek supplies of grace,
　Through the dear Redeemer's name,
Show thy reconciling face—
　Take away our sin and shame;
From our worldly cares set free,—
May we rest this day in thee.

3 Here we come thy name to praise;
　Let us feel thy presence near;
May thy glory meet our eyes,
　While we in thy house appear:
Here afford us, Lord, a taste
Of our everlasting feast.

4 May thy gospel's joyful sound
　Conquer sinners, comfort saints;
Make the fruits of grace abound,
　Bring relief for all complaints:
Thus let all our Sabbaths prove,
Till we rest in thee above.

14 *Morning.* C. WESLEY.

CHRIST, whose glory fills the skies,
  Christ, the true, the only light,
Sun of Righteousness, arise,
  Triumph o'er the shades of night;
Day-spring from on high, be near,
Day-star in my heart appear.

2 Dark and cheerless is the morn,
  If thy light is hid from me;
Joyless is the day's return,
  Till thy mercy's beams I see;
Till they inward light impart,
Warmth and gladness to my heart.

3 Visit, then, this soul of mine,
  Pierce the gloom of sin and grief;
Fill me, radiant Sun divine!
  Scatter all my unbelief;
More and more thyself display,
Shining to the perfect day.

15 *Evening.* T. HASTINGS.

Now, FROM labor and from care,
  Evening shades have set me free;
In the work of praise and prayer,
  Lord! I would converse with thee:
Oh, behold me from above,
Fill me with a Saviour's love.

2 Sin and sorrow, guilt and woe,
  Wither all my earthly joys;
Naught can charm me here below,
  But my Saviour's melting voice;
Lord! forgive—thy grace restore,
Make me thine for evermore.

3 For the blessings of this day,
  For the mercies of this hour,
For the gospel's cheering ray,
  For the Spirit's quickening power,—
Grateful notes to thee I raise;
Oh, accept my song of praise.

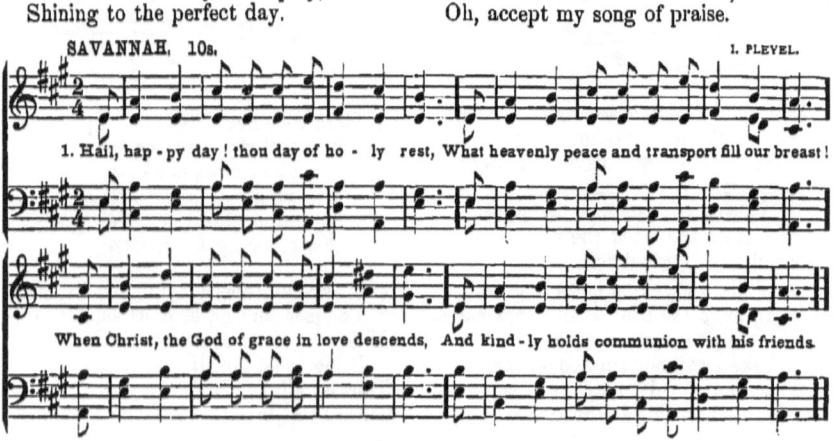

THE LORD'S DAY.

MENDEBRAS. 7s & 6s. D. LOWELL MASON, arr.

1. O day of rest and gladness, O day of joy and light,
O balm of care and sadness, Most beauti-ful, most bright;
On thee, the high and low-ly, Bend-ing be-fore the throne,
Sing Ho-ly, Ho-ly, Ho-ly, To the Great Three in One.

16   *"Day of Rest"*   C. WORDSWORTH.

O DAY of rest and gladness,
  O day of joy and light,
O balm of care and sadness,
  Most beautiful, most bright;
On thee, the high and lowly,
  Bending before the throne,
Sing, Holy, Holy, Holy,
  To the Great Three in One.

2 To-day on weary nations
  The heavenly manna falls;
To holy convocations
  The silver trumpet calls,
Where gospel light is glowing
  With pure and radiant beams,
And living water flowing
  With soul-refreshing streams.

3 New graces ever gaining
  From this our day of rest,
We reach the rest remaining
  To spirits of the blest.

To Holy Ghost be praises,
  To Father and to Son;
The Church her voice upraises
  To thee, blest Three in One.

17   *"Thine holy day."*   RAY PALMER.

THINE holy day's returning,
  Our hearts exult to see;
And with devotion burning,
  Ascend, O God, to thee!
To-day with purest pleasure,
  Our thoughts from earth withdraw.
We search for heavenly treasure,
  We learn thy holy law.

2 We join to sing thy praises,
  Lord of the Sabbath day;
Each voice in gladness raises
  Its loudest, sweetest lay!
Thy richest mercies sharing,
  Inspire us with thy love,
By grace our souls preparing
  For nobler praise above.

---

18   10S.   *Communion in love.*   P. H. BROWN.

HAIL, happy day! thou day of holy rest,
What heavenly peace and transport fill our breast!
When Christ, the God of grace, in love descends,
And kindly holds communion with his friends.

2 Let earth and all its vanities be gone,
Move from my sight, and leave my soul alone;
Its flattering, fading glories I despise,
And to immortal beauties turn my eyes.

3 Fain would I mount and penetrate the skies,
And on my Saviour's glories fix my eyes:
Oh, meet my rising soul, thou God of love,
And waft it to the blissful realms above!

THE LORD'S DAY.

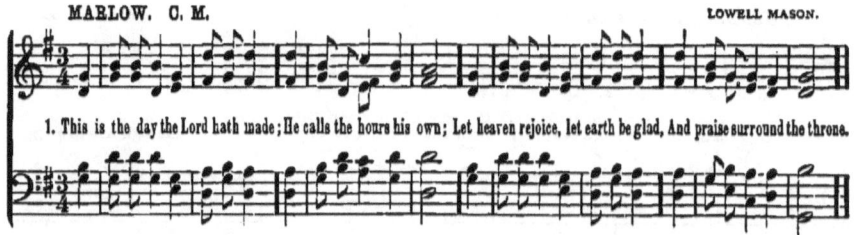

19   Psalm 118.   I. WATTS.

This is the day the Lord hath made;
He calls the hours his own;
Let heaven rejoice, let earth be glad,
And praise surround the throne.

2 To-day he rose, and left the dead,
And Satan's empire fell;
To-day the saints his triumph spread,
And all his wonders tell.

3 Hosanna to the anointed King,
To David's only Son;
Help us, O Lord; descend, and bring
Salvation from thy throne.

4 Blest be the Lord who comes to men
With messages of grace;
Who comes, in God his Father's name,
To save our sinful race.

5 Hosanna in the highest strains
The church on earth can raise;
The highest heavens, in which he reigns,
Shall give him nobler praise.

20   Psalm 122.   I. WATTS.

How did my heart rejoice to hear
My friends devoutly say,—
"In Zion let us all appear,
And keep the solemn day."

2 I love her gates, I love the road;
The Church, adorned with grace,
Stands like a palace built for God,
To show his milder face.

3 Up to her courts, with joys unknown,
The holy tribes repair;
The Son of David holds his throne,
And sits in judgment there.

4 Peace be within this sacred place,
And joy a constant guest;
With holy gifts and heavenly grace,
Be her attendants blest.

5 My soul shall pray for Zion still,
While life or breath remains;
There my best friends, my kindred dwell,
There God, my Saviour reigns.

THE LORD'S DAY.

LANESBORO. C. M.   W. DIXON.

1. Early, my God, without delay, I haste to seek thy face; My thirsty spirit faints away, My thirsty spirit faints away, Without thy cheering grace.

21   *Psalm 63.*   I. WATTS.
Early, my God, without delay,
  I haste to seek thy face;
My thirsty spirit faints away,
  Without thy cheering grace.

2 I've seen thy glory and thy power
  Through all thy temple shine;
My God, repeat that heavenly hour,
  That vision so divine.

3 Not life itself, with all its joys,
  Can my best passions move,
Or raise so high my cheerful voice,
  As thy forgiving love.

4 Thus, till my last expiring day,
  I'll bless my God and King;
Thus will I lift my hands to pray,
  And tune my lips to sing.

BEMERTON. C. M.   H. W. GREATOREX.

1. Lord! when we bend before thy throne, And our confessions pour, Oh, may we feel the sins we own, And hate what we deplore.

22   *Sincerity.*   J. D. CARLYLE.
Lord! when we bend before thy throne,
  And our confessions pour,
Oh, may we feel the sins we own,
  And hate what we deplore.

2 Our contrite spirits pitying see;
  True penitence impart:
And let a healing ray from thee
  Beam hope on every heart.

3 When we disclose our wants in prayer,
  May we our wills resign;
Nor let a thought our bosom share,
  Which is not wholly thine.

4 Let faith each meek petition fill,
  And waft it to the skies;
And teach our heart 'tis goodness still
  That grants it or denies.

THE LORD'S DAY.

OAKSVILLE. C. M.   C. ZEUNER.

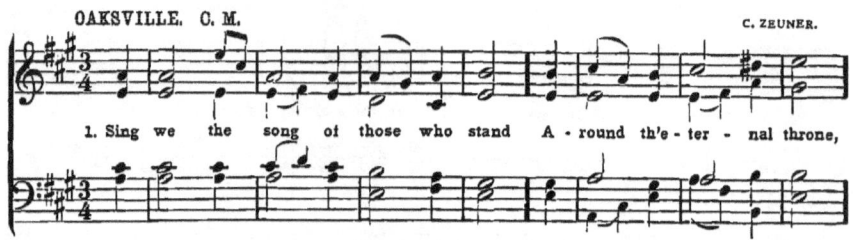
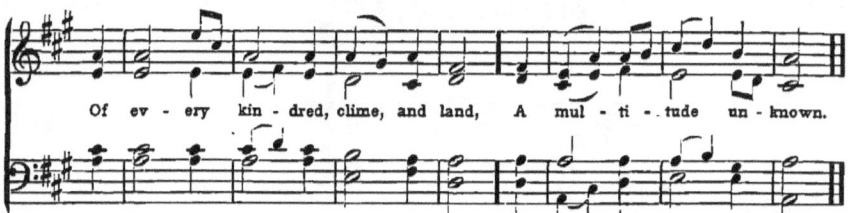

1. Sing we the song of those who stand Around th' eternal throne, Of every kindred, clime, and land, A multitude unknown.

23   "*Worthy the Lamb!*"   J. MONTGOMERY.

SING we the song of those who stand
  Around the eternal throne,
Of every kindred, clime, and land,
  A multitude unknown.

2 Life's poor distinctions vanish here:
  To-day the young, the old,
Our Saviour and his flock appear
  One Shepherd and one fold.

3 Toil, trial, sufferings still await
  On earth the pilgrim throng;
Yet learn we in our low estate
  The Church Triumphant's song.

4 "Worthy the Lamb for sinners slain,"—
  Cry the redeemed above,
"Blessing and honor to obtain,
  And everlasting love!"

5 "Worthy the Lamb," on earth we sing,
  "Who died our souls to save!
Henceforth, O Death! where is thy sting?
  Thy victory, O Grave!"

24   *Psalm 122.*   H. F. LYTE.

WITH joy we hail the sacred day
  Which God hath called his own;
With joy the summons we obey
  To worship at his throne.

2 Thy chosen temple, Lord, how fair!
  Where willing votaries throng
To breathe the humble, fervent prayer,
  And pour the choral song.

3 Spirit of grace! oh, deign to dwell
  Within thy church below;
Make her in holiness excel,
  With pure devotion glow.

4 Let peace within her walls be found;
  Let all her sons unite
To spread with grateful zeal around
  Her clear and shining light.

5 Great God, we hail the sacred day
  Which thou hast called thine own;
With joy the summons we obey
  To worship at thy throne.

25   "*The Rising Day.*"   I. WATTS.

ONCE more, my soul, the rising day
  Salutes thy waking eyes;
Once more, my voice, thy tribute pay
  To him that rules the skies.

2 Night unto night his name repeats,
  The day renews the sound,
Wide as the heaven on which he sits
  To turn the seasons round.

3 'Tis he supports my mortal frame;
  My tongue shall speak his praise;
My sins would rouse his wrath to flame,
  And yet his wrath delays.

4 Great God, let all my hours be thine,
  While I enjoy the light;
Then shall my sun in smiles decline,
  And bring a pleasant night.

26 *Psalm 84.* I. WATTS.

My soul, how lovely is the place,
  To which thy God resorts!
'Tis heaven to see his smiling face,
  Though in his earthly courts.

2 There the great Monarch of the skies
    His saving power displays;
  And light breaks in upon our eyes,
    With kind and quickening rays.

3 With his rich gifts the heavenly Dove
    Descends and fills the place;
  While Christ reveals his wondrous love,
    And sheds abroad his grace.

4 There, mighty God, thy words declare
    The secrets of thy will;
  And still we seek thy mercy there,
    And sing thy praises still.

27 *Psalm 25:14.* C. WESLEY, *alt.*

Speak to me, Lord, thyself reveal,
  While here on earth I rove;
Speak to my heart, and let me feel
  The kindling of thy love.

2 With thee conversing, I forget
    All time and toil and care;
  Labor is rest, and pain is sweet,
    If thou, my God, art here.

3 Thou callest me to seek thy face;
    Thy face, O God, I seek,—
  Attend the whispers of thy grace,
    And hear thee inly speak.

4 Let this my every hour employ,
    Till I thy glory see,
  Enter into my Master's joy,
    And find my heaven in thee.

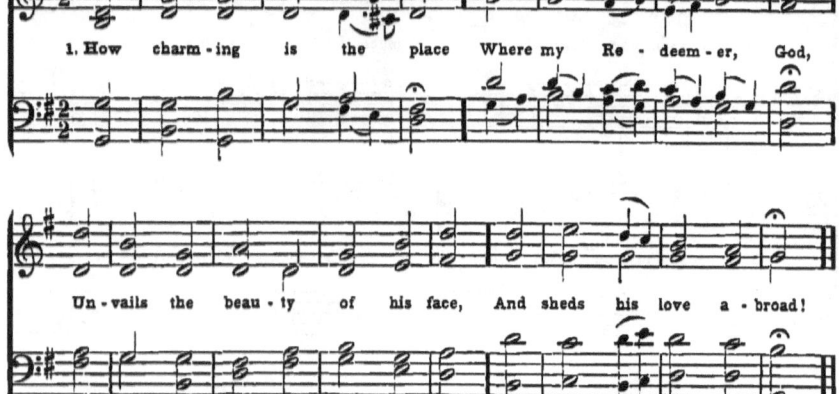

28
The Sanctuary.   S. STENNETT.

How CHARMING is the place
Where my Redeemer, God,
Unvails the beauty of his face,
And sheds his love abroad!

2 Not the fair palaces,
To which the great resort,
Are once to be compared with this,
Where Jesus holds his court.

3 Here on the mercy-seat,
With radiant glory crowned,
Our joyful eyes behold him sit
And smile on all around.

4 Give me, O Lord, a place
Within thy blest abode,
Among the children of thy grace,
The servants of my God.

29
Psalm 63.   I. WATTS.

My God! permit my tongue
This joy, to call thee mine;
And let my early cries prevail
To taste thy love divine.

2 My thirsty fainting soul
Thy mercy doth implore;
Not travelers, in desert lands,
Can pant for water more.

3 For life, without thy love,
No relish can afford;
No joy can be compared to this,—
To serve and please the Lord.

4 In wakeful hours at night,
I call my God to mind;
I think how wise thy counsels are,
And all thy dealings kind.

5 Since thou hast been my help,
To thee my spirit flies;
And, on thy watchful providence,
My cheerful hope relies.

6 The shadow of thy wings
My soul in safety keeps;
I follow where my Father leads,
And he supports my steps.

30
Psalm 84.   I. WATTS.

WELCOME, sweet day of rest,
That saw the Lord arise!
Welcome to this reviving breast,
And these rejoicing eyes!

2 The King himself comes near,
And feasts his saints to-day;
Here may we sit and see him here,
And love, and praise, and pray.

3 One day, amid the place
Where my dear Lord hath been,
Is sweeter than ten thousand days
Within the tents of sin.

4 My willing soul would stay
In such a frame as this,
And sit and sing herself away
To everlasting bliss.

THE LORD'S DAY.

GLORY. S. M. — RALPH HARRISON.

1. Come, we who love the Lord, And let our joys be known; Join in a song with sweet ac-cord, And thus sur-round the throne.

31 *"Immanuel's ground."* I. WATTS.

Come, we who love the Lord,
And let our joys be known;
Join in a song of sweet accord,
And thus surround the throne.

2 Let those refuse to sing
Who never knew our God;
But children of the heavenly King
May speak their joys abroad.

3 The men of grace have found
Glory begun below;
Celestial fruits on earthly ground
From faith and hope may grow.

4 The hill of Zion yields
A thousand sacred sweets
Before we reach the heavenly fields,
Or walk the golden streets.

5 Then let our songs abound,
And every tear be dry;
We're marching through Immanuel's ground
To fairer worlds on high.

32 Rev. 15:3. W. HAMMOND.

Awake, and sing the song
Of Moses and the Lamb;
Wake, every heart and every tongue,
To praise the Saviour's name.

2 Sing of his dying love;
Sing of his rising power;
Sing, how he intercedes above
For those whose sins he bore.

3 Ye pilgrims! on the road
To Zion's city, sing!
Rejoice ye in the Lamb of God,—
In Christ, the eternal King.

4 Soon shall we hear him say,—
"Ye blessèd children! come;"
Soon will he call us hence away,
And take his wanderers home.

5 There shall each raptured tongue
His endless praise proclaim;
And sweeter voices tune the song
Of Moses and the Lamb.

LISBON. S. M. — DANIEL READ.

1. Welcome, sweet day of rest, That saw the Lord a-rise, Welcome to this re-viving breast, And these rejoic-ing eyes.

THE LORD'S DAY.

PACKINGTON. S. M.   J. BLACK.

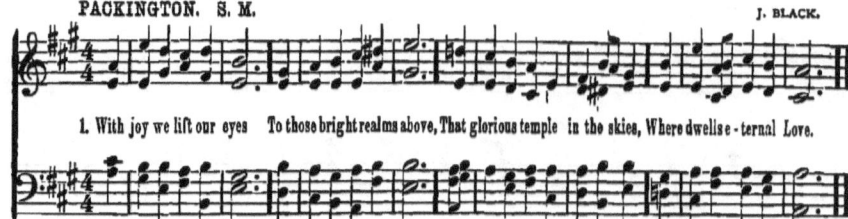

1. With joy we lift our eyes To those bright realms above, That glorious temple in the skies, Where dwells eternal Love.

33   *Hymn of praise.*   T. JERVIS.

WITH joy we lift our eyes
  To those bright realms above,
That glorious temple in the skies,
  Where dwells eternal Love.

2 Before thy throne we bow,
  O thou almighty King;
Here we present the solemn vow,
  And hymns of praise we sing.

3 While in thy house we kneel,
  With trust and holy fear,
Thy mercy and thy truth reveal,
  And lend a gracious ear.

4 Lord, teach our hearts to pray,
  And tune our lips to sing;
Nor from thy presence cast away
  The sacrifice we bring.

34   *Christian outlook.*   P. DODDRIDGE.

NOW LET our voices join
  To raise a sacred song;
Ye pilgrims! in Jehovah's ways,
  With music pass along.

2 See—flowers of paradise,
  In rich profusion, spring;
The sun of glory gilds the path,
  And dear companions sing.

3 See—Salem's golden spires,
  In beauteous prospect, rise;
And brighter crowns than mortals wear,
  Which sparkle through the skies.

4 All honor to his name,
  Who marks the shining way,—
To him who leads the pilgrims on
  To realms of endless day.

STATE STREET. S. M.   J. C. WOODMAN.

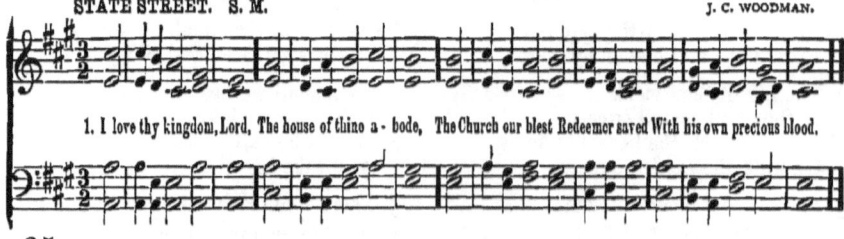

1. I love thy kingdom, Lord, The house of thine abode, The Church our blest Redeemer saved With his own precious blood.

35   *Psalm 137.*   T. DWIGHT.

I LOVE thy kingdom, Lord,
  The house of thine abode,
The Church our blest Redeemer saved
  With his own precious blood.

2 I love thy Church, O God!
  Her walls before thee stand,
Dear as the apple of thine eye,
  And graven on thine hand.

3 For her my tears shall fall,
  For her my prayers ascend;

To her my cares and toils be given,
  Till toils and cares shall end.

4 Beyond my highest joy
  I prize her heavenly ways,
Her sweet communion, solemn vows,
  Her hymns of love and praise.

5 Sure as thy truth shall last,
  To Zion shall be given
The brightest glories earth can yield,
  And brighter bliss of heaven.

WARWICK. C. M.   S. STANLEY.

1. Lord! in the morning thou shalt hear My voice as-cend-ing high; To thee will I di-

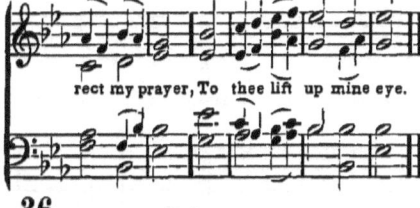

rect my prayer, To thee lift up mine eye.

36   *Psalm 5.*   I. WATTS.

LORD! in the morning thou shalt hear
My voice ascending high;
To thee will I direct my prayer,
To thee lift up mine eye;—

2 Up to the hills, where Christ has gone
To plead for all his saints,
Presenting, at his Father's throne,
Our songs and our complaints.

3 Thou art a God, before whose sight
The wicked shall not stand;
Sinners shall ne'er be thy delight,
Nor dwell at thy right hand.

4 But to thy house will I resort,
To taste thy mercies there;
I will frequent thy holy court,
And worship in thy fear.

5 Oh, may thy Spirit guide my feet,
In ways of righteousness;
Make every path of duty straight,
And plain before my face.

HYMN. C. M.   MODERN HARP.

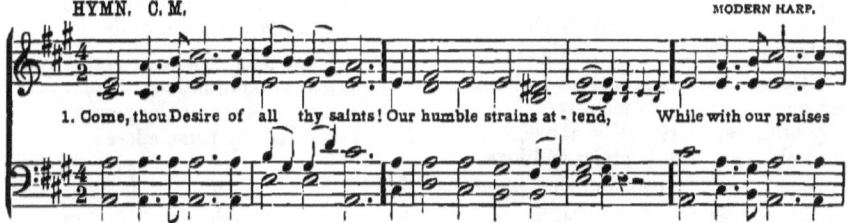

1. Come, thou Desire of all thy saints! Our humble strains at-tend, While with our praises

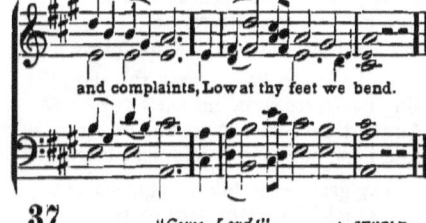

and complaints, Low at thy feet we bend.

37   *"Come, Lord!"*   A. STEELE.

COME, thou Desire of all thy saints!
Our humble strains attend,
While with our praises and complaints,
Low at thy feet we bend.

2 How should our songs, like those above,
With warm devotion rise!
How should our souls, on wings of love,
Mount upward to the skies!

3 Come, Lord! thy love alone can raise
In us the heavenly flame;
Then shall our lips resound thy praise,
Our hearts adore thy name.

4 Dear Saviour, let thy glory shine,
And fill thy dwellings here,
Till life, and love, and joy divine
A heaven on earth appear.

5 Then shall our hearts enraptured say,
Come, great Redeemer! come,
And bring the bright, the glorious day,
That calls thy children home.

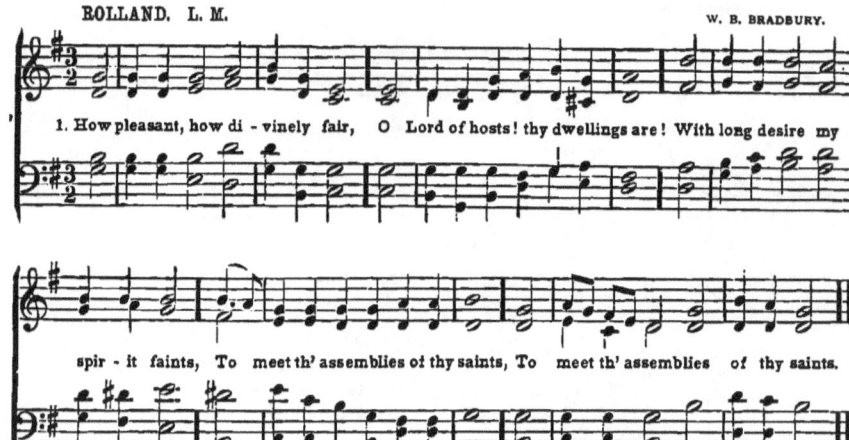

ROLLAND. L. M.   W. B. BRADBURY.

1. How pleasant, how divinely fair, O Lord of hosts! thy dwellings are! With long desire my spirit faints, To meet th' assemblies of thy saints, To meet th' assemblies of thy saints.

38   Psalm 84.   I. WATTS.

How PLEASANT, how divinely fair,
O Lord of hosts! thy dwellings are!
With long desire my spirit faints,
To meet the assemblies of thy saints.

2 My flesh would rest in thine abode,
My panting heart cries out for God;
My God! my King! why should I be
So far from all my joys, and thee?

3 Blest are the saints who sit on high,
Around thy throne of majesty;
Thy brightest glories shine above,
And all their work is praise and love.

4 Blest are the souls who find a place
Within the temple of thy grace;
There they behold thy gentler rays,
And seek thy face, and learn thy praise.

5 Cheerful they walk with growing strength,
Till all shall meet in heaven at length;
Till all before thy face appear,
And join in nobler worship there.

39   Psalm 84.   I. WATTS.

GREAT God! attend, while Zion sings
The joy that from thy presence springs;
To spend one day with thee on earth
Exceeds a thousand days of mirth.

2 Might I enjoy the meanest place
Within thy house, O God of grace!
Nor tents of ease, nor thrones of power,
Should tempt my feet to leave thy door.

3 God is our sun, he makes our day;
God is our shield, he guards our way
From all the assaults of hell and sin,
From foes without, and foes within.

4 All needful grace will God bestow,
And crown that grace with glory, too;
He gives us all things, and withholds
No real good from upright souls.

5 O God, our King, whose sovereign sway
The glorious hosts of heaven obey,
Display thy grace, exert thy power,
Till all on earth thy name adore!

40   Morning Hymn.   J. CHANDLER, tr.

O CHRIST! with each returning morn
Thine image to our hearts be borne;
And may we ever clearly see
Our God and Saviour, Lord, in thee!

2 All hallowed be our walk this day;
May meekness form our early ray,
And faithful love our noontide light,
And hope our sunset, calm and bright.

3 May grace each idle thought control,
And sanctify our wayward soul;
May guile depart, and malice cease,
And all within be joy and peace.

4 Our daily course, O Jesus, bless;
Make plain the way of holiness:
From sudden falls our feet defend,
And cheer at last our journey's end.

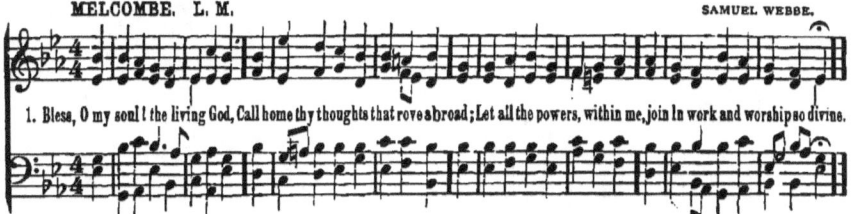

MELCOMBE. L. M. SAMUEL WEBBE.

1. Bless, O my soul! the living God, Call home thy thoughts that rove abroad; Let all the powers, within me, join in work and worship so divine.

41 *Psalm 103.* I. WATTS.

BLESS, O my soul! the living God,
Call home thy thoughts that rove abroad;
Let all the powers, within me, join
In work and worship so divine.

2 Bless, O my soul! the God of grace;
His favors claim thy highest praise:
Why should the wonders he hath wrought
Be lost in silence and forgot?

3 'Tis he, my soul! who sent his Son
To die for crimes which thou hast done:
He owns the ransom, and forgives
The hourly follies of our lives.

4 Let the whole earth his power confess,
Let the whole earth adore his grace;
The Gentile with the Jew shall join
In work and worship so divine.

42 *Psalm 135.* I. WATTS.

PRAISE ye the Lord; exalt his name,
While in his earthly courts ye wait,
Ye saints, that to his house belong,
Or stand attending at his gate.

2 Praise ye the Lord, the Lord is good;
To praise his name is sweet employ:
Israel he chose of old, and still
His church is his peculiar joy

3 Bless ye the Lord who taste his love,
People and priests exalt his name;
Among his saints he ever dwells;
His church is his Jerusalem.

MIGDOL. L. M. LOWELL MASON.

1. Sweet is the work, my God, my King, To praise thy name, give thanks, and sing; To show thy love by morning light, And talk of all thy truth at night.

43 *Psalm 92.* I. WATTS.

SWEET is the work, my God, my King,
To praise thy name, give thanks and sing;
To show thy love by morning light,
And talk of all thy truth at night.

2 Sweet is the day of sacred rest;
No mortal care shall seize my breast;
Oh, may my heart in tune be found,
Like David's harp of solemn sound!

3 My heart shall triumph in my Lord,
And bless his works and bless his word;
Thy works of grace, how bright they shine!
How deep thy counsels! how divine!

4 Lord, I shall share a glorious part,
When grace hath well refined my heart,
And fresh supplies of joy are shed,
Like holy oil to cheer my head.

5 Then shall I see, and hear, and know
All I desired or wished below;
And every power find sweet employ,
In that eternal world of joy.

ANVERN. L. M.   LOWELL MASON, arr.

44   *"A nobler Rest."*   P. DODDRIDGE.

THINE earthly Sabbaths, Lord, we love,
But there's a nobler rest above;
To that our longing souls aspire,
With cheerful hope and strong desire.

2 No more fatigue, no more distress,
Nor sin nor death shall reach the place;
No groans shall mingle with the songs
That warble from immortal tongues.

3 No rude alarms of raging foes,
No cares to break the long repose,
No midnight shade, no clouded sun,
But sacred, high, eternal noon.

4 O long-expected day, begin!
Dawn on these realms of woe and sin;
Fain would we leave this weary road,
And sleep in death, to rest with God.

45   *Invocation.*   I. WATTS.

COME, gracious Lord, descend and dwell,
By faith and love, in every breast;
Then shall we know, and taste, and feel
The joys that cannot be expressed.

2 Come, fill our hearts with inward strength,
Make our enlargéd souls possess,
And learn the height, and breadth, and length
Of thine eternal love and grace.

3 Now to the God whose power can do
More than our thoughts and wishes know,
Be everlasting honors done,
By all the Church, through Christ his Son.

46   *Morning.*   J. HUTTON.

MY opening eyes with rapture see
The dawn of thy returning day;
My thoughts, O God, ascend to thee,
While thus my early vows I pay.

2 Oh, bid this trifling world retire,
And drive each carnal thought away;
Nor let me feel one vain desire—
One sinful thought through all the day.

3 Then, to thy courts when I repair,
My soul shall rise on joyful wing,
The wonders of thy love declare,
And join the strains which angels sing.

47   *"Return, my soul!"*   J. STENNETT.

ANOTHER six days' work is done,
Another Sabbath is begun;
Return, my soul! enjoy thy rest,
Improve the day thy God hath blessed.

2 Oh, that our thoughts and thanks may rise,
As grateful incense to the skies;
And draw from heaven that sweet repose,
Which none, but he that feels it, knows.

3 This heavenly calm, within the breast,
Is the dear pledge of glorious rest,
Which for the church of God remains—
The end of cares, the end of pains.

4 In holy duties, let the day,
In holy pleasures, pass away;
How sweet a Sabbath thus to spend,
In hope of one that ne'er shall end.

THE LORD'S DAY.

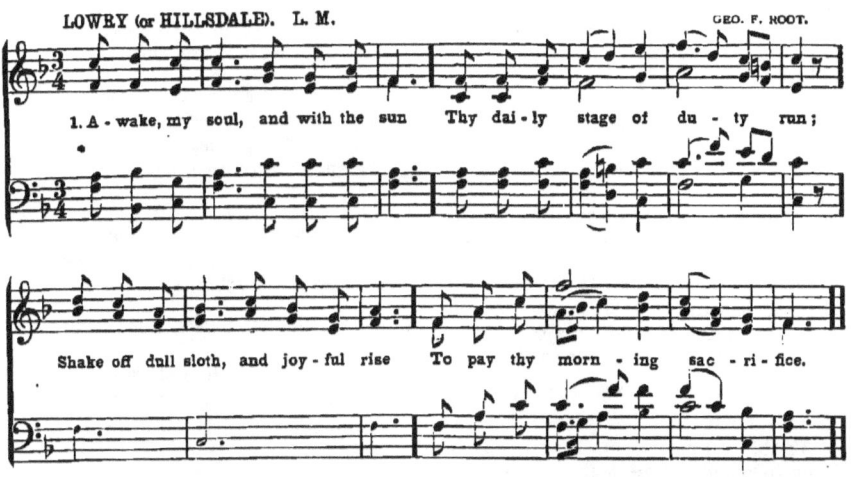

LOWRY (or HILLSDALE). L. M.   GEO. F. ROOT.

1. A-wake, my soul, and with the sun Thy dai-ly stage of du-ty run; Shake off dull sloth, and joy-ful rise To pay thy morn-ing sac-ri-fice.

48   *Morning.*   T. KEN.

Awake, my soul, and with the sun
Thy daily stage of duty run;
Shake off dull sloth, and joyful rise
To pay thy morning sacrifice.

2 Awake, lift up thyself, my heart,
And with the angels bear thy part,
Who all night long unwearied sing
High praises to the eternal King.

3 Glory to thee, who safe hast kept,
And hast refreshed me when I slept;
Grant, Lord, when I from death shall wake,
I may of endless life partake.

4 Lord, I my vows to thee renew:
Scatter my sins as morning dew;
Guard my first springs of thought and will,
And with thyself my spirit fill.

5 Direct, control, suggest, this day,
All I design, or do, or say;
That all my powers, with all their might,
In thy sole glory may unite.

49   *Psalm 65.*   H. F. LYTE.

Praise, Lord, for thee in Zion waits;
Prayer shall besiege thy temple gates;
All flesh shall to thy throne repair,
And find, through Christ, salvation there.

2 How blest thy saints! how safely led!
How surely kept! how richly fed!
Saviour of all in earth and sea,
How happy they who rest in thee!

3 Thy hand sets fast the mighty hills,
Thy voice the troubled ocean stills!
Evening and morning hymn thy praise,
And earth thy bounty wide displays.

4 The year is with thy goodness crowned;
Thy clouds drop wealth the world around;
Through thee the deserts laugh and sing,
And nature smiles and owns her king.

5 Lord, on our souls thy Spirit pour;
The moral waste within restore;
Oh, let thy love our spring-tide be,
And make us all bear fruit to thee.

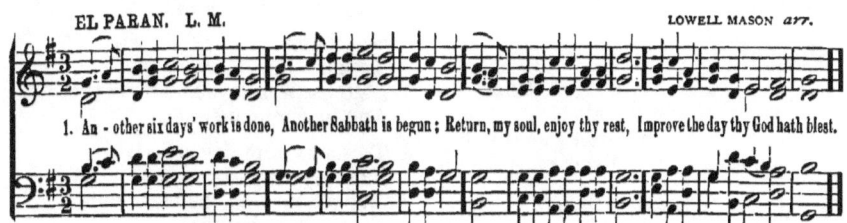

EL PARAN. L. M.   LOWELL MASON arr.

1. An-other six days' work is done, Another Sabbath is begun; Return, my soul, enjoy thy rest, Improve the day thy God hath blest.

50 7s. *Redeeming Love.* G. BURDER.
Sweet the time, exceeding sweet,
When the saints together meet;
When the Saviour is the theme,
When they join to sing of him.

2 Sing we then eternal love,
Such as did the Father move:
He beheld the world undone,
Loved the world, and gave his Son.

3 Sing the Son's amazing love:
How he left the realms above,
Took our nature and our place,
Lived and died to save our race.

4 Sing we, too, the Spirit's love:
With our wretched hearts he strove,
Took the things of Christ, and showed
How to reach his blest abode.

5 Sweet the place, exceeding sweet,
Where the saints in glory meet;
Where the Saviour's still the theme,
Where they see, and sing of him.

51 C. M. *The Mercy-Seat.* A. STEELE.
Dear Father, to thy mercy-seat
　My soul for shelter flies:
'T is here I find a safe retreat
　When storms and tempests rise.

2 My cheerful hope can never die,
　If thou, my God, art near;
Thy grace can raise my comforts high,
　And banish every fear.

3 My great Protector, and my Lord!
　Thy constant aid impart;
Oh! let thy kind, thy gracious word
　Sustain my trembling heart.

4 Oh! never let my soul remove
　From this divine retreat;
Still let me trust thy power and love,
　And dwell beneath thy feet.

52 C. M. *Retirement.* W. COWPER.
Far from the world, O Lord, I flee,
　From strife and tumult far;
From scenes where Satan wages still
　His most successful war.

2 The calm retreat, the silent shade,
　With prayer and praise agree;

And seem by thy sweet bounty made
　For those who follow thee.

3 There, if thy Spirit touch the soul,
　And grace her mean abode,
Oh! with what peace, and joy, and love,
　She then communes with God.

4 Author and Guardian of my life!
　Sweet Source of light divine,
And—all harmonious names in one—
　My Saviour!—thou art mine!

5 What thanks I owe thee, and what
　　love—
A boundless, endless store—
Shall echo through the realms above,
　When time shall be no more.

53 C. M. *Public Worship.* A. L. BARBAULD.
When, as returns this solemn day,
　Man comes to meet his God,
What rites, what honors shall he pay?
　How spread his praise abroad?

2 From marble domes and gilded spires
　Shall clouds of incense rise?
And gems, and gold, and garlands deck
　The costly sacrifice?

3 Vain, sinful man! creation's Lord
　Thy offerings well may spare;
But give thy heart, and thou shalt find
　Thy God will hear thy prayer.

54 S. M. *Psalm 92.* H. AUBER.
Sweet is the work, O Lord,
　Thy glorious name to sing;
To praise and pray—to hear thy word,
　And grateful offerings bring.

2 Sweet—at the dawning light,
　Thy boundless love to tell;
And, when approach the shades of night,
　Still on the theme to dwell.

3 Sweet—on this day of rest,
　To join in heart and voice,
With those who love and serve thee best,
　And in thy name rejoice.

4 To songs of praise and joy
　Be every Sabbath given,
That such may be our blest employ
　Eternally in heaven.

THE LORD'S DAY.

55 L. M. *Hour of Prayer.* T. RAFFLES.
Blest hour! when mortal man retires
 To hold communion with his God,
To send to heaven his warm desires,
 And listen to the sacred word.
2 Blest hour! when earthly cares resign
 Their empire o'er his anxious breast,
While all around, the calm divine
 Proclaims the holy day of rest.
3 Blest hour! when God himself draws nigh,
 Well pleased his people's voice to hear,
To hush the penitential sigh,
 And wipe away the mourner's tear.
4 Blest hour! for where the Lord resorts,
 Foretastes of future bliss are given;
And mortals find his earthly courts
 The house of God, the gate of Heaven!

56 L. M. *"Gate of Heaven."* T. KELLY.
How sweet to leave the world awhile,
 And seek the presence of our Lord!
Dear Saviour! on thy people smile,
 And come, according to thy word.
2 From busy scenes we now retreat,
 That we may here converse with thee
Ah, Lord! behold us at thy feet;
 Let this the "gate of heaven" be.
3 "Chief of ten thousand!" now appear,
 That we by faith may see thy face:
Oh, speak, that we thy voice may hear,
 And let thy presence fill this place.

57 8s, 7s, 4s. *"We draw near."* T. KELLY.
In thy name, O Lord, assembling,
 We, thy people, now draw near;
Teach us to rejoice with trembling;
 Speak, and let thy servants hear;
  Hear with meekness—
 Hear thy word with godly fear.
2 While our days on earth are lengthened,
 May we give them, Lord, to thee;
Cheered by hope, and daily strengthened,
 May we run, nor weary be,
  Till thy glory
 Without cloud in heaven we see.
3 There, in worship purer, sweeter,
 All thy people shall adore;
Tasting of enjoyment greater
 Than they could conceive before;
  Full enjoyment,
 Full and pure for evermore.

58 L. M. *Invocation.* I. WATTS.
Far from my thoughts, vain world, begone!
Let my religious hours alone:
Fain would mine eyes my Saviour see:
I wait a visit, Lord, from thee.
2 My heart grows warm with holy fire,
 And kindles with a pure desire:
Come, my dear Jesus! from above,
 And feed my soul with heavenly love.
3 Blest Saviour! what delicious fare,
 How sweet thine entertainments are!
Never did angels taste, above,
 Redeeming grace and dying love.
4 Hail, great Immanuel, all-divine!
 In thee thy Father's glories shine:
Thou brightest, sweetest, fairest One
 That eyes have seen, or angels known!

59 L. M. *"Two or Three."* S. STENNETT.
Where two or three, with sweet accord,
 Obedient to their sovereign Lord,
Meet to recount his acts of grace,
 And offer solemn prayer and praise;—
2 There will the gracious Saviour be,
 To bless the little company;
There, to unvail his smiling face,
 And bid his glories fill the place.
3 We meet at thy command, O Lord!
 Relying on thy faithful word;
Now send the Spirit from above,
 And fill our hearts with heavenly love.

60 S. M. *Invitation.* E. TAYLOR.
Come to the house of prayer,
 O thou afflicted, come;
The God of peace shall meet thee there—
 He makes that house his home.
2 Come to the house of praise,
 Ye who are happy now;
In sweet accord your voices raise,
 In kindred homage bow.
3 Ye aged, hither come,
 For ye have felt his love;
Soon shall your trembling tongues be dumb,
 Your lips forget to move.
4 Ye young, before his throne,
 Come, bow; your voices raise;
Let not your hearts his praise disown
 Who gives the power to praise.

THE HOUSE OF PRAYER.

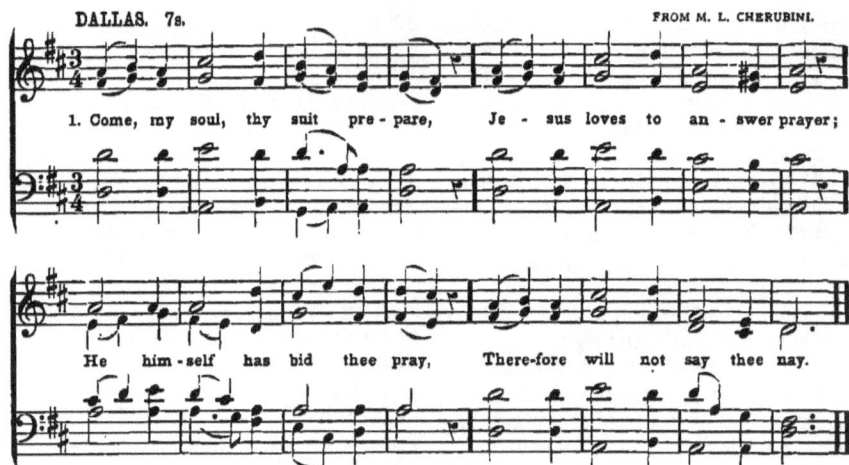

61 *A Prayer in Need.* J. NEWTON.

COME, my soul, thy suit prepare,
Jesus loves to answer prayer;
He himself has bid thee pray,
Therefore will not say thee nay.

2 With my burden I begin:—
Lord! remove this load of sin;
Let thy blood, for sinners spilt,
Set my conscience free from guilt.

3 Lord! I come to thee for rest;
Take possession of my breast:
There, thy blood-bought right maintain,
And, without a rival, reign.

4 While I am a pilgrim here,
Let thy love my spirit cheer;
As my Guide, my Guard, my Friend,
Lead me to my journey's end.

5 Show me what I have to do,
Every hour my strength renew;
Let me live a life of faith,
Let me die thy people's death.

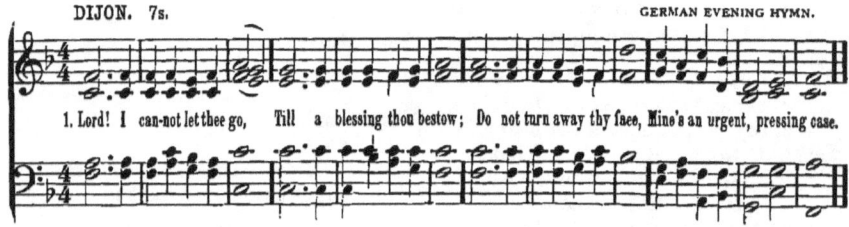

62 *The Case Argued.* J. NEWTON.

LORD! I cannot let thee go,
Till a blessing thou bestow;
Do not turn away thy face,
Mine's an urgent, pressing case.

2 Once a sinner, near despair,
Sought thy mercy-seat by prayer;
Mercy heard and set him free—
Lord! that mercy came to me.

3 Many days have passed since then,
Many changes I have seen;
Yet have been upheld till now;
Who could hold me up but thou?

4 Thou hast helped in every need—
This emboldens me to plead;
After so much mercy past,
Canst thou let me sink at last?

5 No—I must maintain my hold;
'Tis thy goodness makes me bold;
I can no denial take,
Since I plead for Jesus' sake.

THE HOUSE OF PRAYER.

DIX. 7s. 6l. WILLIAM HENRY MONK, arr.

1. As with gladness men of old Did the guiding star behold;
As with joy they hailed its light, Leading onward, beaming bright; So, most gracious Lord, may we Evermore be led to thee.

63   *The Guiding Star.*   W. C. DIX.

As WITH gladness men of old
Did the guiding star behold,
As with joy they hailed its light,
Leading onward, beaming bright;
So, most gracious Lord, may we
Evermore be led to thee.

2 As with joyful steps they sped,
Saviour, to thy manger bed,
There to bend the knee before
Thee whom heaven and earth adore;
So may we with willing feet
Ever seek the mercy-seat.

3 As they offered gifts most rare
At thy cradle rude and bare,
So may we with holy joy,
Pure and free from sin's alloy,
All our costliest treasures bring,
Christ, to thee our heavenly King.

4 Holy Jesus, every day
Keep us in the narrow way;
And, when earthly things are past,
Bring our ransomed souls at last
Where they need no star to guide,
Where no clouds thy glory hide.

HEROLD. 7s. A. J. F. HEROLD.

1. They who seek the throne of grace Find that throne in ev-ery place;
If we live a life of prayer, God is pres-ent ev-ery-where.

64   *God everywhere.*   O. HOLDEN.

THEY who seek the throne of grace
Find that throne in every place;
If we live a life of prayer,
God is present everywhere.

2 In our sickness and our health,
In our want, or in our wealth,
If we look to God in prayer,
God is present everywhere.

3 When our earthly comforts fail,
When the foes of life prevail,
'Tis the time for earnest prayer;
God is present everywhere.

4 Then, my soul, in every strait,
To thy Father come, and wait;
He will answer every prayer:
God is present everywhere.

THE HOUSE OF PRAYER.

WOODSTOCK. C. M. — D. DUTTON.

1. I love to steal a-while a-way From ev-ery cum-bering care, And spend the hours of set-ting day In hum-ble, grate-ful prayer.

65 *Retirement.* F. H. BROWN.

I LOVE to steal awhile away
From every cumbering care,
And spend the hours of setting day
In humble, grateful prayer.

2 I love in solitude to shed
The penitential tear,
And all his promises to plead,
Where none but God can hear.

3 I love to think on mercies past,
And future good implore,
And all my cares and sorrows cast
On him whom I adore.

4 I love by faith to take a view
Of brighter scenes in heaven;
The prospect doth my strength renew,
While here by tempests driven.

5 Thus, when life's toilsome day is o'er,
May its departing ray
Be calm as this impressive hour,
And lead to endless day.

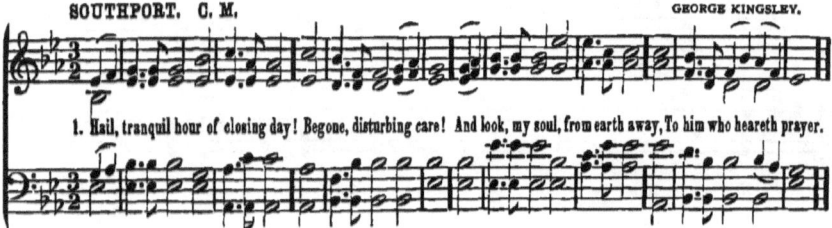

SOUTHPORT. C. M. — GEORGE KINGSLEY.

1. Hail, tranquil hour of closing day! Begone, disturbing care! And look, my soul, from earth away, To him who heareth prayer.

66 *"Tranquil hour."* L. BACON.

HAIL, tranquil hour of closing day!
Begone, disturbing care!
And look, my soul, from earth away,
To him who heareth prayer.

2 How sweet the tear of penitence,
Before his throne of grace,
While, to the contrite spirit's sense,
He shows his smiling face.

3 How sweet, thro' long remembered years,
His mercies to recall;
And, pressed with wants, and griefs, and fears,
To trust his love for all.

4 How sweet to look, in thoughtful hope,
Beyond this fading sky,
And hear him call his children up
To his fair home on high.

5 Calmly the day forsakes our heaven
To dawn beyond the west;
So let my soul, in life's last even,
Retire to glorious rest.

THE HOUSE OF PRAYER.

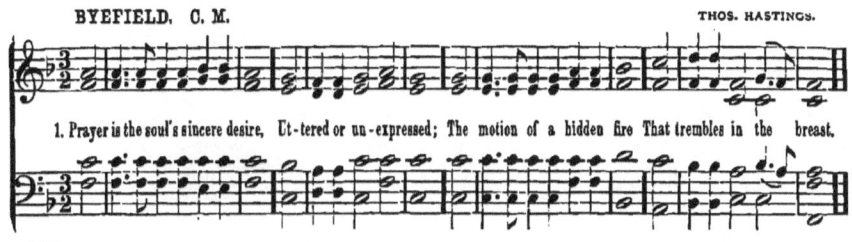

BYEFIELD. C. M. — THOS. HASTINGS.

1. Prayer is the soul's sincere desire, Uttered or unexpressed; The motion of a hidden fire That trembles in the breast.

67   *What prayer is.*   J. MONTGOMERY.

Prayer is the soul's sincere desire,
  Uttered or unexpressed;
The motion of a hidden fire
  That trembles in the breast.

2 Prayer is the burden of a sigh,
  The falling of a tear,
The upward glancing of an eye,
  When none but God is near.

3 Prayer is the simplest form of speech
  That infant lips can try;
Prayer the sublimest strains that reach
  The Majesty on high.

4 Prayer is the Christian's vital breath,
  The Christian's native air:
His watchword at the gates of death—
  He enters heaven with prayer.

5 Prayer is the contrite sinner's voice,
  Returning from his ways;
While angels in their songs rejoice,
  And cry—"Behold he prays!"

6 O thou, by whom we come to God—
  The Life, the Truth, the Way;
The path of prayer thyself hast trod;
  Lord! teach us how to pray.

68   *"The sacred fire."*   B. BEDDOME.

Prayer is the breath of God in man,
  Returning whence it came;
Love is the sacred fire within,
  And prayer the rising flame.

2 It gives the burdened spirit ease,
  And soothes the troubled breast;
Yields comfort to the mourning soul,
  And to the weary rest.

3 When God inclines the heart to pray,
  He hath an ear to hear;
To him there's music in a sigh,
  And beauty in a tear.

4 The humble suppliant cannot fail
  To have his wants supplied,
Since He for sinners intercedes,
  Who once for sinners died.

COLCHESTER. C. M. — H. PURCELL.

1. Prayer is the breath of God in man, Returning whence it came; Love is the sacred fire within, And prayer the rising flame.

THE HOUSE OF PRAYER.

RETREAT. L. M. THOS. HASTINGS.

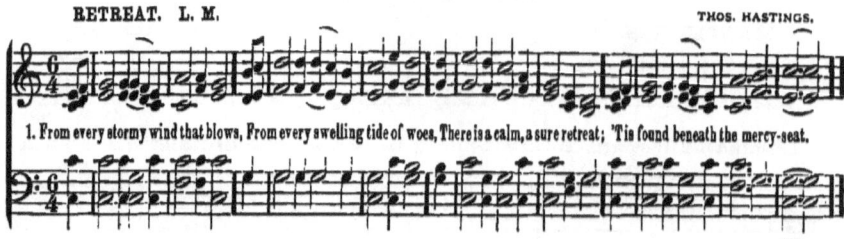

1. From every stormy wind that blows, From every swelling tide of woes, There is a calm, a sure retreat; 'Tis found beneath the mercy-seat.

69
The mercy-seat. H. STOWELL.

From every stormy wind that blows,
From every swelling tide of woes,
There is a calm, a sure retreat;
'Tis found beneath the mercy-seat.

2 There is a place where Jesus sheds
The oil of gladness on our heads,—
A place than all besides more sweet;
It is the blood-bought mercy-seat.

3 There is a scene where spirits blend,
Where friend holds fellowship with friend;
Though sundered far, by faith they meet
Around one common mercy-seat.

4 There, there, on eagle wings we soar,
And sense and sin molest no more,
And heaven comes down our souls to greet,
And glory crowns the mercy-seat.

5 Oh, let my hand forget her skill,
My tongue be silent, cold, and still,
This throbbing heart forget to beat,
If I forget the mercy-seat.

STOWELL. L. M. SOLON WILDER.

SOLO.—SOPRANO.

1. From every stormy wind that blows, From ev-ery swell-ing tide of woes,

CHORUS.

1. From every stormy wind that blows, From ev-ery swell-ing tide of woes,

There is.... a calm, a sure re-treat; 'Tis found be-neath the mer-cy-seat.

There is.... a calm, a sure re-treat; 'Tis found be-neath the mer-cy-seat.

THE HOUSE OF PRAYER.

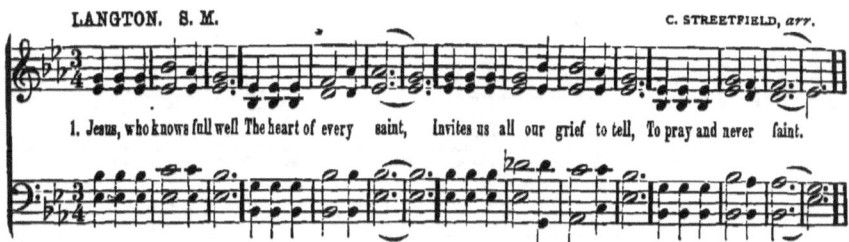

70 *Importunity.* J. NEWTON.

Jesus, who knows full well
The heart of every saint,
Invites us all our grief to tell,
To pray and never faint.

2 He bows his gracious ear,—
We never plead in vain;
Then let us wait till he appear,
And pray, and pray again.

3 Jesus, the Lord, will hear
His chosen when they cry;
Yes, though he may a while forbear,
He'll help them from on high.

4 Then let us earnest cry,
And never faint in prayer;
He sees, he hears, and, from on high,
Will make our cause his care.

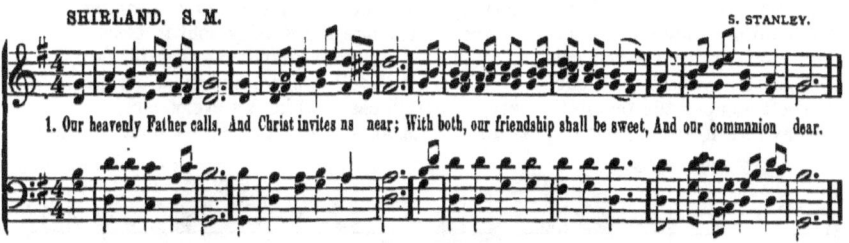

71 "God pities." P. DODDRIDGE.

Our heavenly Father calls.
And Christ invites us near;
With both, our friendship shall be sweet,
And our communion dear.

2 God pities all our griefs:
He pardons every day;
Almighty to protect our souls,
And wise to guide our way.

3 How large his bounties are!
What various stores of good,
Diffused from our Redeemer's hand,
And purchased with his blood!

4 Jesus, our living Head,
We bless thy faithful care;
Our Advocate before the throne,
And our Forerunner there.

5 Here fix, my roving heart!
Here wait, my warmest love!
Till the communion be complete,
In nobler scenes above.

72 "The throne of grace." J. NEWTON.

Behold the throne of grace!
The promise calls me near;
There Jesus shows a smiling face,
And waits to answer prayer.

2 That rich atoning blood,
Which sprinkled round I see,
Provides for those who come to God
An all-prevailing plea.

3 My soul! ask what thou wilt;
Thou canst not be too bold:
Since his own blood for thee he spilt,
What else can he withhold?

4 Thine image, Lord, bestow,
Thy presence and thy love;
I ask to serve thee here below,
And reign with thee above.

5 Teach me to live by faith;
Conform my will to thine:
Let me victorious be in death,
And then in glory shine.

THE HOUSE OF PRAYER.

73 *"Sweet hour."* W. W. WALFORD.

SWEET hour of prayer! sweet hour of prayer!
That calls me from a world of care,
And bids me, at my Father's throne,
Make all my wants and wishes known:
In seasons of distress and grief,
My soul has often found relief,
And oft escaped the tempter's snare,
By thy return, sweet hour of prayer!

2 Sweet hour of prayer! sweet hour of prayer!
Thy wings shall my petition bear
To him, whose truth and faithfulness
Engage the waiting soul to bless:
And, since he bids me seek his face,
Believe his word, and trust his grace,
I'll cast on him my every care,
And wait for thee, sweet hour of prayer!

74 *The mercy-seat.* W. COWPER.

JESUS, where'er thy people meet,
There they behold thy mercy-seat;
Where'er they seek thee thou art found,
And every place is hallowed ground.

2 For thou, within no walls confined,
Inhabitest the humble mind;
Such ever bring thee where they come,
And going, take thee to their home.

3 Great Shepherd of thy chosen few,
Thy former mercies here renew;
Here to our waiting hearts proclaim
The sweetness of thy saving name.

4 Here may we prove the power of prayer,
To strengthen faith and sweeten care,
To teach our faint desires to rise,
And bring all heaven before our eyes.

THE HOUSE OF PRAYER.

OBERLIN. L. M.   THOS. HASTINGS, arr.

1. Where high the heavenly tem-ple stands, The house of God not made with hands, A great High Priest our na-ture wears,—The Guardian of man-kind ap-pears.

75   *"The evil hour."*   M. BRUCE.

Where high the heavenly temple stands,
The house of God not made with hands,
A great High Priest our nature wears,—
The Guardian of mankind appears.

2 Though now ascended up on high,
He bends on earth a brother's eye;
Partaker of the human name,
He knows the frailty of our frame.

3 Our Fellow-sufferer yet retains
A fellow-feeling of our pains;
And still remembers, in the skies,
His tears, his agonies, and cries.

4 In every pang that rends the heart,
The Man of Sorrows had a part;
He sympathizes with our grief,
And to the sufferer sends relief.

5 With boldness, therefore, at the throne,
Let us make all our sorrows known;
And ask the aid of heavenly power,
To help us in the evil hour.

76   *"What thou wilt."*   J. NEWTON.

And dost thou say, "Ask what thou wilt?"
Lord, I would seize the golden hour:
I pray to be released from guilt,
And freed from sin and Satan's power.

2 More of thy presence, Lord, impart;
More of thine image let me bear:
Erect thy throne within my heart,
And reign without a rival there.

3 Give me to read my pardon sealed,
And from thy joy to draw my strength:
Oh, be thy boundless love revealed
In all its height and breadth and length.

4 Grant these requests—I ask no more,
But to thy care the rest resign:
Sick, or in health, or rich, or poor,
All shall be well, if thou art mine.

77   *Prayers hindered.*   W. COWPER.

What various hindrances we meet
In coming to a mercy-seat!
Yet who that knows the worth of prayer
But wishes to be often there?

2 Prayer makes the darkened cloud withdraw;
Prayer climbs the ladder Jacob saw,
Gives exercise to faith and love,
Brings every blessing from above.

3 Restraining prayer, we cease to fight;
Prayer makes the Christian's armor bright;
And Satan trembles when he sees
The weakest saint upon his knees.

4 Have you no words? ah! think again;
Words flow apace when you complain,
And fill a fellow-creature's ear
With the sad tale of all your care.

5 Were half the breath thus vainly spent
To heaven in supplication sent,
Our cheerful song would oftener be,
"Hear what the Lord hath done for me!"

THE SACRIFICE OF PRAISE.

OLD HUNDRED. L. M. — GUILLAUME FRANC.

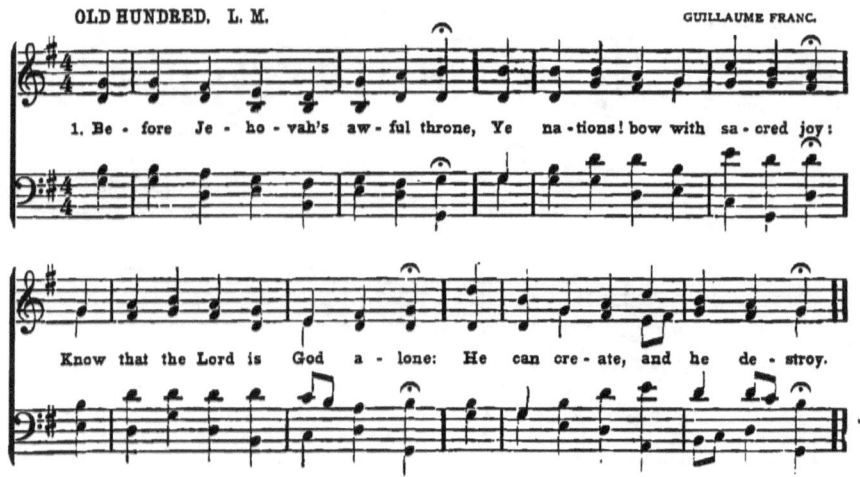

1. Be-fore Je-ho-vah's aw-ful throne, Ye na-tions! bow with sa-cred joy: Know that the Lord is God a-lone: He can cre-ate, and he de-stroy.

78   *Psalm 100.*   I. WATTS.

BEFORE Jehovah's awful throne,
  Ye nations! bow with sacred joy:
Know that the Lord is God alone:
  He can create, and he destroy.

2 His sovereign power, without our aid,
  Made us of clay, and formed us men;
And when, like wandering sheep, we strayed,
  He brought us to his fold again.

3 We are his people, we his care,—
  Our souls, and all our mortal frame:
What lasting honors shall we rear,
  Almighty Maker! to thy name?

4 We'll crowd thy gates with thankful songs,
  High as the heavens our voices raise;
And earth, with her ten thousand tongues,
  Shall fill thy courts with sounding praise.

5 Wide as the world is thy command,
  Vast as eternity, thy love;
Firm as a rock thy truth must stand,
  When rolling years shall cease to move.

79   *Psalm 100.*   W. KETHE.

ALL people that on earth do dwell,
  Sing to the Lord with cheerful voice:
Him serve with mirth, his praise forth tell,
  Come ye before him and rejoice.

2 Know that the Lord is God indeed;
  Without our aid he did us make:
We are his flock, he doth us feed,
  And for his sheep he doth us take.

3 Oh, enter then his gates with praise,
  Approach with joy his courts unto:
Praise, laud, and bless his name always,
  For it is seemly so to do.

4 For why? the Lord our God is good,
  His mercy is for ever sure;
His truth at all times firmly stood,
  And shall from age to age endure.

80   *Doxology.*   T. KEN.

PRAISE God, from whom all blessings flow,
Praise him, all creatures here below;
Praise him above, ye heavenly host;
Praise Father, Son, and Holy Ghost.

81   *Doxology.*   I. WATTS.

To GOD the Father, God the Son,
And God the Spirit, Three in One,
Be honor, praise, and glory given,
By all on earth, and all in heaven.

82   *Psalm 117.*   I. WATTS.

FROM all that dwell below the skies,
Let the Creator's praise arise:
Let the Redeemer's name be sung,
Through every land, by every tongue.

2 Eternal are thy mercies, Lord!
Eternal truth attends thy word:
Thy praise shall sound from shore to shore,
Till suns shall rise and set no more.

THE SACRIFICE OF PRAISE.

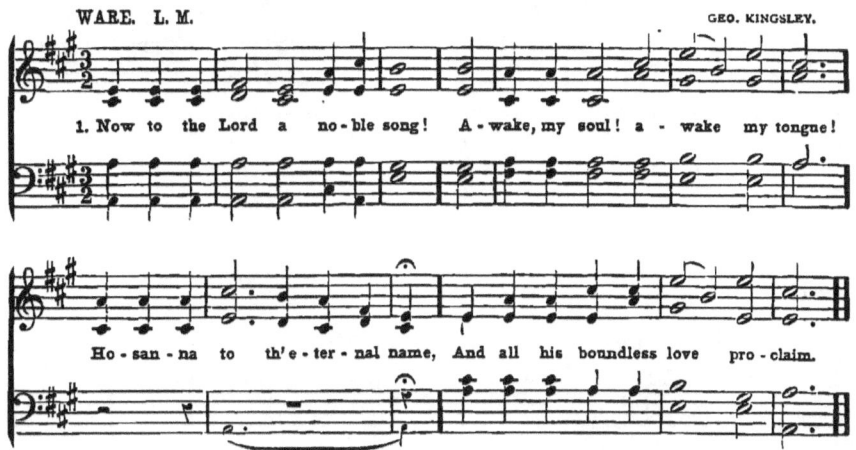

WARE. L. M.   GEO. KINGSLEY.

1. Now to the Lord a no-ble song! A-wake, my soul! a-wake my tongue! Ho-san-na to th' e-ter-nal name, And all his boundless love pro-claim.

83   *God's grace.*   I. WATTS.

Now to the Lord a noble song!
Awake, my soul! awake, my tongue!
Hosanna to the eternal name,
And all his boundless love proclaim.

2 See where it shines in Jesus' face,—
The brightest image of his grace!
God, in the person of his Son,
Hath all his mightiest works outdone.

3 Grace!—'tis a sweet, a charming theme:
My thoughts rejoice at Jesus' name:
Ye angels! dwell upon the sound:
Ye heavens! reflect it to the ground.

4 Oh, may I reach that happy place,
Where he unvails his lovely face,
Where all his beauties you behold,
And sing his name to harps of gold.

84   *Psalm 36.*   I. WATTS.

High in the heavens, eternal God!
Thy goodness in full glory shines;
Thy truth shall break through every cloud
That vails and darkens thy designs.

2 For ever firm thy justice stands,
As mountains their foundations keep:
Wise are the wonders of thy hands;
Thy judgments are a mighty deep.

3 My God, how excellent thy grace!
Whence all our hope and comfort springs;
The sons of Adam, in distress,
Fly to the shadow of thy wings.

4 From the provisions of thy house
We shall be fed with sweet repast;
There, mercy like a river flows,
And brings salvation to our taste.

5 Life, like a fountain rich and free,
Springs from the presence of my Lord;
And in thy light our souls shall see
The glories promised in thy word.

85   *"Te Deum."*   T. COTTERILL, *alt.*

Lord God of Hosts, by all adored!
Thy name we praise with one accord;
The earth and heavens are full of thee,
Thy light, thy love, thy majesty.

2 Loud hallelujahs to thy name
Angels and seraphim proclaim;
Eternal praise to thee is given
By all the powers and thrones in heaven.

3 The apostles join the glorious throng,
The prophets aid to swell the song,
The noble and triumphant host
Of martyrs make of thee their boast.

4 The holy church in every place
Throughout the world exalts thy praise;
Both heaven and earth do worship thee,
Thou Father of eternity!

5 From day to day, O Lord, do we
Highly exalt and honor thee;
Thy name we worship and adore,
World without end for evermore.

THE SACRIFICE OF PRAISE.

GILEAD. L. M.   ETIENNE HENRI MEHUL.

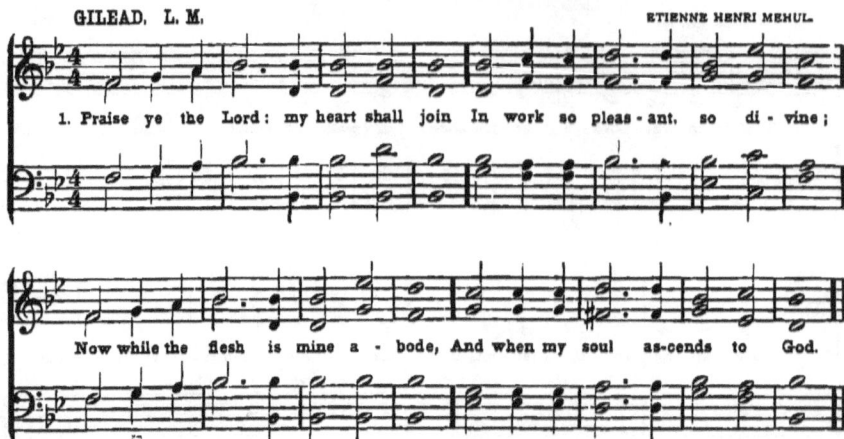

86
Psalm 146.   I. WATTS.

PRAISE ye the Lord: my heart shall join
In work so pleasant, so divine;
Now while the flesh is mine abode,
And when my soul ascends to God.

2 Praise shall employ my noblest powers,
While immortality endures;
My days of praise shall ne'er be past,
While life, and thought, and being last.

3 Happy the man whose hopes rely
On Israel's God: he made the sky,
And earth, and seas, with all their train;
And none shall find his promise vain.

4 His truth for ever stands secure;
He saves the oppressed, he feeds the poor;
He helps the stranger in distress,
The widow and the fatherless.

5 He loves his saints, he knows them well,
But turns the wicked down to hell;
Thy God, O Zion, ever reigns;
Praise him in everlasting strains.

87
Psalm 147.   I. WATTS.

PRAISE ye the Lord!—'tis good to raise
Our hearts and voices in his praise;
His nature and his works invite
To make this duty our delight.

2 The Lord builds up Jerusalem,
And gathers nations to his name;
His mercy melts the stubborn soul,
And makes the broken spirit whole.

3 He formed the stars—those heavenly flames,
He counts their numbers, calls their names:
His wisdom's vast, and knows no bound,—
A deep, where all our thoughts are drowned.

4 Great is our Lord, and great his might,
And all his glories infinite:
He crowns the meek, rewards the just,
And treads the wicked to the dust.

5 But saints are lovely in his sight;
He views his children with delight;
He sees their hope, he knows their fear,
And looks, and loves his image there.

88
Psalm 29.   I. WATTS.

GIVE to the Lord, ye sons of fame,
  Give to the Lord renown and power;
Ascribe due honors to his name,
  And his eternal might adore.

2 The Lord proclaims his power aloud,
  O'er all the ocean and the land;
His voice divides the watery cloud,
  And lightnings blaze at his command.

3 The Lord sits Sovereign on the flood;
  The Thunderer reigns for ever King;
But makes his church his blest abode,
  Where we his awful glories sing.

4 In gentler language, there the Lord
  The counsels of his grace imparts:
Amid the raging storm, his word
  Speaks peace and courage to our hearts.

THE SACRIFICE OF PRAISE. 35

89 L. M. *Psalm 145.* I. WATTS.

My God, my King, thy various praise
Shall fill the remnant of my days:
Thy grace employ my humble tongue
Till death and glory raise the song.

2 The wings of every hour shall bear
Some thankful tribute to thine ear;
And every setting sun shall see
New works of duty done for thee.

3 Thy works with sovereign glory shine,
And speak thy majesty divine:
Let Zion in her courts proclaim
The sound and honor of thy name.

4 But who can speak thy wondrous deeds?
Thy greatness all our thoughts exceeds:
Vast and unsearchable thy ways;
Vast and immortal be thy praise.

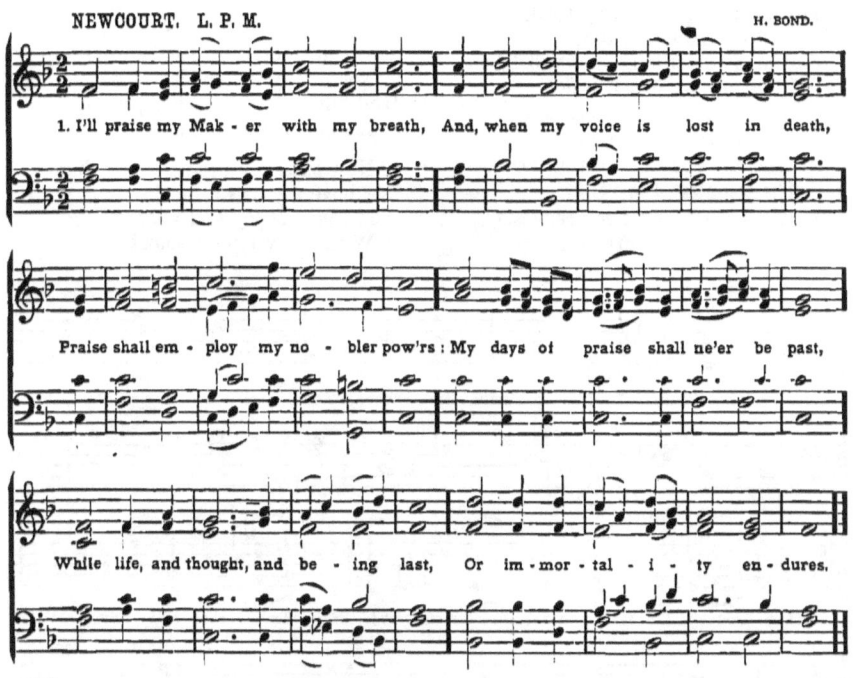

NEWCOURT. L. P. M. H. BOND.

1. I'll praise my Mak-er with my breath, And, when my voice is lost in death, Praise shall em-ploy my no-bler pow'rs: My days of praise shall ne'er be past, While life, and thought, and be-ing last, Or im-mor-tal-i-ty en-dures.

90 *Psalm 146.* I. WATTS.

I'll praise my Maker with my breath,
And, when my voice is lost in death,
  Praise shall employ my nobler powers:
My days of praise shall ne'er be past,
While life, and thought, and being last,
  Or immortality endures.

2 Happy the man, whose hopes rely
On Israel's God ;—he made the sky,
  And earth, and seas, with all their train:
His truth for ever stands secure ;
He saves the oppressed, he feeds the poor ;
  And none shall find his promise vain.

3 He loves his saints—he knows them well,
But turns the wicked down to hell:
  Thy God, O Zion ! ever reigns;
Let every tongue, let every age,
In this exalted work engage:
  Praise him in everlasting strains.

4 I'll praise him while he lends me breath,
And, when my voice is lost in death,
  Praise shall employ my nobler powers:
My days of praise shall ne'er be past,
While life, and thought, and being last,
  Or immortality endures.

THE SACRIFICE OF PRAISE.

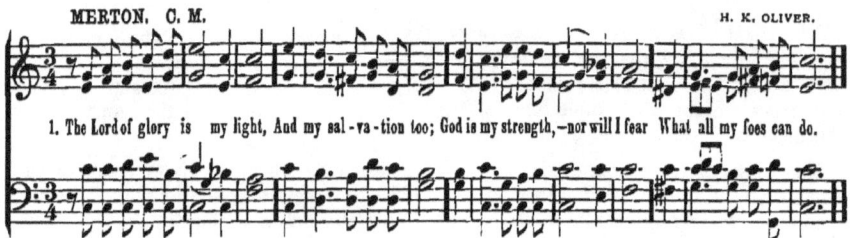

MERTON. C. M. — H. K. OLIVER.

1. The Lord of glory is my light, And my sal-va-tion too; God is my strength,—nor will I fear What all my foes can do.

91
Psalm 27.   I. WATTS.

The Lord of glory is my light,
  And my salvation too;
God is my strength,—nor will I fear
  What all my foes can do.

2 One privilege my heart desires,—
  Oh, grant me an abode
Among the churches of thy saints,—
  The temples of my God.

3 There shall I offer my requests,
  And see thy beauty still;
Shall hear thy messages of love,
  And there inquire thy will.

4 When troubles rise and storms appear,
  There may his children hide;
God has a strong pavilion, where
  He makes my soul abide.

5 Now shall my head be lifted high
  Above my foes around;
And songs of joy and victory
  Within thy temple sound.

HENRY. C. M. — S. B. POND.

1. Praise waits in Zi-on, Lord! for thee; There shall our vows be paid; Thou hast an ear when sin-ners pray; All flesh shall seek thine aid.

92
Psalm 65.   I. WATTS.

Praise waits in Zion, Lord! for thee;
  There shall our vows be paid;
Thou hast an ear when sinners pray;
  All flesh shall seek thine aid.

2 O Lord! our guilt and fears prevail,
  But pardoning grace is thine;
And thou wilt grant us power and skill,
  To conquer every sin.

3 Blest are the men, whom thou wilt choose
  To bring them near thy face;
Give them a dwelling in thy house,
  To feast upon thy grace.

4 In answering what thy church requests,
  Thy truth and terror shine;
And works of dreadful righteousness
  Fulfill thy kind design.

5 Thus shall the wondering nations see
  The Lord is good and just;
The distant isles shall fly to thee,
  And make thy name their trust.

THE SACRIFICE OF PRAISE.

SILVER STREET. S. M. I. SMITH.

1. Come, sound his praise a-broad, And hymns of glo - ry sing: Je - ho - vah is the sov - 'reign God, The u - ni - ver - sal King.

93 *Psalm 95.* I. WATTS.
Come, sound his praise abroad,
 And hymns of glory sing:
Jehovah is the sovereign God,
 The universal King.

2 He formed the deeps unknown;
 He gave the seas their bound;
The watery worlds are all his own,
 And all the solid ground.

3 Come, worship at his throne,
 Come, bow before the Lord:
We are his work, and not our own,
 He formed us by his word.

4 To-day attend his voice,
 Nor dare provoke his rod;
Come, like the people of his choice,
 And own our gracious God.

94 *Psalm 81.* H. F. LYTE.
Sing to the Lord, our Might,
 With holy fervor sing;
Let hearts and instruments unite
 To praise our heavenly King.

2 The Sabbath to our sires
 In mercy first was given;
The Church her Sabbaths still requires
 To speed her on to heaven.

3 We still, like them of old,
 Are in the wilderness;
And God is still as near his fold,
 To pity and to bless.

4 Then let us open wide
 Our hearts for him to fill;
And he, that Israel then supplied,
 Will help his Israel still.

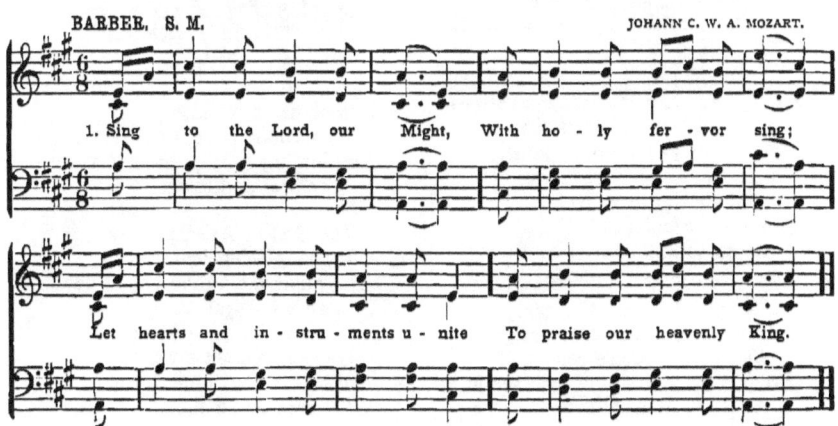

BARBER. S. M. JOHANN C. W. A. MOZART.

1. Sing to the Lord, our Might, With ho - ly fer - vor sing; Let hearts and in - stru - ments u - nite To praise our heavenly King.

95
"I Am." T. OLIVERS.

The God of Abraham praise,
  Who reigns enthroned above,
Ancient of everlasting days,
  And God of love!
Jehovah! great I AM!
  By earth and heaven confessed;
I bow and bless the sacred name,
  For ever blest!

2 The God of Abraham praise!
  At whose supreme command
From earth I rise, and seek the joys
  At his right hand:
I all on earth forsake,
  Its wisdom, fame, and power,
And him my only portion make,
  My shield and tower.

3 The God of Abraham praise!
  Whose all-sufficient grace
Shall guide me all my happy days
  In all my ways:
He calls a worm his friend!
  He calls himself my God!
And he shall save me to the end
  Through Jesus' blood!

THE SACRIFICE OF PRAISE. 39

96 P. M. *The triune God.* R. HEBER.

Holy, holy, holy, Lord God Almighty!
Early in the morning our song shall rise
  to thee;
Holy, holy, holy, merciful and mighty,
  God in three persons, blessèd Trinity!
2 Holy, holy, holy! all the saints adore
    thee,
  Casting down their golden crowns
    around the glassy sea;
  Cherubim and seraphim falling down be-
    fore thee,
  Which wert and art and evermore shalt be

3 Holy, holy, holy! though the darkness
    hide thee,
  Though the eye of sinful man thy glory
    may not see;
  Only thou art holy; there is none beside
    thee,
  Perfect in power, in love and purity.

4 Holy, holy, holy! Lord God Almighty!
  All thy works shall praise thy name, in
    earth and sky and sea;
  Holy, holy, holy, merciful and mighty;
  God in three persons, blessèd Trinity!

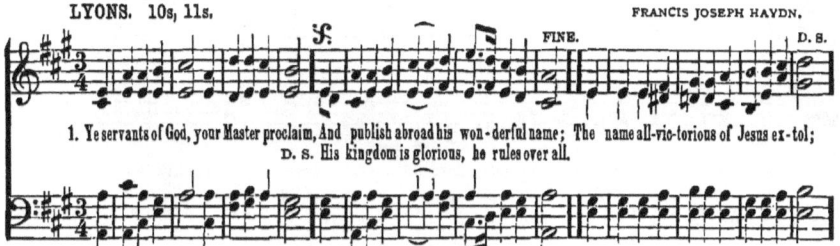

LYONS. 10s, 11s. FRANCIS JOSEPH HAYDN.

1. Ye servants of God, your Master proclaim, And publish abroad his won-derful name; The name all-vic-torious of Jesus ex-tol;
  D. S. His kingdom is glorious, he rules over all.

97 *"Salvation to God."* C. WESLEY.

Ye servants of God, your Master pro-
  claim,
And publish abroad his wonderful name;
The name all-victorious of Jesus extol;
His kingdom is glorious, he rules over all.

2 God ruleth on high, almighty to save;
  And still he is nigh—his presence we have;
  The great congregation his triumph shall
    sing,
  Ascribing salvation to Jesus our King.

3 Salvation to God, who sits on the throne,
  Let all cry aloud and honor the Son;
  The praises of Jesus the angels proclaim,
  Fall down on their faces and worship the
    Lamb.

4 Then let us adore and give him his right,
  All glory, and power, and wisdom and
    might;
  All honor and blessing, with angels above,
  And thanks never ceasing, and infinite love.

98 *"Worship the King."* R. GRANT.

Oh, worship the King, all-glorious above,
And gratefully sing his wonderful love;

Our Shield and Defender, the Ancient of
    days,
Pavilioned in splendor, and girded with
    praise.

2 Oh, tell of his might and sing of his
    grace,
  Whose robe is the light, whose canopy
    space;
  His chariots of wrath the deep thunder-
    clouds form,
  And dark is his path on the wings of the
    storm.

3 Thy bountiful care what tongue can
    recite?
  It breathes in the air, it shines in the light,
  It streams from the hills, it descends to the
    plain,
  And sweetly distils in the dew and the
    rain.

4 Frail children of dust, and feeble as
    frail,
  In thee do we trust, nor find thee to fail;
  Thy mercies how tender! how firm to the
    end!
  Our Maker, Defender, Redeemer and
    Friend.

THE SACRIFICE OF PRAISE.

HAMLIN. 7s. D. J. DOWLAND.

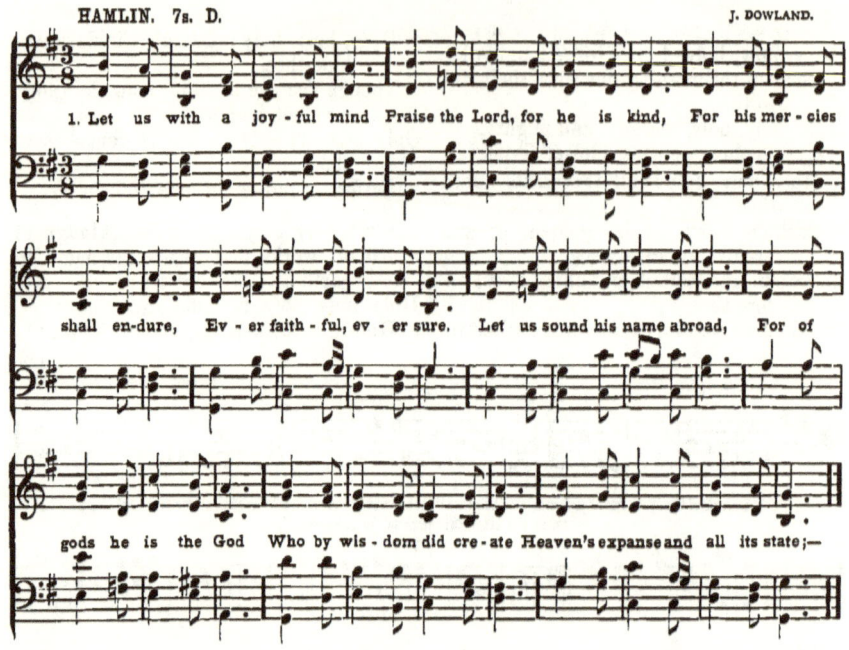

99 *"Ever faithful."* J. MILTON.

Let us with a joyful mind
Praise the Lord, for he is kind,
For his mercies shall endure,
Ever faithful, ever sure.
Let us sound his name abroad,
For of gods he is the God
Who by wisdom did create
Heaven's expanse and all its state;—

2 Did the solid earth ordain
How to rise above the main;
Who, by his commanding might,
Filled the new-made world with light:
Caused the golden-tresséd sun
All the day his course to run;
And the moon to shine by night,
'Mid her spangled sisters bright.

3 All his creatures God doth feed,
His full hand supplies their need;
Let us, therefore, warble forth
His high majesty and worth.
He his mansion hath on high,
'Bove the reach of mortal eye;
And his mercies shall endure,
Ever faithful, ever sure.

100 *Psalm 107.* J. MONTGOMERY.

Thank and praise Jehovah's name;
For his mercies firm and sure,
From eternity the same,
To eternity endure.
Let the ransomed thus rejoice,
Gathered out of every land,
As the people of his choice,
Plucked from the destroyer's hand.

2 In the wilderness astray
Hither, thither, while they roam,
Hungry, fainting by the way,
Far from refuge, shelter, home,—
Then unto the Lord they cry;
He inclines a gracious ear,
Sends deliverance from on high,
Rescues them from all their fear.

3 To a pleasant land he brings,
Where the vine and olive grow,
Where from flowery hills the springs
Through luxuriant valleys flow.
Oh, that men would praise the Lord
For his goodness to their race;
For the wonders of his word,
And the riches of his grace.

THE SACRIFICE OF PRAISE.

ONIDO. 7s, D. LOWELL MASON, arr.

1. God eternal, Lord of all! Lowly at thy feet we fall: All the world doth worship thee; We amidst the throng would be. All the holy angels cry, Hail, thrice-holy, God most high! Lord of all the heavenly pow'rs, Be the same loud anthem ours.

101 *"Te Deum."* J. E. MILLARD, tr.

GOD eternal, Lord of all!
Lowly at thy feet we fall:
All the world doth worship thee;
We amidst the throng would be.
All the holy angels cry,
Hail, thrice-holy, God most high!
Lord of all the heavenly powers,
Be the same loud anthem ours.

2 Glorified apostles raise,
Night and day, continual praise;
Hast thou not a mission too
For thy children here to do?
With the prophets' goodly line
We in mystic bond combine;
For thou hast to babes revealed
Things that to the wise were sealed.

3 Martyrs, in a noble host,
Of thy cross are heard to boast;
Since so bright the crown they wear,
We with them thy cross would bear.
All thy church, in heaven and earth,
Jesus! hail thy spotless birth;—
Seated on the judgment-throne,
Number us among thine own!

102 *"In Excelsis."* C. WESLEY.

GLORY be to God on high,—
God, whose glory fills the sky;
Peace on earth to man forgiven,—
Man, the well-beloved of heaven.
Sovereign Father, Heavenly King!
Thee we now presume to sing;
Glad thine attributes confess,
Glorious all, and numberless.

2 Hail, by all thy works adored!
Hail, the everlasting Lord!
Thee with thankful hearts we prove,—
God of power, and God of love!
Christ our Lord and God we own,—
Christ the Father's only Son;
Lamb of God, for sinners slain,
Saviour of offending man.

3 Jesus! in thy name we pray,
Take, oh, take our sins away!
Powerful Advocate with God!
Justify us by thy blood.
Hear, for thou, O Christ! alone,
Art with thy great Father one;
One the Holy Ghost with thee;—
One supreme eternal Three.

103 7s, D.   *"God on High."*   G. SANDYS.

Thou who art enthroned above,
Thou by whom we live and move!
Oh, how sweet, with joyful tongue,
To resound thy praise in song!
When the morning paints the skies,
When the sparkling stars arise,
All thy favors to rehearse,
And give thanks in grateful verse.

2 Sweet the day of sacred rest,
When devotion fills the breast,
When we dwell within thy house,
Hear thy word, and pay our vows;
Notes to heaven's high mansions raise,
Fill its courts with joyful praise;
With repeated hymns proclaim
Great Jehovah's awful name.

3 From thy works our joys arise,
O thou only good and wise!
Who thy wonders can declare?
How profound thy counsels are!
Warm our hearts with sacred fire;
Grateful fervors still inspire;
All our powers, with all their might,
Ever in thy praise unite.

104 8s, 7s.   *"Praise to Thee."*   J. FAWCETT.

Praise to thee, thou great Creator!
  Praise to thee from every tongue;
Join, my soul, with every creature,
  Join the universal song.

2 Father! source of all compassion!
  Pure, unbounded grace is thine:
Hail the God of our salvation,
  Praise him for his love divine!

3 For ten thousand blessings given,
  For the hope of future joy,
Sound his praise thro' earth and heaven,
  Sound Jehovah's praise on high!

4 Praise to God, the great Creator,
  Father, Son, and Holy Ghost;
Praise him, every living creature,
  Earth and heaven's united host.

5 Joyfully on earth adore him,
  Till in heaven our song we raise;
Then enraptured fall before him,
  Lost in wonder, love, and praise!

105 11s.   *"Alleluia."*   ANON.

Oh, join ye the anthems of triumph that rise
From the throne of the blest, from the hosts of the skies;
Alleluia, they sing in rapturous strains,
Alleluia, the Lord God omnipotent reigns!

2 He gave to the light its beneficent wings;
He controlleth the councils of senates and kings;
From his throne in the clouds the lightnings are hurled,
And he ruleth the factions that rage through the world.

3 Rejoice, ye that love him; his power cannot fail;
His omnipotent goodness shall surely prevail;
The triumph of evil will shortly be passed,
The omnipotent King shall conquer at last.

106 7s, 6s.   *Psalm 150.*   C. WESLEY.

Praise the Lord, who reigns above,
  And keeps his courts below;
Praise him for his boundless love,
  And all his greatness show!
Praise him for his noble deeds;
  Praise him for his matchless power;
Him, from whom all good proceeds,
  Let earth and heaven adore.

2 Publish, spread to all around,
  The great Immanuel's name;
Let the gospel trumpet sound,
  The Prince of Peace proclaim!
Praise him, every tuneful string;
  All the reach of heavenly art,
All the power of music bring,
  The music of the heart.

3 Him, in whom they move and live,
  Let every creature sing;
Glory to our Saviour give,
  And homage to our King:
Hallowed be his name beneath,
  As in heaven, on earth adored;
Praise the Lord in every breath,
  Let all things praise the Lord.

107 7s, d. *Singing to God.* j. montgomery.

Songs of praise the angels sang,
Heaven with hallelujahs rang,
When Jehovah's work begun,
When he spake, and it was done.
Songs of praise awoke the morn,
When the Prince of Peace was born;
Songs of praise arose, when he
Captive led captivity.

2 Heaven and earth must pass away—
Songs of praise shall crown that day;
God will make new heavens and earth—
Songs of praise shall hail their birth.
And shall man alone be dumb,
Till that glorious kingdom come?
No; the Church delights to raise
Psalms and hymns and songs of praise.

3 Saints below, with heart and voice,
Still in songs of praise rejoice;
Learning here, by faith and love,
Songs of praise to sing above.
Borne upon their latest breath
Songs of praise shall conquer death;
Then, amid eternal joy,
Songs of praise their powers employ.

108 c. m. *"Hearts to Pray."* j. newton.

Again our earthly cares we leave,
And to thy courts repair;
Again with joyful feet we come,
To meet our Saviour here.

2 Great Shepherd of thy people, hear!
Thy presence now display;
We bow within thy house of prayer;
Oh, give us hearts to pray!

3 The clouds which vail thee from our sight,
In pity, Lord, remove;
Dispose our minds to hear aright
The message of thy love.

4 The feeling heart, the melting eye,
The humble mind, bestow;
And shine upon us from on high,
To make our graces grow.

5 Show us some token of thy love,
Our fainting hopes to raise;
And pour thy blessing from above,
To aid our feeble praise.

109 l. m. *Psalm 39.* i. watts.

Jehovah reigns; his throne is high;
His robes are light and majesty;
His glory shines with beams so bright,
No mortal can sustain the sight.

2 His terrors keep the world in awe;
His justice guards his holy law;
Yet love reveals a smiling face,
And truth and promise seal the grace.

3 Through all his works his wisdom shines,
And baffles Satan's deep designs;
His power is sovereign to fulfill
The noblest counsels of his will.

4 And will this glorious Lord descend
To be my Father and my Friend?
Then let my songs with angels join;
Heaven is secure, if God be mine.

110 l. m. *"God is Here."* j. wesley, tr.

Lo, God is here!—let us adore!
And own how dreadful is this place!
Let all within us feel his power,
And, silent, bow before his face.

2 Lo, God is here!—him day and night
United choirs of angels sing:
To him, enthroned above all height,
Let saints their humble worship bring.

3 Lord God of hosts! oh, may our praise
Thy courts with grateful incense fill!
Still may we stand before thy face,
Still hear and do thy sovereign will.

111 c. m. *"Light in thy Light."* c. wesley.

Eternal Sun of righteousness,
Display thy beams divine,
And cause the glory of thy face
Upon my heart to shine.

2 Light, in thy light, oh, may I see,
Thy grace and mercy prove,
Revived, and cheered, and blest by thee
The God of pardoning love.

3 Lift up thy countenance serene,
And let thy happy child
Behold, without a cloud between,
The Father reconciled.

4 On me thy promised peace bestow,
The peace by Jesus given;—
The joys of holiness below,
And then the joys of heaven.

CLOSE OF WORSHIP.

112   *"Sun of my soul!"*   J. KEBLE.

SUN of my soul! thou Saviour dear,
It is not night if thou be near:
Oh, may no earth-born cloud arise
To hide thee from thy servant's eyes!

2 When soft the dews of kindly sleep
My wearied eyelids gently steep,
Be my last thought—how sweet to rest
For ever on my Saviour's breast!

3 Abide with me from morn till eve,
For without thee I cannot live;
Abide with me when night is nigh,
For without thee I dare not die.

4 Be near to bless me when I wake,
Ere through the world my way I take;
Abide with me till in thy love
I lose myself in heaven above.

113   *Evening song.*   T. KEN.

GLORY to thee, my God, this night,
For all the blessings of the light;
Keep me, oh, keep me, King of kings!
Beneath thine own almighty wings.

2 Forgive me, Lord, for thy dear Son,
The ill which I this day have done;
That with the world, myself, and thee,
I, ere I sleep, at peace may be.

3 Teach me to live, that I may dread
The grave as little as my bed:
Teach me to die, that so I may
Rise glorious at the judgment-day.

4 Oh, let my soul on thee repose,
And may sweet sleep mine eyelids close!
Sleep, which shall me more vigorous make,
To serve my God when I awake.

OVERBERG. L. M.   J. C. H. RINK.

1. Great God! to thee my evening song With humble gratitude I raise; Oh, let thy mercy tune my tongue, And fill my heart with lively praise.

114   *Twilight.*   A. STEELE.

GREAT God! to thee my evening song
  With humble gratitude I raise;
Oh, let thy mercy tune my tongue,
  And fill my heart with lively praise.

2 My days unclouded as they pass,
  And every gentle, rolling hour,
Are monuments of wondrous grace,
  And witness to thy love and power.

3 Seal my forgiveness in the blood
  Of Jesus; his dear name alone
I plead for pardon, gracious God!
  And kind acceptance at thy throne.

115   *Benediction.*   J. NEWTON.

THE peace which God alone reveals,
  And by his word of grace imparts,
Which only the believer feels,
  Direct, and keep, and cheer our hearts!

2 And may the holy Three in One,
  The Father, Word, and Comforter,
Pour an abundant blessing down
  On every soul assembled here!

3 Praise God, from whom all blessings flow:
  Praise him, all creatures here below;
Praise him above, ye heavenly host!
  Praise Father, Son, and Holy Ghost.

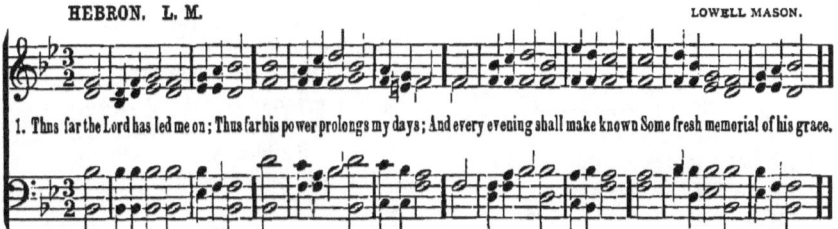

HEBRON. L. M.   LOWELL MASON.

1. Thus far the Lord has led me on; Thus far his power prolongs my days; And every evening shall make known Some fresh memorial of his grace.

116   *Evening.*   I. WATTS.

THUS far the Lord has led me on;
  Thus far his power prolongs my days;
And every evening shall make known
  Some fresh memorial of his grace.

2 Much of my time has run to waste,
  And I, perhaps, am near my home,
But he forgives my follies past,
  And gives me strength for days to come.

3 I lay my body down to sleep;
  Peace is the pillow for my head;
While well-appointed angels keep
  Their watchful stations round my bed.

4 Thus when the night of death shall come,
  My flesh shall rest beneath the ground,
And wait thy voice to break my tomb,
  With sweet salvation in the sound.

117   *Dismissal.*   J. HART.

DISMISS us with thy blessing, Lord!
  Help us to feed upon thy word;
All that has been amiss, forgive,
  And let thy truth within us live.

2 Though we are guilty, thou art good;
  Wash all our works in Jesus' blood;
Give every burdened soul release,
  And bid us all depart in peace.

CLOSE OF WORSHIP.

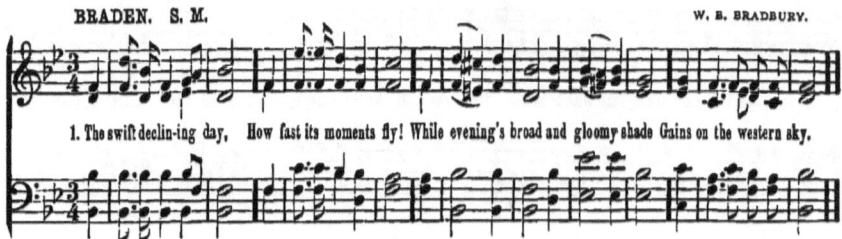

BRADEN. S. M.   W. B. BRADBURY.

1. The swift declin-ing day, How fast its moments fly! While evening's broad and gloomy shade Gains on the western sky.

118   *Evening.*   P. DODDRIDGE.

THE swift declining day,
  How fast its moments fly!
While evening's broad and gloomy shade
  Gains on the western sky.

2 Ye mortals, mark its pace,
  And use the hours of light;
And know, its Maker can command
  At once eternal night.

3 Give glory to the Lord,
  Who rules the whirling sphere;
Submissive at his footstool bow,
  And seek salvation there.

4 Then shall new lustre break
  Through death's impending gloom,
And lead you to unchanging light,
  In your celestial home.

119   *"Abide with us."*   J. M. NEALE.

THE day, O Lord, is spent;
  Abide with us, and rest;
Our hearts' desires are fully bent
  On making thee our guest.

2 We have not reached that land,
  That happy land, as yet,
Where holy angels round thee stand,
  Whose sun can never set.

3 Our sun is sinking now,
  Our day is almost o'er;
O Sun of Righteousness, do thou
  Shine on us evermore!

120   *"Still with thee."*   J. D. BURNS.

STILL, still with thee, my God,
  I would desire to be:
By day, by night, at home, abroad,
  I would be still with thee.

2 With thee when dawn comes in,
  And calls me back to care,
Each day returning to begin
  With thee my God in prayer.

3 With thee when day is done,
  And evening calms the mind;
The setting, as the rising, sun
  With thee my heart would find.

4 With thee, in thee, by faith
  Abiding I would be;
By day, by night, in life, in death,
  I would be still with thee.

121   *Doxology.*   I. WATTS.

To GOD the only wise,
  Who keeps us by his word,
Be glory now and evermore,
  Through Jesus Christ our Lord.

2 Hosanna to the Word,
  Who from the Father came;
Ascribe salvation to the Lord,
  And ever bless his name.

3 The grace of Christ our Lord,
  The Father's boundless love,
The Spirit's blest communion, too,
  Be with us from above.

122   *The final rest.*   W. J. BLEW.

THE day is past and gone,
  Great God, we bow to thee;
Again, as shades of night steal on,
  Unto thy side we flee.

2 Oh, when shall that day come,
  Ne'er sinking in the west,
That country and that happy home,
  Where none shall break our rest;—

3 Where all things shall be peace,
  And pleasure without end,
And golden harps, that never cease,
  With joyous hymns shall blend;—

4 Where we, preserved beneath
  The shelter of thy wing,
For evermore thy praise shall breathe,
  And of thy mercy sing.

CLOSE OF WORSHIP.

EVENING. S. M. — A. CHAPIN.

1. The day is past and gone, The evening shades appear; Oh, may we all re-member well The night of death draws near.

123 *Home Hymn.* J. LELAND.

THE day is past and gone,
 The evening shades appear;
Oh, may we all remember well
 The night of death draws near!

2 We lay our garments by,
 Upon our beds to rest;
So death will soon disrobe us all
 Of what we here possessed.

3 Lord, keep us safe this night,
 Secure from all our fears;
May angels guard us while we sleep,
 Till morning light appears.

4 And when we early rise,
 And view the unwearied sun,
May we set out to win the prize,
 And after glory run.

5 And when our days are past,
 And we from time remove,
Oh, may we in thy bosom rest,
 The bosom of thy love!

124 *"Closing hour."* E. T. FITCH.

LORD, at this closing hour,
 Establish every heart
Upon thy word of truth and power,
 To keep us when we part.

2 Peace to our brethren give;
 Fill all our hearts with love;
In faith and patience may we live,
 And seek our rest above.

3 Through changes, bright or drear,
 We would thy will pursue;
And toil to spread thy kingdom here,
 Till we its glory view.

4 To God, the only wise,
 In every age adored,
Let glory from the church arise
 Through Jesus Christ our Lord!

125 *Sabbath ended.* J. ELLERTON.

THE day of praise is done;
 The evening shadows fall;
Yet pass not from us with the sun,
 True Light that lightenest all!

2 Around thy throne on high,
 Where night can never be,
The white-robed harpers of the sky
 Bring ceaseless hymns to thee.

3 Too faint our anthems here;
 Too soon of praise we tire;
But oh, the strains how full and clear
 Of that eternal choir!

4 Yet, Lord! to thy dear will
 If thou attune the heart,
We in thine angels' music still
 May bear our lower part.

5 Shine thou within us, then,
 A day that knows no end,
Till songs of angels and of men
 In perfect praise shall blend.

126 *At Dismission.* J. HART.

ONCE more, before we part,
 Oh, bless the Saviour's name!
Let every tongue and every heart
 Adore and praise the same.

2 Lord, in thy grace we came,
 That blessing still impart;
We met in Jesus' sacred name,
 In Jesus' name we part.

3 Still on thy holy word
 Help us to feed, and grow,
Still to go on to know the Lord,
 And practice what we know.

4 Now, Lord, before we part,
 Help us to bless thy name:
Let every tongue and every heart
 Adore and praise the same.

EVENTIDE. 10s.   WM. H. MONK.

127   "Abide with us."   H. F. LYTE.

ABIDE with me! Fast falls the eventide,
The darkness deepens—Lord, with me abide!
When other helpers fail, and comforts flee,
Help of the helpless, oh, abide with me!

2 Swift to its close ebbs out life's little day;
Earth's joys grow dim, its glories pass away;
Change and decay in all around I see;
O thou, who changest not, abide with me!

3 I need thy presence every passing hour,
What but thy grace can foil the tempter's power?
Who, like thyself, my guide and stay can be?
Thro' cloud and sunshine, oh, abide with me!

4 Hold thou thy cross before my closing eyes;
Shine through the gloom, and point me to the skies;
Heaven's morning breaks, and earth's vain shadows flee!
In life, in death, O Lord, abide with me!

PAX DEI. 10s.   J. B. DYKES.

128   "Go in peace."   J. ELLERTON.

SAVIOUR, again to thy dear name we raise
With one accord our parting hymn of praise;
We rise to bless thee ere our worship cease,
And now, departing, wait thy word of peace.

2 Grant us thy peace upon our homeward way;
With thee began, with thee shall end the day;
Guard thou the lips from sin, the hearts from shame,
That in this house have called upon thy name.

3 Grant us thy peace, Lord, through the coming night;
Turn thou for us its darkness into light;
From harm and danger keep thy children free,
For dark and light are both alike to thee.

4 Grant us thy peace throughout our earthly life,
Our balm in sorrow, and our stay in strife;
Then, when thy voice shall bid our conflict cease,
Call us, O Lord, to thine eternal peace.

129
Evening. G. W. DOANE.

SOFTLY now the light of day
Fades upon my sight away;
Free from care, from labor free,
Lord, I would commune with thee.

2 Thou, whose all-pervading eye
Naught escapes without, within,
Pardon each infirmity,
Open fault, and secret sin.

3 Soon, for me, the light of day
Shall for ever pass away;
Then, from sin and sorrow free,
Take me, Lord, to dwell with thee.

4 Thou who, sinless, yet hast known
All of man's infirmity;
Then from thine eternal throne,
Jesus, look with pitying eye.

130
"Foretastes." J. MONTGOMERY.

FOR the mercies of the day,
For this rest upon our way,
Thanks to thee alone be given,
Lord of earth and King of heaven!

2 Cold our services have been,
Mingled every prayer with sin:
But thou canst and wilt forgive;
By thy grace alone we live.

3 While this thorny path we tread,
May thy love our footsteps lead;
When our journey here is past,
May we rest with thee at last.

4 Let these earthly Sabbaths prove
Foretastes of our joys above;
While their steps thy children bend
To the rest which knows no end.

CLOSE OF WORSHIP.

NIGHTFALL. 11s, 5s.   J. BARNBY.

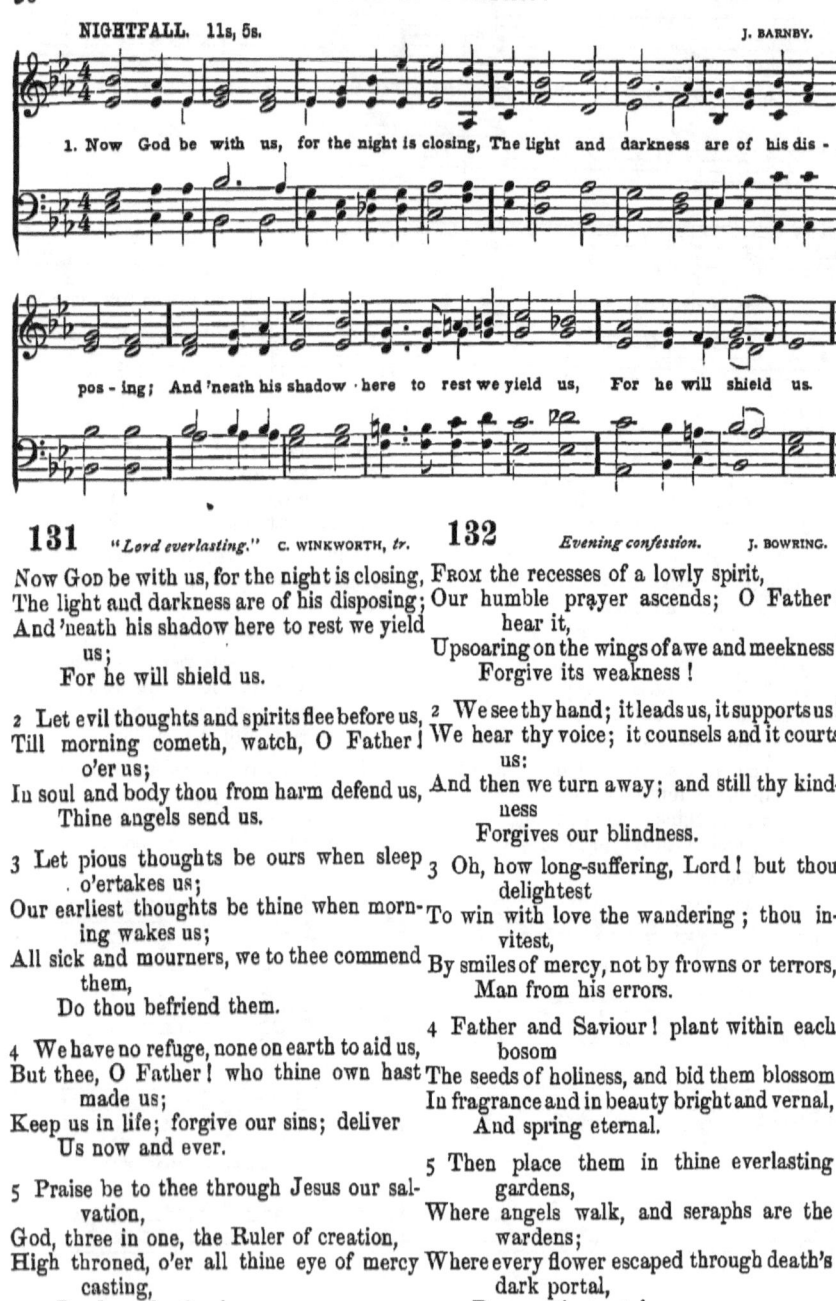

1. Now God be with us, for the night is closing, The light and darkness are of his disposing; And 'neath his shadow here to rest we yield us, For he will shield us.

131   *"Lord everlasting."*   C. WINKWORTH, *tr.*

Now GOD be with us, for the night is closing,
The light and darkness are of his disposing;
And 'neath his shadow here to rest we yield
   us;
   For he will shield us.

2 Let evil thoughts and spirits flee before us,
Till morning cometh, watch, O Father!
   o'er us;
In soul and body thou from harm defend us,
   Thine angels send us.

3 Let pious thoughts be ours when sleep
   o'ertakes us;
Our earliest thoughts be thine when morning wakes us;
All sick and mourners, we to thee commend
   them,
   Do thou befriend them.

4 We have no refuge, none on earth to aid us,
But thee, O Father! who thine own hast
   made us;
Keep us in life; forgive our sins; deliver
   Us now and ever.

5 Praise be to thee through Jesus our salvation,
God, three in one, the Ruler of creation,
High throned, o'er all thine eye of mercy
   casting,
   Lord everlasting!

132   *Evening confession.*   J. BOWRING.

FROM the recesses of a lowly spirit,
Our humble prayer ascends; O Father!
   hear it,
Upsoaring on the wings of awe and meekness!
   Forgive its weakness!

2 We see thy hand; it leads us, it supports us!
We hear thy voice; it counsels and it courts
   us:
And then we turn away; and still thy kindness
   Forgives our blindness.

3 Oh, how long-suffering, Lord! but thou
   delightest
To win with love the wandering; thou invitest,
By smiles of mercy, not by frowns or terrors,
   Man from his errors.

4 Father and Saviour! plant within each
   bosom
The seeds of holiness, and bid them blossom
In fragrance and in beauty bright and vernal,
   And spring eternal.

5 Then place them in thine everlasting
   gardens,
Where angels walk, and seraphs are the
   wardens,
Where every flower escaped through death's
   dark portal,
   Becomes immortal.

133   *"The Last Beam."*   HUNTINGTON.

FADING, still fading, the last beam is shining,
Father in heaven, the day is declining;
Safety and innocence fly with the light,
Temptation and danger walk forth with the night:
From the fall of the shade till the morning bells chime,
Shield me from danger, save me from crime!—REF.

2 Father in heaven, oh, hear when we call!
Hear, for Christ's sake, who is Saviour of all;
Feeble and fainting, we trust in thy might;
In doubting and darkness, thy love be our light;
Let us sleep on thy breast while the night taper burns,
Wake in thine arms when morning returns.—REF.

CLOSE OF WORSHIP.

SEGUR. 8s, 7s, 4s.   J. P. HOLBROOK.

1. Guide me, O thou great Jehovah, Pilgrim through this barren land; I am weak, but thou art mighty; Hold me with thy powerful hand; Bread of heaven, Bread of heaven, Feed me till I want no more.

134   *Guidance.*   P. WILLIAMS.

GUIDE me, O thou great Jehovah,
  Pilgrim through this barren land;
I am weak, but thou art mighty;
  Hold me with thy powerful hand;
    Bread of heaven,
Feed me till I want no more.

2 Open thou the crystal fountain
  Whence the healing streams do flow;
Let the fiery, cloudy pillar
  Lead me all my journey through;
    Strong Deliverer,
Be thou still my Strength and Shield.

3 When I tread the verge of Jordan,
  Bid my anxious fears subside;
Death of death! and hell's Destruction!
  Land me safe on Canaan's side;
    Songs of praises
I will ever give to thee.

135   *"Lead us!"*   J. EDMESTON.

LEAD us, heavenly Father, lead us
  O'er the world's tempestuous sea;
Guard us, guide us, keep us, feed us,
  For we have no help but thee;
    Yet possessing Every blessing,
If our God our Father be.

2 Saviour, breathe forgiveness o'er us;
  All our weakness thou dost know;
Thou didst tread this earth before us;
  Thou didst feel its keenest woe;
    Lone and dreary, Faint and weary,
Through the desert thou didst go.

3 Spirit of our God, descending,
  Fill our hearts with heavenly joy;
Love with every passion blending,
  Pleasure that can never cloy;
    Thus provided, Pardoned, guided,
Nothing can our peace destroy.

OLIPHANT. 8s, 7s, 4s.   LOWELL MASON, arr.

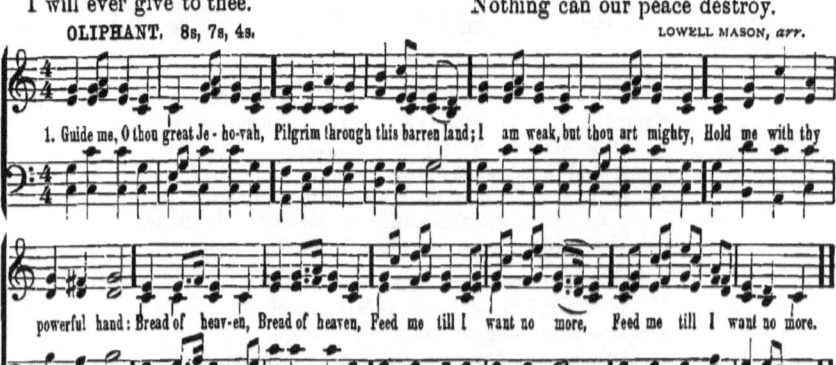

1. Guide me, O thou great Jehovah, Pilgrim through this barren land; I am weak, but thou art mighty, Hold me with thy powerful hand: Bread of heaven, Bread of heaven, Feed me till I want no more, Feed me till I want no more.

CLOSE OF WORSHIP.

GREENVILLE. 8s, 7s, 4s. J. J. ROUSSEAU.

1. Lord, dismiss us with thy blessing, Fill our hearts with joy and peace; Let us each thy love pos-sess-ing,
D. C. Oh, re-fresh us, Oh, re-fresh us, Traveling through this wilderness. Tri-umph in re-deeming (omit) grace;

136 *Dismissal.* J. FAWCETT.
LORD, dismiss us with thy blessing,
  Fill our hearts with joy and peace;
Let us each, thy love possessing,
  Triumph in redeeming grace;
    Oh, refresh us,
  Traveling through this wilderness.

2 Thanks we give, and adoration,
  For thy gospel's joyful sound,
May the fruits of thy salvation
  In our hearts and lives abound;
    May thy presence
  With us evermore be found.

3 So, whene'er the signal's given,
  Us from earth to call away;
Borne on angels' wings to heaven,
  Glad to leave our cumbrous clay,
    May we, ready,
  Rise and reign in endless day.

137 *"Keep us safe."* T. KELLY.
GOD of our salvation! hear us;
  Bless, oh, bless us, ere we go;
When we join the world, be near us,
  Lest we cold and careless grow.
    Saviour! keep us;
  Keep us safe from every foe.

2 As our steps are drawing nearer
  To our everlasting home,
May our view of heaven grow clearer,
  Hope more bright of joys to come;
    And, when dying,
  May thy presence cheer the gloom.

138 *Benediction.* J. NEWTON.
MAY the grace of Christ our Saviour,
  And the Father's boundless love,
With the Holy Spirit's favor,
  Rest upon us from above!

2 Thus may we abide in union
  With each other and the Lord;
And possess in sweet communion,
  Joys which earth cannot afford.

139 *Evening blessing.* J. EDMESTON.
SAVIOUR, breathe an evening blessing,
  Ere repose our spirits seal;
Sin and want we come confessing;
  Thou canst save, and thou canst heal.

2 Though destruction walk around us,
  Though the arrow near us fly,
Angel guards from thee surround us,
  We are safe if thou art nigh.

3 Though the night be dark and dreary,
  Darkness cannot hide from thee;
Thou art he who, never weary,
  Watcheth where thy people be.

4 Should swift death this night o'ertake us,
  And our couch become our tomb,
May the morn in heaven awake us,
  Clad in light and deathless bloom.

STOCKWELL. 8s, 7s. D. E. JONES.

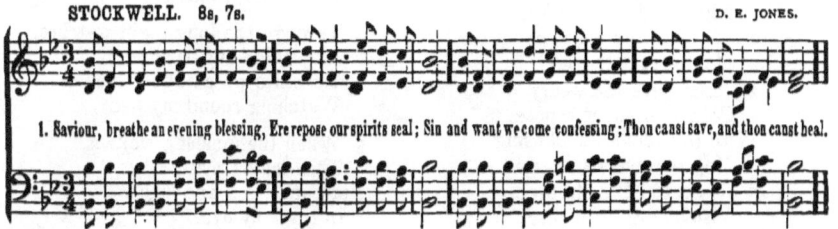

1. Saviour, breathe an evening blessing, Ere repose our spirits seal; Sin and want we come confessing; Thou canst save, and thou canst heal.

CLOSE OF WORSHIP.

140 *"One More Day."*   A. WARNER.

One more day's work for Jesus,
  One less of life for me!
But heaven is nearer, And Christ is dearer,
  Than yesterday, to me;
    His love and light
  Fill all my soul to-night.—CHO.

2 One more day's work for Jesus!
  How sweet the work has been,
To tell the story, To show the glory,
  Where Christ's flock enter in!
    How it did shine
  In this poor heart of mine!—CHO.

3 One more day's work for Jesus—
  Oh, yes, a weary day;
But heaven shines clearer, And rest comes nearer,
  At each step of the way;
    And Christ in all—
  Before his face I fall.—CHO.

4 Oh, blesséd work for Jesus!
  Oh, rest at Jesus' feet!
There toil seems pleasure, My wants are treasure,
  And pain for him is sweet.
    Lord, if I may,
  I'll serve another day!—CHO.

EMMELAR. 6s, 5s.   J. BARNBY.

141 *Day is over.*   S. BARING-GOULD.

Now THE day is over,
  Night is drawing nigh,
Shadows of the evening
  Steal across the sky.

2 Jesus, give the weary
  Calm and sweet repose;
With thy tenderest blessing
  May our eyelids close.

3 Grant to little children
  Visions bright of thee;
Guard the sailors tossing
  On the deep blue sea.

4 Through the long night-watches,
  May thine angels spread
Their white wings above me,
  Watching round my bed.

5 When the morning wakens,
  Then may I arise,
Pure and fresh and sinless
  In thy holy eyes.

CLOSE OF WORSHIP.

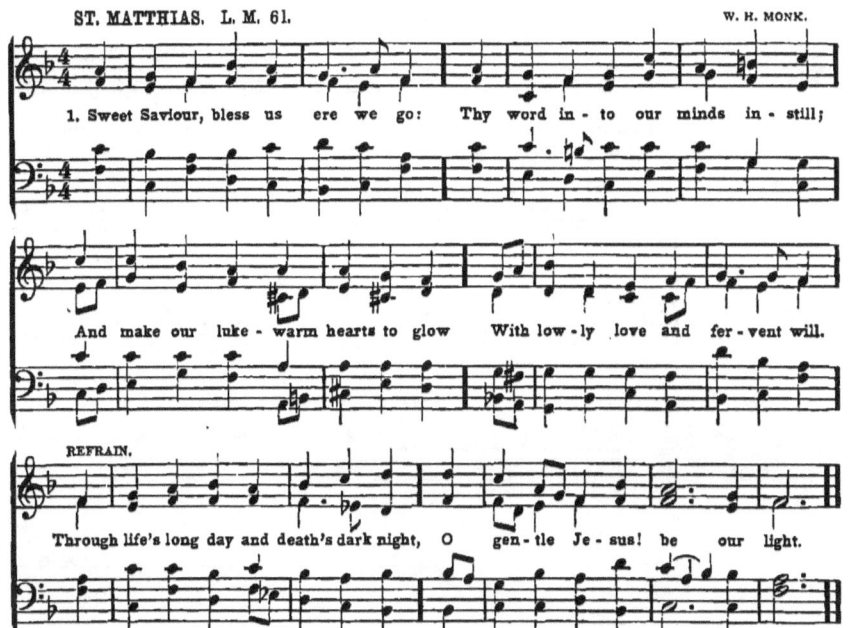

142   *"Ere we go."*   F. W. FABER.

SWEET Saviour, bless us ere we go:
Thy word into our minds instill:
And make our lukewarm hearts to glow
   With lowly love and fervent will.—REF.

2 The day is gone, its hours have run,
And thou hast taken count of all—
The scanty triumphs grace hath won,
   The broken vow, the frequent fall.—REF.

3 Do more than pardon; give us joy,
Sweet fear, and sober liberty,
And simple hearts without alloy
   That only long to be like thee.—REF.

4 For all we love, the poor, the sad,
The sinful, unto thee we call;
Oh, let thy mercy make us glad:
   Thou art our Jesus, and our all.—REF.

THE LORD'S PRAYER.

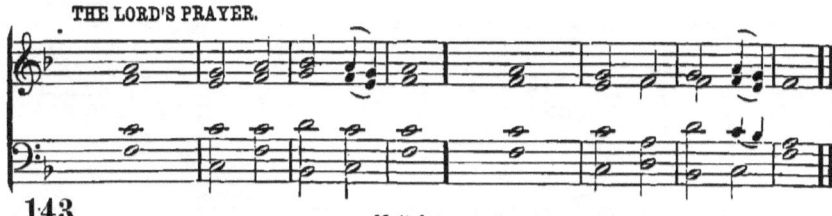

143   *Matt. 6 : 9—13.*

1 OUR FATHER, who art in heaven, | hallowed | be thy | name; || thy kingdom come, thy will be done on | earth, as it | is in | heaven;

2 Give us this | day our | daily | bread; || and forgive us our trespasses, as we forgive | them that | trespass a- | gainst us.

3 And lead us not into temptation, but de- | liver | us from | evil; || for thine is the kingdom, and the power, and the | glory, for- | ever. A- | men.

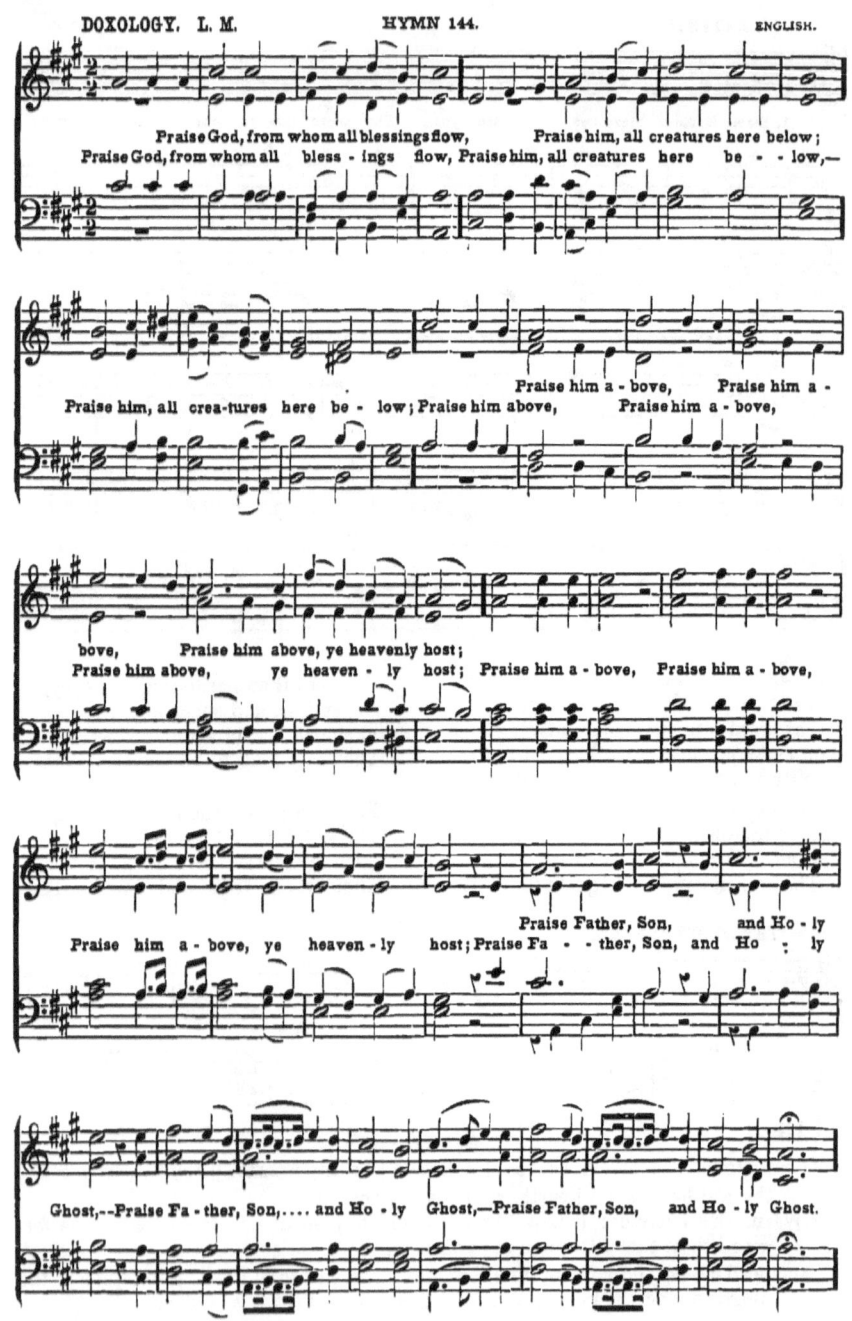

145   'By Galilee."   M. A. LATHBURY.

BREAK thou the bread of life,
  Dear Lord, to me,
As thou didst break the loaves
  Beside the sea;
Beyond the sacred page
  I seek thee, Lord;
My spirit pants for thee,
  O living Word!

2 Bless thou the truth, dear Lord,
  To me—to me—
As thou didst bless the bread
  By Galilee;
Then shall all bondage cease,
  All fetters fall;
And I shall find my peace,
  My All-in-All!

CLOSE OF WORSHIP.

146 S. M. *The Lord's Prayer.* J. MONTGOMERY.
Our Heavenly Father, hear
  The prayer we offer now:—
"Thy name be hallowed far and near,
  To thee all nations bow.

2 "Thy kingdom come; thy will
  On earth be done in love,
As saints and seraphim fulfill
  Thy perfect law above.

3 "Our daily bread supply,
  While by thy word we live;
The guilt of our iniquity
  Forgive, as we forgive.

4 "From dark temptation's power
  Our feeble hearts defend;
Deliver in the evil hour,
  And guide us to the end.

5 "Thine, then, for ever be
  Glory and power divine;
The sceptre, throne, and majesty
  Of heaven and earth are thine."

147 7s. *The Holy Spirit.* C. WESLEY.
Light of life, seraphic Fire,
  Love divine, thyself impart;
Every fainting soul inspire;
  Enter every drooping heart;—

2 Every mournful sinner cheer;
  Scatter all our guilty gloom;
Father! in thy grace appear,
  To thy human temples come.

3 Come, in this accepted hour,
  Bring thy heavenly kingdom in;
Fill us with thy glorious power,
  Set us free from all our sin.

4 Nothing more can we require,
  We will covet nothing less;
Be thou all our heart's desire,
  All our joy, and all our peace.

148 8s, 7s. *Dismissal.* R. HAWKER.
Lord, dismiss us with thy blessing;
  Bid us now depart in peace;
Still on heavenly manna feeding,
  Let our faith and love increase.

2 Fill each breast with consolation;
  Up to thee our hearts we raise;
When we reach our blissful station,
  Then we'll give thee nobler praise.

149 L. M. *Sabbath Eve.* J. EDMESTON.
Sweet is the light of Sabbath eve,
  And soft the sunbeams lingering there;
For these blest hours the world I leave,
  Wafted on wings of faith and prayer.

2 The time, how lovely and how still!
  Peace shines and smiles on all below;
The plain, the stream, the wood, the hill,
  All fair with evening's setting glow.

3 Season of rest! the tranquil soul
  Feels the sweet calm, and melts to love;
And while these sacred moments roll,
  Faith sees the smiling heaven above.

4 Nor will our days of toil be long;
  Our pilgrimage will soon be trod;
And we shall join the ceaseless song,
  The endless Sabbath of our God.

150 H. M. *God's Word.* P. DODDRIDGE.
The promises I sing,
  Which sovereign love hath spoke;
Nor will the Eternal King
  His words of grace revoke;
They stand secure | Not Zion's hill
And steadfast still; | Abides so sure.

2 The mountains melt away
  When once the Judge appears,
And sun and moon decay,
  That measure mortal years;
But still the same,|The promise shines
In radiant lines |Through all the flame.

3 Their harmony shall sound
  Through my attentive ears,
When thunders cleave the ground
  And dissipate the spheres;
Midst all the shock | I stand serene,
Of that dread scene, | Thy word my rock.

151 C. M. *"Hear and Know."* I. WATTS.
Blest are the souls that hear and know
  The gospel's joyful sound;
Peace shall attend the path they go,
  And light their steps surround.

2 Their joy shall bear their spirits up,
  Through their Redeemer's name;
His righteousness exalts their hope,
  Nor Satan dares condemn.

3 The Lord, our glory and defence,
  Strength and salvation gives;
Israel! thy King for ever reigns,
  Thy God for ever lives.

152 7s. *Hymn at Parting.* E. L. FOLLEN.

Thou, from whom we never part,
 Thou, whose love is everywhere,
 Thou, who seest every heart,
  Listen to our evening prayer.

2 Father, fill our hearts with love,
 Love unfailing, full and free;
 Love that no alarm can move,
  Love that ever rests on thee.

3 Heavenly Father! through the night
 Keep us safe from every ill;
 Cheerful as the morning light,
  May we wake to do thy will.

153 8s, 7s, 4s. *"Hear us!"* D. C. COLESWORTHY.

While we lowly bow before thee,
 Wilt thou, gracious Saviour, hear?
We are poor and needy sinners,
 Full of doubt and full of fear;
  Gracious Saviour,
 Make us humble and sincere.

2 Fill us with thy Holy Spirit;
 Sanctify us by thy grace;
Oh, incline us more to love thee,
 And in dust our souls abase.
  Hear us, Saviour,
 And unvail thy glorious face.

3 None in vain did ever ask thee
 For the Spirit of thy love;
Hear us, then, dear Saviour, hear us;
 Grant an answer from above;
  Blessèd Saviour,
 Hear and answer from above.

154 8s, 7s, 4s. *Invocation.* J. PIERPONT.

God Almighty and All-seeing!
 Holy One, in whom we all
Live, and move, and have our being,
 Hear us when on thee we call;
  Father, hear us,
 As before thy throne we fall.

2 Of all good art thou the Giver;
 Weak and wandering ones are we;
Then for ever, yea, for ever,
 In thy presence would we be;
  Oh, be near us,
 That we wander not from thee.

155 7s. *Separation.* J. NEWTON.

For a season called to part,
 Let us now ourselves commend
To the gracious eye and heart
 Of our ever present Friend.

2 Jesus! hear our humble prayer,
 Tender Shepherd of thy sheep!
Let thy mercy and thy care
 All our souls in safety keep.

3 Then if thou thy help afford,
 Joyful songs to thee shall rise,
And our souls shall praise the Lord,
 Who regards our humble cries.

156 S. M. *"Bless the Lord!"* J. MONTGOMERY.

Stand up, and bless the Lord,
 Ye people of his choice;
Stand up and bless the Lord your God,
 With heart and soul and voice.

2 Though high above all praise,
 Above all blessing high,
Who would not fear his holy name,
 And laud, and magnify?

3 Oh, for the living flame
 From his own altar brought,
To touch our lips, our souls inspire,
 And wing to heaven our thought!

4 God is our strength and song,
 And his salvation ours:
Then be his love in Christ proclaimed,
 With all our ransomed powers.

5 Stand up, and bless the Lord;
 The Lord your God adore;
Stand up, and bless his glorious name,
 Henceforth, for evermore.

157 8s, 7s, 4s. *"Lord, keep us."* T. KELLY.

Keep us, Lord, oh, keep us ever:
 Vain our hope, if left by thee;
We are thine; oh, leave us never,
 Till thy glorious face we see;
  Then to praise thee
 Through a bright eternity.

2 Precious is thy word of promise,
 Precious to thy people here;
Never take thy presence from us,
 Jesus, Saviour, still be near:
  Living, dying,
 May thy name our spirits cheer.

THE SCRIPTURES.

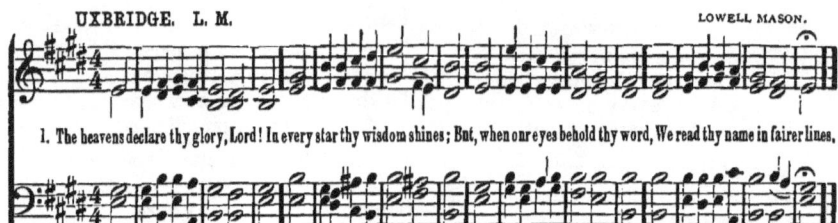

UXBRIDGE. L. M.   LOWELL MASON.

1. The heavens declare thy glory, Lord! In every star thy wisdom shines; But, when our eyes behold thy word, We read thy name in fairer lines.

158   Psalm 19.   I. WATTS.

The heavens declare thy glory, Lord!
  In every star thy wisdom shines;
But, when our eyes behold thy word,
  We read thy name in fairer lines.

2 The rolling sun, the changing light,
  And nights and days thy power confess;
But the blest volume thou hast writ
  Reveals thy justice and thy grace.

3 Sun, moon, and stars convey thy praise
  Round the whole earth, and never stand;
So, when thy truth began its race,
  It touched and glanced on every land.

4 Nor shall thy spreading gospel rest,
  Till through the world thy truth has run,
Till Christ has all the nations blessed,
  That see the light, or feel the sun.

5 Great Sun of righteousness! arise;
  Bless the dark world with heavenly light;
Thy gospel makes the simple wise,
  Thy laws are pure, thy judgments right.

6 Thy noblest wonders here we view,
  In souls renewed, and sins forgiven:
Lord! cleanse my sins, my soul renew,
  And make thy word my guide to heaven.

159   Inspiration.   I. WATTS.

'Twas by an order from the Lord
The ancient prophets spoke his word!
His Spirit did their tongues inspire,
And warmed their hearts with heavenly fire.

2 The works and wonders which they wrought
Confirmed the messages they brought:
The prophet's pen succeeds his breath,
To save the holy words from death.

3 Great God, mine eyes with pleasure look
On the dear volume of thy book;
There my Redeemer's face I see,
And read his name who died for me.

160   The Gospel Word.   B. BEDDOME.

God, in the gospel of his Son,
Makes his eternal counsels known:
Where love in all its glory shines,
And truth is drawn in fairest lines.

2 Here sinners, of an humble frame,
May taste his grace, and learn his name;
May read, in characters of blood,
The wisdom, power, and grace of God.

3 The prisoner here may break his chains;
The weary rest from all his pains;
The captive feel his bondage cease;
The mourner find the way of peace.

4 Here faith reveals to mortal eyes
A brighter world beyond the skies;
Here shines the light which guides our way
From earth to realms of endless day.

5 Oh, grant us grace, Almighty Lord,
To read and mark thy holy word;
Its truth with meekness to receive,
And by its holy precepts live.

161   Psalm 19.   R. GRANT.

The starry firmament on high,
And all the glories of the sky,
Yet shine not to thy praise, O Lord,
So brightly as thy written word.

2 The hopes that holy word supplies,
Its truths divine and precepts wise,
In each a heavenly beam I see,
And every beam conducts to thee.

3 Almighty Lord, the sun shall fail,
The moon forget her nightly tale,
And deepest silence hush on high
The radiant chorus of the sky;—

4 But fixed for everlasting years,
Unmoved, amid the wreck of spheres,
Thy word shall shine in cloudless day,
When heaven and earth have passed away.

THE SCRIPTURES.

WILLINGTON. L. M. — GREATOREX COLL.

1. Now let my soul, eternal King, To thee its grateful tribute bring; My knee with humble homage bow, My tongue perform its solemn vow.

162   *"Nature sings."*   O. HEGINBOTHAM.

Now let my soul, eternal King,
To thee its grateful tribute bring;
My knee with humble homage bow,
My tongue perform its solemn vow.

2 All nature sings thy boundless love,
In worlds below and worlds above;
But in thy blesséd word I trace
Diviner wonders of thy grace.

3 Here Jesus bids my sorrows cease,
And gives my laboring conscience peace;
Here lifts my grateful passions high,
And points to mansions in the sky.

4 For love like this, oh, let my song,
Through endless years, thy praise prolong;
Let distant climes thy name adore,
Till time and nature are no more.

CAPELLO. L. M. — RUDOLF KREUTZER.

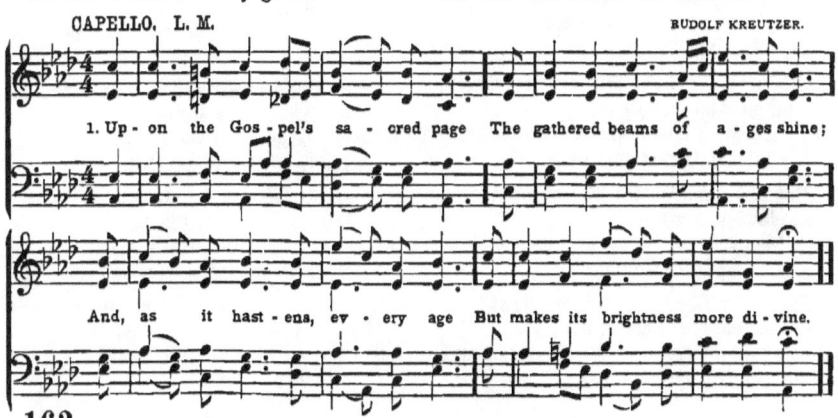

1. Upon the Gospel's sacred page The gathered beams of ages shine; And, as it hastens, every age But makes its brightness more divine.

163   *"And be glorified."*   J. BOWRING.

Upon the Gospel's sacred page
The gathered beams of ages shine;
And, as it hastens, every age
But makes its brightness more divine.

2 On mightier wing, in loftier flight,
From year to year does knowledge soar;
And, as it soars, the Gospel light
Becomes effulgent more and more.

3 More glorious still, as centuries roll,
New regions blest, new powers unfurled,
Expanding with the expanding soul,
Its radiance shall o'erflow the world,—

4 Flow to restore, but not destroy;
As when the cloudless lamp of day
Pours out its floods of light and joy,
And sweeps the lingering mist away.

THE SCRIPTURES.

HAVEN. C. M. — THOS. HASTINGS.

1. Thou lovely Source of true delight, Whom I unseen adore! Unvail thy beauties to my sight, That I may love thee more.

164 *Christ in the Word.* A. STEELE.

THOU lovely Source of true delight,
  Whom I unseen adore!
Unvail thy beauties to my sight,
  That I may love thee more.

2 Thy glory o'er creation shines;—
  But in thy sacred word,
I read, in fairer, brighter lines,
  My bleeding, dying Lord.

3 'Tis here, whene'er my comforts droop,
  And sin and sorrow rise,
Thy love, with cheering beams of hope,
  My fainting heart supplies.

4 But ah! too soon the pleasing scene
  Is clouded o'er with pain;
My gloomy fears rise dark between,
  And I again complain.

5 Jesus, my Lord, my life, my light!
  Oh, come with blissful ray;
Break radiant through the shades of night,
  And chase my fears away.

6 Then shall my soul with rapture trace
  The wonders of thy love:
But the full glories of thy face
  Are only known above.

165 *Psalm 119.* J. FAWCETT.

How PRECIOUS is the book divine,
  By inspiration given!
Bright as a lamp its doctrines shine,
  To guide our souls to heaven.

2 O'er all the strait and narrow way
  Its radiant beams are cast;
A light whose never weary ray
  Grows brightest at the last.

3 It sweetly cheers our drooping hearts,
  In this dark vale of tears;
Life, light, and joy it still imparts,
  And quells our rising fears.

4 This lamp, through all the tedious night
  Of life, shall guide our way,
Till we behold the clearer light
  Of an eternal day.

KNOX. C. M. — TEMPLE MELODIES.

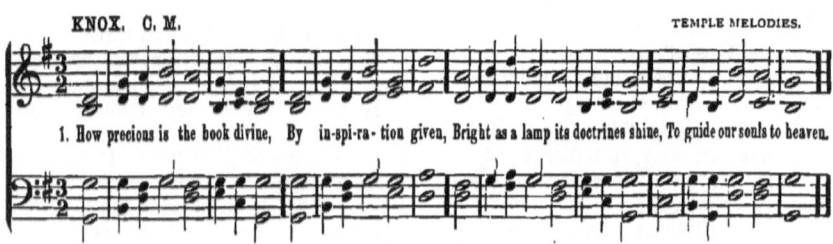

1. How precious is the book divine, By in-spi-ra-tion given, Bright as a lamp its doctrines shine, To guide our souls to heaven.

THE SCRIPTURES.

ELIZABETHTOWN. C. M.   GEORGE KINGSLEY.

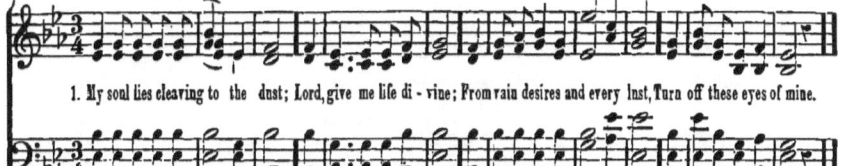

1. My soul lies cleaving to the dust; Lord, give me life di-vine; From vain desires and every lust, Turn off these eyes of mine.

166   *Psalm 119.*   I. WATTS.

My soul lies cleaving to the dust;
  Lord, give me life divine;
From vain desires and every lust,
  Turn off these eyes of mine.

2 I need the influence of thy grace
  To speed me in thy way,
Lest I should loiter in my race
  Or turn my feet astray.

3 Are not thy mercies sovereign still,
  And thou a faithful God?
Wilt thou not grant me warmer zeal
  To run the heavenly road?

4 Does not my heart thy precepts love,
  And long to see thy face?
And yet how slow my spirits move
  Without enlivening grace!

5 Then shall I love thy gospel more,
  And ne'er forget thy word,
When I have felt its quickening power
  To draw me near the Lord.

167   *Dull of Heart.*   I. WATTS.

Laden with guilt, and full of fears,
  I fly to thee, my Lord,
And not a glimpse of hope appears,
  But in thy written word.

2 This is the field where hidden lies
  The pearl of price unknown;
That merchant is divinely wise,
  Who makes the pearl his own.

3 This is the judge that ends the strife,
  Where wit and reason fail;
My guide to everlasting life,
  Through all this gloomy vale.

4 Oh, may thy counsels, mighty God!
  My roving feet command;
Nor I forsake the happy road,
  That leads to thy right hand.

168   *Psalm 119.*   I. WATTS.

Oh, how I love thy holy law!
  'Tis daily my delight;
And thence my meditations draw
  Divine advice by night.

2 How doth thy word my heart engage!
  How well employ my tongue!
And in my tiresome pilgrimage
  Yields me a heavenly song.

3 Am I a stranger, or at home,
  'Tis my perpetual feast:
Not honey dropping from the comb,
  So much allures the taste.

4 No treasures so enrich the mind,
  Nor shall thy word be sold
For loads of silver well-refined,
  Nor heaps of choicest gold.

5 When nature sinks, and spirits droop,
  Thy promises of grace
Are pillars to support my hope,
  And there I write thy praise.

169   *Psalm 119.*   I. WATTS.

Lord! I have made thy word my choice,
  My lasting heritage;
There shall my noblest powers rejoice,
  My warmest thoughts engage.

2 I'll read the histories of thy love,
  And keep thy laws in sight,
While through the promises I rove,
  With ever-fresh delight.

3 'Tis a broad land of wealth unknown,
  Where springs of life arise;
Seeds of immortal bliss are sown,
  And hidden glory lies:—

4 The best relief that mourners have;
  It makes our sorrows blest:—
Our fairest hope beyond the grave,
  And our eternal rest.

THE SCRIPTURES.

IOLA. C. M.
D. G. MASON.

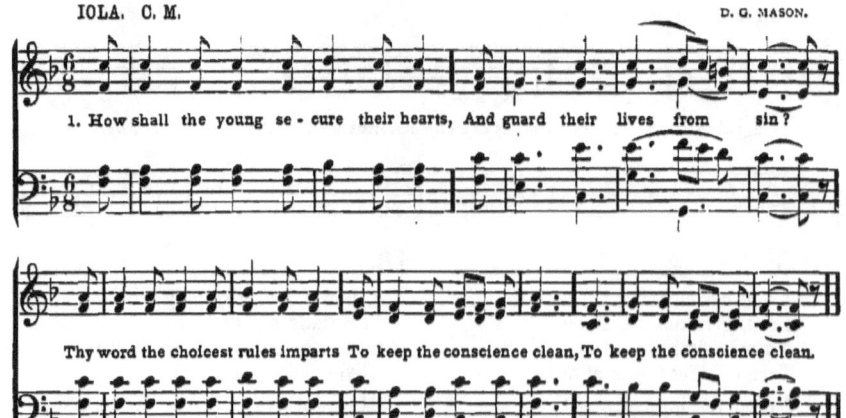

1. How shall the young secure their hearts, And guard their lives from sin? Thy word the choicest rules imparts To keep the conscience clean, To keep the conscience clean.

170 *Psalm* 119.   I. WATTS.

How shall the young secure their hearts,
And guard their lives from sin?
Thy word the choicest rules imparts
To keep the conscience clean.

2 When once it enters to the mind,
It spreads such light abroad;
The meanest souls instruction find,
And raise their thoughts to God.

3 'Tis like the sun, a heavenly light,
That guides us all the day;
And, through the dangers of the night,
A lamp to lead our way.

4 Thy precepts make me truly wise;
I hate the sinner's road;
I hate my own vain thoughts that rise,
But love thy law, my God!

5 Thy word is everlasting truth;
How pure is every page!
That holy book shall guide our youth,
And well support our age.

171 *Psalm* 119.   I. WATTS.

Oh, that the Lord would guide my ways
To keep his statutes still:
Oh, that my God would grant me grace
To know and do his will.

2 Oh, send thy Spirit down, to write
Thy law upon my heart;
Nor let my tongue indulge deceit,
Or act the liar's part.

3 From vanity turn off my eyes;
Let no corrupt design,
Nor covetous desires, arise
Within this soul of mine.

4 Order my footsteps by thy word,
And make my heart sincere;
Let sin have no dominion, Lord!
But keep my conscience clear.

5 Make me to walk in thy commands—
'Tis a delightful road;
Nor let my head, or heart, or hands,
Offend against my God.

YORK. C. M.
SCOTCH PSALTER.

1. Oh, that the Lord would guide my ways To keep his statutes still; Oh, that my God would grant me grace To know and do his will.

THE SCRIPTURES

CHIMES. C. M. — LOWELL MASON.

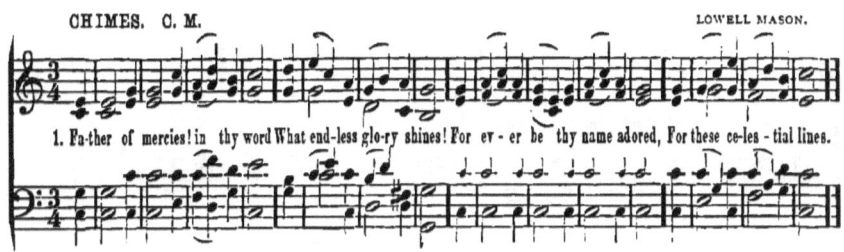

1. Fa-ther of mercies! in thy word What end-less glo-ry shines! For ev-er be thy name adored, For these ce-les-tial lines.

172   *"Endless glory."*   A. STEELE.

Father of mercies! in thy word
What endless glory shines!
For ever be thy name adored.
For these celestial lines.

2 Here, the fair tree of knowledge grows,
And yields a free repast;
Sublimer sweets than nature knows
Invite the longing taste.

3 Here, the Redeemer's welcome voice
Spreads heavenly peace around;
And life and everlasting joys
Attend the blissful sound.

4 Oh, may these heavenly pages be
My ever dear delight;
And still new beauties may I see,
And still increasing light.

5 Divine Instructor, gracious Lord!
Be thou for ever near;
Teach me to love thy sacred word,
And view my Saviour there.

173   *Psalm 119.*   W. COWPER.

The Spirit breathes upon the word,
And brings the truth to sight;
Precepts and promises afford
A sanctifying light.

2 A glory gilds the sacred page,
Majestic, like the sun;
It gives a light to every age;—
It gives, but borrows none.

3 The hand, that gave it, still supplies
The gracious light and heat;
Its truths upon the nations rise,—
They rise, but never set.

4 Let everlasting thanks be thine,
For such a bright display,
As makes a world of darkness shine
With beams of heavenly day.

5 My soul rejoices to pursue
The steps of him I love,
Till glory breaks upon my view,
In brighter worlds above.

DEVIZES. C. M. — I. TUCKER.

1. The Spirit breathes up-on the word, And brings the truth to sight; Pre-cepts and prom-is-es af-ford A sanc-ti-fy-ing light, A sanc-ti-fy-ing light.

THE SCRIPTURES.

CHENIES. 7s, 6s. D.   T. R. MATTHEWS.

1. O Word of God in-car-nate, O Wis-dom from on high, O Truth unchanged, un-chang-ing, O Light of our dark sky! We praise thee for the ra-diance That from the hal-lowed page, A lan-tern to our foot-steps, Shines on from age to age.

174   *The Church's Gift.*   W. W. HOW.

O WORD of God incarnate,
  O Wisdom from on high,
O Truth unchanged, unchanging,
  O Light of our dark sky!
We praise thee for the radiance
  That from the hallowed page,
A lantern to our footsteps,
  Shines on from age to age.

2 The Church from her dear Master
  Received the gift divine,
And still that light she lifteth
  O'er all the earth to shine.
It is the golden casket
  Where gems of truth are stored,
It is the heaven-drawn picture
  Of Christ the living Word.

3 Oh, make thy Church, dear Saviour,
  A lamp of burnished gold,
To bear before the nations
  Thy true light as of old;
Oh, teach thy wandering pilgrims
  By this their path to trace,
Till, clouds and darkness ended,
  They see thee face to face.

175   *Psalm 19.*   J. CONDER.

THE heavens declare his glory,
  Their Maker's skill the skies;
Each day repeats the story,
  And night to night replies.
Their silent proclamation
  Throughout the earth is heard;
The record of creation,
  The page of nature's word.

2 So pure, so soul-restoring,
  Is truth's diviner ray;
A brighter radiance pouring
  Than all the pomp of day:
The wanderer surely guiding,
  It makes the simple wise;
And, evermore abiding,
  Unfailing joy supplies.

3 Thy word is richer treasure
  Than lurks within the mine;
And daintiest fare less pleasure
  Yields than this food divine.
How wise each kind monition!
  Led by thy counsels, Lord,
How safe the saints' condition,
  How great is their reward!

GOD:—ATTRIBUTES.

MIRIAM. 7s & 6s. D.   J. P. HOLBROOK.

1. O God, the Rock of Ages, Who evermore hast been, What time the tempest rages,
Our dwelling-place serene: Before thy first creations, O Lord, the same as now,
D.S.—To endless generations, The Everlasting thou!

176   *Everlasting.—Ps. 90.*   E. BICKERSTETH.

O GOD, the Rock of Ages,
Who evermore hast been,
What time the tempest rages,
Our dwelling-place serene:
Before thy first creations,
O Lord, the same as now,
To endless generations,
The Everlasting thou!

2 Our years are like the shadows
On sunny hills that lie,
Or grasses in the meadows
That blossom but to die:
A sleep, a dream, a story,
By strangers quickly told,
An unremaining glory
Of things that soon are old.

3 O thou who canst not slumber,
Whose light grows never pale,
Teach us aright to number
Our years before they fail!
On us thy mercy lighten,
On us thy goodness rest,
And let thy Spirit brighten
The hearts thyself hast blessed!

177   *Omnipresent.*   DUTCH HYMN.

ON mountains and in valleys
Where'er we go is God;
The cottage and the palace,
Alike are his abode.
With watchful eye abiding
Upon us with delight;
Our souls, in him confiding,
He keeps both day and night.

2 Above me and beside me,
My God is ever near,
To watch, protect, and guide me,
Whatever ills appear.
Though other friends may fail me;
In sorrow's dark abode,
Though death itself assail me,
I'm ever safe with God.

178   *Sovereign Love.*   J. CONDER.

'TIS NOT that I did choose thee,
For, Lord! that could not be;
This heart would still refuse thee;
But thou hast chosen me;—
Hast, from the sin that stained me,
Washed me and set me free,
And to this end ordained me,
That I should live to thee.

2 'Twas sovereign mercy called me,
And taught my opening mind;
The world had else enthralled me,
To heavenly glories blind.
My heart owns none above thee;
For thy rich grace I thirst;
This knowing,—if I love thee,
Thou must have loved me first.

GOD:—THE FATHER.

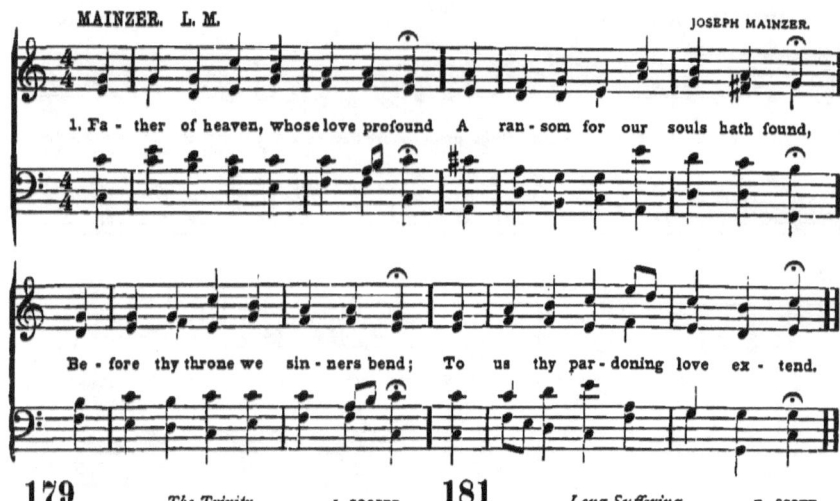

MAINZER. L. M.   JOSEPH MAINZER.

1. Father of heaven, whose love profound / A ransom for our souls hath found, / Before thy throne we sinners bend; / To us thy pardoning love extend.

179   *The Trinity.*   J. COOPER.

Father of heaven, whose love profound
A ransom for our souls hath found,
Before thy throne we sinners bend;
To us thy pardoning love extend.

2 Almighty Son—incarnate Word—
Our Prophet, Priest, Redeemer, Lord!
Before thy throne we sinners bend;
To us thy saving grace extend.

3 Eternal Spirit! by whose breath
The soul is raised from sin and death,—
Before thy throne we sinners bend;
To us thy quickening power extend.

4 Jehovah!—Father, Spirit, Son!
Mysterious Godhead!—Three in One!
Before thy throne we sinners bend;
Grace, pardon, life to us extend.

180   *Unsearchableness.*   E. BUTCHER.

With deepest reverence at thy throne,
Jehovah, peerless and unknown!
Our feeble spirits strive, in vain,
A glimpse of thee, great God! to gain.

2 Who, by the closest search, can find
The eternal, uncreated Mind?
Nor men, nor angels can explore
Thy heights of love, thy depths of power.

3 That power we trace on every side;
Oh, may thy wisdom be our guide!
And while we live, and when we die,
May thine almighty love be nigh.

181   *Long-Suffering.*   E. SCOTT.

God of my life, to thee belong
The grateful heart, the joyful song;
Touched by thy love, each tuneful chord
Resounds the goodness of the Lord.

2 Yet why, dear Lord, this tender care?
Why doth thy hand so kindly rear
A useless cumberer of the ground,
On which so little fruit is found?

3 Still let the barren fig-tree stand
Upheld and fostered by thy hand;
And let its fruit and verdure be
A grateful tribute, Lord, to thee.

182   *Mystery.*   B. BEDDOME.

Wait, O my soul! thy Maker's will;
Tumultuous passions, all be still!
Nor let a murmuring thought arise;
His ways are just, his counsels wise.

2 He in the thickest darkness dwells,
Performs his work, the cause conceals;
But, though his methods are unknown,
Judgment and truth support his throne.

3 In heaven, and earth, and air, and seas,
He executes his firm decrees;
And by his saints it stands confessed,
That what he does is ever best.

4 Wait, then, my soul! submissive wait,
Prostrate before his awful seat;
And, 'mid the terrors of his rod,
Trust in a wise and gracious God.

ATTRIBUTES.

CREATION. L. M. D.   F. J. HAYDN.

1. { The spacious firma-ment on high, With all the blue e-the-real sky, }
   { And spangled heavens, a shining frame, Their great O-rig-i-nal (Omit)... } pro-claim:

Th' unwea-ried sun, from day to day, Does his Cre-a-tor's power dis-play;

And pub-lish-es to ev-'ry land The work of an al-might-y hand.

183   *In Nature.—Ps.* 19.   J. ADDISON.

THE spacious firmament on high,
With all the blue ethereal sky,
And spangled heavens, a shining frame,
Their great Original proclaim:
The unwearied sun, from day to day,
Does his Creator's power display;
And publishes to every land
The work of an almighty hand.

2 Soon as the evening shades prevail,
The moon takes up the wondrous tale;
And nightly, to the listening earth,
Repeats the story of her birth;
While all the stars that round her burn,
And all the planets in their turn,
Confirm the tidings as they roll,
And spread the truth from pole to pole.

3 What though in solemn silence, all
Move round the dark terrestrial ball,—
What though no real voice nor sound
Amid their radiant orbs be found,—
In reason's ear they all rejoice,
And utter forth a glorious voice,
For ever singing as they shine,—
"The hand that made us is divine."

184   *In the Seasons.*   P. DODDRIDGE.

ETERNAL Source of every joy,
Well may thy praise our lips employ,
While in thy temple we appear,
To hail thee, sovereign of the year!
Wide as the wheels of nature roll,
Thy hand supports and guides the whole,
The sun is taught by thee to rise,
And darkness when to vail the skies.

2 The flowery spring at thy command,
Perfumes the air, adorns the land;
The summer rays with vigor shine,
To raise the corn, to cheer the vine.
Thy hand, in autumn, richly pours,
Through all our coasts redundant stores:
And winters, softened by thy care,
No more the face of horror wear.

3 Seasons and months, and weeks and days,
Demand successive songs of praise;
And be the grateful homage paid,
With morning light and evening shade.
Here in thy house let incense rise,
And circling Sabbaths bless our eyes,
Till to those lofty heights we soar,
Where days and years revolve no more.

GOD:—THE FATHER.

185 *Providence.* H. M. WILLIAMS.

WHILE thee I seek, protecting Power!
 Be my vain wishes stilled;
And may this consecrated hour
 With better hopes be filled;
Thy love the power of thought bestowed;
 To thee my thoughts would soar:
Thy mercy o'er my life has flowed;
 That mercy I adore.

2 In each event of life how clear
 Thy ruling hand I see!
Each blessing to my soul more dear
 Because conferred by thee.
In every joy that crowns my days,
 In every pain I bear,
My heart shall find delight in praise
 Or seek relief in prayer.

3 When gladness wings my favored hour,
 Thy love my thoughts shall fill;
Resigned, when storms of sorrow lower,
 My soul shall meet thy will.

My lifted eye, without a tear,
 The gathering storm shall see;
My steadfast heart shall know no fear;
 That heart will rest on thee.

186 *Psalm 116.* I. WATTS.

WHAT shall I render to my God,
 For all his kindness shown?
My feet shall visit thine abode,
 My songs address thy throne.

2 Among the saints that fill thine house,
 My offering shall be paid;
There shall my zeal perform the vows,
 My soul in anguish made.

3 How much is mercy thy delight,
 Thou ever blessèd God!
How dear thy servants in thy sight!
 How precious is their blood!

4 How happy all thy servants are!
 How great thy grace to me!
My life, which thou hast made thy care,
 Lord, I devote to thee.

ATTRIBUTES. 71

187 *Continued help.* J. ADDISON.
WHEN all thy mercies, O my God!
My rising soul surveys,
Transported with the view, I'm lost
In wonder, love, and praise.

2 Unnumbered comforts, to my soul,
Thy tender care bestowed,
Before my infant heart conceived
From whom those comforts flowed.

3 When, in the slippery paths of youth,
With heedless steps, I ran,
Thine arm, unseen, conveyed me safe,
And led me up to man.

4 Ten thousand thousand precious gifts
My daily thanks employ;
Nor is the least a cheerful heart,
That tastes those gifts with joy.

5 Through every period of my life,
Thy goodness I'll pursue;
And after death, in distant worlds,
The glorious theme renew.

6 Through all eternity, to thee
A joyful song I'll raise:
For, oh, eternity's too short
To utter all thy praise!

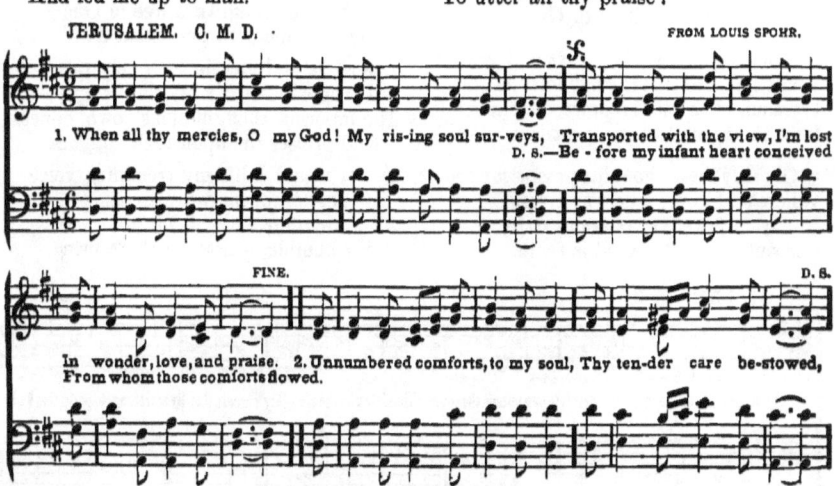

GOD:—THE FATHER.

TRURO. L. M. — CHARLES BURNEY.

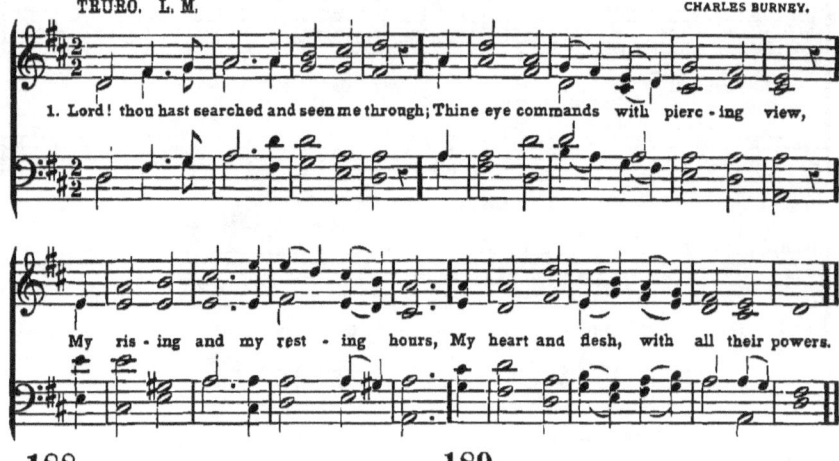

1. Lord! thou hast searched and seen me through; Thine eye commands with piercing view, My rising and my resting hours, My heart and flesh, with all their powers.

188   *Omniscience.—Ps. 139.*   I. WATTS.

LORD! thou hast searched and seen me thro';
Thine eye commands, with piercing view,
My rising and my resting hours,
My heart and flesh, with all their powers.

2 My thoughts, before they are my own,
Are to my God distinctly known;
He knows the words I mean to speak,
Ere from my opening lips they break.

3 Within thy circling power I stand;
On every side I find thy hand;
Awake, asleep, at home, abroad,
I am surrounded still with God.

4 Amazing knowledge, vast and great!
What large extent! what lofty height!
My soul, with all the powers I boast,
Is in the boundless prospect lost.

5 Oh, may these thoughts possess my breast,
Where'er I rove, where'er I rest;
Nor let my weaker passions dare
Consent to sin, for God is there.

189   *Faithfulness.*   I. WATTS.

OH, for a strong, a lasting faith
To credit what the Almighty saith!
To embrace the message of his Son!
And call the joys of heaven our own!

2 Then, should the earth's old pillars shake,
And all the wheels of nature break,
Our steady souls should fear no more
Than solid rocks when billows roar.

190   *Unsearchableness.*   E. SCOTT.

WHAT finite power, with ceaseless toil,
Can fathom the eternal Mind?
Or who the almighty Three in One
By searching, to perfection find?

2 Angels and men in vain may raise,
Harmonious their adoring songs;
The laboring thought sinks down, opprest,
And praises die upon their tongues.

3 Yet would I lift my trembling voice
A portion of his ways to sing;
And mingling with his meanest works,
My humble, grateful tribute bring.

FOREST. L. M. — A. CHAPIN.

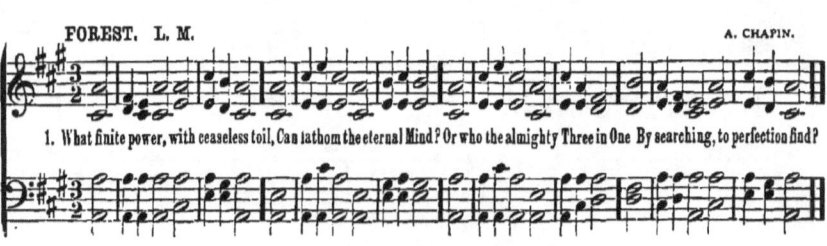

1. What finite power, with ceaseless toil, Can fathom the eternal Mind? Or who the almighty Three in One By searching, to perfection find?

ATTRIBUTES.

LOUVAN. L. M. V. C. TAYLOR.

1. Lord of all be-ing; throned a-far, Thy glo-ry flames from sun and star; Cen-tre and soul of ev-ery sphere, Yet to each lov-ing heart how near!

191 *Omnipresence.* O. W. HOLMES.

Lord of all being; throned afar,
Thy glory flames from sun and star;
Centre and soul of every sphere,
Yet to each loving heart how near!

2 Sun of our life, thy quickening ray
Sheds on our path the glow of day;
Star of our hope, thy softened light
Cheers the long watches of the night.

3 Our midnight is thy smile withdrawn;
Our noontide is thy gracious dawn;
Our rainbow arch thy mercy's sign;
All, save the clouds of sin, are thine!

4 Lord of all life, below, above,
Whose light is truth, whose warmth is love,
Before thy ever-blazing throne
We ask no lustre of our own.

5 Grant us thy truth to make us free,
And kindling hearts that burn for thee,
Till all thy living altars claim
One holy light, one heavenly flame!

192 *Providence.* A. STEELE.

Lord, how mysterious are thy ways!
How blind are we, how mean our praise!
Thy steps no mortal eyes explore;
'Tis ours to wonder and adore.

2 Great God! I do not ask to see
What in futurity shall be;
Let light and bliss attend my days,
And then my future hours be praise.

3 Are darkness and distress my share?
Give me to trust thy guardian care;
Enough for me, if love divine
At length through every cloud shall shine.

4 Yet this my soul desires to know,
Be this my only wish below;
That Christ is mine!—this great request,
Grant, bounteous God, and I am blest.

193 *Sovereignty.* RAY PALMER.

Lord, my weak thought in vain would climb
To search the starry vault profound;
In vain would wing her flight sublime,
To find creation's outmost bound.

2 But weaker yet that thought must prove
To search thy great eternal plan,—
Thy sovereign counsels, born of love
Long ages ere the world began.

3 When my dim reason would demand
Why that, or this, thou dost ordain,
By some vast deep I seem to stand,
Whose secrets I must ask in vain.

4 When doubts disturb my troubled breast,
And all is dark as night to me,
Here, as on solid rock, I rest;
That so it seemeth good to thee.

5 Be this my joy, that evermore
Thou rulest all things at thy will:
Thy sovereign wisdom I adore,
And calmly, sweetly, trust thee still.

GOD:—THE FATHER.

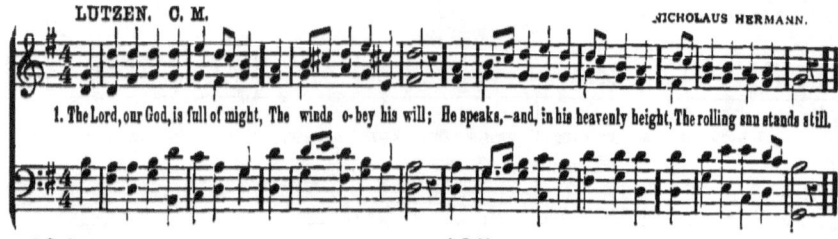
LUTZEN. C. M.   NICHOLAUS HERMANN.

1. The Lord, our God, is full of might, The winds o-bey his will; He speaks,—and, in his heavenly height, The rolling sun stands still.

194   *Power.*   H. K. WHITE.

THE Lord, our God, is full of might,
The winds obey his will;
He speaks,—and, in his heavenly height,
The rolling sun stands still.

2 Rebel, ye waves, and o'er the land
With threatning aspect roar;
The Lord uplifts his awful hand,
And chains you to the shore.

3 Howl, winds of night, your force combine;
Without his high behest,
Ye shall not, in the mountain pine,
Disturb the sparrow's nest.

4 His voice sublime is heard afar,
In distant peals it dies;
He yokes the whirlwind to his car,
And sweeps the howling skies.

5 Ye nations, bend—in reverence bend;
Ye monarchs, wait his nod,
And bid the choral song ascend
To celebrate your God.

195   *Providence.*   I. WATTS.

KEEP silence, all created things!
And wait your Maker's nod;
My soul stands trembling, while she sings
The honors of her God.

2 Life, death, and hell, and worlds unknown,
Hang on his firm decree;
He sits on no precarious throne,
Nor borrows leave to be.

3 His providence unfolds the book,
And makes his counsels shine;
Each opening leaf, and every stroke,
Fulfills some deep design.

4 My God! I would not long to see
My fate, with curious eyes—
What gloomy lines are writ for me,
Or what bright scenes may rise.

5 In thy fair book of life and grace,
Oh, may I find my name
Recorded in some humble place,
Beneath my Lord, the Lamb.

ST. ANN'S. C. M.   WM. CROFT.

1. The Lord, our God, is full of might, The winds o-bey his will; He speaks,—and, in his heaven-ly height, The roll-ing sun stands still.

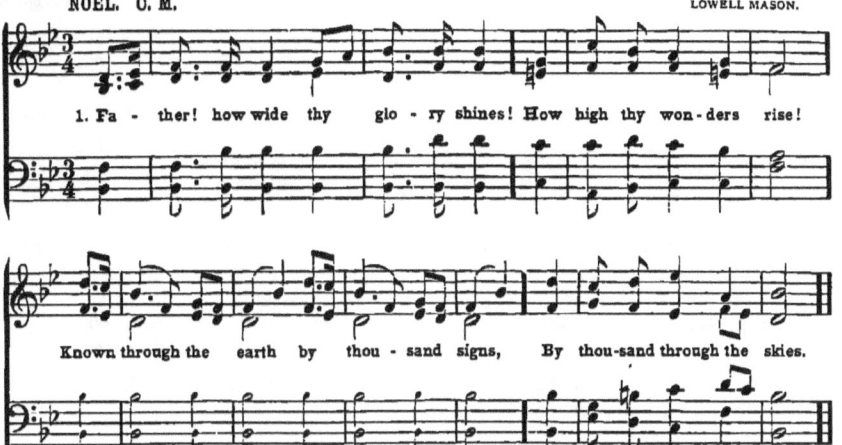

NOEL. C. M.   LOWELL MASON.

1. Father! how wide thy glory shines! How high thy wonders rise! Known through the earth by thousand signs, By thousand through the skies.

196   *Nature and Grace.*   I. WATTS.

Father! how wide thy glory shines!
How high thy wonders rise!
Known through the earth by thousand signs,
By thousand through the skies.

2 Those mighty orbs proclaim thy power,
Their motions speak thy skill;
And on the wings of every hour,
We read thy patience still.

3 But, when we view thy strange design
To save rebellious worms,
Where vengeance and compassion join
In their divinest forms,—

4 Here the whole Deity is known;
Nor dares a creature guess
Which of the glories brightest shone,
The justice, or the grace.

5 Now the full glories of the Lamb
Adorn the heavenly plains;
Bright seraphs learn Immanuel's name,
And try their choicest strains.

6 Oh, may I bear some humble part,
In that immortal song;
Wonder and joy shall tune my heart,
And love command my tongue.

197   *Goodness.—Ps.* 145.   I. WATTS.

Sweet is the memory of thy grace,
My God, my heavenly King;
Let age to age thy righteousness
In sounds of glory sing.

2 God reigns on high; but ne'er confines
His goodness to the skies:
Through the whole earth his bounty shines
And every want supplies.

3 With longing eyes thy creatures wait
On thee for daily food;
Thy liberal hand provides their meat,
And fills their mouth with good.

4 How kind are thy compassions, Lord!
How slow thine anger moves!
But soon he sends his pardoning word
To cheer the souls he loves.

198   *In Nature.*   A. STEELE.

Lord, when my raptured thought surveys
Creation's beauties o'er,
All nature joins to teach thy praise,
And bid my soul adore.

2 Where'er I turn my gazing eyes,
Thy radiant footsteps shine;
Ten thousand pleasing wonders rise,
And speak their source divine.

3 On me thy providence has shone
With gentle smiling rays;
Oh, let my lips and life make known
Thy goodness and thy praise.

4 All-bounteous Lord, thy grace impart!
Oh, teach me to improve
Thy gifts with humble, grateful heart,
And crown them with thy love.

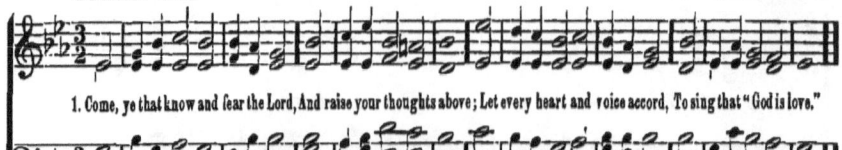

DOWNS. C. M.   LOWELL MASON.

1. Come, ye that know and fear the Lord, And raise your thoughts above; Let every heart and voice accord, To sing that "God is love."

199   *Love.*   G. BURDER.

Come, ye that know and fear the Lord,
  And raise your thoughts above:
Let every heart and voice accord,
  To sing that " God is love."

2 This precious truth his word declares,
  And all his mercies prove;
Jesus, the gift of gifts, appears,
  To show that " God is love."

3 Behold his patience, bearing long
  With those who from him rove;
Till mighty grace their hearts subdues,
  To teach them—" God is love."

4 Oh, may we all, while here below,
  This best of blessings prove;
Till warmer hearts, in brighter worlds,
  Proclaim that "God is love."

200   *Omnipresence.—Ps.* 139.   I. WATTS.

In all my vast concerns with thee,
  In vain my soul would try
To shun thy presence, Lord! or flee
  The notice of thine eye.

2 Thine all-surrounding sight surveys
  My rising and my rest,
My public walks, my private ways,
  And secrets of my breast.

3 My thoughts lie open to the Lord,
  Before they're formed within;
And, ere my lips pronounce the word,
  He knows the sense I mean.

4 Oh, wondrous knowledge, deep and high,
  Where can a creature hide?
Within thy circling arms I lie,
  Enclosed on every side.

5 So let thy grace surround me still,
  And like a bulwark prove,
To guard my soul from every ill,
  Secured by sovereign love.

201   *In Nature.*   J. KEBLE.

There is a book that all may read,
  Which heavenly truth imparts,
And all the lore its scholars need,
  Pure eyes and Christian hearts.

2 The works of God above, below,
  Within us and around,
Are pages in that book, to show
  How God himself is found.

3 The glorious sky, embracing all,
  Is like the Maker's love,
Wherewith encompassed, great and small
  In peace and order move.

4 The dew of heaven is like thy grace,
  It steals in silence down;
But where it lights, the favored place
  By richest fruits is known.

5 Thou, who hast given me eyes to see,
  And love this sight so fair,
Give me a heart to find out thee,
  And read thee everywhere.

202   *Omniscience.—Ps.* 139.   I. WATTS.

Lord! where shall guilty souls retire,
  Forgotten and unknown?
In hell they meet thy dreadful fire—
  In heaven thy glorious throne.

2 If, winged with beams of morning light,
  I fly beyond the west,
Thy hand, which must support my flight,
  Would soon betray my rest.

3 If, o'er my sins, I think to draw
  The curtains of the night,
Those flaming eyes, that guard thy law,
  Would turn the shades to light.

4 The beams of noon, the midnight hour,
  Are both alike to thee:
Oh, may I ne'er provoke that power,
  From which I cannot flee.

ATTRIBUTES.

203 *"Te Deum."* TATE—BRADY.

O God! we praise thee, and confess
That thou the only Lord
And everlasting Father art,
By all the earth adored.

2 To thee all angels cry aloud;
To thee the powers on high,
Both cherubim and seraphim,
Continually do cry:—

3 O holy, holy, holy Lord,
Whom heavenly hosts obey,
The world is with the glory filled
Of thy majestic sway!

4 The apostles' glorious company,
And prophets crowned with light,
With all the martyrs' noble host,
Thy constant praise recite.

5 The holy church throughout the world,
O Lord, confesses thee,
That thou the eternal Father art,
Of boundless majesty.

204 *Eternity.* I. WATTS.

Great God! how infinite art thou!
What worthless worms are we!
Let the whole race of creatures bow,
And pay their praise to thee.

2 Thy throne eternal ages stood,
Ere seas or stars were made:
Thou art the ever-living God,
Were all the nations dead.

3 Eternity, with all its years,
Stands present in thy view;
To thee there's nothing old appears—
Great God! there's nothing new.

4 Our lives through various scenes are drawn,
And vexed with trifling cares;
While thine eternal thought moves on
Thine undisturbed affairs.

5 Great God! how infinite art thou!
What worthless worms are we!
Let the whole race of creatures bow,
And pay their praise to thee.

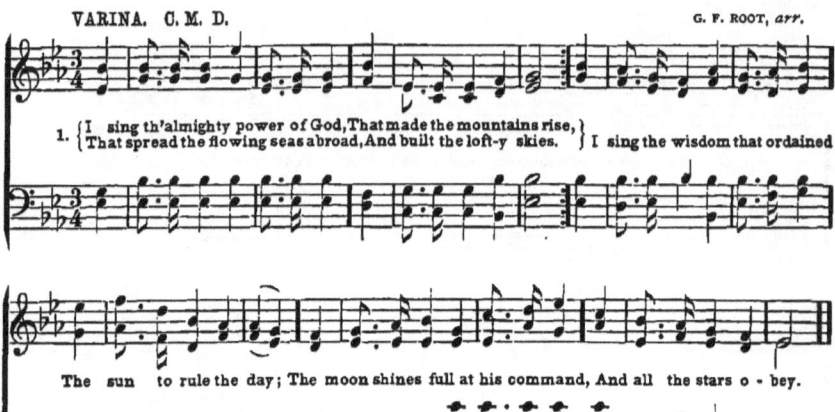

205
Perfections.   L. WATTS.

I SING the almighty power of God,
  That made the mountains rise,
That spread the flowing seas abroad,
  And built the lofty skies.
I sing the wisdom that ordained
  The sun to rule the day;
The moon shines full at his command,
  And all the stars obey.

2 I sing the goodness of the Lord,
  That filled the earth with food;
He formed the creatures with his word,
  And then pronounced them good.
Lord! how thy wonders are displayed
  Where'er I turn mine eye!
If I survey the ground I tread,
  Or gaze upon the sky!

3 There's not a plant or flower below
  But makes thy glories known;
And clouds arise, and tempests blow
  By order from thy throne.
Creatures that borrow life from thee
  Are subject to thy care;
There's not a place where we can flee,
  But God is present there.

206
Mystery.   J. FAWCETT.

THY way, O Lord, is in the sea;
  Thy paths I cannot trace,
Nor comprehend the mystery
  Of thine unbounded grace.

As, through a glass, I dimly see
  The wonders of thy love;
How little do I know of thee,
  Or of the joys above!

2 'Tis but in part I know thy will;
  I bless thee for the sight:
When will thy love the rest reveal,
  In glory's clearer light?
With rapture shall I then survey
  Thy providence and grace;
And spend an everlasting day
  In wonder, love, and praise.

207
Omniscience.—Ps. 139.   J. THOMPSON.

JEHOVAH God! thy gracious power
  On every hand we see;
Oh, may the blessings of each hour
  Lead all our thoughts to thee.
Thy power is in the ocean deeps,
  And reaches to the skies;
Thine eye of mercy never sleeps,
  Thy goodness never dies.

2 From morn till noon, till latest eve,
  The hand of God we see;
And all the blessings we receive,
  Ceaseless proceed from thee.
In all the varying scenes of time,
  On thee our hopes depend;
In every age, in every clime,
  Our Father and our Friend.

ATTRIBUTES.

MANOAH. C. M. — FROM G. ROSSINI.

1. Be-gin, my tongue, some heavenly theme, And speak some boundless thing;
The might-y works, or mightier name, Of our e-ter-nal King.

208 *Faithfulness.* L. WATTS.

BEGIN, my tongue, some heavenly theme,
And speak some boundless thing;
The mighty works or mightier name
Of our eternal King.

2 Tell of his wondrous faithfulness,
And sound his power abroad;
Sing the sweet promise of his grace,
And the performing God.

3 His very word of grace is strong,
As that which built the skies;
The voice that rolls the stars along,
Speaks all the promises.

4 Oh, might I hear thy heavenly tongue
But whisper, "Thou art mine!"
Those gentle words should raise my song
To notes almost divine.

209 *Providence.* W. COWPER.

GOD moves in a mysterious way
His wonders to perform;
He plants his footsteps in the sea,
And rides upon the storm.

2 Deep in unfathomable mines
Of never-failing skill,
He treasures up his bright designs,
And works his sovereign will.

3 Ye fearful saints, fresh courage take!
The clouds ye so much dread,
Are big with mercy, and will break
In blessings on your head.

4 Judge not the Lord by feeble sense,
But trust him for his grace;
Behind a frowning providence
He hides a smiling face.

5 His purposes will ripen fast,
Unfolding every hour;
The bud may have a bitter taste,
But sweet will be the flower.

6 Blind unbelief is sure to err,
And scan his work in vain;
God is his own interpreter,
And he will make it plain.

210 *Holiness.* J. NEEDHAM.

HOLY and reverend is the name
Of our eternal King,
Thrice holy Lord! the angels cry;
Thrice holy! let us sing.

2 The deepest reverence of the mind,
Pay, O my soul! to God;
Lift with thy hands a holy heart
To his sublime abode.

3 With sacred awe pronounce his name,
Whom words nor thoughts can reach;
A broken heart shall please him more
Than the best forms of speech.

4 Thou holy God! preserve our souls
From all pollution free;
The pure in heart are thy delight,
And they thy face shall see.

GOD:—THE FATHER.

FABEN. 8s, 7s. D.   J. H. WILCOX.

1. Lord, thy glo-ry fills the heaven; Earth is with its fullness stored; Un-to thee be glo-ry giv-en, Ho-ly, ho-ly, ho-ly Lord! Heaven is still with anthems ring-ing; Earth takes up the an-gels' cry, Ho-ly, ho-ly, ho-ly, singing, Lord of hosts, thou Lord most high.

211   *Holiness.*   R. MANT.

LORD, thy glory fills the heaven;
  Earth is with its fullness stored;
Unto thee be glory given,
  Holy, holy, holy Lord!
Heaven is still with anthems ringing;
  Earth takes up the angels' cry,
Holy, holy, holy, singing,
  Lord of hosts, thou Lord most high.

2 Ever thus in God's high praises,
  Brethren, let our tongues unite,
While our thoughts his greatness raises,
  And our love his gifts excite:
With his seraph train before him,
  With his holy church below,
Thus unite we to adore him,
  Bid we thus our anthem flow.

3 Lord, thy glory fills the heaven,
  Earth is with its fullness stored;
Unto thee be glory given,
  Holy, holy, holy Lord!
Thus thy glorious name confessing,
  We adopt the angels' cry,
Holy, holy, holy, blessing
  Thee, the Lord our God most high!

212   *Grace.*   F. S. KEY.

LORD, with glowing heart I'd praise thee
  For the bliss thy love bestows;
For the pardoning grace that saves me,
  And the peace that from it flows:
Help, O God, my weak endeavor;
  This dull soul to rapture raise;
Thou must light the flame, or never
  Can my soul be warmed to praise.

2 Praise, my soul, the God that sought thee,
  Wretched wanderer, far astray;
Found thee lost, and kindly brought thee
  From the paths of death away;
Praise, with love's devoutest feeling,
  Him who saw thy guilt-born fear,
And, the light of hope revealing,
  Bade the blood-stained cross appear.

3 Lord, this bosom's ardent feeling
  Vainly would my lips express:
Low before thy footstool kneeling,
  Deign thy suppliant's prayer to bless;
Let thy grace, my soul's chief treasure,
  Love's pure flame within me raise;
And, since words can never measure,
  Let my life show forth thy praise.

ATTRIBUTES.

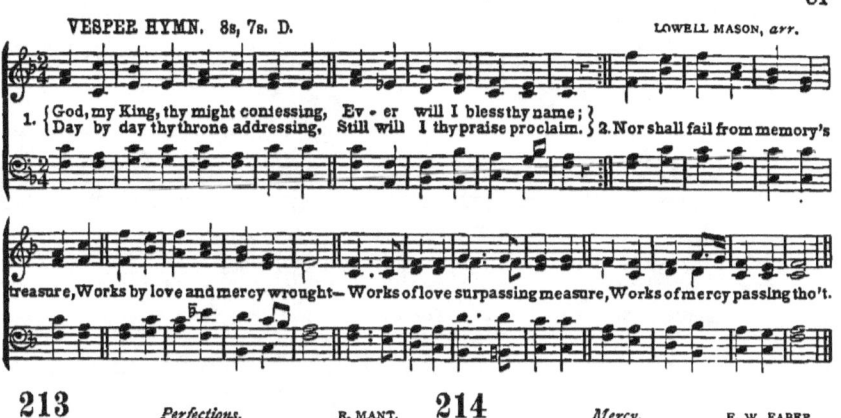

VESPER HYMN. 8s, 7s. D.   LOWELL MASON, arr.

1. { God, my King, thy might confessing, Ev-er will I bless thy name; }
  { Day by day thy throne addressing, Still will I thy praise proclaim. } 2. Nor shall fail from memory's treasure, Works by love and mercy wrought— Works of love surpassing measure, Works of mercy passing tho't.

213   *Perfections.*   R. MANT.

God, my King, thy might confessing,
  Ever will I bless thy name;
Day by day thy throne addressing,
  Still will I thy praise proclaim.
2 Nor shall fail from memory's treasure,
  Works by love and mercy wrought—
Works of love surpassing measure,
  Works of mercy passing thought
3 Full of kindness and compassion,
  Slow of anger, vast in love,
God is good to all creation;
  All his works his goodness prove.
4 All thy works, O Lord, shall bless thee,
  Thee shall all thy saints adore;
King supreme shall they confess thee,
  And proclaim thy sovereign power

214   *Mercy.*   F. W. FABER

There's a wideness in God's mercy,
  Like the wideness of the sea:
There's a kindness in his justice,
  Which is more than liberty.
2 There is welcome for the sinner,
  And more graces for the good;
There is mercy with the Saviour;
  There is healing in his blood.
3 For the love of God is broader
  Than the measure of man's mind;
And the heart of the Eternal
  Is most wonderfully kind.
4 If our love were but more simple,
  We should take him at his word;
And our lives would be all sunshine
  In the sweetness of our Lord.

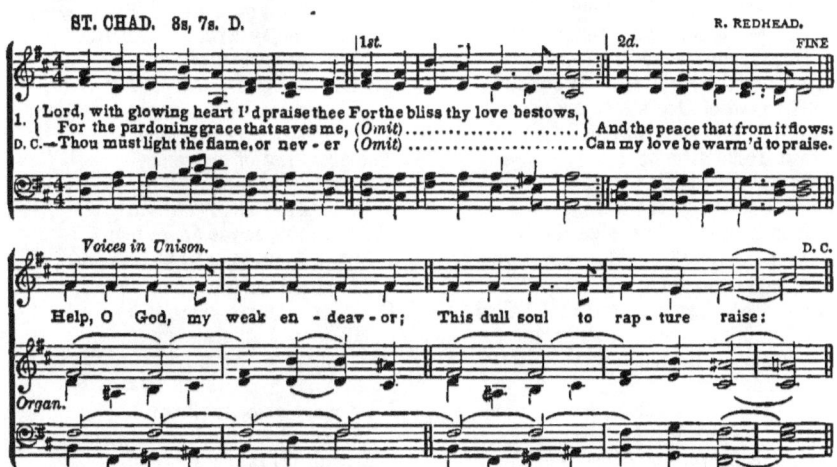

ST. CHAD. 8s, 7s. D.   R. REDHEAD.

1. { Lord, with glowing heart I'd praise thee For the bliss thy love bestows, }
  { For the pardoning grace that saves me, (Omit) } And the peace that from it flows:
D. C.—Thou must light the flame, or nev-er (Omit) Can my love be warm'd to praise.

Voices in Unison.
Help, O God, my weak en-deav-or; This dull soul to rap-ture raise:

82   GOD:—THE FATHER.

EIN' FESTE BURG. P. M.   MARTIN LUTHER.

1. A mighty fortress is our God, A bulwark never fail-ing; Our Helper he, a-mid the flood Of mor-tal ills pre-vail-ing. For still our ancient foe Doth seek to work his woe; His craft and power are great, And armed with cruel hate, On earth is not his e-qual.

215   *"A Mighty Fortress."*   F. H. HEDGE, *tr.*

A MIGHTY fortress is our God,
   A bulwark never failing:
Our Helper he, amid the flood
   Of mortal ills prevailing.
For still our ancient foe
Doth seek to work his woe;
His craft and power are great,
And armed with cruel hate,
   On earth is not his equal.

2 Did we in our own strength confide,
   Our striving would be losing;
Were not the right man on our side,
   The man of God's own choosing.
Dost ask who that may be?
Christ Jesus, it is he;
Lord Sabaoth is his name,
From age to age the same,
   And he must win the battle.

3 And though this world, with devils filled,
   Should threaten to undo us;
We will not fear, for God hath willed
   His truth to triumph through us.
The prince of darkness grim,—
We tremble not for him;
His rage we can endure,
For lo! his doom is sure,—
   One little word shall fell him!

4 That word above all earthly powers—
   No thanks to them—abideth;
The Spirit and the gifts are ours
   Through him who with us sideth.
Let goods and kindred go,
This mortal life also:
The body they may kill:
God's truth abideth still,
   His kingdom is for ever.

216   *"God alone."*   H. W. BAKER.

REJOICE to-day with one accord,
   Sing out with exultation;
Rejoice and praise our mighty Lord,
   Whose arm hath brought salvation;
His works of love proclaim
The greatness of his name;
For he is God alone,
Who hath his mercy shown;
   Let all his saints adore him.

2 When in distress to him we cried,
   He heard our sad complaining;
Oh, trust in him, whate'er betide,
   His love is all sustaining;
Triumphant songs of praise
To him our hearts shall raise;
Now every voice shall say,
"Oh, praise our God alway;"
   Let all his saints adore him.

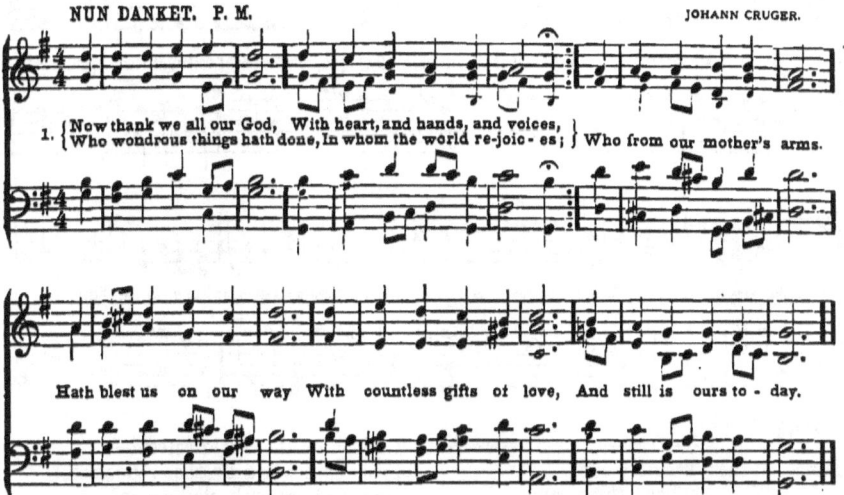

217
Bounteous Care. C. WINKWORTH, *tr.*

Now THANK we all our God,
  With heart, and hands, and voices,
Who wondrous things hath done,
  In whom the world rejoices ;
Who from our mother's arms
  Hath blessed us on our way
With countless gifts of love,
  And still is ours to-day.

2 Oh, may this bounteous God
  Through all our life be near us,
With ever joyful hearts
  And blessèd peace to cheer us;
To keep us in his grace,
  And guide us when perplexed,
And free us from all ills
  In this world and the next.

218
Eternity. C. WINKWORTH, *tr.*

O THOU essential Word,
  Who wast from everlasting
With God, for thou wast God;
  On thee our burden casting,
O Saviour of our race,
  Welcome indeed thou art,
Redeemer, Fount of Grace,
  To this my longing heart.

2 Come, self-existent Word,
  And speak thou in my spirit;
The soul where thou art heard,
  Doth endless peace inherit.

Thou Light that lightenest all,
  Abide through faith in me,
Nor let me from thee fall,
  Nor seek a guide but thee.

219
Beneficence. A. T. PIERSON.

To THEE, O God, we raise
  Our voice in choral singing ;
We come with prayer and praise,
  Our hearts' oblations bringing;
Thou art our fathers' God,
  And ever shalt be ours;
Our lips and lives shall laud
  Thy name, with all our powers.

2 Thy goodness, like the dew
  On Hermon's hill descending,
Is every morning new,
  And tells of love unending.
We bless thy tender care
  That led our wayward feet,
Past every fatal snare,
  To streams and pastures sweet.

3 We bless thy Son, who bore
  The cross, for sinners dying;
Thy Spirit we adore,
  The precious blood applying.
Let work and worship send
  Their incense unto thee;
Till song and service blend,
  Beside the crystal sea,

220
The Trinity.   H. BONAR.

Holy Father, hear my cry;
  Holy Saviour, bend thine ear;
Holy Spirit, come thou nigh:
  Father, Saviour, Spirit, hear!
Father, save me from my sin;
  Saviour, I thy mercy crave;
Gracious Spirit, make me clean:
  Father, Son, and Spirit, save!

2 Father, let me taste thy love;
  Saviour, fill my soul with peace;
Spirit, come my heart to move:
  Father, Son, and Spirit, bless!
Father, Son, and Spirit—thou
  One Jehovah, shed abroad
All thy grace within me now;
  Be my Father and my God!

221
"Holy, holy, holy."   J. MONTGOMERY.

Holy, holy, holy Lord
  God of Hosts! when heaven and earth,
Out of darkness, at thy word
  Issued into glorious birth,
All thy works before thee stood,
And thine eye beheld them good,
While they sung with sweet accord,
Holy, holy, holy Lord!

2 Holy, holy, holy! thee,
  One Jehovah evermore,
Father, Son, and Spirit! we,
  Dust and ashes, would adore:
Lightly by the world esteemed,
From that world by thee redeemed,
Sing we here with glad accord,
Holy, holy, holy Lord!

3 Holy, holy, holy! all
  Heaven's triumphant choir shall sing,
While the ransomed nations fall
  At the footstool of their King:
Then shall saints and seraphim,
Harps and voices, swell one hymn,
Blending in sublime accord,
Holy, holy, holy Lord!

222
Divine Presence.   R. GRANT.

Lord of earth! thy forming hand
Well this beauteous frame hath planned;
Woods that wave, and hills that tower,
Ocean rolling in his power:
Yet, amid this scene so fair,
Should I cease thy smile to share,
What were all its joys to me?
Whom have I on earth but thee?

2 Lord of heaven! beyond our sight
Shines a world of purer light;
There in love's unclouded reign
Parted hands shall meet again:
Oh, that world is passing fair!
Yet, if thou wert absent there,
What were all its joys to me?
Whom have I in heaven but thee?

ATTRIBUTES.

ITALIAN HYMN. 6s, 4s. F. GIARDINI.

223 *"One in Three."* C. WESLEY.

Come, thou almighty King,
  Help us thy name to sing,
    Help us to praise:
  Father! all-glorious,
  O'er all victorious,
  Come, and reign over us,
    Ancient of Days!

2 Come, thou incarnate Word,
  Gird on thy mighty sword;
    Our prayer attend;
  Come, and thy people bless,
  And give thy word success—
    Spirit of holiness!
      On us descend

3 Come, holy Comforter!
  Thy sacred witness bear,
    In this glad hour:
  Thou, who almighty art,
  Now rule in every heart,
  And ne'er from us depart,
    Spirit of power!

4 To the great One in Three,
  The highest praises be,
    Hence evermore!
  His sovereign majesty
  May we in glory see,
  And to eternity
    Love and adore.

ELLACOMBE. 7s, 6s. D. ST. GALL'S COLLECTION.

224 *"Show mercy."—Ps. 67.* ANON.

O God, to us show mercy,
  And bless us in thy grace;
Cause thou to shine upon us
  The brightness of thy face:
That so throughout all nations
  Thy way may be well known,
And unto every people
  Thy saving health be shown.

2 O God, let people praise thee,
  Let all the people praise;
Oh, let the nations joyful
  Their songs of gladness raise:
For thou shalt judge the people
  In truth and righteousness;
And on the earth all nations
  Shall thy just rule confess.

3 O God, let people praise thee:
  Thy praises let them sing;
And then in rich abundance
  The earth her fruit shall bring:
The Lord our God shall bless us,
  God shall his blessing send;
And people all shall fear him
  To earth's remotest end.

225 8s, 7s.   *Wisdom and Love.*   J. BOWRING.

GOD is love; his mercy brightens
All the path in which we rove;
Bliss he wakes and woe he lightens;
God is wisdom, God is love.

2 Chance and change are busy ever;
Man decays, and ages move;
But his mercy waneth never;
God is wisdom, God is love.

3 Ev'n the hour that darkest seemeth,
Will his changeless goodness prove;
From the gloom his brightness streameth;
God is wisdom, God is love.

4 He with earthly cares entwineth
Hope and comfort from above;
Everywhere his glory shineth;
God is wisdom, God is love.

226 L. M.   *The Trinity.*   H. W. BAKER.

BLEST Trinity! from mortal sight
Vailed in thine own eternal light!
We thee confess, in thee believe;
To thee with loving hearts we cleave.

2 O Father! thou Most Holy One!
O God of God! Eternal Son!
O Holy Ghost! thou Love Divine!
To join them both is ever thine.

3 The Father is in God the Son,
And with the Father he is one;
In both the Spirit doth abide,
And with them both is glorified.

4 Eternal Father! thee we praise;
To thee, O Son! our hymns we raise;
O Holy Ghost! we thee adore!
One mighty God for evermore.

227 C. M. 6 l.   *Omnipresence.*   J. CONDER.

BEYOND, beyond the boundless sea,
Above that dome of sky,
Further than thought itself can flee,
Thy dwelling is on high:
Yet dear the awful thought to me,
That thou, my God! art nigh:—

2 Art nigh, and yet my laboring mind
Feels after thee in vain—
Thee in these works of power to find,
Or to thy seat attain;
Thy messenger—the stormy wind;
Thy path—the trackless main.

3 These speak of thee with loud acclaim;
They thunder forth thy praise—
The glorious honor of thy name,
The wonders of thy ways;
But thou art not in tempest-flame,
Nor in the noon-day blaze.

4 We hear thy voice, when thunders roll
Through the wide fields of air:
The waves obey thy dread control;
Yet still thou art not there:
Where shall I find him, O my soul!
Who yet is everywhere?

5 Oh, not in circling depth or height,
But in the conscious breast,
Present by faith, though vailed from sight,
There doth his Spirit rest:
Oh, come, thou Presence infinite!
And make thy creature blest.

228 L. M.   *Goodness.*   P. DODDRIDGE.

TRIUMPHANT Lord, thy goodness reigns
Through all the wide celestial plains;
And its full streams unceasing flow
Down to the abodes of men below.

2 Through nature's work its glories shine;
The cares of providence are thine;
And grace erects our ruined frame
A fairer temple to thy name.

3 Oh, give to every human heart
To taste, and feel how good thou art;
With grateful love and reverent fear,
To know how blest thy children are.

229 L. M.   *Glory.*   T. BLACKLOCK.

COME, O my soul! in sacred lays
Attempt thy great Creator's praise:
But, oh, what tongue can speak his fame?
What mortal verse can reach the theme?

2 Enthroned amid the radiant spheres,
He glory like a garment wears;
To form a robe of light divine,
Ten thousand suns around him shine.

3 In all our Maker's grand designs,
Almighty power with wisdom shines;
His works thro' all this wondrous frame,
Declare the glory of his name.

4 Raised on devotion's lofty wing,
Do thou, my soul, his glories sing;
And let his praise employ thy tongue,
Till listening worlds shall join the song!

230 H. M. *The Trinity* I. WATTS.

We give immortal praise
  For God the Father's love,
For all our comforts here,
  And better hopes above:
He sent his own eternal Son
To die for sins that we had done.

2 To God the Son belongs
  Immortal glory too,
Who bought us with his blood
  From everlasting woe:
And now he lives, and now he reigns,
And sees the fruit of all his pains.

3 To God the Spirit's name
  Immortal worship give,
Whose new-creating power
  Makes the dead sinner live:
His work completes the great design,
And fills the soul with joy divine.

4 Almighty God! to thee
  Be endless honors done,
The undivided Three,
  The great and glorious One:
Where reason fails, with all her powers,
There faith prevails, and love adores.

231 C. M. *Majesty.—Ps. 18.* T. STERNHOLD.

The Lord descended from above,
  And bowed the heavens most high:
And underneath his feet he cast
  The darkness of the sky.

2 On cherub and on cherubim,
  Full royally he rode;
And on the wings of mighty winds
  Came flying all abroad.

3 He sat serene upon the floods,
  Their fury to restrain;
And he, as sovereign Lord and King,
  For evermore shall reign.

4 The Lord will give his people strength,
  Whereby they shall increase;
And he will bless his chosen flock
  With everlasting peace.

5 Give glory to his awful name,
  And honor him alone;
Give worship to his majesty,
  Upon his holy throne.

232 H. M. *Love.* J. YOUNG.

Oh, for a shout of joy,
  Worthy the theme we sing;
To this divine employ
  Our hearts and voices bring;
Sound, sound, thro' all the earth abroad,
The love, the eternal love of God.

2 Unnumbered myriads stand,
  Of seraphs bright and fair,
Or bow at thy right hand,
  And pay their homage there;
But strive in vain with loudest chord,
To sound thy wondrous love, O Lord.

3 Yet sinners saved by grace,
  In songs of lower key,
In every age and place,
  Have sung the mystery,—
Have told in strains of sweet accord,
Thy love, thy sovereign love, O Lord.

4 Though earth and hell assail,
  And doubts and fears arise,
The weakest shall prevail,
  And grasp the heavenly prize,
And through an endless age record
Thy love, thy changeless love, O Lord.

233 L. M. *Grace.—Ps. 138.* I. WATTS.

With all my powers of heart and tongue
I'll praise my Maker in my song:
Angels shall hear the notes I raise,
Approve the song, and join the praise.

2 I'll sing thy truth and mercy, Lord;
I'll sing the wonders of thy word;
Not all the works and names below,
So much thy power and glory show.

3 To God I cried when troubles rose;
He heard me, and subdued my foes;
He did my rising fears control,
And strength diffused thro' all my soul.

4 Amidst a thousand snares I stand,
Upheld and guarded by thy hand;
Thy words my fainting soul revive,
And keep my dying faith alive.

5 Grace will complete what grace begins,
To save from sorrows and from sins;
The work that wisdom undertakes,
Eternal mercy ne'er forsakes.

THE LORD JESUS CHRIST.

REGENT SQUARE. 8s, 7s.   H. SMART.

1. Hark! what mean those holy voices, Sweetly warbling in the skies? Sure, th' angelic host re-joic-es,— Loudest hal-le-lu-jahs rise, Sure, th' angelic host re-joic-es, Loudest hal-le-lu-jahs rise.

234   *"Those holy Voices."*   J. CAWOOD.

HARK! what mean those holy voices,
  Sweetly warbling in the skies?
Sure, the angelic host rejoices—
  Loudest hallelujahs rise.

2 Listen to the wondrous story,
  Which they chant in hymns of joy;—
"Glory in the highest, glory;
  Glory be to God most high!

3 "Peace on earth, good-will from heaven,
  Reaching far as man is found;
Souls redeemed, and sins forgiven;—
  Loud our golden harps shall sound.

4 "Christ is born, the great Anointed;
  Heaven and earth his glory sing:
Glad, receive whom God appointed,
  For your Prophet, Priest, and King.

5 "Hasten, mortals! to adore him,
  Learn his name and taste his joy;
Till in heaven you sing before him,—
  Glory be to God most high!"

6 Let us learn the wondrous story
  Of our great Redeemer's birth,
Spread the brightness of his glory,
  Till it cover all the earth.

ANTIOCH. C. M.   LOWELL MASON, arr.

1. Joy to the world—the Lord is come; Let earth receive her King; Let eve-ry heart pre-pare him room, And heav'n and nature sing, And heav'n and nature sing,......... And heav'n and na-ture sing.

INCARNATION AND BIRTH.

HARK. P. M.   W. F. SHERWIN.

235   *The heavenly Host.*   F. W. FABER.

Hark! hark, my soul; angelic songs are swelling
O'er earth's green fields and ocean's wave-beat shore:
How sweet the truth those blessèd strains are telling
Of that new life when sin shall be no more.—Cho.

2 Onward we go, for still we hear them singing,
"Come, weary souls, for Jesus bids you come:"
And, through the dark its echoes sweetly ringing,
The music of the gospel leads us home.—Cho.

3 Far, far away, like bells at evening pealing,
The voice of Jesus sounds o'er land and sea,
And laden souls by thousands meekly stealing,
Kind Shepherd, turn their weary steps to thee.—Cho.

4 Angels, sing on! your faithful watches keeping;
Sing us sweet fragments of the songs above,
Till morning's joy shall end the night of weeping,
And life's long shadows break in cloudless love.—Cho.

---

236   C. M.   *Psalm 98.*   I. WATTS.

Joy to the world,—the Lord is come;
Let earth receive her King;
Let every heart prepare him room,
And heaven and nature sing.

2 Joy to the earth,—the Saviour reigns;
Let men their songs employ;
While fields and floods, rocks, hills and plains,
Repeat the sounding joy.

3 No more let sin and sorrow grow,
Nor thorns infest the ground,
He comes to make his blessings flow,
Far as the curse is found.

4 He rules the world with truth and grace,
And makes the nations prove
The glories of his righteousness,
And wonders of his love.

THE LORD JESUS CHRIST.

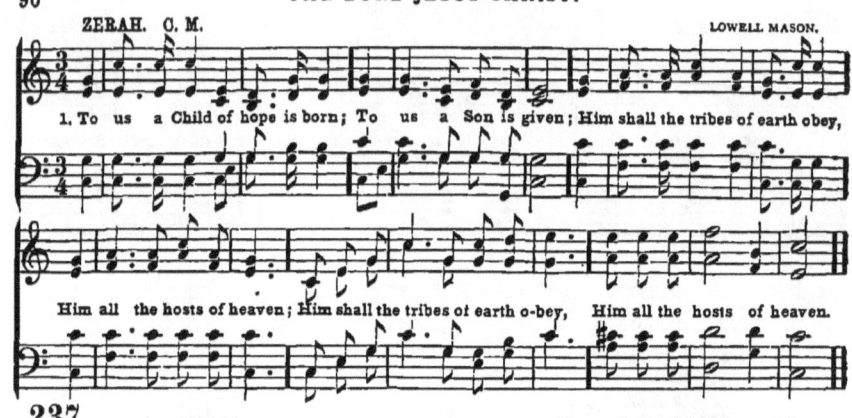

ZERAH. C. M.   LOWELL MASON.

1. To us a Child of hope is born; To us a Son is given; Him shall the tribes of earth obey,
Him all the hosts of heaven; Him shall the tribes of earth o-bey, Him all the hosts of heaven.

237   *Isaiah* 9:6.   J. MORRISON.
To us a Child of hope is born;
To us a Son is given;
Him shall the tribes of earth obey,
Him all the hosts of heaven.
2 His name shall be the Prince of Peace,
For evermore adored,

The Wonderful, the Counselor,
The great and mighty Lord!
3 His power increasing still shall spread,
His reign no end shall know:
Justice shall guard his throne above,
And peace abound below.

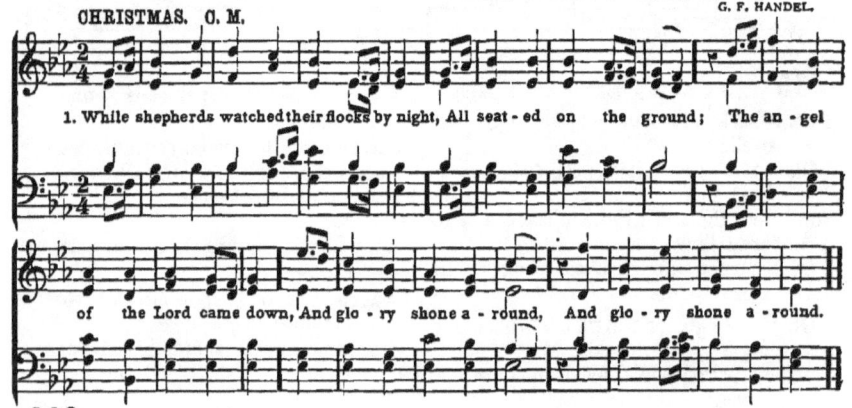

CHRISTMAS. C. M.   G. F. HANDEL.

1. While shepherds watched their flocks by night, All seat-ed on the ground; The an-gel
of the Lord came down, And glo-ry shone a-round, And glo-ry shone a-round.

238   *Bethlehem Song.*   TATE—BRADY.
While shepherds watched their flocks by
  All seated on the ground; [night,
The angel of the Lord came down,
  And glory shone around.
2 "Fear not," said he,—for mighty dread
  Had seized their troubled mind,—
"Glad tidings of great joy I bring,
  To you and all mankind.
3 "To you in David's town this day,
  Is born of David's line,
The Saviour, who is Christ, the Lord,
  And this shall be the sign;—

4 "The heavenly babe you there shall find
  To human view displayed,
All meanly wrapped in swathing bands,
  And in a manger laid."
5 Thus spake the seraph—and forthwith
  Appeared a shining throng
Of angels, praising God, who thus
  Addressed their joyful song:—
6 "All glory be to God on high,
  And to the earth be peace;
Good-will henceforth from heaven to men
  Begin, and never cease!"

INCARNATION AND BIRTH.

239   *"Glory to God."*   W. HURN.

Angels rejoiced and sweetly sung
At our Redeemer's birth;
Mortals! awake; let every tongue
Proclaim his matchless worth.

2 Glory to God, who dwells on high,
And sent his only Son
To take a servant's form, and die,
For evils we had done!

3 Good-will to men; ye fallen race!
Arise, and shout for joy;
He comes, with rich abounding grace
To save and not destroy.

4 Lord! send the gracious tidings forth,
And fill the world with light,
That Jew and Gentile, through the earth,
May know thy saving might.

240   *Angels' music.*   E. H. SEARS.

Calm on the listening ear of night,
Come heaven's melodious strains,
Where wild Judea stretches far
Her silver-mantled plains.

2 Celestial choirs, from courts above,
Shed sacred glories there,
And angels, with their sparkling lyres,
Make music on the air.

3 The answering hills of Palestine
Send back the glad reply;
And greet, from all their holy heights,
The day-spring from on high.

4 O'er the blue depths of Galilee
There comes a holier calm,
And Sharon waves, in solemn praise,
Her silent groves of palm.

5 "Glory to God!" the sounding skies
Loud with their anthems ring—
"Peace to the earth, good-will to men,
From heaven's eternal King!"

THE LORD JESUS CHRIST.

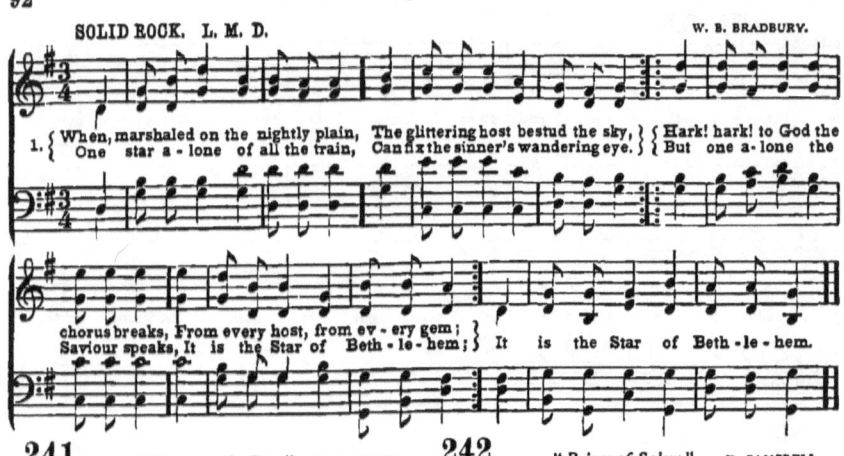

241   "*They saw the Star.*"   H. K. WHITE.

WHEN, marshaled on the nightly plain,
  The glittering host bestud the sky,
One star alone, of all the train,
  Can fix the sinner's wandering eye.
Hark! hark! to God the chorus breaks
  From every host, from every gem;
But one alone the Saviour speaks,—
  It is the Star of Bethlehem.

2 Once on the raging seas I rode,
  The storm was loud, the night was dark,
The ocean yawned, and rudely blowed
  The wind that tossed my foundering bark.
Deep horror then my vitals froze;
  Death-struck, I ceased the tide to stem;
When suddenly a star arose,
  It was the Star of Bethlehem!

3 It was my guide, my light, my all;
  It bade my dark forebodings cease,
And through the storm and danger's thrall
  It led me to the port of peace.
Now safely moored, my perils o'er,
  I'll sing, first in night's diadem,
For ever and for evermore,
  The Star, the Star of Bethlehem!

242   "*Prince of Salem.*"   T. CAMPBELL.

WHEN Jordan hushed his waters still,
  And silence slept on Zion's hill;
When Salem's shepherds thro' the night
  Watched o'er their flocks by starry light;

2 Hark! from the midnight hills around,
  A voice of more than mortal sound
In distant hallelujahs stole,
  Wild murmuring o'er the raptured soul.

3 On wheels of light, on wings of flame,
  The glorious hosts to Zion came;
High heaven with songs of triumph rung,
  While thus they struck their harps and sung:

4 "O Zion! lift thy raptured eye;
  The long expected hour is nigh:
The joys of nature rise again,
  The Prince of Salem comes to reign.

5 "He comes to cheer the trembling heart,
  Bids Satan and his host depart;
Again the Daystar gilds the gloom,
  Again the bowers of Eden bloom."

6 O Zion! lift thy raptured eye;
  The long-expected hour is nigh;
The joys of nature rise again:
  The Prince of Salem comes to reign.

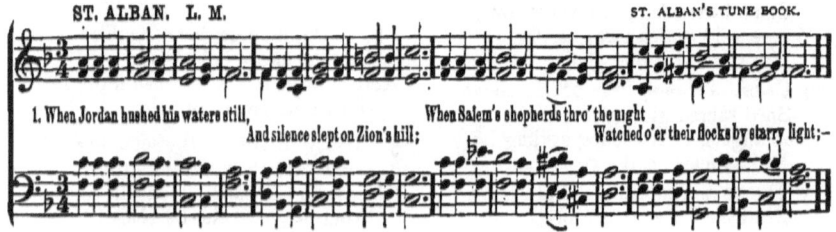

INCARNATION AND BIRTH.

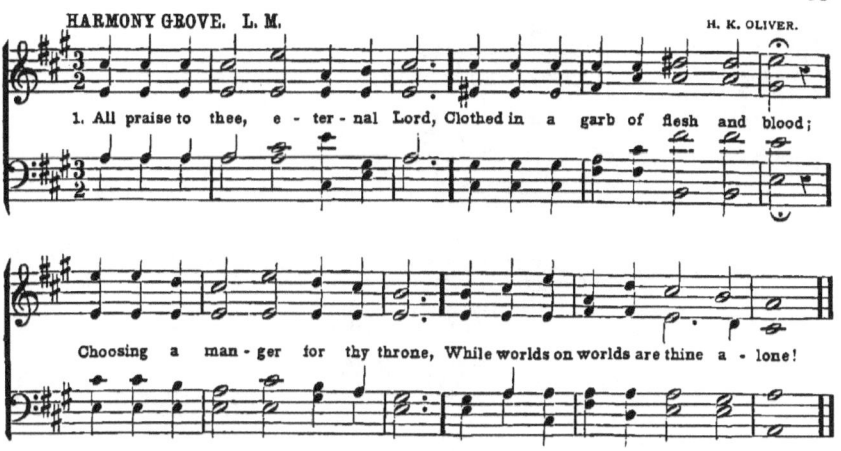

243 *The child Christ.* M. LUTHER.

ALL praise to thee, eternal Lord,
  Clothed in a garb of flesh and blood;
Choosing a manger for thy throne,
  While worlds on worlds are thine alone!

2 Once did the skies before thee bow;
  A virgin's arms contain thee now;
Angels, who did in thee rejoice,
  Now listen for thine infant voice.

3 A little child, thou art our guest,
  That weary ones in thee may rest;
Forlorn and lowly is thy birth,
  That we may rise to heaven from earth.

4 Thou comest in the darksome night
  To make us children of the light;
To make us, in the realms divine,
  Like thine own angels round thee shine.

5 All this for us thy love hath done;
  By this to thee our love is won;
For this we tune our cheerful lays,
  And shout our thanks in ceaseless praise.

244 *Incarnation.* I. WATTS.

BEFORE the heavens were spread abroad,
  From everlasting was the Word;
With God he was, the Word was God!
  And must divinely be adored.

2 Ere sin was born, or Satan fell,
  He led the host of morning stars:
His generation who can tell,
  Or count the number of his years?

3 But lo, he leaves those heavenly forms:
  The Word descends and dwells in clay,
That he may converse hold with worms,
  Dressed in such feeble flesh as they.

4 Mortals with joy behold his face,
  The eternal Father's only Son:
How full of truth, how full of grace,
  When in his eyes the Godhead shone!

5 Archangels leave their high abode,
  To learn new mysteries here, and tell
The love of our descending God,
  The glories of Immanuel.

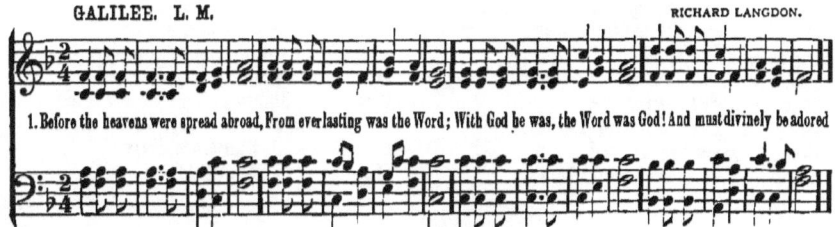

THE LORD JESUS CHRIST.

245 *The Nativity.* C. WESLEY.

HARK! the herald angels sing
"Glory to the new-born King;
Peace on earth, and mercy mild,
God and sinners reconciled!"
Joyful, all ye nations, rise,
Join the triumph of the skies;
With the angelic host proclaim,
Christ is born in Bethlehem!

2 Christ, by highest heaven adored;
Christ, the everlasting Lord;
Late in time behold him come,
Offspring of the Virgin's womb:
Vailed in flesh the Godhead see;
Hail the incarnate Deity,
Pleased as man with men to dwell;
Jesus, our Immanuel!

3 Hail! the heaven-born Prince of Peace!
Hail the Sun of Righteousness!
Light and life to all he brings,
Risen with healing in his wings:
Mild he lays his glory by,
Born that man no more may die:
Born to raise the sons of earth,
Born to give them second birth.

246 *"The Christ of God."* H. BONAR.

HE has come! the Christ of God
Left for us his glad abode;
Stooping from his throne of bliss,
To this darksome wilderness.
He has come! the Prince of Peace;
Come to bid our sorrows cease;
Come to scatter with his light
All the shadows of our night.

2 He the mighty King has come!
Making this poor earth his home;
Come to bear our sin's sad load;
Son of David, Son of God!
He has come, whose name of grace
Speaks deliverance to our race;
Left for us his glad abode;
Son of Mary, Son of God!

3 Unto us a child is born!
Ne'er has earth beheld a morn,
Among all the morns of time,
Half so glorious in its prime.
Unto us a Son is given!
He has come from God's own heaven,
Bringing with him from above
Holy peace and holy love.

INCARNATION AND BIRTH.

247 *The Glad Tidings.* W. A. MUHLENBERG.

Cho.—Shout the glad tidings, exultingly sing;
  Jerusalem triumphs, Messiah is King.

ZION, the marvelous story be telling,
  The Son of the Highest, how lowly his birth;
The brightest archangel in glory excelling,
  He stoops to redeem thee, he reigns upon earth.
    Cho—Shout the glad tidings, etc.

    Cho.—Shout the glad tidings, etc.

2 Tell how he cometh; from nation to nation,
  The heart-cheering news let the earth echo round;
How free to the faithful he offers salvation!
  How his people with joy everlasting are crowned!
    Cho.—Shout the glad tidings, etc.

    Cho.—Shout the glad tidings, etc.

3 Mortals, your homage be gratefully bringing,
  And sweet let the gladsome hosanna arise;
Ye angels, the full hallelujah be singing;
  One chorus resound through the earth and the skies.
    Cho.—Shout the glad tidings, etc.

THE LORD JESUS CHRIST.

248 c. m. d. *"The Age of Gold."* e. h. sears.

It came upon the midnight clear,
 That glorious song of old,
From angels bending near the earth
 To touch their harps of gold;
"Peace to the earth, good-will to man,
 From heaven's all-gracious King:"
The earth in solemn stillness lay,
 To hear the angels sing.

2 Still through the cloven skies they
 With peaceful wings unfurled; [come,
And still celestial music floats
 O'er all the weary world;
Above its sad and lowly plains
 They bend on heavenly wing,
And ever o'er its Babel sounds,
 The blessèd angels sing.

3 O ye, beneath life's crushing load,
 Whose forms are bending low,
Who toil along the climbing way,
 With painful steps and slow;—
Look up! for glad and golden hours
 Come swiftly on the wing;
Oh, rest beside the weary road,
 And hear the angels sing!

4 For lo! the days are hastening on,
 By prophet-bards foretold,
When with the ever-circling years
 Comes round the age of gold!
When peace shall over all the earth
 Its final splendors fling,
And the whole world send back the song
 Which now the angels sing!

249 7s, d. *"All hail the morn!"* german.

Hail the night, all hail the morn,
When the Prince of Peace was born!
When, amid the wakeful fold,
Tidings good the angels told
Now our solemn chant we raise
Duly to the Saviour's praise
Now with carol hymns we bless
Christ the Lord, our righteousness.

2 While resounds the joyful cry,
"Glory be to God on high,
Peace on earth, good-will to men!"
Gladly we respond, "Amen!"
Thus we greet this holy day,
Pouring forth our festive lay;
Thus we tell, with saintly mirth,
Of Immanuel's wondrous birth.

250 11s, 10s. *"Star of the East."* r. heber.

Brightest and best of the sons of the
 morning!
Dawn on our darkness and lend us
 thine aid;
Star of the East, the horizon adorning,
 Guide where our infant Redeemer is
 laid.

2 Cold on his cradle the dew-drops are
 shining;
Low lies his head with the beasts of
 the stall:
Angels adore him, in slumber reclining,
 Maker, and Monarch, and Saviour of
 all!

3 Say shall we yield him, in costly devotion,
 Odors of Edom, and offerings divine?
Gems of the mountain, and pearls of the
 ocean,
Myrrh from the forest, or gold from
 the mine?

4 Vainly we offer each ample oblation,
 Vainly with gold would his favor secure:
Richer, by far, is the heart's adoration;
 Dearer to God are the prayers of the
 poor.

5 Brightest and best of the sons of the
 morning!
Dawn on our darkness and lend us
 thine aid·
Star of the East the horizon adorning,
 Guide where our infant Redeemer is
 laid.

251 7s. *Immanuel.* s. slinn.

God with us! oh, glorious name!
Let it shine in endless fame;
God and man in Christ unite;
Oh, mysterious depth and height!

2 God with us! the eternal Son
Took our soul, our flesh, and bone;
Now, ye saints, his grace admire,
Swell the song with holy fire.

3 God with us! but tainted not
With the first transgressor's blot;
Yet did he our sins sustain,
Bear the guilt, the curse, the pain.

4 God with us! oh, wondrous grace!
Let us see him face to face;
That we may Immanuel sing,
As we ought, our God and King!

252 C. M. *Incarnation.* A. STEELE.

AWAKE, awake the sacred song
  To our incarnate Lord!
Let every heart and every tongue
  Adore the eternal Word.

2 That awful Word, that sovereign Power,
  By whom the worlds were made—
Oh, happy morn! illustrious hour!—
  Was once in flesh arrayed!

3 Then shone almighty power and love,
  In all their glorious forms,
When Jesus left his throne above,
  To dwell with sinful worms.

4 Adoring angels tuned their songs
  To hail the joyful day;
With rapture then let mortal tongues
  Their grateful worship pay.

253 C. M. *The Promised Lord.* P. DODDRIDGE.

HARK, the glad sound! the Saviour comes,
  The Saviour promised long;
Let every heart prepare a throne,
  And every voice a song.

2 He comes, the prisoner to release,
  In Satan's bondage held;
The gates of brass before him burst,
  The iron fetters yield.

3 He comes, from thickest films of vice
  To clear the mental ray,
And, on the eyes long closed in night,
  To pour celestial day.

4 He comes, the broken heart to bind,
  The bleeding soul to cure,
And, with the treasures of his grace,
  Enrich the humble poor.

5 Our glad hosannas, Prince of Peace,
  Thy welcome shall proclaim,
And heaven's eternal arches ring
  With thy belovéd name.

254 C. M. *The Gospel Song.* S. MEDLEY.

MORTALS, awake, with angels join
  And chant the solemn lay;
Joy, love, and gratitude combine
  To hail the auspicious day.

2 In heaven the rapturous song began,
  And sweet seraphic fire
Through all the shining legions ran,
  And strung and tuned the lyre.

3 Swift through the vast expanse it flew,
  And loud the echo rolled;
The theme, the song, the joy, was new,
  'T was more than heaven could hold.

4 Down through the portals of the sky
  The impetuous torrent ran;
And angels flew, with eager joy,
  To bear the news to man.

5 Hark! the cherubic armies shout,
  And glory leads the song;
"Good-will and peace" are heard thro'-
  Th' harmonious angel-throng. [out

6 With joy the chorus we'll repeat,—
  "Glory to God on high!
Good-will and peace are now complete;
  Jesus was born to die!"

255 L. M. *Jesus' Birth.* ANON.

WAKE, O my soul, and hail the morn,
  For unto us a Saviour's born;
See! how the angels wing their way,
  To usher in the glorious day!

2 Hark! what sweet music, what a song,
  Sounds from the bright, celestial throng!
Sweet song, whose melting sounds impart
  Joy to each raptured, listening heart.

3 Come, join the angels in the sky,
  Glory to God, who reigns on high;
Let peace and love on earth abound,
  While time revolves and years roll round.

256 H. M. *"The notes of joy."* A. REED.

HARK! hark!—the notes of joy
  Roll o'er the heavenly plains,
And seraphs find employ
  For their sublimest strains;
Some new delight in heaven is known;
Loud sound the harps around the throne.

2 Hark! hark!—the sounds draw nigh,
  The joyful hosts descend;
Jesus forsakes the sky,
  To earth his footsteps bend;
He comes to bless our fallen race;
He comes with messages of grace.

3 Bear—bear the tidings round;
  Let every mortal know
What love in God is found,
  What pity he can show;
Ye winds that blow! ye waves that roll!
Bear the glad news from pole to pole.

THE LORD JESUS CHRIST.

CRAWFORD. L. M.   J. P. HOLBROOK, arr.

1. How sweetly flowed the gospel sound From lips of gen-tle-ness and grace, When listening thousands gath-ered round, And joy and gladness filled the place! And joy and gladness filled the place!

257 *The Great Teacher.* J. BOWRING.

How SWEETLY flowed the gospel sound
From lips of gentleness and grace,
When listening thousands gathered round,
And joy and gladness filled the place!

2 From heaven he came, of heaven he spoke,
To heaven he led his followers' way;
Dark clouds of gloomy night he broke,
Unvailing an immortal day.

3 "Come, wanderers, to my Father's home,
Come, all ye weary ones, and rest:"
Yes, sacred Teacher, we will come,
Obey thee, love thee, and be blest!

4 Decay then, tenements of dust;
Pillars of earthly pride, decay:
A nobler mansion waits the just,
And Jesus has prepared the way.

258 *"Holy, harmless."* A. C. COXE.

How BEAUTEOUS were the marks divine,
That in thy meekness used to shine,
That lit thy lonely pathway, trod
In wondrous love, O Son of God!

2 Oh, who like thee, so calm, so bright,
So pure, so made to live in light?
Oh, who like thee did ever go
So patient through a world of woe?

3 Oh, who like thee so humbly bore
The scorn, the scoffs of men, before?
So meek, forgiving, godlike, high,
So glorious in humility?

4 Even death, which sets the prisoner free,
Was pang, and scoff, and scorn to thee;
Yet love through all thy torture glowed,
And mercy with thy life-blood flowed.

5 Oh, in thy light be mine to go,
Illuming all my way of woe!
And give me ever on the road
To trace thy footsteps, Son of God.

259 *"He healed them."* J. MONTGOMERY.

WHEN, like a stranger on our sphere,
The lowly Jesus wandered here,
Where'er he went, affliction fled,
And sickness reared her fainting head

2 The eye that rolled in irksome night,
Beheld his face—for God is light;
The opening ear, the loosened tongue,
His precepts heard, his praises sung.

3 With bounding steps the halt and lame,
To hail their great Deliverer came;
O'er the cold grave he bowed his head,
He spake the word, and raised the dead.

4 Despairing madness, dark and wild,
In his inspiring presence smiled;
The storm of horror ceased to roll,
And reason lightened through the soul.

5 Through paths of loving-kindness led,
Where Jesus triumphed we would tread;
To all, with willing hands dispense
The gifts of our benevolence.

LIFE AND CHARACTER.

ROCKINGHAM. L. M.   LOWELL MASON.

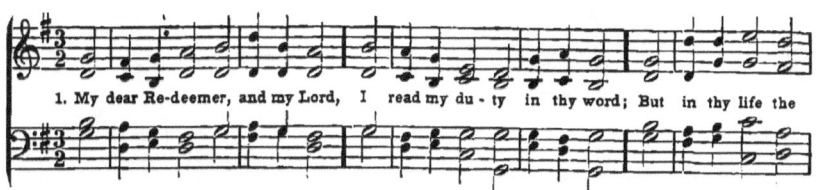

260   *The Divine Pattern.*   I. WATTS.

My dear Redeemer, and my Lord,
I read my duty in thy word;
But in thy life the law appears,
Drawn out in living characters.

2 Such was thy truth and such thy zeal,
Such deference to thy Father's will,
Such love, and meekness so divine,
I would transcribe and make them mine.

3 Cold mountains and the midnight air
Witnessed the fervor of thy prayer;
The desert thy temptations knew,
Thy conflict and thy victory too.

4 Be thou my pattern; make me bear
More of thy gracious image here;
Then God, the Judge, shall own my name
Among the followers of the Lamb.

GERMANY. L. M.   LUDWIG VON BEETHOVEN.

261   *"How shall I copy?"*   J. CONDER.

How SHALL I follow him I serve?
How shall I copy him I love?
Nor from those blessed footsteps swerve,
Which lead me to his seat above?

2 Lord, should my path through suffering lie,
Forbid it I should e'er repine;
Still let me turn to Calvary,
Nor heed my griefs, remembering thine.

3 Oh, let me think how thou didst leave
Untasted every pure delight,
To fast, to faint, to watch, to grieve,
The toilsome day, the homeless night:—

4 To faint, to grieve, to die for me!
Thou camest not thyself to please:
And, dear as earthly comforts be,
Shall I not love thee more than these?

8

THE LORD JESUS CHRIST.

TRENT. C. M.   GREATOREX COLL.

1. Behold, where, in a mortal form, Appears each grace divine! The virtues, all in Jesus met, With mildest radiance shine.

262   *"All in Jesus."*   WM. ENFIELD.
BEHOLD, where, in a mortal form,
  Appears each grace divine!
The virtues, all in Jesus met,
  With mildest radiance shine.

2 To spread the rays of heavenly light,
  To give the mourner joy,
To preach glad tidings to the poor,
  Was his divine employ.

3 'Mid keen reproach and cruel scorn,
  He meek and patient stood;
His foes, ungrateful, sought his life,
  Who labored for their good.

4 In the last hour of deep distress,
  Before his Father's throne,
With soul resigned he bowed and said,—
  "Thy will, not mine, be done!"

5 Be Christ our pattern, and our guide,
  His image may we bear;
Oh, may we tread his holy steps,—
  His joy and glory share.

263   *A lonely life.*   E. DENNY.
A PILGRIM through this lonely world,
  The blessèd Saviour passed;
A mourner all his life was he,
  A dying Lamb at last.

2 That tender heart that felt for all,
  For all its life-blood gave;
It found on earth no resting-place,
  Save only in the grave.

3 Such was our Lord; and shall we fear
  The cross, with all its scorn?
Or love a faithless evil world,
  That wreathed his brow with thorn?

4 No! facing all its frowns or smiles,
  Like him, obedient still,
We homeward press through storm or calm,
  To Zion's blessèd hill.

264   *For our example.*   E. DENNY.
WHAT grace, O Lord, and beauty shone
  Around thy steps below;
What patient love was seen in all
  Thy life and death of woe.

2 For, ever on thy burdened heart
  A weight of sorrow hung;
Yet no ungentle, murmuring word
  Escaped thy silent tongue.

3 Thy foes might hate, despise, revile,
  Thy friends unfaithful prove;
Unwearied in forgiveness still,
  Thy heart could only love.

4 Oh, give us hearts to love like thee!
  Like thee, O Lord, to grieve
Far more for others' sins, than all
  The wrongs that we receive.

5 One with thyself, may every eye,
  In us, thy brethren, see
The gentleness and grace that spring
  From union, Lord! with thee.

LIFE AND CHARACTER.

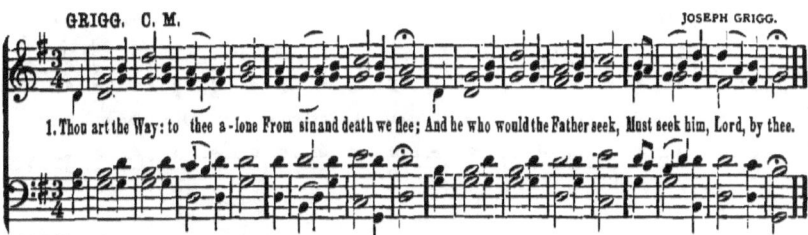

GRIGG. C. M.   JOSEPH GRIGG.

1. Thou art the Way: to thee a-lone From sin and death we flee; And he who would the Father seek, Must seek him, Lord, by thee.

265   *"Way, Truth, and Life."*   G. W. DOANE.

THOU art the Way: to thee alone
From sin and death we flee;
And he who would the Father seek,
Must seek him, Lord, by thee.

2 Thou art the Truth: thy word alone
True wisdom can impart;
Thou only canst inform the mind,
And purify the heart.

3 Thou art the Life: the rending tomb
Proclaims thy conquering arm;
And those who put their trust in thee
Nor death nor hell shall harm.

4 Thou art the Way, the Truth, the Life:
Grant us that Way to know;
That Truth to keep, that Life to win,
Whose joys eternal flow.

HELENA. C. M.   W. B. BRADBURY.

1. Lord, as to thy dear cross we flee, And pray to be for-given, So let thy life our pattern be, And form our souls for heaven.

266   *Pattern of Forgiveness.*   J. H. GURNEY.

LORD, as to thy dear cross we flee,
And pray to be forgiven,
So let thy life our pattern be,
And form our souls for heaven.

2 Help us, through good report and ill,
Our daily cross to bear;
Like thee, to do our Father's will,
Our brother's griefs to share.

3 Let grace our selfishness expel,
Our earthliness refine;
And kindness in our bosoms dwell
As free and true as thine.

4 If joy shall at thy bidding fly,
And grief's dark day come on,
We, in our turn, would meekly cry,
"Father, thy will be done!"

5 Kept peaceful in the midst of strife,
Forgiving and forgiven,
Oh, may we lead the pilgrim's life,
And follow thee to heaven!

267   *"Shall we forget."*   W. MITCHELL.

JESUS! thy love shall we forget,
And never bring to mind
The grace that paid our hopeless debt,
And bade us pardon find?

2 Shall we thy life of grief forget,
Thy fasting and thy prayer;
Thy locks with mountain vapors wet,
To save us from despair?

3 Gethsemane can we forget—
Thy struggling agony
When night lay dark on Olivet,
And none to watch with thee?

4 Our sorrows and our sins were laid
On thee, alone on thee;
Thy precious blood our ransom paid—
Thine all the glory be!

5 Life's brightest joys we may forget—
Our kindred cease to love;
But he who paid our hopeless debt,
Our constancy shall prove.

THE LORD JESUS CHRIST.

ORTONVILLE. C. M. — THOS. HASTINGS.

1. Ma-jes-tic sweetness sits enthroned Up-on the Saviour's brow; His head with radiant glories crowned, His lips with grace o'er-flow, His lips with grace o'er-flow.

268 *"Altogether Lovely."* S. STENNETT.

MAJESTIC sweetness sits enthroned
  Upon the Saviour's brow;
His head with radiant glories crowned,
  His lips with grace o'erflow.

2 No mortal can with him compare,
  Among the sons of men;
Fairer is he than all the fair
  That fill the heavenly train.

3 He saw me plunged in deep distress,
  He flew to my relief;
For me he bore the shameful cross,
  And carried all my grief.

4 To him I owe my life and breath,
  And all the joys I have;
He makes me triumph over death,
  He saves me from the grave.

5 To heaven, the place of his abode,
  He brings my weary feet;
Shows me the glories of my God,
  And makes my joy complete.

6 Since from his bounty I receive
  Such proofs of love divine,
Had I a thousand hearts to give,
  Lord! they should all be thine.

269 *"His free ways."* F. W. FABER.

OH, see how Jesus trusts himself
  Unto our childish love!
As though by his free ways with us
  Our earnestness to prove.

2 His sacred name a common word
  On earth he loves to hear;
There is no majesty in him
  Which love may not come near.

3 The light of love is round his feet,
  His paths are never dim;
And he comes nigh to us when we
  Dare not come nigh to him.

4 Let us be simple with him then,
  Not backward, stiff, nor cold,
As though our Bethlehem could be
  What Sinai was of old.

270 *The name "Jesus."* A. STEELE.

THE Saviour! oh, what endless charms
  Dwell in the blissful sound!
Its influence every fear disarms,
  And spreads sweet comfort round.

2 The almighty Former of the skies
  Stooped to our vile abode;
While angels viewed with wondering eyes
  And hailed the incarnate God.

3 Oh, the rich depths of love divine!
  Of bliss a boundless store!
Dear Saviour, let me call thee mine;
  I cannot wish for more.

4 On thee alone my hope relies,
  Beneath thy cross I fall;
My Lord, my Life, my Sacrifice,
  My Saviour, and my All!

LIFE AND CHARACTER. 103

INVITATION. C. M.   W. V. WALLACE.

1. We may not climb the heavenly steeps To bring the Lord Christ down; In vain we search the low-est deeps, For him no depths can drown.

271   *The true Test.*   J. G. WHITTIER.

WE may not climb the heavenly steeps
  To bring the Lord Christ down;
In vain we search the lowest deeps,
  For him no depths can drown.

2 But warm, sweet, tender, even yet
  A present help is he;
And faith has yet its Olivet,
  And love its Galilee.

3 The healing of the seamless dress
  Is by our beds of pain;

We touch him in life's throng and press,
  And we are whole again.

4 Through him the first fond prayers are said
  Our lips of childhood frame;
The last low whispers of our dead
  Are burdened with his name.

5 O Lord and Master of us all,
  Whate'er our name or sign,
We own thy sway, we hear thy call,
  We test our lives by thine!

ST. JOSEPH. 8s, 7s, 7s.   H. H. STATHAM.

1. { Jesus wept! those tears are over, But his heart is still the same; }
   { Kinsman, Friend, and elder Brother, Is his ev-er-lasting name. } Saviour, who can love like thee, Gracious One of Betha-ny?

272   *"Jesus wept."*   E. DENNY.

JESUS wept! those tears are over,
  But his heart is still the same;
Kinsman, Friend, and elder Brother,
  Is his everlasting name.
    Saviour, who can love like thee,
    Gracious One of Bethany?

2 When the pangs of trial seize us,
  When the waves of sorrow roll,
I will lay my head on Jesus,
  Pillow of the troubled soul.
    Surely, none can feel like thee,
    Weeping One of Bethany!

3 Jesus wept! and still in glory,
  He can mark each mourner's tear;
Living to retrace the story
  Of the hearts he solaced here.
    Lord, when I am called to die,
    Let me think of Bethany.

4 Jesus wept! that tear of sorrow
  Is a legacy of love;
Yesterday, to-day, to-morrow,
  He the same doth ever prove.
    Thou art all in all to me,
    Living One of Bethany!

THE LORD JESUS CHRIST.

OLIVE'S BROW. L. M.
W. B. BRADBURY.

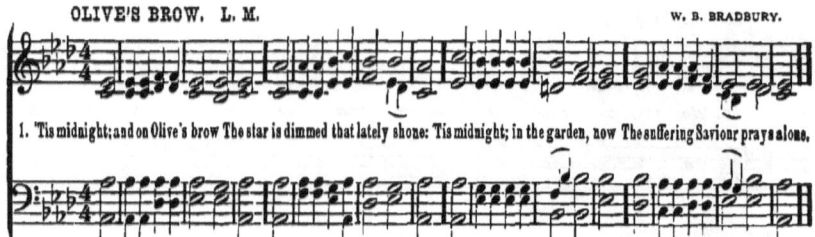

1. 'Tis midnight; and on Olive's brow The star is dimmed that lately shone: 'Tis midnight; in the garden, now The suffering Saviour prays alone.

273 *Gethsemane.* W. B. TAPPAN.

'TIS midnight; and on Olive's brow
The star is dimmed that lately shone:
'Tis midnight; in the garden, now
The suffering Saviour prays alone.

2 'Tis midnight; and from all removed,
The Saviour wrestles lone with fears;
Ev'n that disciple whom he loved
Heeds not his Master's grief and tears.

3 'Tis midnight; and for others' guilt
The Man of Sorrows weeps in blood;
Yet he that hath in anguish knelt
Is not forsaken by his God.

4 'Tis midnight; and from ether-plains
Is borne the song that angels know;
Unheard by mortals are the strains
That sweetly soothe the Saviour's woe.

274 *"'Tis finished!"* S. STENNETT.

"'TIS finished!"—so the Saviour cried,
And meekly bowed his head and died:
"'Tis finished!"—yes, the race is run,
The battle fought, the victory won.

2 'Tis finished!—all that heaven foretold
By prophets in the days of old;
And truths are opened to our view
That kings and prophets never knew.

3 'Tis finished!—Son of God, thy power
Hath triumphed in this awful hour;
And yet our eyes with sorrow see
That life to us was death to thee.

4 'Tis finished!—let the joyful sound
Be heard through all the nations round:
'Tis finished!—let the triumph rise,
And swell the chorus of the skies.

SOLITUDE. L. M.
V. C. TAYLOR.

1. 'Tis midnight; and on Ol-ive's brow The star is dimmed that lately shone: 'Tis midnight; in the gar-den now The suffering Sav-iour prays a-lone.

SUFFERINGS AND DEATH.

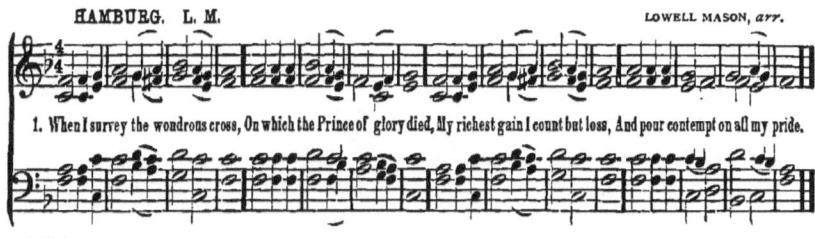

275   *"The wondrous Cross."*   I. WATTS.

WHEN I survey the wondrous cross,
   On which the Prince of glory died,
My richest gain I count but loss,
   And pour contempt on all my pride.

2 Forbid it, Lord! that I should boast,
   Save in the death of Christ, my God;
All the vain things that charm me most
   I sacrifice them to his blood.

3 See, from his head, his hands, his feet,
   Sorrow and love flow mingled down;
Did e'er such love and sorrow meet,
   Or thorns compose so rich a crown?

4 His dying crimson, like a robe,
   Spreads o'er his body on the tree;
Then I am dead to all the globe,
   And all the globe is dead to me.

5 Were the whole realm of nature mine,
   That were a present far too small;
Love so amazing, so divine,
   Demands my soul, my life, my all.

276   *"For me."*   H. BONAR.

JESUS, whom angel hosts adore,
   Became a man of griefs for me;
In love, though rich, becoming poor,
   That I through him enriched might be.

2 Though Lord of all, above, below,
   He went to Olivet for me:
There drank my cup of wrath and woe,
   When bleeding in Gethsemane.

3 The ever-blessèd Son of God
   Went up to Calvary for me;
There paid my debt, there bore my load.
   In his own body on the tree.

4 Jesus, whose dwelling is the skies,
   Went down into the grave for me;
There overcame my enemies,
   There won the glorious victory.

5 'T is finished all: the vail is rent,
   The welcome sure, the access free:—
Now then, we leave our banishment,
   O Father, to return to thee!

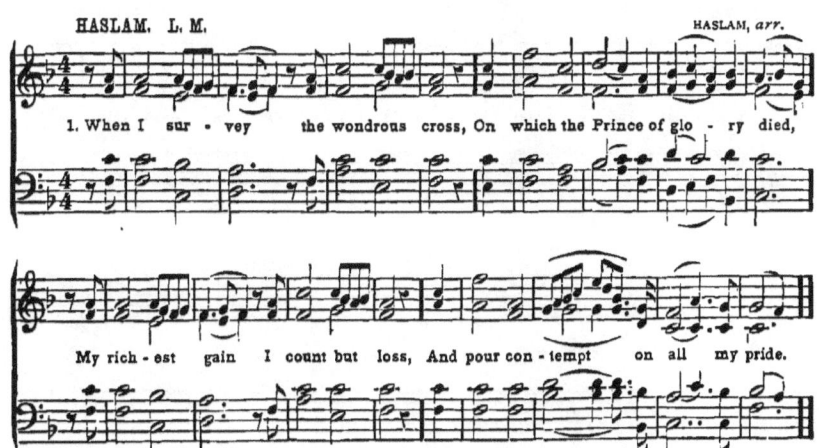

THE LORD JESUS CHRIST.

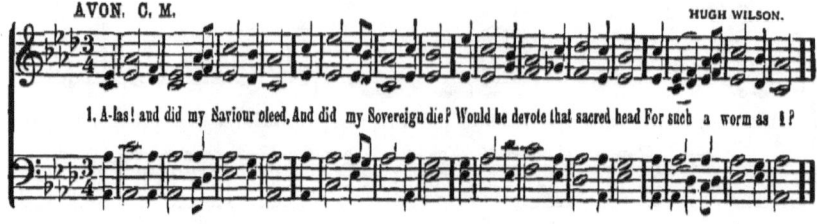

AVON. C. M.   HUGH WILSON.

1. A-las! and did my Saviour bleed, And did my Sovereign die? Would he devote that sacred head For such a worm as I?

277   *"Grace unknown."*   L. WATTS.

Alas! and did my Saviour bleed,
  And did my Sovereign die?
Would he devote that sacred head
  For such a worm as I?

2 Was it for crimes that I had done
  He groaned upon the tree?
Amazing pity! grace unknown!
  And love beyond degree!

3 Well might the sun in darkness hide,
  And shut his glories in,
When Christ, the great Creator, died
  For man, the creature's sin.

4 Thus might I hide my blushing face
  While his dear cross appears;
Dissolve my heart in thankfulness,
  And melt my eyes to tears.

5 But drops of grief can ne'er repay
  The debt of love I owe;
Here, Lord, I give myself away,
  'Tis all that I can do.

278   *Suffered for sin.*   L. WATTS.

Oh, if my soul were formed for woe,
  How would I vent my sighs!
Repentance should like rivers flow
  From both my streaming eyes.

2 'Twas for my sins my dearest Lord
  Hung on the cursed tree,
And groaned away a dying life
  For thee, my soul! for thee.

3 Oh, how I hate these lusts of mine
  That crucified my Lord;
Those sins that pierced and nailed his flesh
  Fast to the fatal wood!

4 Yes, my Redeemer—they shall die;
  My heart has so decreed;
Nor will I spare the guilty things
  That made my Saviour bleed.

5 While with a melting, broken heart,
  My murdered Lord I view,
I'll raise revenge against my sins,
  And slay the murderers too.

COMMUNION. C. M.   STEPHEN JENKS.

1. A-las! and did my Sav-iour bleed, And did my Sove-reign die? Would he de-vote that sa-cred head For such a worm as I?

SUFFERINGS AND DEATH.

MANOAH. C. M. — FROM G. ROSSINI.

1. I saw One hang-ing on a tree, In ag-o-ny and blood;
Who fixed his lan-guid eyes on me, As near the cross I stood.

279 *The two Looks.* J. NEWTON.

I saw One hanging on a tree,
  In agony and blood;
Who fixed his languid eyes on me,
  As near the cross I stood.

2 Sure, never, till my latest breath,
  Can I forget that look:
It seemed to charge me with his death,
  Though not a word he spoke.

3 Alas! I knew not what I did,—
  But now my tears are vain;
Where shall my trembling soul be hid,
  For I the Lord have slain!

4 A second look he gave, that said,
  "I freely all forgive:
This blood is for thy ransom paid;
  I die that thou may'st live."

5 Thus while his death my sin displays
  In all its blackest hue,
Such is the mystery of grace,
  It seals my pardon too!

280 *"He remembers Calvary."* I. WATTS.

How condescending and how kind
  Was God's eternal Son!
Our misery reached his heavenly mind,
  And pity brought him down.

2 He sunk beneath our heavy woes,
  To raise us to his throne;
There's ne'er a gift his hand bestows,
  But cost his heart a groan.

3 This was compassion, like a God,
  That when the Saviour knew
The price of pardon was his blood,
  His pity ne'er withdrew.

4 Now, though he reigns exalted high,
  His love is still as great;
Well he remembers Calvary,
  Nor let his saints forget.

281 *"O Christ of God!"* RAY PALMER.

O Jesus, sweet the tears I shed,
  While at thy cross I kneel,
Gaze on thy wounded, fainting head,
  And all thy sorrows feel.

2 My heart dissolves to see thee bleed,
  This heart so hard before;
I hear thee for the guilty plead,
  And grief o'erflows the more.

3 I know this cleansing blood of thine
  Was shed, dear Lord, for me:
For me, for all,—oh, grace divine!—
  Who look by faith on thee.

4 O Christ of God, O spotless Lamb,
  By love my soul is drawn;
Henceforth, for ever, thine I am;
  Here life and peace are born.

5 In patient hope, the cross I'll bear,
  Thine arm shall be my stay;
And thou, enthroned, my soul shalt spare,
  On thy great judgment-day.

THE LORD JESUS CHRIST.

HYMN OF JOY. 8s, 7s, D.   LUDWIG VON BEETHOVEN.

1. Hail, thou once despised Jesus! Crowned in mockery a king! Thou didst suffer to release us; Thou didst free salvation bring. Hail, thou agonizing Saviour, Bearer of our sin and shame! By thy merits we find favor; Life is given thro' thy name.

282   *Mocked.*   J. BAKEWELL.

Hail, thou once despiséd Jesus!
  Crowned in mockery a king!
Thou didst suffer to release us;
  Thou didst free salvation bring.
Hail, thou agonizing Saviour,
  Bearer of our sin and shame!
By thy merits we find favor;
  Life is given through thy name.

2 Paschal Lamb, by God appointed,
  All our sins on thee were laid;
By Almighty Love anointed,
  Thou hast full atonement made:
All thy people are forgiven
  Through the virtue of thy blood;
Opened is the gate of heaven,
  Peace is made 'twixt man and God.

283   *On the cross.*   R. LEE.

When I view my Saviour bleeding,
  For my sins, upon the tree;
Oh, how wondrous!—how exceeding
  Great his love appears to me!
Floods of deep distress and anguish,
  To impede his labors, came;
Yet they all could not extinguish
  Love's eternal, burning flame.

2 Now redemption is completed,
  Full salvation is procured;
Death and Satan are defeated,
  By the sufferings he endured.

Now the gracious Mediator
  Risen to the courts of bliss,
Claims for me, a sinful creature,
  Pardon, righteousness, and peace!

3 Sure such infinite affection
  Lays the highest claims to mine;
All my powers, without exception,
  Should in fervent praises join.
Jesus, fit me for thy service;
  Form me for thyself alone;
I am thy most costly purchase,—
  Take possession of thine own.

284   *Reproached.*   MORAVIAN.

Cross, reproach, and tribulation!
  Ye to me are welcome guests,
When I have this consolation,
  That my soul in Jesus rests.
The reproach of Christ is glorious!
  Those who here his burden bear,
In the end shall prove victorious,
  And eternal gladness share.

2 Bonds and stripes, and evil story,
  Are our honorable crowns;
Pain is peace, and shame is glory,
  Gloomy dungeons are as thrones.
Bear, then, the reproach of Jesus,
  Ye who live a life of faith!
Lift triumphant songs and praises
  Ev'n in martyrdom and death.

SUFFERINGS AND DEATH.

STABAT MATER. P. M.   ANON.

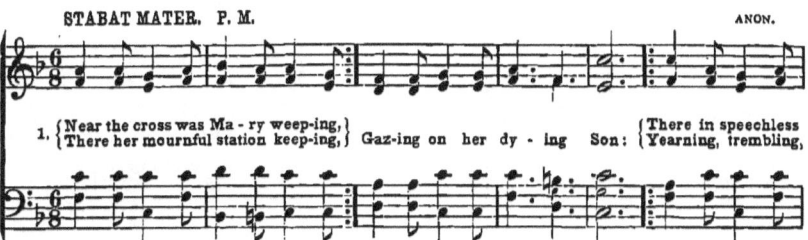

1. Near the cross was Mary weeping, / There her mournful station keeping, / Gazing on her dying Son: / There in speechless / Yearning, trembling,

anguish groaning, / sighing, moaning, / Through her soul the sword had [gone.

285   *"Near the Cross."*   J. W. ALEXANDER, *tr.*

NEAR the cross was Mary weeping,
There her mournful station keeping,
  Gazing on her dying Son:
There in speechless anguish groaning,
Yearning, trembling, sighing, moaning,
  Through her soul the sword had gone!

2 But we have no need to borrow
Motives from the mother's sorrow,
  At our Saviour's cross to mourn:
'Twas our sins brought him from heaven,
These the cruel nails had driven:
  All his griefs for us were borne.

3 When no eye its pity gave us,
When there was no arm to save us,
  He his love and power displayed:
By his stripes he wrought our healing,
By his death, our life revealing,
  He for us the ransom paid.

4 Jesus, may thy love constrain us,
That from sin we may refrain us,
  In thy griefs may deeply grieve:
Thee our best affections giving,
To thy glory ever living,
  May we in thy glory live.

286   *"It is finished."*   H. BONAR.

FROM the cross the blood is falling,
And to us a voice is calling

Like a trumpet silver-clear:
'Tis the voice announcing pardon—
It is finished, is its burden,
  Pardon to the far and near.

2 Peace that glorious blood is sealing,
All our wounds for ever healing,
  And removing every load;
Words of peace that voice has spoken,
Peace that shall no more be broken,
  Peace between the soul and God.

287   *"Day of darkness."*   F. H. HEDGE, *tr.*

'TWAS the day when God's Anointed
Died for us the death appointed,
  Bleeding on the dreadful cross;
Day of darkness, day of terror,
Deadly fruit of ancient error,
  Nature's fall, and Eden's loss!

2 Haste, prepare the bitter chalice!
Gentile hate and Jewish malice
  Lift the royal Victim high;
Like the serpent, wonder-gifted,
Which the prophet once uplifted,
  For a sinful world to die.

3 Conscious of the deed unholy,
Nature's pulses beat more slowly,
  And the sun his light denied;
Darkness wrapped the sacred city,
And the earth with fear and pity
  Trembled, when the Just One died

4 Not in vain for us uplifted,
Man of sorrows, wonder-gifted,
  May that sacred symbol be;
Eminent amid the ages,
Guide of heroes and of sages,
  May it guide us still to thee.

THE LORD JESUS CHRIST.

PASSION CHORALE. 7s, 6s. D. — J. S. BACH, *arr.*

1. O sacred Head, now wounded, With grief and shame weighed down,
Now scornfully surrounded, With thorns thine only crown;
O sacred Head, what glory, What bliss, till now was thine!
Yet, though despised and gory, I joy to call thee mine.

---

288   *"Upon the cross."*   ANON.

O Jesus, we adore thee,
  Upon the cross, our King:
We bow our hearts before thee;
  Thy gracious Name we sing:
That Name hath brought salvation,
  That Name, in life our stay;
Our peace, our consolation
  When life shall fade away.

2 Yet doth the world disdain thee,
  Still pressing by thy cross:
Lord, may our hearts retain thee;
  All else we count but loss.
The grief thy soul enduréd,
  Who can that grief declare?
Thy pains have thus assuréd
  That thou thy foes wilt spare.

3 Ah, Lord, our sins arraigned thee,
  And nailed thee to the tree:
Our pride, O Lord, disdained thee;—
  Yet deign our hope to be.
O glorious King, we bless thee,
  No longer pass thee by;
O Jesus, we confess thee
  Our Lord enthroned on high.

---

289   *The Lamb of God.*   J. G. DECK.

O Lamb of God! still keep me
  Near to thy wounded side;
'Tis only there in safety
  And peace I can abide!
What foes and snares surround me,
  What doubts and fears within!
The grace that sought and found me,
  Alone can keep me clean.

2 'Tis only in thee hiding
  I know my life secure—
Only in thee abiding,
  The conflict can endure:
Thine arm the victory gaineth
  O'er every hateful foe;
Thy love my heart sustaineth
  In all its care and woe.

3 Soon shall my eyes behold thee,
  With rapture, face to face;
One half hath not been told me
  Of all thy power and grace:
Thy beauty, Lord, and glory,
  The wonders of thy love,
Shall be the endless story
  Of all the saints above.

SUFFERINGS AND DEATH.

290 *At the Cross.* J. W. ALEXANDER, *tr.*

O SACRED Head, now wounded,
  With grief and shame weighed down,
Now scornfully surrounded
  With thorns, thine only crown;
O sacred Head, what glory,
  What bliss, till now was thine!
Yet, though despised and gory,
  I joy to call thee mine.

2 What thou, my Lord, hast suffered
  Was all for sinners' gain:
Mine, mine was the transgression,
  But thine the deadly pain;
Lo, here I fall, my Saviour!
  'Tis I deserved thy place;
Look on me with thy favor,
  Vouchsafe to me thy grace.

3 What language shall I borrow,
  To thank thee, dearest Friend,
For this, thy dying sorrow,
  Thy pity without end?
Lord, make me thine for ever,
  Nor let me faithless prove:
Oh, let me never, never,
  Abuse such dying love.

4 Be near when I am dying,
  Oh, show thy cross to me!
And for my succor flying,
  Come, Lord, and set me free!
These eyes, new faith receiving,
  From Jesus shall not move;
For he who dies believing,
  Dies safely—through thy love.

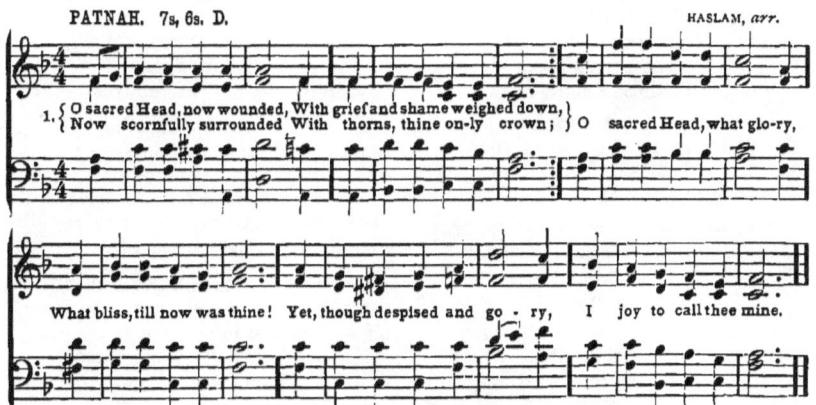

291 C. L. M.　　*Gethsemane.*　　F. D. HEMANS.

HE knelt, the Saviour knelt and prayed,
　When but his Father's eye
Looked through the lonely garden's shade,
　On that dread agony;
The Lord of all above, beneath,
Was bowed with sorrow unto death.

2 The sun set in a fearful hour,
　The skies might well grow dim,
When this mortality had power
　So to o'ershadow him!
That he who gave man's breath, might know
The very depths of human woe. [know

3 He knew them all; the doubt, the
　The faint, perplexing dread; [strife,
The mists that hang o'er parting life,
　All darkened round his head;
And the Deliverer knelt to pray;
Yet passed it not, that cup, away.

4 It passed not, though the stormy wave
　Had sunk beneath his tread;
It passed not, though to him the grave
　Had yielded up its dead.
But there was sent him from on high,
A gift of strength for man to die.

5 And was his mortal hour beset
　With anguish and dismay?
How may we meet our conflict yet,
　In the dark, narrow way?
How but through him, that path who
Save or we perish, Son of God! [trod?

292 L. M.　　*Christ in the Desert.*　　J. F. THRUPP.

AWHILE in spirit, Lord, to thee
Into the desert would we flee;
Awhile upon the barren steep
Thy fast with thee in spirit keep;—

2 Awhile from thy temptation learn
The daily snares of sin to spurn,
And in our hearts to feel and own
Man liveth not by bread alone.

3 And while at thy command we pray,
Give us our bread from day to day,
May we with thee, O Christ, be fed,
Thou Word of God, thou Living Bread.

4 Incarnate Lord, we come to thee,
Thou knowest our infirmity;
Be thou our Helper in the strife,
Be thou our true, our inward Life.

293 7s.　　"*Jesus, Saviour.*"　　J. D. BURNS.

THOU who didst on Calvary bleed,
Thou who dost for sinners plead,
Help me in my time of need,
　Jesus, Saviour, hear my cry!

2 In my darkness and my grief,
With my heart of unbelief,
I, who am of sinners chief,
　Jesus, lift to thee mine eye!

3 Foes without and fears within,
With no plea thy grace to win,
But that thou canst save from sin,
　Jesus, to thy cross I fly!

4 There on thee I cast my care,
There to thee I raise my prayer,
Jesus, save me from despair,
　Save me, save me, or I die!

5 When the storms of trial lower,
When I feel temptation's power,
In the last and darkest hour,
　Jesus, Saviour, be thou nigh!

294 7s, 6 l.　　"*Lamb of God.*"　　RAY PALMER.

JESUS, Lamb of God, for me
　Thou, the Lord of life, didst die;
Whither—whither, but to thee,
　Can a trembling sinner fly!
Death's dark waters o'er me roll,
Save, oh, save my sinking soul!

2 Never bowed a martyr's head
　Weighed with equal sorrow down;
Never blood so rich was shed,
　Never king wore such a crown;
To thy cross and sacrifice
Faith now lifts her tearful eyes.

3 All my soul, by love subdued,
　Melts in deep contrition there;
By thy mighty grace renewed,
　New-born hope forbids despair:
Lord! thou canst my guilt forgive,
Thou hast bid me look and live.

4 While with broken heart I kneel,
　Sinks the inward storm to rest;
Life—immortal life—I feel
　Kindled in my throbbing breast;
Thine—for ever thine—I am!
Glory to thee, bleeding Lamb!

295 L. M.   *"He lives again."*   I. WATTS.

He dies!—the friend of sinners dies;
  Lo! Salem's daughters weep around;
A solemn darkness vails the skies;
  A sudden trembling shakes the ground.

2 Here's love and grief beyond degree:
  The Lord of glory dies for men;
But lo! what sudden joys we see,
  Jesus, the dead, revives again.

3 The rising God forsakes the tomb;
  Up to his Father's court he flies;
Cherubic legions guard him home,
  And shout him welcome to the skies.

4 Break off your tears, ye saints, and tell
  How high our great Deliverer reigns;
Sing how he spoiled the hosts of hell,
  And led the tyrant Death in chains.

5 Say—live for ever, glorious King,
  Born to redeem, and strong to save!
Where now, O Death, where is thy sting?
  And where thy victory, boasting Grave?

296 C. M.   *"Died for me."*   A. STEELE.

To our Redeemer's glorious name,
  Awake the sacred song!
Oh, may his love—immortal flame—
  Tune every heart and tongue!

2 His love, what mortal thought can reach?
  What mortal tongue display?
Imagination's utmost stretch,
  In wonder, dies away.

3 Dear Lord! while we adoring pay
  Our humble thanks to thee,
May every heart with rapture say,—
  "The Saviour died for me!"

4 Oh, may the sweet, the blissful theme,
  Fill every heart and tongue,
Till strangers love thy charming name,
  And join the sacred song.

297 7s.   *The Resurrection.*   T. SCOTT.

Angels! roll the rock away;
Death! yield up thy mighty prey;
See! the Saviour leaves the tomb,
Glowing with immortal bloom.

2 Hark! the wondering angels raise
Louder notes of joyful praise;
Let the earth's remotest bound
Echo with the blissful sound.

3 Saints on earth, lift up your eyes,—
Now to glory see him rise
In long triumph through the sky,
Up to waiting worlds on high.

4 Heaven unfolds its portals wide!
Mighty Conqueror! through them ride;
King of glory! mount thy throne,
Boundless empire is thine own.

298 6s, 4s.   *"Worthy the Lamb!"*   J. ALLEN.

Glory to God on high!
  Let heaven and earth reply,
    "Praise ye his name!"
His love and grace adore,
Who all our sorrows bore;
Sing loud for evermore,
    "Worthy the Lamb!"

2 While they around the throne
Cheerfully join in one,
    Praising his name,—
Ye who have felt his blood
Sealing your peace with God,
Sound his dear name abroad,
    "Worthy the Lamb!"

3 Join, all ye ransomed race,
Our Lord and God to bless;
    Praise ye his name!
In him we will rejoice,
And make a joyful noise,
Shouting with heart and voice,
    "Worthy the Lamb!"

299 H. M.   *"Rejoice!"*   C. WESLEY.

Rejoice! the Lord is King;
  Your Lord and King adore:
Mortals, give thanks and sing,
  And triumph evermore!
Lift up your heart, lift up your voice;
Rejoice!—again I say, rejoice!

2 Jesus, the Saviour, reigns,
  The God of truth and love;
When he had purged our stains,
  He took his seat above:
Lift up your heart, lift up your voice;
Rejoice!—again I say, rejoice!

3 Rejoice in glorious hope:
  Jesus, the Judge, shall come
And take his servants up
  To their eternal home:
We soon shall hear the archangel's voice;
The trump of God shall sound, Rejoice!

THE LORD JESUS CHRIST.

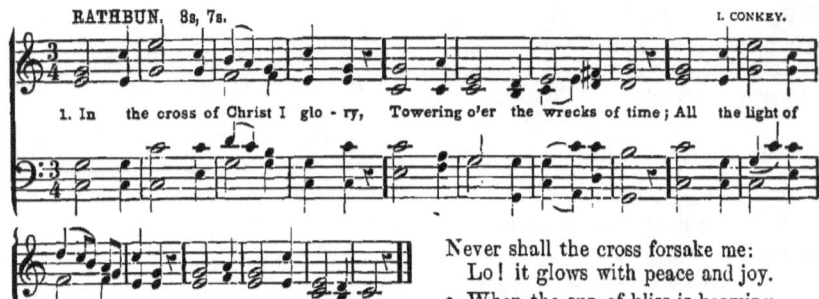

RATHBUN. 8s, 7s.   I. CONKEY.

1. In the cross of Christ I glory, Towering o'er the wrecks of time; All the light of sacred story Gathers round its head sublime.

300   *Glorying in the Cross.*   J. BOWRING.

In the cross of Christ I glory,
  Towering o'er the wrecks of time;
All the light of sacred story
  Gathers round its head sublime.

2 When the woes of life o'ertake me,
  Hopes deceive, and fears annoy,
Never shall the cross forsake me:
  Lo! it glows with peace and joy.

3 When the sun of bliss is beaming
  Light and love upon my way,
From the cross the radiance, streaming,
  Adds more lustre to the day.

4 Bane and blessing, pain and pleasure,
  By the cross are sanctified;
Peace is there, that knows no measure,
  Joys that through all time abide.

5 In the cross of Christ I glory,
  Towering o'er the wrecks of time;
All the light of sacred story
  Gathers round its head sublime.

CARTHAGE. 8s, 7s.   G. F. ROOT, *arr.*

1. Christ, above all glory seated! King eternal, strong to save! To thee, Death, by death defeated, Triumph high and glory gave.

301   *"Many crowns."*   J. R. WOODFORD.

Christ, above all glory seated!
  King eternal, strong to save!
To thee, Death, by death defeated,
  Triumph high and glory gave.

2 Thou art gone where now is given
  What no mortal might could gain,
On the eternal throne of heaven,
  In thy Father's power to reign.

3 We, O Lord! with hearts adoring,
  Follow thee above the sky:
Hear our prayers thy grace imploring,
  Lift our souls to thee on high.

4 So when thou again in glory
  On the clouds of heaven shall shine,
We thy flock shall stand before thee,
  Owned for evermore as thine.

RESURRECTION AND REIGN. 115

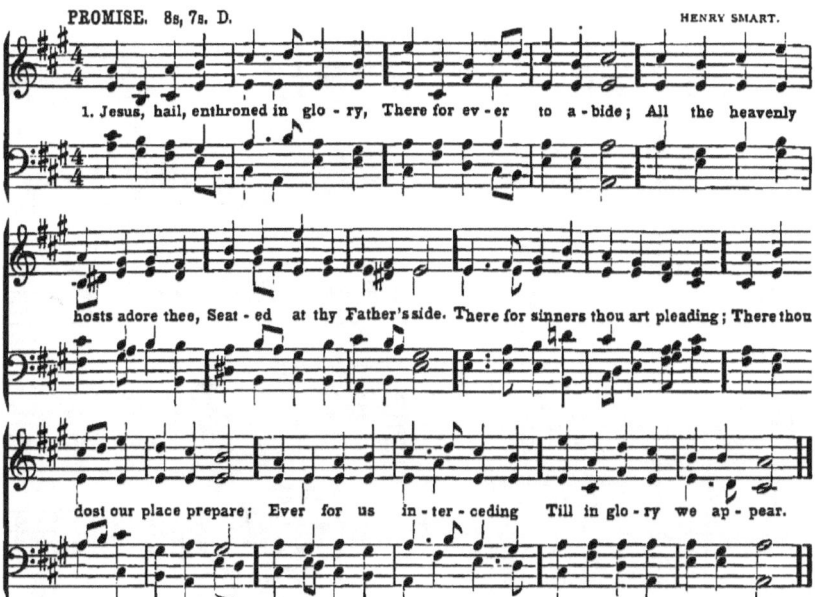

302 *"Enthroned in glory."* J. BAKEWELL.

JESUS, hail, enthroned in glory,
　There for ever to abide;
All the heavenly hosts adore thee,
　Seated at thy Father's side.
There for sinners thou art pleading;
　There thou dost our place prepare ;
Ever for us interceding
　Till in glory we appear.

2 Worship, honor, power and blessing,
　Thou art worthy to receive;
Loudest praises, without ceasing,
　Meet it is for us to give.
Help, ye bright angelic spirits,
　Bring your sweetest, noblest lays;
Help to sing our Saviour's merits,
　Help to chant Immanuel's praise.

303 *"The blood that speaketh."* C. WESLEY.

FATHER, hear the blood of Jesus,
　Speaking in thine ears above:
From impending wrath release us;
　Manifest thy pardoning love.
Oh, receive us to thy favor,—
　For his only sake receive;
Give us to the bleeding Saviour,
　Let us by his dying live.

2 "To thy pardoning grace receive them,"
　Once he prayed upon the tree;
Still his blood cries out "Forgive them;
　All their sins were laid on me."
Still our Advocate in heaven
　Prays the prayer on earth begun,—
"Father, show their sins forgiven;
　Father, glorify thy Son!"

304 *"Shall see his face."* M. PYPER.

"WE shall see Him," in our nature,
　Seated on his lofty throne,
Loved, adored, by every creature,
　Owned as God, and God alone !
There the hosts of shining spirits
　Strike their harps, and loudly sing
To the praise of Jesus' merits,
　To the glory of their King.

2 When we pass o'er death's dark river,
　"We shall see him as he is,"
Resting in his love and favor,
　Owning all the glory his.
There to cast our crowns before him,
　Oh, what bliss the thought affords !
There for ever to adore him,
　King of kings, and Lord of lords !

305   *He lives again.*   C. WESLEY.

CHRIST, the Lord, is risen to-day,
Sons of men, and angels, say;
Raise your joys and triumphs high!
Sing, ye heavens! and earth, reply!

2 Love's redeeming work is done,
Fought the fight, the battle won;
Lo, our Sun's eclipse is o'er;
Lo, he sets in blood no more.

3 Vain the stone, the watch, the seal;
Christ hath burst the gates of hell;
Death in vain forbids his rise;
Christ hath opened Paradise.

4 Lives again our glorious King;
"Where, O Death, is now thy sting?"
Once he died our souls to save;
"Where's thy victory, boasting Grave?"

5 Soar we now where Christ has led,
Following our exalted Head;
Made like him, like him we rise;
Ours the cross, the grave, the skies!

306   *Joy in the Lord.*   T. KELLY.

JOYFUL be the hours to-day;
Joyful let the seasons be;
Let us sing, for well we may:
Jesus! we will sing of thee.

2 Should thy people silent be,
Then the very stones would sing:
What a debt we owe to thee,
Thee our Saviour, thee our King!

3 Joyful are we now to own,
Rapture thrills us as we trace
All the deeds thy love hath done,
All the riches of thy grace.

4 'Tis thy grace alone can save;
Every blessing comes from thee—
All we have, and hope to have,
All we are, and hope to be.

5 Thine the Name to sinners dear!
Thine the Name all names before!
Blessèd here and everywhere;
Blessèd now and evermore!

RESURRECTION AND REIGN.

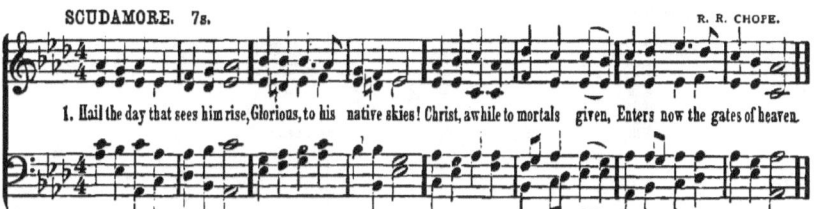

SCUDAMORE. 7s.   R. R. CHOPE.

1. Hail the day that sees him rise, Glorious, to his native skies! Christ, awhile to mortals given, Enters now the gates of heaven.

307   *The Lord's Day.*   C. WESLEY.

Hail the day that sees him rise,
Glorious, to his native skies!
Christ, awhile to mortals given,
Enters now the gates of heaven.

2 There the glorious triumph waits;
Lift your heads, eternal gates!
Christ hath vanquished death and sin;
Take the King of glory in.

3 See, the heaven its Lord receives!
Yet he loves the earth he leaves:
Though returning to his throne,
Still he calls mankind his own.

4 Still for us he intercedes,
His prevailing death he pleads;
Near himself prepares a place,
Great Forerunner of our race.

5 What, though parted from our sight,
Far above yon starry height;
Thither our affections rise,
Following him beyond the skies.

MOZART. 7.   FROM J. C. W. A. MOZART.

1. Christ the Lord is risen a-gain; Christ hath broken ev-ery chain; Hark! an-gel-ic voic-es cry, Singing ev-er-more on high, Hal-le-lu-jah! Praise the Lord!

308   *"Hallelujah."*   C. WINKWORTH, tr.

Christ the Lord is risen again,
Christ hath broken every chain;
Hark! angelic voices cry,
Singing evermore on high,
  Hallelujah! Praise the Lord!

2 He who bore all pain and loss,
Comfortless, upon the cross,
Lives in glory now on high,
Pleads for us, and hears our cry:
  Hallelujah! Praise the Lord!

3 He who slumbered in the grave
Is exalted now to save;
Now through Christendom it rings
That the Lamb is King of kings:
  Hallelujah! Praise the Lord!

4 Now he bids us tell abroad
How the lost may be restored,
How the penitent forgiven,
How we, too, may enter heaven:
  Hallelujah! Praise the Lord!

THE LORD JESUS CHRIST.

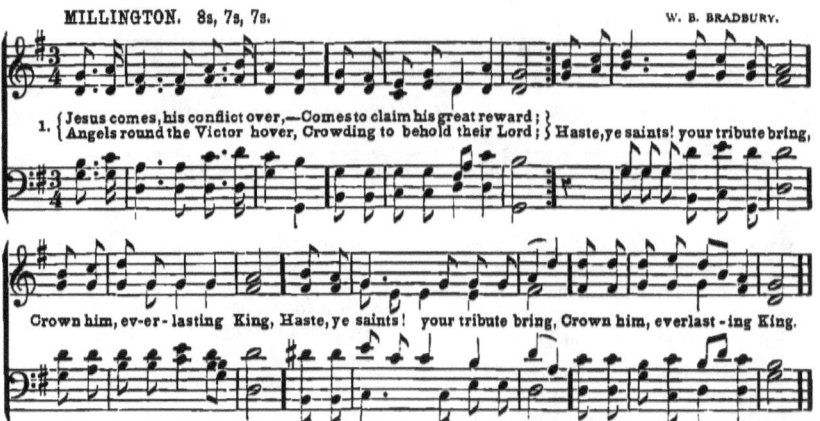

MILLINGTON. 8s, 7s, 7s.   W. B. BRADBURY.

1. { Jesus comes, his conflict over,—Comes to claim his great reward;
 { Angels round the Victor hover, Crowding to behold their Lord; } Haste, ye saints! your tribute bring, Crown him, ev-er-lasting King, Haste, ye saints! your tribute bring, Crown him, everlast-ing King.

309   *The Return to Heaven.*   T. KELLY.

JESUS comes, his conflict over,—
  Comes to claim his great reward;
Angels round the Victor hover,
  Crowding to behold their Lord;
Haste, ye saints! your tribute bring,
Crown him, everlasting King.

2 Yonder throne for him erected,
  Now becomes the Victor's seat;
Lo, the Man on earth rejected!
  Angels worship at his feet:
Haste, ye saints! your tribute bring,
Crown him, everlasting King.

3 Day and night they cry before him,—
  "Holy, holy, holy Lord!"
All the powers of heaven adore him,
  All obey his sovereign word;
Haste, ye saints! your tribute bring,
Crown him, everlasting King.

310   *Isaiah* 63: 1.   T. KELLY.

WHO is this that comes from Edom,
  All his raiment stained with blood;
To the slave proclaiming freedom;
  Bringing and bestowing good:
Glorious in the garb he wears,
Glorious in the spoils he bears?

2 'Tis the Saviour, now victorious,
  Travelling onward in his might;
'Tis the Saviour, oh, how glorious
  To his people is the sight!
Jesus now is strong to save;
Mighty to redeem the slave.

3 Why that blood his raiment staining?
  'Tis the blood of many slain;
Of his foes there's none remaining,
  None the contest to maintain:
Fallen they, no more to rise,
All their glory prostrate lies.

4 Mighty Victor, reign for ever;
  Wear the crown so dearly won;
Never shall thy people, never
  Cease to sing what thou hast done;
Thou hast fought thy people's foes;
Thou hast healed thy people's woes.

311   *All glory to Christ.*   T. KELLY.

GLORY, glory to our King!
  Crowns unfading wreathe his head;
Jesus is the name we sing,—
  Jesus, risen from the dead;
Jesus, Conqueror o'er the grave;
Jesus, mighty now to save.

2 Jesus is gone up on high:
  Angels come to meet their King;
Shouts triumphant rend the sky,
  While the Victor's praise they sing:
"Open now, ye heavenly gates!
'Tis the King of glory waits."

3 Now behold him high enthroned,
  Glory beaming from his face,
By adoring angels owned,
  God of holiness and grace!
Oh, for hearts and tongues to sing—
"Glory, glory to our King!"

RESURRECTION AND REIGN.

312 *"Jesus reigns."* T. KELLY.

HARK! ten thousand harps and voices
 Sound the note of praise above;
Jesus reigns, and heaven rejoices;
 Jesus reigns, the God of love:
See, he sits on yonder throne;
 Jesus rules the world alone.

2 King of glory! reign for ever—
 Thine an everlasting crown;
Nothing, from thy love, shall sever
 Those whom thou hast made thine own;—
Happy objects of thy grace,
Destined to behold thy face.

3 Saviour! hasten thine appearing;
 Bring, oh, bring the glorious day,
When, the awful summons hearing,
 Heaven and earth shall pass away;—
Then, with golden harps, we'll sing,—
"Glory, glory to our King!"

313 *We live in Him.* C. WORDSWORTH.

SEE, the Conqueror mounts in triumph!
 See the King in royal state,
Riding on the clouds, his chariot,
 To his heavenly palace gate!
Hark! the choirs of angel voices
 Joyful hallelujahs sing,
And the portals high are lifted
 To receive their heavenly King.

2 Who is this that comes in glory,
 With the trump of jubilee?

Lord of battles, God of armies,
 He has gained the victory;
He, who on the cross did suffer,
 He, who from the grave arose,
He has vanquished sin and Satan,
 He by death has spoiled his foes.

3 Thou hast raised our human nature,
 On the clouds to God's right hand;
There we sit in heavenly places,
 There with thee in glory stand;
Jesus reigns, adored by angels;
 Man with God is on the throne;
Mighty Lord! in thine ascension,
 We by faith behold our own.

4 Lift us up from earth to heaven,
 Give us wings of faith and love,
Gales of holy aspirations,
 Wafting us to realms above;
That, with hearts and minds uplifted,
 We with Christ our Lord may dwell,
Where he sits enthroned in glory,
 In the heavenly citadel.

5 So at last, when he appeareth,
 We from out our graves may spring,
With our youth renewed like eagles',
 Flocking round our heavenly King,
Caught up on the clouds of heaven,
 And may meet him in the air—
Rise to realms where he is reigning,
 And may reign for ever there.

RESURRECTION AND REIGN.

FARLAND. 8s, 7s, 4s. — THOS. HASTINGS.

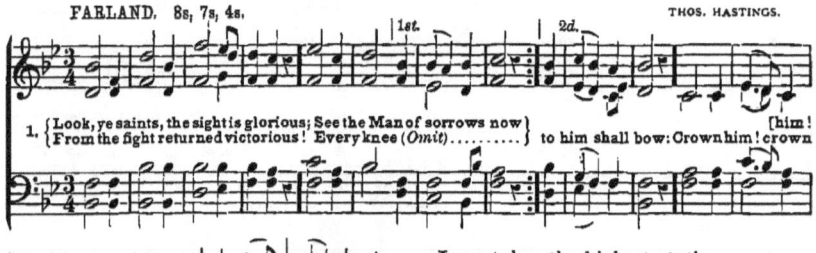

1. Look, ye saints, the sight is glorious; See the Man of sorrows now
   From the fight returned victorious! Every knee (*Omit*)......
   to him shall bow: Crown him! crown him! crown him! crown him! Crowns become the Victor's [brow.

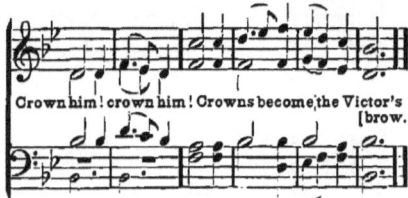

314   "*Crown him!*"   T. KELLY.

Look, ye saints, the sight is glorious;
See the Man of sorrows now
From the fight returned victorious!
Every knee to him shall bow:
   Crown him! crown him!
Crowns become the victor's brow.

2 Crown the Saviour, angels, crown him!
Rich the trophies Jesus brings;
In the seat of power enthrone him,
While the vault of heaven rings:
   Crown him! crown him!
Crown the Saviour King of kings!

3 Hark, those bursts of acclamation!
Hark, those loud, triumphant chords!
Jesus takes the highest station;
Oh, what joy the sight affords!
   Crown him! crown him!
King of kings and Lord of lords!

315   "*It is finished?*"   J. EVANS.

HARK! the voice of love and mercy
Sounds aloud from Calvary;
See! it rends the rocks asunder,
Shakes the earth, and vails the sky:
   "It is finished!"
Hear the dying Saviour cry.

2 "It is finished!" oh, what pleasure
Do these charming words afford!
Heavenly blessings, without measure,
Flow to us from Christ, the Lord:
   "It is finished!"
Saints, the dying words record.

3 Tune your harps anew, ye seraphs;
Join to sing the pleasing theme:
All on earth and all in heaven,
Join to praise Immanuel's name:
   Hallelujah!
Glory to the bleeding Lamb!

CALVARY. 8s, 7s, 4s. — SAMUEL STANLEY.

1. Hark! the voice of love and mercy Sounds aloud from Calvary; See! it rends the rocks asunder, Shakes the earth, and vails the sky; "It is finished:" "It is finished:" Hear the dying Saviour cry.

RESURRECTION AND REIGN. 121

AUTUMN. 8s, 7s. D.   SPANISH; FROM MARECHIO.

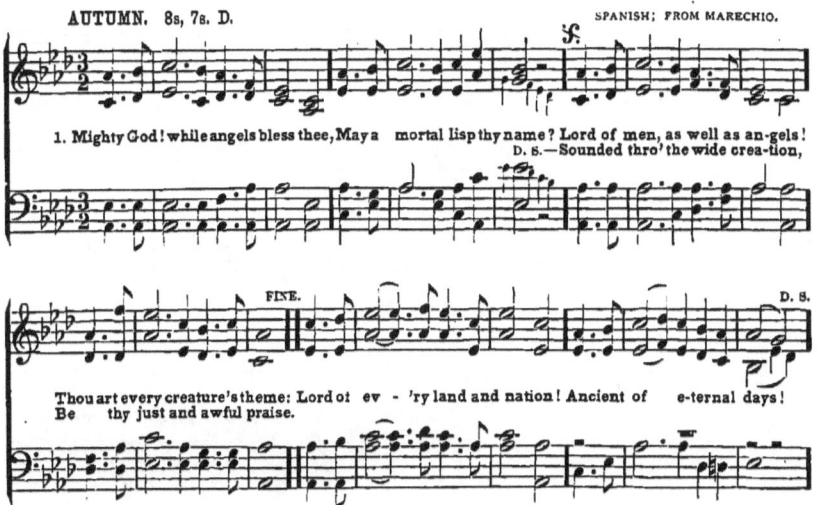

1. Mighty God! while angels bless thee, May a mortal lisp thy name? Lord of men, as well as an-gels!
D. S.—Sounded thro' the wide crea-tion,
Thou art every creature's theme: Lord of ev - 'ry land and nation! Ancient of e-ternal days!
Be thy just and awful praise.

---

316   *Christ is God.*   R. ROBINSON.

MIGHTY God! while angels bless thee,
 May a mortal lisp thy name?
Lord of men, as well as angels!
 Thou art every creature's theme:
Lord of every land and nation!
 Ancient of eternal days!
Sounded through the wide creation—
 Be thy just and awful praise.

2 For the grandeur of thy nature,—
 Grand, beyond a seraph's thought;
For the wonders of creation,
 Works with skill and kindness wrought;
For thy providence, that governs
 Through thine empire's wide domain,
Wings an angel, guides a sparrow;—
 Blessèd be thy gentle reign.

3 For thy rich, thy free redemption,
 Bright, though vailed in darkness long,
Thought is poor, and poor expression;
 Who can sing that wondrous song?
Brightness of the Father's glory!
 Shall thy praise unuttered lie?
Break, my tongue! such guilty silence,
 Sing the Lord who came to die:—

4 From the highest throne of glory,
 To the cross of deepest woe,
Came to ransom guilty captives!—
 Flow, my praise! for ever flow:

Re-ascend, immortal Saviour!
 Leave thy footstool, take thy throne;
Thence return and reign for ever;—
 Be the kingdom all thine own!

317   *"Lo, Jehovah!"*   W. GOODE.

CROWN his head with endless blessing,
 Who, in God the Father's name,
With compassions never ceasing,
 Comes salvation to proclaim.
Hail, ye saints, who know his favor,
 Who within his gates are found;
Hail, ye saints, the exalted Saviour,
 Let his courts with praise resound.

2 Lo, Jehovah, we adore thee;
 Thee our Saviour! thee our God!
From his throne his beams of glory
 Shine through all the world abroad.
In his word his light arises,
 Brightest beams of truth and grace;
Bind, oh, bind your sacrifices,
 In his courts your offerings place.

3 Jesus, thee our Saviour hailing,
 Thee our God in praise we own;
Highest honors, never failing,
 Rise eternal round thy throne;
Now, ye saints, his power confessing,
 In your grateful strains adore;
For his mercy, never ceasing,
 Flows, and flows for evermore.

THE LORD JESUS CHRIST.

BENJAMIN. S. M. D — FROM F. J. HAYDN.

318 *"Risen indeed."* T. KELLY.

"THE Lord is risen indeed!"
  And are the tidings true?
Yes, they beheld the Saviour bleed,
  And saw him living too.
"The Lord is risen indeed!"
  Then justice asks no more;
Mercy and truth are now agreed,
  Who stood opposed before.

2 "The Lord is risen indeed!"
  Then is his work performed;
The mighty Captive now is freed,
  And death, our foe, disarmed.
"The Lord is risen indeed!"
  He lives to die no more;
He lives, the sinner's cause to plead,
  Whose curse and shame he bore.

3 "The Lord is risen indeed!"
  Attending angels! hear;
Up to the courts of heaven, with speed
  The joyful tidings bear.
Then wake your golden lyres,
  And strike each cheerful chord;
Join, all ye bright, celestial choirs!
  To sing our risen Lord.

319 *"Lead us to thee!"* E. TOKE.

THOU art gone up on high
  To mansions in the skies,
And round thy throne unceasingly
  The songs of praise arise.
But we are lingering here
  With sin and care oppressed:
Lord! send thy promised Comforter,
  And lead us to thy rest!

2 Thou art gone up on high:
  But thou didst first come down,
Through earth's most bitter misery
  To pass unto thy crown.
And girt with griefs and fears
  Our onward course must be;
But only let that path of tears
  Lead us at last to thee!

3 Thou art gone up on high:
  But thou shalt come again
With all the bright ones of the sky
  Attendant in thy train.
Oh, by thy saving power
  So make us live and die,
That we may stand in that dread hour
  At thy right hand on high!

RESURRECTION AND REIGN.

DIADEMATA. S. M. D. SIR GEORGE J. ELVEY.

1. Crown him with ma-ny crowns, The Lamb upon his throne; Hark! how the heavenly an-them drowns All mu-sic but its own! A-wake, my soul, and sing Of him who died for thee; And hail him as thy matchless King Through all e-ter-ni-ty.

320 *"Many Crowns."* M. BRIDGES.

CROWN him with many crowns,
 The Lamb upon his throne;
Hark! how the heavenly anthem drowns
 All music but its own!
Awake, my soul, and sing
 Of him who died for thee;
And hail him as thy matchless King
 Through all eternity.

2 Crown him the Lord of love!
 Behold his hands and side,—
Those wounds, yet visible above,
 In beauty glorified:
No angel in the sky
 Can fully bear that sight,
But downward bends his wondering eye
 At mysteries so bright.

3 Crown him the Lord of heaven!
 One with the Father known,—
And the blest Spirit through him given
 From yonder Triune throne!
All hail, Redeemer, hail!
 For thou hast died for me:
Thy praise and glory shall not fail
 Throughout eternity.

321 *"The work is done."* J. FANCH, alt.

BEYOND the starry skies,
 Far as the eternal hills,
There in the boundless world of light
 Our great Redeemer dwells.
Around him angels fair
 In countless armies shine;
And ever, in exalted lays,
 They offer songs divine.

2 "Hail, Prince of life!" they cry,
 "Whose unexampled love,
Moved thee to quit these glorious realms
 And royalties above."
And when he stooped to earth,
 And suffered rude disdain,
They cast their honors at his feet,
 And waited in his train.

3 They saw him on the cross,
 While darkness vailed the skies,
And when he burst the gates of death,
 They saw the conqueror rise.
They thronged his chariot wheels,
 And bore him to his throne;
Then swept their golden harps and sung,—
 "The glorious work is done."

THE LORD JESUS CHRIST.

DORT. 6s, 4s. — LOWELL MASON.

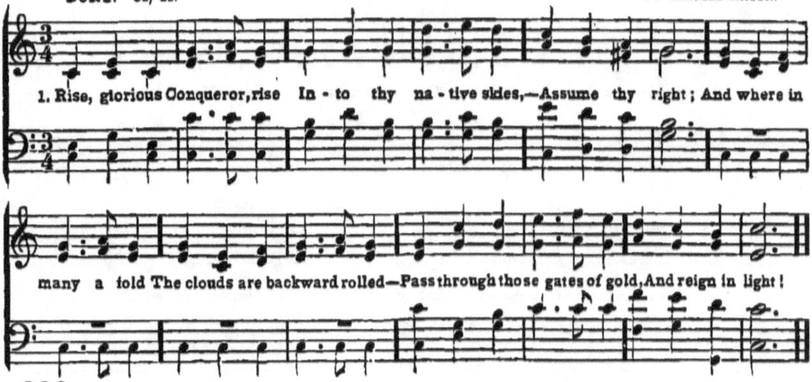

1. Rise, glorious Conqueror, rise In-to thy na-tive skies,—Assume thy right; And where in many a fold The clouds are backward rolled—Pass through those gates of gold, And reign in light!

322   *"Lion of Judah."*   M. BRIDGES.

Rise, glorious Conqueror, rise
Into thy native skies,—
  Assume thy right;
And where in many a fold
The clouds are backward rolled—
Pass through those gates of gold,
  And reign in light!

2 Victor o'er death and hell!
Cherubic legions swell
  Thy radiant train:
Praises all heaven inspire;
Each angel sweeps his lyre,
And waves his wings of fire,—
  Thou Lamb once slain!

3 Enter, incarnate God!—
No feet but thine, have trod
  The serpent down;

Blow the full trumpets, blow!
Wider yon portals throw!
  Saviour triumphant—go,
  And take thy crown!

4 Lion of Judah—Hail!
And let thy name prevail
  From age to age;
Lord of the rolling years!
Claim for thine own the spheres,
For thou has bought with tears
  Thy heritage.

5 And then was heard afar
Star answering to star—
  "Lo! these have come,
Followers of him who gave
His life their lives to save;
And now their palms they wave,
  Brought safely home."

RIGHINI. 6s, 4s. — V. RIGHINI.

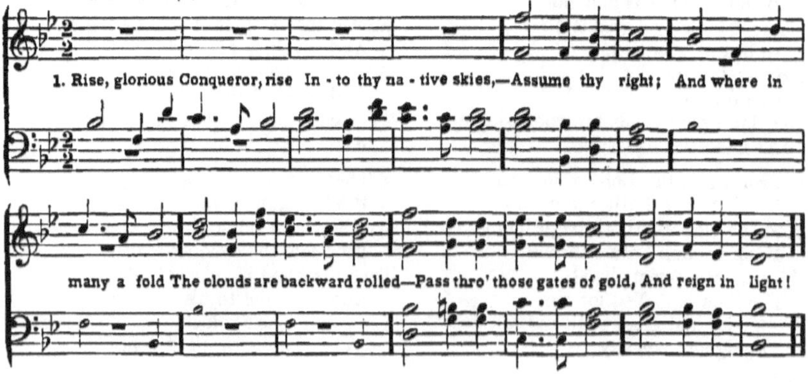

1. Rise, glorious Conqueror, rise In-to thy na-tive skies,—Assume thy right; And where in many a fold The clouds are backward rolled—Pass thro' those gates of gold, And reign in light!

RESURRECTION AND REIGN.

323 *Job 19:25.* C. WESLEY.
I KNOW that my Redeemer lives,
  And ever prays for me:
A token of his love he gives,
  A pledge of liberty.

2 I find him lifting up my head;
  He brings salvation near:
His presence makes me free indeed,
  And he will soon appear.

3 He wills that I should holy be:
  What can withstand his will?
The counsel of his grace in me,
  He surely shall fulfill.

4 Jesus, I hang upon thy word:
  I steadfastly believe
Thou wilt return, and claim me, Lord,
  And to thyself receive.

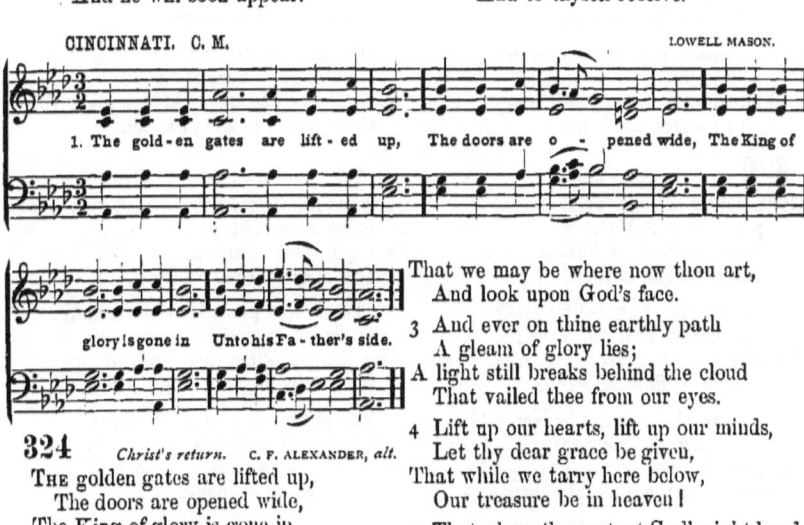

324 *Christ's return.* C. F. ALEXANDER, *alt.*
THE golden gates are lifted up,
  The doors are opened wide,
The King of glory is gone in
  Unto his Father's side.

2 Thou art gone up before us, Lord,
  To make for us a place,
That we may be where now thou art,
  And look upon God's face.

3 And ever on thine earthly path
  A gleam of glory lies;
A light still breaks behind the cloud
  That vailed thee from our eyes.

4 Lift up our hearts, lift up our minds,
  Let thy dear grace be given,
That while we tarry here below,
  Our treasure be in heaven!

5 That where thou art, at God's right hand,
  Our hope, our love may be;
Dwell thou in us, that we may dwell
  For evermore in thee!

THE LORD JESUS CHRIST.

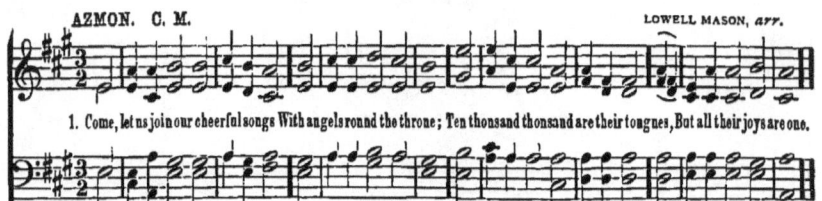

AZMON. C. M.   LOWELL MASON, arr.

1. Come, let us join our cheerful songs With angels round the throne; Ten thousand thousand are their tongues, But all their joys are one.

325   "Worthy the Lamb!"   I. WATTS.

Come, let us join our cheerful songs
  With angels round the throne;
Ten thousand thousand are their tongues,
  But all their joys are one.

2 "Worthy the Lamb that died," they cry,
  "To be exalted thus!"
"Worthy the Lamb!" our lips reply,
  "For he was slain for us."

3 Jesus is worthy to receive
  Honor and power divine;
And blessings, more than we can give,
  Be, Lord, for ever thine!

4 Let all that dwell above the sky,
  And air, and earth, and seas,
Conspire to lift thy glories high,
  And speak thine endless praise.

5 The whole creation join in one,
  To bless the sacred name
Of him who sits upon the throne,
  And to adore the Lamb!

326   Reconciliation.   I. WATTS.

Come, let us lift our joyful eyes,
  Up to the courts above,
And smile to see our Father there,
  Upon a throne of love.

2 Now we may bow before his feet,
  And venture near the Lord:
No fiery cherub guards his seat,
  Nor double flaming sword.

3 The peaceful gates of heavenly bliss
  Are opened by the Son;
High let us raise our notes of praise,
  And reach the almighty throne.

4 To thee ten thousand thanks we bring,
  Great Advocate on high,
And glory to the eternal King,
  Who lays his anger by.

327   Christ, our Priest.   A. PIRRIE.

Come, let us join our songs of praise
  To our ascended Priest;
He entered heaven with all our names
  Engraven on his breast.

2 Below he washed our guilt away,
  By his atoning blood;
Now he appears before the throne,
  And pleads our cause with God.

3 Clothed with our nature still, he knows
  The weakness of our frame,
And how to shield us from the foes
  Which he himself o'ercame.

4 Nor time, nor distance, e'er shall quench
  The fervor of his love;
For us he died in kindness here,
  For us he lives above.

5 Oh! may we ne'er forget his grace,
  Nor blush to bear his name;
Still may our hearts hold fast his faith—
  Our lips his praise proclaim.

328   "Crowned with honor."   T. KELLY.

The head that once was crowned with thorns,
  Is crowned with glory now;
A royal diadem adorns
  The mighty Victor's brow.

2 The highest place that heaven affords,
  Is his by sovereign right;
The King of kings, and Lord of lords,
  He reigns in glory bright;—

3 The joy of all who dwell above,
  The joy of all below,
To whom he manifests his love,
  And grants his name to know.

4 To them the cross with all its shame,
  With all its grace, is given;
Their name—an everlasting name,
  Their joy—the joy of heaven.

EXALTATION AND OFFICES.

CORONATION. C. M. — OLIVER HOLDEN.

329   *"Lord of all."*   E. PERRONET.

ALL hail the power of Jesus' name!
  Let angels prostrate fall;
Bring forth the royal diadem,
  And crown him Lord of all.

2 Crown him, ye martyrs of our God,
  Who from his altar call;
Extol the stem of Jesse's rod,
  And crown him Lord of all.

3 Ye chosen seed of Israel's race,
  Ye ransomed from the fall;
Hail him, who saves you by his grace,
  And crown him Lord of all.

4 Sinners, whose love can ne'er forget
  The wormwood and the gall;
Go, spread your trophies at his feet,
  And crown him Lord of all.

5 Let every kindred, every tribe,
  On this terrestrial ball,
To him all majesty ascribe,
  And crown him Lord of all.

6 Oh, that with yonder sacred throng,
  We at his feet may fall;
We'll join the everlasting song,
  And crown him Lord of all.

MILES LANE. C. M. — W. SHRUBSOLE.

THE LORD JESUS CHRIST.

PORTUGUESE HYMN. L. M. J. READING.

1. O Christ, the Lord of heaven! to thee, Clothed with all ma-jes-ty di-vine, E-ternal power and glory be! E-ter-nal praise, of right, is thine, E-ter-nal praise, of right, is thine.

330 *"Lord of heaven."* RAY PALMER.

O CHRIST, the Lord of heaven! to thee,
 Clothed with all majesty divine,
Eternal power and glory be!
 Eternal praise, of right, is thine.

2 Reign, Prince of life! that once thy brow
 Didst yield to wear the wounding thorn;
Reign, throned beside the Father now,
 Adored the Son of God first-born.

3 From angel hosts that round thee stand,
 With forms more pure than spotless snow,
From the bright burning seraph band,
 Let praise in loftiest numbers flow.

4 To thee, the Lamb, our mortal songs,
 Born of deep fervent love, shall rise;
All honor to thy name belongs,
 Our lips would sound it to the skies.

5 "Jesus!"—all earth shall speak the word;
 "Jesus!"—all heaven resound it still;
Immanuel, Saviour, Conqueror, Lord!
 Thy praise the universe shall fill.

331 *Psalm 45.* I. WATTS.

Now BE my heart inspired to sing
 The glories of my Saviour King,—
Jesus the Lord; how heavenly fair
 His form! how bright his beauties are!

2 O'er all the sons of human race,
 He shines with a superior grace:
Love from his lips divinely flows,
 And blessings all his state compose.

3 Thy throne, O God, for ever stands;
 Grace is the sceptre in thy hands;
Thy laws and works are just and right;
 Justice and grace are thy delight.

4 God, thine own God, has richly shed
 His oil of gladness on thy head;
And with his Sacred Spirit blessed
 His first-born Son above the rest.

332 *"King, Creator, Lord."* RAY PALMER, tr.

O CHRIST! our King, Creator, Lord!
 Saviour of all who trust thy word!
To them who seek thee ever near,
 Now to our praises bend thine ear.

2 In thy dear cross a grace is found,—
 It flows from every streaming wound,—
Whose power our inbred sin controls,
 Breaks the firm bond, and frees our souls.

3 Thou didst create the stars of night;
 Yet thou hast vailed in flesh thy light,
Hast deigned a mortal form to wear.
 A mortal's painful lot to bear.

4 When thou didst hang upon the tree,
 The quaking earth acknowledged thee;
When thou didst there yield up thy breath,
 The world grew dark as shades of death.

5 Now in the Father's glory high,
 Great Conqueror! never more to die,
Us by thy mighty power defend,
 And reign through ages without end.

333 *Christ, our Advocate.* A. STEELE.

He lives! the great Redeemer lives!
What joy the blest assurance gives!
And now, before his Father, God,
Pleads the full merits of his blood.

2 Repeated crimes awake our fears,
And justice armed with frowns appears;
But in the Saviour's lovely face
Sweet mercy smiles, and all is peace.

3 In every dark, distressful hour,
When sin and Satan join their power,
Let this dear hope repel the dart,
That Jesus bears us on his heart.

4 Great Advocate, almighty Friend!
On him our humble hopes depend;
Our cause can never, never fail,
For Jesus pleads, and must prevail.

334 *"Behold the Way!"* J. CENNICK.

Jesus, my All, to heaven is gone,
He whom I fix my hopes upon;
His track I see, and I'll pursue
The narrow way till him I view.

2 The way the holy prophets went,
The road that leads from banishment,
The King's highway of holiness,
I'll go for all his paths are peace.

3 This is the way I long had sought,
And mourned because I found it not;
My grief, my burden, long had been
Because I could not cease from sin.

4 The more I strove against its power,
I sinned and stumbled but the more;
Till late I heard my Saviour say,
"Come hither, soul, I am the Way!"

5 Lo! glad I come; and thou, dear Lamb,
Shalt take me to thee as I am,
Nothing but sin I thee can give;
Nothing but love shall I receive.

6 Then will I tell, to sinners round,
What a dear Saviour I have found;
I'll point to thy redeeming blood,
And say, "Behold the way to God!"

335 *Atonement made.* I. WATTS.

Now to the power of God supreme
  Be everlasting honors given;
He saves from hell,—we bless his name,—
  He guides our wandering feet to heaven.

2 'Twas his own purpose that began
  To rescue rebels doomed to die:
He gave us grace in Christ, his Son,
  Before he spread the starry sky.

3 Jesus, the Lord, appears at last,
  And makes his Father's counsels known;
Declares the great transactions past,
  And brings immortal blessings down.

4 He dies; and in that dreadful night
  Doth all the powers of hell destroy;
Rising, he brings our heaven to light,
  And takes possession of the joy.

THE LORD JESUS CHRIST.

SAMSON. L. M.   G. F. HANDEL.

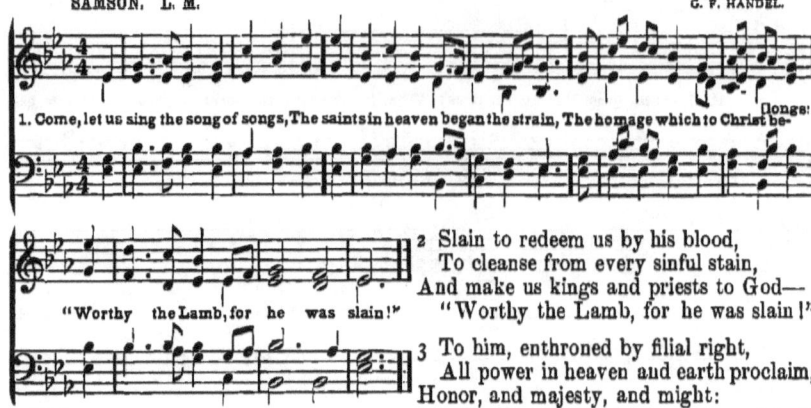

1. Come, let us sing the song of songs, The saints in heaven began the strain, The homage which to Christ be-longs:

2 Slain to redeem us by his blood,
To cleanse from every sinful stain,
And make us kings and priests to God—
"Worthy the Lamb, for he was slain!"

3 To him, enthroned by filial right,
All power in heaven and earth proclaim,
Honor, and majesty, and might:
"Worthy the Lamb, for he was slain!"

336   *"The Song of Songs."*   J. MONTGOMERY.

COME, let us sing the song of songs,—
The saints in heaven began the strain—
The homage which to Christ belongs:
"Worthy the Lamb, for he was slain!"

4 Long as we live, and when we die,
And while in heaven with him we reign:
This song, our song of songs shall be:
Worthy the Lamb, for he was slain!"

ALL SAINTS. L. M.   WILLIAM KNAPP.

1. Now to the Lord, who makes us know The won-ders of his dy-ing love,
Be hum-ble hon-ors paid be-low, And strains of no-bler praise a-bove.

337   *The atoning Priest.*   I. WATTS.

Now TO the Lord, who makes us know
The wonders of his dying love,
Be humble honors paid below,
And strains of nobler praise above.

'Twas he who cleansed our foulest sins,
And washed us in his precious blood;
'Tis he who makes us priests and kings,
And brings us rebels near to God.

3 To Jesus, our atoning Priest,
To Jesus, our eternal King,

Be everlasting power confessed!
Let every tongue his glory sing.

4 Behold! on flying clouds he comes,
And every eye shall see him move;
Though with our sins we pierced him once,
He now displays his pardoning love.

5 The unbelieving world shall wail,
While we rejoice to see the day;
Come, Lord! nor let thy promise fail,
Nor let thy chariot long delay.

EXALTATION AND OFFICES.

338 *Christ is God.* L. WATTS.

WHAT equal honors shall we bring
To thee, O Lord our God, the Lamb,
When all the notes that angels sing,
Are far inferior to thy name?

2 Worthy is he that once was slain,
The Prince of Peace that groaned and died,
Worthy to rise, and live, and reign
At his almighty Father's side.

3 All riches are his native right,
Yet he sustained amazing loss;
To him ascribe eternal might,
Who left his weakness on the cross.

4 Honor immortal must be paid,
Instead of scandal and of scorn;
While glory shines around his head,
And a bright crown without a thorn.

5 Blessings for ever on the Lamb,
Who bore the curse for wretched men;
Let angels sound his sacred name,
And every creature say, Amen.

BENNINGTON. L. M. D.   FROM PERCIVAL.

1. Our Lord is ris-en from the dead, Our Jesus is gone up on high; The powers of hell are captive led, Dragged to the por-tals of the sky. There his triumphal cha-riot waits, And angels chant the solemn lay:—"Lift up your heads,.... ye heav'nly gates! Ye ever-last-ing doors! give way!

339 *Psalm 24.* C. WESLEY.

OUR Lord is risen from the dead,
Our Jesus is gone up on high;
The powers of hell are captive led,
Dragged to the portals of the sky.
There his triumphal chariot waits,
And angels chant the solemn lay:
"Lift up your heads, ye heavenly gates!
Ye everlasting doors! give way."

2 Loose all your bars of massy light,
And wide unfold the ethereal scene:
He claims these mansions as his right;
Receive the King of glory in.

Who is this King of glory—who?
The Lord who all our foes o'ercame;
Who sin, and death, and hell o'erthrew;
And Jesus is the conqueror's name.

3 Lo! his triumphal chariot waits,
And angels chant the solemn lay:—
"Lift up your heads, ye heavenly gates!
Ye everlasting doors! give way."
Who is this King of glory—who?
The Lord of boundless power possessed;
The King of saints and angels, too,
God over all, for ever blessed.

10

340 7s, 6s, d. *The Lord's Day.* J. M. NEALE, tr.

The day of resurrection,
  Earth, tell it out abroad:
The Passover of gladness,
  The Passover of God.
From death to life eternal,
  From earth unto the sky,
Our Christ hath brought us over,
  With hymns of victory.

2 Our hearts be pure from evil,
  That we may see aright
The Lord in rays eternal
  Of resurrection-light;
And, listening to his accents,
  May hear, so calm and plain,
His own " All hail!" and, hearing,
  May raise the victor-strain.

341 C. M. *Psalm 45.* I. WATTS.

I'll speak the honors of my King,—
  His form divinely fair;
None of the sons of mortal race
  May with the Lord compare.

2 Sweet is thy speech, and heavenly
  Upon thy lips is shed; [grace
Thy God, with blessings infinite,
  Hath crowned thy sacred head.

3 Gird on thy sword, victorious Prince!
  Ride with majestic sway;
Thy terrors shall strike through thy foes,
  And make the world obey.

4 Thy throne, O God! for ever stands;
  Thy word of grace shall prove
A peaceful sceptre in thy hands,
  To rule the saints by love.

5 Justice and truth attend thee still,
  But mercy is thy choice;
And God, thy God, thy soul shall fill
  With most peculiar joys.

342 L. M. *"Full Equality."* I. WATTS.

Bright King of glory, dreadful God!
  Our spirits bow before thy feet:
To thee we lift an humble thought,
  And worship at thine awful seat.

2 A thousand seraphs strong and bright
  Stand round the glorious Deity;
But who, among those sons of light,
  Pretends comparison with thee?

3 Yet there is One of human frame,
  Jesus, arrayed in flesh and blood,
Thinks it no robbery to claim
  A full equality with God.

4 Then let the name of Christ our King
  With equal honors be adored;
His praise let every angel sing,
  And all the nations own their Lord.

343 7s. *The Risen Redeemer.* ANON.

Christ, the Lord, is risen to-day,
  Our triumphant holy-day:
He endured the cross and grave,
  Sinners to redeem and save.

2 Lo! he rises, mighty King!
  Where, O Death! is now thy sting?
Lo! he claims his native sky!
  Grave! where is thy victory?

3 Sinners, see your ransom paid,
  Peace with God for ever made:
With your risen Saviour rise;
  Claim with him the purchased skies.

4 Christ, the Lord, is risen to-day,
  Our triumphant holy-day;
Loud the song of victory raise;
  Shout the great Redeemer's praise.

344 H. M. *"The Debt of Love."* S. STENNETT.

Come, every pious heart,
  That loves the Saviour's name,
Your noblest powers exert
  To celebrate his fame;
Tell all above, and all below,
The debt of love to him you owe.

2 He left his starry crown,
  And laid his robes aside,
On wings of love came down,
  And wept, and bled, and died;
What he endured, oh, who can tell,
To save our souls from death and hell?

3 From the dark grave he rose,
  The mansion of the dead,
And thence his mighty foes
  In glorious triumph led;
Up through the sky the Conqueror rode,
And reigns on high, the Saviour God.

345 L. M. *Psalm 45.* I. WATTS.

The King of saints,—how fair his face!
Adorned with majesty and grace,
He comes, with blessings from above,
And wins the nations to his love.

2 At his right hand, our eyes behold
The queen, arrayed in purest gold;
The world admires her heavenly dress,
Her robe of joy and righteousness.

3 Oh, happy hour, when thou shalt rise
To his fair palace in the skies;
And all thy sons, a numerous train,
Each, like a prince, in glory reign.

4 Let endless honors crown his head;
Let every age his praises spread;
While we, with cheerful songs, approve
The condescension of his love.

346 C. M. D. *"The Fairest Face."* P. STRYKER.

I heard a voice, the sweetest voice
That mortal ever heard;
Oh! how it made my heart rejoice,
And every feeling stirred!
'T was Jesus spoke to me so mild;
He called me to his side,
And said, although with heart defiled,
I might in him confide.

2 I saw his face, the fairest face
That mortal ever saw;
I longed the Saviour to embrace,
From him new life to draw.
"Come unto me," he kindly said,
"And I will give thee rest;
The ransom-price I fully paid—
Repent! believe! be blest!"

3 I felt his love, the strongest love
That mortal ever felt;
Oh! how it drew my soul above,
And made my hard heart melt!
My burden at his feet I laid,
And knew the joy of heaven,
As in my willing ear he said
The blessèd word, "*Forgiven!*"

347 C. M. *Psalm 47.* I. WATTS.

Oh, for a shout of sacred joy
To God, the sovereign King;
Let every land their tongues employ,
And hymns of triumph sing.

2 Jesus, our God, ascends on high;
His heavenly guards around
Attend him rising through the sky,
With trumpets' joyful sound.

3 While angels shout and praise their
Let mortals learn their strains; [King,
Let all the earth his honor sing;—
O'er all the earth he reigns.

4 Rehearse his praise with awe pro-
Let knowledge lead the song; [found;
Nor mock him with a solemn sound
Upon a thoughtless tongue.

5 In Israel stood his ancient throne:—
He loved that chosen race;
But now he calls the world his own;
The heathen taste his grace.

348 C. M. *Psalm 71.* I. WATTS.

My Saviour! my almighty Friend:
When I begin thy praise,
Where will the growing numbers end,—
The numbers of thy grace?

2 Thou art my everlasting trust;
Thy goodness I adore;
And, since I knew thy graces first,
I speak thy glories more.

3 My feet shall travel all the length
Of the celestial road;
And march, with courage, in thy strength,
To see my Father God.

4 How will my lips rejoice to tell
The victories of my King!
My soul, redeemed from sin and hell,
Shall thy salvation sing.

349 C. M. *Our High-Priest.* P. DODDRIDGE.

Now let our cheerful eyes survey
Our great High-Priest above,
And celebrate his constant care,
And sympathetic love.

2 Though raised to a superior throne,
Where angels bow around,
And high o'er all the shining train,
With matchless honors crowned;—

3 The names of all his saints he bears
Engraven on his heart;
Nor shall a name once treasured there
E'er from his care depart.

4 So, gracious Saviour! on my breast
May thy dear name be worn,
A sacred ornament and guard,
To endless ages borne.

THE HOLY SPIRIT.

WIMBORNE. L. M. — J. WHITAKER.

1. E-ter-nal Spir-it, we con-fess And sing the won-ders of thy grace: Thy pow'r con-veys our bless-ings down From God the Fa-ther and the Son.

350 *"Inward Teachings."* I. WATTS.

ETERNAL Spirit, we confess
And sing the wonders of thy grace:
Thy power conveys our blesssings down
From God the Father and the Son.

2 Enlightened by thy heavenly ray,
Our shades and darkness turn to day;
Thine inward teachings make us know
Our danger and our refuge too.

3 Thy power and glory work within,
And break the chains of reigning sin;
All our imperious lusts subdue,
And form our wretched hearts anew.

351 *"Veni, Creator!"* E. CASWALL, tr.

COME, O Creator Spirit blest!
And in our souls take up thy rest;
Come, with thy grace, and heavenly aid,
To fill the hearts which thou hast made.

2 Great Comforter! to thee we cry;
O highest gift of God most high!
O fount of life! O fire of love!
Send sweet anointing from above!

3 Kindle our senses from above,
And make our hearts o'erflow with love;
With patience firm, and virtue high,
The weakness of our flesh supply.

4 Far from us drive the foe we dread,
And grant us thy true peace instead;
So shall we not, with thee for guide,
Turn from the path of life aside.

352 *"The book unfold."* B. BEDDOME.

COME, blesséd Spirit! source of light!
Whose power and grace are unconfined,
Dispel the gloomy shades of night—
The thicker darkness of the mind.

2 To mine illumined eyes, display
The glorious truths thy word reveals;
Cause me to run the heavenly way,
Thy book unfold, and loose the seals.

3 Thine inward teachings make me know
The mysteries of redeeming love,
The vanity of things below,
And excellence of things above.

4 While through this dubious maze I stray,
Spread, like the sun, thy beams abroad,
To show the dangers of the way,
And guide my feeble steps to God.

353 *Spirit of grace.* P. DODDRIDGE.

COME, sacred Spirit, from above,
And fill the coldest heart with love:
Oh, turn to flesh the flinty stone,
And let thy sovereign power be known.

2 Speak thou, and from the haughtiest eyes
Shall floods of contrite sorrow rise;
While all their glowing souls are borne
To seek that grace which now they scorn.

3 Oh, let a holy flock await
In crowds around thy temple-gate!
Each pressing on with zeal to be
A living sacrifice to thee.

THE HOLY SPIRIT.

PRINCE. L. M.   FELIX MENDELSSOHN-BARTHOLDY.

1. Come, gracious Spir-it, heaven-ly Dove, With light and comfort from a - bove:
D. S.—O'er every thought and step pre - side.

Be thou our guardian, thou our guide!

354   *Invocation.*   S. BROWNE, alt.

Come, gracious Spirit, heavenly Dove,
With light and comfort from above:
Be thou our guardian, thou our guide!
O'er every thought and step preside.

2 To us the light of truth display,
And make us know and choose thy way;
Plant holy fear in every heart,
That we from God may ne'er depart.

3 Lead us to holiness—the road
That we must take to dwell with God;
Lead us to Christ, the living way,
Nor let us from his precepts stray.

4 Lead us to God, our final rest,
To be with him for ever blest;
Lead us to heaven, its bliss to share—
Fullness of joy for ever there!

ZEPHYR. L. M.   W. B. BRADBURY.

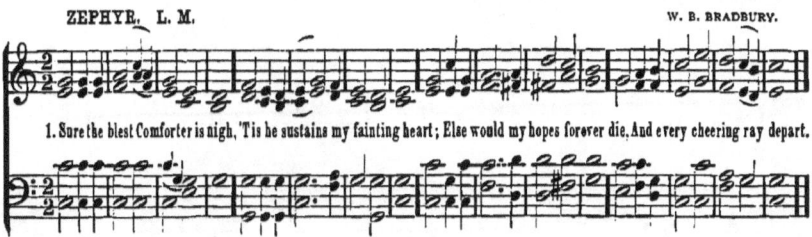

1. Sure the blest Comforter is nigh, 'Tis he sustains my fainting heart; Else would my hopes forever die, And every cheering ray depart.

355   *The Spirit near.*   A. STEELE.

Sure the blest Comforter is nigh,
'Tis he sustains my fainting heart;
Else would my hopes for ever die,
And every cheering ray depart.

2 Whene'er, to call the Saviour mine,
With ardent wish my heart aspires,—
Can it be less than power divine,
That animates these strong desires?

3 And, when my cheerful hope can say,—
I love my God and taste his grace,—
Lord! is it not thy blissful ray,
That brings this dawn of sacred peace?

4 Let thy good Spirit in my heart
For ever dwell, O God of love!

And light and heavenly peace impart,—
Sweet earnest of the joys above.

356   *Giver of Rest.*   STEWART.

Come, Holy Spirit! calm my mind,
And fit me to approach my God;
Remove each vain, each worldly thought,
And lead me to thy blest abode.

2 Hast thou imparted to my soul
A living spark of holy fire?
Oh, kindle now the sacred flame;
Make me to burn with pure desire.

3 A brighter faith and hope impart,
And let me now my Saviour see;
Oh, soothe and cheer my burdened heart,
And bid my spirit rest in thee

THE HOLY SPIRIT.

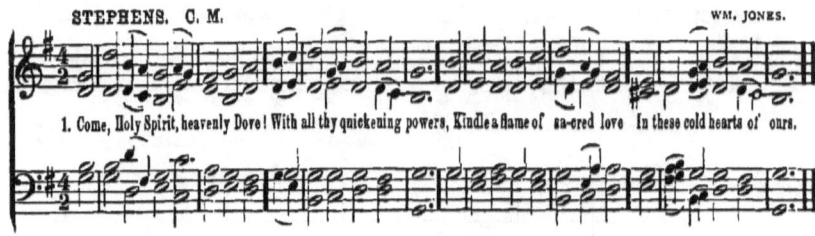
STEPHENS. C. M.   WM. JONES.

1. Come, Holy Spirit, heavenly Dove! With all thy quickening powers, Kindle a flame of sacred love In these cold hearts of ours.

357   *Invocation.*   I. WATTS.

Come, Holy Spirit, heavenly Dove!
  With all thy quickening powers,
Kindle a flame of sacred love
  In these cold hearts of ours.

2 Look! how we grovel here below,
  Fond of these trifling toys!
Our souls can neither fly nor go
  To reach eternal joys.

3 In vain we tune our formal songs;
  In vain we strive to rise;
Hosannas languish on our tongues,
  And our devotion dies.

4 Dear Lord, and shall we ever live
  At this poor dying rate—
Our love so faint, so cold to thee,
  And thine to us so great?

5 Come, Holy Spirit, heavenly Dove!
  With all thy quickening powers;
Come, shed abroad a Saviour's love,
  And that shall kindle ours.

CHESTER. C. M.   THOS. HASTINGS.

1. O Ho-ly Ghost, the Com-fort-er, How is thy love de-spised, While the heart longs for sym-pa-thy And friends are i-dol-ized, And friends are i-dol-ized.

358   *The Comforter's love.*   J. E. SAXBY.

O Holy Ghost, the Comforter,
  How is thy love despised,
While the heart longs for sympathy
  And friends are idolized.

2 O Spirit of the living God,
  Brooding with dove-like wings
Over the helpless and the weak
  Among created things!

3 Where should our feebleness find strength,
  Our helplessness a stay,
Didst thou not bring us hope and help,
  And comfort, day by day?

4 Great are thy consolations, Lord.
  And mighty is thy power,
In sickness and in solitude,
  In sorrow's darkest hour.

5 Oh, if the souls that now despise
  And grieve thee, heavenly Dove,
Would seek thee, and would welcome thee,
  How would they prize thy love!

THE HOLY SPIRIT.

359 *Assurance.* I. WATTS.

Why should the children of a King
 Go mourning all their days?
Great Comforter, descend, and bring
 Some tokens of thy grace.

2 Dost thou not dwell in all the saints,
 And seal the heirs of heaven?
When wilt thou banish my complaints,
 And show my sins forgiven?

3 Assure my conscience of her part
 In the Redeemer's blood;
And bear thy witness with my heart,
 That I am born of God.

4 Thou art the earnest of his love,
 The pledge of joys to come;
And thy soft wings, celestial Dove,
 Will safe convey me home.

360 *Sanctification.* T. COTTERILL.

Eternal Spirit, God of truth,
 Our contrite hearts inspire;
Revive the flame of heavenly love,
 And feed the pure desire.

2 'Tis thine to soothe the sorrowing mind,
 With guilt and fear oppressed;
'Tis thine to bid the dying live,
 And give the weary rest.

3 Subdue the power of every sin,
 Whate'er that sin may be,
That we, with humble, holy heart,
 May worship only thee.

4 Then with our spirits witness bear
 That we are sons of God,
Redeemed from sin, from death and hell,
 Through Christ's atoning blood.

THE HOLY SPIRIT.

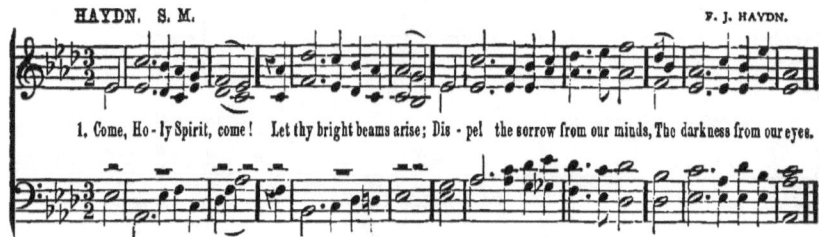

HAYDN. S. M.   F. J. HAYDN.

1. Come, Ho-ly Spirit, come! Let thy bright beams arise; Dis-pel the sorrow from our minds, The darkness from our eyes.

361   *Giver of Grace.*   J. HART.

Come, Holy Spirit, come!
Let thy bright beams arise;
Dispel the sorrow from our minds,
The darkness from our eyes.

2 Convince us of our sin;
Then lead to Jesus' blood,
And to our wondering view reveal
The mercies of our God.

3 Revive our drooping faith,
Our doubts and fears remove,
And kindle in our breasts the flame
Of never-dying love.

4 'Tis thine to cleanse the heart,
To sanctify the soul,
To pour fresh life in every part,
And new-create the whole.

5 Come, Holy Spirit, come;
Our minds from bondage free;
Then shall we know, and praise, and love,
The Father, Son, and thee.

MORNINGTON. S. M.   G. W. MORNINGTON.

1. Blest Com-fort-ter di-vine, Whose rays of heavenly love
A-mid our gloom and dark-ness shine, And point our souls a-bove;—

362   *"Still small voice."*   L. H. SIGOURNEY.

Blest Comforter divine,
Whose rays of heavenly love
Amid our gloom and darkness shine,
And point our souls above;—

2 Thou, who with "still small voice,"
Dost stop the sinner's way,
And bid the mourning saint rejoice,
Though earthly joys decay;—

3 Thou, whose inspiring breath
Can make the cloud of care,
And ev'n the gloomy vale of death,
A smile of glory wear;—

4 Thou, who dost fill the heart
With love to all our race;—
Blest Comforter, to us impart
The blessings of thy grace.

THE HOLY SPIRIT.

WHITEFIELD. S. M.   EDWARD MILLER.

1. Come, Holy Spirit, come, With energy divine; And on this poor benighted soul, With beams of mercy shine.

363   *The heart melted.*   B. BEDDOME.

Come, Holy Spirit, come,
  With energy divine;
And on this poor benighted soul,
  With beams of mercy shine.

2 Oh, melt this frozen heart;
  This stubborn will subdue;
Each evil passion overcome,
  And form me all anew.

3 Mine will the profit be,
  But thine shall be the praise;
And unto thee will I devote
  The remnant of my days.

364   *Teaching Truth.*   B. BEDDOME.

Come, Spirit, source of light,
  Thy grace is unconfined;
Dispel the gloomy shades of night,
  The darkness of the mind.

2 Now to our eyes display
  The truth thy words reveal;
Cause us to run the heavenly way,
  Delighting in thy will.

3 Thy teachings make us know
  The mysteries of thy love,
The vanity of things below,
  The joy of things above.

4 While through this maze we stray,
  Oh, spread thy beams abroad;
Disclose the dangers of the way,
  And guide our steps to God.

365   *He works in us.*   J. MONTGOMERY.

'Tis God the Spirit leads
  In paths before unknown;
The work to be performed is ours,
  The strength is all his own.

2 Supported by his grace
  We still pursue our way;
And hope at last to reach the prize,
  Secure in endless day.

3 'Tis he that works to will,
  'Tis he that works to do;
His is the power by which we act,
  His be the glory too.

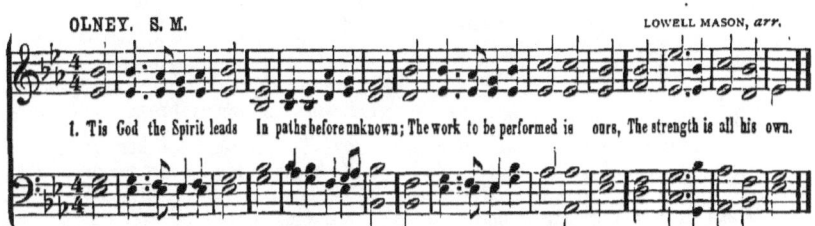

OLNEY. S. M.   LOWELL MASON, *arr.*

1. 'Tis God the Spirit leads In paths before unknown; The work to be performed is ours, The strength is all his own.

THE HOLY SPIRIT.

MERCY. 7s. E. P. PARKER, arr.

366 *All-divine.* A. REED.

HOLY Ghost! with light divine,
Shine upon this heart of mine;
Chase the shades of night away,
Turn my darkness into day.

2 Holy Ghost! with power divine,
Cleanse this guilty heart of mine;
Long hath sin, without control,
Held dominion o'er my soul.

3 Holy Ghost! with joy divine,
Cheer this saddened heart of mine;
Bid my many woes depart,
Heal my wounded, bleeding heart.

4 Holy Spirit! all-divine,
Dwell within this heart of mine;
Cast down every idol-throne,
Reign supreme—and reign alone.

FULTON. 7s. W. B. BRADBURY.

367 *"Keep me, Lord!"* J. STOCKER.

GRACIOUS Spirit, Love divine!
Let thy light within me shine;
All my guilty fears remove,
Fill me with thy heavenly love.

2 Speak thy pardoning grace to me,
Set the burdened sinner free;
Lead me to the Lamb of God;
Wash me in his precious blood.

3 Life and peace to me impart,
Seal salvation on my heart;
Breathe thyself into my breast,—
Earnest of immortal rest.

4 Let me never from thee stray,
Keep me in the narrow way;
Fill my soul with joy divine,
Keep me, Lord! for ever thine.

THE HOLY SPIRIT.

NEW HAVEN. 6s, 4s.   THOS. HASTINGS.

1. Come, Holy Ghost! in love, Shed on us, from above, Thine own bright ray: Divinely good thou art; Thy sacred gifts impart, To gladden each sad heart; Oh, come to-day!

368   *"Oh, come to-day."*   RAY PALMER, *tr.*

Come, Holy Ghost! in love,
Shed on us, from above,
  Thine own bright ray:
Divinely good thou art;
Thy sacred gifts impart,
To gladden each sad heart;
  Oh, come to-day!

2 Come, tenderest Friend, and best,
Our most delightful Guest!
  With sooothing power;
Rest, which the weary know;
Shade, 'mid the noontide glow;
Peace, when deep griefs o'erflow;
  Cheer us, this hour!

3 Come, Light serene! and still
Our inmost bosoms fill;
  Dwell in each breast:
We know no dawn but thine;
Send forth thy beams divine,
On our dark souls to shine,
  And make us blest.

4 Exalt our low desires;
Extinguish passion's fires;
  Heal every wound;
Our stubborn spirits bend;
Our icy coldness end;
Our devious steps attend,
  While heavenward bound.

5 Come, all the faithful bless,
Let all, who Christ confess,
  His praise employ:
Give virtue's rich reward;
Victorious death accord,
And, with our glorious Lord,
  Eternal joy!

369   *"Let there be light."*   J. MARRIOTT.

Thou! whose almighty word
Chaos and darkness heard,
  And took their flight,
Hear us, we humbly pray,
And, where the gospel's day
Sheds not its glorious ray,
  "Let there be light!"

2 Thou! who didst come to bring,
On thy redeeming wing,
  Healing and sight,
Health to the sick in mind,
Sight to the inly blind,—
Oh, now to all mankind,
  "Let there be light!"

3 Spirit of truth and love,
Life-giving holy Dove!
  Speed forth thy flight:
Move o'er the waters' face,
Bearing the lamp of grace,
And in earth's darkest place,
  "Let there be light!"

4 Blessèd and holy Three,
All-glorious Trinity,—
  Wisdom, Love, Might!
Boundless as ocean's tide
Rolling in fullest pride,
Through the world, far and wide,—
  "Let there be light!"

THE HOLY SPIRIT.

370 C. M. *Pentecost.* J. KEBLE.
WHEN God, of old, came down from heaven,
　In power and wrath he came;
Before his feet the clouds were riven,
　Half darkness and half flame.

2 But when he came the second time,
　He came in power and love;
Softer than gales at morning prime,
　Hovered his holy Dove.

3 The fires that rushed on Sinai down
　In sudden torrents dread,
Now gently light a glorious crown
　On every sainted head.

4 Like arrows went those lightnings forth,
　Winged with the sinner's doom;
But these, like tongues, o'er all the earth
　Proclaiming life to come.

371 7s. *"The things of Christ."* W. HAMMOND.
HOLY Spirit! gently come,
　Raise us from our fallen state;
Fix thy everlasting home
　In the hearts thou didst create.

2 Now thy quickening influence bring,
　On our spirits sweetly move;
Open every mouth to sing
　Jesus' everlasting love.

3 Take the things of Christ, and show
　What our Lord for us hath done;
May we God the Father know
　Through his well-belovèd Son.

372 7s, 6s, 8s. *The Witness.* A. M. TOPLADY.
BLESSED Comforter, come down,
　And live and move in me;
Make my every deed thy own,
　In all things led by thee;
Bid my every lust depart,
　And now with me, vouchsafe to dwell;
Faithful Witness, in my heart
　Thy perfect love reveal.

2 Let me in thy love rejoice,
　Thy shrine, thy pure abode;
Tell me, by thine inward voice,
　I am a child of God:
Lord, I choose the better part;
　Jesus, I wait thy peace to feel;
Send the witness, in my heart
　The Holy Ghost reveal.

373 C. M. *The Promise.* H. AUBER.
OUR blest Redeemer, ere he breathed
　His tender, last farewell,
A Guide, a Comforter bequeathed,
　With us on earth to dwell.

2 He came in tongues of living flame,
　To teach, convince, subdue;
All powerful as the wind he came,
　And all as viewless, too.

3 He came, sweet influence to impart,
　A gracious, willing Guest,
While he can find one humble heart
　Wherein to fix his rest.

4 And every virtue we possess,
　And every victory won,
And every thought of holiness,
　Is his and his alone.

5 Spirit of purity and grace!
　Our weakness pitying see;
Oh, make our hearts thy dwelling-place,
　Purer and worthier thee!

374 7s, 5s. *"Comforter Divine!"* G. RAWSON.
HOLY Ghost, the Infinite!
Shine upon our nature's night
With thy blessèd inward light,
　Comforter Divine!

2 We are sinful: cleanse us, Lord;
We are faint: thy strength afford;
Lost,—until by thee restored,
　Comforter Divine!

3 Like the dew, thy peace distill;
Guide, subdue our wayward will,
Things of Christ unfolding still,
　Comforter Divine!

4 In us, for us, intercede,
And, with voiceless groanings, plead
Our unutterable need,
　Comforter Divine!

5 In us "Abba, Father," cry,—
Earnest of our bliss on high,
Seal of immortality,—
　Comforter Divine!

6 Search for us the depths of God;
Bear us up the starry road,
To the height of thine abode,
　Comforter Divine!

375 S. M.   *The Light.*   W. H. BATHURST.

LORD, bid thy light arise
  On all thy people here,
And when we raise our longing eyes,
  Oh, may we find thee near!

2 Thy Holy Spirit send,
  To quicken every soul;
And hearts, the most rebellious, bend
  To thy divine control.

3 Let all that own thy name
  Thy sacred image bear;
And light in every heart the flame
  Of watchfulness and prayer.

4 Since in thy love we see
  Our only sure relief,
Oh, raise our earthly minds to thee,
  And help our unbelief.

376 L. M.   *Quiet Influence.*   T. GIBBONS.

AS when in silence vernal showers
Descend and cheer the fainting flowers,
So, in the secrecy of love,
Falls the sweet influence from above.

2 That heavenly influence let me find
In holy silence of the mind,
While every grace maintains its bloom,
Diffusing wide its rich perfume.

3 Nor let these blessings be confined
To me, but poured on all mankind,
Till earth's wild wastes in verdure rise,
And a young Eden bless our eyes.

377 L. M.   *Veni, Creator.*   J. DRYDEN, tr

CREATOR Spirit, by whose aid
The world's foundations first were laid,
Come, visit every waiting mind;
Come, pour thy joys on human-kind.

2 Thrice holy Fount, thrice holy Fire,
Our hearts with heavenly love inspire;
Come, and thy sacred unction bring
To sanctify us, while we sing.

3 O Source of uncreated light,
The Father's promised Paraclete,—
From sin and sorrow set us free,
And make us temples worthy thee!

4 Make us eternal truths receive,
And practise all that we believe;
Give us thyself, that we may see
The Father and the Son, by thee.

378 C. M.   *Invocation.*   C. WESLEY.

COME, Holy Ghost! our hearts inspire,
  Let us thine influence prove;
Source of the old prophetic fire!
  Fountain of life and love!

2 Water with heavenly dew thy word,
  In this appointed hour;
Attend it with thy presence, Lord,
  And bid it come with power.

3 Open the hearts of them that hear,
  To make the Saviour room;
Now let us find redemption near;
  Let faith by hearing come.

379 H. M.   *Luke* 11: 13.   J. BURTON.

O THOU that hearest prayer!
  Attend our humble cry;
And let thy servants share
  Thy blessing from on high:
We plead the promise of thy word,
Grant us thy Holy Spirit, Lord!

2 If earthly parents hear
  Their children when they cry;
If they, with love sincere,
  Their children's wants supply;
Much more wilt thou thy love display,
And answer when thy children pray.

3 Our heavenly Father, thou,—
  We—children of thy grace,—
Oh, let thy Spirit now
  Descend and fill the place;
That all may feel the heavenly flame
And all unite to praise thy name.

380 L. M.   *"Baptize the Nations!"*   J. MONTGOMERY.

O SPIRIT of the living God,
  In all thy plenitude of grace,
Where'er the foot of man hath trod,
  Descend on our apostate race.

2 Give tongues of fire and hearts of love,
  To preach the reconciling word;
Give power and unction from above,
  Where'er the joyful sound is heard.

3 Be darkness, at thy coming, light;
  Confusion, order, in thy path;
Souls without strength inspire with
    might;
  Bid mercy triumph over wrath.

4 Baptize the nations! far and nigh,
  The triumphs of the cross record;
The name of Jesus glorify,
  Till every people call him Lord.

THE GOSPEL OF GRACE.

381 *Deut.* 30: 19. J. MONTGOMERY.

Oh, where shall rest be found—
  Rest for the weary soul?
'Twere vain the ocean depths to sound,
  Or pierce to either pole.

2 The world can never give
  The bliss for which we sigh:
'Tis not the whole of life to live,
  Nor all of death to die.

3 Beyond this vale of tears
  There is a life above,
Unmeasured by the flight of years;
  And all that life is love.

4 There is a death whose pang
  Outlasts the fleeting breath:
Oh, what eternal horrors hang
  Around the second death!

5 Lord God of truth and grace!
  Teach us that death to shun;
Lest we be banished from thy face,
  And evermore undone.

382 *"None other name."* I. WATTS.

Not all the blood of beasts
  On Jewish altars slain,
Could give the guilty conscience peace,
  Or wash away the stain.

2 But Christ the heavenly Lamb
  Takes all our sins away,
A sacrifice of nobler name
  And richer blood than they.

3 My faith would lay her hand
  On that dear head of thine,
While like a penitent I stand,
  And there confess my sin.

4 My soul looks back to see
  The burdens thou didst bear,
When hanging on the cursèd tree,
  And hopes her guilt was there.

5 Believing, we rejoice
  To see the curse remove;
We bless the Lamb with cheerful voice,
  And sing his dying love.

MAN'S LOST CONDITION.

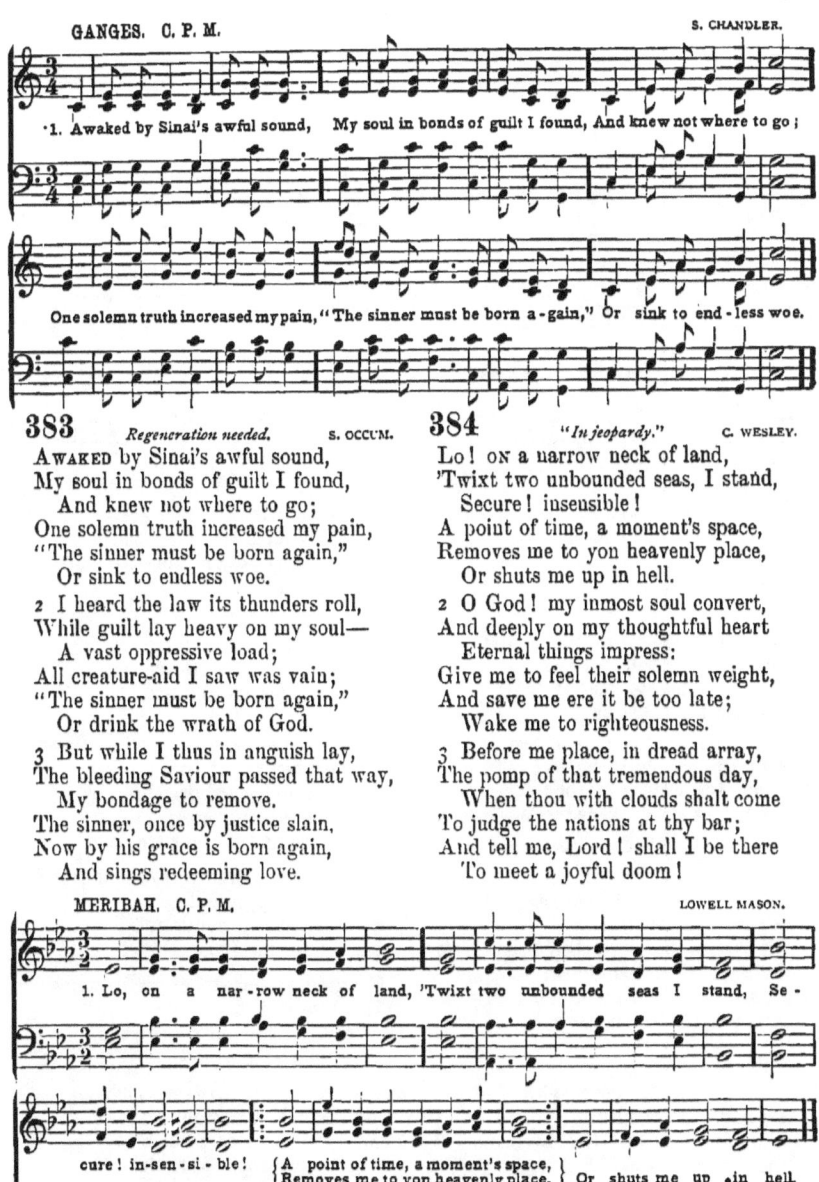

383 *Regeneration needed.* S. OCCUM.

Awaked by Sinai's awful sound,
My soul in bonds of guilt I found,
  And knew not where to go;
One solemn truth increased my pain,
"The sinner must be born again,"
  Or sink to endless woe.

2 I heard the law its thunders roll,
While guilt lay heavy on my soul—
  A vast oppressive load;
All creature-aid I saw was vain;
"The sinner must be born again,"
  Or drink the wrath of God.

3 But while I thus in anguish lay,
The bleeding Saviour passed that way,
  My bondage to remove.
The sinner, once by justice slain,
Now by his grace is born again,
  And sings redeeming love.

384 *"In jeopardy."* C. WESLEY.

Lo! on a narrow neck of land,
'Twixt two unbounded seas, I stand,
  Secure! insensible!
A point of time, a moment's space,
Removes me to yon heavenly place,
  Or shuts me up in hell.

2 O God! my inmost soul convert,
And deeply on my thoughtful heart
  Eternal things impress:
Give me to feel their solemn weight,
And save me ere it be too late;
  Wake me to righteousness.

3 Before me place, in dread array,
The pomp of that tremendous day,
  When thou with clouds shalt come
To judge the nations at thy bar;
And tell me, Lord! shall I be there
  To meet a joyful doom!

THE GOSPEL OF GRACE.

MONSON. C. M.   S. R. BROWN.

1. How help-less guilt-y na-ture lies, Un-con-scious of its load! The heart, un-changed, can nev-er rise To hap-pi-ness and God.

385   *The load of Sin.*   A. STEELE.
How HELPLESS guilty nature lies,
  Unconscious of its load!
The heart, unchanged, can never rise
  To happiness and God.

2 Can aught, beneath a power divine,
  The stubborn will subdue?
'Tis thine, almighty Spirit! thine,
  To form the heart anew.

3 'Tis thine, the passions to recall,
  And upward bid them rise;
To make the scales of error fall
  From reason's darkened eyes;—

4 To chase the shades of death away,
  And bid the sinner live;
A beam of heaven, a vital ray,
  'Tis thine alone to give.

5 Oh change these wretched hearts of ours,
  And give them life divine;
Then shall our passions and our powers,
  Almighty Lord! be thine.

386   *No escape.*   I. WATTS.
IN vain we seek for peace with God
  By methods of our own:
Nothing, O Saviour! but thy blood
  Can bring us near the throne.

2 The threatenings of the broken law
  Impress the soul with dread:
If God his sword of vengeance draw,
  It strikes the spirit dead.

3 But thine illustrious sacrifice
  Hath answered these demands;
And peace and pardon from the skies
  Are offered by thy hands.

4 'Tis by thy death we live, O Lord!
  'Tis on thy cross we rest:
For ever be thy love adored,
  Thy name for ever blessed.

387   *"Sin revived: I died."*   I. WATTS.
LORD, how secure my conscience was,
  And felt no inward dread!
I was alive without the law,
  And thought my sins were dead.

2 My hopes of heaven were firm and bright;
  But since the precept came
With a convincing power and light,
  I find how vile I am.

3 My guilt appeared but small before,
  Till terribly I saw
How perfect, holy, just, and pure,
  Was thine eternal law.

4 Then felt my soul the heavy load;
  My sins revived again:
I had provoked a dreadful God,
  And all my hopes were slain.

5 My God, I cry with every breath
  For some kind power to save,
To break the yoke of sin and death,
  And thus redeem the slave.

MAN'S LOST CONDITION.

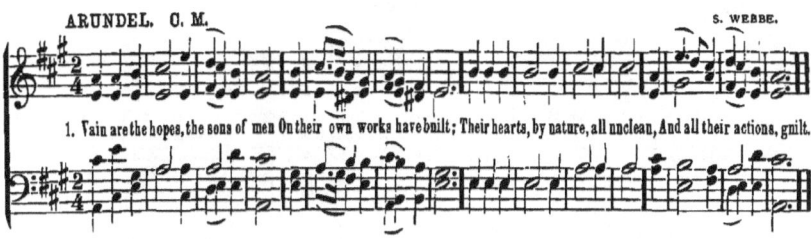

ARUNDEL. C. M. S. WEBBE.

1. Vain are the hopes, the sons of men On their own works have built; Their hearts, by nature, all unclean, And all their actions, guilt.

388 *"All Guilty."* I. WATTS.
VAIN are the hopes, the sons of men
 On their own works have built;
Their hearts, by nature, all unclean,
 And all their actions, guilt.

2 Let Jew and Gentile stop their mouths,
 Without a murmuring word;
And the whole race of Adam stand
 Guilty before the Lord.

3 Jesus! how glorious is thy grace;—
 When in thy name we trust,
Our faith receives a righteousness,
 That makes the sinner just.

389 *The Strait Way.* I. WATTS.
STRAIT is the way, the door is strait,
 That leads to joys on high;
'Tis but a few that find the gate
 While crowds mistake and die.

2 Beloved self must be denied,
 The mind and will renewed,
Passion suppressed, and patience tried,
 And vain desires subdued.

3 Lord! can a feeble, helpless worm,
 Fulfill a task so hard!
Thy grace must all my work perform,
 And give the free reward.

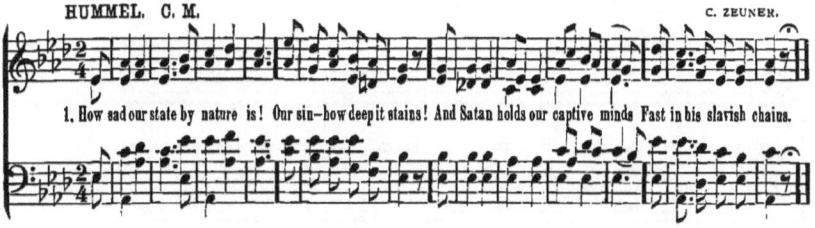

HUMMEL. C. M. C. ZEUNER.

1. How sad our state by nature is! Our sin—how deep it stains! And Satan holds our captive minds Fast in his slavish chains.

390 *The Soul ruined.* I. WATTS.
How SAD our state by nature is!
 Our sin—how deep it stains!
And Satan holds our captive minds
 Fast in his slavish chains.

2 But there's a voice of sovereign grace,
 Sounds from the sacred word;
"Ho! ye despairing sinners, come,
 And trust a pardoning Lord."

3 My soul obeys the almighty call,
 And runs to this relief;
I would believe thy promise, Lord:
 Oh, help my unbelief!

4 A guilty, weak, and helpless worm,
 On thy kind arms I fall;
Be thou my Strength and Righteousness,
 My Saviour and my All.

391 *Utter helplessness.* I. WATTS.
NOT all the outward forms on earth,
 Nor rites that God has given,
Nor will of man, nor blood, nor birth,
 Can raise a soul to heaven.

2 The sovereign will of God alone
 Creates us heirs of grace;
Born in the image of his Son,
 A new, peculiar race.

3 The Spirit, like some heavenly wind,
 Breathes on the sons of flesh,
New-models all the carnal mind,
 And forms the man afresh.

4 Our quickened souls awake and rise
 From the long sleep of death;
On heavenly things we fix our eyes,
 And praise employs our breath.

11

THE GOSPEL OF GRACE.

WELLS. L. M.   ISRAEL HOLDROYD, arr.

1. Broad is the road that leads to death, And thousands walk to-geth-er there;
But wis-dom shows a nar-row path, With here and there a tra-vel-er.

392   *The narrow path.*   I. WATTS.

Broad is the road that leads to death,
  And thousands walk together there;
But wisdom shows a narrow path,
  With here and there a traveler.

2 "Deny thyself and take thy cross,"—
  Is the Redeemer's great command:
Nature must count her gold but dross,
  If she would gain this heavenly land.

3 The fearful soul that tires and faints,
  And walks the ways of God no more,
Is but esteemed almost a saint,
  And makes his own destruction sure.

4 Lord! let not all my hopes be vain:
  Create my heart entirely new;
Which hypocrites could ne'er attain,
  Which false apostates never knew.

REPENTANCE. L. M.   THEO. E. PERKINS.

1. Je-sus, en-grave it on my heart, That thou the one thing need-ful art;
I could from all things part-ed be, But nev-er, nev-er, Lord, from thee.

393   *"One thing needful."*   S. MEDLEY.

Jesus, engrave it on my heart,
That thou the one thing needful art;
I could from all things parted be,
But never, never, Lord, from thee.

2 Needful is thy most precious blood,
To reconcile my soul to God;
Needful is thy indulgent care;
Needful thy all-prevailing prayer.

3 Needful art thou, my guide, my stay,
Through all life's dark and weary way;
Nor less in death thou'lt needful be,
To bring my spirit home to thee.

4 Then needful still, my God, my King,
Thy name eternally I'll sing!
Glory and praise be ever his,—
The one thing needful Jesus is!

MAN'S LOST CONDITION.

PRAYER. S. M. — LEONARD MARSHALL.

1. Can sinners hope for heaven, Who love this world so well? Or dream of future happiness, While on the road to hell?

394 *Pardon and Purity.* B. BEDDOME.
Can sinners hope for heaven,
  Who love this world so well?
Or dream of future happiness,
  While on the road to hell?
2 Shall they hosannas sing,
  With an unhallowed tongue?
Shall palms adorn the guilty hand
  Which does its neighbor wrong?
3 Thy grace, O God, alone,
  Good hope can e'er afford!
The pardoned and the pure shall see
  The glory of the Lord.

395 *"All downward."* I. WATTS.
Like sheep we went astray,
  And broke the fold of God—
Each wandering in a different way,
  But all the downward road.
2 How dreadful was the hour,
  When God our wanderings laid,
And did at once his vengeance pour
  Upon the Shepherd's head!

3 How glorious was the grace,
  When Christ sustained the stroke!
His life and blood the Shepherd pays,
  A ransom for the flock.
4 But God shall raise his head,
  O'er all the sons of men,
And make him see a numerous seed,
  To recompense his pain.

396 *"Jesus only."* H. BONAR.
Not what these hands have done
  Can save this guilty soul:
Not what this toiling flesh has borne
  Can make my spirit whole.
2 Not what I feel or do
  Can give me peace with God;
Not all my prayers, and sighs, and tears,
  Can bear my awful load.
3 Thy work alone, O Christ,
  Can ease this weight of sin;
Thy blood alone, O Lamb of God,
  Can give me peace within.

IOWA. S. M. — A. CHAPIN.

1. A charge to keep I have, A God to glo-ri-fy, A nev-er-dy-ing soul to save, And fit it for the sky.

397 *Probation.* C. WESLEY.
A charge to keep I have,
  A God to glorify,
A never-dying soul to save,
  And fit it for the sky.
2 To serve the present age,
  My calling to fulfill;
Oh, may it all my powers engage
  To do my Master's will.

3 Arm me with jealous care,
  As in thy sight to live;
And oh, thy servant, Lord, prepare
  A strict account to give.
4 Help me to watch and pray,
  And on thyself rely,
Assured, if I my trust betray,
  I shall for ever die.

THE GOSPEL OF GRACE.

398 *Zech. 13:1.* W. COWPER.

There is a fountain filled with blood,
Drawn from Immanuel's veins;
And sinners, plunged beneath that flood,
Lose all their guilty stains.

2 The dying thief rejoiced to see
That fountain in his day;
And there may I, though vile as he,
Wash all my sins away.

3 Dear dying Lamb, thy precious blood
Shall never lose its power,
Till all the ransomed church of God
Be saved to sin no more.

4 E'er since, by faith, I saw the stream
Thy flowing wounds supply,
Redeeming love has been my theme,
And shall be, till I die.

5 Then in a nobler, sweeter song,
I'll sing thy power to save,
When this poor lisping, stammering tongue
Lies silent in the grave.

399 *The Gospel.* S. MEDLEY.

Oh, what amazing words of grace
Are in the gospel found,
Suited to every sinner's case
Who hears the joyful sound!

2 Come, then, with all your wants and
Your every burden bring; [wounds;
Here love, unchanging love, abounds,—
A deep celestial spring.

3 This spring with living water flows,
And heavenly joy imparts:
Come, thirsty souls! your wants disclose
And drink, with thankful hearts.

THE ATONEMENT.

ARLINGTON. C. M.   T. A. ARNE.

1. A-maz-ing grace! how sweet the sound That saved a wretch like me!
I once was lost, but now am found,— Was blind, but now I see.

400   *"Amazing grace."*   J. NEWTON.

AMAZING grace! how sweet the sound
That saved a wretch like me!
I once was lost, but now am found—
Was blind, but now I see.

2 'Twas grace that taught my heart to fear,
And grace my fears relieved;
How precious did that grace appear,
The hour I first believed!

3 Through many dangers, toils, and snares,
I have already come;
'Tis grace hath brought me safe thus far,
And grace will lead me home.

4 Yea—when this flesh and heart shall fail,
And mortal life shall cease,
I shall possess, within the vail,
A life of joy and peace.

5 The earth shall soon dissolve like snow,
The sun forbear to shine;
But God, who called me here below,
Will be for ever mine.

401   *"Salvation."*   L. WATTS.

SALVATION!—oh, the joyful sound!
'Tis pleasure to our ears;
A sovereign balm for every wound,
A cordial for our fears.

2 Buried in sorrow and in sin,
At hell's dark door we lay;—
But we arise by grace divine,
To see a heavenly day.

3 Salvation!—let the echo fly
The spacious earth around;
While all the armies of the sky
Conspire to raise the sound.

SIMPSON. C. M.   FROM LOUIS SPOHR.

1. Sal-va-tion!—oh, the joy-ful sound! 'Tis pleas-ure to our ears;
A sove-reign balm for ev-ery wound. A cor-dial for our fears.

THE GOSPEL OF GRACE.

SCOTLAND. 12s.   *Small notes for hymn 934.*   J. CLARK.

1. The voice of free grace cries, Escape to the mountain, For A-dam's lost race Christ hath opened a fountain; { *For sin and unclean-ness, and ev-ery transgression, His* / *Halle-lu-jah to the Lamb, who hath purchased our par-don, We'll* } *blood flows most freely in streams of salvation, His blood flows most freely in streams of sal-va-tion.* } *praise him a-gain, when we pass over Jordan, We'll praise him a-gain, when we pass over Jordan.*

402   *"Flee for life!"*   R. BURDSALL.

THE voice of free grace cries, Escape to
   the mountain,
For Adam's lost race Christ hath opened
   a fountain;
For sin and uncleanness, and every transgression,
His blood flows most freely in streams of
   salvation.
       Hallelujah to the Lamb, etc.

2 Ye souls that are wounded! oh, flee to
   the Saviour!
He calls you in mercy, 'tis infinite favor;
Your sins are increasing, escape to the
   mountain—
His blood can remove them, it flows from
   the fountain.
       Hallelujah to the Lamb, etc.

3 With joy shall we stand when escaped
   to the shore;
With harps in our hands we will praise him
   the more!
We'll range the sweet plains on the banks
   of the river,
And sing of salvation for ever and ever!
       Hallelujah to the Lamb, etc.

LOVING-KINDNESS. L. M.   WESTERN MELODY.

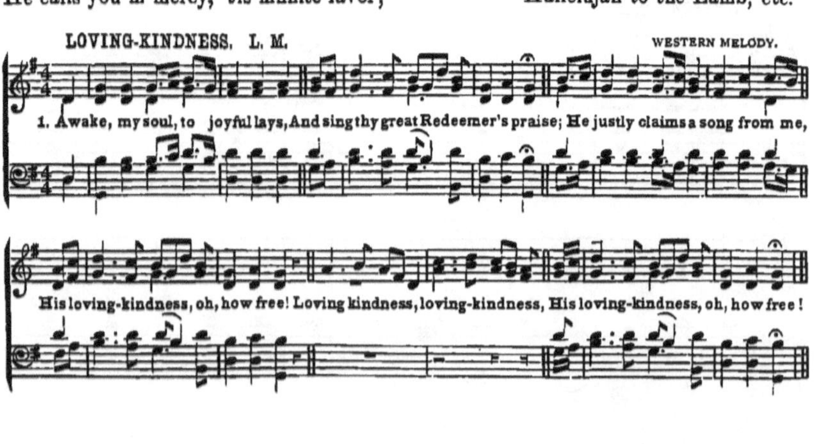

1. Awake, my soul, to joyful lays, And sing thy great Redeemer's praise; He justly claims a song from me, His loving-kindness, oh, how free! Loving kindness, loving-kindness, His loving-kindness, oh, how free!

THE ATONEMENT. 153

THE NINETY AND NINE. P. M.   IRA D. SANKEY.

403   *"To save the lost."*   E. C. CLEPHANE.

There were ninety and nine that safely lay
  In the shelter of the fold,
But one was out on the hills away,
  Far off from the gates of gold—
Away on the mountains wild and bare,
Away from the tender Shepherd's care.

2 "Lord, thou hast here thy ninety and nine:
   Are they not enough for thee?"
But the Shepherd made answer: "This of mine
   Has wandered away from me:
And although the road be rough and steep
I go to the desert to find my sheep."

3 But none of the ransomed ever knew
    How deep were the waters crossed;
  Nor how dark was the night that the Lord
    passed through
  Ere he found his sheep that was lost;
  Out in the desert he heard its cry—
  'Twas helpless and sick, and ready to die.

4 But all through the mountains, thunder-
    And up from the rocky steep,   [riven,
  There rose a cry to the gate of heaven,
    "Rejoice! I have found my sheep!"
  And the angels echoed around the throne,
  "Rejoice, for the Lord brings back his own!"

---

404 L. M. *Loving-kindness.*   S. MEDLEY.

Awake, my soul, to joyful lays,
And sing thy great Redeemer's praise;
He justly claims a song from me:
His loving-kindness, oh, how free!

2 He saw me ruined in the fall,
Yet loved me, notwithstanding all;
He saved me from my lost estate:
His loving-kindness, oh, how great!

3 Though numerous hosts of mighty foes,
Though earth and hell my way oppose,
He safely leads my soul along:
His loving-kindness, oh, how strong!

4 When trouble, like a gloomy cloud,
Has gathered thick and thundered loud,
He near my soul has always stood:
His loving-kindness, oh, how good!

THE GOSPEL OF GRACE.

405 *Our Surety.* C. WESLEY.

Arise, my soul, arise!
Shake off thy guilty fears;
The bleeding Sacrifice
In my behalf appears;
Before the throne my Surety stands:
My name is written on his hands.

2 He ever lives above,
For me to intercede,
His all-redeeming love,
His precious blood to plead;
His blood atoned for all our race,
And sprinkles now the throne of grace.

3 My God is reconciled;
His pardoning voice I hear;
He owns me for his child;
I can no longer fear;
With confidence I now draw nigh,
And Father, Abba, Father, cry.

406 *Year of Jubilee.* C. WESLEY.

Blow ye the trumpet, blow;—
The gladly solemn sound;—
Let all the nations know,
To earth's remotest bound,
The year of jubilee is come:
Return, ye ransomed sinners, home.

2 Jesus, our great High-Priest,
Hath full atonement made;
Ye weary spirits, rest;
Ye mournful souls, be glad:
The year of jubilee is come;
Return, ye ransomed sinners, home.

3 Extol the Lamb of God,
The all-atoning Lamb;
Redemption in his blood
Throughout the world proclaim:
The year of jubilee is come;
Return, ye ransomed sinners, home.

THE ATONEMENT.

ATHENS. C. M. D.   F. GIARDINI.

1. Awake, my heart, arise, my tongue, Prepare a tuneful voice; In God, the life of all my joys,
D. S.—Upon a poor, pollut-ed worm,

A-loud will I re-joice. 'Tis he adorned my nak-ed soul, And made sal-va-tion mine;
He makes his graces shine.

407   "*The Seamless Robe.*"   I. WATTS.

Awake, my heart, arise, my tongue,
  Prepare a tuneful voice;
In God, the life of all my joys,
  Aloud will I rejoice.
'Tis he adorned my naked soul,
  And made salvation mine;
Upon a poor, polluted worm,
  He makes his graces shine.

2 And lest the shadow of a spot
  Should on my soul be found,
He took the robe the Saviour wrought,
  And cast it all around.
How far the heavenly robe exceeds
  What earthly princes wear!
These ornaments, how bright they shine!
  How white the garments are!

3 The Spirit wrought my faith and love,
  And hope and every grace;
But Jesus spent his life to work
  The robe of righteousness.
Strangely, my soul, art thou arrayed,
  By the great sacred Three;
In sweetest harmony of praise,
  Let all thy powers agree.

408   "*Jesus died for me.*"   W. H. BATHURST.

Great God, when I approach thy throne,
  And all thy glory see;
This is my stay, and this alone,
  That Jesus died for me.

2 How can a soul condemned to die,
  Escape the just decree?
Helpless, and full of sin am I,
  But Jesus died for me.

3 Burdened with sin's oppressive chain,
  Oh, how can I get free?
No peace can all my efforts gain,
  But Jesus died for me.

4 And Lord, when I behold thy face,
  This must be all my plea;
Save me by thy almighty grace,
  For Jesus died for me.

409   *Divine compassion.*   A. STEELE.

Jesus,—and didst thou leave the sky,
  To bear our griefs and woes?
And didst thou bleed, and groan and die,
  For thy rebellious foes?

2 Well might the heavens with wonder view
  A love so strange as thine!
No thought of angels ever knew
  Compassion so divine!

3 Is there a heart that will not bend
  To thy divine control?
Descend, O sovereign love, descend,
  And melt that stubborn soul.

4 Oh! may our willing hearts confess
  Thy sweet, thy gentle sway;
Glad captives of thy matchless grace,
  Thy righteous rule obey.

THE GOSPEL OF GRACE.

ALL TO CHRIST. P. M. — J. T. GRAPE.

1. I hear the Saviour say, Thy strength indeed is small; Child of weakness, watch and pray,

CHORUS.

Find in me thine all in all. Jesus paid it all, All to him I owe;

Sin had left a crimson stain; He washed it white as snow.

---

410 *The debt paid.* E. M. HALL.

I hear the Saviour say,
  Thy strength indeed is small;
Child of weakness, watch and pray,
  Find in me thine all in all.
Cho.—Jesus paid it all,
    All to him I owe;
  Sin had left a crimson stain;
    He washed it white as snow.

2 Lord, now indeed I find
  Thy power, and thine alone,
Can change the leper's spots,
  And melt the heart of stone.—Cho.

3 For nothing good have I
  Whereby thy grace to claim—
I'll wash my garment white
  In the blood of Calvary's Lamb.—Cho.

4 When from my dying bed
  My ransomed soul shall rise,
Then "Jesus paid it all"
  Shall rend the vaulted skies.—Cho.

5 And when before the throne
  I stand in him complete,
I'll lay my trophies down,
  All down at Jesus' feet.—Cho.

SPANISH HYMN. 7s, 6l. — SPANISH MELODY.

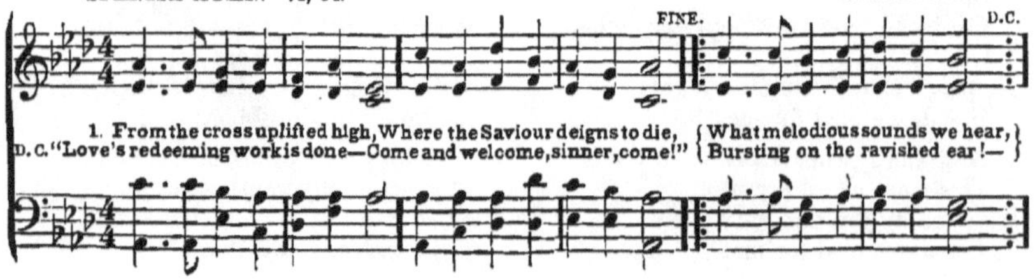

1. From the cross uplifted high, Where the Saviour deigns to die, { What melodious sounds we hear,
D. C. "Love's redeeming work is done—Come and welcome, sinner, come!" { Bursting on the ravished ear!—}

THE ATONEMENT.

411   *"Atoning blood."*   L. HARTSOUGH.

I HEAR thy welcome voice,
  That calls me, Lord, to thee,
For cleansing in thy precious blood,
  That flowed on Calvary.

CHO.—I am coming, Lord!
    Coming now to thee;
  Wash me, cleanse me, in the blood
    That flowed on Calvary!

2 Though coming weak and vile,
  Thou dost my strength assure;
Thou dost my vileness fully cleanse,
  Till spotless all, and pure.—CHO.

3 'Tis Jesus calls me on
  To perfect faith and love,
To perfect hope, and peace, and trust,
  For earth and heaven above.—CHO.

4 All hail! atoning blood!
  All hail! redeeming grace!
All hail! the gift of Christ, our Lord,
  Our Strength and Righteousness.—CHO.

---

412   7s, 6l.   *"Come and welcome."*   T. HAWEIS.

FROM the cross uplifted high,
Where the Saviour deigns to die,
What melodious sounds we hear,
Bursting on the ravished ear!—
"Love's redeeming work is done—
Come and welcome, sinner, come!

2 "Sprinkled now with blood the throne—
Why beneath thy burdens groan?
On my pierced body laid,
Justice owns the ransom paid—
Bow the knee, and kiss the Son—
Come and welcome, sinner, come!

3 "Spread for thee, the festal board
See with richest bounty stored;
To thy Father's bosom pressed,
Thou shalt be a child confessed,
Never from his house to roam;
Come and welcome, sinner, come!

4 "Soon the days of life shall end—
Lo, I come—your Saviour, Friend!
Safe your spirit to convey
To the realms of endless day,
Up to my eternal home—
Come and welcome, sinner, come!"

THE GOSPEL OF GRACE.

413 *The story of the Cross.* K. HANKEY.

TELL me the old, old story
 Of unseen things above,
 Of Jesus and his glory,
 Of Jesus and his love.
Tell me the story simply,
 As to a little child,
For I am weak and weary,
 And helpless and defiled.—CHO.

2 Tell me the story slowly,
 That I may take it in—
That wonderful Redemption,
 God's remedy for sin!
Tell me the story often,
 For I forget so soon!
The "early dew" of morning
 Has passed away at noon!—CHO.

3 Tell me the story softly,
 With earnest tones and grave;
Remember! I'm the sinner
 Whom Jesus came to save.
Tell me that story always,
 If you would really be,
In any time of trouble,
 A comforter to me.—CHO.

4 Tell me the same old story,
 When you have cause to fear
That this world's empty glory
 Is costing me too dear.
Yes, and when that world's glory
 Is dawning on my soul,
Tell me the old, old story:
 "Christ Jesus makes thee whole."—CHO.

THE ATONEMENT.

414 *The old, old story.* K. HANKEY.

I LOVE to tell the story
  Of unseen things above,
Of Jesus and his glory,
  Of Jesus and his love.
I love to tell the story,
  Because I know 'tis true;
It satisfies my longings
  As nothing else can do.—Cho.

2 I love to tell the story:
  'Tis pleasant to repeat
What seems each time I tell it,
  More wonderfully sweet.
I love to tell the story:
  For some have never heard
The message of salvation,
  From God's own holy word.—Cho.

3 I love to tell the story;
  For those who know it best
Seem hungering and thirsting
  To hear it like the rest.
And when, in scenes of glory,
  I sing the NEW, NEW SONG,
'Twill be the OLD, OLD STORY
  That I have loved so long.—Cho.

415 *Jesus' Cross.* ANON.

I SAW the cross of Jesus,
  When burdened with my sin;
I sought the cross of Jesus,
  To give me peace within;
I brought my soul to Jesus,
  He cleansed it in his blood;
And in the cross of Jesus
  I found my peace with God.

Cho.—No righteousness, no merit,
  No beauty can I plead;
Yet in the cross I glory,
  My title there I read.

2 Sweet is the cross of Jesus!
  There let my weary heart
Still rest in peace unshaken,
  Till with him, ne'er to part;
And then in strains of glory
  I'll sing his wondrous power,
Where sin can never enter,
  And death is known no more.

Cho.—I love the cross of Jesus,
  It tells me what I am;
A vile and guilty creature,
  Saved only through the Lamb.

THE GOSPEL:—INVITATIONS.

OWEN. S. M. — J. E. SWEETSER.

1. Did Christ o'er sinners weep, And shall our cheeks be dry? Let floods of penitential grief Burst forth from every eye.

416 *Weeping for sinners.* B. BEDDOME.

Did Christ o'er sinners weep,
And shall our cheeks be dry?
Let floods of penitential grief
Burst forth from every eye.

2 The Son of God in tears
Angels with wonder see;
Be thou astonished, O my soul!
He shed those tears for thee.

3 He wept that we might weep;
Each sin demands a tear:
In heaven alone no sin is found,
And there's no weeping there.

417 *The call of love.* A. B. HYDE.

And canst thou, sinner! slight
The call of love divine?
Shall God, with tenderness, invite,
And gain no thought of thine?

2 Wilt thou not cease to grieve
The Spirit from thy breast,
Till he thy wretched soul shall leave
With all thy sins oppressed?

3 To-day, a pardoning God
Will hear the suppliant pray;
To-day, a Saviour's cleansing blood
Will wash thy guilt away.

DETROIT. S. M. — E. F. HASTINGS.

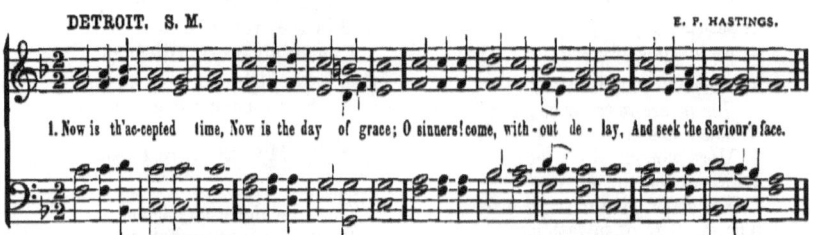

1. Now is th'accepted time, Now is the day of grace; O sinners! come, without delay, And seek the Saviour's face.

418 *The accepted time.* J. DOBELL.

Now is the accepted time,
Now is the day of grace;
O sinners! come, without delay,
And seek the Saviour's face.

2 Now is the accepted time,
The Saviour calls to-day;
To-morrow it may be too late;—
Then why should you delay?

3 Now is the accepted time,
The gospel bids you come;
And every promise in his word
Declares there yet is room.

4 Lord, draw reluctant souls,
And feast them with thy love;
Then will the angels spread their wings
And bear the news above.

THE GOSPEL:—INVITATIONS.

419 *The Prodigal Son.*   T. HASTINGS.

Return, O wanderer, to thy home,
  Thy Father calls for thee:
No longer now an exile roam
  In guilt and misery.
2 Return, O wanderer, to thy home,
  Thy Saviour calls for thee:

"The Spirit and the Bride say, Come;"
  Oh, now for refuge flee!

3 Return, O wanderer, to thy home,
  'Tis madness to delay:
There are no pardons in the tomb;
  And brief is mercy's day!

420   *Esther* 4: 16.   E. JONES.

Come, trembling sinner, in whose breast
  A thousand thoughts revolve;
Come, with your guilt and fear oppressed,
  And make this last resolve;—
2 "I'll go to Jesus, though my sins
  Like mountains round me close;
I know his courts, I'll enter in,
  Whatever may oppose.
3 "Prostrate I'll lie before his throne,
  And there my guilt confess;

I'll tell him I'm a wretch undone,
  Without his sovereign grace.
4 "Perhaps he will admit my plea,
  Perhaps will hear my prayer;
But if I perish, I will pray,
  And perish only there.
5 "I can but perish if I go;
  I am resolved to try;
For if I stay away, I know
  I must for ever die."

THE GOSPEL:—INVITATIONS.

421   *"At the door."*   J. GRIGG.

BEHOLD a Stranger at the door!
He gently knocks, has knocked before,
Has waited long, is waiting still;
You treat no other friend so ill.

2 Oh, lovely attitude! he stands
With melting heart and laden hands;
Oh, matchless kindness! and he shows
This matchless kindness to his foes.

3 But will he prove a friend indeed?
He will, the very friend you need—
The Friend of sinners; yes, 'tis he,
With garments dyed on Calvary.

4 Rise, touched with gratitude divine,
Turn out his enemy and thine,
That soul-destroying monster sin,
And let the heavenly Stranger in.

422   *"God calling yet."*   J. BORTHWICK.

GOD calling yet! shall I not hear?
Earth's pleasures shall I still hold dear?
Shall life's swift passing years all fly,
And still my soul in slumber lie?

2 God calling yet! shall I not rise?
Can I his loving voice despise,
And basely his kind care repay?
He calls me still; can I delay?

3 God calling yet! and shall I give
No heed, but still in bondage live?
I wait, but he does not forsake;
He calls me still; my heart, awake!

4 God calling yet! I cannot stay;
My heart I yield without delay;
Vain world, farewell! from thee I part;
The voice of God hath reached my heart.

THE GOSPEL:—INVITATIONS.

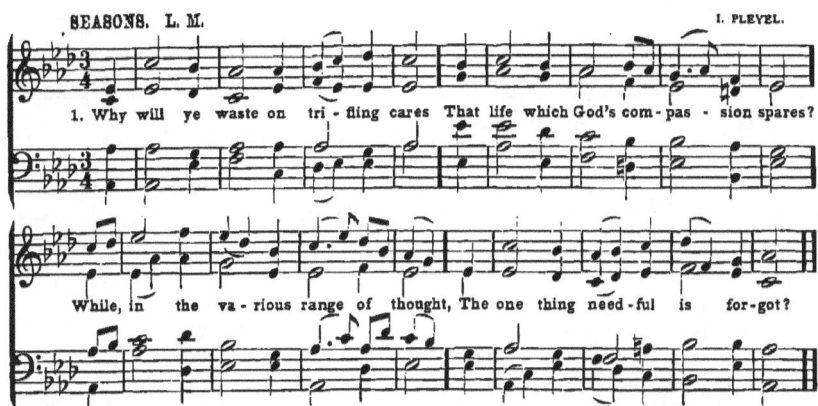

SEASONS. L. M.   I. PLEYEL.

1. Why will ye waste on trifling cares That life which God's compassion spares? While, in the various range of thought, The one thing needful is forgot?

423   *One Thing needful.*   P. DODDRIDGE.

WHY will ye waste on trifling cares
That life which God's compassion spares?
While, in the various range of thought,
The one thing needful is forgot?

2 Shall God invite you from above?
Shall Jesus urge his dying love?
Shall troubled conscience give you pain?
And all these pleas unite in vain?

3 Not so your eyes will always view
Those objects which you now pursue;
Not so will heaven and hell appear,
When death's decisive hour is near.

4 Almighty God! thy grace impart;
Fix deep conviction on each heart:
Nor let us waste on trifling cares
That life which thy compassion spares.

ASHWELL. L. M.   LOWELL MASON.

1. Oh, do not let the word depart, And close thine eyes against the light; Poor sinner, harden not thy heart: Thou wouldst be saved; why not to-night?

424   *"Why not to-night?"*   MRS. E. REED.

OH, do not let the word depart,
   And close thine eyes against the light;
Poor sinner, harden not thy heart:
   Thou wouldst be saved; why not to-night?

2 To-morrow's sun may never rise
   To bless thy long-deluded sight;
This is the time; oh, then be wise!
   Thou wouldst be saved; why not to-night?

3 Our God in pity lingers still;
   And wilt thou thus his love requite?
Renounce at length thy stubborn will;
   Thou wouldst be saved; why not to-night?

4 Our blessèd Lord refuses none
   Who would to him their souls unite;
Then be the work of grace begun:
   Thou wouldst be saved; why not to-night?

THE GOSPEL:—INVITATIONS.

MARTYN. 7s. D. — S. B. MARSH.

425 *Ezekiel* 33:11. C. WESLEY.

Sinners, turn, why will ye die?
God, your Maker, asks you—Why?
God, who did your being give,
Made you with himself to live;
He the fatal cause demands,
Asks the work of his own hands,—
Why, ye thankless creatures, why
Will ye cross his love, and die?

2 Sinners, turn, why will ye die?
God, your Saviour, asks you—Why?
He who did your souls retrieve,
Died himself that ye might live.
Will ye let him die in vain?
Crucify your Lord again?
Why, ye ransomed sinners, why
Will ye slight his grace, and die?

3 Sinners, turn, why will ye die?
God, the Spirit, asks you—Why?
He, who all your lives hath strove,
Urged you to embrace his love:
Will ye not his grace receive?
Will ye still refuse to live?
Why, ye long-sought sinners! why,
Will ye grieve your God, and die?

HORTON. 7s. — XAVIER SCHNYDER VON WARTENSEE.

426 *"Whosoever will."* A. L. BARBAULD.

Come, said Jesus' sacred voice,
Come, and make my paths your choice;
I will guide you to your home,
Weary pilgrim, hither come!

2 Thou who, houseless, sole, forlorn,
Long hast borne the proud world's scorn,
Long hast roamed the barren waste,
Weary pilgrim, hither haste.

3 Ye who, tossed on beds of pain,
Seek for ease, but seek in vain;
Ye, by fiercer anguish torn,
In remorse for guilt who mourn;—

4 Hither come! for here is found
Balm that flows for every wound,
Peace that ever shall endure,
Rest eternal, sacred, sure.

THE GOSPEL:—INVITATIONS.

EXPOSTULATION. 11s. — J. HOPKINS.

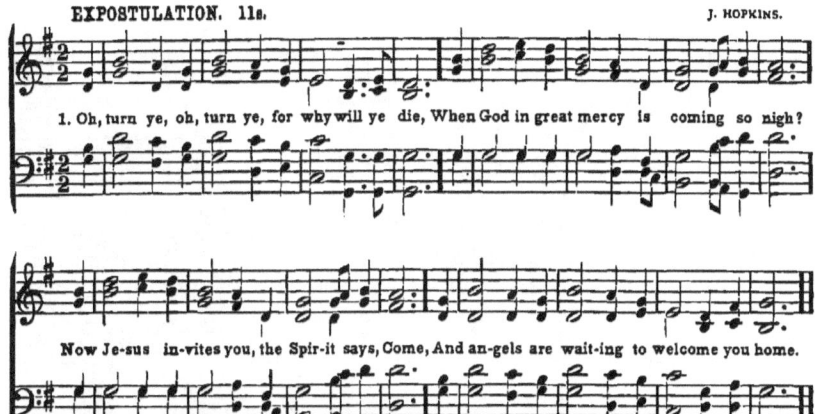

1. Oh, turn ye, oh, turn ye, for why will ye die, When God in great mercy is coming so nigh? Now Jesus invites you, the Spirit says, Come, And angels are waiting to welcome you home.

427   *"Why will ye die?"*   J. HOPKINS.

Oh, turn ye, oh, turn ye, for why will ye die,
When God in great mercy is coming so nigh?
Now Jesus invites you, the Spirit says, Come,
And angels are waiting to welcome you home.

2 In riches, in pleasures, what can you obtain,
To soothe your affliction, or banish your pain?
To bear up your spirit when summoned to die,
Or waft you to mansions of glory on high?

3 And now Christ is ready your souls to receive,
Oh, how can you question, if you will believe?
If sin is your burden, why will you not come?
'Tis you he bids welcome; he bids you come home.

428   *"I made haste."*   T. HASTINGS.

Delay not, delay not, O sinner, draw near,
The waters of life are now flowing for thee;
No price is demanded, the Saviour is here;
Redemption is purchased, salvation is free.

2 Delay not, delay not, O sinner, to come,
For Mercy still lingers and calls thee to-day:
Her voice is not heard in the vale of the tomb;
Her message unheeded will soon pass away.

3 Delay not, delay not, the Spirit of grace,
Long grieved and resisted, may take his sad flight,
And leave thee in darkness to finish thy race,
To sink in the gloom of eternity's night.

4 Delay not, delay not, the hour is at hand,
The earth shall dissolve and the heavens shall fade,
The dead, small and great, in the judgment shall stand;
What power then, O sinner, will lend thee its aid!

429   *"Acquaint thyself."*   KNOX.

Acquaint thyself quickly, O sinner, with God,
And joy, like the sunshine, shall beam on thy road,
And peace, like the dewdrop, shall fall on thy head,
And sleep, like an angel, shall visit thy bed.

2 Acquaint thyself quickly, O sinner, with God,
And he shall be with thee when fears are abroad,
Thy Safeguard in danger that threatens thy path;
Thy Joy in the valley and shadow of death.

430
"No other name." — R. LOWRY.

Weeping will not save me—
Though my face were bathed in tears,
That could not allay my fears,
Could not wash the sins of years,—
Weeping will not save me.—Cho.

2 Working will not save me—
Purest deeds that I can do,
Honest thought and feelings too,
Cannot form my soul anew,—
Working will not save me.—Cho.

3 Waiting will not save me—
Helpless, guilty, lost, I lie;
In my ear is mercy's cry;
If I wait I can but die—
Waiting will not save me.—Cho.

4 Faith in Christ will save me—
Let me trust thy weeping Son;
Trust the work that he has done;
To his arms, Lord, help me run—
Faith in Christ will save me.—Cho.

THE GOSPEL:—INVITATIONS.

COME, YE DISCONSOLATE. 11s, 10s.   S. WEBBE.

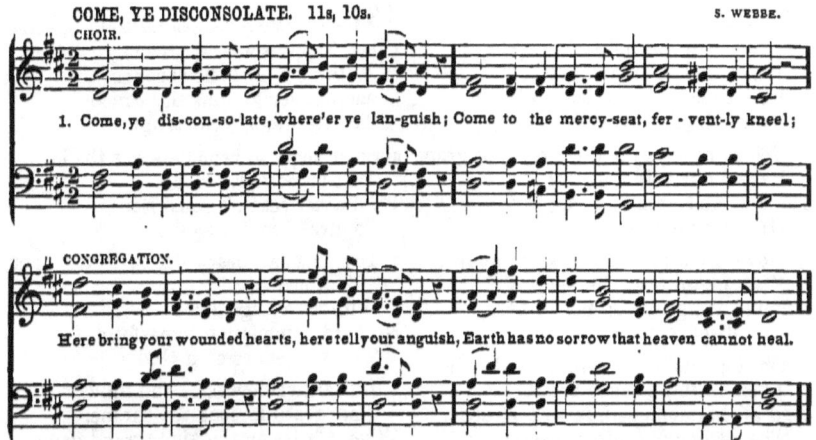

1. Come, ye dis-con-so-late, where'er ye lan-guish; Come to the mercy-seat, fer-vent-ly kneel;

Here bring your wounded hearts, here tell your anguish, Earth has no sorrow that heaven cannot heal.

431   "*Here speaks the Comforter.*"   T. MOORE.

COME, ye disconsolate, where'er ye languish:
  Come to the mercy-seat, fervently kneel;
Here bring your wounded hearts, here tell
    your anguish;
  Earth has no sorrow that heaven cannot
    heal.

2 Joy of the comfortless, light of the straying,
  Hope of the penitent, fadeless and pure;
Here speaks the Comforter tenderly saying—
  Earth has no sorrow that heaven cannot
    cure.

3 Here see the Bread of Life; see waters
    flowing
  Forth from the throne of God, pure from
    above;
Come to the feast of love: come, ever knowing
  Earth has no sorrow but heaven can remove.

---

432   "*Ho, ye needy!*"   J. HART.

COME, ye sinners, poor and wretched,
  Weak and wounded, sick and sore,
Jesus ready stands to save you,
  Full of pity, love and power.
    He is able,
He is willing, doubt no more.

2 Ho, ye needy; come, and welcome;
  God's free bounty glorify!
True belief and true repentance,
  Every grace that brings us nigh,
    Without money,
Come to Jesus Christ, and buy.

3 Let not conscience make you linger,
  Nor of fitness fondly dream;
All the fitness he requireth
  Is to feel your need of him;
    This he gives you;
'Tis the Spirit's rising beam.

433   "*Mercy's Call.*"   J. ALLEN.

SINNERS, will you scorn the message,
  Coming from the courts above?
Mercy beams in every passage;
  Every line is full of love;
    Oh! believe it,
Every line is full of love.

2 Now the heralds of salvation
  Joyful news from heaven proclaim!
Sinners freed from condemnation,
  Through the all-atoning Lamb!
    Life receiving
Through the all-atoning Lamb!

3 O ye angels, hovering round us,
  Waiting spirits, speed your way;
Haste ye to the court of heaven,
  Tidings bear without delay:
    Rebel sinners
Glad the message will obey.

THE GOSPEL:—INVITATIONS.

434 C. M. *"Oh, amazing Love!"* I. WATTS.
PLUNGED in a gulf of dark despair,
  We wretched sinners lay,
Without one cheerful beam of hope,
  Or spark of glimmering day.

2 With pitying eyes the Prince of grace
    Beheld our helpless grief;
  He saw, and—oh, amazing love!—
    He ran to our relief.

3 Down from the shining seats above,
    With joyful haste he fled,
  Entered the grave in mortal flesh,
    And dwelt among the dead.

4 Oh, for this love let rocks and hills
    Their lasting silence break;
  And all harmonious human tongues
    The Saviour's praises speak.

5 Angels! assist our mighty joys;
    Strike all your harps of gold;
  But, when you raise your highest notes,
    His love can ne'er be told.

435 L. M. *Psalm 136.* I. WATTS.
GIVE to our God immortal praise;
  Mercy and truth are all his ways;
  Wonders of grace to God belong;
  Repeat his mercies in your son

2 He sent his Son, with power to save
    From guilt, and darkness, and the grave:
  Wonders of grace to God belong;—
  Repeat his mercies in your song.

3 Through this vain world he guides our feet,
  And leads us to his heavenly seat;
  His mercies ever shall endure,
  When this vain world shall be no more.

436 C. M. *! Every One."* I. WATTS
LET every mortal ear attend,
  And every heart rejoice;
The trumpet of the gospel sounds,
  With an inviting voice.

2 Ho! all ye hungry starving souls,
    That feed upon the wind,
  And vainly strive with earthly toys
    To fill the immortal mind,—

3 Eternal wisdom has prepared
    A soul-reviving feast,
  And bids your longing appetites
    The rich provision taste.

437 C. M. *"Not to Condemn, but Save."* I. WATTS.
COME, happy souls, approach your God
  With new, melodious songs;
Come, render to almighty grace
  The tribute of your tongues.

2 So strange, so boundless was the love
    That pitied dying men,
  The Father sent his equal Son
    To give them life again.

3 Thy hands, dear Jesus, were not armed
    With an avenging rod,
  No hard commission to perform
    The vengeance of a God.

4 But all was merciful and mild,
    And wrath forsook the throne,
  When Christ on the kind errand came,
    And brought salvation down.

5 See, dearest Lord, our willing souls
    Accept thine offered grace;
  We bless the great Redeemer's love,
    And give the Father praise.

438 L. M. *"To Save Sinners."* I. WATTS.
NOT to condemn the sons of men,
  Did Christ, the Son of God, appear;
No weapons in his hands are seen,
  No flaming sword nor thunder there.

2 Such was the pity of our God,
    He loved the race of man so well,
  He sent his Son to bear our load
    Of sins, and save our souls from hell.

3 Sinners, believe the Saviour's word;
    Trust in his mighty name, and live:
  A thousand joys his lips afford,
    His hands a thousand blessings give.

439 S. M. *The Bride says, Come.* J. MONTGOMERY.
COME to the land of peace;
  From shadows come away;
Where all the sounds of weeping cease,
  And storms no more have sway.

2 Fear hath no dwelling here;
    But pure repose and love
  Breathe through the bright, celestial air
    The spirit of the dove.

3 Come to the bright and blest,
    Gathered from every land;
  For here thy soul shall find its rest,
    Amid the shining band.

440 P. M.   *Jesus calls.*   T. HASTINGS.

Drooping souls, no longer mourn,
  Jesus still is precious;
If to him you now return,
  Heaven will be propitious;
Jesus now is passing by,
  Calling wanderers near him;
Drooping souls, you need not die,
  Go to him and hear him!

2 He has pardons, full and free,
  Drooping souls to gladden;
Still he cries—"Come unto me,
  Weary, heavy-laden!"
Though your sins, like mountains high,
  Rise, and reach to heaven,
Soon as you on him rely,
  All shall be forgiven.

3 Precious is the Saviour's name,
  Dear to all that love him;
He to save the dying came;—
  Go to him and prove him!
Wandering sinners, now return;
  Contrite souls, believe him!
Jesus calls you, cease to mourn:
  Worship him; receive him.

441 S. M.   *Spirit and Bride.*   H. U. ONDERDONK.

The Spirit, in our hearts,
  Is whispering, "Sinner, come;"
The bride, the Church of Christ, pro-
  To all his children, "Come!" [claims,

2 Let him that heareth, say
  To all about him, "Come!"
Let him that thirsts for righteousness,
  To Christ, the fountain, come!

3 Yes, whosoever will,
  Oh, let him freely come,
And freely drink the stream of life;
  'T is Jesus bids him come.

4 Lo! Jesus, who invites,
  Declares, "I quickly come;"
Lord, even so; we wait thine hour;
  O blest Redeemer, come!

442 L. M.   *Flee for Life.*   W. B. COLLYER.

Haste, traveler, haste! the night comes
And many a shining hour is gone; [on,
The storm is gathering in the west,
And thou far off from home and rest.

2 The rising tempest sweeps the sky;
The rains descend, the winds are high;
The waters swell, and death and fear
Beset thy path, nor refuge near.

3 Oh, yet a shelter you may gain,
A covert from the wind and rain;
A hiding-place, a rest, a home,
A refuge from the wrath to come!

4 Then linger not in all the plain;
Flee for thy life; the mountain gain;
Look not behind; make no delay;
Oh, speed thee, speed thee on thy way!

443 7s.   *Winning Souls.*   W. HAMMOND.

Would you win a soul to God?
Tell him of a Saviour's blood,
Once for dying sinners spilt,
To atone for all their guilt.

2 Tell him—it was sovereign grace
Led thee first to seek his face;
Made thee choose the better part,
Wrought salvation in thy heart.

3 Tell him of that liberty,
Wherewith Jesus makes thee free!
Sweetly speak of sins forgiven,
Earnest of the joys of heaven.

444 L. M.   *"Only Knock."*   J. B. WATERBURY.

Infinite Love! what precious stores
  Thy mercy has prepared for us!
The costliest gems, the richest ores
  Could never have endowed us thus.

2 But thy soft hand, O gracious Lord!
  Can draw from suffering souls the sting:
And thy rich bounty to our board
  Can bread for hungering sinners bring.

3 How rich the grace! the gift how free!
  'T is only ask—it shall be given;
'T is only knock, and thou shalt see
  The opening door that leads to heaven.

4 Oh! then arise and take the good,
  So full and freely proffered thee,
Remembering that it cost the blood
  Of him who died on Calvary.

THE GOSPEL:—REPENTANCE.

LIFE. 8s, 7s, 7s.   THOS. HASTINGS.

1. Come to Calvary's ho-ly mountain, Sinners, ru-ined by the fall! Here a pure and heal-ing foun-tain, Flows to you, to me, to all,— In a full, per-pet-ual tide, Opened when our Sav-iour died, O-pened when our Saviour died.

445   *A fountain opened.*   J. MONTGOMERY.

COME to Calvary's holy mountain,
  Sinners, ruined by the fall!
Here a pure and healing fountain
  Flows to you, to me, to all,—
In a full, perpetual tide,
Opened when our Saviour died.

2 Come, in sorrow and contrition,
  Wounded, impotent, and blind!
Here the guilty, free remission,
  Here the troubled, peace may find;
Health this fountain will restore,
He that drinks shall thirst no more—

3 He that drinks shall live for ever;
  'Tis a soul-renewing flood:
God is faithful; God will never
  Break his covenant in blood,
Signed when our Redeemer died,
Sealed when he was glorified.

PASS ME NOT. 8s, 5s.   W. H. DOANE.

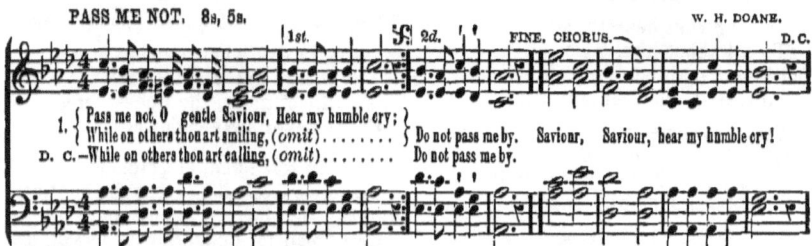

1. Pass me not, O gentle Saviour, Hear my humble cry; While on others thou art smiling, (*omit*) .... Do not pass me by. Saviour, Saviour, hear my humble cry!
D. C.—While on others thou art calling, (*omit*) .... Do not pass me by.

446   *"Do not pass me."*   F. C. VAN ALSTYNE.

PASS me not, O gentle Saviour,
  Hear my humble cry;
While on others thou art smiling,
  Do not pass me by.—CHO.

2 Let me at thy throne of mercy
  Find a sweet relief;
Kneeling there in deep contrition,
  Help my unbelief.—CHO.

3 Trusting only in thy merit,
  Would I seek thy face;
Heal my wounded, broken spirit,
  Save me by thy grace.—CHO.

4 Thou the Spring of all my comfort,
  More than life to me,
Whom on earth have I beside thee,
  Whom in heaven but thee!—CHO.

REPENTANCE UNTO LIFE.

447 *The door of mercy.* U. L. BAILEY.

The mistakes of my life are many,
   The sins of my heart are more,
And I scarce can see for weeping;
   But I knock at the open door.—Cho.

2 I am lowest of those who love him,
   I am weakest of those who pray:
But I come as he has bidden,
   And he will not say me nay.—Cho.

3 My mistakes his free grace will cover,
   My sins he will wash away,
And the feet that shrink and falter,
   Shall walk through the gate of day.—Cho.

448 *"Even me."* E. CODNER.

Lord, I hear of showers of blessing
   Thou art scattering full and free;
Showers the thirsty soul refreshing;
   Let some droppings fall on me!—Ref.

2 Pass me not, O gracious Father!
   Lost and sinful though I be;
Thou might'st curse me, but the rather
   Let thy mercy light on me.—Ref.

3 Have I long in sin been sleeping?
   Long been slighting, grieving thee!
Has the world my heart been keeping,
   Oh! forgive and rescue me!—Ref.

4 Pass me not, O mighty Spirit!
   Thou canst make the blind to see;
Testify of Jesus' merit,
   Speak the word of peace to me.—Ref.

THE GOSPEL:—REPENTANCE.

WILBERFORCE. 7s. 6l.   C. C. CONVERSE, arr.

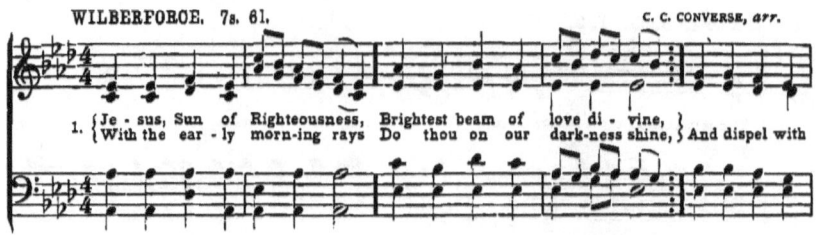

1. Jesus, Sun of Righteousness, Brightest beam of love divine,
With the early morning rays Do thou on our darkness shine, And dispel with

purest light All our night,—all our night.

449   *The melted heart.*   J. BORTHWICK.

Jesus, Sun of Righteousness,
Brightest beam of love divine,
With the early morning rays
Do thou on our darkness shine,
  And dispel with purest light
  All our night,—all our night.

2 Like the sun's reviving ray,
May thy love, with tender glow,
All our coldness melt away,
  Warm and cheer us forth to go;
  Gladly serve thee and obey,
  All the day,—all the day.

3 Thou, our only Life and Guide,
Never leave us nor forsake;
In thy light may we abide
  Till the eternal morning break;
  Moving on to Zion's hill,
  Homeward still,—homeward still.

JESUS, MY ALL. 6s, 4s.   A. BOIELDIEU.

1. Lord, at thy mer-cy-seat, Humbly I fall;
Pleading thy promise sweet, Lord, hear my call; Now let thy work begin, Oh, make me pure with-

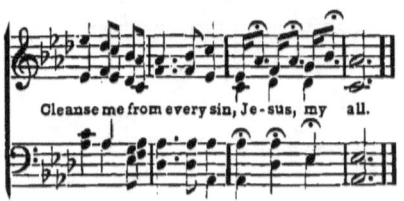

Cleanse me from every sin, Je-sus, my all.

450   *"Jesus, my all."*   F. C. VAN ALSTYNE.

Lord, at thy mercy-seat,
  Humbly I fall;
Pleading thy promise sweet,
  Lord, hear my call;
Now let thy work begin,
Oh, make me pure within,
Cleanse me from every sin,
  Jesus, my all.

2 Hark! how the words of love
  Tenderly fall,
Ere to the realms above,
  Heard is my call;
Now every doubt has flown,
Broken my heart of stone,
Lord, I am thine alone,
  Jesus, my all.

3 Still at thy mercy-seat
  Humbly I fall;
Pleading thy promise sweet,
  Heard is my call;
Faith wings my soul to thee;
This all my hope shall be,
Jesus has died for me,
  Jesus, my all.

REPENTANCE UNTO LIFE.

451 *"Hearer of prayer."* J. CONDER.

O THOU God who hearest prayer
Every hour and everywhere!
For his sake, whose blood I plead,
Hear me in my hour of need:
Only hide not now thy face,
God of all-sufficient grace!

2 Leave me not, my strength, my trust;
Oh, remember I am dust:
Leave me not again to stray;
Leave me not the tempter's prey:
Fix my heart on things above;
Make me happy in thy love.

3 Hear and save me, gracious Lord!
For my trust is in thy word;
Wash me from the stain of sin,
That thy peace may rule within:
May I know myself thy child,
Ransomed, pardoned, reconciled.

452 *Look and live.* A. M. TOPLADY.

SURELY Christ thy griefs hath borne,
Weeping soul, no longer mourn;
View him bleeding on the tree,
Pouring out his life for thee:
There thy every sin he bore;
Weeping soul, lament no more.

2 Weary sinner, keep thine eyes
On the atoning sacrifice:

There the incarnate Deity
Numbered with transgressors see;
There his Father's absence mourns,
Nailed, and bruised, and crowned with thorns.

3 Cast thy guilty soul on him,
Find him mighty to redeem;
At his feet thy burden lay,
Look thy doubts and cares away;
Now by faith the Son embrace,
Plead his promise, trust his grace.

453 *"Chief of sinners."* MC COMB

CHIEF of sinners though I be,
Jesus shed his blood for me;
Died that I might live on high,
Died that I might never die;
As the branch is to the vine,
I am his and he is mine.

2 Oh, the height of Jesus' love!
Higher than the heavens above,
Deeper than the depths of sea,
Lasting as eternity;
Love that found me,—wondrous thought!—
Found me when I sought him not!

3 Chief of sinners though I be,
Christ is all in all to me;
All my wants to him are known,
All my sorrows are his own;
Safe with him from earthly strife,
He sustains my hidden life.

THE GOSPEL:—REPENTANCE.

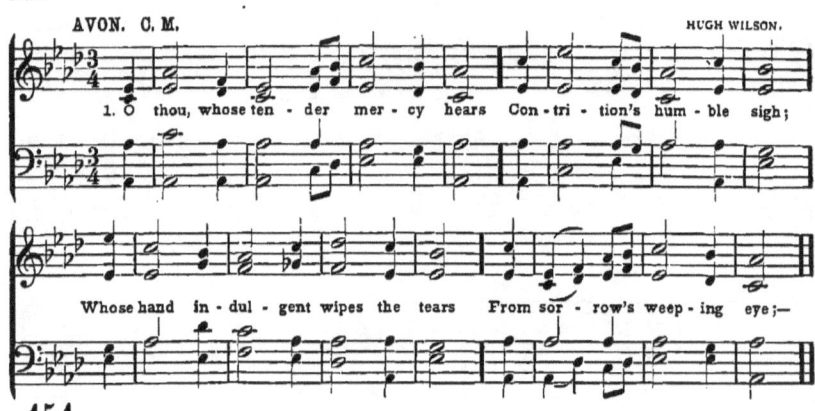

454 *"Return."* A. STEELE.

O THOU, whose tender mercy hears
Contrition's humble sigh;
Whose hand indulgent wipes the tears
From sorrow's weeping eye;—

2 See, Lord, before thy throne of grace,
A wretched wanderer mourn;
Hast thou not bid me seek thy face?
Hast thou not said—"Return?"

3 And shall my guilty fears prevail
To drive me from thy feet?
Oh, let not this dear refuge fail,
This only safe retreat!

4 Oh, shine on this benighted heart,
With beams of mercy shine!
And let thy healing voice impart
The sense of joy divine.

455 *"Remember me."* T. HAWEIS.

O THOU, from whom all goodness flows,
I lift my soul to thee;
In all my sorrows, conflicts, woes,
O Lord, remember me!

2 When on my aching, burdened heart
My sins lie heavily,
Thy pardon grant, new peace impart;
Thus, Lord, remember me!

3 When trials sore obstruct my way,
And ills I cannot flee,
Oh, let my strength be as my day—
Dear Lord, remember me!

4 When in the solemn hour of death
I wait thy just decree:
Be this the prayer of my last breath:
Now, Lord, remember me!

REPENTANCE UNTO LIFE. 175

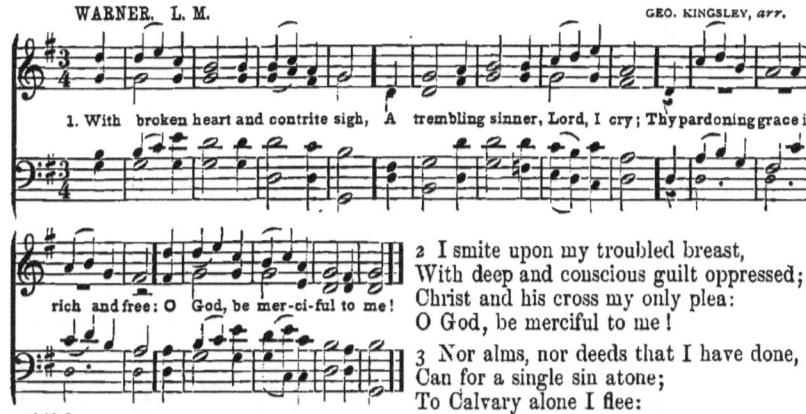

WARNER. L. M.   GEO. KINGSLEY, arr.

1. With broken heart and contrite sigh, A trembling sinner, Lord, I cry; Thy pardoning grace is rich and free: O God, be mer-ci-ful to me!

2 I smite upon my troubled breast,
With deep and conscious guilt oppressed;
Christ and his cross my only plea:
O God, be merciful to me!

3 Nor alms, nor deeds that I have done,
Can for a single sin atone;
To Calvary alone I flee:
O God, be merciful to me!

456   "*Be merciful, O God.*"   C. ELVEN.

WITH broken heart and contrite sigh,
A trembling sinner, Lord, I cry:
Thy pardoning grace is rich and free:
O God, be merciful to me!

4 And when, redeemed from sin and hell,
With all the ransomed throng I dwell,
My raptured song shall ever be,
God hath been merciful to me!

WOODWORTH. L. M.   W. B. BRADBURY.

1. Just as I am, with-out one plea, But that thy blood was shed for me, And that thou bid'st me come to thee, O Lamb of God, I come! I come!

457   "*Lamb of God.*"   C. ELLIOTT.

JUST as I am, without one plea,
But that thy blood was shed for me,
And that thou bid'st me come to thee,
   O Lamb of God, I come!

2 Just as I am, and waiting not
To rid my soul of one dark blot,
To thee whose blood can cleanse each spot,
   O Lamb of God, I come!

3 Just as I am, though tossed about
With many a conflict, many a doubt,

Fightings within, and fears without,
   O Lamb of God, I come!

4 Just as I am—thou wilt receive,
Wilt welcome, pardon, cleanse, relieve;
Because thy promise I believe,
   O Lamb of God, I come!

5 Just as I am—thy love unknown
Hath broken every barrier down;
Now, to be thine, yea, thine alone,
   O Lamb of God, I come!

THE GOSPEL:—REPENTANCE.

PENITENCE. 7s, 6s, 8s.   W. H. OAKLEY.

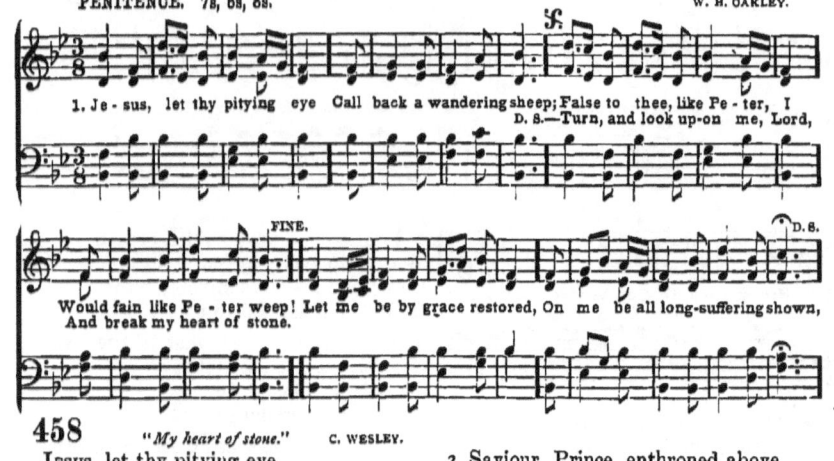

458   "My heart of stone."   C. WESLEY.

Jesus, let thy pitying eye
  Call back a wandering sheep;
False to thee, like Peter, I
  Would fain like Peter weep!
Let me be by grace restored,
  On me be all long-suffering shown,
Turn, and look upon me, Lord,
  And break my heart of stone.

2 Saviour, Prince, enthroned above,
  Repentance to impart,
Give me, through thy dying love,
  The humble, contrite heart:
Give what I have long implored,
  A portion of thy grief unknown;
Turn, and look upon me, Lord!
  And break my heart of stone.

NEAR THE CROSS. P. M.   W. H. DOANE.

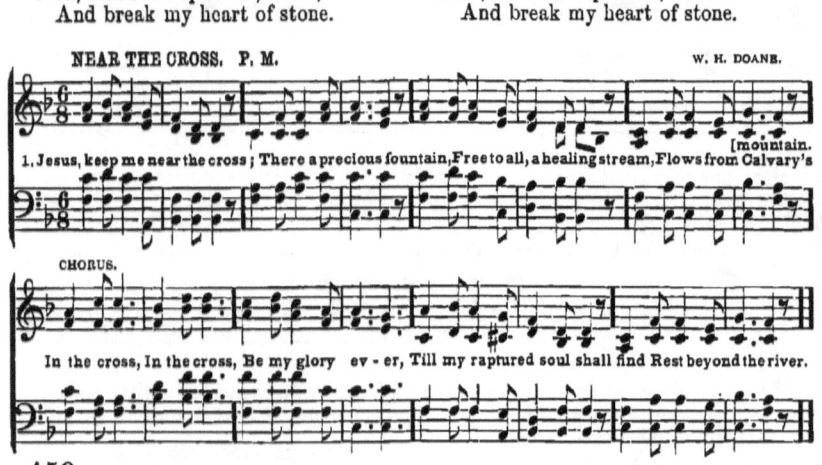

459   "Near the Cross."   F. C. VAN ALSTYNE.

Jesus, keep me near the cross;
  There a precious fountain,
Free to all, a healing stream,
  Flows from Calvary's mountain.—Cho.

2 Near the Cross, a trembling soul,
  Love and mercy found me;
There the bright and morning star
  Sheds its beams around me.—Cho.

3 Near the Cross! oh, Lamb of God,
  Bring its scenes before me;
Help me walk from day to day,
  With its shadow o'er me.—Cho.

REPENTANCE UNTO LIFE. 177

GAYLORD. 8s, 7s. D. J. P. HOLBROOK, arr.

460 "Take me." RAY PALMER.
Take me, O my Father, take me!
Take me, save me, through thy Son;
That which thou wouldst have me, make me,
Let thy will in me be done.
Long from thee my footsteps straying,
Thorny proved the way I trod;
Weary come I now, and praying—
Take me to thy love, my God!

2 Fruitless years with grief recalling,
Humbly I confess my sin;
At thy feet, O Father, falling,
To thy household take me in.
Freely now to thee I proffer
This relenting heart of mine;
Freely life and soul I offer—
Gift unworthy love like thine.

3 Once the world's Redeemer, dying,
Bare our sins upon the tree;
On that sacrifice relying,
Now I look in hope to thee;
Father, take me! all forgiving,
Fold me to thy loving breast;
In thy love for ever living,
I must be for ever blest!

DEPENDENCE. P. M. WM. F. SHERWIN.

461 "I need thee." W. F. SHERWIN.
I NEED thee, O my God,
Thy all-sustaining power;
I need thy cleansing blood
To save me every hour.—Cho.

2 I need thy Spirit, Lord,
My comfort day by day,
To guide my steps aright,
And warn me when I stray.—Cho.

3 I need the sheltering Rock,
Where, from the noon-tide heat,
My soul may rest awhile
Beneath its calm retreat.—Cho.

THE GOSPEL:—REPENTANCE.

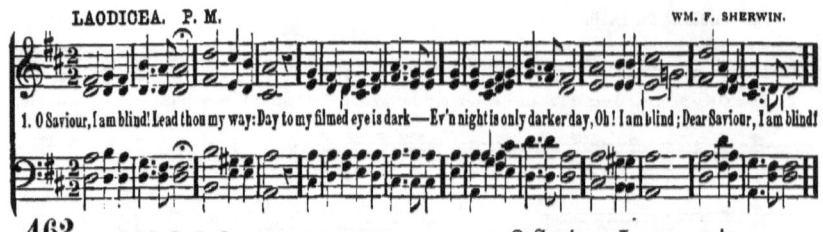

LAODICEA. P. M. — WM. F. SHERWIN.

1. O Saviour, I am blind! Lead thou my way: Day to my filmèd eye is dark—Ev'n night is only darker day, Oh! I am blind; Dear Saviour, I am blind!

462 *The Soul's Cry.* S. S. CUTTING.

O SAVIOUR, I am blind!
  Lead thou my way;
Day to my filmèd eye is dark—
Even night is only darker day;
  Oh! I am blind,
  Dear Saviour, I am blind!

2 O Saviour, I am deaf!
  Unstop my ear:
My heart would turn to thy dear voice,
The voice thy sheep alone will hear;
  Oh! I am deaf,
  Dear Saviour, I am deaf!

3 O Saviour, I am poor!
  Give me to eat:
My hungered heart loathes earthly food,
And heavenly manna craves for meat;
  Oh! I am poor,
  Dear Saviour, I am poor!

4 O Saviour, I believe,
  Blind, deaf and poor!
Sight give me; hearing; heavenly food;
Thou hast them in thy blessèd store.
  Now I believe,
  O Saviour, I believe!

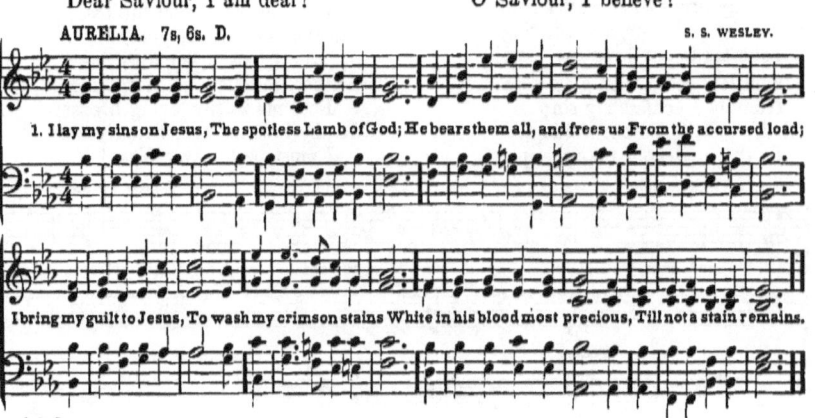

AURELIA. 7s, 6s. D. — S. S. WESLEY.

1. I lay my sins on Jesus, The spotless Lamb of God; He bears them all, and frees us From the accursèd load; I bring my guilt to Jesus, To wash my crimson stains White in his blood most precious, Till not a stain remains.

463 *"None other name."* H. BONAR.

I LAY my sins on Jesus,
  The spotless Lamb of God;
He bears them all, and frees us
  From the accursèd load;
I bring my guilt to Jesus,
  To wash my crimson stains
White in his blood most precious,
  Till not a stain remains.

2 I lay my wants on Jesus;
  All fullness dwells in him;
He healeth my diseases,
  He doth my soul redeem:
I lay my griefs on Jesus,
  My burdens and my cares;
He from them all releases,
  He all my sorrows shares.

3 I long to be like Jesus,
  Meek, loving, lowly, mild;
I long to be like Jesus,
  The Father's holy child:
I long to be with Jesus
  Amid the heavenly throng,
To sing with saints his praises,
  And learn the angels' song.

REPENTANCE UNTO LIFE.

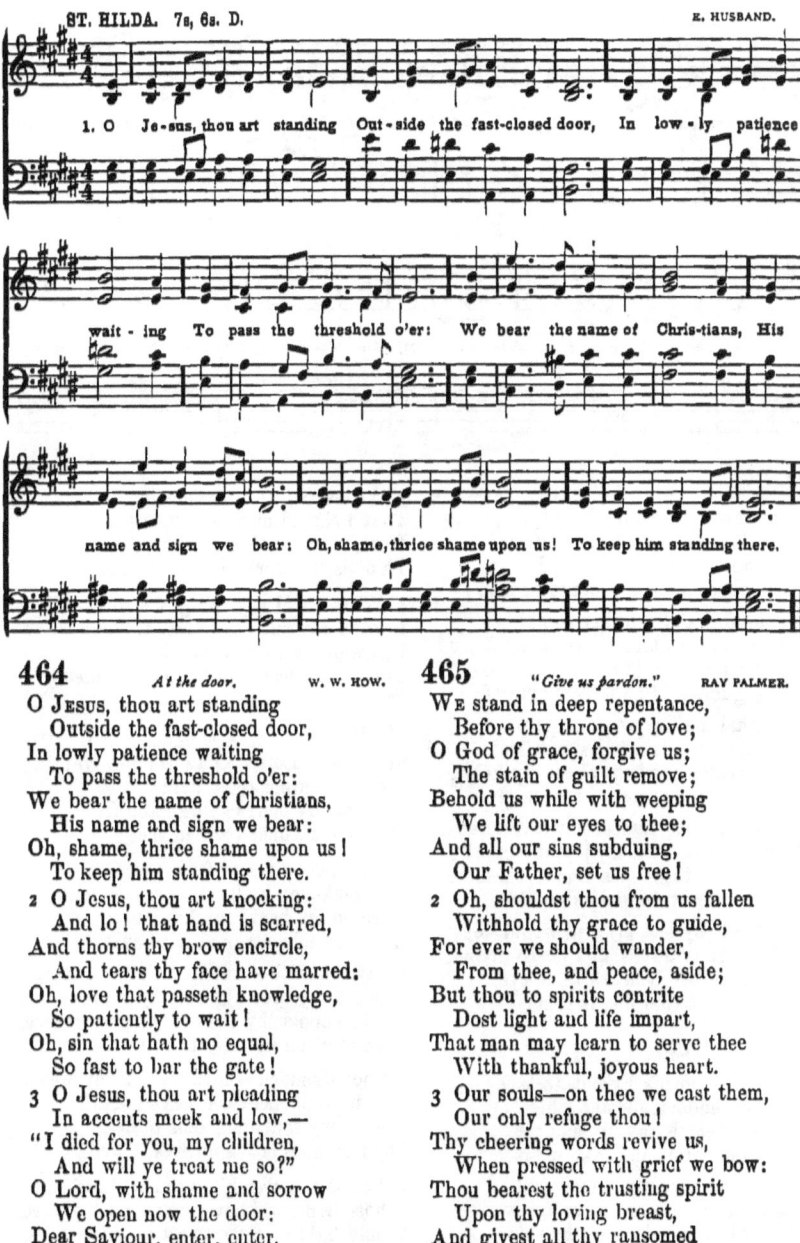

ST. HILDA. 7s, 6s. D. — E. HUSBAND.

1. O Jesus, thou art standing Out-side the fast-closed door, In low-ly patience wait-ing To pass the threshold o'er: We bear the name of Chris-tians, His name and sign we bear: Oh, shame, thrice shame upon us! To keep him standing there.

464 *At the door.* W. W. HOW.

O Jesus, thou art standing
 Outside the fast-closed door,
In lowly patience waiting
 To pass the threshold o'er:
We bear the name of Christians,
 His name and sign we bear:
Oh, shame, thrice shame upon us!
 To keep him standing there.

2 O Jesus, thou art knocking:
 And lo! that hand is scarred,
And thorns thy brow encircle,
 And tears thy face have marred:
Oh, love that passeth knowledge,
 So patiently to wait!
Oh, sin that hath no equal,
 So fast to bar the gate!

3 O Jesus, thou art pleading
 In accents meek and low,—
"I died for you, my children,
 And will ye treat me so?"
O Lord, with shame and sorrow
 We open now the door:
Dear Saviour, enter, enter,
 And leave us nevermore!
13

465 *"Give us pardon."* RAY PALMER.

We stand in deep repentance,
 Before thy throne of love;
O God of grace, forgive us;
 The stain of guilt remove;
Behold us while with weeping
 We lift our eyes to thee;
And all our sins subduing,
 Our Father, set us free!

2 Oh, shouldst thou from us fallen
 Withhold thy grace to guide,
For ever we should wander,
 From thee, and peace, aside;
But thou to spirits contrite
 Dost light and life impart,
That man may learn to serve thee
 With thankful, joyous heart.

3 Our souls—on thee we cast them,
 Our only refuge thou!
Thy cheering words revive us,
 When pressed with grief we bow:
Thou bearest the trusting spirit
 Upon thy loving breast,
And givest all thy ransomed
 A sweet, unending rest.

THE GOSPEL:—REPENTANCE.

BLAKE. L. M.   J. P. HOLBROOK.

1. Thou on-ly Sovereign of my heart, My Ref-uge, my al-might-y Friend—
And can my soul from thee de-part, On whom a-lone my hopes de-pend!

466 *"To whom shall we go!"* A. STEELE.

Thou only Sovereign of my heart,
 My Refuge, my almighty Friend—
And can my soul from thee depart,
 On whom alone my hopes depend!

2 Whither, ah! whither shall I go,
 A wretched wanderer from my Lord?
Can this dark world of sin and woe
 One glimpse of happiness afford?

3 Eternal life thy words impart;
 On these my fainting spirit lives;
Here sweeter comforts cheer my heart,
 Than all the round of nature gives

4 Thy name my inmost powers adore;
 Thou art my life, my joy, my care;
Depart from thee—'tis death, 'tis more;
 'Tis endless ruin, deep despair!

5 Low at thy feet my soul would lie;
 Here safety dwells, and peace divine;
Still let me live beneath thine eye,
 For life, eternal life, is thine.

467 *"Thou hast died."* C. WESLEY.

Jesus, the sinner's Friend, to thee
Lost and undone, for aid I flee;
Weary of earth, myself, and sin,
Open thine arms and take me in.

2 Pity and save my ruined soul;
'Tis thou alone canst make me whole;
Dark, till in me thine image shine,
And lost I am, till thou art mine.

3 At last I own it cannot be
That I should fit myself for thee:
Here, then, to thee I all resign;
Thine is the work, and only thine.

4 What can I say thy grace to move?
Lord, I am sin,—but thou art love:
I give up every plea beside,
Lord, I am lost,—but thou hast died!

468   *Psalm 51.*   I. WATTS.

Show pity, Lord! O Lord! forgive;
 Let a repenting rebel live;
Are not thy mercies large and free?
 May not a sinner trust in thee?

2 Oh, wash my soul from every sin,
And make my guilty conscience clean;
Here on my heart the burden lies,
And past offences pain mine eyes.

3 My lips with shame my sins confess,
Against thy law, against thy grace:
Lord! should thy judgments grow severe,
I am condemned, but thou art clear.

4 Should sudden vengeance seize my breath,
I must pronounce thee just in death;
And, if my soul were sent to hell,
Thy righteous law approves it well.

5 Yet save a trembling sinner, Lord!
Whose hope, still hovering round thy word,
Would light on some sweet promise there,
Some sure support against despair.

REPENTANCE UNTO LIFE.

469 *Philippians 3: 7-10.* I. WATTS.

No more, my God! I boast no more,
  Of all the duties I have done;
I quit the hopes I held before,
  To trust the merits of thy Son.

2 Now for the love I bear his name,
  What was my gain, I count but loss;
My former pride I call my shame,
  And nail my glory to his cross.

3 Yes,—and I must, and will esteem
  All things but loss for Jesus' sake;
Oh, may my soul be found in him,
  And of his righteousness partake.

4 The best obedience of my hands
  Dares not appear before thy throne;
But faith can answer thy demands,
  By pleading what my Lord has done.

470 *"Look unto me!"* S. MEDLEY.

See a poor sinner, dearest Lord,
  Whose soul, encouraged by thy word,
At mercy's footstool would remain,
  And then would look,—and look again.

2 Ah! bring a wretched wanderer home,
  Now to thy footstool let me come,
And tell thee all my grief and pain,
  And wait and look,—and look again!

3 Take courage, then, my trembling soul;
  One look from Christ will make thee whole:
Trust thou in him, 'tis not in vain,
  But wait and look,—and look again!

4 Ere long that happy day will come,
  When I shall reach my blissful home;
And when to glory I attain,
  Oh, then I'll look and look again!

THE GOSPEL:—REPENTANCE.

471 C. M. *Deep Penitence.* S. STENNETT.
PROSTRATE, dear Jesus! at thy feet,
  A guilty rebel lies,
And upwards, to thy mercy-seat,
  Presumes to lift his eyes.

2 Let not thy justice frown me hence;
  Oh, stay the vengeful storm;
Forbid it, that Omnipotence
  Should crush a feeble worm.

3 If tears of sorrow could suffice
  To pay the debt I owe,
Tears should, from both my weeping eyes,
  In ceaseless currents flow.

4 But no such sacrifice I plead
  To expiate my guilt; [shed,—
No tears, but those which thou hast
  No blood, but thou hast spilt.

5 Think of thy sorrows, dearest Lord!
  And all my sins forgive;
Then justice will approve the word,
  That bids the sinner live.

472 L. M. *Pardon Implored.* T. HASTINGS.
FORGIVE us, Lord! to thee we cry,
  Forgive us thro' thy matchless grace;
On thee alone our souls rely,
  Be thou our strength and righteousness.

2 Forgive thou us, as we forgive
  The ills we suffer from our foes;
Restore us, Lord! and bid us live;
  Oh! let us in thine arms repose.

3 Forgive us, for our guilt is great!
  Our wretched souls no merit claim;
For sovereign mercy still we wait,
  And ask but in the Saviour's name.

4 Forgive us,—O thou bleeding Lamb!
  Thou risen, thou exalted Lord!
Thou great High-Priest, our souls redeem,
  And speak the pardon-sealing word.

473 C. M. *Psalm 42.* H. F. LYTE.
As pants the hart for cooling streams,
  When heated in the chase,
So longs my soul, O God, for thee,
  And thy refreshing grace.

2 For thee, my God—the living God,
  My thirsty soul doth pine;
Oh, when shall I behold thy face,
  Thou Majesty divine!

3 Why restless, why cast down, my soul?
  Trust God; who will employ
His aid for thee, and change these sighs
  To thankful hymns of joy.

4 I sigh to think of happier days,
  When thou, O Lord! wast nigh;
When every heart was tuned to praise,
  And none more blest than I.

5 Why restless, why cast down, my soul?
  Hope still; and thou shalt sing
The praise of him who is thy God,
  Thy health's eternal spring.

474 L. M. *Psalm 51.* I. WATTS.
A BROKEN heart, my God, my King,
  Is all the sacrifice I bring:
The God of grace will ne'er despise
  A broken heart for sacrifice.

2 My soul lies humbled in the dust,
  And owns thy dreadful sentence just;
Look down, O Lord, with pitying eye,
  And save the soul condemned to die.

3 Then will I teach the world thy ways;
  Sinners shall learn thy sovereign grace;
I'll lead them to my Saviour's blood,
  And they shall praise a pardoning God.

4 Oh, may thy love inspire my tongue!
  Salvation shall be all my song;
And all my powers shall join to bless
  The Lord, my Strength and Righteousness.

475 C. M. *Submission.* ANON.
BE merciful to me, O God!
  Be merciful to me;
For though I sink beneath thy rod,
  Yet do I trust in thee.

2 Thou art my refuge, and I know
  My burden thou dost bear,
And I would seek, where'er I go,
  To cast on thee my care.

3 Thou knowest, Lord, my flesh how
  Strong though my spirit be; [frail,
Oh, then assist, when foes assail,
  The soul that clings to thee.

4 And, gracious Lord, whate'er befall,
  A thankful heart be mine,—
A heart that answers to thy call,
  One that is wholly thine.

476 8s, 7s, D.   *Contrition.*   C. WESLEY.
FULL of trembling expectation,
 Feeling much, and fearing more,
Mighty God of my salvation!
 I thy timely aid implore;
Suffering Son of Man! be near me,
 All my sufferings to sustain,
By thy sorer griefs to cheer me,
 By thy more than mortal pain.

2 Call to mind that unknown anguish,
 In thy days of flesh below;
When thy troubled soul did languish
 Under a whole world of woe;
When thou didst our curse inherit,
 Groan beneath our guilty load,
Burdened with a wounded spirit,
 Bruised by the wrath of God.

3 By thy most severe temptation,
 In that dark, satanic hour;
By thy last mysterious passion,
 Screen me from the adverse power!
By thy fainting in the garden,
 By thy bloody sweat, I pray,
Write upon my heart the pardon,
 Take my sins and fears away.

477 L. M.   *1 Peter 1: 12.*   A. L. HILLHOUSE.
TREMBLING before thine awful throne,
 O Lord! in dust my sins I own:
Justice and mercy for my life
 Contend! oh, smile and heal the strife!

2 The Saviour smiles! upon my soul
 New tides of hope tumultuous roll—
His voice proclaims my pardon found—
 Seraphic transport wings the sound.

3 Earth has a joy unknown in heaven,
 The new-born peace of sin forgiven!
Tears of such pure and deep delight,
 Ye angels! never dimmed your sight.

4 Ye saw of old, on chaos rise
 The beauteous pillars of the skies:
Ye know where morn exulting springs,
 And evening folds her drooping wings.

5 Bright heralds of the eternal Will,
 Abroad his errands ye fulfill;
Or, throned in floods of beamy day,
 Symphonious, in his presence play.

6 But I amid your choirs shall shine,
 And all your knowledge will be mine:
Ye on your harps must lean to hear
 A secret chord that mine will bear.

478 8s, 7s.   *Matt. 11: 28-30.*   J. E. RANKIN.
LABORING and heavy-laden
 With my sins, O Lord, I roam,
While I know thou hast invited
 All such wanderers to their home.

2 Make my stubborn spirit willing
 To obey thy gracious voice,
At the cross to leave its burden,
 And departing to rejoice.

3 Thy sweet yoke I'd take upon me,
 And would learn, O Lord, of thee;
Thou art meek in heart, and lowly,
 Teach me like thyself to be.

4 Laboring and heavy-laden,
 Lord, no longer will I roam:
Here I fix my habitation,
 In thy sheltering love at home.

479 7s, 6s, 8s.   *"Jesus Only."*   C. WESLEY.
VAIN, delusive world, adieu,
 With all of creature good!
Only Jesus I pursue,
 Who bought me with his blood:
All thy pleasures I forego;
 I trample on thy wealth and pride;
Only Jesus will I know,
 And Jesus crucified.

2 Other knowledge I disdain;
 'T is all but vanity:
Christ, the Lamb of God, was slain,—
 He tasted death for me.
Me to save from endless woe,
 The sin-atoning Victim died:
Only Jesus will I know,
 And Jesus crucified.

480 C. M.   *Surrender.*   F. W. FABER.
THY home is with the humble, Lord!
 The simple are the best;
Thy lodging is in child-like hearts;
 Thou makest there thy rest.

2 Dear Comforter! eternal Love!
 If thou wilt stay with me,
Of lowly thoughts and simple ways,
 I'll build a house for thee.

3 Who made this breathing heart of mine
 But thou, my heavenly Guest?
Let no one have it, then, but thee,
 And let it be thy rest!

CHRISTIAN CONFLICT.

THARAW. 7s, 6l.   H. LAMSON, arr.

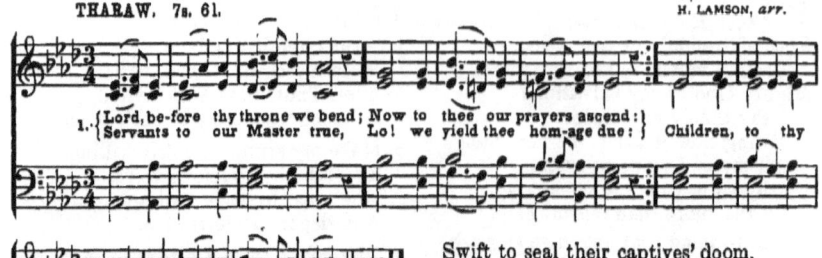

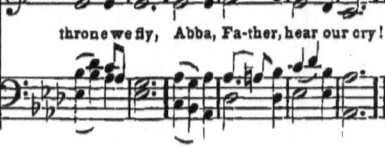

481   *Psalm* 123.   J. BOWDLER.

LORD, before thy throne we bend;
Now to thee our prayers ascend:
Servants to our Master true,
Lo! we yield thee homage due:
Children, to thy throne we fly,
Abba, Father, hear our cry!

2 Low before thee, Lord! we bow;
We are weak—but mighty thou:
Sore distressed, yet suppliant still,
Here we wait thy holy will;
Bound to earth, and rooted here,
Till our Saviour God appear.

3 Leave us not beneath the power
Of temptation's darkest hour:
Swift to seal their captives' doom,
See our foes exulting come!
Jesus, Saviour! yet be nigh,
Lord of life and victory.

482   *Backsliding confessed.*   J. NEWTON.

ONCE I thought my mountain strong,
Firmly fixed no more to move;
Then my Saviour was my song,
Then my soul was filled with love;
Those were happy, golden days,
Sweetly spent in prayer and praise.

2 Little then myself I knew,
Little thought of Satan's power;
Now I feel my sins anew;
Now I feel the stormy hour!
Sin has put my joys to flight;
Sin has turned my day to night.

3 Saviour, shine and cheer my soul,
Bid my dying hopes revive;
Make my wounded spirit whole,
Far away the tempter drive;
Speak the word and set me free,
Let me live alone to thee.

483 *"Weary, Lord."* A. D. F. RANDOLPH.

Weary, Lord, of struggling here
With this constant doubt and fear,
Burdened by the pains I bear,
And the trials I must share—
Help me, Lord, again to flee
To the rest that's found in thee.

Weakened by the wayward will
Which controls, yet cheats me still;
Seeking something undefined
With an earnest, darkened mind—
Help me, Lord, again to flee
To the light that breaks from thee.

3 Fettered by this earthly scope
In the reach and aim of hope,
Fixing thought in narrow bound
Where no living truth is found—
Help me, Lord, again to flee
To the hope that's fixed in thee.

4 Fettered, burdened, wearied, weak,
Lord, once more thy grace I seek;
Turn, oh, turn me not away,
Help me, Lord, to watch and pray—
That I never more may flee
From the rest that's found in thee.

I NEED THEE. P. M. ROBERT LOWRY.

1. I need thee ev-ery hour, Most gra-cious Lord; No ten-der voice like thine
Can peace af-ford. I need thee, oh, I need thee; Ev-ery hour I
need thee; Oh, bless me now, my Sav-iour! I come to thee.

484 *"I need thee."* A. S. HAWKS.

I need thee every hour,
  Most gracious Lord;
No tender voice like thine
  Can peace afford.
Ref.—I need thee, oh, I need thee;
  Every hour I need thee;
Oh, bless me now, my Saviour!
  I come to thee.

2 I need thee every hour;
  Stay thou near by;
Temptations lose their power
  When thou art nigh.—Ref.

3 I need thee every hour,
  In joy or pain;
Come quickly and abide,
  Or life is vain.—Ref.

4 I need thee every hour;
  Teach me thy will;
And thy rich promises
  In me fulfill.—Ref.

5 I need thee every hour,
  Most Holy One;
Oh, make me thine indeed,
  Thou blessèd Son.—Ref.

CHRISTIAN CONFLICT.

BETHANY. 6s, 4s. LOWELL MASON.

485 *Genesis 28: 10-22.* S. F. ADAMS.

Nearer, my God, to thee,
 Nearer to thee!
Ev'n though it be a cross
 That raiseth me!
Still all my song shall be,
Nearer, my God, to thee,
 Nearer to thee!

2 Though, like a wanderer,
 The sun gone down,
Darkness be over me,
 My rest a stone,
Yet in my dreams I'd be
Nearer, my God, to thee,
 Nearer to thee!

3 There let the way appear,
 Steps unto heaven;
All that thou sendest me,
 In mercy given;
Angels to beckon me
Nearer, my God, to thee,
 Nearer to thee!

4 Then, with my waking thoughts
 Bright with thy praise,
Out of my stony griefs
 Bethel I'll raise;
So by my woes to be
Nearer, my God, to thee,
 Nearer to thee!

MORE LOVE. 6s, 4s. T. E. PERKINS.

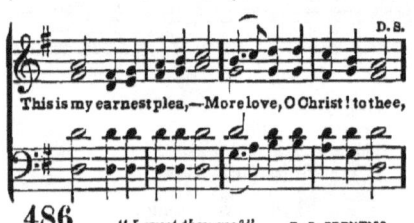

486 *"Lovest thou me?"* E. P. PRENTISS.

More love to thee, O Christ!
 More love to thee!
Hear thou the prayer I make
 On bended knee;
This is my earnest plea,—
More love, O Christ, to thee,
 More love to thee!

2 Once earthly joy I craved,
 Sought peace and rest;
Now thee alone I seek,
 Give what is best:
This all my prayer shall be,—
More love, O Christ, to thee,
 More love to thee!

3 Then shall my latest breath
 Whisper thy praise;
This be the parting cry
 My heart shall raise,—
This still its prayer shall be,—
More love, O Christ, to thee,
 More love to thee!

FIGHTINGS WITHOUT:—FEARS WITHIN.

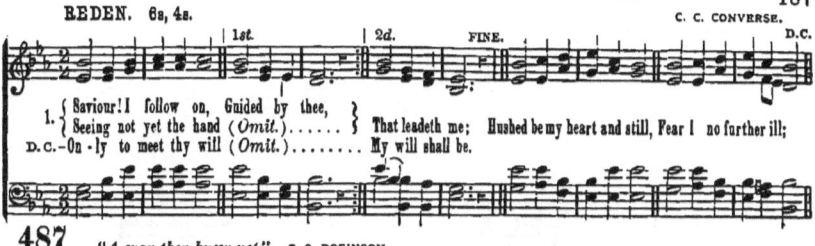

EDEN. 6s, 4s.   C. C. CONVERSE.

487 *"A way they knew not."* C. S. ROBINSON.

SAVIOUR! I follow on,
  Guided by thee,
Seeing not yet the hand
  That leadeth me;
Hushed be my heart and still,
Fear I no further ill;
Only to meet thy will
  My will shall be.

2 Riven the rock for me
  Thirst to relieve,
Manna from heaven falls
  Fresh every eve;
Never a want severe
Causeth my eye a tear,
But thou dost whisper near,
  "Only believe!"

3 Often to Marah's brink
  Have I been brought;
Shrinking the cup to drink,
  Help I have sought;
And with the prayer's ascent,
Jesus the branch hath rent—
Quickly relief hath sent,
  Sweetening the draught.

4 Saviour! I long to walk
  Closer with thee;
Led by thy guiding hand,
  Ever to be;
Constantly near thy side,
Quickened and purified,
Living for him who died
  Freely for me!

SOMETHING FOR JESUS. 6s, 4s. D.   ROBERT LOWRY.

488 *"Something for thee."* S. D. PHELPS.

SAVIOUR, thy dying love
  Thou gavest me:
Nor should I aught withhold,
  Dear Lord, from thee:
In love my soul would bow,
My heart fulfill its vow,
Some offering bring thee now,
  Something for thee.

2 O'er the blest mercy-seat,
  Pleading for me,
My feeble faith looks up,
  Jesus, to thee:
Help me the cross to bear,
Thy wondrous love declare,
Some song to raise, or prayer,
  Something for thee.

3 Give me a faithful heart—
  Likeness to thee,
That each departing day
  Henceforth may see
Some work of love begun,
Some deed of kindness done,
Some wanderer sought and won,
  Something for thee.

489   *"A clean heart."*   C. WESLEY.

Oh, for a heart to praise my God,
  A heart from sin set free;
A heart that always feels thy blood
  So freely shed for me!

2 A heart resigned, submissive, meek,
  My dear Redeemer's throne;
Where only Christ is heard to speak,
  Where Jesus reigns alone!

3 Oh, for a lowly, contrite heart,
  Believing, true, and clean!
Which neither life nor death can part
  From him that dwells within.

4 A heart in every thought renewed,
  And filled with love divine;
Perfect, and right, and pure, and good;
  An image, Lord! of thine.

5 Thy nature, gracious Lord, impart;
  Come quickly from above;
Write thy new name upon my heart,—
  Thy new, best name of Love.

490   *Thanks for victory.*   C. WESLEY.

Oh, for a thousand tongues to sing
  My dear Redeemer's praise!
The glories of my God and King,
  The triumphs of his grace!

2 My gracious Master and my God!
  Assist me to proclaim,
To spread, through all the earth abroad,
  The honors of thy name.

3 Jesus—the name that calms my fears,
  That bids my sorrows cease;
'Tis music to my ravished ears;
  'Tis life, and health, and peace.

4 He breaks the power of canceled sin,
  He sets the prisoner free;
His blood can make the foulest clean;
  His blood availed for me.

5 Let us obey, we then shall know,
  Shall feel our sins forgiven;
Anticipate our heaven below,
  And own that love is heaven.

FIGHTINGS WITHOUT:—FEARS WITHIN.

491 *Greatness in Service.* T. H. GILL

Oh, not to fill the mouth of fame
My longing soul is stirred:
Oh, give me a diviner name!
Call me thy servant, Lord!

2 No longer would my soul be known
As uncontrolled and free;
Oh, not mine own, oh, not mine own!
Lord, I belong to thee!

3 Thy servant,—me thy servant choose;
Naught of thy claim abate!
The glorious name I would not lose,
Nor change the sweet estate.

4 In life, in death, on earth, in heaven,
This is the name for me!
The same sweet style and title given
Through all eternity.

492 *"Trembleth at my word."* C. WESLEY.

Oh, for that tenderness of heart,
That bows before the Lord;
That owns how just and good thou art,
And trembles at thy word.

2 Oh, for those humble, contrite tears,
Which from repentance flow;
That sense of guilt which, trembling, fears
The long-suspended blow!

3 Saviour! to me, in pity give,
For sin, the deep distress;
The pledge thou wilt, at last, receive,
And bid me die in peace.

4 Oh, fill my soul with faith and love,
And strength to do thy will;
Raise my desires and hopes above,—
Thyself to me reveal.

CHRISTIAN CONFLICT.

HERMON. C. M. — LOWELL MASON.

1. Oh, for a closer walk with God, A calm and heavenly frame,— A light to shine upon the road That leads me to the Lamb!

493 *The closer walk.* W. COWPER.

Oh, for a closer walk with God,
A calm and heavenly frame,—
A light to shine upon the road
That leads me to the Lamb!

2 Where is the blessedness I knew
When first I saw the Lord?
Where is the soul-refreshing view
Of Jesus and his word?

3 What peaceful hours I once enjoyed!
How sweet their memory still!
But they have left an aching void
The world can never fill.

4 Return, O holy Dove, return,
Sweet messenger of rest!
I hate the sins that made thee mourn,
And drove thee from my breast.

5 The dearest idol I have known,
Whate'er that idol be,
Help me to tear it from thy throne,
And worship only thee.

6 So shall my walk be close with God,
Calm and serene my frame;
So purer light shall mark the road
That leads me to the Lamb.

494 *"What hourly dangers!"* A. STEELE.

Alas! what hourly dangers rise!
What snares beset my way!
To heaven, oh, let me lift mine eyes,
And hourly watch and pray.

2 How oft my mournful thoughts complain,
And melt in flowing tears!
My weak resistance, ah, how vain!
How strong my foes and fears!

3 O gracious God! in whom I live,
My feeble efforts aid;
Help me to watch, and pray, and strive,
Though trembling and afraid.

4 Increase my faith, increase my hope,
When foes and fears prevail;
And bear my fainting spirit up,
Or soon my strength will fail.

5 Oh, keep me in thy heavenly way,
And bid the tempter flee!
And let me never, never stray
From happiness and thee.

495 *"Search me, O God."* G. P. MORRIS.

Searcher of hearts! from mine erase
All thoughts that should not be,
And in its deep recesses trace
My gratitude to thee!

2 Hearer of prayer! oh, guide aright
Each word and deed of mine;
Life's battle teach me how to fight,
And be the victory thine.

3 Father, and Son, and Holy Ghost!
Thou glorious Three in One!
Thou knowest best what I need most,
And let thy will be done.

FIGHTINGS WITHOUT:—FEARS WITHIN.

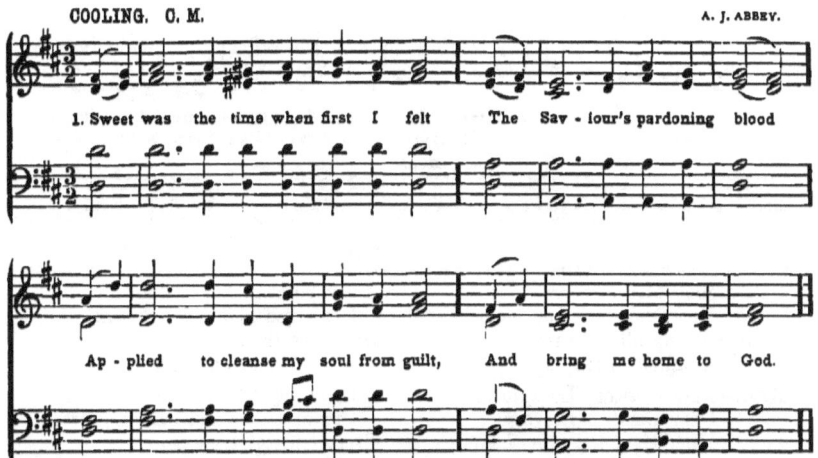

496 *"Where is the blessedness?"* J. NEWTON.

SWEET was the time when first I felt
 The Saviour's pardoning blood
Applied to cleanse my soul from guilt,
 And bring me home to God.

2 Soon as the morn the light revealed,
 His praises tuned my tongue;
And, when the evening shade prevailed,
 His love was all my song.

3 In prayer, my soul drew near the Lord,
 And saw his glory shine;
And when I read his holy word,
 I called each promise mine.

4 Now, when the evening shade prevails,
 My soul in darkness mourns;
And when the morn the light reveals,
 No light to me returns

5 Rise, Saviour! help me to prevail,
 And make my soul thy care;
I know thy mercy cannot fail,
 Let me that mercy share.

497 *"Nearer to thee."* B. CLEVELAND.

OH, could I find, from day to day,
 A nearness to my God,
Then would my hours glide sweet away
 While leaning on his word.

2 Lord, I desire with thee to live
 Anew from day to day,
In joys the world can never give,
 Nor ever take away.

3 Blest Jesus, come and rule my heart,
 And make me wholly thine,
That I may never more depart,
 Nor grieve thy love divine.

4 Thus, till my last, expiring breath,
 Thy goodness I'll adore;
And when my frame dissolves in death,
 My soul shall love thee more.

CHRISTIAN CONFLICT.

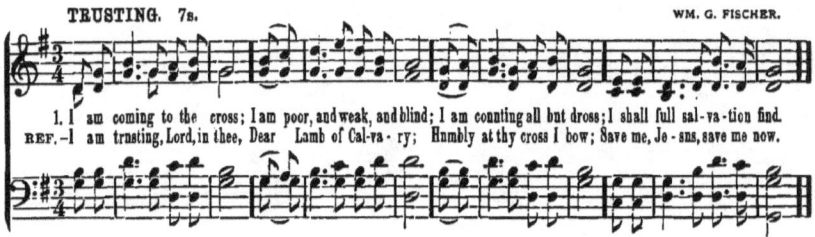

TRUSTING. 7s.   WM. G. FISCHER.

1. I am coming to the cross; I am poor, and weak, and blind; I am counting all but dross; I shall full sal-va-tion find.
REF.—I am trusting, Lord, in thee, Dear Lamb of Cal-va-ry; Humbly at thy cross I bow; Save me, Je-sus, save me now.

498   *"Cleanseth from all sin."*   W. MC DONALD.

I AM coming to the cross;
  I am poor and weak and blind;
I am counting all but dross;
  I shall full salvation find.

REF.—I am trusting, Lord, in thee,
  Dear Lamb of Calvary;
Humbly at thy cross I bow;
  Save me, Jesus, save me now.

2 Long my heart has sighed for thee;
  Long has evil dwelt within ;
Jesus sweetly speaks to me,
  I will cleanse you from all sin.—REF.

3 Here I give my all to thee,—
  Friends and time and earthly store;
Soul and body thine to be—
  Wholly thine for evermore.—REF.

4 In the promises I trust;
  Now I feel the blood applied;
I am prostrate in the dust;
  I with Christ am crucified.—REF.

499   *"Lovest thou Me."*   J. NEWTON.

'TIS a point I long to know,
  Oft it causes anxious thought;
Do I love the Lord, or no?
  Am I his, or am I not?

2 Could my heart so hard remain,
  Prayer a task and burden prove,
Every trifle give me pain,
  If I knew a Saviour's love?

3 Yet I mourn my stubborn will,
  Find my sin a grief and thrall;
Should I grieve for what I feel,
  If I did not love at all?

4 Could I joy with saints to meet,
  Choose the ways I once abhorred,
Find at times the promise sweet,
  If I did not love the Lord?

5 Lord, decide the doubtful case,
  Thou who art thy people's Sun;
Shine upon thy work of grace,
  If it be indeed begun.

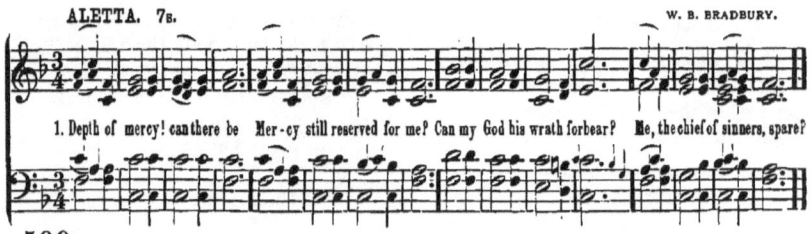

ALETTA. 7s.   W. B. BRADBURY.

1. Depth of mercy! can there be Mer-cy still reserved for me? Can my God his wrath forbear? Me, the chief of sinners, spare?

500   *"My repentings are kindled."*   C. WESLEY.

DEPTH of mercy !—can there be
Mercy still reserved for me?
Can my God his wrath forbear?
Me, the chief of sinners, spare?

2 I have long withstood his grace;
Long provoked him to his face;
Would not hearken to his calls;
Grieved him by a thousand falls.

3 Kindled his relentings are;
Me he now delights to spare;
Cries, How shall I give thee up?—
Lets the lifted thunder drop.

4 There for me the Saviour stands;
Shows his wounds and spreads his hands!
God is love! I know, I feel:
Jesus weeps, and loves me still.

FIGHTINGS WITHOUT:—FEARS WITHIN.

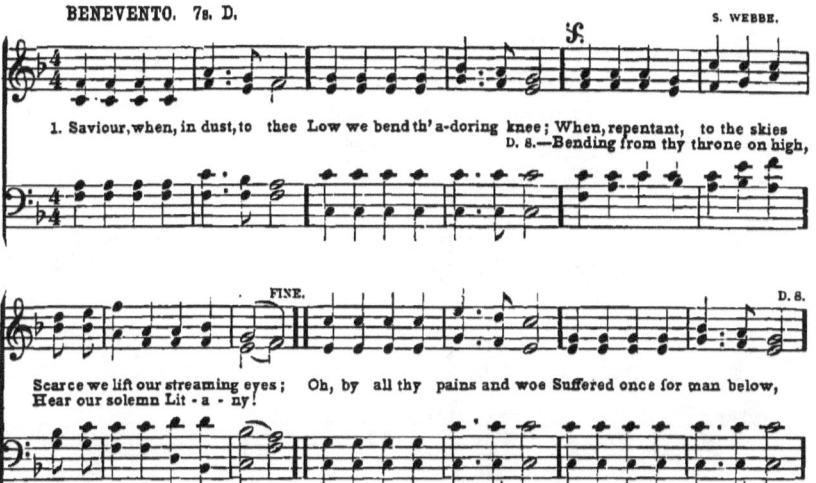

BENEVENTO. 7s. D. S. WEBBE.

1. Saviour, when, in dust, to thee Low we bend th' a-doring knee; When, repentant, to the skies
D. S.—Bending from thy throne on high,

Scarce we lift our streaming eyes; Oh, by all thy pains and woe Suffered once for man below,
Hear our solemn Lit-a-ny!

501   *The Ancient Litany.*   R. GRANT.
SAVIOUR, when, in dust, to thee
Low we bend the adoring knee;
When, repentant, to the skies
Scarce we lift our weeping eyes;
Oh, by all thy pains and woe
Suffered once for man below,
Bending from thy throne on high,
Hear our solemn Litany!

2 By thy helpless infant years,
By thy life of want and tears,
By thy days of sore distress
In the savage wilderness;
By the dread mysterious hour
Of the insulting tempter's power,—
Turn, oh, turn a favoring eye;
Hear our solemn Litany!

3 By thine hour of dire despair;
By thine agony of prayer;
By the cross, the nail, the thorn,
Piercing spear, and torturing scorn;
By the gloom that vailed the skies
O'er the dreadful sacrifice;—
Listen to our humble cry,
Hear our solemn Litany!

4 By thy deep expiring groan;
By the sad sepulchral stone;
By the vault whose dark abode
Held in vain the rising God;—

Oh, from earth to heaven restored,
Mighty re-ascended Lord!
Listen, listen to the cry
Of our solemn Litany!

502   *A hard heart.*   H. BONAR.
OH, this soul, how dark and blind!
Oh, this foolish, earthly mind!
Oh, this froward, selfish will,
Which refuses to be still!
Oh, these ever-roaming eyes,
Upward that refuse to rise!
Oh, these wayward feet of mine,
Found in every path but thine!

2 Oh, this stubborn, prayerless knee,
Hands so seldom clasped to thee,
Longings of the soul, that go
Like the wild wind, to and fro!
To and fro, without an aim,
Turning idly whence they came,
Bringing in no joy, no bliss,
Only adding weariness!

3 Giver of the heavenly peace!
Bid, oh, bid these tumults cease;
Minister thy holy balm;
Fill me with thy Spirit's calm:
Thou, the Life, the Truth, the Way,
Leave me not in sin to stay;
Bearer of the sinner's guilt,
Lead me, lead me, as thou wilt.

CHRISTIAN CONFLICT.

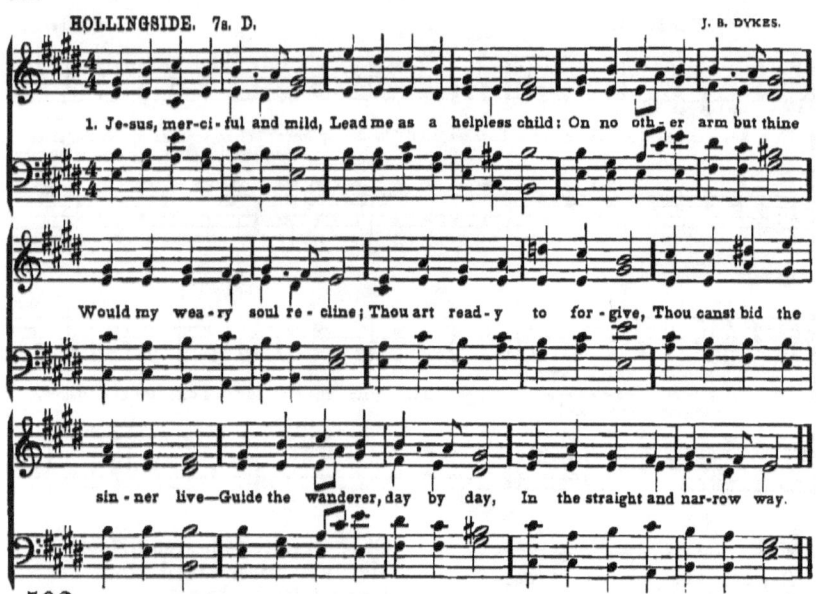

503   *"Lead me."*   T. HASTINGS.

Jesus, merciful and mild,
Lead me as a helpless child:
On no other arm but thine
Would my weary soul recline;
Thou art ready to forgive,
Thou canst bid the sinner live—
Guide the wanderer day by day,
In the strait and narrow way.

2 Thou canst fit me by thy grace
For the heavenly dwelling-place;
All thy promises are sure,
Ever shall thy love endure;
Then what more could I desire,
How to greater bliss aspire?
All I need, in thee I see,
Thou art all in all to me.

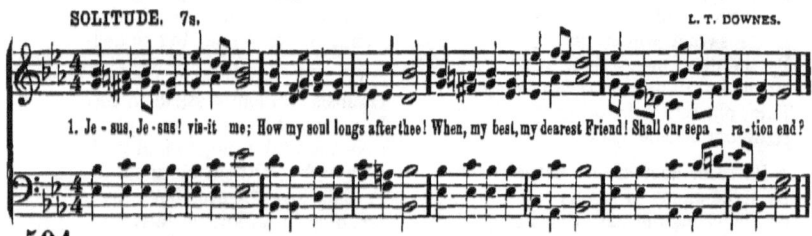

504   *"Jesus, visit me."*   R. P. DUNN, tr.

Jesus, Jesus! visit me;
How my soul longs after thee!
When, my best, my dearest Friend!
Shall our separation end?

2 Lord! my longings never cease;
Without thee I find no peace;
'Tis my constant cry to thee,—
Jesus, Jesus! visit me.

3 Mean the joys of earth appear,
All below is dark and drear;
Naught but thy beloved voice
Can my wretched heart rejoice.

4 Thou alone, my gracious Lord!
Art my shield and great reward;
All my hope, my Saviour thou,—
To thy sovereign will I bow.

FIGHTINGS WITHOUT:—FEARS WITHIN.

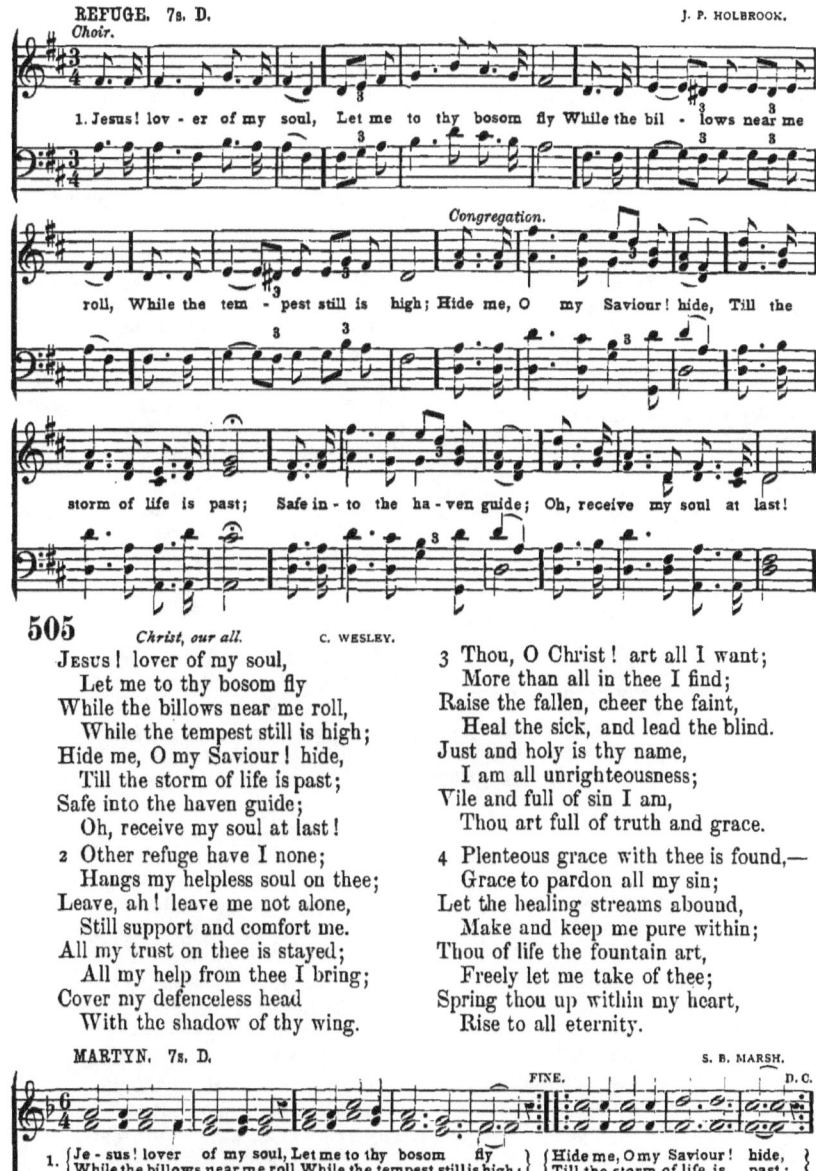

505 *Christ, our all.* C. WESLEY.

Jesus! lover of my soul,
  Let me to thy bosom fly
While the billows near me roll,
  While the tempest still is high;
Hide me, O my Saviour! hide,
  Till the storm of life is past;
Safe into the haven guide;
  Oh, receive my soul at last!

2 Other refuge have I none;
  Hangs my helpless soul on thee;
Leave, ah! leave me not alone,
  Still support and comfort me.
All my trust on thee is stayed;
  All my help from thee I bring;
Cover my defenceless head
  With the shadow of thy wing.

3 Thou, O Christ! art all I want;
  More than all in thee I find;
Raise the fallen, cheer the faint,
  Heal the sick, and lead the blind.
Just and holy is thy name,
  I am all unrighteousness;
Vile and full of sin I am,
  Thou art full of truth and grace.

4 Plenteous grace with thee is found,—
  Grace to pardon all my sin;
Let the healing streams abound,
  Make and keep me pure within;
Thou of life the fountain art,
  Freely let me take of thee;
Spring thou up within my heart,
  Rise to all eternity.

506 L. M. *Backsliding deplored.* P. DODDRIDGE
Return, my roving heart, return,
And life's vain shadows chase no more;
Seek out some solitude to mourn,
And thy forsaken God implore.

2 O thou great God! whose piercing eye
Distinctly marks each deep retreat,
In these sequestered hours draw nigh,
And let me here thy presence meet.

3 Through all the windings of my heart,
My search let heavenly wisdom guide;
And still its beams unerring dart,
Till all be known and purified.

4 Then let the visits of thy love,
My inmost soul be made to share,
Till every grace combine to prove
That God has fixed his dwelling there.

507 L. M. *Psalm 51.* J. MERRICK.
Oh, turn, great Ruler of the skies!
Turn from my sin thy searching eyes;
Nor let the offences of my hand
Within thy book recorded stand.

2 Give me a will to thine subdued,—
A conscience pure, a soul renewed;
Nor let me, wrapt in endless gloom,
An outcast from thy presence roam.

3 Oh, let thy Spirit to my heart
Once more his quickening aid impart;
My mind from every fear release, [peace.
And soothe my troubled thoughts to

508 L. M. *"Come to Me!"* C. ELLIOTT.
With tearful eyes I look around;
Life seems a dark and stormy sea;
Yet, 'mid the gloom, I hear a sound,
A heavenly whisper, "Come to me."

2 It tells me of a place of rest;
It tells me where my soul may flee:
Oh, to the weary, faint, oppressed,
How sweet the bidding, "Come to me!"

3 "Come, for all else must fail and die!
Earth is no resting-place for thee;
To heaven direct thy weeping eye,
I am thy portion; come to me."

4 O voice of mercy! voice of love!
In conflict, grief, and agony,
Support me, cheer me from above!
And gently whisper, "Come to me."

509 L. M. *Our Companion.* I. WATTS.
My God! permit me not to be
A stranger to myself and thee;
Amidst a thousand thoughts I rove,
Forgetful of my highest love.

2 Why should my passions mix with earth,
And thus debase my heavenly birth?
Why should I cleave to things below,
And let my God, my Saviour, go?

3 Call me away from flesh and sense;
One sovereign word can draw me thence;
I would obey the voice divine,
And all inferior joys resign.

4 Be earth, with all her scenes, with-
Let noise and vanity be gone; [drawn,
In secret silence of the mind,
My heaven, and there my God, I find.

510 L. M. *"Give me thine heart."* A. STEELE.
Jesus demands this heart of mine,
Demands my love, my joy, my care;
But ah! how dead to things divine,
How cold my best affections are!

2 'Tis sin, alas! with dreadful power,
Divides my Saviour from my sight;
Oh, for one happy, cloudless hour
Of sacred freedom, sweet delight!

3 Come, gracious Lord! thy love can raise
My captive powers from sin and death,
And fill my heart and life with praise,
And tune my last expiring breath.

511 C. M. *"His great love."* S. BROWNE.
Lord! at thy feet we sinners lie,
And knock at mercy's door:
With heavy heart and downcast eye,
Thy favor we implore.

2 On us the vast extent display
Of thy forgiving love;
Take all our heinous guilt away;
This heavy load remove.

3 'T is mercy—mercy we implore;
We would thy pity move:
Thy grace is an exhaustless store,
And thou thyself art love.

4 Oh, for thine own, for Jesus' sake,
Our numerous sins forgive!
Thy grace our rocky hearts can break:
Heal us, and bid us live.

512 L. M., 6 l. 1 John 4: 18. ANON.
"Perfect in love!" Lord, can it be,
Amid this state of doubt and sin?
While foes so thick without, I see,
With weakness, pain, disease within;
Can perfect love inhabit here,
And, strong in faith, extinguish fear?

2 O Lord! amid this mental night,
Amid the clouds of dark dismay,
Arise! arise! shed forth thy light,
And kindle love's meridian day:
My Saviour God, to me appear,
So love shall triumph over fear.

513 L. M. Psalm 130. I. WATTS.
From deep distress and troubled thoughts,
To thee, my God, I raise my cries;
If thou severely mark our faults,
No flesh can stand before thine eyes.

2 But thou hast built thy throne of grace,
Free to dispense thy pardons there;
That sinners may approach thy face,
And hope and love, as well as fear.

3 As the benighted pilgrims wait,
And long, and wish for breaking day,
So waits my soul before thy gate:
When will my God his face display?

4 My trust is fixed upon thy word,
Nor shall I trust thy word in vain;
Let mourning souls address the Lord,
And find relief from all their pain.

5 Great is his love, and large his grace,
Through the redemption of his Son;
He turns our feet from sinful ways,
And pardons what our hands have done.

514 7s. Psalm 13. W. GOODE.
Lord of mercy, just and kind!
Wilt thou ne'er my guilt forgive?
Never shall my troubled mind,
In thy kind remembrance, live?

2 Lord! how long shall Satan's art
Tempt my harassed soul to sin,
Triumph o'er my humbled heart,—
Fears without and guilt within?

3 Lord, my God! thine ear incline,
Bending to the prayer of faith;
Cheer my eyes with light divine,
Lest I sleep the sleep of death.

515 C. M. "Weary, Heavy-laden." J. NEWTON.
Approach, my soul! the mercy-seat,
Where Jesus answers prayer;
There humbly fall before his feet,
For none can perish there.

2 Thy promise is my only plea,
With this I venture nigh:
Thou callest burdened souls to thee,
And such, O Lord! am I.

3 Bowed down beneath a load of sin,
By Satan sorely pressed;
By war without, and fears within,
I come to thee for rest.

4 Be thou my shield and hiding-place,
That, sheltered near thy side,
I may my fierce accuser face,
And tell him—thou hast died.

5 Oh, wondrous Love—to bleed and die,
To bear the cross and shame
That guilty sinners, such as I,
Might plead thy gracious name!

516 7s, 6s, 8s. "Without Care." C. WESLEY.
Thou, O Lord, in tender love,
Dost all my burdens bear;
Lift my heart to things above,
And fix it ever there!
Calm in tumult's whirl I sit,
'Midst busy multitudes alone;
Sweetly waiting at thy feet,
Till all thy will be done.

2 Careful without care I am,
Nor feel my happy toil!
Kept in peace by Jesus' name,
Supported by his smile.
Joyful thus my faith to show,
I find his service my reward;
Every work I do below,
I do it to the Lord.

3 To the desert or the cell,
Let others blindly fly,
In this evil world I dwell,
Unhurt, unspotted, I.
Here I find a house of prayer,
To which I inwardly retire;
Walking unconcerned in care,
And unconsumed in fire.

CHRISTIAN COURAGE AND CHEER.

ST. ALBAN'S. 6s, 5s. D. *FROM F. J. HAYDN.*

1. Brightly gleams our banner, Pointing to the sky, Waving wand'rers onward To their home on high.
Journeying o'er the desert, Gladly thus we pray, And with hearts u-ni-ted Take our heav'nward way.

REFRAIN.
Brightly gleams our banner, Pointing to the sky, Waving wand'rers onward To their home on high.

517 *"Jehovah Nissi."* T. J. POTTER.

BRIGHTLY gleams our banner,
　Pointing to the sky,
Waving wanderers onward
　To their home on high.
Journeying o'er the desert,
　Gladly thus we pray,
And with hearts united,
　Take our heavenward way.—REF.

2 Jesus, Lord and Master,
　At thy sacred feet,
Here with hearts rejoicing
　See thy children meet;
Often have we left thee,
　Often gone astray;
Keep us, mighty Saviour,
　In the narrow way.—REF.

3 All our days direct us
　In the way we go;
Lead us on victorious
　Over every foe:
Bid thine angels shield us
　When the storm-clouds lower,
Pardon thou and save us
　In the last dread hour.—REF.

WALES. 8s, 4s. *WELSH AIR.*

1. Through the love of God our Saviour, All will be well: Free and changeless is his fa-vor;
D. S.—Strong the hand stretched out to shield us:
FINE.
All, all is well. Precious is the blood that healed us; Perfect is the grace that sealed us;
All must be well.

CHRISTIAN COURAGE AND CHEER.

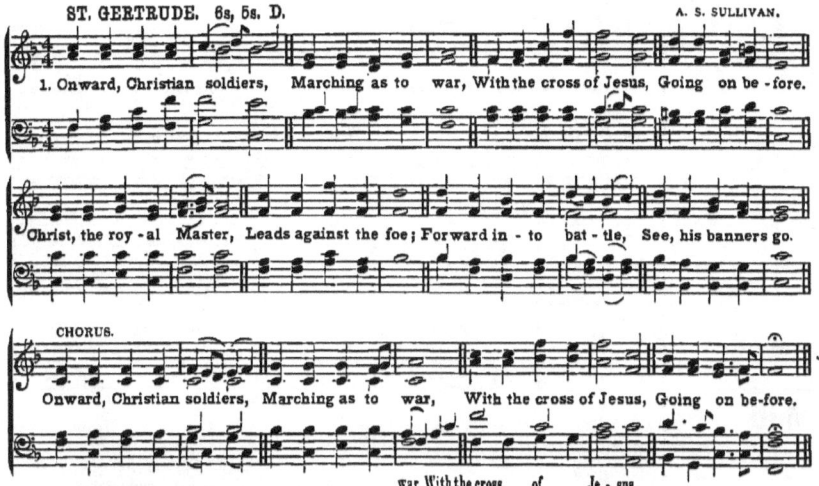

ST. GERTRUDE. 6s, 5s. D.   A. S. SULLIVAN.

518   *"Fight the good fight."*   S. BARING-GOULD.

ONWARD, Christian soldiers,
  Marching as to war,
With the cross of Jesus
  Going on before.
Christ, the royal Master,
  Leads against the foe;
Forward into battle,
  See, his banners go.—CHO.

2 Like a mighty army,
  Moves the Church of God;
Brothers, we are treading
  Where the saints have trod;
We are not divided,
  All one body we,
One in hope and doctrine,
  One in charity.—CHO.

3 Crowns and thrones may perish,
  Kingdoms rise and wane,
But the Church of Jesus
  Constant will remain;
Gates of hell can never
  'Gainst that Church prevail;
We have Christ's own promise,
  And that cannot fail.—CHO.

4 Onward, then, ye people,
  Join our happy throng;
Blend with ours your voices
  In the triumph-song;
Glory, laud, and honor,
  Unto Christ the King;
This through countless ages,
  Men and angels sing.—CHO.

---

519   8s, 4s.   *"All is well."*   M. B. PETERS.

Through the love of God our Saviour,
  All will be well;
Free and changeless is his favor;
  All, all is well.
Precious is the blood that healed us;
Perfect is the grace that sealed us;
Strong the hand stretched out to shield us;
  All must be well.

2 Though we pass through tribulation,
  All will be well:
Ours is such a full salvation;
  All, all is well.
Happy still in God confiding,
Fruitful, if in Christ abiding,
Holy, through the Spirit's guiding,
  All must be well.

3 We expect a bright to-morrow;
  All will be well;
Faith can sing through days of sorrow,
  All, all is well.
On our Father's love relying,
Jesus every need supplying,
Or in living, or in dying,
  All must be well.

CHRISTIAN COURAGE AND CHEER.

ELLESDIE. 8s, 7s. D.   FROM J. C. W. A. MOZART.

1. Je-sus, I my cross have taken, All to leave and follow thee; Naked, poor, despised, forsaken,
D. S.—Yet how rich is my condi - tion,

Thou, from hence, my all shalt be! Perish, ev-'ry fond am-bition, All I've sought, or hoped, or known,
God and heaven are still my own!

520   *Bearing the Cross.*   H. F. LYTE.

Jesus, I my cross have taken,
  All to leave, and follow thee;
Naked, poor, despised, forsaken,
  Thou, from hence, my all shalt be!
Perish, every fond ambition,
  All I've sought, or hoped, or known,
Yet how rich is my condition,
  God and heaven are still my own!

2 Let the world despise and leave me,
  They have left my Saviour, too;
Human hearts and looks deceive me—
  Thou art not, like them, untrue;
Oh, while thou dost smile upon me,
  God of wisdom, love, and might,
Foes may hate, and friends disown me,
  Show thy face, and all is bright.

3 Man may trouble and distress me,
  'T will but drive me to thy breast;
Life with trials hard may press me;
  Heaven will bring me sweeter rest!
Oh, 'tis not in grief to harm me,
  While thy love is left to me;
Oh, 'twere not in joy to charm me,
  Were that joy unmixed with thee.

4 Go then, earthly fame and treasure!
  Come disaster, scorn, and pain!
In thy service pain is pleasure,
  With thy favor, loss is gain.
I have called thee—Abba, Father!
  I have stayed my heart on thee!
Storms may howl, and clouds may gather,
  All must work for good to me.

ESSEX. 8s, 7s.   THOMAS CLARK.

1. Soul, then know thy full salvation,   Joy, to find in every station Something still to do or bear,
Rise o'er sin, and fear, and care;   Something still to do or bear.

521   *The crown coming.*   H. F. LYTE.

Soul, then know thy full salvation,
  Rise o'er sin, and fear, and care;
Joy, to find in every station
  Something still to do or bear.
2 Think what Spirit dwells within thee;
  Think what Father's smiles are thine;
Think that Jesus died to win thee!
  Child of heaven, canst thou repine?

3 Haste thee on from grace to glory,
  Armed by faith and winged by prayer!
Heaven's eternal day's before thee,
  God's own hand shall guide thee there:
4 Soon shall close thy earthly mission,
  Soon shall pass thy pilgrim days,
Hope shall change to glad fruition,
  Faith to sight, and prayer to praise.

CHRISTIAN COURAGE AND CHEER.

AUSTRIA. 8s, 7s. D. F. J. HAYDN.

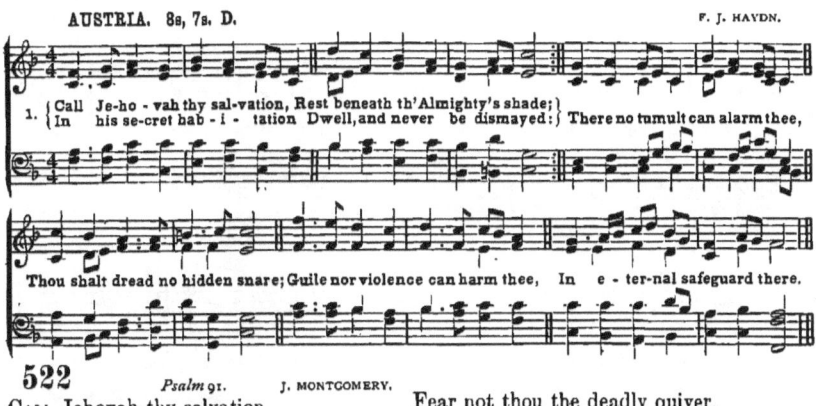

522 *Psalm 91.* J. MONTGOMERY.

CALL Jehovah thy salvation,
Rest beneath the Almighty's shade;
In his secret habitation
Dwell, and never be dismayed:
There no tumult can alarm thee,
Thou shalt dread no hidden snare;
Guile nor violence can harm thee,
In eternal safeguard there.

2 From the sword, at noon-day wasting,
From the noisome pestilence,
In the depth of midnight, blasting,
God shall be thy sure defence:
Fear not thou the deadly quiver,
When a thousand feel the blow;
Mercy shall thy soul deliver,
Though ten thousand be laid low.

3 Since, with pure and firm affection,
Thou on God hast set thy love,
With the wings of his protection,
He will shield thee from above;
Thou shalt call on him in trouble,
He will hearken, he will save;
Here, for grief reward thee double,
Crown with life beyond the grave.

ALL THE DAYS. P. M. WM. F. SHERWIN.

523 *"Always."—Matt. 28 : 20.* A. COLES.

FROM thee, begetting sure conviction,
Sound out, O risen Lord, always
Those faithful words of valediction,
"Lo! I am with you all the days."—REF.

2 What things shall happen on the morrow
Thou kindly hidest from our gaze;
But tellest us, in joy or sorrow,
"Lo! I am with you all the days."—REF.

3 When round our head the tempest rages,
And sink our feet in miry ways,
Thy voice comes floating down the ages—
"Lo! I am with you all the days."—REF

4 O thou who art our life and meetness!
Not death shall daunt us or amaze,
Hearing those words of power and sweetness,
"Lo! I am with you all the days."—REF.

CHRISTIAN COURAGE AND CHEER.

WIMBORNE. L. M. — J. WHITAKER.

1. Stand up, my soul, shake off thy fears, And gird the gospel armor on; March to the gates of endless joy, Where Jesus, thy great Captain's gone.

524 *Ephesians* 6 : 14. I. WATTS.

STAND up, my soul, shake off thy fears,
 And gird the gospel armor on;
March to the gates of endless joy,
 Where Jesus, thy great Captain's gone.

2 Hell and thy sins resist thy course,
 But hell and sin are vanquished foes;
Thy Saviour nailed them to the cross,
 And sung the triumph when he rose.

3 Then let my soul march boldly on,—
 Press forward to the heavenly gate;
There peace and joy eternal reign,
 And glittering robes for conquerors wait.

4 There shall I wear a starry crown,
 And triumph in almighty grace,
While all the armies of the skies
 Join in my glorious Leader's praise.

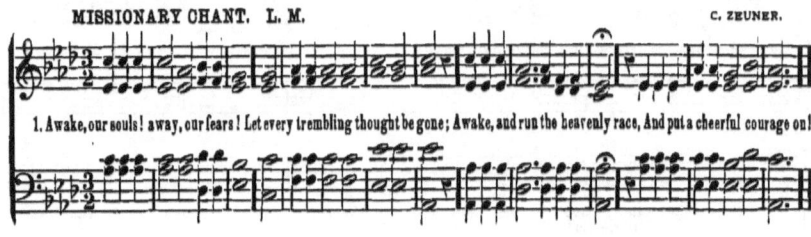

MISSIONARY CHANT. L. M. — C. ZEUNER.

1. Awake, our souls! away, our fears! Let every trembling thought be gone; Awake, and run the heavenly race, And put a cheerful courage on!

525 *Isaiah* 40 : 28-31. I. WATTS.

AWAKE, our souls! away, our fears!
 Let every trembling thought be gone;
Awake, and run the heavenly race,
 And put a cheerful courage on!

2 True, 'tis a strait and thorny road,
 And mortal spirits tire and faint;
But they forget the mighty God,
 Who feeds the strength of every saint—

3 The mighty God, whose matchless power
 Is ever new and ever young,
And firm endures, while endless years
 Their everlasting circles run.

4 From thee, the overflowing spring,
 Our souls shall drink a fresh supply;
While such as trust their native strength
 Shall melt away, and droop, and die.

5 Swift as an eagle cuts the air,
 We'll mount aloft to thine abode;
On wings of love our souls shall fly,
 Nor tire amid the heavenly road!

CHRISTIAN COURAGE AND CHEER.

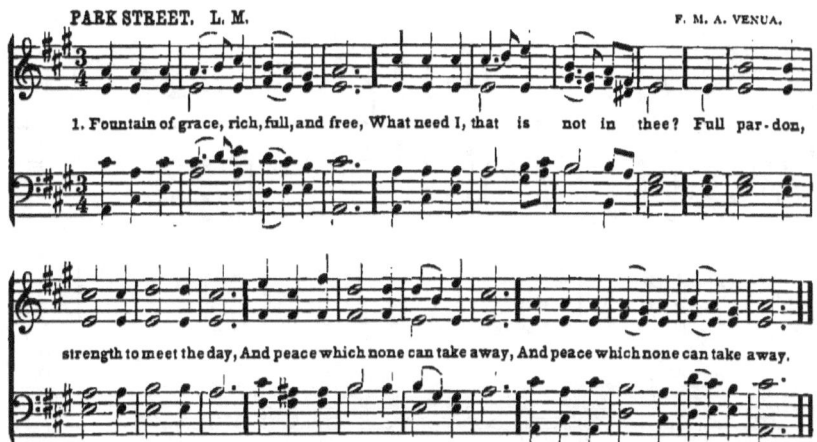

PARK STREET. L. M. F. M. A. VENUA.

1. Fountain of grace, rich, full, and free, What need I, that is not in thee? Full pardon, strength to meet the day, And peace which none can take away, And peace which none can take away.

526   *"My springs in thee."*   J. EDMESTON.

FOUNTAIN of grace, rich, full, and free,
What need I, that is not in thee?
Full pardon, strength to meet the day,
And peace which none can take away.

2 Doth sickness fill my heart with fear,
'Tis sweet to know that thou art near;
Am I with dread of justice tried,
'Tis sweet to know that Christ hath died.

3 In life, thy promises of aid
Forbid my heart to be afraid;
In death, peace gently vails the eyes,—
Christ rose, and I shall surely rise.

527   *Jesus is forever mine.*   A. STEELE.

WHEN sins and fears, prevailing, rise,
And fainting hope almost expires,
To thee, O Lord, I lift my eyes;
To thee I breathe my soul's desires.

2 Art thou not mine, my living Lord?
And can my hope, my comfort die?
'Tis fixed on thine almighty word—
That word which built the earth and sky.

3 If my immortal Saviour lives,
Then my immortal life is sure;
His word a firm foundation gives;
Here may I build and rest secure.

4 Here, O my soul, thy trust repose;
If Jesus is for ever mine,
Not death itself—that last of foes—
Shall break a union so divine.

528   *"Complete in Him."*   G. W. HINSDALE.

MY soul complete in Jesus stands!
It fears no more the law's demands;
The smile of God is sweet within,
Where all before was guilt and sin.

2 My soul at rest in Jesus lives;
Accepts the peace his pardon gives;
Receives the grace his death secured,
And pleads the anguish he endured.

3 My soul its every foe defies,
And cries—'Tis God that justifies!
Who charges God's elect with sin?
Shall Christ, who died their peace to win?

4 A song of praise my soul shall sing,
To our eternal, glorious King!
Shall worship humbly at his feet,
In whom alone it stands complete.

529   2 Cor. 12: 9.   I. WATTS.

LET me but hear my Saviour say,
"Strength shall be equal to thy day;"
Then I rejoice in deep distress,
Leaning on all-sufficient grace.

2 I can do all things—or can bear
All suffering, if my Lord be there;
Sweet pleasures mingle with the pains,
While he my sinking head sustains.

3 I glory in infirmity,
That Christ's own power may rest on me;
When I am weak, then am I strong;
Grace is my shield, and Christ my song.

MESSIAH. 7s. D.

GEO. KINGSLEY, arr.

1. Brethren, while we sojourn here, Fight we must, but should not fear; Foes we have, but we've a Friend, One that loves us to the end: Forward, then, with courage go; Long we shall not dwell below; Soon the joyful news will come, "Child, your Father calls—come home!"

530 *"Come home."* J. SWAIN.

BRETHREN, while we sojourn here,
Fight we must, but should not fear;
Foes we have, but we've a Friend,
One that loves us to the end:
Forward, then, with courage go;
Long we shall not dwell below;
Soon the joyful news will come,
"Child, your Father calls—come home!"

2 In the way a thousand snares
Lie, to take us unawares;
Satan, with malicious art,
Watches each unguarded part:
But, from Satan's malice free,
Saints shall soon victorious be;
Soon the joyful news will come,
"Child, your Father calls—come home!"

3 But of all the foes we meet,
None so oft mislead our feet,
None betray us into sin,
Like the foes that dwell within;
Yet let nothing spoil our peace,
Christ shall also conquer these;
Soon the joyful news will come,
"Child, your Father calls—come home!"

VIENNA. 7s.

W. H. HAVERGAL.

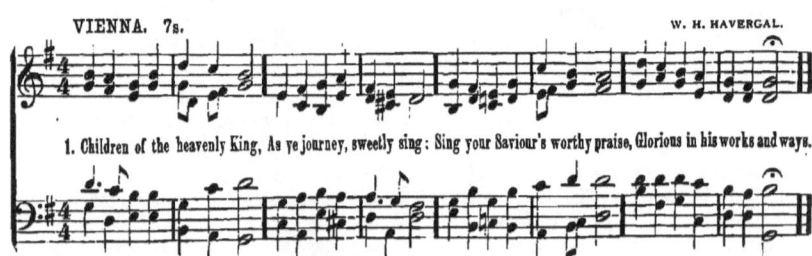

1. Children of the heavenly King, As ye journey, sweetly sing: Sing your Saviour's worthy praise, Glorious in his works and ways.

CHRISTIAN COURAGE AND CHEER.

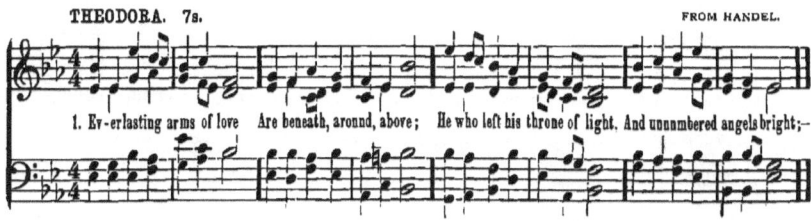

THEODORA. 7s.   FROM HANDEL.

531 *"The everlasting arms."*   J. R. MACDUFF.

EVERLASTING arms of love
Are beneath, around, above;
He who left his throne of light,
And unnumbered angels bright;—

2 He who on the accursèd tree
Gave his precious life for me;
He it is that bears me on,
His the arm I lean upon.

3 All things hasten to decay,
Earth and sea will pass away;
Soon will yonder circling sun
Cease his blazing course to run.

4 Scenes will vary, friends grow strange,
But the Changeless cannot change:
Gladly will I journey on,
With his arm to lean upon.

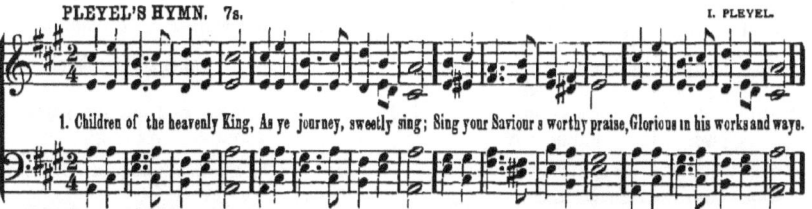

PLEYEL'S HYMN. 7s.   I. PLEYEL.

532   *Isaiah 35 : 8—10.*   J. CENNICK.

CHILDREN of the heavenly King,
As ye journey, sweetly sing;
Sing your Saviour's worthy praise,
Glorious in his works and ways.

2 Ye are traveling home to God
In the way the fathers trod;
They are happy now, and ye
Soon their happiness shall see.

3 Shout, ye little flock, and blest!
You on Jesus' throne shall rest;
There your seat is now prepared;
There your kingdom and reward.

4 Fear not, brethren; joyful stand
On the borders of your land;
Jesus Christ, your Father's Son,
Bids you undismayed go on.

5 Lord, submissive make us go,
Gladly leaving all below;
Only thou our Leader be,
And we still will follow thee.

533   *Redeeming Love.*   J. LANGFORD.

Now begin the heavenly theme,
Sing aloud in Jesus' name;
Ye who Jesus' kindness prove,
Triumph in redeeming love.

2 Ye who see the Father's grace
Beaming in the Saviour's face,
As to Canaan on ye move,
Praise and bless redeeming love.

3 Mourning souls, dry up your tears;
Banish all your guilty fears;
See your guilt and curse remove,
Canceled by redeeming love.

4 Welcome, all by sin opprest,
Welcome to his sacred rest;
Nothing brought him from above,
Nothing but redeeming love.

5 Hither, then, your music bring,
Strike aloud each joyful string;
Mortals, join the host above,
Join to praise redeeming love.

CHRISTIAN COURAGE AND CHEER.

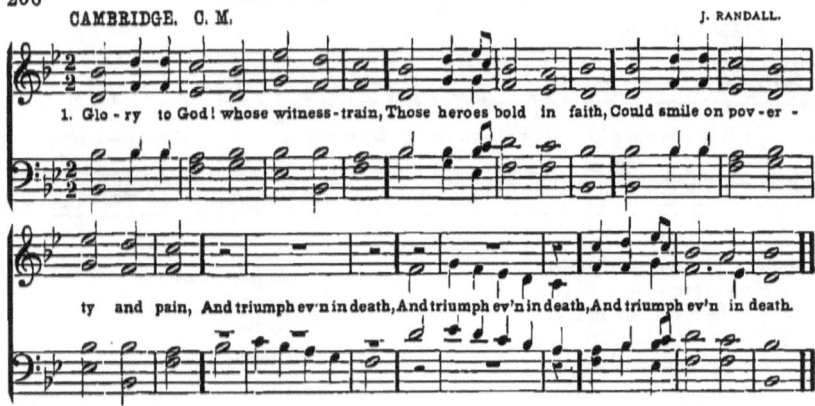

CAMBRIDGE. C. M. — J. RANDALL.

1. Glo-ry to God! whose witness-train, Those heroes bold in faith, Could smile on pov-er-ty and pain, And triumph ev'n in death, And triumph ev'n in death, And triumph ev'n in death.

534 *Martyr-faith.* MORAVIAN.

GLORY to God! whose witness-train,
 Those heroes bold in faith,
Could smile on poverty and pain,
 And triumph ev'n in death.

2 Oh, may that faith our hearts sustain,
 Wherein they fearless stood,
When, in the power of cruel men,
 They poured their willing blood.

3 God whom we serve, our God, can save,
 Can damp the scorching flame,
Can build an ark, can smooth the wave,
 For such as love his name.

4 Lord! if thine arm support us still
 With its eternal strength,
We shall o'ercome the mightiest ill,
 And conquerors prove at length.

535 *"The elders."* J. NEEDHAM.

RISE, O my soul, pursue the path
 By ancient worthies trod;
Aspiring, view those holy men
 Who lived and walked with God.

2 Though dead, they speak in reason's ear,
 And in example live;
Their faith, and hope, and mighty deeds
 Still fresh instruction give.

3 'Twas thro' the Lamb's most precious blood
 They conquered every foe;
And to his power and matchless grace
 Their crowns of life they owe.

4 Lord, may I ever keep in view
 The patterns thou hast given,
And ne'er forsake the blesséd road
 That led them safe to heaven.

WIRTH. C. M. — W. B. BRADBURY.

1. In time of fear, when trouble's near, I look to thine a-bode; Though help-ers fail, and foes pre-vail,...... I'll put my trust in God.

CHRISTIAN COURAGE AND CHEER.

ARCADIA. C. M.   THOS. HASTINGS.

1. In time of fear, when trouble's near, I look to thine abode; Though helpers fail, and foes prevail, I'll put my trust in God, I'll put my trust.... in God.

536   *"What time I am afraid."*   T. HASTINGS.

In time of fear, when trouble's near,
  I look to thine abode;
Though helpers fail, and foes prevail,
  I'll put my trust in God.

2 And what is life, 'mid toil and strife?
  What terror has the grave?
Thine arm of power, in peril's hour,
  The trembling soul will save.

3 In darkest skies, though storms arise,
  I will not be dismayed:
O God of light, and boundless might,
  My soul on thee is stayed!

537   *"I shall be with Him."*   R. BAXTER.

LORD, it belongs not to my care
  Whether I die or live;
To love and serve thee is my share,
  And this thy grace must give.

2 If life be long, I will be glad
  That I may long obey;
If short, yet why should I be sad
  To soar to endless day?

3 Christ leads me through no darker rooms
  Than he went through before;
No one into his kingdom comes,
  But through his opened door.

4 Come, Lord, when grace has made me meet
  Thy blessèd face to see;
For if thy work on earth be sweet,
  What will thy glory be?

5 Then shall I end my sad complaints,
  And weary, sinful days,
And join with all triumphant saints
  Who sing Jehovah's praise.

6 My knowledge of that life is small;
  The eye of faith is dim;
But 'tis enough that Christ knows all,
  And I shall be with him.

538   *"If God be for us."*   F. W. FABER.

GOD'S glory is a wondrous thing,
  Most strange in all its ways,
And of all things on earth, least like
  What men agree to praise.

2 Oh, blest is he to whom is given
  The instinct that can tell
That God is on the field, when he
  Is most invisible!

3 And blest is he who can divine
  Where real right doth lie,
And dares to take the side that seems
  Wrong to man's blindfold eye!

4 Oh, learn to scorn the praise of men!
  Oh, learn to lose with God!
For Jesus won the world through shame,
  And beckons thee his road.

5 And right is right, since God is God;
  And right the day must win;
To doubt would be disloyalty,
  To falter would be sin!

CHRISTMAS. C. M.   G. F. HANDEL.

539   *The Race.*   P. DODDRIDGE.

AWAKE, my soul, stretch every nerve,
    And press with vigor on;
A heavenly race demands thy zeal,
    And an immortal crown.

2 A cloud of witnesses around
    Hold thee in full survey;
Forget the steps already trod,
    And onward urge thy way.

3 'Tis God's all-animating voice,
    That calls thee from on high,
'Tis his own hand presents the prize
    To thine aspiring eye.

4 Blest Saviour, introduced by thee
    Have I my race begun;
And, crowned with victory, at thy feet
    I'll lay my honors down.

540   *The Warfare.*   I. WATTS.

AM I a soldier of the cross,
    A follower of the Lamb?
And shall I fear to own his cause,
    Or blush to speak his name?

2 Must I be carried to the skies
    On flowery beds of ease?
While others fought to win the prize,
    And sailed through bloody seas?

3 Are there no foes for me to face?
    Must I not stem the flood?
Is this vile world a friend to grace,
    To help me on to God?

4 Sure I must fight, if I would reign;
    Increase my courage, Lord!
I'll bear the toil, endure the pain,
    Supported by thy word.

5 Thy saints, in all this glorious war,
    Shall conquer, though they die;
They view the triumph from afar,
    And seize it with their eye.

6 When that illustrious day shall rise,
    And all thine armies shine
In robes of victory through the skies,
    The glory shall be thine.

541   *"I'm not ashamed.*   I. WATTS.

I'M NOT ashamed to own my Lord,
    Or to defend his cause;
Maintain the honor of his word,
    The glory of his cross.

2 Jesus, my God!—I know his name—
    His name is all my trust;
Nor will he put my soul to shame,
    Nor let my hope be lost.

3 Firm as his throne his promise stands,
    And he can well secure
What I've committed to his hands,
    Till the decisive hour.

4 Then will he own my worthless name
    Before his Father's face,
And in the new Jerusalem
    Appoint my soul a place.

CHRISTIAN COURAGE AND CHEER.

542 *Isaiah 35: 8-10.*   P. DODDRIDGE.

Sing, all ye ransomed of the Lord,
  Your great Deliverer sing;
Ye pilgrims, now for Zion bound,
  Be joyful in your King.

2 His hand divine shall lead you on,
  Through all the blissful road;
Till to the sacred mount you rise,
  And see your gracious God.

3 Bright garlands of immortal joy
  Shall bloom on every head;
While sorrow, sighing, and distress,
  Like shadows, all are fled.

4 March on in your Redeemer's strength;
  Pursue his footsteps still;
And let the prospect cheer your eye
  While laboring up the hill.

543 *No cross, no crown.* T. SHEPHERD, *alt.*

Must Jesus bear the cross alone,
  And all the world go free?
No, there's a cross for every one,
  And there's a cross for me.

2 How happy are the saints above,
  Who once went sorrowing here!
But now they taste unmingled love,
  And joy without a tear.

3 The consecrated cross I'll bear,
  Till death shall set me free;
And then go home my crown to wear,
  For there's a crown for me.

4 Upon the crystal pavement, down
  At Jesus' piercéd feet,
Joyful, I'll cast my golden crown,
  And his dear name repeat.

5 And palms shall wave, and harps shall ring,
  Beneath heaven's arches high;
The Lord that lives, the ransomed sing,
  That lives no more to die.

6 Oh, precious cross! oh, glorious crown!
  Oh, resurrection day!
Ye angels, from the stars come down,
  And bear my soul away.

CHRISTIAN COURAGE AND CHEER.

RENOVATION. S. M. — J. H. HUMMEL.

1. The people of the Lord Are on their way to heaven; There they obtain their great reward; The prize will there be given.

544 *Christian Pilgrims.* T. KELLY.

THE people of the Lord
  Are on their way to heaven;
There they obtain their great reward;
  The prize will there be given.

2 'Tis conflict here below;
  'Tis triumph there, and peace:
On earth we wrestle with the foe;
  In heaven our conflicts cease.

3 'Tis gloom and darkness here;
  'Tis light and joy above;
There all is pure, and all is clear;
  There all is peace and love.

4 There rest shall follow toil,
  And ease succeed to care:
The victors there divide the spoil;
  They sing and triumph there.

5 Then let us joyful sing;
  The conflict is not long:
We hope in heaven to praise our King
  In one eternal song.

545 *"Jehovah Jireh."* J. SWAIN.

I STAND on Zion's mount,
  And view my starry crown;
No power on earth my hope can shake,
  Nor hell can thrust me down.

2 The lofty hills and towers,
  That lift their heads on high,
Shall all be leveled low in dust—
  Their very names shall die.

3 The vaulted heavens shall fall,
  Built by Jehovah's hands;
But firmer than the heavens, the Rock
  Of my salvation stands!

546 *"Goeth forth weeping."* G. BURGESS.

THE harvest dawn is near,
  The year delays not long;
And he who sows with many a tear,
  Shall reap with many a song.

2 Sad to his toil he goes,
  His seed with weeping leaves;
But he shall come, at twilight's close,
  And bring his golden sheaves.

LABAN. S. M. — LOWELL MASON.

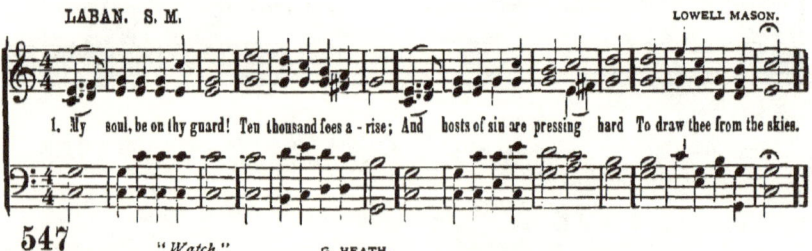

1. My soul, be on thy guard! Ten thousand foes a-rise; And hosts of sin are pressing hard To draw thee from the skies.

547 *"Watch."* G. HEATH.

MY soul, be on thy guard,
  Ten thousand foes arise;
And hosts of sin are pressing hard
  To draw thee from the skies.

2 Oh, watch, and fight, and pray!
  The battle ne'er give o'er;
Renew it boldly every day,
  And help divine implore.

3 Ne'er think the victory won,
  Nor lay thine armor down;
Thine arduous work will not be done,
  Till thou obtain thy crown.

4 Fight on, my soul, till death
  Shall bring thee to thy God!
He'll take thee at thy parting breath,
  Up to his blest abode.

548 "Weigh not thy life." L. SWAIN.

My soul, weigh not thy life
Against thy heavenly crown;
Nor suffer Satan's deadliest strife
To beat thy courage down.

2 With prayer and crying strong,
Hold on the fearful fight,
And let the breaking day prolong
The wrestling of the night.

3 The battle soon will yield,
If thou thy part fulfill;
For strong as is the hostile shield,
Thy sword is stronger still.

4 Thine armor is divine,
Thy feet with victory shod;
And on thy head shall quickly shine
The diadem of God.

549 "He careth." P. DODDRIDGE.

How GENTLE God's commands!
How kind his precepts are!
Come, cast your burdens on the Lord,
And trust his constant care.

2 Beneath his watchful eye
His saints securely dwell;
That hand which bears creation up
Shall guard his children well.

3 Why should this anxious load
Press down your weary mind?
Haste to your heavenly Father's throne,
And sweet refreshment find.

4 His goodness stands approved,
Unchanged from day to day:
I'll drop my burden at his feet,
And bear a song away.

CHRISTIAN COURAGE AND CHEER.

LEIGHTON. S. M.   H. W. GREATOREX.

1. Mine eyes and my desire Are ever to the Lord;
I love to plead his promises, And rest upon his word.

550   *Psalm 25.*   I. WATTS.

MINE eyes and my desire
  Are ever to the Lord;
I love to plead his promises,
  And rest upon his word.

2 Lord, turn to thee my soul;
  Bring thy salvation near:
When will thy hand release my feet
  From sin's destructive snare?

3 When shall the sovereign grace
  Of my forgiving God
Restore me from those dangerous ways
  My wandering feet have trod?

4 Oh, keep my soul from death,
  Nor put my hope to shame!
For I have placed my only trust
  In my Redeemer's name.

5 With humble faith I wait
  To see thy face again;
Of Israel it shall ne'er be said,
  He sought the Lord in vain.

551   *Psalm 60.*   T. KELLY.

ARISE, ye saints, arise!
  The Lord our Leader is;
The foe before his banner flies,
  And victory is his.

2 We follow thee, our Guide,
  Our Saviour, and our King!
We follow thee, through grace supplied
  From heaven's eternal spring.

3 We soon shall see the day
  When all our toils shall cease;
When we shall cast our arms away,
  And dwell in endless peace.

4 This hope supports us here;
  It makes our burdens light;
'T will serve our drooping hearts to cheer.
  Till faith shall end in sight.

5 Till, of the prize possessed,
  We hear of war no more;
And ever with our Leader rest,
  On yonder peaceful shore.

552   *Psalm 31.*   H. F. LYTE.

MY spirit on thy care,
  Blest Saviour, I recline;
Thou wilt not leave me to despair,
  For thou art love divine.

2 In thee I place my trust;
  On thee I calmly rest:
I know thee good, I know thee just,
  And count thy choice the best.

3 Whate'er events betide,
  Thy will they all perform;
Safe in thy breast my head I hide,
  Nor fear the coming storm.

4 Let good or ill befall,
  It must be good for me,—
Secure of having thee in all,
  Of having all in thee.

CHRISTIAN COURAGE AND CHEER.

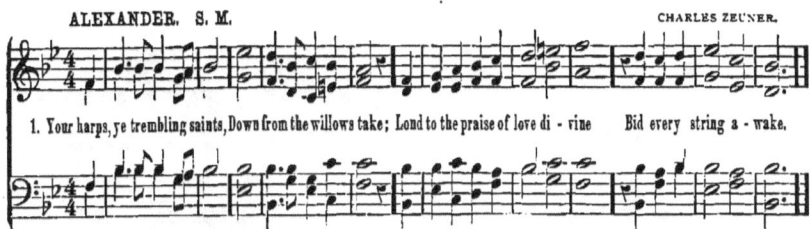

ALEXANDER. S. M.   CHARLES ZEUNER.

1. Your harps, ye trembling saints, Down from the willows take; Loud to the praise of love di-vine Bid every string a-wake.

553   *Our Salvation near.*   A. M. TOPLADY.

Your harps, ye trembling saints,
  Down from the willows take:
Loud to the praise of love divine
  Bid every string awake.

2 Though in a foreign land,
  We are not far from home;
And nearer to our house above
  We every moment come.

3 His grace will to the end
  Stronger and brighter shine;
Nor present things, nor things to come,
  Shall quench the spark divine.

4 When we in darkness walk,
  Nor feel the heavenly flame,
Then is the time to trust our God,
  And rest upon his name.

5 Soon shall our doubts and fears
  Subside at his control;
His loving-kindness shall break through
  The midnight of the soul.

6 Blest is the man, O God,
  Who stays himself on thee;
Who waits for thy salvation, Lord,
  Shall thy salvation see.

554   *"Be of good courage."*   J. WESLEY, tr.

Give to the winds thy fears;
  Hope, and be undismayed;
God hears thy sighs and counts thy tears;
  God shall lift up thy head.

2 Through waves, and clouds, and storms,
  He gently clears thy way;
Wait thou his time; so shall this night
  Soon end in joyous day.

3 What though thou rulest not!
  Yet heaven, and earth, and hell
Proclaim, God sitteth on the throne,
  And ruleth all things well.

4 Far, far above thy thought
  His counsel shall appear,
When fully he the work has wrought,
  That caused thy needless fear.

OLMUTZ. S. M.   LOWELL MASON, arr.

1. Your harps, ye trem-bling saints, Down from the wil-lows take: Loud to the praise of love di-vine Bid ev-ery string a-wake.

555 *Matthew 6 : 25-34.*   W. COWPER.

Sometimes a light surprises
  The Christian while he sings;
It is the Lord who rises
  With healing in his wings:
When comforts are declining,
  He grants the soul again
A season of clear shining,
  To cheer it after rain.

2 In holy contemplation,
  We sweetly then pursue
The theme of God's salvation,
  And find it ever new:
Set free from present sorrow,
  We cheerfully can say,
Let the unknown to-morrow
  Bring with it what it may.

3 It can bring with it nothing,
  But he will bring us through;
Who gives the lilies clothing,
  Will clothe his people too:
Beneath the spreading heavens,
  No creature but is fed;
And he who feeds the ravens,
  Will give his children bread.

4 Though vine nor fig-tree neither,
  Their wonted fruit should bear,
Though all the fields should wither,
  Nor flocks, nor herds be there;
Yet God the same abiding,
  His praise shall tune my voice,
For while in him confiding,
  I cannot but rejoice.

556   *Perfect peace.*   A. E. WARING.

In heavenly love abiding,
  No change my heart shall fear,
And safe is such confiding,
  For nothing changes here:
The storm may roar without me,
  My heart may low be laid,
But God is round about me,
  And can I be dismayed?

2 Wherever he may guide me,
  No want shall turn me back;
My Shepherd is beside me,
  And nothing can I lack:
His wisdom ever waketh,
  His sight is never dim:
He knows the way he taketh,
  And I will walk with him.

3 Green pastures are before me,
  Which yet I have not seen;
Bright skies will soon be o'er me,
  Where darkest clouds have been:
My hope I cannot measure;
  My path to life is free;
My Saviour has my treasure,
  And he will walk with me.

CHRISTIAN COURAGE AND CHEER.

557 *"Having done all, stand."* G. DUFFIELD.

STAND up!—stand up for Jesus!
 Ye soldiers of the cross;
Lift high his royal banner,
 It must not suffer loss:
From victory unto victory
 His army shall he lead,
Till every foe is vanquished,
 And Christ is Lord indeed.

2 Stand up!—stand up for Jesus!
 The trumpet call obey;
Forth to the mighty conflict,
 In this his glorious day:
"Ye that are men, now serve him,"
 Against unnumbered foes;
Let courage rise with danger,
 And strength to strength oppose.

3 Stand up!—stand up for Jesus!
 Stand in his strength alone;
The arm of flesh will fail you—
 Ye dare not trust your own:
Put on the gospel armor,
 And, watching unto prayer,
Where duty calls, or danger,
 Be never wanting there.

4 Stand up!—stand up for Jesus!
 The strife will not be long;
This day, the noise of battle,
 The next, the victor's song:
To him that overcometh,
 A crown of life shall be;
He with the King of glory
 Shall reign eternally!

CHRISTIAN COURAGE AND CHEER.

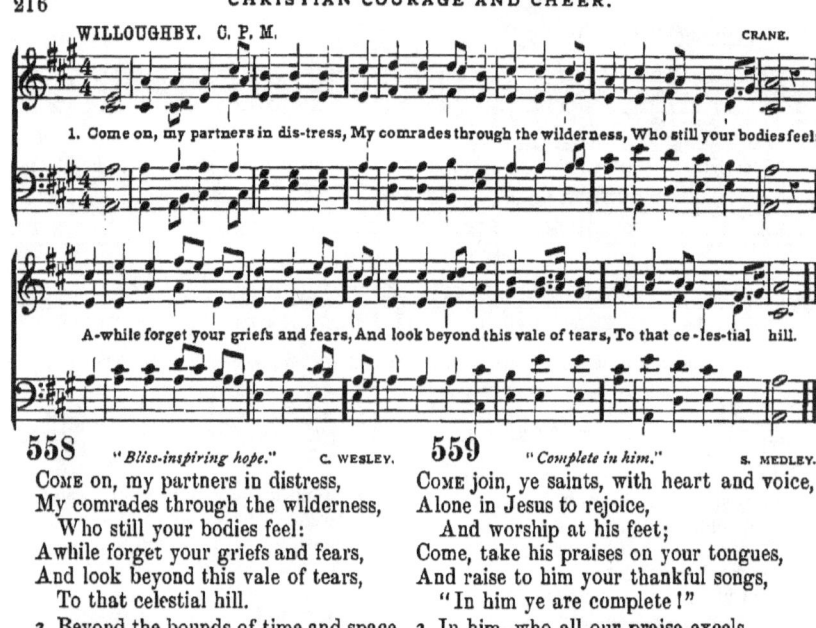

558 *"Bliss-inspiring hope."* C. WESLEY.

Come on, my partners in distress,
My comrades through the wilderness,
  Who still your bodies feel:
Awhile forget your griefs and fears,
And look beyond this vale of tears,
  To that celestial hill.

2 Beyond the bounds of time and space,
Look forward to that heavenly place,
  The saints' secure abode;
On faith's strong eagle-pinions rise,
And force your passage to the skies,
  And scale the mount of God.

3 Who suffer with our Master here,
We shall before his face appear,
  And by his side sit down;
To patient faith the prize is sure;
And all that to the end endure
  The cross, shall wear the crown.

559 *"Complete in him."* S. MEDLEY.

Come join, ye saints, with heart and voice,
Alone in Jesus to rejoice,
  And worship at his feet;
Come, take his praises on your tongues,
And raise to him your thankful songs,
  "In him ye are complete!"

2 In him, who all our praise excels,
The fullness of the Godhead dwells,
  And all perfections meet:
The head of all celestial powers,
Divinely theirs, divinely ours;—
  "In him ye are complete!"

3 Still onward urge your heavenly way,
Dependent on him day by day,
  His presence still entreat;
His precious name for ever bless,
Your glory, strength, and righteousness,—
  "In him ye are complete!"

CHRISTIAN COURAGE AND CHEER.

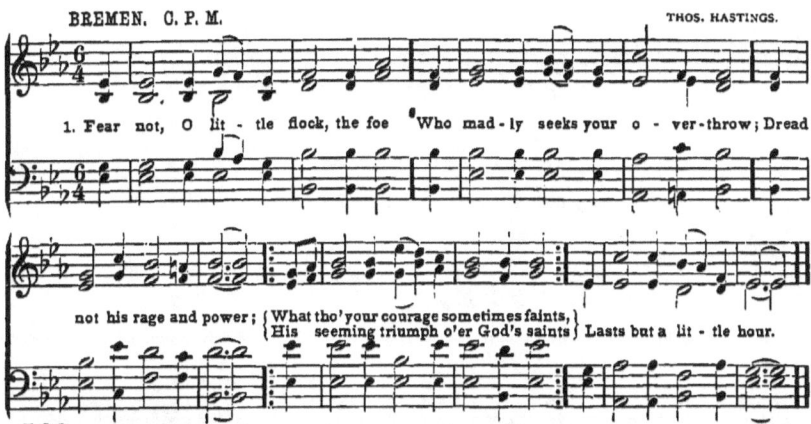

BREMEN. C. P. M.   THOS. HASTINGS.

1. Fear not, O little flock, the foe Who madly seeks your overthrow; Dread not his rage and power; { What tho' your courage sometimes faints, / His seeming triumph o'er God's saints } Lasts but a little hour.

560 *"Fear not, little flock."* C. WINKWORTH, tr.

FEAR not, O little flock, the foe
Who madly seeks your overthrow;
  Dread not his rage and power;
What tho' your courage sometimes faints,
His seeming triumph o'er God's saints
  Lasts but a little hour.

2 Be of good cheer; your cause belongs
To him who can avenge your wrongs;
  Leave it to him, our Lord!
Though hidden yet from mortal eyes,
He sees the Gideon that shall rise
  To save us, and his word.

3 As true as God's own word is true,
Not earth nor hell with all their crew
  Against us shall prevail;
A jest and by-word are they grown;
God is with us, we are his own,
  Our victory cannot fail!

4 Amen, Lord Jesus, grant our prayer!
Great Captain, now thine arm make bare,
  Fight for us once again!
So shall thy saints and martyrs raise
A mighty chorus to thy praise,
  World without end: Amen!

561 *"Casting all care on God."* J. ANSTICE

O LORD! how happy should we be,
If we could cast our care on thee,
  If we from self could rest;
And feel, at heart, that One above,
In perfect wisdom, perfect love,
  Is working for the best!

2 How far from this our daily life,
Ever disturbed by anxious strife,
  By sudden, wild alarms!
Oh, could we but relinquish all
Our earthly props, and simply fall
  On thine almighty arms!

562 P. M. *"Lead on."* J. BORTHWICK, tr.

JESUS still lead on,
  Till our rest be won;
And although the way be cheerless,
We will follow, calm and fearless;
  Guide us by thy hand
    To our Fatherland.

2 If the way be drear,
  If the foe be near,
Let not faithless fears o'ertake us,
Let not faith and hope forsake us;
  For, through many a foe,
    To our home we go.

3 When we seek relief
  From a long-felt grief,
When temptations come, alluring,
Make us patient and enduring;
  Show us that bright shore
    Where we weep no more.

4 Jesus, still lead on,
  Till our rest be won;
Heavenly Leader, still direct us,
Still support, console, protect us,
  Till we safely stand
    In our Fatherland.

CHRISTIAN COURAGE AND CHEER.

PORTUGUESE HYMN. 11s. J. READING.

1. How firm a foundation, ye saints of the Lord! Is laid for your faith in his excellent word! What more can he say, than to you he hath said,—To you, who for refuge to Jesus have fled, To you, who for refuge to Jesus have fled?

563 *"Fear Not."* G. KEITH.

How FIRM a foundation, ye saints of the Lord!
Is laid for your faith in his excellent word!
What more can he say, than to you he hath said,—
To you, who for refuge to Jesus have fled?

2 "Fear not, I am with thee, oh, be not dismayed,
For I am thy God, I will still give thee aid;
I'll strengthen thee, help thee, and cause thee to stand,
Upheld by my gracious, omnipotent hand.

3 "When through the deep waters I call thee to go,
The rivers of sorrow shall not overflow;
For I will be with thee thy trouble to bless,
And sanctify to thee thy deepest distress.

4 "When through fiery trials thy pathway shall lie,
My grace, all-sufficient, shall be thy supply;
The flame shall not hurt thee; I only design
Thy dross to consume, and thy gold to refine.

5 "Ev'n down to old age all my people shall prove
My sovereign, eternal, unchangeable love;
And then, when gray hairs shall their temples adorn,
Like lambs they shall still in my bosom be borne.

6 "The soul that on Jesus hath leaned for repose,
I will not—I will not desert to his foes;
That soul—though all hell should endeavor to shake,
I'll never—no never—no never forsake!"

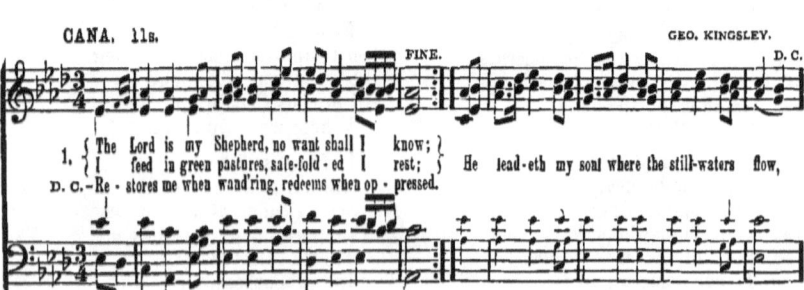

CANA. 11s. GEO. KINGSLEY.

1. The Lord is my Shepherd, no want shall I know; I feed in green pastures, safe-fold-ed I rest; He lead-eth my soul where the still-waters flow,
D. C.—Re-stores me when wand'ring, redeems when op-pressed.

CHRISTIAN COURAGE AND CHEER.

GOSHEN. 11s.   THOS. HASTINGS, arr.

1. The Lord is my Shepherd, no want shall I know; I feed in green pas-tures, safe-folded I rest; He leadeth my soul where the still waters flow, Restores me when wand'ring, redeems when oppressed.

564   *Psalm 23.*   J. MONTGOMERY.

THE Lord is my Shepherd, no want shall
  I know;
I feed in green pastures, safe-folded I rest;
He leadeth my soul where the still waters flow,
Restores me when wandering, redeems
  when oppressed.

2 Through the valley and shadow of death
  though I stray,
Since thou art my Guardian, no evil I fear;
Thy rod shall defend me, thy staff be my stay;
No harm can befall, with my Comforter near.

3 In the midst of affliction, my table is spread;
With blessings unmeasured my cup run-
  neth o'er;
With perfume and oil thou anointest my head;
Oh, what shall I ask of thy providence
  more?

4 Let goodness and mercy, my bountiful God!
Still follow my steps till I meet thee above;
I seek, by the path which my forefathers trod
Through the land of their sojourn, thy
  kingdom of love.

565   *"Faint, yet pursuing."*   J. N. DARBY.

THOUGH faint, yet pursuing, we go on our way;
The Lord is our Leader, his word is our stay;
Tho' suffering, and sorrow, and trial be near,
The Lord is our Refuge, and whom can we fear?

2 He raiseth the fallen, he cheereth the faint;
The weak, and oppressed—he will hear
  their complaint;
The way may be weary, and thorny the road,
But how can we falter?—our help is in God!

3 And to his green pastures our footsteps
  he leads;
His flock in the desert how kindly he feeds!
The lambs in his bosom he tenderly bears,
And brings back the wanderers all safe from
  the snares.

4 Though clouds may surround us, our God
  is our light;
Though storms rage around us, our God is
  our might;
So, faint yet pursuing, still onward we come;
The Lord is our Leader, and heaven is our
  home!

CHRISTIAN COURAGE AND CHEER

LOVE DIVINE. 8s, 7s. D.   JOHN ZUNDEL.

1. Love di-vine, all love ex-cell-ing,—Joy of heaven, to earth come down! Fix in us thy humble dwelling;
D. S.—Vis-it us with thy sal-va-tion,

All thy faithful mercies crown. Jesus! thou art all com-pas-sion, Pure, unbounded love thou art;
En-ter ev-ery trembling heart.

566
       C. WESLEY.
"Finish thy new creation."

Love divine, all love excelling,—
  Joy of heaven, to earth come down!
Fix in us thy humble dwelling,
  All thy faithful mercies crown:
Jesus! thou art all compassion,
  Pure, unbounded love thou art;
Visit us with thy salvation,
  Enter every trembling heart.
2 Breathe, oh, breathe thy loving Spirit
  Into every troubled breast!
Let us all in thee inherit,
  Let us find the promised rest:

Come, almighty to deliver,
  Let us all thy life receive!
Speedily return, and never,
  Never more thy temples leave!
3 Finish then thy new creation,
  Pure, unspotted may we be:
Let us see our whole salvation
  Perfectly secured by thee!
Changed from glory into glory,
  Till in heaven we take our place;
Till we cast our crowns before thee,
  Lost in wonder, love, and praise.

BAYLEY. 8s, 7s. D.   J. P. HOLBROOK, *arr.*

1. {Love di-vine, all love ex-cell - ing,—Joy of heaven, to earth come down! }
   {Fix in us thy hum-ble dwelling, All thy faith-ful (Omit)........ } mer - cies crown;
D. C.—Vis - it us with thy sal-va - tion, En - ter ev - ery (Omit)........ trem-bling heart.

Je - sus! thou art all com-pas - sion, Pure, un - bound-ed love thou art;

567 *What a Friend.* ANON.

WHAT a Friend we have in Jesus,
  All our sins and griefs to bear!
What a privilege to carry
  Everything to God in prayer!
Oh, what peace we often forfeit,
  Oh, what needless pain we bear,
All because we do not carry
  Everything to God in prayer!

2 Have we trials and temptations?
  Is there trouble anywhere?
We should never be discouraged,—
  Take it to the Lord in prayer.
Can we find a friend so faithful,
  Who will all our sorrows share?
Jesus knows our every weakness—
  Take it to the Lord in prayer.

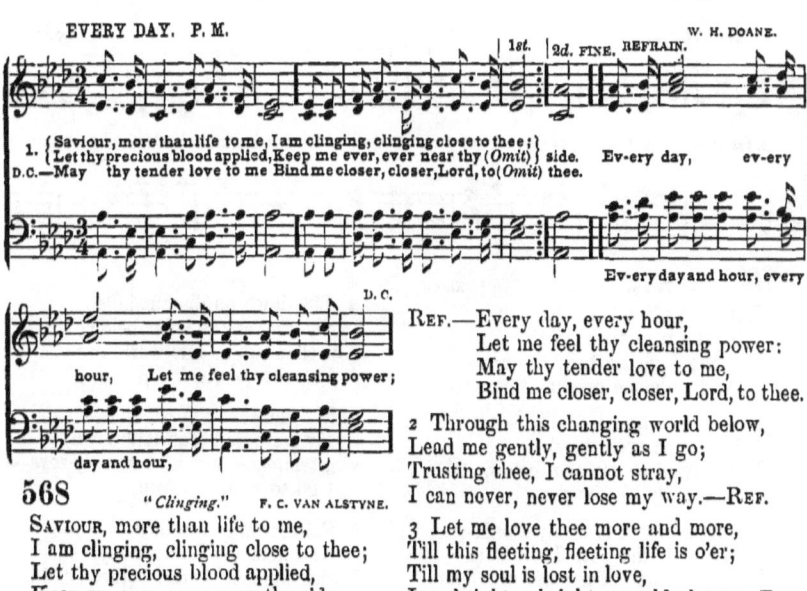

568 *"Clinging."* F. C. VAN ALSTYNE.

SAVIOUR, more than life to me,
  I am clinging, clinging close to thee;
Let thy precious blood applied,
  Keep me ever, ever near thy side.

REF.—Every day, every hour,
  Let me feel thy cleansing power:
May thy tender love to me,
  Bind me closer, closer, Lord, to thee.

2 Through this changing world below,
  Lead me gently, gently as I go;
Trusting thee, I cannot stray,
  I can never, never lose my way.—REF.

3 Let me love thee more and more,
  Till this fleeting, fleeting life is o'er;
Till my soul is lost in love,
  In a brighter, brighter world above.—REF.

CHRISTIAN COURAGE AND CHEER.

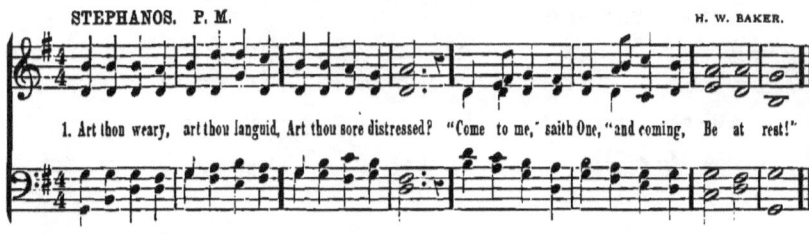

STEPHANOS. P. M.   H. W. BAKER.

1. Art thou weary, art thou languid, Art thou sore distressed? "Come to me," saith One, "and coming, Be at rest!"

569   *Our Master.*   J. M. NEALE, tr.

Art thou weary, art thou languid,
  Art thou sore distressed?
"Come to me," saith One, "and coming,
  Be at rest."

2 Hath he marks to lead me to him,
  If he be my Guide?—
"In his feet and hands are wound-prints,
  And his side."

3 Is there diadem, as Monarch,
  That his brow adorns?—
"Yea, a crown, in very surety;
  But of thorns."

4 If I find him, if I follow,
  What his guerdon here?—

"Many a sorrow, many a labor,
  Many a tear."

5 If I still hold closely to him,
  What hath he at last?—
"Sorrow vanquished, labor ended,
  Jordan passed."

6 If I ask him to receive me,
  Will he say me nay?—
"Not till earth, and not till heaven
  Pass away."

7 Finding, following, keeping, struggling,
  Is he sure to bless?—
"Saints, apostles, prophets, martyrs,
  Answer, Yes."

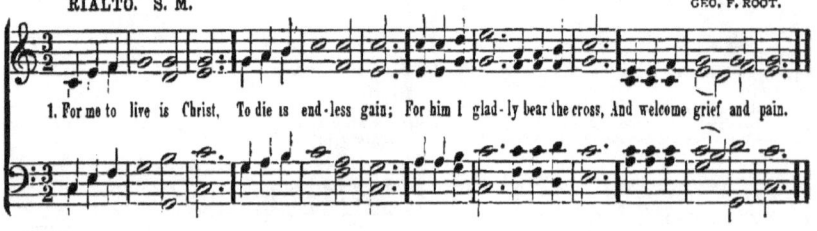

RIALTO. S. M.   GEO. F. ROOT.

1. For me to live is Christ, To die is end-less gain; For him I glad-ly bear the cross, And welcome grief and pain.

570   *"To live is Christ."*   ANON.

For me to live is Christ,
  To die is endless gain;
For him I gladly bear the cross,
  And welcome grief and pain.

2 A pilgrimage my lot,
  My home is in the skies;
I nightly pitch my tent below,
  And daily higher rise.

3 I fare with Christ my Lord;
  His path the path I choose;
They joy who suffer most with him—
  They win who with him lose.

4 The dawn on distant hills
  Shines o'er the vales below;
The shadows of this world are lost
  In light to which I go.

5 My journey soon will end,
  My scrip and staff laid down:
Oh, tempt me not with earthly toys—
  I go to wear a crown.

6 Faithful may I endure,
  And hear my Saviour say,
Thrice welcome home, belovéd child,
  Inherit endless day!

CHRISTIAN COURAGE AND CHEER.

571 *Psalm 125.* I. WATTS.
UNSHAKEN as the sacred hill,
And fixed as mountains be,
Firm as a rock the soul shall rest,
That leans, O Lord, on thee!

2 Not walls nor hills could guard so well
Old Salem's happy ground,
As those eternal arms of love,
That every saint surround.

3 Deal gently, Lord, with souls sincere,
And lead them safely on
To the bright gates of Paradise,
Where Christ, their Lord, is gone.

572 *"Nearer to thee"* CAREY
ALONG the mountain track of life,
Along the weary lea,
In rocks, in storms, in joy, in strife,
Let this my heart-cry be,—
"Nearer to thee—nearer to thee."

2 This pilgrim-path by thee was trod,
Jesus,—my King, by thee,
Traced by thy tears, thy feet, thy blood,
In love, in death, for me:
Oh, bring my soul nearer to thee.

3 Let every step, let every thought
Sweet memories bear of thee;
And hear the soul thy love hath bought,
Whose every cry shall be—
"Nearer to thee—nearer to thee."

4 Thou wilt! thou dost!—a still small voice
Whispers of faith in thee,
Of hope that might in grief rejoice,
If still the way-cry be,—
"Nearer to thee—nearer to thee."

CHRISTIAN COURAGE AND CHEER.

LEAD ME ON. P. M. — C. C. CONVERSE.

1. Trav'ling to the bet-ter land, O'er the desert's scorching sand, Father! let me grasp thy hand; Lead me on, lead me on!

573 *"Lead me on."* ANON.

Traveling to the better land,
O'er the desert's scorching sand,
Father! let me grasp thy hand;
  Lead me on, lead me on!

2 When at Marah, parched with heat,
I the sparkling fountain greet,
Make the bitter water sweet;
  Lead me on!

3 When the wilderness is drear,
Show me Elim's palm-grove near,
And her wells, as crystal clear:
  Lead me on!

4 Through the water, through the fire,
Never let me fall or tire,
Every step brings Canaan nigher:
  Lead me on!

5 Bid me stand on Nebo's height,
Gaze upon the land of light,
Then, transported with the sight,
  Lead me on!

6 When I stand on Jordan's brink,
Never let me fear or shrink;
Hold me, Father, lest I sink:
  Lead me on!

7 When the victory is won,
And eternal life begun,
Up to glory lead me on!
  Lead me on, lead me on!

HOUGHTON. 10s, 11s. — WM. GARDINER.

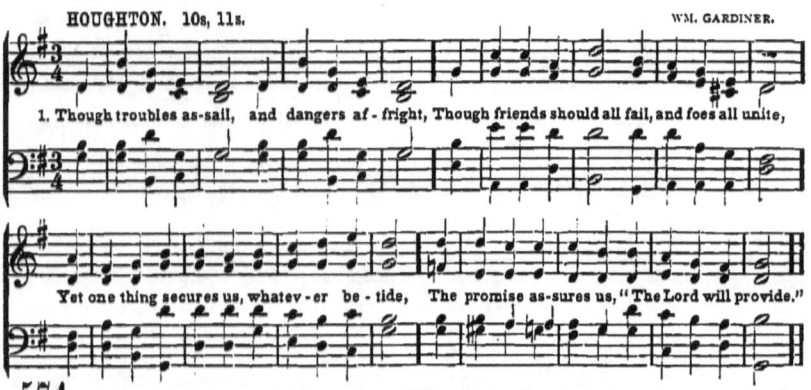

1. Though troubles as-sail, and dangers af-fright, Though friends should all fail, and foes all unite, Yet one thing secures us, whatev-er be-tide, The promise as-sures us, "The Lord will provide."

574 *The Lord will provide.* J. NEWTON.

Though troubles assail, and dangers affright,
Though friends should all fail, and foes all unite,
Yet one thing secures us, whatever betide,
The promise assures us, "The Lord will provide."

2 The birds, without barn or store-house, are fed;
From them let us learn to trust for our bread:
His saints what is fitting shall ne'er be denied,
So long as 'tis written, "The Lord will provide."

3 When life sinks apace, and death is in view,
The word of his grace shall comfort us through:
Not fearing or doubting, with Christ on our side,
We hope to die shouting, "The Lord will provide."

CHRISTIAN COURAGE AND CHEER.

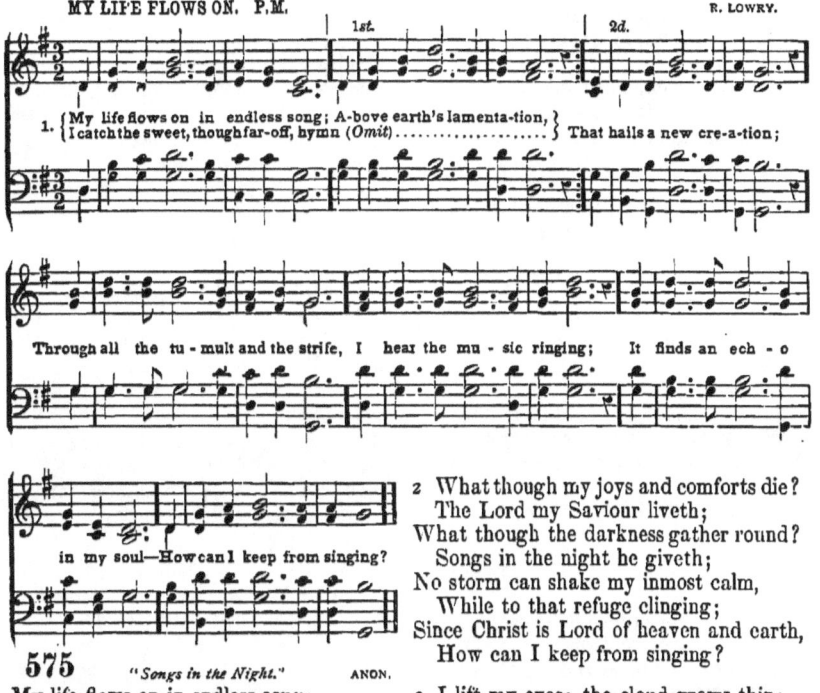

MY LIFE FLOWS ON. P.M.   R. LOWRY.

1. My life flows on in endless song; A-bove earth's lamenta-tion,
I catch the sweet, though far-off, hymn (Omit)........ That hails a new cre-a-tion;
Through all the tu-mult and the strife, I hear the mu-sic ringing; It finds an ech-o
in my soul—How can I keep from singing?

575   *"Songs in the Night."*   ANON.

My life flows on in endless song;
  Above earth's lamentation,
I catch the sweet, though far-off, hymn
  That hails a new creation;
Through all the tumult and the strife,
  I hear the music ringing;
It finds an echo in my soul—
  How can I keep from singing?

2 What though my joys and comforts die?
  The Lord my Saviour liveth;
What though the darkness gather round?
  Songs in the night he giveth;
No storm can shake my inmost calm,
  While to that refuge clinging;
Since Christ is Lord of heaven and earth,
  How can I keep from singing?

3 I lift my eyes; the cloud grows thin;
  I see the blue above it;
And day by day this pathway smooths,
  Since first I learned to love it;
The peace of Christ makes fresh my heart,
  A fountain ever springing;
All things are mine since I am his—
  How can I keep from singing?

576   10s, 11s.   *Christ with us.*   J. NEWTON.

BEGONE, unbelief, my Saviour is near,
And for my relief will surely appear;
By prayer let me wrestle, and he will per-
  form,   [storm.
With Christ in the vessel, I smile at the

2 Though dark be my way, since he is my
  guide,
'Tis mine to obey, 'tis his to provide;
Though cisterns be broken, and creatures
  all fail,   [vail.
The word he has spoken shall surely pre-

3 His love in time past forbids me to think
He'll leave me at last in trouble to sink;
Each sweet Ebenezer I have in review,
Confirms his good pleasure to help me quite
  through.

4 Since all that I meet shall work for my
  good,
The bitter is sweet, the medicine is food;
Though painful at present, 't will cease be-
  fore long,   [song!
And then, oh, how pleasant the conqueror's

577 9s, 8s. *Rom.* 13: 11, 12. J. RUSLING.

CHRISTIAN, the morn breaks sweetly o'er
    thee,
And all the midnight shadows flee,
Tinged are the distant skies with glory,
    A beacon-light hung out for thee;
Arise! arise! the light breaks o'er thee;
    Thy name is graven on the throne;
Thy home is in the world of glory,
    Where thy Redeemer reigns alone.

2 Tossed on time's rude, relentless
    surges,
Calmly composed, and dauntless stand,
For lo! beyond those scenes emerges
    The height that bounds the promised
    land:
Behold! behold! the land is nearing,
    Where the wild sea-storm's rage is o'er;
Hark! how the heavenly hosts are cheer-
    ing,
See in what throngs they range the
    shore!

3 Cheer up! cheer up! the day breaks
    o'er thee,
Bright as the summer's noon-tide ray,
The star-gemmed crowns and realms of
    Invite thy happy soul away; [glory
Away! away! leave all for glory,
    Thy name is graven on the throne;
Thy home is in that world of glory,
    Where thy Redeemer reigns alone.

578 S. M. *Psalm* 23. A. STEELE.

WHILE my Redeemer's near,
    My Shepherd and my guide,
I bid farewell to anxious fear:
    My wants are all supplied.

2 To ever fragrant meads,
    Where rich abundance grows,
His gracious hand indulgent leads,
    And guards my sweet repose.

3 Dear Shepherd, if I stray,
    My wandering feet restore;
To thy fair pastures guide my way,
    And let me rove no more.

4 Unworthy, as I am,
    Of thy protecting care,
Jesus, I plead thy gracious name,
    For all my hopes are there.

579 S. M. *The Warfare.* C. WESLEY.

SOLDIERS of Christ, arise,
    And put your armor on,
Strong is the strength which God sup-
    Through his eternal Son. [plies

2 Strong in the Lord of hosts,
    And in his mighty power,
Who in the strength of Jesus trusts
    Is more than conqueror.

3 Stand then in his great might,
    With all his strength endued,
And take, to arm you for the fight,
    The panoply of God.

4 Till, having all things done,
    And all your conflicts past,
You may o'ercome, through Christ alone,
    And stand entire at last.

5 From strength to strength go on;
    Wrestle, and fight, and pray;
Tread all the powers of darkness down,
    And win the well-fought day.

6 Still let the Spirit cry
    In all his soldiers, come!
Till Christ the Lord descend from high,
    And take the conquerors home.

580 7s, 6s, D. *Psalm* 77. J. MONTGOMERY.

IN time of tribulation,
    Hear, Lord! my feeble cries;
With humble supplication
    To thee my spirit flies:
My heart with grief is breaking;
    Scarce can my voice complain:
Mine eyes, with tears kept waking,
    Still watch and weep in vain.

2 Thee, with the tribes assembled,
    O God, the billows saw;
They saw thee and they trembled,
    Turned, and stood still with awe;
The clouds shot hail,—they lightened,—
    The earth reeled to and fro;
The fiery pillar brightened
    The gulf of gloom below.

3 Thy way is in great waters:
    Thy footsteps are not known:
Let Adam's sons and daughters
    Confide in thee alone:
Through the wild sea thou leddest
    Thy chosen flock of yore:
Still on the waves thou treadest,
    And thy redeemed pass o'er.

581 6s, 5s.   *Growth by Conflict.*

Purer yet and purer
  I would be in mind,
Dearer yet and dearer
  Every duty find;
Hoping still and trusting
  God without a fear,
Patiently believing
  He will make all clear.

2 Calmer yet and calmer
  Trial bear and pain,
Surer yet and surer
  Peace at last to gain;
Suffering still and doing,
  To his will resigned,
And to God subduing
  Heart and will and mind.

3 Higher yet and higher
  Out of clouds and night,
Nearer yet and nearer
  Rising to the light—
Light serene and holy,
  Where my soul may rest,
Purified and lowly,
  Sanctified and blest.

4 Quicker yet and quicker
  Ever onward press,
Firmer yet and firmer
  Step as I progress:
Oft these earnest longings
  Swell within my breast,
Yet their inner meaning
  Ne'er can be expressed.

582 H. M.   1 Tim. 6: 12.   J. MONTGOMERY.

Fight the good fight! lay hold
  Upon eternal life;
Keep but thy shield,—be bold!
  Stand through the hottest strife:
With thy great Captain on the field,
Thou canst not fail, unless thou yield.

2 No force of earth or hell,
  Though fiends with men unite,
Truth's champion can compel,
  However pressed, to flight:
He stands unmoved upon the field;
He cannot fall, unless he yield.

3 Great words are these, and strong;
  Yet, Lord, I look to thee;

ANON.

To whom alone belong
  Valor and victory:
With thee, my Captain, in the field,
I must prevail—I cannot yield!

583 C. M. D.   *"Wake thy heart!"*   J. BOWDLER.

Children of God, who, faint and slow,
  Your pilgrim-path pursue,
In strength and weakness, joy and woe,
  To God's high calling true!—
Why move ye thus, with lingering tread,
  A doubting, mournful band?
Why faintly hangs the drooping head?
  Why fails the feeble hand?

2 Oh, weak to know a Saviour's power,
  To feel a Father's care!
A moment's toil, a passing shower,
  Is all the grief ye share.
The orb of light, though clouds awhile
  May hide his noon-tide ray,
Shall soon in lovelier beauty smile
  To gild the closing day,—

3 And, bursting through the dusky shroud
  That dared his power invest,
Ride throned in light o'er every cloud,
  Triumphant to his rest.
Then, Christian, dry the falling tear,
  The faithless doubt remove;
Redeemed at last from guilt and fear,
  Oh! wake thy heart to love.

584 7s.   Deut. 33: 25.   W. F. LLOYD.

Wait, my soul, upon the Lord,
  To his gracious promise flee,
Laying hold upon his word,
  "As thy days thy strength shall be."

2 If the sorrows of thy case
  Seem peculiar still to thee,
God has promised needful grace—
  "As thy days thy strength shall be."

3 Days of trial, days of grief,
  In succession thou mayst see;
This is still thy sweet relief—
  "As thy days thy strength shall be."

4 Rock of Ages, I'm secure,
  With thy promise full and free;
Faithful, positive, and sure—
  "As thy days thy strength shall be."

LOVE, AND COMMUNION WITH CHRIST.

BARTIMEUS. 8s, 7s.   STEPHEN JENKS.

1. One there is, above all others, Well deserves the name of Friend;
His is love beyond a brother's, Costly, free, and knows no end.

585   *"Closer than a brother."*   J. NEWTON.

One there is, above all others,
  Well deserves the name of Friend;
His is love beyond a brother's,
  Costly, free, and knows no end.

2 Which of all our friends, to save us,
  Could or would have shed his blood?
But our Jesus died to have us
  Reconciled in him to God.

3 When he lived on earth abaséd,
  Friend of sinners was his name;
Now above all glory raiséd,
  He rejoices in the same.

4 Oh, for grace our hearts to soften!
  Teach us, Lord, at length, to love;
We, alas! forget too often
  What a friend we have above.

586   *"Jesus only."*   E. NASON.

Jesus only, when the morning
  Beams upon the path I tread;
Jesus only, when the darkness
  Gathers round my weary head.

2 Jesus only, when the billows
  Cold and sullen o'er me roll;
Jesus only, when the trumpet
  Rends the tomb and wakes the soul.

3 Jesus only, when, adoring,
  Saints their crowns before him bring;
Jesus only, I will, joyous,
  Through eternal ages sing.

587   *None but Jesus.*   A. R. COUSIN.

None but Christ: his merit hides me,
  He was faultless—I am fair;
None but Christ, his wisdom guides me,
  He was out-cast—I'm his care.

2 None but Christ: his Spirit seals me,
  Gives me freedom with control;
None but Christ, his bruising heals me,
  And his sorrow soothes my soul.

3 None but Christ: his life sustains me,
  Strength and song to me he is;
None but Christ, his love constrains me,
  He is mine and I am his.

588   *"With you always."*   E. H. NEVIN.

Always with us, always with us—
  Words of cheer and words of love;
Thus the risen Saviour whispers,
  From his dwelling-place above.

2 With us when we toil in sadness,
  Sowing much and reaping none;
Telling us that in the future
  Golden harvests shall be won.

3 With us when the storm is sweeping
  O'er our pathway dark and drear;
Waking hope within our bosoms,
  Stilling every anxious fear.

4 With us in the lonely valley,
  When we cross the chilling stream—
Lighting up the steps to glory
  With salvation's radiant beam.

LOVE, AND COMMUNION WITH CHRIST.

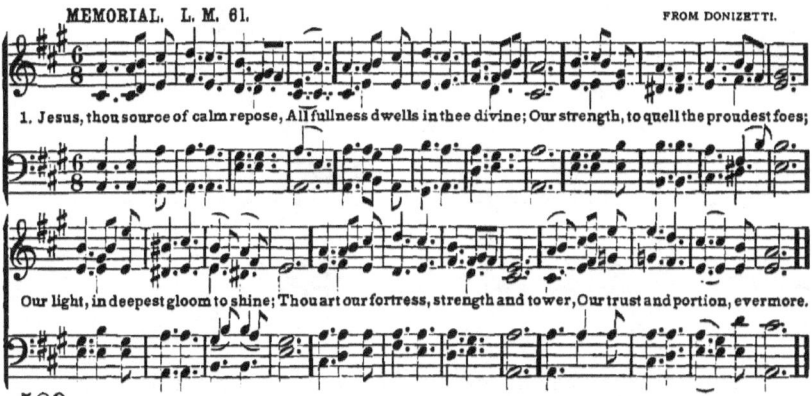

MEMORIAL. L. M. 6l. FROM DONIZETTI.

1. Jesus, thou source of calm repose, All fullness dwells in thee divine; Our strength, to quell the proudest foes; Our light, in deepest gloom to shine; Thou art our fortress, strength and tower, Our trust and portion, evermore.

589 *"All fullness."* C. WESLEY.

Jesus, thou source of calm repose,
All fullness dwells in thee divine;
Our strength to quell the proudest foes;
Our light, in deepest gloom to shine;
Thou art our fortress, strength, and tower,
Our trust and portion, evermore.

2 Jesus, our Comforter thou art;
Our rest in toil, our ease in pain;
The balm to heal each broken heart,
In storms our peace, in loss our gain;
Our joy, beneath the worldling's frown;
In shame, our glory and our crown;—

3 In want, our plentiful supply;
In weakness, our almighty power;
In bonds, our perfect liberty;
Our refuge in temptation's hour;
Our comfort when in grief and thrall;
Our life in death; our all in all.

590 *"Just such as I."* J. EDMESTON.

As oft with worn and weary feet,
We tread earth's rugged valley o'er,
The thought, how comforting and sweet,
Christ trod this very path before!
Our wants and weaknesses he knows,
From life's first dawning till its close.

2 If Satan tempt our hearts to stray,
And whisper evil things within,
So did he, in the desert way,
Assail our Lord with thoughts of sin:
When worn, and in a feeble hour,
The tempter came with all his power.

3 Just such as I, this earth he trod,
With every human ill but sin;
And, though indeed the very God,
As I am now, so he has been:
My God, my Saviour! look on me
With pity, love, and sympathy.

591 *"My Strength, my Tower."* J. WESLEY, *tr.*

Thee will I love, my Strength, my Tower!
Thee will I love, my Joy, my Crown;
Thee will I love, with all my power,
In all thy works, and thee alone:
Thee will I love, till the pure fire
Fill my whole soul with chaste desire.

2 Thee will I love, my Joy, my Crown!
Thee will I love, my Lord, my God!
Thee will I love, beneath thy frown
Or smile, thy sceptre or thy rod.
What though my heart and flesh decay?
Thee shall I love in endless day.

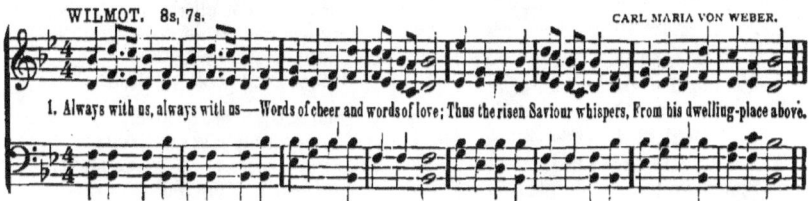

WILMOT. 8s, 7s. CARL MARIA VON WEBER.

1. Always with us, always with us—Words of cheer and words of love; Thus the risen Saviour whispers, From his dwelling-place above.

LOVE, AND COMMUNION WITH CHRIST.

CARLISLE. S. M. — CHARLES LOCKHART.

1. Dear Lord and Master mine! Thy happy servant see;
My Conqu'ror! with what joy divine Thy captive clings to thee!

592   *"Master mine!"*   T. H. GILL.

DEAR Lord and Master mine!
  Thy happy servant see;
My Conqueror! with what joy divine
  Thy captive clings to thee!

2 I would not walk alone,
  But still with thee, my God,
At every step my blindness own,
  And ask of thee the road.

3 The weakness I enjoy
  That casts me on thy breast;
The conflicts that thy strength employ
  Make me divinely blest.

4 Dear Lord and Master mine!
  Still keep thy servant true;
My Guardian and my Guide divine!
  Bring, bring thy pilgrim through.

5 My Conqueror and my King!
  Still keep me in thy train;
And with thee thy glad captive bring
  When thou return'st to reign.

STILLINGFLEET. S. M. — SWISS COLL.

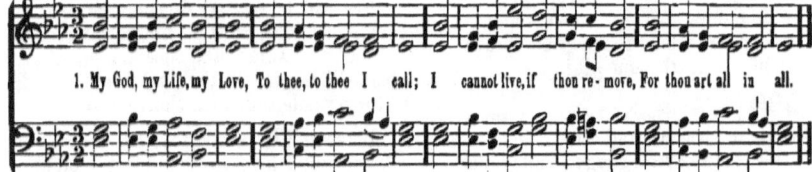

1. My God, my Life, my Love, To thee, to thee I call; I cannot live, if thou remove, For thou art all in all.

593   *None but Jesus.*   I. WATTS.

MY God, my Life, my Love,
  To thee, to thee I call;
I cannot live, if thou remove,
  For thou art all in all.

2 To thee, and thee alone,
  The angels owe their bliss;
They sit around thy gracious throne,
  And dwell where Jesus is.

3 Not all the harps above
  Can make a heavenly place,
If God his residence remove,
  Or but conceal his face.

4 Nor earth, nor all the sky,
  Can one delight afford—
No, not a drop of real joy
  Without thy presence, Lord.

5 Thou art the sea of love,
  Where all my pleasures roll;
The circle where my passions move,
  And centre of my soul.

LOVE, AND COMMUNION WITH CHRIST. 231

594 *"Jesus is my friend."* C. WINKWORTH, *tr.*
SINCE Jesus is my friend,
　And I to him belong,
It matters not what foes intend,
　However fierce and strong.

2 He whispers in my breast
　Sweet words of holy cheer,
How they who seek in God their rest
　Shall ever find him near;—

3 How God hath built above
　A city fair and new,
Where eye and heart shall see and prove
　What faith has counted true.

4 My heart for gladness springs;
　It cannot more be sad;
For very joy it smiles and sings,—
　Sees naught but sunshine glad.

5 The sun that lights mine eyes
　Is Christ, the Lord I love;
I sing for joy of that which lies
　Stored up for me above.

595　*Psalm 23.*　I. WATTS.
THE Lord my Shepherd is,
　I shall be well supplied;
Since he is mine, and I am his,
　What can I want beside?

2 He leads me to the place
　Where heavenly pasture grows,
Where living waters gently pass,
　And full salvation flows.

3 If e'er I go astray,
　He doth my soul reclaim;
And guide me in his own right way,
　For his most holy name.

4 While he affords his aid,
　I cannot yield to fear;
Tho' I should walk thro' death's dark shade,
　My Shepherd's with me there.

5 In spite of all my foes,
　Thou dost my table spread;
My cup with blessings overflows,
　And joy exalts my head.

6 The bounties of thy love
　Shall crown my future days;
Nor from thy house will I remove,
　Nor cease to speak thy praise.

596　*Unseen, we love.*　I. WATTS.
NOT with our mortal eyes
　Have we beheld the Lord;
Yet we rejoice to hear his name;
　And love him in his word.

2 On earth we want the sight
　Of our Redeemer's face;
Yet, Lord, our inmost thoughts delight
　To dwell upon thy grace.

3 And when we taste thy love,
　Our joys divinely grow
Unspeakable, like those above,
　And heaven begins below.

232   LOVE, AND COMMUNION WITH CHRIST.

FEDERAL STREET. L. M. — H. K. OLIVER.

1. Jesus! and shall it ever be, A mortal man ashamed of thee?
A-shamed of thee, whom angels praise, Whose glories shine through endless days?

597   *"Ashamed of me."*   J. GRIGG.

Jesus! and shall it ever be,
A mortal man ashamed of thee?
Ashamed of thee, whom angels praise,
Whose glories shine through endless days?

2 Ashamed of Jesus! sooner far
Let evening blush to own a star;
He sheds the beams of light divine
O'er this benighted soul of mine.

3 Ashamed of Jesus! that dear Friend
On whom my hopes of heaven depend!
No; when I blush, be this my shame,
That I no more revere his name.

4 Ashamed of Jesus! yes, I may,
When I've no guilt to wash away;
No tear to wipe, no good to crave,
No fears to quell, no soul to save.

5 Till then—nor is my boasting vain—
Till then, I boast a Saviour slain!
And, oh, may this my glory be
That Christ is not ashamed of me!

598   *Jesus all in all.*   RAY PALMER, tr.

Jesus, thou Joy of loving hearts,
Thou Fount of life! thou Light of men!
From the best bliss that earth imparts,
We turn unfilled to thee again.

2 Thy truth unchanged hath ever stood;
Thou savest those that on thee call;
To them that seek thee thou art good,
To them that find thee, All in All.

3 We taste thee, O thou Living Bread,
And long to feast upon thee still;
We drink of thee, the Fountain Head,
And thirst our souls from thee to fill!

4 Our restless spirits yearn for thee,
Where'er our changeful lot is cast;
Glad, when thy gracious smile we see,
Blest, when our faith can hold thee fast.

5 O Jesus, ever with us stay;
Make all our moments calm and bright;
Chase the dark night of sin away,
Shed o'er the world thy holy light!

599   *"Not your own."*   S. F. SMITH.

Oh, not my own these verdant hills,
And fruits, and flowers, and stream, and wood;
But his who all with glory fills,
Who bought me with his precious blood.

2 Oh, not my own this wondrous frame,
Its curious work, its living soul;
But his who for my ransom came;
Slain for my sake, he claims the whole.

3 Oh, not my own the grace that keeps
My feet from fierce temptations free;
Oh, not my own the thought that leaps,
Adoring, blessèd Lord, to thee.

4 Oh, not my own; I'll soar and sing,
When life, with all its toils, is o'er,
And thou thy trembling lamb shalt bring
Safe home, to wander nevermore.

LOVE, AND COMMUNION WITH CHRIST.

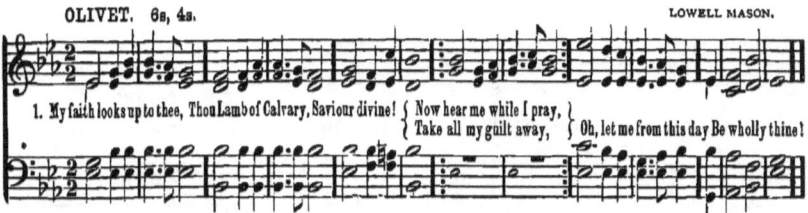

OLIVET. 6s, 4s. LOWELL MASON.

1. My faith looks up to thee, Thou Lamb of Calvary, Saviour divine! { Now hear me while I pray, / Take all my guilt away, } Oh, let me from this day Be wholly thine!

600 "Look unto Me." RAY PALMER.

My faith looks up to thee,
Thou Lamb of Calvary,
 Saviour divine!
Now hear me while I pray
Take all my guilt away,
Oh, let me from this day
 Be wholly thine!

2 May thy rich grace impart
Strength to my fainting heart;
 My zeal inspire;
As thou hast died for me,
Oh, may my love to thee
Pure, warm, and changeless be,
 A living fire!

3 While life's dark maze I tread,
And griefs around me spread,
 Be thou my guide;
Bid darkness turn to day,
Wipe sorrow's tears away,
Nor let me ever stray
 From thee aside.

4 When ends life's transient dream,
When death's cold, sullen stream
 Shall o'er me roll,
Blest Saviour! then, in love,
Fear and distrust remove;
Oh, bear me safe above,
 A ransomed soul!

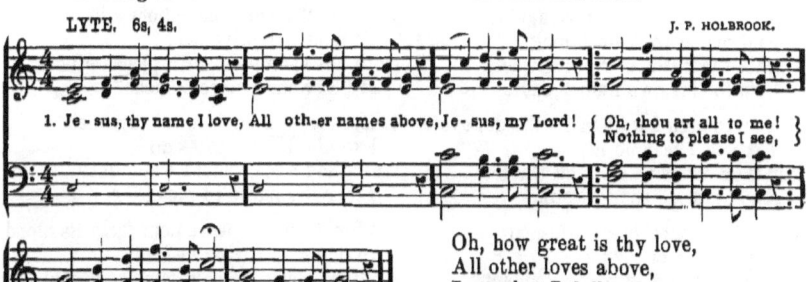

LYTE. 6s, 4s. J. P. HOLBROOK.

1. Je-sus, thy name I love, All oth-er names above, Je-sus, my Lord! { Oh, thou art all to me! / Nothing to please I see, }

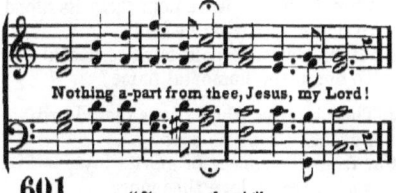

Nothing a-part from thee, Jesus, my Lord!

601 "Jesus my Lord!" J. G. DECK.

Jesus, thy name I love,
All other names above,
 Jesus, my Lord!
Oh, thou art all to me!
Nothing to please I see,
Nothing apart from thee,
 Jesus, my Lord!

2 Thou, blessèd Son of God,
Hast bought me with thy blood,
 Jesus, my Lord!

Oh, how great is thy love,
All other loves above,
Love that I daily prove,
 Jesus, my Lord!

3 When unto thee I flee,
Thou wilt my refuge be,
 Jesus, my Lord!
What need I now to fear?
What earthly grief or care,
Since thou art ever near?
 Jesus, my Lord!

4 Soon thou wilt come again!
I shall be happy then,
 Jesus, my Lord!
Then thine own face I'll see,
Then I shall like thee be,
Then evermore with thee,
 Jesus, my Lord!

LOVE, AND COMMUNION WITH CHRIST.

LA MIRA. C. M.
W. B. BRADBURY.

1. The Lord's my shepherd, I'll not want: He makes me down to lie In pas-tures green; he lead-eth me The qui-et wa-ters by.

602   *Psalm 23.*   SCOTCH VERS.

The Lord's my shepherd, I'll not want:
He makes me down to lie
In pastures green; he leadeth me
The quiet waters by.

2 My soul he doth restore again;
And me to walk doth make
Within the paths of righteousness,
Ev'n for his own name's sake.

3 Yea, though I walk in death's dark vale,
Yet will I fear no ill;
For thou art with me, and thy rod
And staff me comfort still.

4 My table thou hast furnishéd
In presence of my foes;
My head thou dost with oil anoint,
And my cup overflows.

5 Goodness and mercy, all my life,
Shall surely follow me;
And in God's house for evermore
My dwelling-place shall be.

603   *Loving and Beloved.*   P. DODDRIDGE.

Do not I love thee, O my Lord?
Behold my heart, and see;
And turn the dearest idol out
That dares to rival thee.

2 Is not thy name melodious still
To mine attentive ear?
Doth not each pulse with pleasure bound,
My Saviour's voice to hear?

3 Hast thou a lamb in all thy flock
I would disdain to feed?
Hast thou a foe, before whose face
I fear thy cause to plead?

4 Would not my heart pour forth its blood
In honor of thy name?
And challenge the cold hand of death
To damp the immortal flame?

5 Thou knowest that I love thee, Lord;
But, oh, I long to soar
Far from the sphere of mortal joys,
And learn to love thee more.

ARMENIA. C. M.
S. B. POND.

1. {Do not I love thee, O my Lord? Be-hold my heart, and see;}
   {And turn the dearest i-dol out (Omit).................} That dares to ri-val thee.

LOVE, AND COMMUNION WITH CHRIST.

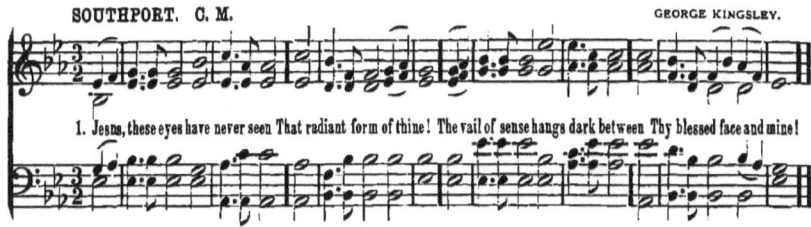

SOUTHPORT. C. M.   GEORGE KINGSLEY.

1. Jesus, these eyes have never seen That radiant form of thine! The vail of sense hangs dark between Thy blessed face and mine!

604   *"Whom unseen, we love."* RAY PALMER.

JESUS, these eyes have never seen
   That radiant form of thine!
The vail of sense hangs dark between
   Thy blessèd face and mine!

2 I see thee not, I hear thee not,
   Yet art thou oft with me;
And earth hath ne'er so dear a spot,
   As where I meet with thee.

3 Like some bright dream that comes un-
   When slumbers o'er me roll, [sought,
Thine image ever fills my thought,
   And charms my ravished soul.

4 Yet though I have not seen, and still
   Must rest in faith alone;
I love thee, dearest Lord!—and will,
   Unseen, but not unknown.

5 When death these mortal eyes shall seal,
   And still this throbbing heart,
The rending vail shall thee reveal,
   All glorious as thou art!

605   *Strength, Fortress, Refuge.* A. STEELE.

DEAR Refuge of my weary soul,
   On thee, when sorrows rise,
On thee, when waves of trouble roll,
   My fainting hope relies.

2 To thee I tell each rising grief,
   For thou alone canst heal;
Thy word can bring a sweet relief
   For every pain I feel.

3 But oh, when gloomy doubts prevail,
   I fear to call thee mine;
The springs of comfort seem to fail,
   And all my hopes decline.

4 Yet, gracious God, where shall I flee?
   Thou art my only trust;
And still my soul would cleave to thee,
   Though prostrate in the dust.

5 Thy mercy-seat is open still,
   Here let my soul retreat,
With humble hope attend thy will,
   And wait beneath thy feet.

GEER. C. M.   H. W. GREATOREX.

1. Dear Ref-uge of my wea-ry soul, On thee, when sor-rows rise, On thee, when waves of troub-le roll, My faint-ing hope re-lies.

LOVE, AND COMMUNION WITH CHRIST.

606 *Immanuel.* RAY PALMER.

OH, sweetly breathe the lyres above,
  When angels touch the quivering string,
And wake, to chant Immanuel's love,
  Such strains as angel-lips can sing!

2 And sweet, on earth, the choral swell,
  From mortal tongues, of gladsome lays;
When pardoned souls their raptures tell,
  And, grateful, hymn Immanuel's praise.

3 Jesus, thy name our souls adore;
  We own the bond that makes us thine;
And carnal joys that charmed before,
  For thy dear sake we now resign.

4 Our hearts, by dying love subdued,
  Accept thine offered grace to-day;
Beneath the cross, with blood bedewed,
  We bow, and give ourselves away.

5 In thee we trust,—on thee rely;
  Though we are feeble, thou art strong;
Oh, keep us till our spirits fly
  To join the bright, immortal throng!

607 *Robe of Righteousness.* J. WESLEY, tr.

JESUS, thy Blood and Righteousness
  My beauty are, my glorious dress;
'Midst flaming worlds, in these arrayed,
  With joy shall I lift up my head.

2 Lord, I believe thy precious blood,—
  Which, at the mercy-seat of God,
For ever doth for sinners plead,—
  For me, ev'n for my soul, was shed.

3 When from the dust of death I rise
  To claim my mansion in the skies—
Ev'n then, this shall be all my plea:
  Jesus hath lived, hath died for me.

4 This spotless robe the same appears,
  When ruined nature sinks in years;
No age can change its glorious hue,
  The robe of Christ is ever new.

5 Oh, let the dead now hear thy voice:
  Bid, Lord, thy mourning ones rejoice;
Their beauty this, their glorious dress,
  Jesus, the Lord our Righteousness.

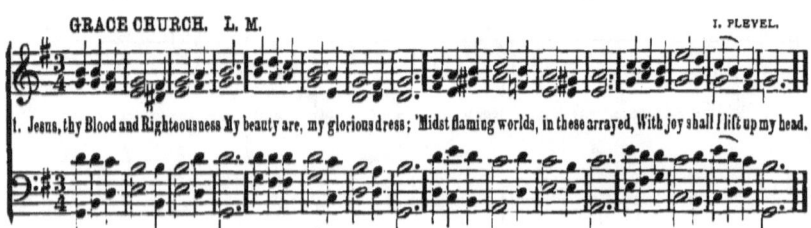

LOVE, AND COMMUNION WITH CHRIST.

HOSANNA. L. M.   CHARLES ZEUNER.

1. A-way from earth my spir-it turns, A-way from ev-ery tran-sient good; With strong de-sire my bo-som burns, To feast on heaven's di-vin-er food.

608   *"The living bread."*   RAY PALMER.

Away from earth my spirit turns,
  Away from every transient good;
With strong desire my bosom burns,
  To feast on heaven's diviner food.

2 Thou, Saviour, art the living bread;
  Thou wilt my every want supply:
By thee sustained, and cheered, and led,
  I'll press through dangers to the sky.

3 What though temptations oft distress,
  And sin assails and breaks my peace;
Thou wilt uphold, and save, and bless,
  And bid the storms of passion cease.

4 Then let me take thy gracious hand,
  And walk beside thee onward still;
Till my glad feet shall safely stand,
  For ever firm, on Zion's hill.

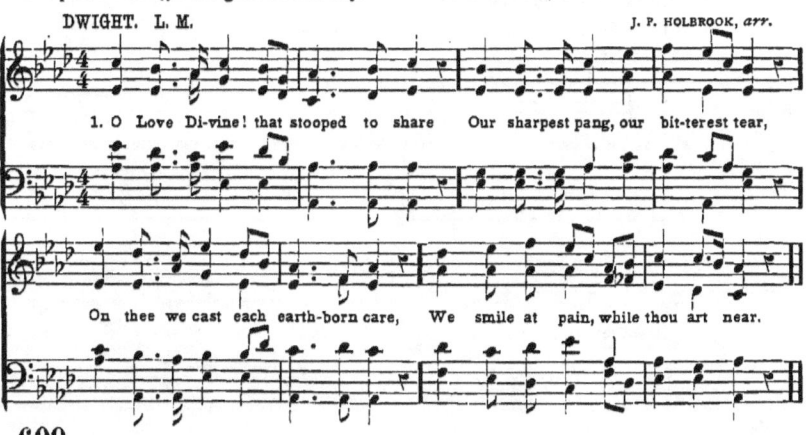

DWIGHT. L. M.   J. P. HOLBROOK, arr.

1. O Love Di-vine! that stooped to share Our sharpest pang, our bit-ter-est tear, On thee we cast each earth-born care, We smile at pain, while thou art near.

609   *"Thou art near."*   O. W. HOLMES.

O Love Divine! that stooped to share
  Our sharpest pang, our bitterest tear,
On thee we cast each earth-born care,
  We smile at pain, while thou art near.

2 Though long the weary way we tread,
  And sorrow crown each lingering year,
No path we shun, no darkness dread,
  Our hearts still whispering, thou art near.

3 When drooping pleasure turns to grief,
  And trembling faith is changed to fear,
The murmuring wind, the quivering leaf,
  Shall softly tell us thou art near.

4 On thee we fling our burdening woe,
  O Love Divine, for ever dear;
Content to suffer while we know,
  Living or dying, thou art near!

LOVE, AND COMMUNION WITH CHRIST.

610   *"Altogether Lovely."*   I. WATTS.

My God! the spring of all my joys,
  The life of my delights,
The glory of my brightest days,
  And comfort of my nights!

2 In darkest shades if he appear,
  My dawning is begun:
He is my soul's sweet morning star,
  And he my rising sun.

3 The opening heavens around me shine
  With beams of sacred bliss,
While Jesus shows his heart is mine,
  And whispers, I am his!

4 My soul would leave this heavy clay,
  At that transporting word;
Run up with joy the shining way,
  To embrace my dearest Lord!

611   *"To live is Christ."*   J. NEWTON.

Jesus, who on his glorious throne
  Rules heaven, and earth, and sea,
Is pleased to claim me for his own
  And give himself to me.

2 His person fixes all my love,
  His blood removes my fear;
And while he pleads for me above,
  His arm preserves me here.

3 His word of promise is my food,
  His Spirit is my guide;
Thus daily is my strength renewed,
  And all my wants supplied.

4 For him I count as gain each loss,
  Disgrace for him renown;
Well may I glory in my cross,
  While he prepares my crown.

LOVE, AND COMMUNION WITH CHRIST.

HOLY CROSS. C. M.   FROM MENDELSSOHN.

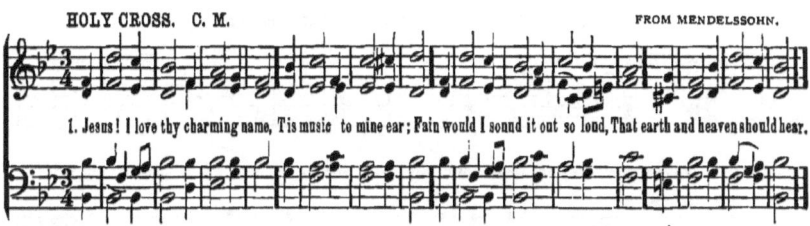

1. Jesus! I love thy charming name, 'Tis music to mine ear; Fain would I sound it out so loud, That earth and heaven should hear.

612   "His name Jesus."   P. DODDRIDGE.

Jesus! I love thy charming name,
  'Tis music to mine ear;
Fain would I sound it out so loud,
  That earth and heaven should hear.

2 Yes!—thou art precious to my soul,
  My transport and my trust;
Jewels, to thee, are gaudy toys,
  And gold is sordid dust.

3 All my capacious powers can wish,
  In thee doth richly meet;
Not to mine eyes is light so dear,
  Nor friendship half so sweet.

4 Thy grace still dwells upon my heart,
  And sheds its fragrance there;—
The noblest balm of all its wounds,
  The cordial of its care.

HEBER. C. M.   GEO. KINGSLEY.

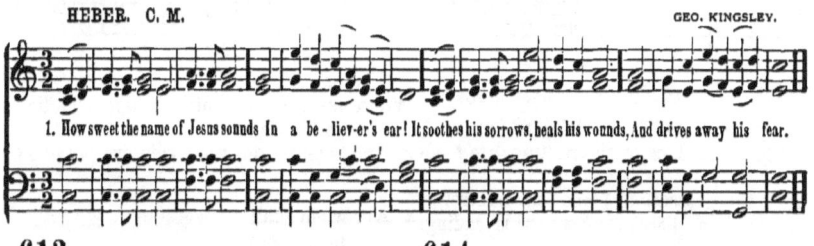

1. How sweet the name of Jesus sounds In a be-liev-er's ear! It soothes his sorrows, heals his wounds, And drives away his fear.

613   "He is precious."   J. NEWTON.

How sweet the name of Jesus sounds
  In a believer's ear!
It soothes his sorrows, heals his wounds,
  And drives away his fear.

2 It makes the wounded spirit whole,
  And calms the troubled breast;
'Tis manna to the hungry soul,
  And to the weary, rest.

3 Jesus! my Shepherd, Guardian, Friend,
  My Prophet, Priest, and King;
My Lord, my Life, my Way, my End,
  Accept the praise I bring.

4 Weak is the effort of my heart,
  And cold my warmest thought;
But when I see thee as thou art,
  I'll praise thee as I ought.

5 Till then I would thy love proclaim,
  With every fleeting breath;
And may the music of thy name,
  Refresh my soul in death.

614   "Jesus only."   E. CASWALL, tr.

Jesus, the very thought of thee,
  With sweetness fills my breast;
But sweeter far thy face to see
  And in thy presence rest.

2 Nor voice can sing, nor heart can frame,
  Nor can the memory find
A sweeter sound than thy blest name,
  O Saviour of mankind!

3 O Hope of every contrite heart!
  O Joy of all the meek!
To those who fall, how kind thou art!
  How good to those who seek!

4 But what to those who find? Ah! this,
  Nor tongue nor pen can show;
The love of Jesus, what it is,
  None but his loved ones know.

5 Jesus, our only joy be thou,
  As thou our prize wilt be;
Jesus, be thou our glory now.
  And through eternity.

LOVE, AND COMMUNION WITH CHRIST.

STILL WATER. 10s, 11s.   THOS. HASTINGS.

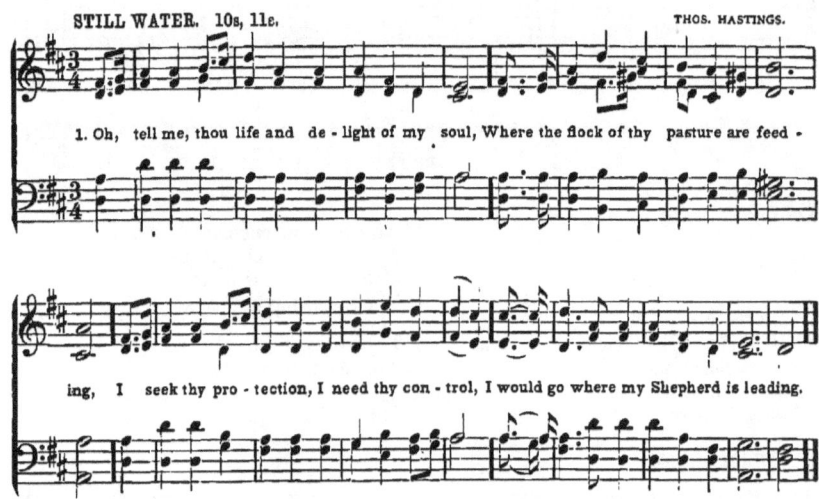

615
Cant. i: 7, 8.   THOS. HASTINGS.

Oh, tell me, thou life and delight of my soul,
  Where the flock of thy pasture are feeding;
I seek thy protection, I need thy control,
  I would go where my Shepherd is leading.

2 Oh, tell me the place where thy flock are at rest,
  Where the noontide will find them reposing;
The tempest now rages, my soul is distressed,
  And the pathway of peace I am losing.

3 And why should I stray with the flocks of thy foes,
  In the desert where now they are roving,
Where hunger and thirst, where affliction and woes,
  And temptations their ruin are proving?

4 Ah, when shall my woes and my wanderings cease,
  And the follies that fill me with weeping?
Thou Shepherd of Israel, restore me that peace,
  Thou dost give to the flock thou art keeping.

5 A voice from the Shepherd now bids me return
  By the way where the footprints are lying;
No longer to wander, no longer to mourn:
  And homeward my spirit is flying.

SPANISH HYMN. 7s. 61.   SPANISH MELODY.

LOVE, AND COMMUNION WITH CHRIST. 241

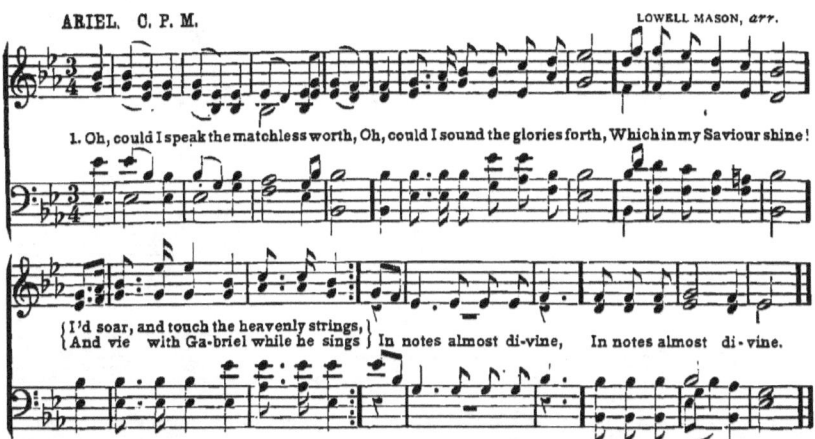

ARIEL. C. P. M.   LOWELL MASON, arr.

1. Oh, could I speak the matchless worth, Oh, could I sound the glories forth, Which in my Saviour shine! I'd soar, and touch the heavenly strings, And vie with Ga-briel while he sings In notes almost di-vine, In notes almost di-vine.

616   "*He is precious.*"   S. MEDLEY.

OH, could I speak the matchless worth,
Oh, could I sound the glories forth,
   Which in my Saviour shine!
I'd soar, and touch the heavenly strings,
And vie with Gabriel while he sings
   In notes almost divine.

2 I'd sing the precious blood he spilt,
My ransom from the dreadful guilt
   Of sin and wrath divine!
I'd sing his glorious righteousness,
In which all-perfect heavenly dress
   My soul shall ever shine.

3 I'd sing the characters he bears,
And all the forms of love he wears,
   Exalted on his throne:
In loftiest songs of sweetest praise,
I would to everlasting days
   Make all his glories known.

4 Well—the delightful day will come,
When my dear Lord will bring me home,
   And I shall see his face:
Then with my Saviour, Brother, Friend,
A blest eternity I'll spend,
   Triumphant in his grace.

617   7s, 6L   "*Only thee.*"   G. DUFFIELD.

BLESSED Saviour! thee I love,
All my other joys above;
All my hopes in thee abide,
Thou my hope, and naught beside:
   Ever let my glory be,
   Only, only, only thee.

2 Once again beside the cross,
All my gain I count but loss;
Earthly pleasures fade away,—
Clouds they are that hide my day:
Hence, vain shadows! let me see
Jesus, crucified for me.

3 Blessèd Saviour, thine am I,
Thine to live, and thine to die;
Height, or depth, or earthly power,
Ne'er shall hide my Saviour more:
   Ever shall my glory be
   Only, only, only thee!

618   7s, 6L   "*I am thine.*"   F. R. HAVERGAL.

JESUS, Master, whose I am,
   Purchased thine alone to be,
By thy blood, O spotless Lamb,
   Shed so willingly for me;
Let my heart be all thine own,
Let me live to thee alone.

2 Other lords have long held sway;
   Now thy name alone to bear,
Thy dear voice alone obey,
   Is my daily, hourly prayer.
Whom have I in heaven but thee?
Nothing else my joy can be.

3 Jesus, Master, I am thine;
   Keep me faithful, keep me near;
Let thy presence in me shine
   All my homeward way to cheer.
Jesus, at thy feet I fall,
Oh, be thou my All in all.

LOVE, AND COMMUNION WITH CHRIST.

GOSHEN. 11s.   THOS. HASTINGS, arr.

1. I once was a stranger to grace and to God; I knew not my
D.S.—Je-ho-vah, my

dan-ger, and felt not my load; Though friends spoke in rap-ture of Christ on the tree,
Sav-iour, seemed nothing to me.

619   *Love and assurance.*   R. M. MC CHEYNE.

I ONCE was a stranger to grace and to God;
I knew not my danger, and felt not my load;
Though friends spoke in rapture of Christ
   on the tree,
Jehovah, my Saviour, seemed nothing to me.

2 When free grace awoke me by light from
   on high,
Then legal fears shook me: I trembled to die:
No refuge, no safety, in self could I see:
Jehovah, thou only my Saviour must be!

3 My terrors all vanished before his sweet
   name;
My guilty fears banished, with boldness I
   came
To drink at the fountain, so copious and free:
Jehovah, my Saviour, is all things to me.

4 Jehovah, the Lord, is my treasure and
   boast;
Jehovah, my Saviour, I ne'er can be lost;
In thee I shall conquer, by flood and by
   field,
Jehovah my anchor, Jehovah my shield!

620   *"Looking unto Jesus."*   J. N. DARBY.

O EYES that are weary, and hearts that
   are sore!
Look off unto Jesus, now sorrow no more!
The light of his countenance shineth so
   bright,
That here, as in heaven, there need be no
   night.

2 While looking to Jesus, my heart cannot fear;
I tremble no more when I see Jesus near;
I know that his presence my safeguard
   will be,
For, "Why are you troubled?" he saith
   unto me.

3 Still looking to Jesus, oh, may I be found,
When Jordan's dark waters encompass me
   round:
They bear me away in his presence to be:
I see him still nearer whom always I see.

4 Then, then shall I know the full beauty
   and grace
Of Jesus, my Lord, when I stand face to face;
Shall know how his love went before me
   each day,
And wonder that ever my eyes turned away.

LOVE, AND COMMUNION WITH CHRIST.

MAGILL. 11s.　　　　　　　　　　　　　　T. E. PERKINS.

1. Come, Jesus, Redeemer, abide thou with me; Come, gladden my spirit, that waiteth for thee; Thy smile every shadow shall chase from my heart, And soothe every sorrow though keen be the smart.

621   *"I will come to you."*   RAY PALMER.

COME, Jesus, Redeemer, abide thou with me;
Come, gladden my spirit that waiteth for thee;
Thy smile every shadow shall chase from my heart,
And soothe every sorrow though keen be the smart.

2 Without thee but weakness, with thee I am strong;
By day thou shalt lead me, by night be my song ;
Though dangers surround me, I still every fear,
Since thou, the Most Mighty, my Helper, art near.

3 Thy love, oh, how faithful! so tender, so pure !
Thy promise, faith's anchor, how steadfast and sure !
That love, like sweet sunshine, my cold heart can warm,
That promise make steady my soul in the storm.

4 Breathe, breathe on my spirit, oft ruffled, thy peace:
From restless, vain wishes, bid thou my heart cease;
In thee all its longings henceforward shall end,
Till, glad, to thy presence my soul shall ascend.

17

5 Oh, then, blessèd Jesus, who once for me died,
Made clean in the fountain that gushed from thy side,
I shall see thy full glory, thy face shall behold,
And praise thee with raptures for ever untold !

622   *"Distresses for Christ's sake."*   C. FRY.

FOR what shall I praise thee, my God and my King,
For what blessings the tribute of gratitude bring?
Shall I praise thee for pleasure, for health, or for ease,
For the sunshine of youth, for the garden of peace?

2 For this I should praise; but if only for this,
I should leave half untold the donation of bliss !
I thank thee for sickness, for sorrow, and care,
For the thorns I have gathered, the anguish I bear;—

3 For nights of anxiety, watching, and tears,
A present of pain, a prospective of fears;
I praise thee, I bless thee, my Lord and my God,
For the good and the evil thy hand hath bestowed !

244. LOVE, AND COMMUNION WITH CHRIST.

DE FLEURY. 8s. D. — LEWIS EDSON.

623
"Whom have I but thee?" J. NEWTON.

How TEDIOUS and tasteless the hours,
  When Jesus no longer I see!
The woodlands, the fields, and the flowers,
  Have lost all their sweetness to me.
His name yields the richest perfume,
  And softer than music his voice;
His presence can banish my gloom,
  And bid all within me rejoice.

2 Dear Lord! if indeed I am thine,
  And thou art my light and my song;
Say, why do I languish and pine,
  And why are my winters so long?
Oh, drive these dark clouds from the sky,
  Thy soul-cheering presence restore;
Or bid me soar upward on high,
  Where winters and storms are no more.

624
"Altogether lovely." B. FRANCIS.

My gracious Redeemer I love,
  His praises aloud I'll proclaim:
And join with the armies above,
  To shout his adorable name.
To gaze on his glories divine
  Shall be my eternal employ;
To see them incessantly shine,
  My boundless, ineffable joy.

2 He freely redeemed with his blood
  My soul from the confines of hell,
To live on the smiles of my God,
  And in his sweet presence to dwell:—
To shine with the angels in light,
  With saints and with seraphs to sing,
To view, with eternal delight,
  My Jesus, my Saviour, my King!

VERNON. 8s. D. — GERMAN.

LOVE, AND COMMUNION WITH CHRIST.

MADISON. 8s. D.   S. B. POND.

1. Ye angels! who stand round the throne, And view my Immanuel's face,—In rapturous songs make him known, Oh, tune your soft harps to his praise: He formed you the spirits you are, So hap-py, so no-ble, so good; When oth-ers sank down in despair, Confirmed by his pow-er, ye stood.

625 *Philippians* 1:23. M. DE FLEURY.

YE angels! who stand round the throne,
And view my Immanuel's face,—
In rapturous songs make him known,
Oh, tune your soft harps to his praise:
He formed you the spirits you are,
So happy, so noble, so good;
When others sank down in despair,
Confirmed by his power, ye stood.

2 Ye saints! who stand nearer than they,
And cast your bright crowns at his feet,
His grace and his glory display,
And all his rich mercy repeat;
He snatched you from hell and the grave,
He ransomed from death and despair:
For you he was mighty to save,
Almighty to bring you safe there.

3 Oh, when will the period appear
When I shall unite in your song?
I'm weary of lingering here,
And I to your Saviour belong!
I want—oh, I want to be there,
To sorrow and sin bid adieu—
Your joy and your friendship to share—
To wonder, and worship with you!

626 *"Not seen, ye love."* W. COWPER.

MY Saviour, whom absent I love,
Whom, not having seen, I adore,
Whose name is exalted above
All glory, dominion, and power,—
Dissolve thou these bands that detain
My soul from her portion in thee;
Ah, strike off this adamant chain,
And make me eternally free!

2 When that happy era begins,
When arrayed in thy glories I shine,
Nor grieve any more, by my sins,
The bosom on which I recline,
Oh, then shall the vail be removed,
And round me thy brightness be poured!
I shall meet him, whom absent I loved,
I shall see, whom unseen I adored.

3 And then, nevermore shall the fears,
The trials, temptations, and woes,
Which darken this valley of tears,
Intrude on my blissful repose:
To Jesus, the crown of my hope,
My soul is in haste to be gone;
Oh, bear me, ye cherubim, up,
And waft me away to his throne!

LOVE, AND COMMUNION WITH CHRIST.

KARL. 7s. GEO. KINGSLEY, arr.

1. Earth has nothing sweet or fair, Lovely forms or beauties rare, But before my eyes they bring Christ, of beauty Source and Spring.

627 *"Altogether lovely."* F. E. COX, tr.
EARTH has nothing sweet or fair,
Lovely forms or beauties rare,
But before my eyes they bring
Christ, of beauty Source and Spring.

2 When the morning paints the skies,
When the golden sunbeams rise,
Then my Saviour's form I find
Brightly imaged on my mind.

3 When the star-beams pierce the night,
Oft I think on Jesus' light;
Think how bright that light will be,
Shining through eternity.

4 Come, Lord Jesus! and dispel
This dark cloud in which I dwell,
And to me the power impart
To behold thee as thou art.

628 *"Immanuel."* J. NEWTON.
SWEETER sounds than music knows
Charm me in Immanuel's name;
All her hopes my spirit owes
To his birth, and cross, and shame.

2 When he came the angels sung,
"Glory be to God on high:"
Lord, unloose my stammering tongue;
Who should louder sing than I?

3 Did the Lord a man become,
That he might the law fulfill,
Bleed and suffer in my room,—
And canst thou, my tongue, be still?

4 No; I must my praises bring,
Though they worthless are, and weak;
For should I refuse to sing,
Sure the very stones would speak.

5 O my Saviour! Shield, and Sun,
Shepherd, Brother, Lord, and Friend—
Every precious name in one!
I will love thee without end.

629 *"To live is Christ."* R. WARDLAW.
CHRIST, of all my hopes the Ground,
Christ, the Spring of all my joy,
Still in thee let me be found,
Still for thee my powers employ.

2 Fountain of o'erflowing grace!
Freely from thy fullness give;
Till I close my earthly race,
Be it "Christ for me to live!"

3 Firmly trusting in thy blood,
Nothing shall my heart confound;
Safely I shall pass the flood,
Safely reach Immanuel's ground.

4 When I touch the blessèd shore,
Back the closing waves shall roll!
Death's dark stream shall nevermore
Part from thee my ravished soul.

5 Thus—oh, thus an entrance give
To the land of cloudless sky;
Having known it "Christ to live,"
Let me know it "gain to die."

LOVE, AND COMMUNION WITH CHRIST.

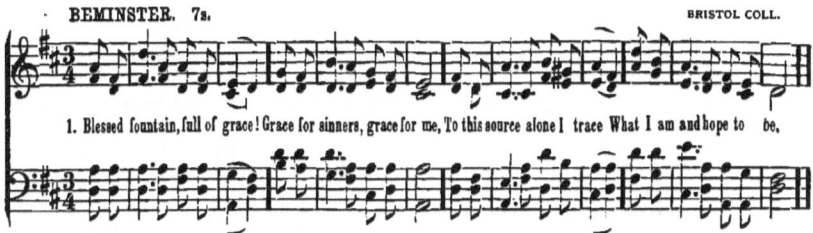

BEMINSTER. 7s. BRISTOL COLL.

1. Blessed fountain, full of grace! Grace for sinners, grace for me, To this source alone I trace What I am and hope to be.

630 *"I am what I am."* T. KELLY.

BLESSED fountain, full of grace!
Grace for sinners, grace for me,
To this source alone I trace
What I am, and hope to be.

2 What I am, as one redeemed,
Saved and rescued by the Lord;
Hating what I once esteemed,
Loving what I once abhorred.

3 What I hope to be ere long,
When I take my place above;
When I join the heavenly throng;
When I see the God of love.

4 Then I hope like him to be,
Who redeemed his saints from sin,
Whom I now obscurely see,
Through a vail that stands between.

5 Blessèd fountain, full of grace!
Grace for sinners, grace for me;
To this source alone I trace
What I am, and hope to be.

FULTON. 7s. W. B. BRADBURY.

1. Sav-iour! teach me day by day, Love's sweet les-son to o-bey; Sweet-er les-son can-not be, Lov-ing-him who first loved me.

631 *"Who first loved us."* J. E. LEESON.

SAVIOUR! teach me, day by day,
Love's sweet lesson to obey;
Sweeter lesson cannot be,
Loving him who first loved me.

2 With a childlike heart of love,
At thy bidding may I move;
Prompt to serve and follow thee,
Loving him who first loved me.

3 Teach me all thy steps to trace,
Strong to follow in thy grace;
Learning how to love from thee,
Loving him who first loved me.

4 Love in loving finds employ—
In obedience all her joy;
Ever new that joy will be,
Loving him who first loved me.

5 Thus may I rejoice to show
That I feel the love I owe;
Singing, till thy face I see,
Of his love who first loved me.

632 C. M.   *"He is precious."*   O. HEGINBOTHAM.

Blest Jesus! when my soaring thoughts
  O'er all thy graces rove,
How is my soul in transport lost,—
  In wonder, joy, and love!

2 Not softest strains can charm my ears,
  Like thy belovéd name;
Nor aught beneath the skies inspire
  My heart with equal flame.

3 Where'er I look, my wondering eyes
  Unnumbered blessings see;
But what is life, with all its bliss,
  If once compared with thee?

4 Hast thou a rival in my breast?
  Search, Lord, for thou canst tell
If aught can raise my passions thus,
  Or please my soul so well.

5 No; thou art precious to my heart,
  My portion and my joy:
For ever let thy boundless grace
  My sweetest thoughts employ.

633 C. M. D.   *Jesus' Words.*   H. BONAR.

I heard the voice of Jesus say,—
  "Come unto me and rest:
Lay down, thou weary one, lay down
  Thy head upon my breast!"
I came to Jesus as I was,
  Weary, and worn, and sad,
I found in him a resting-place,
  And he hath made me glad.

2 I heard the voice of Jesus say,—
  "Behold I freely give
The living water; thirsty one,
  Stoop down, and drink, and live!"
I came to Jesus, and I drank
  Of that life-giving stream;
My thirst was quenched, my soul re-
  And now I live in him.   [vived,

3 I heard the voice of Jesus say,—
  "I am this dark world's light;
Look unto me, thy morn shall rise
  And all thy day be bright!"
I looked to Jesus, and I found
  In him my Star, my Sun;
And in that light of life I'll walk,
  Till all my journey's done.

634 7s, 6 l.   *Psalm 23.*   ANON.

Shepherd! with thy tenderest love,
Guide me to thy fold above;
Let me hear thy gentle voice;
More and more in thee rejoice;
From thy fullness grace receive,
Ever in thy Spirit live.

2 Filled by thee my cup o'erflows,
For thy love no limit knows:
Guardian angels, ever nigh,
Lead and draw my soul on high;
Constant to my latest end,
Thou my footsteps wilt attend.

3 Jesus, with thy presence blest,
Death is life, and labor rest;
Guide me while I draw my breath,
Guard me through the gate of death;
And at last, oh, let me stand,
With the sheep at thy right hand.

635 L. M. D.   *"I love thee, Lord!"*   R. HEBER.

Though sorrows rise and dangers roll,
In waves of darkness o'er my soul;
Though friends are false, and love de-
And few and evil are my days;   [cays,
Though conscience, fiercest of my foes,
Swells with remembered guilt my woes;
Yet ev'n in nature's utmost ill,
I love thee, Lord! I love thee still!

2 Though Sinai's curse, in thunder dread,
Peals o'er mine unprotected head,
And memory points, with busy pain,
To grace and mercy given in vain;
Till nature, shrinking in the strife,
Would fly to hell to 'scape from life;
Though every thought has power to kill,
I love thee, Lord! I love thee still!

3 Oh, by the pangs thyself hast borne,
The ruffian's blow, the tyrant's scorn,
By Sinai's curse, whose dreadful doom
Was buried in thy guiltless tomb;
By these my pangs, whose healing smart,
Thy grace hath planted in my heart—
I know, I feel thy bounteous will,
Thou lov'st me, Lord! thou lov'st me still!

LOVE, AND COMMUNION WITH CHRIST.

636 C. M. D. *Psalm 23.* I. WATTS.

My Shepherd will supply my need,
  Jehovah is his name;
In pastures fresh he makes me feed,
  Beside the living stream.
He brings my wandering spirit back,
  When I forsake his ways;
And leads me, for his mercy's sake,
  In paths of truth and grace.

2 When I walk through the shades of
    Thy presence is my stay;   [death,
A word of thy supporting breath
  Drives all my fears away.
Thy hand, in sight of all my foes,
  Doth still my table spread;
My cup with blessings overflows,
  Thine oil anoints my head.

3 The sure provisions of my God
  Attend me all my days;
Oh, may thy house be mine abode,
  And all my works be praise:
There would I find a settled rest,
  While others go and come,—
No more a stranger, or a guest,
  But like a child at home.

637 C. M. *Christ, our Model.* E. CASWALL, *tr.*

O Jesus! King most wonderful,
  Thou Conqueror renowned,
Thou sweetness most ineffable,
  In whom all joys are found!

2 When once thou visitest the heart,
  Then truth begins to shine,
Then earthly vanities depart,
  Then kindles love divine.

3 O Jesus, Light of all below!
  Thou Fount of life and fire!
Surpassing all the joys we know,
  All that we can desire,—

4 May every heart confess thy name,
  And ever thee adore;
And, seeking thee, itself inflame
  To seek thee more and more.

5 Thee may our tongues for ever bless:
  Thee may we love alone;
And ever in our life express
  The image of thine own.

638 C. M. *Christ above all.* J. NEWTON.

Let worldly minds the world pursue—
  It has no charms for me;
Once I admired its trifles too,
  But grace hath set me free.

2 Its joys can now no longer please,
  Nor ev'n content afford:
Far from my heart be joys like these,
  For I have seen the Lord.

3 As by the light of opening day
  The stars are all concealed,
So earthly pleasures fade away
  When Jesus is revealed.

4 Creatures no more divide my choice—
  I bid them all depart;
His name, his love, his gracious voice,
  Have fixed my roving heart.

5 And may I hope that thou wilt own
  A worthless worm like me?
Dear Lord! I would be thine alone,
  And wholly live to thee.

639 7s, 6s, D. *"God, our Saviour."* T. HAWEIS.

To thee, my God and Saviour!
  My heart exulting sings,
Rejoicing in thy favor,
  Almighty King of kings!
I'll celebrate thy glory,
  With all thy saints above,
And tell the joyful story
  Of thy redeeming love.

2 Soon as the morn with roses
  Bedecks the dewy east,
And when the sun reposes
  Upon the ocean's breast,
My voice, in supplication,
  Well-pleased the Lord shall hear:
Oh, grant me thy salvation,
  And to my soul draw near.

3 By thee, through life supported,
  I'll pass the dangerous road,
With heavenly hosts escorted,
  Up to thy bright abode;
Then cast my crown before thee,
  And, all my conflicts o'er,
Unceasingly adore thee:—
  What could an angel more?

CHRISTIAN EXPERIENCE AND GRACES.

ROSEFIELD. 7s. 6l. — C. H. A. MALAN.

1. Bless-ed are the sons of God, They are bought with Christ's own blood; They are ransomed from the grave; Life e-ter-nal they shall have: With them numbered may we be, Here, and in e-ter-ni-ty.

640   *Brotherly Love.*   J. HUMPHREYS.

BLESSED are the sons of God,
They are bought with Christ's own blood;
They are ransomed from the grave;
Life eternal they shall have:
With them numbered may we be,
Here, and in eternity.

2 They are justified by grace,
They enjoy the Saviour's peace;
All their sins are washed away;
They shall stand in God's great day:
With them numbered may we be,
Here, and in eternity.

3 They are lights upon the earth,
Children of a heavenly birth,—

One with God, with Jesus one:
Glory is in them begun:
With them numbered may we be,
Here, and in eternity.

641   *Charity.*   C. WINKWORTH, tr.

THOUGH I speak with angel tongues
Bravest words of strength and fire,
They are but as idle songs,
If no love my heart inspire;
All the eloquence shall pass
As the noise of sounding brass.

2 Though I lavish all I have
On the poor in charity,
Though I shrink not from the grave,
Or unmoved the stake can see,—
Till by love the work be crowned,
All shall profitless be found.

3 Come, thou Spirit of pure love,
Who didst forth from God proceed,
Never from my heart remove;
Let me all thy impulse heed;
Let my heart henceforward be
Moved, controlled, inspired by thee.

GUIDE. 7s. 6l. — M. M. WELLS.

1. Qui-et, Lord, my fro-ward heart; Make me teach-a-ble and mild,
D.C.—From dis-trust and en-vy free, Pleased with all that pleas-es thee.

Up-right, sim-ple, free from art; Make me as a wean-ed child;

CHRISTIAN EXPERIENCES AND GRACES.

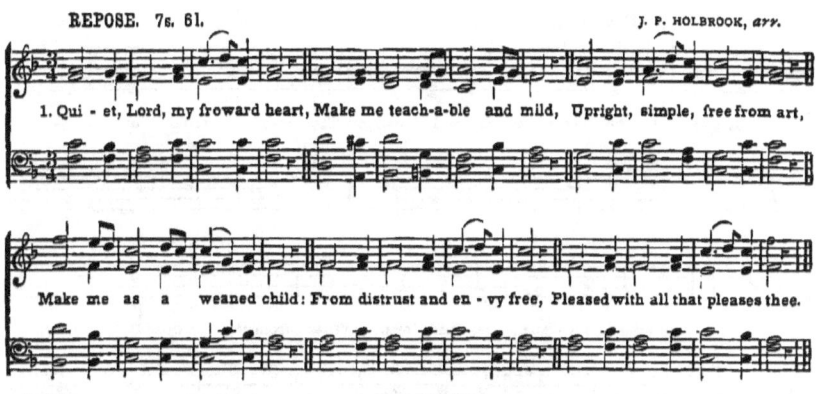

642 *Psalm 131.* J. NEWTON.
Quiet, Lord, my froward heart,
 Make me teachable and mild,
Upright, simple, free from art,
 Make me as a weanéd child:
From distrust and envy free,
Pleased with all that pleases thee.

2 What thou shalt to-day provide,
 Let me as a child receive;
What to-morrow may betide,
 Calmly to thy wisdom leave:
'Tis enough that thou wilt care;
Why should I the burden bear?

3 As a little child relies
 On a care beyond his own,
Knows he's neither strong nor wise,
 Fears to stir a step alone;—
Let me thus with thee abide,
As my Father, Guard, and Guide.

643 *Trust.* E. H. NEVIN.
Saviour, happy would I be,
 If I could but trust in thee;
Trust thy wisdom me to guide;
Trust thy goodness to provide;
Trust thy saving love and power;
Trust thee every day and hour:—

2 Trust thee as the only light
 In the darkest hour of night;
Trust in sickness, trust in health;
Trust in poverty and wealth;
Trust in joy and trust in grief;
Trust thy promise for relief:—

3 Trust thy blood to cleanse my soul;
Trust thy grace to make me whole;
Trust thee living, dying too;
Trust thee all my journey through;
Trust thee till my feet shall be
Planted on the crystal sea.

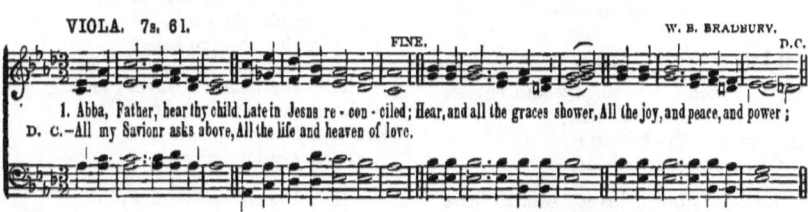

644 *Spirituality.* C. WESLEY.
Abba, Father, hear thy child,
Late in Jesus reconciled;
Hear, and all the graces shower,
All the joy, and peace, and power;
All my Saviour asks above,
All the life and heaven of love.

2 Holy Ghost, no more delay;
Come, and in thy temple stay:
Now, thine inward witness bear,
Strong, and permanent, and clear:
Spring of life, thyself impart;
Rise eternal in my heart.

CHRISTIAN EXPERIENCES AND GRACES.

MOUNT AUBURN. C. M.   GEO. KINGSLEY.

1. Lord, I be-lieve; thy power I own; Thy word I would o-bey;
I wan-der com-fort-less and lone, When from thy truth I stray.

645   *Faith.*   J. R. WREFORD.

LORD, I believe; thy power I own;
Thy word I would obey;
I wander comfortless and lone,
When from thy truth I stray.

2 Lord, I believe; but gloomy fears
Sometimes bedim my sight;
I look to thee with prayers and tears,
And cry for strength and light.

3 Lord, I believe; but oft, I know,
My faith is cold and weak:
My weakness strengthen, and bestow
The confidence I seek.

4 Yes! I believe; and only thou
Canst give my soul relief:
Lord, to thy truth my spirit bow;
"Help thou mine unbelief!"

646   *Meekness.*   T. H. GILL.

LORD! when I all things would possess,
I crave but to be thine;
Oh, lowly is the loftiness
Of these desires divine.

2 Each gift but helps my soul to learn
How boundless is thy store;
I go from strength to strength, and yearn
For thee, my Helper, more.

3 How can my soul divinely soar,
How keep the shining way,
And not more tremblingly adore,
And not more humbly pray!

4 The more I triumph in thy gifts,
The more I wait on thee;
The grace that mightily uplifts
Most sweetly humbleth me.

5 The heaven where I would stand complete
My lowly love shall see,
And stronger grow the yearning sweet,
My holy One! for thee.

647   *Calmness.*   H. BONAR.

CALM me, my God, and keep me calm;
Let thine outstretchéd wing
Be like the shade of Elim's palm,
Beside her desert spring.

2 Yes, keep me calm, though loud and rude
The sounds my ear that greet,—
Calm in the closet's solitude,
Calm in the bustling street,—

3 Calm in the hour of buoyant health,
Calm in my hour of pain,
Calm in my poverty or wealth,
Calm in my loss or gain,—

4 Calm in the sufferance of wrong,
Like him who bore my shame,
Calm 'mid the threatening, taunting throng,
Who hate thy holy name.

5 Calm me, my God, and keep me calm,
Soft resting on thy breast;
Soothe me with holy hymn and psalm,
And bid my spirit rest.

CHRISTIAN EXPERIENCE AND GRACES.

CORINTH. C. M.   LOWELL MASON.

1. My God, how wonderful thou art, Thy majesty how bright! How glorious is thy mercy-seat, In depths of burning light!

648   *"Herein is Love."*   F. W. FABER.

My God, how wonderful thou art,
  Thy majesty how bright!
How glorious is thy mercy seat,
  In depths of burning light!

2 Yet I may love thee too, O Lord,
  Almighty as thou art;
For thou hast stooped to ask of me
  The love of my poor heart.

3 No earthly father loves like thee,
  No mother half so mild
Bears and forbears, as thou hast done
  With me, thy sinful child.

4 My God, how wonderful thou art,
  Thou everlasting Friend!
On thee I stay my trusting heart,
  Till faith in vision end.

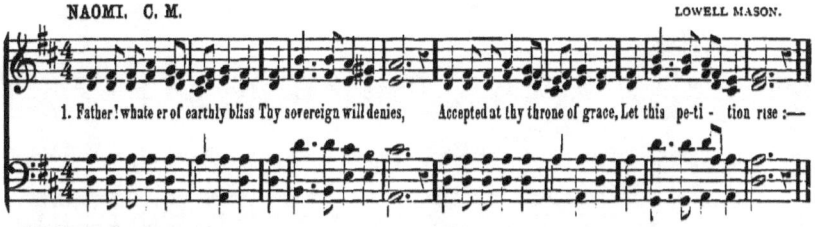

NAOMI. C. M.   LOWELL MASON.

1. Father! whate'er of earthly bliss Thy sovereign will denies, Accepted at thy throne of grace, Let this petition rise:—

649   *Humble Devotion.*   A. STEELE.

FATHER! whate'er of earthly bliss
  Thy sovereign will denies,
Accepted at thy throne of grace,
  Let this petition rise:—

2 "Give me a calm, a thankful heart,
  From every murmur free;
The blessings of thy grace impart,
  And make me live to thee.

3 "Let the sweet hope that thou art mine:
  My life and death attend;
Thy presence through my journey shine,
  And crown my journey's end."

650   *Growth in grace.*   A. NETTLETON.

COME, Holy Ghost, my soul inspire;
  This one great gift impart—
What most I need, and most desire,
  An humble, holy heart.

2 Bear witness I am born again,
  My many sins forgiven:
Nor let a gloomy doubt remain
  To cloud my hope of heaven.

3 More of myself grant I may know,
  From sin's deceit be free;
In all the Christian graces grow,
  And live alone to thee.

CHRISTIAN EXPERIENCES AND GRACES.

ONTARIO. S. M.   LONDON TUNE BOOK.

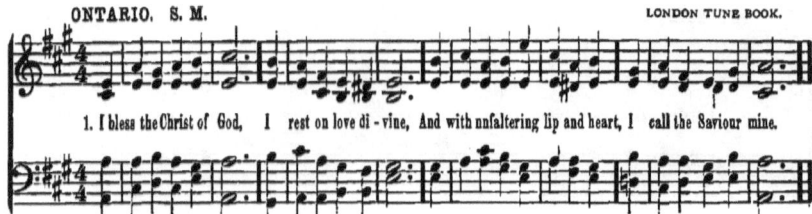

1. I bless the Christ of God, I rest on love di-vine, And with unfaltering lip and heart, I call the Saviour mine.

651   *Grateful Confidence.*   H. BONAR.

I BLESS the Christ of God,
  I rest on love divine,
And with unfaltering lip and heart,
  I call this Saviour mine.

2 His cross dispels each doubt;
  I bury in his tomb
Each thought of unbelief and fear,
  Each lingering shade of gloom.

3 I praise the God of peace;
  I trust his truth and might;
He calls me his, I call him mine,
  My God, my joy, my light.

4 'Tis he who saveth me,
  And freely pardon gives:
I love because he loveth me;
  I live because he lives.

5 My life with him is hid,
  My death has passed away,
My clouds have melted into light,
  My midnight into day.

652   *Purity.*   J. KEBLE.

BLEST are the pure in heart,
  For they shall see their God;
The secret of the Lord is theirs;
  Their soul is Christ's abode.

2 He to the lowly soul
  Doth still himself impart,
And for his dwelling, and his throne,
  Chooseth the pure in heart.

3 Lord! we thy presence seek:
  May ours this blessing be;
Oh, give the pure and lowly heart,—
  A temple meet for thee.

GOOD CHEER. S. M.   T. E. PERKINS.

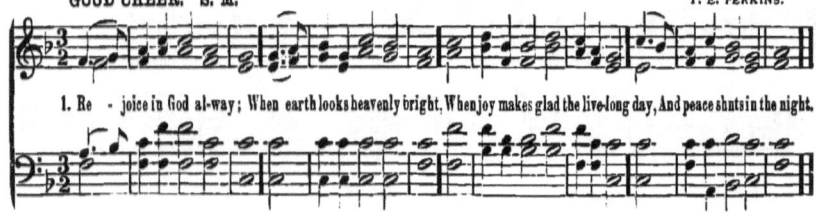

1. Re - joice in God al-way; When earth looks heavenly bright, When joy makes glad the live-long day, And peace shuts in the night.

653   *Joy.*   MOULTRIE.

REJOICE in God alway;
  When earth looks heavenly bright,
When joy makes glad the livelong day,
  And peace shuts in the night.

2 Rejoice when care and woe
  The fainting soul oppress;
When tears at wakeful midnight flow,
  And morn brings heaviness.

3 Rejoice in hope and fear;
  Rejoice in life and death;

Rejoice when threatening storms are near,
  And comfort languisheth.

4 When should not they rejoice,
  Whom Christ his brethren calls,
Who hear and know his guiding voice,
  When on their hearts it falls?

5 So, though our path is steep,
  And many a tempest lowers,
Shall his own peace our spirits keep,
  And Christ's dear love be ours.

CHRISTIAN EXPERIENCE AND GRACES.

VALENTIA. C. M.   GEO. KINGSLEY, arr.

1. Oh, gift of gifts! oh, grace of faith! My God! how can it be
That thou, who hast dis-cern-ing love, Shouldst give that gift to me?

654   *Faith.*   F. W. FABER.

Oh, gift of gifts! oh, grace of faith!
  My God! how can it be
That thou, who hast discerning love,
  Shouldst give that gift to me?

2 How many hearts thou mightst have had
  More innocent than mine!
How many souls more worthy far
  Of that sweet touch of thine!

3 Ah, grace! into unlikeliest hearts
  It is thy boast to come,
The glory of thy light to find
  In darkest spots a home.

4 The crowd of cares, the weightiest cross,
  Seem trifles less than light—
Earth looks so little and so low
  When faith shines full and bright.

5 Oh, happy, happy that I am!
  If thou canst be, O Faith,
The treasure that thou art in life,
  What wilt thou be in death!

655   *Godly sincerity.*   BARTON.

Walk in the light! so shalt thou know
  That fellowship of love,
His Spirit only can bestow,
  Who reigns in light above.

2 Walk in the light! and thou shalt find
  Thy heart made truly his,
Who dwells in cloudless light enshrined,
  In whom no darkness is.

3 Walk in the light! and ev'n the tomb
  No fearful shade shall wear;
Glory shall chase away its gloom,
  For Christ hath conquered there.

4 Walk in the light! and thou shalt see
  Thy path, though thorny, bright,
For God by grace shall dwell in thee,
  And God himself is light.

656   *Faith.*   D. TURNER.

Faith adds new charms to earthly bliss,
  And saves me from its snares;
Its aid, in every duty, brings,
  And softens all my cares.

2 The wounded conscience knows its power
  The healing balm to give;
That balm the saddest heart can cheer;
  And make the dying live.

3 Wide it unvails celestial worlds,
  Where deathless pleasures reign;
And bids me seek my portion there,
  Nor bids me seek in vain.

4 It shows the precious promise sealed
  With the Redeemer's blood;
And helps my feeble hope to rest
  Upon a faithful God.

5 There—there unshaken would I rest,
  Till this frail body dies;
And then, on faith's triumphant wings,
  To endless glory rise.

CHRISTIAN EXPERIENCE AND GRACES.

GRATITUDE. L. M. THOS. HASTINGS, arr.

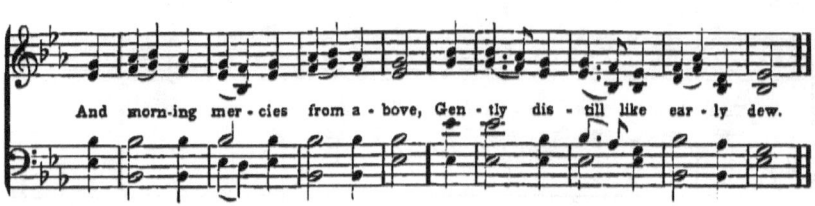

1. My God, how endless is thy love! Thy gifts are every evening new; And morning mercies from above, Gently distill like early dew.

657   *Gratitude.*   I. WATTS.

My God, how endless is thy love!
  Thy gifts are every evening new;
And morning mercies from above,
  Gently distill like early dew.

2 Thou spread'st the curtains of the night,
  Great Guardian of my sleeping hours;
Thy sovereign word restores the light,
  And quickens all my drowsy powers.

3 I yield my powers to thy command;
  To thee I consecrate my days;
Perpetual blessings from thine hand
  Demand perpetual songs of praise.

658   *Faith.*   J. NEWTON.

By faith in Christ I walk with God,
  With heaven, my journey's end, in view;
Supported by his staff and rod,
  My road is safe and pleasant too.

2 Though snares and dangers throng my path,
  And earth and hell my course withstand,
I triumph over all by faith,
  Guarded by his almighty hand.

3 The wilderness affords no food,
  But God for my support prepares,
Provides me every needful good,
  And frees my soul from wants and cares.

4 With him sweet converse I maintain;
  Great as he is, I dare be free;
I tell him all my grief and pain,
  And he reveals his love to me.

659   *Contentment.*   W. COWPER, tr.

O LORD, how full of sweet content
  Our years of pilgrimage are spent!
Where'er we dwell, we dwell with thee,
  In heaven, in earth, or on the sea.

2 To us remains nor place nor time:
  Our country is in every clime:
We can be calm and free from care
  On any shore, since God is there.

3 While place we seek, or place we shun,
  The soul finds happiness in none;
But with our God to guide our way,
  'Tis equal joy to go or stay.

4 Could we be cast where thou art not,
  That were indeed a dreadful lot;
But regions none remote we call,
  Secure of finding God in all.

660   *Voiceless Prayer.*   GREEK HYMN.

O BLESSED God, to thee I raise
  My voice in thankful hymns of praise;
And when my voice shall silent be,
  My silence shall be praise to thee.

2 For voice and silence doth impart
  The filial homage of my heart;
And both alike are understood
  By thee, thou Parent of all good—

3 Whose grace is all unsearchable,
  Whose care for me no tongue can tell,
Who loves my loudest praise to hear,
  And loves to bless my voiceless prayer.

CHRISTIAN EXPERIENCE AND GRACES.

DUKE STREET. L. M. — J. HATTON.

1. 'Tis by the faith of joys to come, We walk through deserts dark as night; Till we arrive at heaven, our home, Faith is our guide, and faith our light.

661 *Faith.* I. WATTS.

'Tis by the faith of joys to come,
  We walk through deserts dark as night;
Till we arrive at heaven, our home,
  Faith is our guide, and faith our light.

2 The want of sight she well supplies;
  She makes the pearly gates appear;
Far into distant worlds she pries,
  And brings eternal glories near.

3 Cheerful we tread the desert through,
  While faith inspires a heavenly ray;
Though lions roar, and tempests blow,
  And rocks and dangers fill the way.

662 *Self-denial.* J. KEBLE.

If on our daily course our mind
  Be set, to hallow all we find,
New treasures still, of countless price,
  God will provide for sacrifice.

2 Old friends, old scenes, will lovelier be,
  As more of heaven in each we see;
Some softening gleam of love and prayer
  Shall dawn on every cross and care.

3 The trivial round, the common task,
  Will furnish all we ought to ask;—
Room to deny ourselves, a road
  To bring us daily nearer God.

4 Only, O Lord, in thy dear love,
  Fit us for perfect rest above;
And help us, this and every day,
  To live more nearly as we pray.

663 *Love.* I. WATTS.

Had I the tongues of Greeks and Jews,
  And nobler speech than angels use,
If love be absent, I am found
  Like tinkling brass, an empty sound.

2 Were I inspired to preach and tell
  All that is done in heaven and hell—
Or could my faith the world remove,
  Still I am nothing without love.

3 Should I distribute all my store
  To feed the hungry, clothe the poor;
Or give my body to the flame,
  To gain a martyr's glorious name:—

4 If love to God and love to men
  Be absent, all my hopes are vain;
Nor tongues, nor gifts, nor fiery zeal,
  The work of love can e'er fulfill.

664 *Consistency.* I. WATTS.

So let our lips and lives express
  The holy gospel we profess;
So let our works and virtues shine,
  To prove the doctrine all divine.

2 Thus shall we best proclaim abroad
  The honors of our Saviour God;
When his salvation reigns within,
  And grace subdues the power of sin.

3 Religion bears our spirits up,
  While we expect that blessed hope,—
The bright appearance of the Lord:
  And faith stands leaning on his word.

665 C. M. *Docility.—Ps.* 131. I. WATTS.

Is there ambition in my heart?
  Search, gracious God, and see;
Or do I act a haughty part?
  Lord, I appeal to thee.

2 I charge my thoughts, be humble still,
  And all my carriage mild;
Content, my Father, with thy will,
  And quiet as a child.

3 The patient soul, the lowly mind,
  Shall have a large reward;
Let saints in sorrow lie resigned,
  And trust a faithful Lord.

666 C. M. *" The Head, even Christ."* C. WESLEY.

BLEST be the dear, uniting love,
  That will not let us part:
Our bodies may far off remove;
  We still are one in heart.

2 Joined in one spirit to our Head,
  Where he appoints we go;
We still in Jesus' footsteps tread,
  And show his praise below.

3 Oh, may we ever walk in him,
  And nothing know beside!
Nothing desire, nothing esteem,
  But Jesus crucified!

4 Partakers of the Saviour's grace,
  The same in mind and heart,
Not joy nor grief nor time nor place
  Nor life nor death can part.

667 C. M. *" Watch and Pray."* T. HASTINGS.

THE Saviour bids thee watch and pray
  Through life's momentous hour;
And grants the Spirit's quickening ray
  To those who seek his power.

2 The Saviour bids thee watch and pray,
  Maintain a warrior's strife;
O Christian! hear his voice to-day:
  Obedience is thy life.

3 The Saviour bids thee watch and pray;
  For soon the hour will come
That calls thee from the earth away
  To thy eternal home.

4 The Saviour bids thee watch and pray,
  Oh, hearken to his voice,
And follow where he leads the way,
  To heaven's eternal joys!

668 L. M. *Living to Christ.* P. DODDRIDGE.

MY gracious Lord, I own thy right
  To every service I can pay,
And call it my supreme delight
  To hear thy dictates and obey.

2 What is my being, but for thee,
  Its sure support, its noblest end?
Thine ever-smiling face to see,
  And serve the cause of such a Friend.

3 I would not breathe for worldly joy,
  Or to increase my worldly good;
Nor future days nor powers employ
  To spread a sounding name abroad.

4 'T is to my Saviour I would live,
  To him who for my ransom died;
Nor could the bowers of Eden give
  Such bliss as blossoms at his side.

5 His work my hoary age shall bless,
  When youthful vigor is no more;
And my last hour of life confess
  His dying love, his saving power.

669 S. M. *Psalm* 103. I. WATTS.

OH, bless the Lord, my soul!
  Let all within me join,
And aid my tongue to bless his name,
  Whose favors are divine.

2 Oh, bless the Lord, my soul,
  Nor let his mercies lie
Forgotten in unthankfulness,
  And without praises die.

3 'T is he forgives thy sins,
  'T is he relieves thy pain,
'T is he that heals thy sicknesses,
  And makes thee young again.

4 He crowns thy life with love,
  When ransomed from the grave;
He that redeemed my soul from hell,
  Hath sovereign power to save.

5 He fills the poor with good;
  He gives the sufferers rest:
The Lord hath judgments for the proud,
  And justice for the oppressed.

6 His wondrous works and ways
  He made by Moses known;
But sent the world his truth and grace
  By his belovéd Son.

670
7s, 6 l.   *Acknowledgment.*   R. M. MC CHEYNE.

Chosen not for good in me,
Waked from coming wrath to flee,
Hidden in the Saviour's side,
By the Spirit sanctified—
Teach me, Lord, on earth to show,
By my love, how much I owe.

2 Oft I walk beneath the cloud,
Dark as midnight's gloomy shroud:
But, when fear is at the height,
Jesus comes, and all is light;
Blessèd Jesus! bid me show
Doubting saints how much I owe.

3 Oft the nights of sorrow reign—
Weeping, sickness, sighing, pain;
But a night thine anger burns—
Morning comes, and joy returns:
God of comforts! bid me show
To thy poor how much I owe.

4 When in flowery paths I tread,
Oft by sin I'm captive led;
Oft I fall, but still arise—
Jesus comes—the tempter flies:
Blessèd Jesus! bid me show
Weary sinners all I owe.

671
C. M.   *Psalm* 34.   TATE-BRADY.

Through all the changing scenes of life,
  In trouble, and in joy,
The praises of my God shall still
  My heart and tongue employ.

2 Of his deliverance I will boast,
  Till all, who are distressed,
From my example comfort take,
  And charm their griefs to rest.

3 Oh, magnify the Lord with me,
  With me exalt his name!
When in distress to him I called,
  He to my rescue came.

4 The hosts of God encamp around
  The dwellings of the just;
Deliverance he affords to all,
  Who on his succor trust.

5 Oh, make but trial of his love;
  Experience will decide,
How blest are they, and only they,
  Who in his truth confide.

672
7s.   *Psalm* 131.   C. WESLEY.

Lord, if thou thy grace impart,
Poor in spirit, meek in heart,
I shall as my Master be,—
Rooted in humility!

2 Simple, teachable, and mild,
Changed into a little child;
Pleased with all the Lord provides,
Weaned from all the world besides.

3 Father, fix my soul on thee;
Every evil let me flee;
Nothing want, beneath, above,
Happy in thy precious love.

4 Oh, that all may seek and find
Every good in Jesus joined!
Him let Israel still adore,
Trust him, praise him evermore.

673
S. M.   *Phil.* 2: 13.   ANON.

Heirs of unending life,
  While yet we sojourn here,
Oh, let us our salvation work
  With trembling and with fear.

2 God will support our hearts,
  With might before unknown;
The work to be performed is ours,
  The strength is all his own.

3 'T is he that works to will,
  'T is he that works to do;
His is the power by which we act,
  His be the glory too!

674
L. M.   "*Of one heart.*"   A. L. BARBAULD.

How blest the sacred tie that binds,
In union sweet, according minds!
How swift the heavenly course they run,
Whose hearts and faith and hopes are one.

2 To each the soul of each how dear!
What jealous care, what holy fear!
How doth the generous flame within,
Refine from earth and cleanse from sin!

3 Their streaming tears together flow,
For human guilt and human woe;
Their ardent prayers united rise,
Like mingling flames in sacrifice.

4 Nor shall the glowing flame expire
'Mid nature's drooping, sickening fire:
Soon shall they meet in realms above—
A heaven of joy, because of love.

PRIVILEGES OF BELIEVERS.

BLOOMFIELD CHANT. L. M.
W. B. BRADBURY.

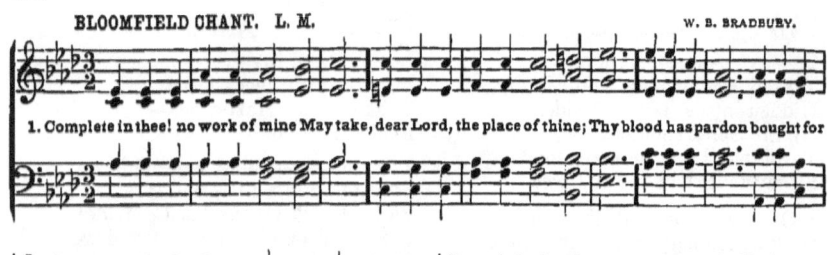

1. Complete in thee! no work of mine May take, dear Lord, the place of thine; Thy blood has pardon bought for

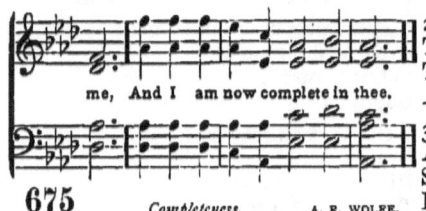

me, And I am now complete in thee.

675   *Completeness.*   A. R. WOLFE.

COMPLETE in thee! no work of mine
May take, dear Lord, the place of thine;
Thy blood has pardon bought for me,
And I am now complete in thee.

2 Complete in thee—no more shall sin,
Thy grace has conquered, reign within;
Thy voice will bid the tempter flee,
And I shall stand complete in thee.

3 Complete in thee—each want supplied,
And no good thing to me denied,
Since thou my portion, Lord, wilt be,
I ask no more—complete in thee.

4 Dear Saviour! when, before thy bar,
All tribes and tongues assembled are,
Among thy chosen may I be
At thy right hand—complete in thee.

SPOHR. L. M.
FROM L. SPOHR.

1. Not all the no-bles of the earth, Who boast the hon-ors of their birth, So high a dig-ni-ty can claim, As those who bear the Chris-tian name.

676   *Adoption.*   S. STENNETT.

NOT all the nobles of the earth,
Who boast the honors of their birth,
So high a dignity can claim,
As those who bear the Christian name.

2 To them the privilege is given
To be the sons and heirs of heaven;
Sons of the God who reigns on high,
And heirs of joy beyond the sky.

3 His will he makes them early know,
And teaches their young feet to go;
Whispers instruction to their minds,
And on their hearts his precepts binds.

4 Their daily wants his hands supply,
Their steps he guards with watchful eye;
Leads them from earth to heaven above,
And crowns them with eternal love.

PRIVILEGES OF BELIEVERS.

WARRINGTON. L. M. — R. HARRISON.

1. Lord, how secure and blest are they Who feel the joys of pardoned sin! Should storms of wrath shake earth and sea, Their minds have heaven and peace within.

677 *Security and rest.* I. WATTS.

LORD, how secure and blest are they
  Who feel the joys of pardoned sin!
Should storms of wrath shake earth and sea,
  Their minds have heaven and peace within.

2 The day glides sweetly o'er their heads,
  Made up of innocence and love;
And soft and silent as the shades,
  Their nightly minutes gently move

3 Quick as their thoughts their joys come on,
  But fly not half so swift away:
Their souls are ever bright as noon,
  And calm as summer evenings be.

4 How oft they look to heavenly hills,
  Where streams of living pleasures flow;
And longing hopes and cheerful smiles
  Sit undisturbed upon their brow!

5 They scorn to seek earth's golden toys,
  But spend the day, and share the night,
In numbering o'er the richer joys
  That heaven prepares for their delight.

678 *Remembrance.* J. BOWRING.

EARTH's transitory things decay;
  Its pomps, its pleasures pass away;
But the sweet memory of the good
  Survives in the vicissitude.

2 As, 'mid the ever-rolling sea,
  The eternal isles established be,
'Gainst which the surges of the main
  Fret, dash, and break themselves in vain;—

3 As in the heavens, the urns divine
  Of golden light for ever shine;
Tho' clouds may darken, storms may rage,
  They still shine on from age to age;—

4 So, through the ocean tide of years,
  The memory of the just appears;
So, through the tempest and the gloom,
  The good man's virtues light the tomb.

679 *Perseverance.* I. WATTS.

WHO shall the Lord's elect condemn?
  'Tis God who justifies their souls;
And mercy, like a mighty stream,
  O'er all their sins divinely rolls.

2 Who shall adjudge the saints to hell?
  'Tis Christ who suffered in their stead;
And their salvation to fulfill,
  Behold him rising from the dead!

3 He lives! he lives! and sits above,
  For ever interceding there:
Who shall divide us from his love,
  Or what shall tempt us to despair?

4 Shall persecution or distress,
  Famine, or sword, or nakedness?
He who hath loved us bears us through,
  And makes us more than conquerors too.

5 Not all that men on earth can do,
  Nor powers on high, nor powers below,
Shall cause his mercy to remove,
  Or wean our hearts from Christ, our love.

PRIVILEGES OF BELIEVERS.

BRIDGMAN. C. M. GEO. KINGSLEY, arr.

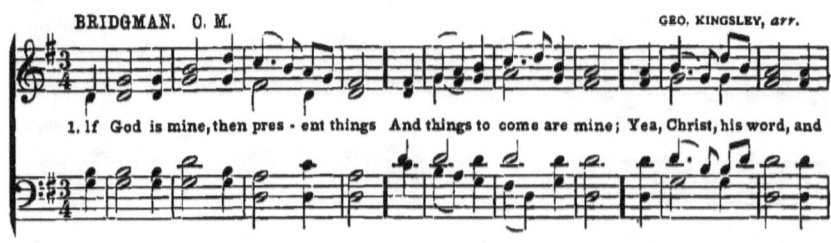

1. If God is mine, then pres-ent things And things to come are mine; Yea, Christ, his word, and

Spir-it too, And glo-ry all divine.

Sure he who giveth me himself
Is more than these to me.
4 Oh, tell me, Lord, that thou art mine;
What can I wish beside?
My soul shall at the fountain live,
When all the streams are dried.

680 "*Saints' Inventory.*" B. BEDDOME.

If God is mine, then present things
And things to come are mine;
Yea, Christ, his word, and Spirit too,
And glory all divine.
2 If he is mine, then from his love
He every trouble sends;
All things are working for my good,
And bliss his rod attends.
3 If he is mine, let friends forsake,
Let wealth and honor flee:

681 *Perseverance.* I. WATTS.

Firm as the earth thy gospel stands,
My Lord, my hope, my trust;
If I am found in Jesus' hands,
My soul can ne'er be lost.
2 His honor is engaged to save
The meanest of his sheep;
All, whom his heavenly Father gave,
His hands securely keep.
3 Nor death nor hell shall e'er remove
His favorites from his breast;
In the dear bosom of his love
They must for ever rest.

BROWN. C. M. W. B. BRADBURY.

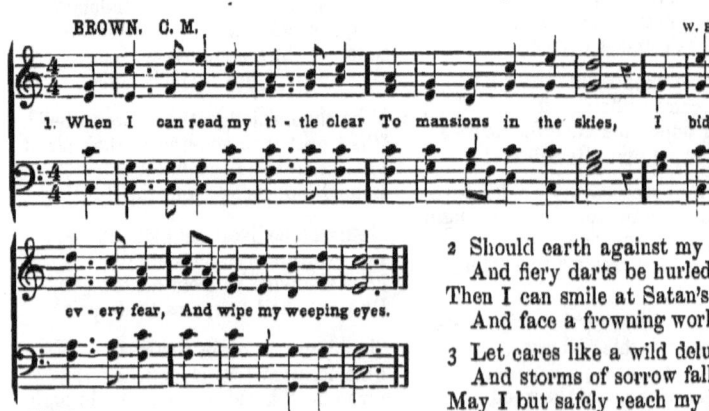

1. When I can read my ti-tle clear To mansions in the skies, I bid farewell to
ev-ery fear, And wipe my weeping eyes.

2 Should earth against my soul engage,
And fiery darts be hurled,
Then I can smile at Satan's rage,
And face a frowning world.
3 Let cares like a wild deluge come,
And storms of sorrow fall,
May I but safely reach my home,
My God, my heaven, my all!—

682 *Assurance.* I. WATTS.

When I can read my title clear
To mansions in the skies,
I bid farewell to every fear,
And wipe my weeping eyes.

4 There shall I bathe my weary soul
In seas of heavenly rest;
And not a wave of trouble roll
Across my peaceful breast.

PRIVILEGES OF BELIEVERS.

683 *Security.* H. F. LYTE.

There is a safe and secret place,
  Beneath the wings divine,
Reserved for all the heirs of grace,—
  Oh, be that refuge mine!

2 The least and feeblest there may bide,
  Uninjured and unawed;
While thousands fall on every side,
  He rests secure in God.

3 He feeds in pastures large and fair,
  Of love and truth divine;
O child of God, O glory's heir!
  How rich a lot is thine!

4 A hand almighty to defend,
  An ear for every call,
An honored life, a peaceful end,
  And heaven to crown it all!

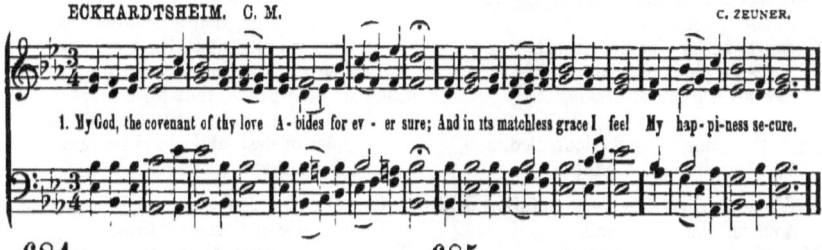

684 *The Covenant.* P. DODDRIDGE.

My God, the covenant of thy love
  Abides for ever sure;
And in its matchless grace I feel
  My happiness secure.

2 Since thou, the everlasting God,
  My Father art become,
Jesus my Guardian and my Friend,
  And heaven my final home;—

3 I welcome all thy sovereign will,
  For all that will is love;
And when I know not what thou dost,
  I wait the light above.

685 *Adoption.* P. DODDRIDGE.

My Father, God! how sweet the sound!
  How tender and how dear!
Not all the melody of heaven
  Could so delight the ear.

2 Come, sacred Spirit, seal the name
  On my expanding heart;
And show, that in Jehovah's grace
  I share a filial part.

3 Cheered by a signal so divine,
  Unwavering I believe;
My spirit Abba, Father! cries,
  Nor can the sign deceive.

PRIVILEGES OF BELIEVERS.

GREENPORT. C. M. D.   FROM S. THALBERG.

1. Thou art my hid-ing-place, O Lord! In thee I put my trust; En-couraged by thy ho-ly word, A fee-ble child of dust: I have no ar-gu-ment be-side, I urge no oth-er plea; And 'tis enough my Saviour died, My Saviour died for me!

686 *Hiding-place.* T. RAFFLES.

Thou art my hiding-place, O Lord!
 In thee I put my trust;
Encouraged by thy holy word,
 A feeble child of dust:
I have no argument beside,
 I urge no other plea;
And 'tis enough my Saviour died,
 My Saviour died for me!

2 When storms of fierce temptation beat,
 And furious foes assail,
My refuge is the mercy-seat,
 My hope within the vail:
From strife of tongues, and bitter words,
 My spirit flies to thee;
Joy to my heart the thought affords,
 My Saviour died for me!

3 And when thine awful voice commands
 This body to decay,
And life in its last lingering sands,
 Is ebbing fast away;—
Then, though it be in accents weak,
 My voice shall call on thee,
And ask for strength in death to speak,
 "My Saviour died for me."

687 *Union to Christ.* J. G. DECK.

Lord Jesus, are we one with thee?
 Oh, height! oh, depth of love!
With thee we died upon the tree,
 In thee we live above.
Such was thy grace, that for our sake
 Thou didst from heaven come down,
Thou didst of flesh and blood partake,
 In all our sorrows one.

2 Our sins, our guilt, in love divine,
 Confessed and borne by thee;
The gall, the curse, the wrath, were thine,
 To set thy members free.
Ascended now, in glory bright,
 Still one with us thou art;
Nor life, nor death, nor depth, nor height,
 Thy saints and thee can part.

3 Oh, teach us, Lord, to know and own
 This wondrous mystery,
That thou with us art truly one,
 And we are one with thee!
Soon, soon shall come that glorious day,
 When, seated on thy throne,
Thou shalt to wondering worlds display,
 That thou with us art one.

PRIVILEGES OF BELIEVERS.

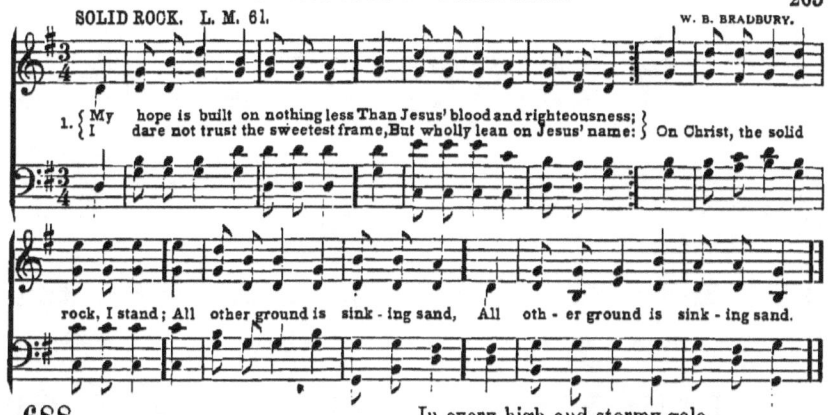

688 *In Christ alone.* E. MOTE.

My hope is built on nothing less
Than Jesus' blood and righteousness;
I dare not trust the sweetest frame,
But wholly lean on Jesus' name:
  On Christ, the solid rock, I stand;
  All other ground is sinking sand.

2 When darkness seems to vail his face,
I rest on his unchanging grace;
In every high and stormy gale,
My anchor holds within the vail;
  On Christ, the solid rock, I stand;
  All other ground is sinking sand.

3 His oath, his covenant, and blood,
Support me in the whelming flood:
When all around my soul gives way,
He then is all my hope and stay:
  On Christ, the solid rock, I stand;
  All other ground is sinking sand.

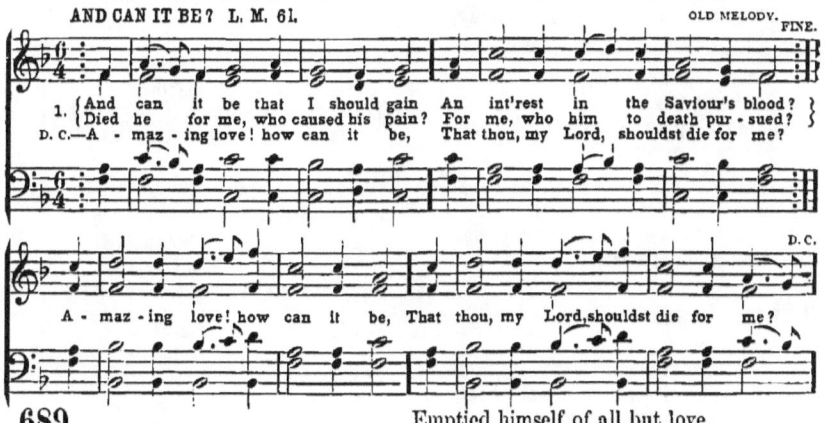

689 *"No condemnation."* C. WESLEY.

And can it be that I should gain
  An interest in the Saviour's blood?
Died he for me, who caused his pain?
  For me, who him to death pursued?
Amazing love! how can it be,
That thou, my Lord, shouldst die for me?

2 He left his Father's throne above;
  (So free, so infinite his grace!)
Emptied himself of all but love,
  And bled for Adam's helpless race;
'Tis mercy all, immense and free,
For, O my God, it found out me!

3 No condemnation now I dread,—
  Jesus, with all in him, is mine;
Alive in him, my living Head,
  And clothed in righteousness divine,
Bold I approach the eternal throne,
And claim the crown, thro' Christ my own.

PRIVILEGES OF BELIEVERS.

LUTHER. S. M. THOS. HASTINGS.

1. Grace! 'tis a charm-ing sound! Harmonious to mine ear! Heav'n with the ech - o shall resound, And all the earth shall hear, And all the earth shall hear.

690 *Grace.* P. DODDRIDGE.

Grace! 'tis a charming sound!
  Harmonious to mine ear!
Heaven with the echo shall resound,
  And all the earth shall hear.

2 Grace first contrived a way
  To save rebellious man;
And all the steps that grace display,
  Which drew the wondrous plan.

3 Grace led my roving feet
  To tread the heavenly road;
And new supplies each hour I meet
  While pressing on to God.

4 Grace all the work shall crown,
  Through everlasting days;
It lays in heaven the topmost stone,
  And well deserves the praise.

691 *God our Father.* C. WINKWORTH, tr.

Here I can firmly rest;
  I dare to boast of this,
That God, the highest and the best,
  My Friend and Father is.

2 Naught have I of my own,
  Naught in the life I lead;
What Christ hath given, that alone
  I dare in faith to plead.

3 I rest upon the ground
  Of Jesus and his blood;
It is through him that I have found
  My soul's eternal good.

4 At cost of all I have,
  At cost of life and limb,
I cling to God who yet shall save;
  I will not turn from him.

5 His Spirit in me dwells,
  O'er all my mind he reigns;
My care and sadness he dispels,
  And soothes away my pains.

6 He prospers day by day
  His work within my heart,
Till I have strength and faith to say,
  "Thou, God, my Father art!"

692 *"It is well."* J. KENT.

What cheering words are these;
  Their sweetness who can tell?
In time, and to eternal days,
  "'Tis with the righteous well!"

2 Well when they see his face,
  Or sink amidst the flood;
Well in affliction's thorny maze,
  Or on the mount with God.

3 'Tis well when joys arise,
  'Tis well when sorrows flow,
'Tis well when darkness vails the skies,
  And strong temptations grow.

4 'Tis well when Jesus calls,—
  "From earth and sin arise,
To join the hosts of ransomed souls,
  Made to salvation wise!"

PRIVILEGES OF BELIEVERS.

FERGUSON. S. M. GEO. KINGSLEY.

1. Behold what wondrous grace The Father has bestowed On sinners of a mortal race, To call them sons of God!

693 *Adoption.* I. WATTS.

BEHOLD! what wondrous grace
　The Father has bestowed
On sinners of a mortal race,
　To call them sons of God!

2 Nor doth it yet appear
　How great we must be made;
But when we see our Saviour here,
　We shall be like our Head.

3 A hope so much divine
　May trials well endure,
May purge our souls from sense and sin,
　As Christ the Lord is pure.

4 If in my Father's love
　I share a filial part,
Send down thy Spirit, like a dove,
　To rest upon my heart.

5 We would no longer lie
　Like slaves beneath the throne;
Our faith shall Abba, Father! cry,
　And thou the kindred own.

694 *Peace.* C. WESLEY.

THOU very present Aid
　In suffering and distress,
The mind which still on thee is stayed,
　Is kept in perfect peace.

2 The soul by faith reclined
　On the Redeemer's breast,
'Mid raging storms, exults to find
　An everlasting rest.

3 Sorrow and fear are gone,
　Whene'er thy face appears;
It stills the sighing orphan's moan,
　And dries the widow's tears.

4 Jesus, to whom I fly,
　Doth all my wishes fill;
What though created streams are dry?
　I have the fountain still.

5 Stripped of each earthly friend,
　I find them all in One,
And peace and joy which never end,
　And heaven, in Christ, alone.

THATCHER. S. M. FROM G. F. HANDEL.

1. Thou very present Aid In suffering and distress, The mind which still on thee is stayed, Is kept in perfect peace.

695 L. M. *Psalm 91.* I. WATTS.

He that hath made his refuge God,
  Shall find a most secure abode;
Shall walk all day beneath his shade,
  And there, at night, shall rest his head.

2 Then will I say, "My God! thy power
  Shall be my fortress and my tower;
I, who am formed of feeble dust,
  Make thine almighty arm my trust."

3 Thrice happy man! thy Maker's care
  Shall keep thee from the fowler's snare;—
Satan, the fowler, who betrays
  Unguarded souls a thousand ways.

4 If burning beams of noon conspire
  To dart a pestilential fire;
God is thy life,—his wings are spread,
  To shield thee with a healthful shade.

5 If vapors, with malignant breath,
  Rise thick and scatter midnight death,
Israel is safe, the poisoned air
  Grows pure, if Israel's God be there.

696 L. M. *Psalm 85.* I. WATTS.

Salvation is for ever nigh
  The souls that fear and trust the Lord;
And grace, descending from on high,
  Fresh hopes of glory shall afford.

2 Mercy and truth on earth are met,
  Since Christ, the Lord, came down from
By his obedience so complete   [heaven;
  Justice is pleased, and peace is given.

3 Now truth and honor shall abound,
  Religion dwell on earth again,
And heavenly influence bless the ground
  In our Redeemer's gentle reign.

4 His righteousness is gone before,
  To give us free access to God;
Our wandering feet shall stray no more,
  But mark his steps and keep the road.

697 C. M. *God's Peace.* ANON.

We bless thee for thy peace, O God!
  Deep as the soundless sea,
Which falls like sunshine on the road
  Of those who trust in thee.

2 We ask not, Father, for repose
  Which comes from outward rest,
If we may have through all life's woes
  Thy peace within our breast;—

3 That peace which suffers and is strong,
  Trusts where it cannot see,
Deems not the trial way too long,
  But leaves the end with thee;—

4 That peace which flows serene and
  A river in the soul,   [deep—
Whose banks a living verdure keep:
  God's sunshine o'er the whole!

5 Such, Father, give our hearts such
  Whate'er the outward be,   [peace,
Till all life's discipline shall cease,
  And we go home to thee.

698 8s, 7s, D. *The Pilgrim.* T. HASTINGS.

Gently, Lord, oh, gently lead us,
  Through this lonely vale of tears;
Through the changes thou'st decreed us,
  Till our last great change appears.
When temptation's darts assail us,
  When in devious paths we stray,
Let thy goodness never fail us,
  Lead us in thy perfect way.

2 In the hour of pain and anguish,
  In the hour when death draws near,
Suffer not our hearts to languish,
  Suffer not our souls to fear.
And when mortal life is ended,
  Bid us in thine arms to rest,
Till, by angel bands attended,
  We awake among the blest.

699 S. M. *Psalm 61.* I. WATTS.

When, overwhelmed with grief,
  My heart within me dies;
Helpless, and far from all relief,
  To heaven I lift mine eyes.

2 Oh, lead me to the rock,
  That's high above my head;
And make the covert of thy wings
  My shelter and my shade.

3 Within thy presence, Lord;
  For ever I'll abide;
Thou art the tower of my defence,
  The refuge where I hide.

4 Thou givest me the lot
  Of those that fear thy name;
If endless life be their reward,
  I shall possess the same.

700 L. M. 6 l. *"Thy boundless love."* J. WESLEY, *tr.*

Jesus, thy boundless love to me
  No thought can reach, no tongue declare;
Oh, knit my thankful heart to thee,
  And reign without a rival there:
Thine wholly, thine alone, I am;
Be thou alone my constant flame.

2 Oh, grant that nothing in my soul
  May dwell, but thy pure love alone:
Oh, may thy love possess me whole,—
  My joy, my treasure, and my crown:
Strange flames far from my heart remove;
My every act, word, thought, be love.

3 O Love! how cheering is thy ray!
  All pain before thy presence flies;
Care, anguish, sorrow, melt away,
  Where'er thy healing beams arise:
O Jesus! nothing may I see,
Nothing desire, or seek but thee!

701 H. M. *Protection.—Psalm* 121. I. WATTS.

Upward I lift mine eyes,
  From God is all my aid;
The God who built the skies,
  And earth and nature made:
God is the tower | His grace is nigh
To which I fly; | In every hour.

2 My feet shall never slide,
  Nor fall in fatal snares,
Since God, my guard and guide,
  Defends me from my fears:
Those wakeful eyes | Shall Israel keep
That never sleep, | When dangers rise.

3 No burning heats by day,
  Nor blasts of evening air,
Shall take my health away,
  If God be with me there;
Thou art my sun, | To guard my head
And thou my shade, | By night or noon.

4 Hast thou not given thy word
  To save my soul from death?
And I can trust my Lord
  To keep my mortal breath:
I'll go and come, | Till, from on high
Nor fear to die, | Thou call me home.

702 L. M. *At Jesus' Feet.* MRS. E. REED.

Oh, that I could for ever dwell,
  Delighted at the Saviour's feet;
Behold the form I love so well,
  And all his tender words repeat!

2 The world shut out from all my soul,
  And heaven brought in with all its bliss,—
Oh! is there aught, from pole to pole,
  One moment to compare with this?

3 This is the hidden life I prize—
  A life of penitential love;
When most my follies I despise,
  And raise my highest thoughts above;

4 When all I am I clearly see,
  And freely own, with deepest shame;
When the Redeemer's love to me
  Kindles within a deathless flame.

5 Thus would I live till nature fail,
  And all my former sins forsake;
Then rise to God within the vail,
  And of eternal joys partake.

703 C. M. *Our Father.—Psalm* 31. A. STEELE.

My God, my Father!—blissful name!
  Oh, may I call thee mine?
May I, with sweet assurance, claim
  A portion so divine?

2 This only can my fears control,
  And bid my sorrows fly:
What harm can ever reach my soul,
  Beneath my Father's eye?

3 Whate'er thy providence denies,
  I calmly would resign
For thou art just, and good, and wise;
  Oh, bend my will to thine.

4 Whate'er thy sacred will ordains,
  Oh, give me strength to bear;
And let me know my Father reigns,
  And trust his tender care.

5 If pain and sickness rend this frame,
  And life almost depart,
Is not thy mercy still the same,
  To cheer my drooping heart?

6 My God, my Father! be thy name
  My solace and my stay;
Oh, wilt thou seal my humble claim,
  And drive my fears away?

DISCIPLINE AND SORROW.

PALESTINE. L. M. 6l. — J. MAZZINGHI.

1. Peace, troubled soul, whose plaintive moan Hath taught each scene the notes of woe;
Cease thy complaint, suppress thy groan, And let thy tears forget to flow;
Behold, the precious balm is found, To lull thy pain, to heal thy wound.

704 "Balm in Gilead." W. SHIRLEY.

PEACE, troubled soul, whose plaintive moan
Hath taught each scene the notes of woe,
Cease thy complaint, suppress thy groan,
And let thy tears forget to flow;
Behold, the precious balm is found,
To lull thy pain, to heal thy wound.

2 Come, freely come, by sin oppressed;
On Jesus, cast thy weighty load;
In him thy refuge find, thy rest,
Safe in the mercy of thy God;
Thy God's thy Saviour—glorious word!
For ever love and praise the Lord.

705 "Eben-ezer." J. NEWTON.

BE still, my heart! these anxious cares
To thee are burdens, thorns, and snares;
They cast dishonor on thy Lord,
And contradict his gracious word;
Brought safely by his hand thus far,
Why wilt thou now give place to fear?

2 When first before his mercy-seat
Thou didst to him thy all commit,
He gave thee warrant from that hour
To trust his wisdom, love, and power:
Did ever trouble yet befall
And he refuse to hear thy call?

3 He who has helped thee hitherto,
Will help thee all thy journey through;
Though rough and thorny be the road,
It leads thee home, apace, to God;
Then count thy present trials small,
For heaven will make amends for all.

706 "As thy days." L. H. SIGOURNEY.

WHEN adverse winds and waves arise,
And in my heart despondence sighs;
When life her throng of cares reveals,
And weakness o'er my spirit steals,
Grateful I hear the kind decree,
That "as my day, my strength shall be."

2 One trial more must yet be past,
One pang—the keenest and the last;
And when, with brow convulsed and pale,
My feeble, quivering heart-strings fail,
Redeemer! grant my soul to see
That "as my day, my strength shall be."

DISCIPLINE AND SORROW. 271

HANDY. L. M. 6l. J. P. HOLBROOK.

1. At evening time let there be light; Life's little day draws near its close; A-round me fall the shades of night, The night of death, the grave's repose; To crown my joys, to end my woes, At evening time let there be light.

707   *"At evening time."*   ANON.

At evening time let there be light;
 Life's little day draws near its close;
Around me fall the shades of night,
 The night of death, the grave's repose;
To crown my joys, to end my woes,
At evening time let there be light.

2 At evening time let there be light;
 Stormy and dark hath been my day—
Yet rose the morn divinely bright;
 Dews, birds, and blossoms cheered the way;—
Oh, for one sweet, one parting ray!
At evening time let there be light.

3 At evening time there shall be light!
 For God hath spoken; it must be;
Fear, doubt, and anguish take their flight;
 His glory now is risen on me;
Mine eyes shall his salvation see;
'T is evening time, and there is light!

708   *"Jesus wept."*   R. GRANT.

WHEN gathering clouds around I view,
And days are dark, and friends are few,
On him I lean, who, not in vain,
Experienced every human pain;
He sees my wants, allays my fears,
And counts and treasures up my tears.

2 If aught should tempt my soul to stray
From heavenly virtue's narrow way,—
To fly the good I would pursue,
Or do the sin I would not do,—
Still he, who felt temptation's power,
Shall guard me in that dangerous hour.

3 When sorrowing o'er some stone, I bend,
Which covers all that was a friend,
And from his voice, his hand, his smile,
Divides me, for a little while,
My Saviour sees the tears I shed,
For Jesus wept o'er Lazarus dead.

4 And, oh, when I have safely passed
Through every conflict, but the last,—
Still, still unchanging, watch beside
My painful bed,—for thou hast died;
Then point to realms of cloudless day,
And wipe my latest tear away.

DISCIPLINE AND SORROW.

709 *Thanks for all.* J. CREWDSON.

O THOU, whose bounty fills my cup
   With every blessing meet!
I give thee thanks for every drop—
   The bitter and the sweet.

2 I praise thee for the desert road,
   And for the river-side;
For all thy goodness hath bestowed,
   And all thy grace denied.

3 I thank thee for both smile and frown,
   And for the gain and loss;
I praise thee for the future crown,
   And for the present cross.

4 I thank thee for the wing of love,
   Which stirred my worldly nest;
And for the stormy clouds which drove
   The flutterer to thy breast.

5 I bless thee for the glad increase,
   And for the waning joy;
And for this strange, this settled peace,
   Which nothing can destroy.

710 *"I firmly trust."* J. MONTGOMERY.

ONE prayer I have—all prayers in one—
   When I am wholly thine;
Thy will, my God, thy will be done,
   And let that will be mine.

2 All-wise, almighty, and all-good,
   In thee I firmly trust;
Thy ways, unknown or understood,
   Are merciful and just.

3 May I remember that to thee
   Whate'er I have I owe;
And back, in gratitude, from me
   May all thy bounties flow.

4 And though thy wisdom takes away,
   Shall I arraign thy will?
No, let me bless thy name, and say,
   "The Lord is gracious still."

5 A pilgrim through the earth I roam,
   Of nothing long possessed;
And all must fail when I go home,
   For this is not my rest.

711 *"Sweet to lie passive."* A. M. TOPLADY.

WHEN languor and disease invade
   This trembling house of clay,
'Tis sweet to look beyond my pain,
   And long to fly away;—

2 Sweet to look inward, and attend
   The whispers of his love;
Sweet to look upward to the place
   Where Jesus pleads above;—

3 Sweet on his faithfulness to rest,
   Whose love can never end;
Sweet on his covenant of grace
   For all things to depend;—

4 Sweet, in the confidence of faith,
   To trust his firm decrees;
Sweet to lie passive in his hands,
   And know no will but his.

DISCIPLINE AND SORROW.

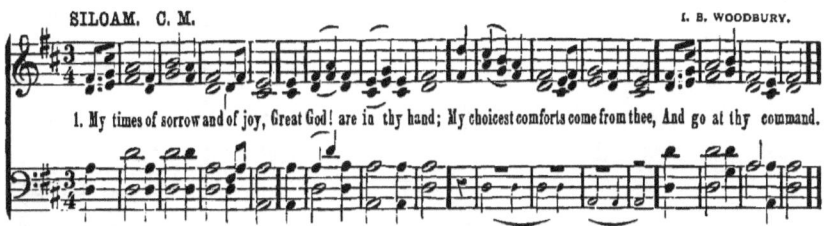

SILOAM. C. M. — I. B. WOODBURY.

1. My times of sorrow and of joy, Great God! are in thy hand; My choicest comforts come from thee, And go at thy command.

712   *"My times."*   B. BEDDOME.

My times of sorrow and of joy,
  Great God! are in thy hand;
My choicest comforts come from thee,
  And go at thy command.

2 If thou shouldst take them all away,
  Yet would I not repine;
Before they were possessed by me,
  They were entirely thine.

3 Nor would I drop a murmuring word,
  Though the whole world were gone,
But seek enduring happiness,
  In thee, and thee alone.

713   *A pierced hand.*   J. EDMESTON.

O THOU, whose mercy guides my way,
  Though now it seems severe,
Forbid my unbelief to say
  There is no mercy here!

2 Oh, may I, Lord, desire the pain
  That comes in kindness down,
Far more than sweetest earthly gain,
  Succeeded by a frown.

3 Then though thou bend my spirit low,
  Love only shall I see;
The gracious hand that strikes the blow,
  Was wounded once for me.

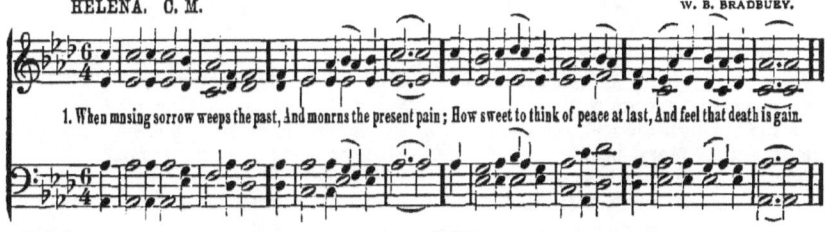

HELENA. C. M. — W. B. BRADBURY.

1. When musing sorrow weeps the past, And mourns the present pain; How sweet to think of peace at last, And feel that death is gain.

714   *"To die is gain."*   G. T. NOEL.

WHEN musing sorrow weeps the past,
  And mourns the present pain;
How sweet to think of peace at last,
  And feel that death is gain!

2 'Tis not that murmuring thoughts arise,
  And dread a Father's will;
'Tis not that meek submission flies,
  And would not suffer still.

3 It is that heaven-born faith surveys
  The path that leads to light,
And longs her eagle plumes to raise,
  And lose herself in sight.

4 Oh, let me wing my hallowed flight
  From earth-born woe and care,
And soar above these clouds of night,
  My Saviour's bliss to share!

715   *"It is I."*   C. ELLIOTT.

WHEN waves of trouble round me swell,
  My soul is not dismayed;
I hear a voice I know full well,—
  "'T is I; be not afraid."

2 When black the threatening skies appear,
  And storms my path invade,
Those accents tranquilize each fear,—
  "'T is I; be not afraid."

3 There is a gulf that must be crossed:
  Saviour, be near to aid!
Whisper, when my frail bark is tossed,—
  "'T is I; be not afraid."

4 There is a dark and fearful vale,
  Death hides within its shade;
Oh, say, when flesh and heart shall fail,—
  "'T is I; be not afraid."

DISCIPLINE AND SORROW.

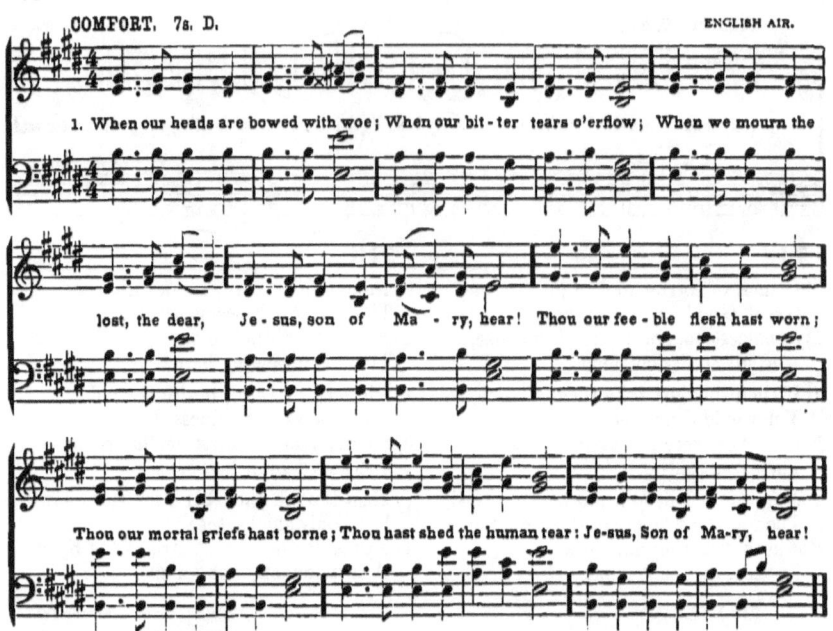

COMFORT. 7s, D. — ENGLISH AIR.

1. When our heads are bowed with woe; When our bitter tears o'erflow; When we mourn the lost, the dear, Jesus, son of Mary, hear! Thou our feeble flesh hast worn; Thou our mortal griefs hast borne; Thou hast shed the human tear: Jesus, Son of Mary, hear!

716   *"Son of Mary."*   H. H. MILMAN.

WHEN our heads are bowed with woe;—
When our bitter tears o'erflow;—
When we mourn the lost, the dear,
Jesus, Son of Mary, hear!
Thou our feeble flesh hast worn;
Thou our mortal griefs hast borne;
Thou hast shed the human tear:
Jesus, Son of Mary, hear!

2 When the heart is sad within,
With the thought of all its sin;
When the spirit shrinks with fear,
Jesus, son of Mary, hear!
Thou the shame, the grief hast known;
Though the sins were not thine own,
Thou hast deigned their load to bear:
Jesus, Son of Mary, hear!

3 When our eyes grow dim in death;
When we heave the parting breath;
When our solemn doom is near,
Jesus, Son of Mary, hear!
Thou hast bowed the dying head;
Thou the blood of life hast shed;
Thou hast filled a mortal bier:
Jesus, Son of Mary, hear!

717   *Looking to Jesus.*   J. G. DECK.

When along life's thorny road,
Faints the soul beneath the load,
By its cares and sins oppressed,
Finds on earth no peace or rest;
When the wily tempter's near,
Filling us with doubt and fear:
Jesus, to thy feet we flee,
Jesus, we will look to thee.

2 Thou, our Saviour, from the throne
List'nest to thy people's moan;
Thou, the living Head, dost share
Every pang thy members bear;
Full of tenderness thou art,
Thou wilt heal the broken heart;
Full of power, thine arm shall quell
All the rage and might of hell.

3 Mighty to redeem and save,
Thou hast overcome the grave;
Thou the bars of death hast riven,
Opened wide the gates of heaven;
Soon in glory thou shalt come,
Taking thy poor pilgrims home;
Jesus, then we all shall be,
Ever—ever—Lord, with thee.

DISCIPLINE AND SORROW. 275

MERCY. 7s.   E. P. PARKER, arr.

1. In the dark and cloud-y day, When earth's rich-es flee a-way,
And the last hope will not stay, Sav-iour, com-fort, com-fort me!

718   *Comfort.*   G. RAWSON.

In the dark and cloudy day,
When earth's riches flee away,
And the last hope will not stay,
  Saviour, comfort me!

2 When the secret idol's gone
That my poor heart yearned upon,—
Desolate, bereft, alone,
  Saviour, comfort me!

3 Thou, who wast so sorely tried,
In the darkness crucified,
Bid me in thy love confide;
  Saviour, comfort me!

4 Comfort me; I am cast down:
'Tis my heavenly Father's frown;
I deserve it all, I own:
  Saviour, comfort me!

5 So it shall be good for me
Much afflicted now to be,
If thou wilt but tenderly,
  Saviour, comfort me!

719   *"For he careth."*   W. HAMMOND.

Cast thy burden on the Lord,
Only lean upon his word;
Thou wilt soon have cause to bless
His unchanging faithfulness.

2 He sustains thee by his hand,
He enables thee to stand;
Those, whom Jesus once hath loved,
From his grace are never moved.

3 Heaven and earth may pass away,
God's free grace shall not decay;
He hath promised to fulfill
All the pleasure of his will.

4 Jesus! guardian of thy flock,
Be thyself our constant rock;
Make us by thy powerful hand,
Firm as Zion's mountain stand.

720   *Love seen in trials.*   W. COWPER.

'Tis my happiness below
  Not to live without the cross,
But the Saviour's power to know,
  Sanctifying every loss.

2 Trials must and will befall;
  But with humble faith to see
Love inscribed upon them all,—
  This is happiness to me.

3 God in Israel sows the seeds
  Of affliction, pain and toil;
These spring up and choke the weeds
  Which would else o'erspread the soil.

4 Did I meet no trials here,
  No chastisement by the way,
Might I not with reason fear
  I should prove a castaway?

5 Trials make the promise sweet;
  Trials give new life to prayer;
Trials bring me to his feet,
  Lay me low, and keep me there.

DISCIPLINE AND SORROW.

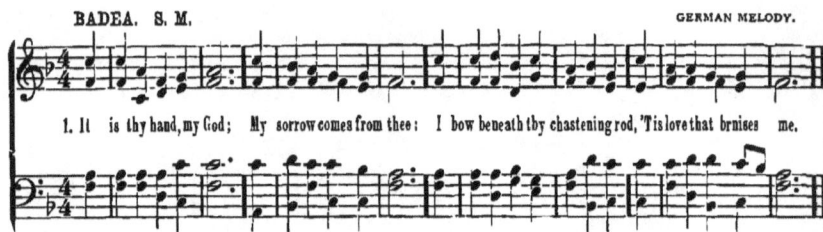

BADEA. S. M.   GERMAN MELODY.

1. It is thy hand, my God; My sorrow comes from thee: I bow beneath thy chastening rod, 'Tis love that bruises me.

721   *"Spare me."*   J. G. DECK.

It is thy hand, my God;
  My sorrow comes from thee:
I bow beneath thy chastening rod,
  'Tis love that bruises me.

2 I would not murmur, Lord;
  Before thee I am dumb:
Lest I should breathe one murmuring word,
  To thee for help I come.

3 My God, thy name is Love;
  A Father's hand is thine;
With tearful eyes I look above,
  And cry, "Thy will be mine!"

4 Jesus for me hath died;
  Thy Son thou didst not spare:
His pierced hands, his bleeding side,
  Thy love for me declare.

5 Here my poor heart can rest;
  My God, it cleaves to thee:
Thy will is love, thine end is blest,
  All work for good to me.

DENNIS. S. M.   LOWELL MASON, arr.

1. A-long my earth-ly way, How ma-ny clouds are spread! Dark-ness, with scarce one cheer-ful ray, Seems gathering o'er my head.

722   *Hereafter.*   J. EDMESTON.

Along my earthly way,
  How many clouds are spread!
Darkness, with scarce one cheerful ray,
  Seems gathering o'er my head.

2 Yet, Father, thou art Love;
  Oh, hide not from my view!
But when I look, in prayer, above,
  Appear in mercy through!

3 My pathway is not hid;
  Thou knowest all my need;
And I would do as Israel did,—
  Follow where thou wilt lead.

4 Lead me, and then my feet
  Shall never, never stray;
But safely I shall reach the seat
  Of happiness and day.

5 And, oh, from that bright throne
  I shall look back, and see,—
The path I went, and that alone
  Was the right path for me.

DISCIPLINE AND SORROW.

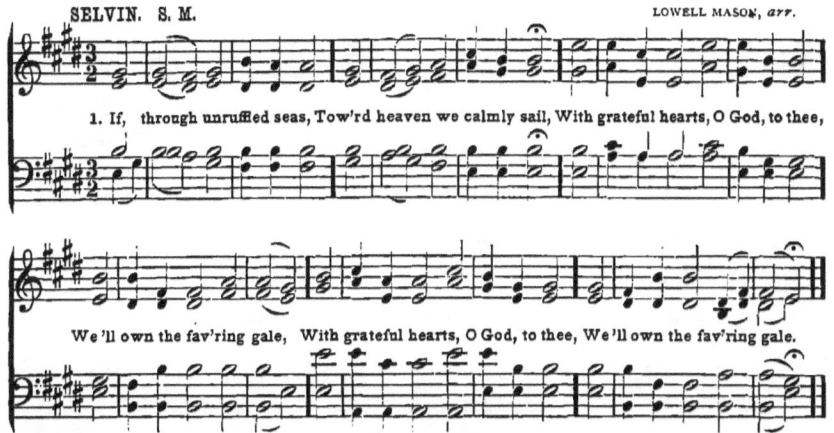

SELVIN. S. M.   LOWELL MASON, arr.

1. If, through unruffled seas, Tow'rd heaven we calmly sail, With grateful hearts, O God, to thee, We'll own the fav'ring gale, With grateful hearts, O God, to thee, We'll own the fav'ring gale.

723   *"We walk by faith."*   A. M. TOPLADY.

IF, through unruffled seas,
  Toward heaven we calmly sail,
With grateful hearts, O God, to thee,
  We'll own the favoring gale.

2 But should the surges rise,
  And rest delay to come,
Blest be the sorrow—kind the storm,
  Which drives us nearer home.

3 Soon shall our doubts and fears
  All yield to thy control:
Thy tender mercies shall illume
  The midnight of the soul.

4 Teach us, in every state,
  To make thy will our own;
And when the joys of sense depart,
  To live by faith alone.

724   *Kindness even in affliction.*   T. HASTINGS.

How tender is thy hand,
  O thou beloved Lord!
Afflictions come at thy command,
  And leave us at thy word.

2 How gentle was the rod
  That chastened us for sin!
How soon we found a smiling God,
  Where deep distress had been!

3 A Father's hand we felt,
  A Father's heart we knew;
With tears of penitence we knelt,
  And found his word was true.

4 We told him all our grief,
  We thought of Jesus' love;
A sense of pardon brought relief,
  And bade our pains remove.

5 Now we will bless the Lord,
  And in his strength confide;
For ever be his name adored;
  For there is none beside.

725   *Psalm 103.*   I. WATTS.

MY soul, repeat his praise,
  Whose mercies are so great;
Whose anger is so slow to rise,
  So ready to abate.

2 God will not always chide;
  And when his strokes are felt,
His strokes are fewer than our crimes,
  And lighter than our guilt.

3 The pity of the Lord
  To those that fear his name,
Is such as tender parents feel:
  He knows our feeble frame.

4 Our days are as the grass,
  Or like the morning flower;
If one sharp blast sweep o'er the field,
  It withers in an hour.

5 But thy compassions, Lord,
  To endless years endure;
And children's children ever find
  Thy words of promise sure.

DISCIPLINE AND SORROW.

JEWETT. 6s. D.   J. P. HOLBROOK, arr.

1. My Je-sus, as thou wilt! Oh, may thy will be mine! In-to thy hand of love I would my all re-sign; Through sor-row, or through joy, Con-duct me as thine own, And help me still to say, My Lord, thy will be done!

726   "*Not my will, but thine.*"   J. BORTHWICK, tr.

My Jesus, as thou wilt!
  Oh, may thy will be mine;
Into thy hand of love
  I would my all resign;
Through sorrow, or through joy,
  Conduct me as thine own,
And help me still to say,
  My Lord, thy will be done!

2 My Jesus, as thou wilt!
  Though seen through many a tear,
Let not my star of hope
  Grow dim or disappear;
Since thou on earth hast wept,
  And sorrowed oft alone,
If I must weep with thee,
  My Lord, thy will be done!

3 My Jesus, as thou wilt!
  All shall be well for me;
Each changing future scene
  I gladly trust with thee:
Straight to my home above
  I travel calmly on,
And sing, in life or death,
  My Lord, thy will be done!

727   "*He knoweth the way.*"   H. BONAR.

Thy way, not mine, O Lord,
  However dark it be!
Lead me by thine own hand;
  Choose out my path for me.
I dare not choose my lot:
  I would not, if I might;
Choose thou for me, my God,
  So shall I walk aright.

2 The kingdom that I seek
  Is thine: so let the way
That leads to it be thine,
  Else I must surely stray.
Take thou my cup, and it
  With joy or sorrow fill,
As best to thee may seem;
  Choose thou my good and ill.

3 Choose thou for me my friends,
  My sickness or my health;
Choose thou my cares for me,
  My poverty or wealth.
Not mine, not mine the choice,
  In things or great or small;
Be thou my Guide, my Strength,
  My Wisdom and my All.

DISCIPLINE AND SORROW.

FLEMMING. 8s, 6s. F. FLEMMING.

1. O Holy Saviour! Friend unseen, Since on thine arm thou bid'st me lean, Help me, throughout life's changing scene, By faith to cling to thee.

728 *Clinging to Christ.* C. ELLIOTT.

O Holy Saviour! Friend unseen,
Since on thine arm thou bid'st me lean,
Help me, throughout life's changing scene,
    By faith to cling to thee!

2 What though the world deceitful prove,
And earthly friends and hopes remove;
With patient, uncomplaining love,
    Still would I cling to thee.

3 Though oft I seem to tread alone
Life's dreary waste, with thorns o'ergrown,
Thy voice of love, in gentlest tone,
    Still whispers, "Cling to me!"

4 Though faith and hope are often tried,
I ask not, need not, aught beside;
So safe, so calm, so satisfied,
    The soul that clings to thee!

729 *A will resigned.* J. G. WHITTIER.

I ask not now for gold to gild,
    With mocking shine, an aching frame;
The yearning of the mind is stilled—
    I ask not now for fame.

2 But, bowed in lowliness of mind,
    I make my humble wishes known;
I only ask a will resigned,
    O Father, to thine own.

3 In vain I task my aching brain,
    In vain the sage's thoughts I scan;
I only feel how weak I am,
    How poor and blind is man.

4 And now my spirit sighs for home,
    And longs for light whereby to see;
And, like a weary child, would come,
    O Father, unto thee.

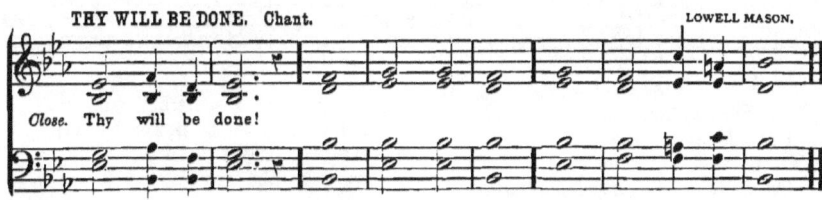

THY WILL BE DONE. Chant. LOWELL MASON.

Close. Thy will be done!

730 *Mark* 14 : 36. J. BOWRING.

"Thy will be | done!" || In devious way
The hurrying stream of | life may | run; ||
Yet still our grateful hearts shall say, |
    "Thy will be | done."

2 "Thy will be | done!" || If o'er us shine
A gladdening and a | prosperous | sun, ||
This prayer will make it more divine—|
    "Thy will be | done!"

3 "Thy will be | done!" || Tho' shrouded o'er
Our | path with | gloom, | one comfort—one
Is ours:—to breathe, while we adore, |
    "Thy will be | done."

DISCIPLINE AND SORROW.

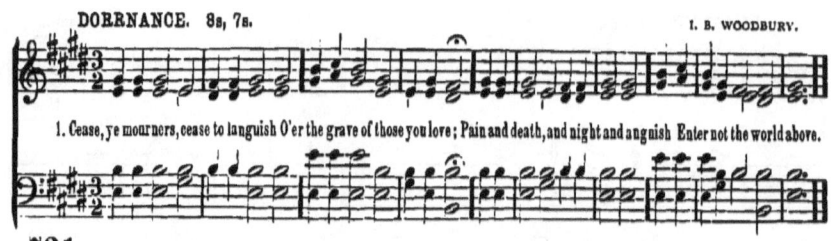

DORRNANCE. 8s, 7s. I. B. WOODBURY.

731 *Comfort.* W. B. COLLYER.

Cease, ye mourners, cease to languish
O'er the grave of those you love;
Pain and death, and night and anguish
Enter not the world above.

2 While our silent steps are straying
Lonely through night's deepening shade,
Glory's brightest beams are playing
Round the happy Christian's head.

3 Light and peace at once deriving
From the hand of God most high,
In his glorious presence living,
They shall never, never die.

4 Now, ye mourners, cease to languish
O'er the grave of those you love;
Far removed from pain and anguish,
They are chanting hymns above.

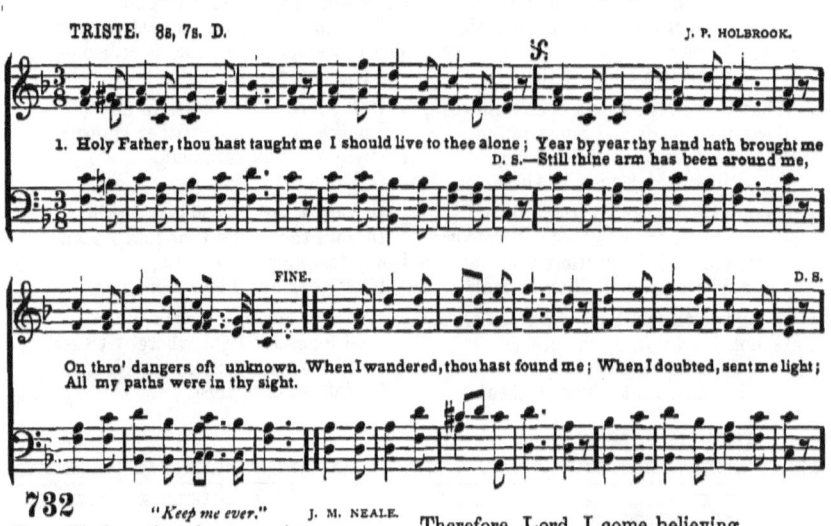

TRISTE. 8s, 7s. D. J. P. HOLBROOK.

732 *"Keep me ever."* J. M. NEALE.

Holy Father, thou hast taught me
I should live to thee alone;
Year by year thy hand hath brought me
On through dangers oft unknown.
When I wandered, thou hast found me;
When I doubted, sent me light;
Still thine arm has been around me,
All my paths were in thy sight.

2 In the world will foes assail me,
Craftier, stronger far than I;
And the strife may never fail me,
Well I know, before I die.

Therefore, Lord, I come believing
Thou canst give the power I need;
Through the prayer of faith receiving
Strength—the Spirit's strength, indeed.

3 I would trust in thy protection,
Wholly rest upon thine arm;
Follow wholly thy direction,
Thou, mine only guard from harm!
Keep me from mine own undoing,
Help me turn to thee when tried,
Still my footsteps, Father, viewing,
Keep me ever at thy side.

DISCIPLINE AND SORROW.

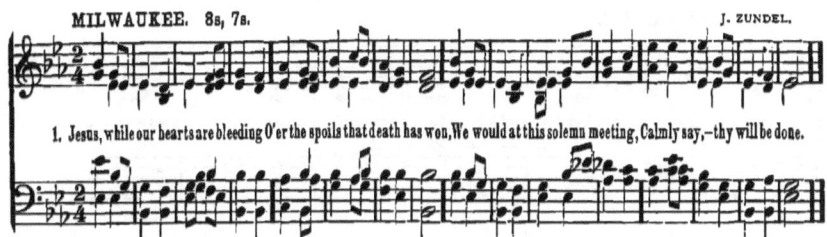

MILWAUKEE. 8s, 7s.   J. ZUNDEL.

1. Jesus, while our hearts are bleeding O'er the spoils that death has won, We would at this solemn meeting, Calmly say,—thy will be done.

733   *"Thy will be done."*   T. HASTINGS.

JESUS, while our hearts are bleeding
  O'er the spoils that death has won,
We would at this solemn meeting,
  Calmly say,—thy will be done.

2 Though cast down, we're not forsaken;
  Though afflicted, not alone;
Thou didst give, and thou hast taken;
  Blessèd Lord,—thy will be done.

3 Though to-day we're filled with mourning,
  Mercy still is on the throne;
With thy smiles of love returning,
  We can sing—thy will be done.

4 By thy hands the boon was given,
  Thou hast taken but thine own:
Lord of earth, and God of heaven,
  Evermore,—thy will be done!

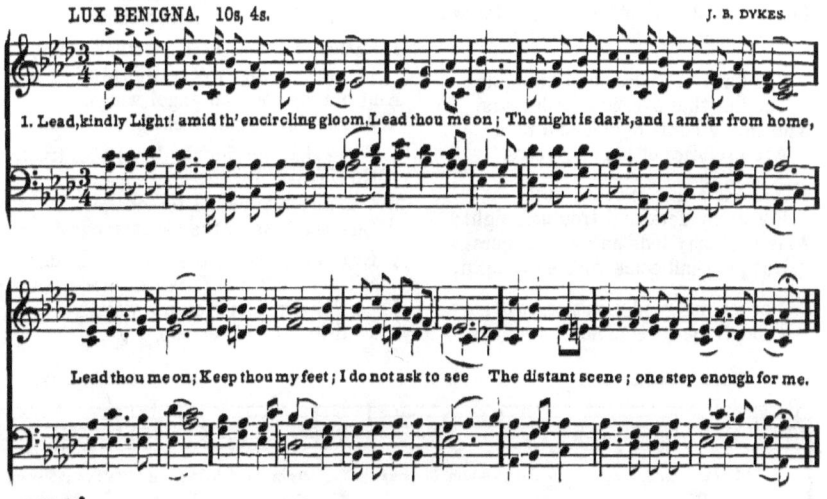

LUX BENIGNA. 10s, 4s.   J. B. DYKES.

1. Lead, kindly Light! amid th' encircling gloom, Lead thou me on; The night is dark, and I am far from home, Lead thou me on; Keep thou my feet; I do not ask to see The distant scene; one step enough for me.

734   *"Lead thou me on!"*   J. H. NEWMAN.

LEAD, kindly Light! amid the encircling
  Lead thou me on;   [gloom,
The night is dark, and I am far from home,
  Lead thou me on;
Keep thou my feet; I do not ask to see
The distant scene; one step enough for me.

2 I was not ever thus, nor prayed that thou
  Shouldst lead me on;
I loved to choose and see my path; but now
  Lead thou me on:

I loved the garish day, and spite of fears,
Pride ruled my will. Remember not past
  years.

3 So long thy power has blessed me, sure
  Will lead me on   [it still
O'er moor and fen, o'er crag and torrent, till
  The night is gone;
And with the morn those angel faces smile
Which I have loved long since, and lost
  awhile!

DISCIPLINE AND SORROW.

BEETHOVEN. L. M. — GEO. KINGSLEY, arr.

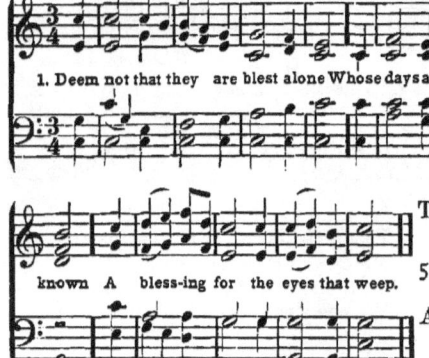

735 — *Blessing for mourners.* W. C. BRYANT.

DEEM not that they are blest alone
 Whose days a peaceful tenor keep;
The anointed Son of God makes known
 A blessing for the eyes that weep.

2 The light of smiles shall fill again
 The lids that overflow with tears;
And weary hours of woe and pain
 Are promises of happier years.

3 There is a day of sunny rest
 For every dark and troubled night;
And grief may bide an evening guest,
 But joy shall come with early light.

4 Nor let the good man's trust depart,
 Though life its common gifts deny,
Though with a pierced and broken heart,
 And spurned of men, he goes to die.

5 For God has marked each sorrowing day,
 And numbered every secret tear;
And heaven's long age of bliss shall pay
 For all his children suffer here.

736 — *Resignation.* J. ROSCOE.

THY will be done! I will not fear
 The fate provided by thy love;
Though clouds and darkness shroud me here,
 I know that all is bright above.

2 Father, forgive the heart that clings,
 Thus trembling, to the things of time;
And bid my soul, on angel wings,
 Ascend into a purer clime.

3 There shall no doubts disturb its trust,
 No sorrows dim celestial love;
But these afflictions of the dust,
 Like shadows of the night, remove.

4 Ev'n now, above, there's radiant day,
 While clouds and darkness brood below;
Then, Father, joyful on my way
 To drink the bitter cup, I go.

DISCIPLINE AND SORROW.

737 *"He leadeth me."* J. H. GILMORE.

He leadeth me! oh, blessèd thought,
Oh, words with heavenly comfort fraught!
Whate'er I do, where'er I be,
Still 'tis God's hand that leadeth me.—
         REF.

2 Sometimes 'mid scenes of deepest gloom,
Sometimes where Eden's bowers bloom,
By waters still, o'er troubled sea,—
Still 'tis his hand that leadeth me!—REF.

3 Lord! I would clasp thy hand in mine,
Nor ever murmur nor repine;
Content whatever lot I see,
Since 'tis my God that leadeth me.—REF.

4 And when my task on earth is done,
When by thy grace the victory's won,
Ev'n death's cold wave I will not flee,
Since God through Jordan leadeth me.—
         REF.

738 *"Thy will be done."* C. ELLIOTT.

My God, my Father, while I stray
Far from my home, on life's rough way,
Oh, teach me from my heart to say,
"Thy will be done, thy will be done!"

2 What though in lonely grief I sigh
For friends beloved no longer nigh;
Submissive still would I reply,
"Thy will be done, thy will be done!"

3 If thou shouldst call me to resign
What most I prize,—it ne'er was mine;
I only yield thee what was thine:
"Thy will be done, thy will be done!"

4 If but my fainting heart be blest
With thy sweet Spirit for its guest,
My God, to thee I leave the rest;
"Thy will be done, thy will be done!"

5 Renew my will from day to day;
Blend it with thine, and take away
Whate'er now makes it hard to say,
"Thy will be done, thy will be done!"

6 Then when on earth I breathe no more
The prayer oft mixed with tears before,
I'll sing, upon a happier shore,
"Thy will be done, thy will be done!"

739 6s, D.   "Thy Father."   T. HASTINGS.

Be tranquil, O my soul,
  Be quiet, every fear!
Thy Father hath control,
  And he is ever near.
Ne'er of thy lot complain,
  Whatever may befall;
Sickness, or care, or pain,
  'T is well-appointed all.

2 A Father's chastening hand
  Is leading thee along;
Nor distant is the land,
  Where swells the immortal song.
Oh, then, my soul, be still!
  Await heaven's high decree;
Seek but thy Father's will,
  It shall be well with thee.

740 S. M.   Trusting.   W. F. LLOYD.

"My times are in thy hand:"
  My God! I wish them there;
My life, my soul, my all, I leave
  Entirely to thy care.

2 "My times are in thy hand;"
  Whatever they may be;
Pleasing or painful, dark or bright,
  As best may seem to thee.

3 "My times are in thy hand;"—
  Why should I doubt or fear?
My Father's hand will never cause
  His child a needless tear.

4 "My times are in thy hand;"
  I'll always trust in thee;
Till I possess the promised land,
  And all thy glory see.

741 C. M.   Psalm 73.   I. WATTS.

God, my supporter and my hope,
  My help for ever near,
Thine arm of mercy held me up,
  When sinking in despair.

2 Thy counsels, Lord, shall guide my
  Through this dark wilderness; [feet
Thine hand conduct me near thy seat,
  To dwell before thy face.

3 Were I in heaven, without my God,
  'T would be no joy to me;

And while the earth is my abode,
  I long for none but thee.

4 What if the springs of life were broke,
  And flesh and heart should faint,
Thou art my soul's eternal rock,
  The strength of every saint.

5 Then to draw near to thee, my God,
  Shall be my sweet employ;
My tongue shall sound thy works abroad,
  And tell the world my joy.

742 L. M.   Psalm 90: 12.   GUYON.

If life in sorrow must be spent,
  So be it; I am well content;
And meekly wait my last remove,
  Desiring only trustful love.

2 No bliss I'll seek, but to fulfill
  In life, in death, thy perfect will;
No succor in my woes I want,
  But what my Lord is pleased to grant.

3 Our days are numbered: let us spare
  Our anxious hearts a needless care;
'Tis thine to number out our days;
  'Tis ours to give them to thy praise.

4 Faith is our only business here—
  Faith, simple, constant, and sincere;
Oh, blessèd days thy servants see!
  Thus spent O Lord! in pleasing thee.

743 C. M.   "Be ye also ready."   A. REED.

There is an hour when I must part
  With all I hold most dear;
And life, with its best hopes, will then
  As nothingness appear.

2 There is an hour when I must sink
  Beneath the stroke of death;
And yield to him, who gave it first,
  My struggling vital breath.

3 There is an hour when I must stand
  Before the judgment-seat;
And all my sins, and all my foes,
  In awful vision meet.

4 There is an hour when I must look
  On one eternity;
And nameless woe, or blissful life,
  My endless portion be.

5 O Saviour, then, in all my need
  Be near, be near to me:
And let my soul, by steadfast faith,
  Find life and heaven in thee.

DISCIPLINE AND SORROW.

744 s. m. *Tell Jesus.* ANON.

In every trying hour
My soul to Jesus flies;
I trust in his almighty power,
When swelling billows rise.

2 His comforts bear me up;
I trust a faithful God;
The sure foundation of my hope
Is in my Saviour's blood.

3 Loud hallelujahs sing
To our Redeemer's name;
In joy or sorrow—life or death—
His love is still the same.

745 l. m. *"Afterwards."* A. R. WOLFE.

I BLESS thee, Lord, for sorrows sent
To break the dream of human power,
For now my shallow cistern's spent,
I find thy fount and thirst no more.

2 I take thy hand and fears grow still:
Behold thy face, and doubts remove;
Who would not yield his wavering will
To perfect truth and boundless love!

3 That truth gives promise of a dawn,
Beneath whose light I am to see,
When all these blinding vails are drawn,
This was the wisest path for me.

4 That love this restless soul doth teach
The strength of thy eternal calm;
And tunes its sad and broken speech,
To sing ev'n now the angels' psalm.

746 l. m. *God is love.* J. BOWRING.

I CANNOT always trace the way
Where thou, Almighty One, dost move;
But I can always, always say,
That God is love, that God is love.

2 When fear her chilling mantle flings
O'er earth, my soul to heaven above,
As to her native home, upsprings,
For God is love, for God is love.

3 When mystery clouds my darkened path,
I'll check my dread, my doubts reprove;
In this my soul sweet comfort hath,
That God is love, that God is love.

4 Yes, God is love;—a thought like this
Can every gloomy thought remove,
And turn all tears, all woes, to bliss,
For God is love, for God is love.

747 8s, 7s. *Life's Evening.* C. P. SMITH, *alt.*

TARRY with me, O my Saviour!
For the day is passing by;
See! the shades of evening gather,
And the night is drawing nigh.

2 Deeper, deeper grow the shadows,
Paler now the glowing west,
Swift the night of death advances;
Shall it be the night of rest?

3 Lonely seems the vale of shadow;
Sinks my heart with troubled fear;
Give me faith for clearer vision,
Speak thou, Lord, in words of cheer.

4 Let me hear thy voice behind me,
Calming all these wild alarms;
Let me, underneath my weakness,
Feel the everlasting arms.

5 Feeble, trembling, fainting, dying,
Lord, I cast myself on thee;
Tarry with me through the darkness;
While I sleep, still watch by me.

6 Tarry with me, O my Saviour!
Lay my head upon thy breast
Till the morning; then awake me—
Morning of eternal rest!

748 6s, d. *More like God.* H. BONAR.

I DID thee wrong, my God,
I wronged thy truth and love;
I fretted at the rod,—
Against thy power I strove.
Come nearer, nearer still;
Let not thy light depart;
Bend, break this stubborn will;
Dissolve this iron heart!

2 Less wayward let me be,
More pliable and mild;
In glad simplicity
More like a trustful child.
Less, less of self each day,
And more, my God, of thee;
Oh, keep me in the way,
However rough it be.

3 Less of the flesh each day,
Less of the world and sin:
More of thy Son, I pray,
More of thyself within.
More moulded to thy will,
Lord, let thy servant be;
Higher and higher still,
More, and still more, like thee!

749 *The Ministry.* I. WATTS.

How BEAUTEOUS are their feet
  Who stand on Zion's hill!
Who bring salvation on their tongues,
  And words of peace reveal.
How charming is their voice!
  How sweet their tidings are!
"Zion, behold thy Saviour King;
  He reigns and triumphs here."

2 How happy are our ears,
  That hear this joyful sound!
Which kings and prophets waited for,
  And sought, but never found.
How blessèd are our eyes,
  That see this heavenly light!
Prophets and kings desired it long,
  But died without the sight.

3 The watchmen join their voice,
  And tuneful notes employ;
Jerusalem breaks forth in songs,
  And deserts learn the joy.
The Lord makes bare his arm
  Through all the earth abroad;
Let every nation now behold
  Their Saviour and their God!

750 *More Laborers.* C. WESLEY.

LORD of the harvest! hear
  Thy needy servants cry;
Answer our faith's effectual prayer,
  And all our wants supply.
On thee we humbly wait;
  Our wants are in thy view;
The harvest truly, Lord! is great,
  The laborers are few.

2 Convert and send forth more
  Into thy Church abroad;
And let them speak thy word of power,
  As workers with their God.
Give the pure Gospel-word,
  The word of general grace;
Thee let them preach, the common Lord,
  The Saviour of our race.

3 Oh, let them spread thy name;
  Their mission fully prove;
Thy universal grace proclaim
  Thy all-redeeming love.
On all mankind forgiven,
  Empower them still to call,
And tell each creature under heaven,
  That thou hast died for all.

THE CHURCH:—INSTITUTIONS. 287

751 *Corner-stone.* J. CHANDLER, *tr.*

CHRIST is our Corner-stone;
On him alone we build;
With his true saints alone
The courts of heaven are filled:
On his great love | Of present grace
Our hopes we place, | And joys above.

2 Oh, then with hymns of praise
These hallowed courts shall ring!
Our voices we will raise,
The Three in One to sing;
And thus proclaim | Both loud and long,
In joyful song, | That glorious Name.

3 Here may we gain from heaven
The grace which we implore,
And may that grace once given,
Be with us evermore,—
Until that day | To endless rest
When all the blest | Are called away.

752 *The Church one.* G. ROBINSON.

ONE sole baptismal sign,
One Lord below, above,
One faith, one hope divine,
One only watchword, love;
From different temples though it rise,
One song ascendeth to the skies.

2 Our sacrifice is one;
One Priest before the throne,
The slain, the risen Son,
Redeemer, Lord alone;
And sighs from contrite hearts that spring
Our chief, our choicest offering.

3 Head of thy church beneath,
The catholic, the true,
On all her members breathe,
Her broken frame renew;
Then shall thy perfect will be done
When Christians love and live as one.

THE CHURCH:—INSTITUTIONS.

STOUGHTON. 8s, 7s. D.   J. P. HOLBROOK.

1. Glo-rious things of thee are spok-en, Zi-on, cit-y of our God!
He, whose word can-not be brok-en, Formed thee for his own a-bode:
D. S.—With sal-va-tion's wall sur-round-ed, Thou may'st smile at all thy foes.
On the Rock of A-ges found-ed, What can shake thy sure re-pose?

753 *"Glorious things."* J. NEWTON.

GLORIOUS things of thee are spoken,
  Zion, city of our God!
He, whose word cannot be broken,
  Formed thee for his own abode:
On the Rock of Ages founded,
  What can shake thy sure repose?
With salvation's walls surrounded,
  Thou may'st smile at all thy foes.

2 See! the streams of living waters,
  Springing from eternal love,
Well supply thy sons and daughters,
  And all fear of want remove:
Who can faint, while such a river
  Ever flows their thirst to assuage?—
Grace, which, like the Lord, the Giver,
  Never fails from age to age.

3 Round each habitation hovering,
  See the cloud and fire appear
For a glory and a covering,
  Showing that the Lord is near!
Thus deriving from their banner,
  Light by night, and shade by day,
Safe they feed upon the manna
  Which he gives them when they pray.

754 *The covenant.* W. COWPER.

HEAR what God, the Lord hath spoken;
  O my people, faint and few,
Comfortless, afflicted, broken,
  Fair abodes I build for you;
Scenes of heartfelt tribulation
  Shall no more perplex your ways;
You shall name your walls "Salvation,"
  And your gates shall all be "Praise."

2 There, like streams that feed the garden,
  Pleasures without end shall flow;
For the Lord, your faith rewarding,
  All his bounty shall bestow.
Still in undisturbed possession
  Peace and righteousness shall reign;
Never shall you feel oppression,
  Hear the voice of war again.

3 Ye, no more your suns descending,
  Waning moons no more shall see,
But, your griefs for ever ending,
  Find eternal noon in me.
God shall rise, and shining o'er you,
  Change to day the gloom of night;
He, the Lord, shall be your Glory,
  God, your everlasting Light.

THE CHURCH:—INSTITUTIONS.

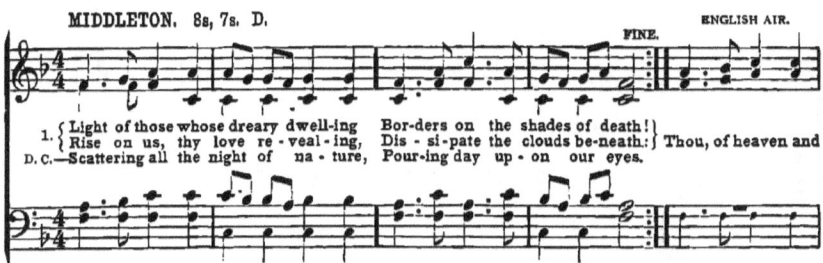

755   *"The true Light."*   C. WESLEY.

LIGHT of those whose dreary dwelling
  Borders on the shades of death!
Rise on us, thy love revealing,
  Dissipate the clouds beneath:
Thou, of heaven and earth Creator,
  In our deepest darkness rise,—
Scattering all the night of nature,
  Pouring day upon our eyes.

2 Still we wait for thine appearing,
  Life and joy thy beams impart,
Chasing all our fears, and cheering
  Every poor benighted heart:
Come, and manifest thy favor
  To the ransomed, helpless race;
Come, thou glorious God and Saviour!
  Come, and bring the gospel grace.

3 Save us, in thy great compassion,
  O thou mild, pacific Prince!
Give the knowledge of salvation,
  Give the pardon of our sins;
By thine all-sufficient merit,
  Every burdened soul release;
Every weary, wandering spirit,
  Guide into thy perfect peace.

756   *"Come quickly."*   C. WESLEY.

COME, thou long-expected Jesus,
  Born to set thy people free;
From our fears and sins release us,
  Let us find our rest in thee.

2 Israel's Strength and Consolation,
  Hope of all the saints thou art:
Dear Desire of every nation,
  Joy of every longing heart.

3 Born, thy people to deliver;
  Born a child, and yet a King!
Born to reign in us for ever,
  Now thy gracious kingdom bring.

4 By thine own eternal Spirit,
  Rule in all our hearts alone;
By thine all-sufficient merit,
  Raise us to thy glorious throne

THE CHURCH:—INSTITUTIONS.

BOND. C. M.   ROOT AND SWEETSER'S COLL.

1. Oh, where are kings and em-pires now, Of old that went and came?
But, Lord, thy church is pray-ing yet, A thou-sand years the same.

757   *A growing kingdom.*   A. C. COXE.

OH, where are kings and empires now,
  Of old that went and came?
But, Lord, thy church is praying yet,
  A thousand years the same.

2 We mark her goodly battlements,
  And her foundations strong;
We hear within the solemn voice
  Of her unending song.

3 For not like kingdoms of the world
  Thy holy church, O God!
Though earthquake shocks are threatening
  And tempests are abroad;—

4 Unshaken as eternal hills,
  Immovable she stands,
A mountain that shall fill the earth,
  A house not made by hands.

758   *"Little Flock."*   H. BONAR.

CHURCH of the ever-living God,
  The Father's gracious choice,
Amid the voices of this earth
  How feeble is thy voice!

2 A little flock!—so calls he thee
  Who bought thee with his blood;
A little flock, disowned of men,
  But owned and loved of God.

3 Not many rich or noble called,
  Not many great or wise;
They whom God makes his kings and priests
  Are poor in human eyes.

4 But the chief Shepherd comes at length;
  Their feeble days are o'er,
No more a handful in the earth,
  A little flock no more.

5 No more a lily among thorns,
  Weary and faint and few;
But countless as the stars of heaven,
  Or as the early dew.

6 Then entering the eternal halls,
  In robes of victory,
That mighty multitude shall keep
  The joyous jubilee.

759   *"Can a mother forget?"*   A. STEELE.

A MOTHER may forgetful be,
  For human love is frail;
But thy Creator's love to thee,
  O Zion, cannot fail.

2 No: thy dear name engraven stands,
  In characters of love,
On thy almighty Father's hands,
  And never shall remove.

3 Before his ever-watchful eye
  Thy mournful state appears,
And every groan, and every sigh,
  Divine compassion hears.

4 O Zion, learn to doubt no more,
  Be every fear suppressed;
Unchanging truth, and love, and power,
  Dwell in thy Saviour's breast.

THE CHURCH:—INSTITUTIONS.

760 *For Dedication.* W. C. BRYANT.

O THOU, whose own vast temple stands,
Built over earth and sea,
Accept the walls that human hands
Have raised to worship thee.

2 Lord, from thine inmost glory send,
Within these courts to bide,
The peace that dwelleth without end,
Serenely by thy side!

3 May erring minds that worship here
Be taught the better way;
And they who mourn and they who fear,
Be strengthened as they pray.

4 May faith grow firm, and love grow warm,
And pure devotion rise,
While round these hallowed walls the storm
Of earth-born passion dies.

761 *The Ministry.* P. DODDRIDGE.

'TIS NOT a cause of small import
The pastor's care demands,
But what might fill an angel's heart,
And filled a Saviour's hands.

2 They watch for souls for whom the Lord
Did heavenly bliss forego—
For souls that must for ever live
In rapture or in woe.

3 All to the great tribunal haste,
The account to render there;
And shouldst thou strictly mark our faults,
Lord! how should we appear?

4 May they that Jesus whom they preach
Their own Redeemer, see,
And watch thou daily o'er their souls,
That they may watch for thee.

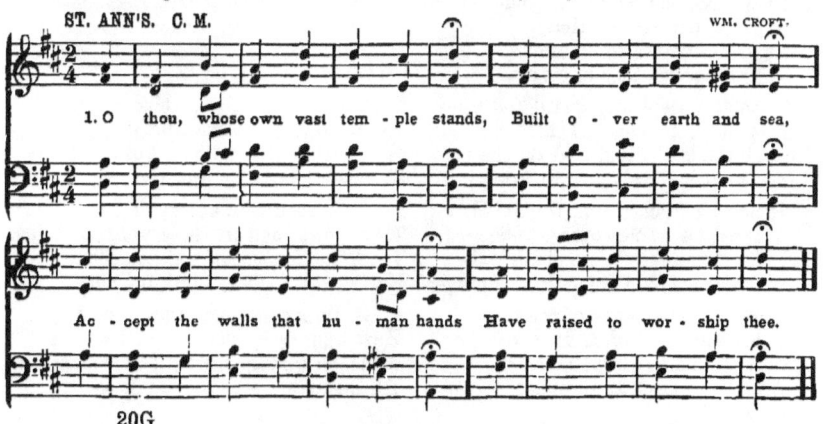

THE CHURCH:—INSTITUTIONS.

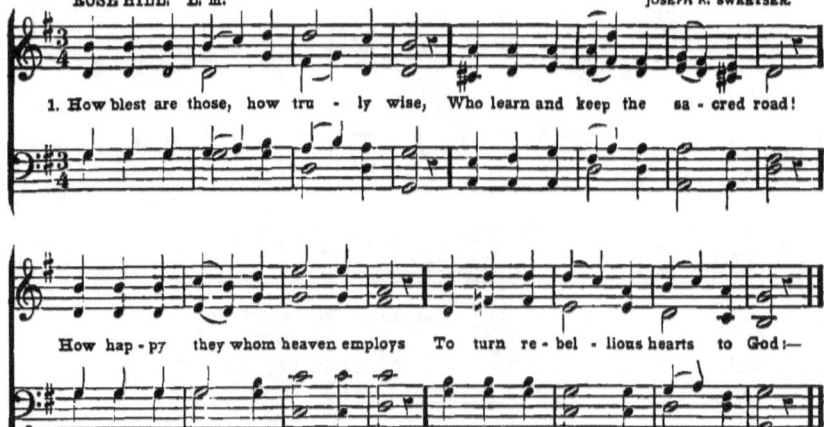

ROSE HILL. L. M.   JOSEPH F. SWEETSER.

1. How blest are those, how tru-ly wise, Who learn and keep the sa-cred road!
How hap-py they whom heaven employs To turn re-bel-lious hearts to God:—

762   *The Ministry.*   A. STEELE.

How BLEST are those, how truly wise,
  Who learn and keep the sacred road!
How happy they whom heaven employs
  To turn rebellious hearts to God:—

2 To win them from the fatal way,
  Where erring folly thoughtless roves,
And that blest righteousness display
  Which Jesus wrought and God approves.

3 The shining firmament shall fade,
  And sparkling stars resign their light;
But these shall know nor change nor shade,
  For ever fair, for ever bright.

763   *Installation.*   J. MONTGOMERY.

WE bid thee welcome in the name
  Of Jesus, our exalted Head;
Come as a servant: so he came,
  And we receive thee in his stead.

2 Come as a shepherd; guard and keep
  This fold from hell, and earth, and sin;
Nourish the lambs, and feed the sheep,
  The wounded heal, the lost bring in.

3 Come as a teacher, sent from God,
  Charged his whole counsel to declare;
Lift o'er our ranks the prophet's rod,
  While we uphold thy hands with prayer.

4 Come as a messenger of peace,
  Filled with the Spirit, fired with love!
Live to behold our large increase,
  And die to meet us all above.
    G

764   *For Dedication.*   N. P. WILLIS.

THE perfect world, by Adam trod,
  Was the first temple,—built by God;
His fiat laid the corner-stone,
  And heaved its pillars, one by one.

2 He hung its starry roof on high—
  The broad, illimitable sky;
He spread its pavement, green and bright,
  And curtained it with morning light.

3 The mountains in their places stood,
The sea—the sky—and "all was good;"
And when its first pure praises rang,
The "morning stars together sang."

4 Lord, 'tis not ours to make the sea,
And earth, and sky, a house for thee;
But in thy sight our offering stands—
An humbler temple, "made with hands."

765   *The Ministry.*   B. BEDDOME.

FATHER of mercies, bow thine ear,
  Attentive to our earnest prayer;
We plead for those who plead for thee;
  Successful may they ever be.

2 Clothe thou with energy divine
  Their words, and let those words be thine;
Teach them immortal souls to gain,
  Nor let them labor, Lord, in vain.

3 Let thronging multitudes around
  Hear from their lips the joyful sound;
And light through distant realms be spread
  Till Zion rears her drooping head.

THE CHURCH:—INSTITUTIONS.

WARE. L. M.   GEO. KINGSLEY.

1. Pour out thy Spir-it from on high; Lord! thine as-sembled ser-vants bless; Gra-ces and gifts to each sup-ply, And clothe thy priests with right-eous-ness.

766   *Convocation.*   J. MONTGOMERY.

Pour out thy Spirit from on high;
  Lord! thine assembled servants bless;
Graces and gifts to each supply,
  And clothe thy priests with righteousness.

2 Wisdom and zeal, and faith impart,
  Firmness with meekness from above,
To bear thy people on our heart,
  And love the souls whom thou dost love:—

3 To watch and pray, and never faint;
  By day and night strict guard to keep;
To warn the sinner, cheer the saint,
  Nourish thy lambs, and feed thy sheep;—

4 Then, when our work is finished here,
  In humble hope our charge resign:
When the chief Shepherd shall appear,
  O God! may they and we be thine!

767   *Seeking a Pastor.*   P. DODDRIDGE.

O Lord, thy pitying eye surveys
Our wandering paths, our trackless ways:
Send forth, in love, thy truth and light,
To guide our doubtful footsteps right.

2 In humble faith, behold we wait:
On thee we call at mercy's gate;
Our drooping hearts, O God, sustain,—
Shall Israel seek thy face in vain?

3 O Lord! in ways of peace return,
Nor let thy flock neglected mourn;
May our blest eyes a shepherd see,
Dear to our souls, and dear to thee.
    G

768   *Prayer for Pastor.*   R. HILL.

With heavenly power, O Lord, defend
Him whom we now to thee commend;
Thy faithful messenger secure,
And make him to the end endure.

2 Gird him with all-sufficient grace;
Direct his feet in paths of peace;
Thy truth and faithfulness fulfill,
And arm him to obey thy will.

769   *Church Dedication.*   J. PIERPONT.

Oh, bow thine ear, Eternal One!
  On thee our heart adoring calls;
To thee the followers of thy Son
  Have raised, and now devote these walls.

2 Here let thy holy days be kept;
  And be this place to worship given,
Like that bright spot where Jacob slept,
  The house of God, the gate of heaven.

3 Here may thine honor dwell; and here,
  As incense, let thy children's prayer,
From contrite hearts and lips sincere,
  Rise on the still and holy air.

4 Here be thy praise devoutly sung;
  Here let thy truth beam forth to save,
As when, of old, thy Spirit hung,
  On wings of light, o'er Jordan's wave.

5 And when the lips, that with thy name
  Are vocal now, to dust shall turn,
On others may devotion's flame
  Be kindled here, and purely burn!

770 s. m.   Psalm 48.   i. watts.

Far as thy name is known,
  The world declares thy praise;
Thy saints, O Lord, before thy throne,
  Their songs of honor raise.

2 With joy thy people stand
  On Zion's chosen hill,
Proclaim the wonders of thy hand,
  And counsels of thy will.

3 Let strangers walk around
  The city where we dwell,
Compass and view thine holy ground,
  And mark the building well—

4 The order of thy house,
  The worship of thy court,
The cheerful songs, the solemn vows;
  And make a fair report.

5 How decent, and how wise!
  How glorious to behold!
Beyond the pomp that charms the eyes,
  And rites adorned with gold.

6 The God we worship now
  Will guide us till we die;
Will be our God, while here below,
  And ours above the sky.

771   7s, 6s.   The Church is Christ's.   s. j. stone.

The Church's one foundation
  Is Jesus Christ her Lord;
She is his new creation
  By water and the word:
From heaven he came and sought her,
  To be his holy bride;
With his own blood he bought her,
  And for her life he died.

2 Elect from every nation,
  Yet one o'er all the earth,
Her charter of salvation
  One Lord, one faith, one birth;
One holy name she blesses,
  Partakes one holy food,
And to one hope she presses,
  With every grace endued.

3 Though with a scornful wonder,
  Men see her sore oppressed,
By schisms rent asunder,
  By heresies distressed,
Yet saints their watch are keeping,
  Their cry goes up, "How long?"
And soon the night of weeping
  Shall be the morn of song.
    G

772 s. m.   Psalm 48.   i. watts.

Great is the Lord our God,
  And let his praise be great;
He makes his churches his abode,
  His most delightful seat.

2 These temples of his grace,
  How beautiful they stand!
The honors of our native place,
  The bulwarks of our land.

3 In Zion God is known,
  A refuge in distress;
How bright has his salvation shone
  Through all her palaces!

4 Oft have our fathers told,
  Our eyes have often seen,
How well our God secures the fold
  Where his own sheep have been.

5 In every new distress
  We'll to his house repair,
We'll think upon his wondrous grace,
  And seek deliverance there.

773   11s, 10s.   "Daughter of Zion!"   anon.

Daughter of Zion! awake from thy sadness:
Awake, for thy foes shall oppress thee no more;
Bright o'er thy hills dawns the day-star of gladness;
Arise! for the night of thy sorrow is o'er.

2 Strong were thy foes, but the arm that subdued them,
And scattered their legions, was mightier far;
They fled, like the chaff, from the scourge that pursued them;
For vain were their steeds and their chariots of war!

3 Daughter of Zion! the Power that hath saved thee,
Extolled with the harp and the timbrel should be:
Shout! for the foe is destroyed that enslaved thee,
Th' oppressor is vanquished, and Zion is free!

774 7s.　　*For Dedication.*　　j. montgomery.

Lord of hosts! to thee we raise
Here a house of prayer and praise:
Thou thy people's hearts prepare,
Here to meet for praise and prayer.

2 Let the living here be fed
With thy word, the heavenly bread:
Here, in hope of glory blest,
May the dead be laid to rest.

3 Here to thee a temple stand,
While the sea shall gird the land:
Here reveal thy mercy sure,
While the sun and moon endure.

4 Hallelujah!—earth and sky
To the joyful sound reply:
Hallelujah! hence ascend
Prayer and praise till time shall end.

775 s. m.　　*The Ministry.*　　mrs. voke.

Ye messengers of Christ!
His sovereign voice obey;
Arise, and follow where he leads,
And peace attend your way.

2 The Master, whom you serve,
Will needful strength bestow;
Depending on his promised aid,
With sacred courage go.

3 Mountains shall sink to plains,
And hell in vain oppose;
The cause is God's—and will prevail,
In spite of all his foes.

776 7s, 6s.　*Departing Missionaries.*　j. edmeston.

Roll on, thou mighty ocean;
And, as thy billows flow,
Bear messengers of mercy
To every land below.
Arise, ye gales, and waft them
Safe to the destined shore;
That man may sit in darkness,
And death's black shade no more.

2 O thou eternal Ruler,
Who holdest in thine arm
The tempests of the ocean,
Protect them from all harm!
Thy presence, Lord, be with them,
Wherever they may be:
Though far from us, who love them,
Still let them be with thee.

G

777 c. m.　　*Church Opening.*　　i. watts.

Arise, O King of grace, arise,
And enter to thy rest;
Lo! thy church waits, with longing eyes,
Thus to be owned and blest.

2 Enter with all thy glorious train,
Thy Spirit and thy word;
All that the ark did once contain
Could no such grace afford.

3 Here, mighty God, accept our vows,
Here let thy praise be spread;
Bless the provisions of thy house,
And fill thy poor with bread.

4 Here let the Son of David reign,
Let God's Anointed shine;
Justice and truth his court maintain,
With love and power divine.

5 Here let him hold a lasting throne,
And as his kingdom grows,
Fresh honors shall adorn his crown,
And shame confound his foes.

778 p. m.　　1 *Pet.* 1: 10, 11.　　f. e. cox, *tr.*

Wake! the welcome day appeareth,
Every heart with joy it cheereth!
Wake! the Lord's great year behold;
That which holy men of old,
Those who throng the sacred pages,
Waited for through countless ages:
　Hallelujah! Hallelujah!

2 Patriarchs erst and priests aspiring,
Kings and prophets long desiring,
Saw not this before they died:—
Lo! the light to them denied!
See its beams to earth directed!
Welcome, O thou long-expected!
　Hallelujah! Hallelujah!

3 In our stead himself he offers,
On the accursèd tree he suffers,
That his death's sweet savor may
Take our curse for aye away;
Cross and curse for us enduring,
Hope and heaven to us securing:
　Hallelujah! Hallelujah!

4 Rent the temple curtain's centre;
Come, ye nations, freely enter
Through the vail the holy place!
Freely stand before his face,
Here your grateful tributes bringing:
Come thou Bride, for ever singing,
　Hallelujah! Hallelujah!

LEIGHTON. S. M. H. W. CREATOREX.

779
Expedition. J. MONTGOMERY.

Work while it is to-day!
This was our Saviour's rule;
With docile minds let us obey,
As learners in his school.

2 Lord Christ, we humbly ask
Of thee the power and will,
With fear and meekness, every task
Of duty to fulfill.

3 At home, by word and deed,
Adorn redeeming grace;
And sow abroad the precious seed
Of truth in every place:—

4 That thus the wilderness
May blossom like the rose,
And trees spring up of righteousness,
Where'er life's river flows.

5 For thee our all to spend,
Still may we watch and pray,
And, persevering to the end,
Work while it is to-day.

780
Contribution. W. W. HOW.

We give thee but thine own,
Whate'er the gift may be:
All that we have is thine alone,
A trust, O Lord, from thee.

2 May we thy bounties thus
As stewards true receive,
And gladly, as thou blessest us,
To thee our first-fruits give.
G

3 To comfort and to bless,
To find a balm for woe,
To tend the lone and fatherless
Is angel's work below.

4 The captive to release,
To God the lost to bring,
To teach the way of life and peace—
It is a Christ-like thing.

5 And we believe thy word,
Though dim our faith may be;
Whate'er for thine we do, O Lord,
We do it unto thee.

781
Reform. ANON.

Mourn for the thousands slain,
The youthful and the strong;
Mourn for the wine-cup's fearful reign,
And the deluded throng.

2 Mourn for the ruined soul,—
Eternal life and light
Lost by the fiery, maddening bowl,
And turned to hopeless night.

3 Mourn for the lost,—but call,
Call to the strong, the free;
Rouse them to shun the dreadful fall,
And to the refuge flee.

4 Mourn for the lost,—but pray,
Pray to our God above,
To break the fell destroyer's sway,
And show his saving love.

CHURCH WORK.

782   *"Harvest home."*   J. MONTGOMERY.

Sow in the morn thy seed,
  At eve hold not thy hand;
To doubt and fear give thou no heed;
  Broad-cast it o'er the land.

2 And duly shall appear
  In verdure, beauty, strength,
The tender blade, the stalk, the ear,
  And the full corn at length.

3 Thou canst not toil in vain;
  Cold, heat, the moist and dry,
Shall foster and mature the grain
  For garners in the sky.

4 Then, when the glorious end,
  The day of God shall come,
The angel-reapers shall descend,
  And heaven sing "Harvest home!"

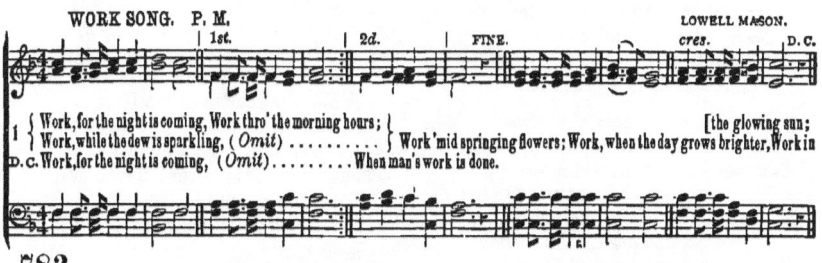

783   *"The night cometh."*   S. DYER.

Work, for the night is coming;
  Work, through the morning hours;
Work, while the dew is sparkling;
  Work, 'mid springing flowers;
Work, when the day grows brighter,
  Work, in the glowing sun;
Work, for the night is coming,
  When man's work is done.

2 Work, for the night is coming,
  Work through the sunny noon;
Fill brightest hours with labor,
  Rest comes sure and soon.
Give every flying minute
  Something to keep in store:
Work, for the night is coming,
  When man works no more.

3 Work, for the night is coming.
  Under the sunset skies;
While their bright tints are glowing,
  Work, for daylight flies.
Work till the last beam fadeth,
  Fadeth to shine no more;
Work while the night is darkening,
  When man's work is o'er.

G

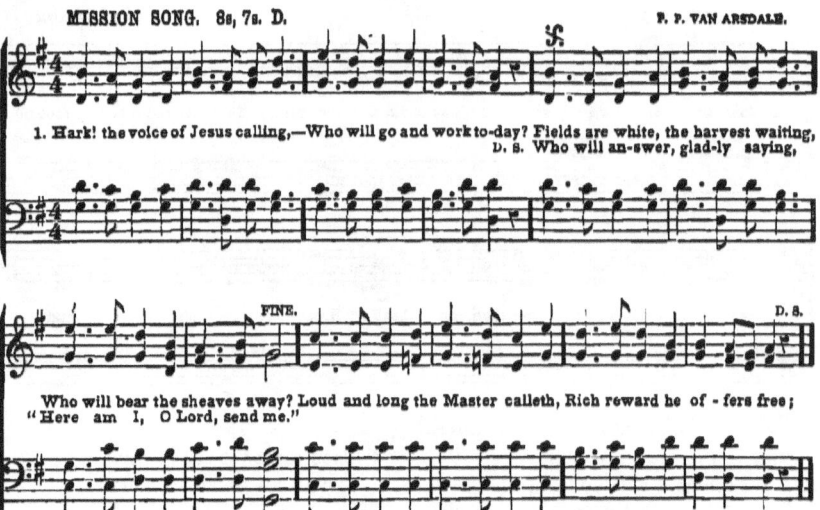

784 "*The Laborers are few.*" D. MARCH.

Hark! the voice of Jesus calling,—
  Who will go and work to-day?
Fields are white, the harvest waiting,—
  Who will bear the sheaves away?
Loud and long the Master calleth,
  Rich reward he offers free;
Who will answer, gladly saying,
  "Here am I, O Lord, send me."

2 If you cannot cross the ocean
    And the heathen lands explore,
  You can find the heathen nearer,
    You can help them at your door;
  If you cannot speak like angels,
    If you cannot preach like Paul,
  You can tell the love of Jesus,
    You can say he died for all.

3 While the souls of men are dying,
    And the Master calls for you,
  Let none hear you idly saying,
    "'There is nothing I can do!"
  Gladly take the task he gives you,
    Let his work your pleasure be;
  Answer quickly when he calleth,
    "Here am I, O Lord, send me."

785 "*What thy hand findeth.*" E. H. GATES.

If you cannot on the ocean
  Sail among the swiftest fleet,
Rocking on the highest billows,
  Laughing at the storms you meet,
You can stand among the sailors,
  Anchored yet within the bay,
You can lend a hand to help them,
  As they launch their boat away.

2 If you are too weak to journey
    Up the mountain steep and high,
  You can stand within the valley,
    While the multitude go by;
  You can chant in happy measure,
    As they slowly pass along;
  Though they may forget the singer,
    They will not forget the song.

3 If you have not gold and silver
    Ever ready to command;
  If you cannot toward the needy
    Reach an ever open hand,
  You can visit the afflicted,
    O'er the erring you can weep;
  You can be a true disciple
    Sitting at the Saviour's feet.

4 If you cannot in the harvest
    Garner up the richest sheaf,
  Many a grain both ripe and golden
    Will the careless reapers leave;
  Go and glean among the briers,
    Growing rank against the wall,
  For it may be that the shadow
    Hides the heaviest wheat of all.

786 8s, 7s. *Christian Union.* T. W. AVELING.

Hail! thou God of grace and glory!
  Who thy name hast magnified,
By redemption's wondrous story,
  By the Saviour crucified;
Thanks to thee for every blessing,
  Flowing from the Fount of love;
Thanks for present good unceasing,
  And for hopes of bliss above.

2 Hear us, as thus bending lowly,
  Near thy bright and burning throne;
We invoke thee, God most holy!
  Through thy well-belovéd Son;
Send the baptism of thy Spirit,
  Shed the pentecostal fire;
Let us all thy grace inherit,
  Waken, crown each good desire.

3 Bind thy people, Lord! in union,
  With the sevenfold cord of love;
Breathe a spirit of communion
  With the glorious hosts above;
Let thy work be seen progressing;
  Bow each heart, and bend each knee;
Till the world, thy truth possessing,
  Celebrates its jubilee.

BEAUTEOUS DAY. P. M. GEO. F. ROOT.

1. We are watching, we are waiting, For the bright prophetic day:
When the shadows, weary shadows, From the world shall roll (*Omit*) a-way. We are waiting for the morning, When the beauteous day is dawning; We are waiting for the morning, For the golden spires of day. Lo! he comes! see the King draws near; Zion, shout! the Lord is here.

787 *We are watching.* W. O. CUSHING.

We are watching, we are waiting,
  For the bright prophetic day:
When the shadows, weary shadows,
  From the world shall roll away.—Cho.

2 We are watching, we are waiting,
  For the star that brings the day:
When the night of sin shall vanish,
  And the shadows melt away.—Cho.

3 We are watching, we are waiting,
  For the beauteous King of day:
For the Chiefest of ten-thousand,
  For the Light, the Truth, the Way.--
    Cho.

CHURCH WORK.

WESTMINSTER. 8s, 7s.   J. F. HOLBROOK.

1. On-ward, Chris-tian, though the re-gion Where thou art be drear and lone; God has set a guar-dian le-gion Ver-y near thee; press thou on.

788   *"Leaving us an example."*   S. JOHNSON.

ONWARD, Christian, though the region
  Where thou art be drear and lone;
God has set a guardian legion
  Very near thee; press thou on.

2 By the thorn-road, and none other,
  Is the mount of vision won;
Tread it without shrinking, brother;
  Jesus trod it; press thou on.

3 Be this world the wiser, stronger,
  For thy life of pain and peace;
While it needs thee, oh, no longer
  Pray thou for thy quick release.

4 Pray thou, Christian, daily rather,
  That thou be a faithful son;
By the prayer of Jesus, "Father,
  Not my will, but thine, be done."

789   *Courage and Faith.*   ANON.

FATHER, hear the prayer we offer!
  Not for ease that prayer shall be,
But for strength that we may ever
  Live our lives courageously.

2 Not for ever by still waters
  Would we idly quiet stay;
But would smite the living fountains
  From the rocks along our way.

3 Be our strength in hours of weakness,
  In our wanderings, be our guide;
Through endeavor, failure, danger,
  Father, be thou at our side!

790   *Progress.*   H. BONAR.

LIKE the eagle, upward, onward,
  Let my soul in faith be borne:
Calmly gazing, skyward, sunward,
  Let my eye unshrinking turn!

2 Where the cross, God's love revealing,
  Sets the fettered spirit free,
Where it sheds its wondrous healing,
  There, my soul, thy rest shall be!

3 Oh, may I no longer, dreaming,
  Idly waste my golden day,
But, each precious hour redeeming,
  Upward, onward, press my way!

791   *Psalm 127.*   H. AUBER

VAINLY, through night's weary hours,
  Keep we watch, lest foes alarm;
Vain our bulwarks, and our towers,
  But for God's protecting arm.

2 Vain were all our toil and labor,
  Did not God that labor bless;
Vain, without his grace and favor.
  Every talent we possess.

3 Vainer still the hope of heaven,
  That on human strength relies;
But to him shall help be given,
  Who in humble faith applies.

4 Seek we, then, the Lord's Anointed;
  He will grant us peace and rest:
Ne'er was suppliant disappointed,
  Who thro' Christ his prayer addressed.

CHURCH WORK.

SOLNEY. 8s, 7s. I. A. P. SCHULZ.

1. Cast thy bread up-on the wa-ters, Thinking not 'tis thrown a-way;
God him-self saith, thou shalt gath-er It a-gain some fu-ture day.

792 *Eccl.* 11 : 1. J. H. HANAFORD.

Cast thy bread upon the waters,
Thinking not 'tis thrown away;
God himself saith, thou shalt gather
It again some future day.

2 Cast thy bread upon the waters;
Wildly though the billows roll,
They but aid thee as thou toilest
Truth to spread from pole to pole.

3 As the seed by billows floated,
To some distant island lone,
So to human souls benighted,
That thou flingest may be borne.

4 Cast thy bread upon the waters;
Why wilt thou still doubting stand?
Bounteous shall God send the harvest,
If thou sow'st with liberal hand.

STOCKWELL. 8s, 7s. D. E. JONES.

1. He that go-eth forth with weep-ing, Bear-ing pre-cious seed in love,
Nev-er tir-ing, nev-er sleep-ing, Find-eth mer-cy from a-bove.

793 *Psalm* 126: 6. T. HASTINGS.

He that goeth forth with weeping,
Bearing precious seed in love,
Never tiring, never sleeping,
Findeth mercy from above.

2 Soft descend the dews of heaven,
Bright the rays celestial shine;
Precious fruits will thus be given,
Through an influence all divine.
G

3 Sow thy seed, be never weary,
Let no fears thy soul annoy;
Be the prospect ne'er so dreary,
Thou shalt reap the fruits of joy.

4 Lo, the scene of verdure brightening!
See the rising grain appear;
Look again! the fields are whitening,
For the harvest time is near.

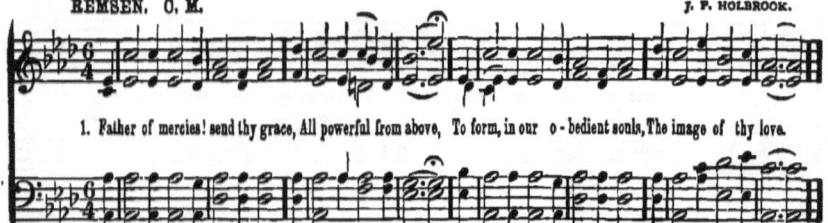

794   *"So Jesus looked."*   P. DODDRIDGE.

FATHER of mercies! send thy grace,
  All powerful from above,
To form in our obedient souls
  The image of thy love.

2 Oh, may our sympathizing breasts
  The generous pleasure know,
Kindly to share in others' joy,
  And weep for others' woe!

3 When the most helpless sons of grief
  In low distress are laid,
Soft be our hearts their pains to feel,
  And swift our hands to aid.

4 So Jesus looked on dying men,
  When throned above the skies;
And mid the embraces of his God,
  He felt compassion rise.

5 On wings of love the Saviour flew,
  To raise us from the ground,
And made the richest of his blood
  A balm for every wound.

795   *God's hidden ones.*   W. CROSWELL.

LORD, lead the way the Saviour went,
  By lane and cell obscure,
And let love's treasures still be spent,
  Like his, upon the poor.

2 Like him, through scenes of deep distress,
  Who bore the world's sad weight,
We, in their crowded loneliness,
  Would seek the desolate.

3 For thou hast placed us side by side
  In this wide world of ill;
And that thy followers may be tried,
  The poor are with us still.

4 Mean are all offerings we can make;
  Yet thou hast taught us, Lord,
If given for the Saviour's sake,
  They lose not their reward.
    G

796   *Minute fidelity.*   ANON.

SCORN not the slightest word or deed,
  Nor deem it void of power;
There's fruit in each wind-wafted seed,
  That waits its natal hour.

2 A whispered word may touch the heart,
  And call it back to life;
A look of love bid sin depart,
  And still unholy strife.

3 No act falls fruitless; none can tell
  How vast its power may be,
Nor what results infolded dwell
  Within it silently.

4 Work on, despair not, bring thy mite,
  Nor care how small it be;
God is with all that serve the right,
  The holy, true, and free.

797   *Psalm 41.*   A. L. BARBAULD.

BLEST is the man whose softening heart
  Feels all another's pain;
To whom the supplicating eye
  Was never raised in vain:—

2 Whose breast expands with generous
  A stranger's woes to feel;   [warmth
And bleeds in pity o'er the wound
  He wants the power to heal.

3 He spreads his kind supporting arms
  To every child of grief;
His secret bounty largely flows,
  And brings unasked relief.

4 To gentle offices of love
  His feet are never slow:
He views, through mercy's melting eye,
  A brother in a foe.

5 Peace from the bosom of his God,
  The Saviour's grace shall give;
And, when he kneels before the throne,
  His trembling soul shall live.

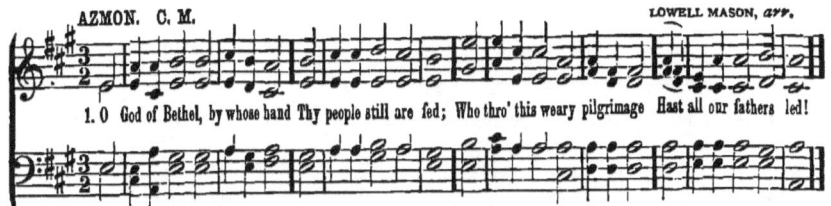

798   *Genesis* 28: 19-22.   P. DODDRIDGE.

O God of Bethel, by whose hand
Thy people still are fed;
Who through this weary pilgrimage
Hast all our fathers led!

2 Our vows, our prayers, we now present
Before thy throne of grace;
God of our fathers! be the God
Of their succeeding race.

3 Through each perplexing path of life
Our wandering footsteps guide;
Give us, each day, our daily bread,
And raiment fit provide.

4 Oh, spread thy covering wings around
Till all our wanderings cease,
And at our Father's loved abode,
Our souls arrive in peace.

5 Such blessings from thy gracious hand
Our humble prayers implore;
And thou shalt be our chosen God,
Our portion evermore.

799   *Christ receiving children.*   P. DODDRIDGE.

See Israel's gentle Shepherd stands,
With all engaging charms!
Hark! how he calls the tender lambs,
And folds them in his arms!

2 "Permit them to approach," he cries,
"Nor scorn their humble name;
For 'twas to bless such souls as these,
The Lord of angels came."

3 We bring them, Lord, in thankful hands,
And yield them up to thee;
Joyful that we ourselves are thine,—
Thine let our offspring be.

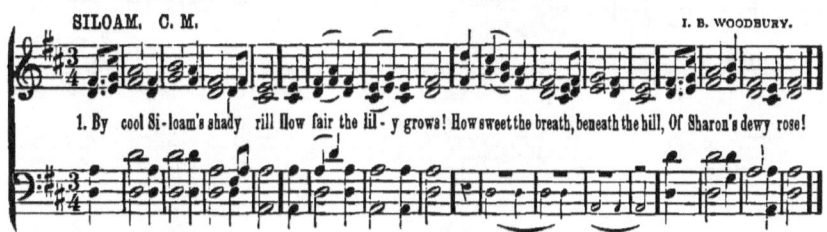

800   *A Christian Child.*   R. HEBER.

By cool Siloam's shady rill
How fair the lily grows!
How sweet the breath, beneath the hill,
Of Sharon's dewy rose!

2 Lo! such the child whose early feet
The paths of peace have trod;
Whose secret heart, with influence sweet,
Is upward drawn to God.

3 By cool Siloam's shady rill
The lily must decay;
The rose that blooms beneath the hill
Must shortly fade away.

4 And soon, too soon, the wintry hour
Of man's maturer age
May shake the soul with sorrow's power
And stormy passion's rage.

5 O thou, whose infant feet were found
Within thy Father's shrine,
Whose years, with changeless virtue crowned,
Were all alike divine!

6 Dependent on thy bounteous breath,
We seek thy grace alone
In childhood, manhood, age and death,
To keep us still thine own.

SUNDAY-SCHOOL.

INVERNESS. S. M. — LOWELL MASON.

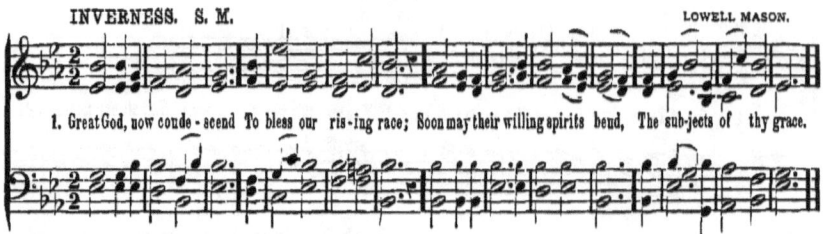

801 *Our children.* J. FELLOWS.

GREAT God, now condescend
To bless our rising race;
Soon may their willing spirits bend,
The subjects of thy grace.

2 Oh, what a pure delight
Their happiness to see;
Our warmest wishes all unite
To lead their souls to thee.

3 Now bless, thou God of love,
The word of truth divine;
Send thy good Spirit from above,
And make these children thine.

802 *"Suffer them to come."* H. U. ONDERDONK.

THE Saviour kindly calls
Our children to his breast;
He folds them in his gracious arms,
Himself declares them blest.

2 "Let them approach," he cries,
"Nor scorn their humble claim;
The heirs of heaven are such as these,
For such as these I came."

3 With joy we bring them, Lord,
Devoting them to thee,
Imploring, that, as we are thine,
Thine may our offspring be.

OLIVET. 6s, 4s. — LOWELL MASON.

803 *Ancient Hymn.* H. M. DEXTER, tr.

SHEPHERD of tender youth,
Guiding in love and truth
 Through devious ways—
Christ, our triumphant King,
We come thy name to sing,
And here our children bring,
 To shout thy praise.

2 Thou art our holy Lord,
The all-subduing Word,
 Healer of strife;
Thou didst thyself abase,
That from sin's deep disgrace
Thou mightest save our race,
 And give us life.

3 Ever be thou our Guide,
Our Shepherd and our pride,
 Our staff and song;
Jesus, thou Christ of God,
By thy perennial word
Lead us where thou hast trod;
 Our faith make strong.

4 So now, and till we die,
Sound we thy praises high,
 And joyful sing:
Let all the holy throng,
Who to thy Church belong,
Unite and swell the song
 To Christ our King!

G

804
Lambs of the Fold.   D. A. THRUPP.

Saviour, like a shepherd lead us:
 Much we need thy tender care;
In thy pleasant pastures feed us,
 For our use thy fold prepare:
We are thine: do thou befriend us,
 Be the guardian of our way;
Keep thy flock, from sin defend us,
 Seek us when we go astray.

2 Thou hast promised to receive us,
 Poor and sinful though we be;
Thou hast mercy to relieve us,
 Grace to cleanse, and power to free:
Early let us seek thy favor,
 Early help us do thy will;
Holy Lord, our only Saviour!
 With thy grace our bosom fill.

805
Sabbath School Meeting.   ANON.

Saviour King, in hallowed union,
 At thy sacred feet we bow;
Heart with heart, in blest communion,
 Join to crave thy favor now!
Though celestial choirs adore thee,
 Let our prayer as incense rise;
And our praise be set before thee,
 Sweet as evening sacrifice.

2 Heavenly Fount, thy streams of blessing,
 Oft have cheered us on our way;
By thy power and grace unceasing,
 We continue to this day:
Raise we then with glad emotion
 Thankful lays: and while we sing,
Vow a pure, a full devotion
 To thy work, O Saviour King!

3 When we tell the wondrous story
 Of thy rich, exhaustless love,
Send thy Spirit, Lord of glory,
 On the youthful heart to move!
Oh, that he, the ever-living,
 May descend, as fruitful rain;
Till the wilderness, reviving,
 Blossoms as the rose again!

806
"These little ones."   W. A. MUHLENBERG.

Saviour! who thy flock art feeding
 With the shepherd's kindest care,
All the feeble gently leading,
 While the lambs thy bosom share;
Now, these little ones receiving,
 Fold them in thy gracious arm;
There, we know, thy word believing,
 Only there, secure from harm.

2 Never, from thy pasture roving,
 Let them be the lion's prey;
Let thy tenderness, so loving,
 Keep them all life's dangerous way:
Then, within thy fold eternal,
 Let them find a resting-place,
Feed in pastures ever vernal,
 Drink the rivers of thy grace.

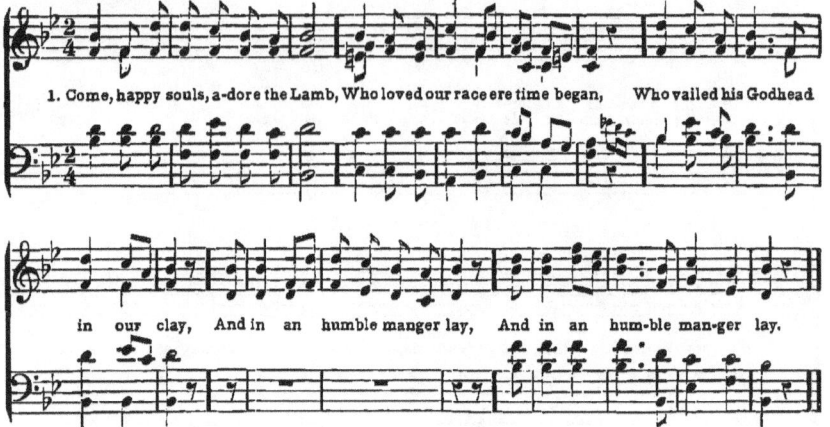

DARLEY. L. M. — W. H. W. DARLEY.

1. Come, happy souls, adore the Lamb, Who loved our race ere time began, Who vailed his Godhead in our clay, And in an humble manger lay, And in an humble manger lay.

807 *Imitation of Christ.* T. BALDWIN.

COME, happy souls, adore the Lamb,
Who loved our race ere time began,
Who vailed his Godhead in our clay,
And in an humble manger lay.

2 To Jordan's stream the Spirit led,
To mark the path his saints should tread;
With joy they trace the sacred way,
To see the place where Jesus lay.

3 Baptized by John in Jordan's wave,
The Saviour left his watery grave;
Heaven owned the deed, approved the way,
And blessed the place where Jesus lay.

4 Come, all who love his precious name,
Come, tread his steps, and learn of him;
Happy beyond expression they
Who find the place where Jesus lay.

808 *"Buried with him."* MORAVIAN.

BURIED in baptism with our Lord,
We rise with him, to life restored;
Not the bare life in Adam lost,
But richer far, for more it cost.

2 Water can cleanse the flesh, we own,
But Christ well knows, and Christ alone,
How dear to him our cleansing stood,
Baptized in fire, and bathed in blood.

3 He by his blood atoned for sin;
This precious blood can wash us clean;
And he arrays us in the dress
Of his unspotted righteousness.

G

809 *The pleasant path.* A. JUDSON.

OUR Saviour bowed beneath the wave,
And meekly sought a watery grave;
Come, see the sacred path he trod,
A path well pleasing to our God.

2 His voice we hear, his footsteps trace,
And hither come to seek his face,
To do his will, to feel his love,
And join our songs with songs above.

3 Hosanna to the Lamb divine!
Let endless glories round him shine!
High o'er the heavens for ever reign,
O Lamb of God, for sinners slain!

810 *Invocation.* A. JUDSON.

COME, Holy Spirit, Dove divine,
On these baptismal waters shine,
And teach our hearts, in highest strain,
To praise the Lamb for sinners slain.

2 We love thy name, we love thy laws,
And joyfully embrace thy cause;
We love thy cross, the shame, the pain,
O Lamb of God, for sinners slain!

3 We sink beneath thy mystic flood,
Oh, bathe us in thy cleansing blood;
We die to sin, and seek a grave
With thee, beneath the yielding wave.

4 And as we rise, with thee to live,
Oh, let the Holy Spirit give
The sealing unction from above,
The breath of life, the fire of love!

BAPTISM.

HAMBURG. L. M.   LOWELL MASON, arr.

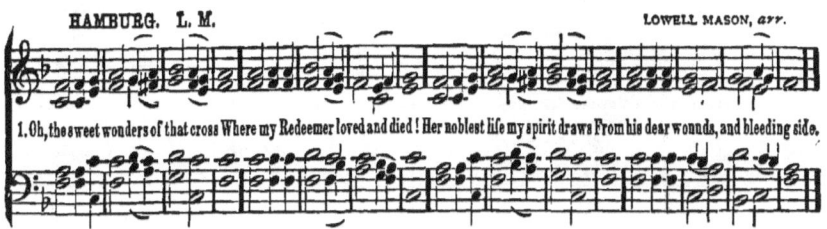

1. Oh, the sweet wonders of that cross Where my Redeemer loved and died! Her noblest life my spirit draws From his dear wounds, and bleeding side.

811   *Parting Song.*   I. WATTS.

OH, the sweet wonders of that cross
  Where my Redeemer loved and died!
Her noblest life my spirit draws
  From his dear wounds, and bleeding side.

2 I would for ever speak his name
  In sounds to mortal ears unknown;
With angels join to praise the Lamb,
  And worship at his Father's throne.

812   *"Bought with a price."*   S. DAVIES.

LORD, I am thine, entirely thine,
  Purchased and saved by blood divine,
With full consent thine I would be,
  And own thy sovereign right in me.

2 Grant one poor sinner more a place
  Among the children of thy grace;
A wretched sinner, lost to God,
  But ransomed by Immanuel's blood.

3 Thine would I live, thine would I die,
  Be thine through all eternity;
The vow is past beyond repeal;
  And now I set the solemn seal.

4 Here at that cross where flows the blood
  That bought my guilty soul for God,
Thee, my new Master now I call,
  And consecrate to thee my all.

HAPPY DAY. L. M.   FROM E. F. RIMBAULT.

1. Oh, happy day, that fixed my choice On thee, my Saviour, and my God!
Well may this glowing heart rejoice, And tell its raptures all abroad. Happy day, happy day, When Jesus wash'd my sins away! He taught me how to watch and pray, And live rejoicing every day;

813   *"Happy Day."*   P. DODDRIDGE.

OH, happy day, that fixed my choice
  On thee, my Saviour, and my God!
Well may this glowing heart rejoice,
  And tell its raptures all abroad.

CHO.—Happy day, happy day,
  When Jesus washed my sins away!
He taught me how to watch and pray,
  And live rejoicing every day:

Happy day, happy day,
  When Jesus washed my sins away!

2 Oh, happy bond, that seals my vows
  To him who merits all my love!
Let cheerful anthems fill his house,
  While to that sacred shrine I move.—CHO.

3 'Tis done, the great transaction's done:
  I am my Lord's, and he is mine:
He drew me, and I followed on,
  Charmed to confess the voice divine—CHO.

BAPTISM.

PAULINA. 11s.   L. W. BACON, arr.

1. O thou who in Jordan didst bow thy meek head, And whelmed in our sorrow didst sink to the dead, Then rose from the darkness to glo-ry a-bove, And claimed for thy chosen the kingdom of love;—

814   *Following Jesus.*   G. W. BETHUNE.

O thou who in Jordan didst bow thy meek head,
And whelmed in our sorrow didst sink to the dead,
Then rose from the darkness to glory above,
And claimed for thy chosen the kingdom of love;—

2 Thy footsteps we follow, to bow in the tide,
And are buried with thee in the death thou hast died,
Then wake with thy likeness to walk in the way
That brightens and brightens to shadowless day.

3 O Jesus, our Saviour, O Jesus, our Lord,
By the life of thy passion, the grace of thy word,
Accept us, redeem us, dwell ever within,
To keep, by thy Spirit, our spirits from sin;—

4 Till, crowned with thy glory, and waving the palm,
Our garments all white from the blood of the Lamb,
We join the bright millions of saints gone before,
And bless thee, and wonder, and praise evermore.

BELIEF. C. M.   ANON. — D. C.

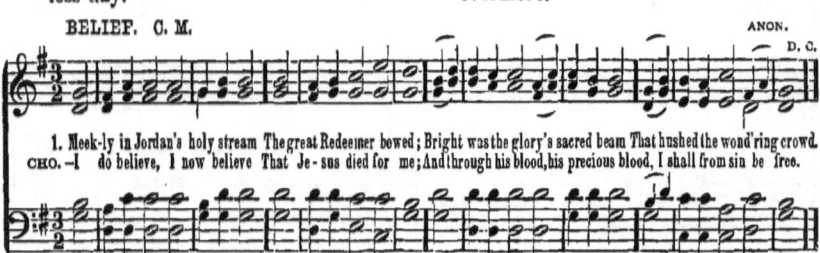

1. Meek-ly in Jordan's holy stream The great Redeemer bowed; Bright was the glory's sacred beam That hushed the wond'ring crowd.
CHO.—I do believe, I now believe That Je-sus died for me; And through his blood, his precious blood, I shall from sin be free.

815   *Jesus' Baptism.*   S. F. SMITH.

MEEKLY in Jordan's holy stream
The great Redeemer bowed;
Bright was the glory's sacred beam
That hushed the wondering crowd.

CHO.—I do believe, I now believe
That Jesus died for me;
And through his blood, his precious blood,
I shall from sin be free.

2 Thus God descended to approve
The deed that Christ had done;
Thus came the emblematic Dove,
And hovered o'er the Son.—CHO.

3 So, blessèd Spirit, come to-day
To our baptismal scene;
Let thoughts of earth be far away,
And every mind serene.—CHO.

G

BAPTISM.

COMMUNION. [No. 2.] C. M. — CHARLES ZEUNER.

1. In all my Lord's appointed ways My journey I'll pur - sue; Hinder me not, ye much-loved saints, For I must go with you.

816   *Gen.* 24: 56.   J. RYLAND.
IN all my Lord's appointed ways
  My journey I'll pursue;
Hinder me not, ye much-loved saints,
  For I must go with you.

2 Through floods and flames, if Jesus lead,
  I'll follow where he goes;
Hinder me not! shall be my cry,
  Though earth and hell oppose.

3 Through duties, and through trials too,
  I'll go at his command;
Hinder me not, for I am bound
  To my Immanuel's land.

4 And when my Saviour calls me home,
  Still this my cry shall be,
Hinder me not! come, welcome death;
  I'll gladly go with thee!

817   *"This is my Son."*   ENG. BAP. COLL.
'TIS God the Father we adore
  In this baptismal sign;
'Tis he whose voice on Jordan's shore
  Proclaimed the Son divine.

2 The Father owned him; let our breath
  In answering praise ascend,
As in the image of his death
  We own our heavenly Friend.

3 We seek the consecrated grave
  Along the path he trod;
Receive us in the hallowed wave,
  Thou holy Son of God.

4 Let earth and heaven our zeal record,
  And future witness bear;
That we to Zion's mighty Lord
  Our full allegiance swear.
  G

818   *"All righteousness."*   B. BEDDOME.
BURIED beneath the yielding wave,
  The great Redeemer lies;
Faith views him in the watery grave,
  And thence beholds him rise.

2 Thus do his willing saints, to-day,
  Their ardent zeal express,
And, in the Lord's appointed way,
  Fulfill all righteousness.

3 With joy we in his footsteps tread,
  And would his cause maintain;
Like him be numbered with the dead,
  And with him rise and reign.

4 Now we, blest Saviour, would to thee
  Our grateful voices raise;
Washed in the fountain of thy blood,
  Our lives shall be thy praise.

819   *Consecration.*   B. BEDDOME.
WITNESS, ye men and angels, now
  Before the Lord we speak;
To him we make our solemn vow,
  A vow we dare not break:—

2 That, long as life itself shall last,
  Ourselves to Christ we yield;
Nor from his cause will we depart,
  Or ever quit the field.

3 We trust not in our native strength,
  But on his grace rely,
That with returning wants the Lord
  Will all our need supply.

4 Oh, guide our doubtful feet aright,
  And keep us in thy ways;
And, while we turn our vows to prayers,
  Turn thou our prayers to praise.

BAPTISM.

OWEN. S. M.   J. E. SWEETSER.
Sing rapidly.

1. Oh, what, if we are Christ's, Is earth-ly shame or loss?
Bright shall the crown of glo-ry be, When we have borne the cross.

820   "*Via crucis, via lucis.*"   H. W. BAKER.
Oh, what, if we are Christ's,
  Is earthly shame or loss?
Bright shall the crown of glory be,
  When we have borne the cross.

2 Keen was the trial once,
  Bitter the cup of woe,
When martyred saints, baptized in blood,
  Christ's sufferings shared below.

3 Bright is their glory now,
  Boundless their joy above,
Where, on the bosom of their God,
  They rest in perfect love.

4 Lord, may that grace be ours!
  Like them in faith to bear
All that of sorrow, grief, or pain,
  May be our portion here!

5 Enough, if thou at last
  The word of blessing give,
And let us rest beneath thy feet,
  Where saints and angels live!

821   "*I can do all things.*"   ANON.
O Saviour, who didst come
  By water and by blood;
Confessed on earth, adored in heaven,
  Eternal Son of God!

2 Jesus, our life and hope,
  To endless years the same;
We plead thy gracious promises;
  And rest upon thy name.
    G

3 By faith in thee we live,
  By faith in thee we stand,
By thee we vanquish sin and death,
  And gain the heavenly land.

4 O Lord, increase our faith;
  Our fearful spirits calm;
Sustain us through this mortal strife,
  Then give the victor's palm!

822   "*I have peace.*"   H. BONAR.
I hear the words of love,
  I gaze upon the blood,
I see the mighty sacrifice,
  And I have peace with God.

2 'Tis everlasting peace,
  Sure as Jehovah's name;
'Tis stable as his steadfast throne,
  For evermore the same.

3 The clouds may go and come,
  And storms may sweep my sky;
This blood-sealed friendship changes not,
  The cross is ever nigh.

4 I change—he changes not;
  The Christ can never die;
His love, not mine, the resting-place;
  His truth, not mine, the tie.

5 My love is ofttimes low,
  My joy still ebbs and flows;
But peace with him remains the same,
  No change Jehovah knows.

CHURCH FELLOWSHIP.

BOYLSTON. S. M.   LOWELL MASON.

1. Blest be the tie that binds Our hearts in Christian love: The fellow-ship of kindred minds Is like to that a - bove.

823   *"Christian Love."*   J. FAWCETT.
BLEST be the tie that binds
  Our hearts in Christian love:
The fellowship of kindred minds
  Is like to that above.

2 Before our Father's throne
  We pour our ardent prayers;
Our fears, our hopes, our aims are one,
  Our comforts and our cares.

3 We share our mutual woes,
  Our mutual burdens bear;
And often for each other flows
  The sympathizing tear.

4 When we asunder part,
  It gives us inward pain;
But we shall still be joined in heart,
  And hope to meet again.

5 This glorious hope revives
  Our courage by the way;
While each in expectation lives,
  And longs to see the day.

6 From sorrow, toil, and pain,
  And sin, we shall be free,
And perfect love and friendship reign
  Through all eternity.

WOOD. S. M.   D. E. JONES.

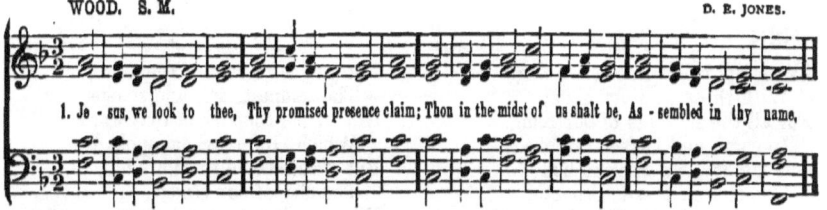

1. Je - sus, we look to thee, Thy promised presence claim; Thou in the midst of us shalt be, As - sembled in thy name.

824   *Christ's Presence.*   C. WESLEY.
JESUS, we look to thee,
  Thy promised presence claim;
Thou in the midst of us shalt be,
  Assembled in thy name.

2 Not in the name of pride
  Or selfishness we meet;
From nature's paths we turn aside,
  And worldly thoughts forget.

3 We meet the grace to take,
  Which thou hast freely given;
We meet on earth for thy dear sake,
  That we may meet in heaven.

4 Present we know thou art,
  But, oh, thyself reveal!
Now, Lord, let every bounding heart
  Thy mighty comfort feel.
G

5 Oh, may thy quickening voice
  The death of sin remove;
And bid our inmost souls rejoice,
  In hope of perfect love.

825   *Christian Union.*   B. BEDDOME.
LET party names no more
  The Christian world o'erspread;
Gentile and Jew, and bond and free,
  Are one in Christ their head.

2 Among the saints on earth,
  Let mutual love be found;
Heirs of the same inheritance,
  With mutual blessings crowned.

3 Thus will the church below
  Resemble that above;
Where streams of pleasure ever flow,
  And every heart is love.

CHURCH FELLOWSHIP.

HEAVENLY FOLD. C. M. D.   WM. F. SHERWIN.

1. Let saints below in concert sing With those to glory gone; For all the servants of our King In earth and heaven are one. One family— we dwell in him— One church above, beneath, Though now divided by the stream, The narrow stream of death;—

826   *"One Family."*   C. WESLEY.

Let saints below in concert sing
  With those to glory gone;
For all the servants of our King
  In earth and heaven are one.
One family—we dwell in him—
  One church above, beneath,
Though now divided by the stream,
  The narrow stream of death;—

2 One army of the living God,
  To his command we bow;
Part of the host have crossed the flood,
  And part are crossing now.
Ev'n now to their eternal home
  Some happy spirits fly;
And we are to the margin come,
  And soon expect to die.

3 Ev'n now, by faith, we join our hands
  With those that went before,
And greet the ransomed, blessèd bands
  Upon the eternal shore.
Lord Jesus! be our constant guide:
  And, when the word is given,
Bid death's cold flood its waves divide,
  And land us safe in heaven.
    G

827   *Hebrews,* 12: 18–24.   I. WATTS.

Not to the terrors of the Lord,
  The tempest, fire, and smoke;
Not to the thunder of that word
  Which God on Sinai spoke;—
But we are come to Zion's hill,
  The city of our God;
Where milder words declare his will,
  And speak his love abroad.

2 Behold the innumerable host
  Of angels clothed in light;
Behold, the spirits of the just,
  Whose faith is turned to sight!
Behold, the blest assembly there,
  Whose names are writ in heaven!
And God, the Judge of all, declare
  Their vilest sins forgiven.

3 The saints on earth, and all the dead,
  But one communion make;
All join in Christ, their living Head,
  And of his grace partake.
In such society as this
  My weary soul would rest;
The man that dwells where Jesus is,
  Must be for ever blest.

CHURCH FELLOWSHIP. 313

BELMONT. C M. S. WEBBE.

828 *"One as we are one."* RAY PALMER.

LORD, thou on earth didst love thine own,
Didst love them to the end;
Oh, still from thy celestial throne,
Let gifts of love descend.

2 The love the Father bears to thee,
His own eternal Son,
Fill all thy saints, till all shall be
In pure affection one.

3 As thou for us didst stoop so low,
Warmed by love's holy flame,
So let our deeds of kindness flow
To all that bear thy name.

4 One blessèd fellowship of love,
Thy living church should stand,
Till, faultless, she at last above
Shall shine at thy right hand.

5 Oh, glorious day, when she, the Bride,
With her dear Lord appears!
Then, robed in beauty at his side,
She shall forget her tears!

829 1 John 4 : 21. J. SWAIN.

How SWEET, how heavenly is the sight,
When those who love the Lord
In one another's peace delight,
And so fulfill his word!

2 When each can feel his brother's sigh,
And with him bear a part!
When sorrow flows from every eye,
And joy from heart to heart!

3 When, free from envy, scorn, and pride,
Our wishes all above,
Each can his brother's failings hide,
And show a brother's love!

4 Let love, in one delightful stream,
Through every bosom flow;
And union sweet, and dear esteem
In every action glow.

5 Love is the golden chain that binds
The happy souls above;
And he's an heir of heaven who finds
His bosom glow with love.

EVAN. C. M. W. H. HAVERGAL, arr.

G

314. WASHING OF SAINTS' FEET.

WORSHIP. 8s, 7s, 4s.   S. W. MOUNTZ.

1. O thou Lamb of God, de-scend-ing To the serv-ant's low-ly place,—
At the feet of mor-tals bend-ing, Mark the Lord of sov'reign grace!
Hum-bly wash-ing, hum-bly wash-ing; Here we meet thee face to face.

830   *Following Christ.*   M. S. NEWCOMER.

O THOU Lamb of God, descending
  To the servant's lowly place,—
At the feet of mortals bending,
  Mark the Lord of sov'reign grace!
    Humbly washing;
Here we meet thee face to face.

2 Shall we stoop to one another?
  Keep the sweet command, "Ye ought,"
Fill the office of a brother,
  And the law our Master taught?
    Lead us, Saviour,
To the cross thy blood hath bought.

3 Thou hast led, and we must follow,
  If we would thy servants be;
Vain profession, loud and hollow,
  Will not bring our souls to thee;
    We are happy
When we yield to thy decree!

4 The example thou hast given
  Is for those who trust and "do;"
For thy footsteps lead to heaven,
  G

And no other way is true,
    Holy Jesus!
Guide us all our journey through!

831   *Love to Saints.*   C. WESLEY, *alt.*
    S. M.

I LOVE the sons of grace,
  The heirs of bliss divine,
Who walk in paths of righteousness,
  And fly from every sin.

2 They Jesus' image bear,
  And his commands obey;
They shall at length with him appear
  In everlasting day.

3 They love the Father's name,
  And gladly do his will;
They humbly follow Christ, the Lamb,
  In purity and zeal.

4 Their footsteps I'll pursue
  With vigor till I die,
Rejoicing in the pleasing view
  Of meeting them on high.

WASHING OF SAINTS' FEET. 315

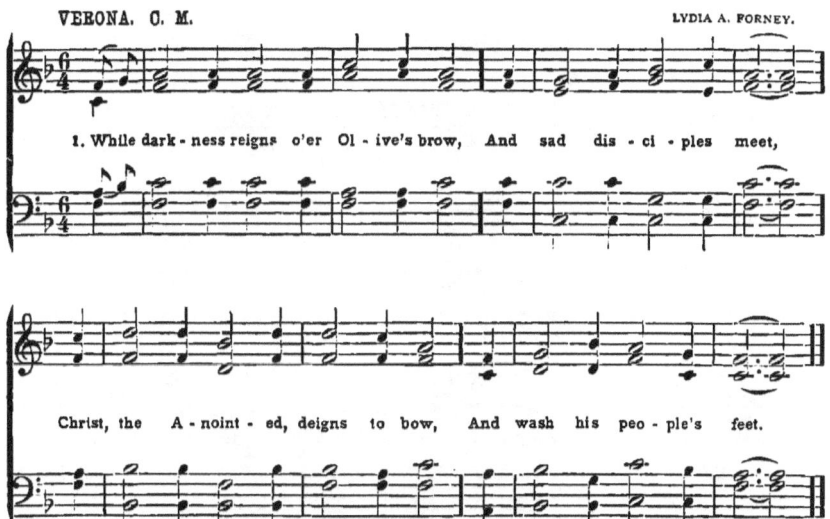

VERONA. C. M.   LYDIA A. FORNEY.

1. While darkness reigns o'er Olive's brow, And sad disciples meet, Christ, the Anointed, deigns to bow, And wash his people's feet.

832 *Christian Obedience.* M. S. NEWCOMER.

WHILE darkness reigns o'er Olive's brow,
  And sad disciples meet,
Christ, the Anointed, deigns to bow,
  And wash his people's feet.

2 Rejoicing with God's only Son,
  We still his words repeat,
Eager to do what he hath done,
  And wash each other's feet.

3 Not mine to ask the reason why,
  If I am Christ's alone;
He speaks, and shall my soul deny
  His sceptre and his throne?

4 Wash me, dear Lord, and mine thou art,
  Wash me with blood again,
And let thy voice, within my heart,
  Repeat the glad amen!

5 Did Christ abase himself for me,
  And shall my heart disdain
To bow itself as low as he,
  The King of endless reign?

6 O God! thou Helper, crucify
  Our selfishness and pride;
And 'neath the glance of Jesus' eye,
  We'll crown the Prince who died!
G

833 *Christ our Example.* JOHN WINEBRENNER.
                L. M.

THE Church of God believes it right
  To think and do as Jesus bade,
When on that dark and doleful night
  He gave his law, and plainly said:—

2 Mark the example which I give;
  Keep it, and show your mutual love:
My precepts do, and you shall live,
  In bliss below, and heaven above.

3 Then, do we love our brethren now?
  And are we bound in union sweet?
If so, like Jesus, let us bow,
  And let us wash each other's feet.

4 Let no one be ashamed of this,—
  Or, Peter-like, turn and say, no;
But as we aim for heavenly bliss,
  We'll in our Master's footsteps go.

5 Now, Lord, we'll wash thy people's feet,
  And here enjoy their fond embrace;
Each with a kiss of friendship greet;
  And hope in love to see thy face.

6 And then we'll feast on heavenly love
  And find our joys to be complete:
Yes, then we'll sing thy praise above,
  And bow, with angels, at thy feet.

WASHING OF SAINTS' FEET.

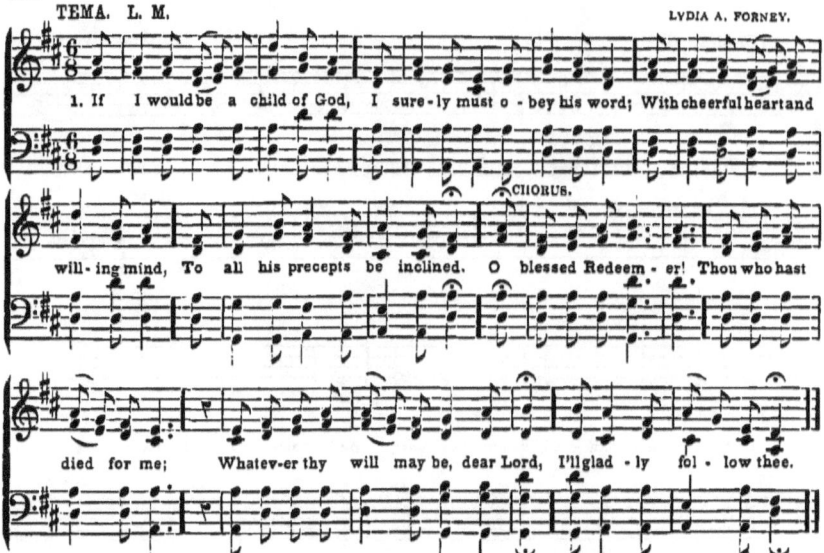

TEMA. L. M. — LYDIA A. FORNEY.

1. If I would be a child of God, I surely must obey his word; With cheerful heart and willing mind, To all his precepts be inclined. O blessed Redeemer! Thou who hast died for me; Whatever thy will may be, dear Lord, I'll gladly follow thee.

834 LYDIA A. FORNEY.

If I would be a child of God,
I surely must obey his word;
With cheerful heart and willing mind,
To all his precepts be inclined.
Cho.—O blessèd Redeemer!
    Thou who hast died for me;
  Whatever thy will may be, dear Lord,
    I'll gladly follow thee.

2 The last great Feast-time having come
Before our Lord was going home—
Adorned in humbleness complete,
He washed his twelve disciples' feet.

3 Then, seated in their midst again,
This new example to explain,
He taught them how to understand,
And to observe this plain command.

4 "Ye call me Lord and Master,—true,
For so I am." Then ought ye too
Be of a meek and lowly mind;
In sweet obedience pleasure find.

5 If I, your Lord, have seen it meet,
To stoop and wash my brethren's feet;
No greater than your Lord are ye;
Then in this act do follow me.

6 Dear Lord, we'll gladly follow thee:
We come in deep humility;
G

Oh, bless us now, while here we meet,
Thy will to do in washing feet.

835 *Feet-washing a Church Ordinance.*
C. M. H. C. S

In Jesus' name once more we meet,
  To honor him who said:
Ye ought to wash each other's feet
  As I the way have led.

2 Shall we forget the sacred rite,
  Our dying Lord ordained,
Upon that dark and solemn night,
  When he our woe-cup drained?

3 With words of love, sublime and sweet,
  He cheered each fainting heart,
And washed and wiped those loved one's feet,
  From whom he soon must part.

4 Girded to serve, the Lord of all
  Thus taught humility;
And still his voice doth on us call,
  "Fear not, but follow me."

5 "If I, your Lord and Master, thought
  A servant's office meet,
Be not ashamed, but know ye ought
  To wash each other's feet."

6 Yea, Lord, we will remember thee,
  And keep this plain command;
Oh, may our hearts obedient be
  In one united band.

836
Entire Purification. C. WESLEY.
C. M.

For ever here my rest shall be,
  Close by thy bleeding side;
This all my hope, and all my plea,—
  For me the Saviour died.

2 My dying Saviour, and my God,
  Fountain for guilt and sin,
Oh, wash me ever with thy blood,
  And cleanse and keep me clean.

3 Wash me, and make me thus thine own;
  Wash me, and mine thou art;
Wash me, but not my feet alone,—
  My hands, my head, my heart.

4 The atonement of thy blood apply,
  Till faith to sight improve;
Till hope in full fruition die,
  And all my soul be love.

837
Christ the Exemplar. C. WESLEY, alt.
7s.

Jesus, all-redeeming Lord,
  Magnify thy faithful word;
In thine ordinance appear;
  Come, and meet thy foll'wers here.

2 In the rite thou hast enjoined,
  Let us now our Saviour find;
Thine example we repeat,
  Washing one another's feet.

3 Thou our faithful hearts prepare;
  Thou thy pard'ning grace declare;
Thou that hast for sinners died,
  Show thyself the Crucified!

4 All the power of sin remove;
  Fill us with thy perfect love:
Stamp us with the stamp divine;
  Seal our souls for ever thine.

838
Full Assurance. HENRY FRANCIS LYTE.
8s & 7s.

Know, my soul! thy full salvation,
  Rise o'er sin, and fear, and care;
Joy to find in every station,
  Something still to do or bear:
Think what Spirit dwells within thee;
  What a Father's smile is thine;
What a Saviour died to win thee!
  Child of heaven! should'st thou repine?

2 Haste thee on from grace to glory,
  Armed by faith and winged by prayer;
G

Heaven's eternal day's before thee,
  God's own hand shall guide thee there.
Soon shall close thy earthly mission,
  Swift shall pass thy pilgrim days,
Hope shall change to glad fruition
  Faith to sight and prayer to praise.

839
C. M.

I'm not ashamed to own my Lord,
  Or to defend his cause;
Maintain the honor of his word,
  The glory of his cross.
Cho.—Help me, dear Saviour, thee to own,
    And ever faithful be,
  And when thou sittest on thy throne,
    O Lord! remember me.
(See Hymn No. 541.)

840
8s & 7s.

One there is above all others,
  Well deserves the name of Friend;
His is love beyond a brother's,
  Costly, free, and knows no end.
Cho.—I love Jesus, Hallelujah!
  I love Jesus, yes, I do; I do love Jesus;
  He's my Saviour, Jesus loves, yes, loves
    me too!
(See Hymn No. 585.)

841
L. M.

Jesus, my All, to heaven is gone,—
  I am bound for the land of Canaan,
He whom I fix my hopes upon,—
  I am bound for the land of Canaan.
Cho.—O Canaan, bright Canaan,
    I am bound for the land of Canaan,
    O Canaan! it is my happy home!
  I am bound for the land of Canaan
(See Hymn No. 334.)

842
S. M.

Come, ye that love the Lord,
  And let your joys be known;
Join in a song with sweet accord
  And thus surround the throne.
Cho.—I'm glad salvation's free!
    I'm glad salvation's free!
  Salvation's free for you and me;
    I'm glad salvation's free!
(See Hymn No. 31.)

THE LORD'S SUPPER.

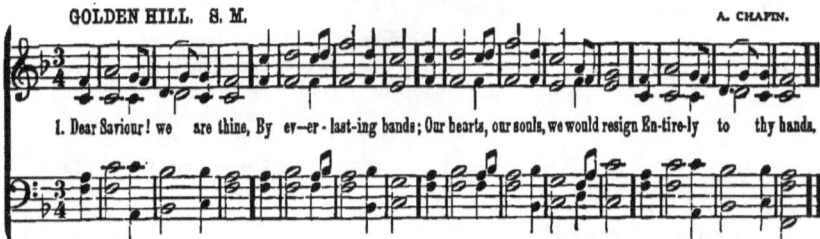

GOLDEN HILL. S. M. — A. CHAPIN.

1. Dear Saviour! we are thine, By ev-er-last-ing bands; Our hearts, our souls, we would resign En-tire-ly to thy hands.

843 *"We are thine."* P. DODDRIDGE.

Dear Saviour! we are thine,
 By everlasting bands;
Our hearts, our souls, we would resign
 Entirely to thy hands.

2 To thee we still would cleave
 With ever-growing zeal;
If millions tempt us Christ to leave,
 Oh, let them ne'er prevail!

3 Thy Spirit shall unite
 Our souls to thee, our Head;
Shall form in us thine image bright,
 And teach thy paths to tread.

4 Death may our souls divide
 From these abodes of clay;
But love shall keep us near thy side,
 Through all the gloomy way.

5 Since Christ and we are one,
 Why should we doubt or fear?
If he in heaven has fixed his throne,
 He'll fix his members there.

844 *At closing.* A. R. WOLFE.

A parting hymn we sing,
 Around thy table, Lord;
Again our grateful tribute bring,
 Our solemn vows record.

2 Here have we seen thy face,
 And felt thy presence here;
So may the savor of thy grace
 In word and life appear.

3 The purchase of thy blood—
 By sin no longer led—
The path our dear Redeemer trod
 May we rejoicing tread.

4 In self-forgetting love
 Be our communion shown,
Until we join the church above,
 And know as we are known.
 G

845 *The invitation.* I. WATTS.

Jesus invites his saints
 To meet around his board;
Here pardoned rebels sit and hold
 Communion with their Lord.

2 This holy bread and wine
 Maintains our fainting breath,
By union with our living Lord,
 And interest in his death.

3 Our heavenly Father calls
 Christ and his members one;
We, the young children of his love,
 And he, the first-born Son.

4 Let all our powers be joined,
 His glorious name to raise;
Pleasure and love fill every mind
 And every voice be praise.

5 To God, the Father, Son,
 And Spirit, glory be,
As was, and is, and shall remain
 Through all eternity!

846 *Great wishes.* C. WESLEY.

Jesus, my strength, my hope,
 On thee I cast my care,
With humble confidence look up,
 And know thou hear'st my prayer.

2 I want a sober mind,
 A self-renouncing will,
That tramples down, and casts behind
 The lures of pleasing ill;—

3 I want a godly fear,
 A quick-discerning eye,
That looks to thee when sin is near,
 And sees the tempter fly;—

4 A spirit still prepared,
 And armed with jealous care,
For ever standing on its guard,
 And watching unto prayer.

THE LORD'S SUPPER. 319

ADRIAN. S. M.   J. E. GOULD.

1. Like Noah's weary dove, That soared the earth around,
But not a resting-place above The cheerless waters found;—

847 *The Ark of God.* W. A. MUHLENBERG.

LIKE Noah's weary dove,
  That soared the earth around,
But not a resting-place above
  The cheerless waters found;—

2 Oh, cease, my wandering soul,
  On restless wing to roam;
All this wide world, to either pole,
  Hath not for thee a home.

3 Behold the ark of God!
  Behold the open door!
Oh, haste to gain that dear abode,
  And rove, my soul, no more.

4 There safe thou shalt abide,
  There sweet shall be thy rest;
And every longing satisfied,
  With full salvation blest.

848 *"This is my blood."* E. DENNY.

BLEST feast of love divine!
  'Tis grace that makes us free
To feed upon this bread and wine,
  In memory, Lord, of thee.

2 That blood which flowed for sin,
  In symbol here we see,
And feel the blessèd pledge within,
  That we are loved of thee.

3 Oh, if this glimpse of love
  Be so divinely sweet,
What will it be, O Lord, above,
  Thy gladdening smile to meet!
G

849 *Christ, our Righteousness.* C. WESLEY, alt.

FOR ever here my rest!
  Close to thy bleeding side;
This all my hope, and all my plea—
  For me the Saviour died.

2 My Saviour, and my God!
  Fountain for guilt and sin!
Sprinkle me ever with thy blood!
  And cleanse and keep me clean.

850 *"The banqueting house."* C. WESLEY.

JESUS, we thus obey
  Thy last and kindest word,
And in thine own appointed way
  We come to meet thee, Lord!

2 Thus we remember thee,
  And take this bread and wine
As thine own dying legacy,
  And our redemption's sign.

3 Thy presence makes the feast;
  Now let our spirits feel
The glory not to be expressed,—
  The joy unspeakable!

4 With high and heavenly bliss
  Thou dost our spirits cheer;
Thy house of banqueting is this,
  And thou hast brought us here.

5 Now let our souls be fed
  With manna from above,
And over us thy banner spread
  Of everlasting love.

THE LORD'S SUPPER.

MONKLAND. 7s. JOHN B. WILKES.

1. At the Lamb's high feast we sing, Praise to our victorious King, Who hath washed us in the tide, Flowing from his wounded side.

851 *"Christ, our Passover."* R. CAMPBELL, tr.

AT the Lamb's high feast we sing
Praise to our victorious King,
Who hath washed us in the tide,
Flowing from his wounded side.

2 Where the Paschal blood is poured,
Death's dark angel sheathes his sword;
Israel's hosts triumphant go
Through the wave that drowns the foe.

3 Christ, our Paschal Lamb, is slain,
Holy victim, without stain;
Death and hell defeated lie,
Heaven unfolds its gates on high.

4 Hymns of glory and of praise,
Father, unto thee we raise;
Risen Lord, all praise to thee,
With the Spirit ever be.

852 *"This is my Body."* J. CONDER.

BREAD of heaven! on thee we feed,
For thy flesh is meat indeed:
Ever let our souls be fed
With this true and living bread!

2 Vine of heaven! thy blood supplies
This blest cup of sacrifice:
Lord! thy wounds our healing give,
To thy cross we look and live.

3 Day by day, with strength supplied,
Through the life of him who died:
Lord of life! oh, let us be,
Rooted, grafted, built on thee!
G

853 *Wounded for us.* ANON.

JESUS, Master! hear me now,
While I would renew my vow,
And record thy dying love;
Hear, and help me from above.

2 Feed me, Saviour, with this bread,
Broken in thy body's stead;
Cheer my spirit with this wine,
Streaming like that blood of thine.

3 And as now I eat and drink,
Let me truly, sweetly think,
Thou didst hang upon the tree,
Broken, bleeding, there—for me!

854 *"Thine for ever."* M. F. MAUDE.

THINE for ever! God of love,
Hear us from thy throne above!
Thine for ever may we be,
Here and in eternity!

2 Thine for ever! oh, how blest
They who find in thee their rest!
Saviour, Guardian, heavenly Friend,
Oh, defend us to the end!

3 Thine for ever! Saviour keep
These thy frail and trembling sheep;
Safe alone beneath thy care,
Let us all thy goodness share.

4 Thine for ever! thou our Guide,—
All our wants by thee supplied,—
All our sins by thee forgiven,—
Lead us, Lord, from earth to heaven!

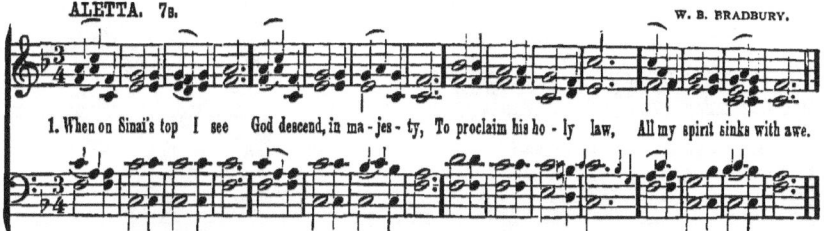

855
Three Mountains. J. MONTGOMERY.

WHEN on Sinai's top I see
God descend, in majesty,
To proclaim his holy law,
All my Spirit sinks with awe.

2 When, in ecstasy sublime,
Tabor's glorious steep I climb,
At the too transporting light,
Darkness rushes o'er my sight.

3 When on Calvary I rest,
God, in flesh made manifest,
Shines in my Redeemer's face,
Full of beauty, truth, and grace.

4 Here I would for ever stay,
Weep and gaze my soul away;
Thou art heaven on earth to me,
Lovely, mournful Calvary!

856
"Lovest thou me?" W. COWPER.

HARK! my soul! it is the Lord;
'Tis thy Saviour—hear his word;
Jesus speaks, and speaks to thee,
"Say, poor sinner, lovest thou me?

2 "I delivered thee when bound,
And when bleeding, healed thy wound:
Sought thee wandering, set thee right,
Turned thy darkness into light.

3 "Can a woman's tender care
Cease towards the child she bare?
Yes, she may forgetful be,
Yet will I remember thee.

4 "Mine is an unchanging love,
Higher than the heights above;
Deeper than the depths beneath—
Free and faithful—strong as death.

5 "Thou shalt see my glory soon,
When the work of grace is done;
Partner of my throne shalt be!
Say, poor sinner! lovest thou me?"

6 Lord! it is my chief complaint,
That my love is weak and faint;
Yet I love thee, and adore;—
Oh, for grace to love thee more.

857
"Thy people shall be my people." J. MONTGOMERY.

PEOPLE of the living God,
I have sought the world around,
Paths of sin and sorrow trod,
Peace and comfort nowhere found.

2 Now to you my spirit turns—
Turns, a fugitive unblest;
Brethren, where your altar burns,
Oh, receive me into rest!

3 Lonely I no longer roam,
Like the cloud, the wind, the wave:
Where you dwell shall be my home,
Where you die shall be my grave;—

4 Mine the God whom you adore,
Your Redeemer shall be mine;
Earth can fill my soul no more,
Every idol I resign.

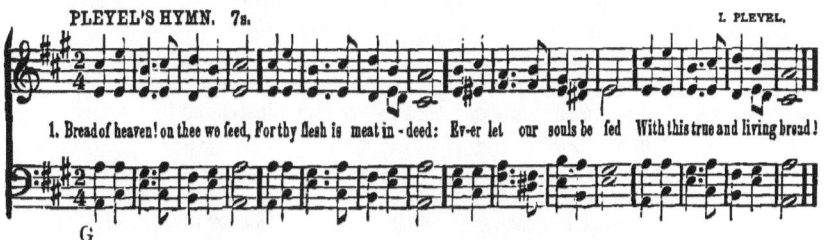

THE LORD'S SUPPER.

OXFORD. C. M. — WILLIAM COOMBS.

1. To-geth-er with these sym-bols, Lord, Thy bless-ed self im-part;
And let thy ho-ly flesh and blood Feed the be-liev-ing heart.

858 *Feeding on Christ.* J. CENNICK.

TOGETHER with these symbols, Lord,
  Thy blessèd self impart;
And let thy holy flesh and blood
  Feed the believing heart.

2 Let us from all our sins be washed
  In thy atoning blood;
And let thy Spirit be the seal
  That we are born of God.

3 Come, Holy Ghost, with Jesus' love,
  Prepare us for this feast;
Oh, let us banquet with our Lord,
  And lean upon his breast.

859 *"Friend of Sinners."* R. BURNHAM.

JESUS! thou art the sinner's Friend;
  As such I look to thee;
Now, in the fullness of thy love,
  O Lord! remember me.

2 Remember thy pure word of grace,—
  Remember Calvary;
Remember all thy dying groans,
  And then remember me.

3 Thou wondrous Advocate with God!
  I yield myself to thee;
While thou art sitting on thy throne,
  Dear Lord! remember me.

4 Lord! I am guilty—I am vile,
  But thy salvation's free;
Then, in thine all-abounding grace,
  Dear Lord! remember me.
  G

860 *"Prepare us, Lord."* T. COTTERILL.

PREPARE us, Lord, to view thy cross,
  Who all our griefs hast borne;
To look on thee, whom we have pierced—
  To look on thee and mourn.

2 While thus we mourn, we would rejoice;
  And as thy cross we see,
Let each exclaim, in faith and hope,
  "The Saviour died for me!"

861 *Persistent Love.* I. WATTS.

HOW SWEET and awful is the place,
  With Christ within the doors,
While everlasting love displays
  The choicest of her stores.

2 While all our hearts, and all our songs,
  Join to admire the feast,
Each of us cries with thankful tongue,—
  "Lord, why was I a guest?"

3 "Why was I made to hear thy voice,
  And enter while there's room,
When thousands make a wretched choice,
  And rather starve than come?"

4 'T was the same love that spread the feast,
  That sweetly drew us in;
Else we had still refused to taste,
  And perished in our sin.

5 Pity the nations, O our God!
  Constrain the earth to come;
Send thy victorious word abroad,
  And bring the strangers home.

THE LORD'S SUPPER.

DEDHAM. C. M. — WM. GARDINER.

1. According to thy gracious word, In meek humility,
This will I do, my dying Lord, I will remember thee.

862 *"I will remember thee."* J. MONTGOMERY.

ACCORDING to thy gracious word,
In meek humility,
This will I do, my dying Lord,
I will remember thee.

2 Thy body, broken for my sake,
My bread from heaven shall be;
Thy testamental cup I take,
And thus remember thee.

3 Gethsemane can I forget?
Or there thy conflict see,
Thine agony and bloody sweat,
And not remember thee?

4 When to the cross I turn mine eyes,
And rest on Calvary,
O Lamb of God, my sacrifice!
I must remember thee:—

5 Remember thee, and all thy pains
And all thy love to me;
Yea, while a breath, a pulse remains,
Will I remember thee.

6 And when these failing lips grow dumb,
And mind and memory flee,
When thou shalt in thy kingdom come,
Then, Lord, remember me!

863 *"The cup of blessing."* C. WESLEY.

JESUS, at whose supreme command,
We now approach to God,
Before us in thy vesture stand,
Thy vesture dipped in blood.

2 Now, Saviour, now thyself reveal,
And make thy nature known;
Affix thy blessed Spirit's seal,
And stamp us for thine own.

3 Obedient to thy gracious word,
We break the hallowed bread,
Commemorate our dying Lord,
And trust on thee to feed.

4 The cup of blessing, blessed by thee,
Let it thy blood impart;
The broken bread thy body be,
To cheer each languid heart.

864 *"Greater love hath no man."* G. T. NOEL.

IF human kindness meets return,
And owns the grateful tie:
If tender thoughts within us burn,
To feel a friend is nigh;—

2 Oh, shall not warmer accents tell
The gratitude we owe
To him, who died our fears to quell—
Who bore our guilt and woe!

3 While yet in anguish he surveyed
Those pangs he would not flee,
What love his latest words displayed,—
"Meet and remember me!"

4 Remember thee—thy death, thy shame,
Our sinful hearts to share!—
O memory! leave no other name
But his recorded there.

THE LORD'S SUPPER.

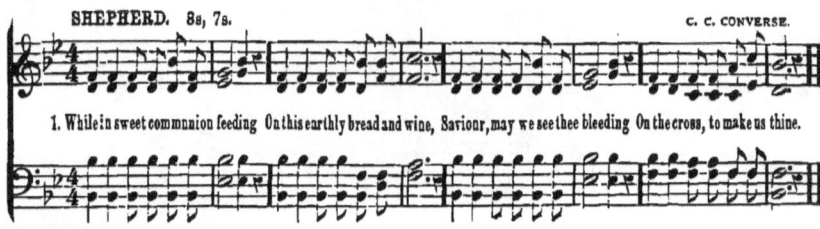

SHEPHERD. 8s, 7s.   C. C. CONVERSE.

1. While in sweet communion feeding On this earthly bread and wine, Saviour, may we see thee bleeding On the cross, to make us thine.

865   *"In remembrance."*   E. DENNY.

While in sweet communion feeding
  On this earthly bread and wine,
Saviour, may we see thee bleeding
  On the cross, to make us thine.

2 Though unseen, now be thou near us,
  With the still small voice of love;
Whispering words of peace to cheer us—
  Every doubt and fear remove.

3 Bring before us all the story,
  Of thy life, and death of woe;
And, with hopes of endless glory,
  Wean our hearts from all below.

866   *"His banner."*   R. PARK.

Jesus spreads his banner o'er us,
  Cheers our famished souls with food;
He the banquet spreads before us,
  Of his mystic flesh and blood.

2 Precious banquet; bread of heaven;
  Wine of gladness, flowing free;
May we taste it, kindly given
  In remembrance, Lord, of thee!

3 In thy trial and rejection;
  In thy sufferings on the tree;
In thy glorious resurrection;
  May we, Lord, remember thee!

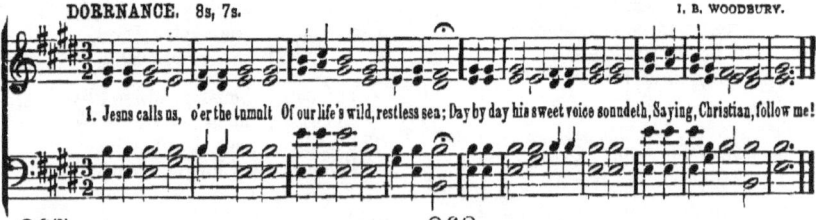

DORRNANCE. 8s, 7s.   I. B. WOODBURY.

1. Jesus calls us, o'er the tumult Of our life's wild, restless sea; Day by day his sweet voice soundeth, Saying, Christian, follow me!

867   *"Follow me."*   C. F. ALEXANDER.

Jesus calls us, o'er the tumult
  Of our life's wild, restless sea;
Day by day his sweet voice soundeth,
  Saying, Christian, follow me!

2 Jesus calls us—from the worship
  Of the vain world's golden store;
From each idol that would keep us,—
  Saying, Christian, love me more!

3 In our joys and in our sorrows,
  Days of toil and hours of ease,
Still he calls, in cares and pleasures,—
  Christian, love me more than these!

4 Jesus calls us! by thy mercies,
  Saviour, may we hear thy call;
Give our hearts to thy obedience,
  Serve and love thee best of all!
    G

868   *"Take my heart."*   ANON.

Take my heart, O Father! take it;
  Make and keep it all thine own;
Let thy Spirit melt and break it—
  This proud heart of sin and stone.

2 Father, make me pure and lowly,
  Fond of peace and far from strife;
Turning from the paths unholy
  Of this vain and sinful life.

3 Ever let thy grace surround me,
  Strengthen me with power divine,
Till thy cords of love have bound me:
  Make me to be wholly thine.

4 May the blood of Jesus heal me,
  And my sins be all forgiven;
Holy Spirit, take and seal me,
  Guide me in the path to heaven.

THE LORD'S SUPPER.

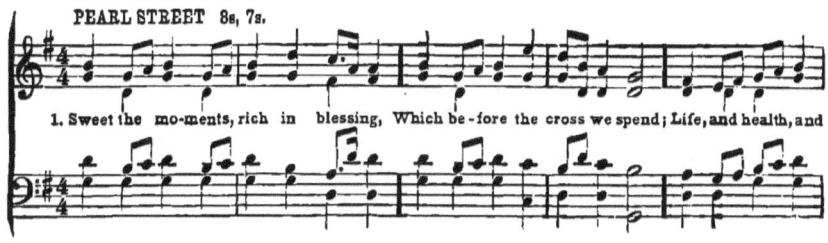

PEARL STREET. 8s, 7s.

1. Sweet the moments, rich in blessing, Which be-fore the cross we spend; Life, and health, and

peace possessing, From the sinner's dying Friend.

869   *Before the cross.*   J. ALLEN.

SWEET the moments, rich in blessing,
  Which before the cross we spend;
Life, and health, and peace possessing,
  From the sinner's dying Friend.

2 Truly blesséd is this station,
  Low before his cross to lie,
While we see divine compassion,
  Beaming in his gracious eye.

3 Love and grief our hearts dividing,
  With our tears his feet we bathe;
Constant still, in faith abiding,
  Life deriving from his death.

4 For thy sorrows we adore thee,
  For the pains that wrought our peace,
Gracious Saviour! we implore thee
  In our souls thy love increase.

5 Here we feel our sins forgiven,
  While upon the Lamb we gaze;
And our thoughts are all of heaven,
  And our lips o'erflow with praise.

6 Still in ceaseless contemplation,
  Fix our hearts and eyes on thee,
Till we taste thy full salvation,
  And, unvailed, thy glories see.

SICILY. 8s, 7s.   SICILIAN MELODY.

1. From the ta-ble now re-tir-ing, Which for us the Lord hath spread, May our souls, refreshment finding, Grow in all things like our Head!

870   *Parting Hymn.*   J. ROWE.

FROM the table now retiring,
  Which for us the Lord hath spread,
May our souls refreshment finding,
  Grow in all things like our Head!

2 His example while beholding,
  May our lives his image bear;
Him our Lord and Master calling,
  His commands may we revere.

3 Love to God and man displaying,
  Walking steadfast in his way,
Joy attend us in believing,
  Peace from God, through endless day.

4 Praise and honor to the Father,
  Praise and honor to the Son,
Praise and honor to the Spirit,
  Ever Three and ever One.

G

THE LORD'S SUPPER.

ROCK OF AGES. 7s, 6l.   THOS. HASTINGS.

1. Rock of Ages, cleft for me! Let me hide my-self in thee;
D.C.—Be of sin the per-fect cure; Save me, Lord! and make me pure.
Let the wa-ter and the blood, From thy wound-ed side that flowed,

871   *The Rock of Ages.*   A. M. TOPLADY.

Rock of Ages, cleft for me!
Let me hide myself in thee;
Let the water and the blood,
From thy wounded side that flowed,
Be of sin the perfect cure;
Save me, Lord! and make me pure.

2 Should my tears for ever flow,
Should my zeal no languor know,
This for sin could not atone,
Thou must save and thou alone:
In my hand no price I bring;
Simply to thy cross I cling.

3 While I draw this fleeting breath,
When mine eye-lids close in death,
When I rise to worlds unknown,
And behold thee on thy throne,
Rock of ages, cleft for me!
Let me hide myself in thee.

872   *"Manifest thyself."*   R. MANT.

Son of God! to thee I cry:
By the holy mystery
Of thy dwelling here on earth,
By thy pure and holy birth,
Lord, thy presence let me see,
Manifest thyself to me.

2 Lamb of God! to thee I cry:
By thy bitter agony,
By thy pangs to us unknown,
By thy spirit's parting groan,
Lord, thy presence let me see,
Manifest thyself to me.
G

3 Prince of Life! to thee I cry:
By thy glorious majesty,
By thy triumph o'er the grave,
Meek to suffer, strong to save,
Lord, thy presence let me see,
Manifest thyself to me.

4 Lord of glory, God most high,
Man exalted to the sky!
With thy love my bosom fill,
Prompt me to perform thy will;
Then thy glory I shall see,
Thou wilt bring me home to thee.

873   *"Till he come."*   E. H. DICKERSTETH.

"TILL He come:" oh, let the words
Linger on the trembling chords;
Let the little while between
In their golden light be seen;
Let us think how heaven and home
Lie beyond that—"Till he come."

2 When the weary ones we love
Enter on their rest above,
Seems the earth so poor and vast,
All our life joy overcast?
Hush, be every murmur dumb;
It is only—"Till he come."

3 See, the feast of love is spread,
Drink the wine, and break the bread;
Sweet memorials,—till the Lord
Call us round his heavenly board;
Some from earth, from glory some,
Severed only—"Till he come."

THE LORD'S SUPPER.

874 *"Wash me, Saviour."*   A. M. TOPLADY.
Rock of Ages, cleft for me!
Let me hide myself in thee;
Let the water and the blood,
From thy wounded side that flowed,
Be of sin the double cure;
Cleanse me from its guilt and power.

2 Not the labor of my hands
Can fulfill the law's demands;
Could my zeal no respite know,
Could my tears for ever flow,
All for sin could not atone;
Thou must save, and thou alone.

3 Nothing in my hand I bring,
Simply to thy cross I cling;
Naked, come to thee for dress,
Helpless, look to thee for grace;
Vile, I to the fountain fly,
Wash me, Saviour, or I die!

4 While I draw this fleeting breath,
When my eyelids close in death,
When I soar to worlds unknown,
See thee on thy judgment throne,
Rock of Ages, cleft for me!
Let me hide myself in thee.
    G

875 *"Take my Heart."*   C. WESLEY.
Father, Son, and Holy Ghost,
One in Three, and Three in One,
As by the celestial host,
Let thy will on earth be done;
Praise by all to thee be given,
Glorious Lord of earth and heaven!

2 Vilest of the fallen race,
Lo, I answer to thy call;
Meanest vessel of thy grace,
Grace divinely free for all;
Lo, I come to do thy will,
All thy counsel to fulfill.

3 If so poor a worm as I
May to thy great glory live,
All my actions sanctify,
All my words and thoughts receive;
Claim me for thy service, claim
All I have, and all I am.

4 Take my soul and body's powers,
Take my memory, mind and will,
All my goods, and all my hours,
All I know and all I feel,
All I think, or speak, or do;
Take my heart, but make it new.

THE LORD'S SUPPER.

NETTLETON. 8s, 7s, D. ANON.

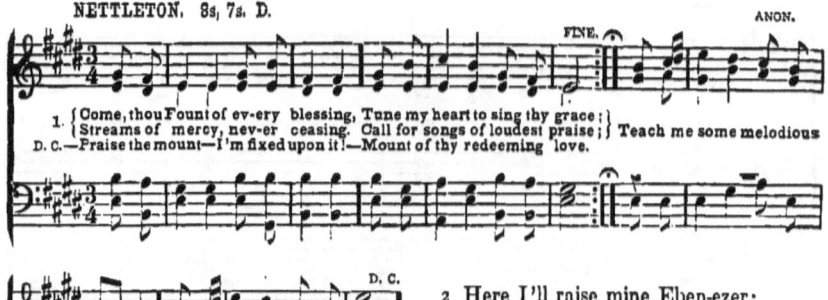

1. Come, thou Fount of ev-ery blessing, Tune my heart to sing thy grace;
Streams of mercy, nev-er ceasing, Call for songs of loudest praise; Teach me some melodious
D. C.—Praise the mount—I'm fixed upon it!—Mount of thy redeeming love.

son-net, Sung by flaming tongues above:

876 *"Eben-ezer."* R. ROBINSON.

Come, thou Fount of every blessing,
  Tune my heart to sing thy grace;
Streams of mercy, never ceasing,
  Call for songs of loudest praise;
Teach me some melodious sonnet,
  Sung by flaming tongues above;
Praise the mount—I'm fixed upon it!—
  Mount of thy redeeming love.

2 Here I'll raise mine Eben-ezer;
  Hither by thy help I'm come;
And I hope, by thy good pleasure,
  Safely to arrive at home.
Jesus sought me when a stranger,
  Wandering from the fold of God;
He, to rescue me from danger,
  Interposed his precious blood.

3 Oh, to grace how great a debtor
  Daily I'm constrained to be!
Let thy goodness, like a fetter,
  Bind my wandering heart to thee;
Prone to wander, Lord, I feel it;
  Prone to leave the God I love;
Here's my heart; oh, take and seal it;
  Seal it for thy courts above.

NAUFORD. P. M. A. S. SULLIVAN.

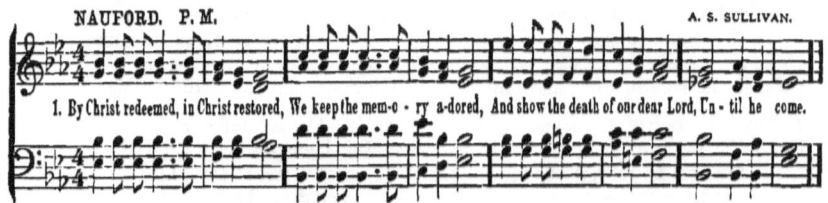

1. By Christ redeemed, in Christ restored, We keep the mem-o-ry a-dored, And show the death of our dear Lord, Un-til he come.

877 *"Till he come."* G. RAWSON.

By Christ redeemed, in Christ restored,
We keep the memory adored,
And show the death of our dear Lord,
  Until he come.

2 His body broken in our stead
Is here, in this memorial bread;
And so our feeble love is fed,
  Until he come.

3 His fearful drops of agony,
His life-blood shed for us we see:
The wine shall tell the mystery,
  Until he come.
  G

4 And thus that dark betrayal night,
With the last advent we unite—
The shame, the glory, by this rite,
  Until he come.

5 Until the trump of God be heard,
Until the ancient graves be stirred,
And with the great commanding word.
  The Lord shall come.

6 Oh, blesséd hope! with this elate,
Let not our hearts be desolate,
But, strong in faith, in patience wait,
  Until he come!

THE LORD'S SUPPER.

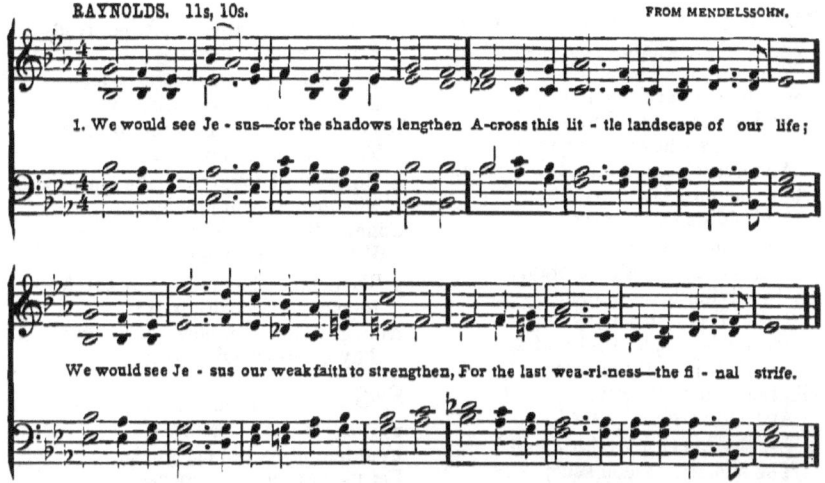

RAYNOLDS. 11s, 10s.   FROM MENDELSSOHN.

1. We would see Jesus—for the shadows lengthen Across this little landscape of our life;
We would see Jesus our weak faith to strengthen, For the last weariness—the final strife.

878   *"We would see Jesus."*   ANON.

WE would see Jesus—for the shadows
   lengthen
Across this little landscape of our life;
We would see Jesus, our weak faith to
   strengthen
For the last weariness—the final strife.

2 We would see Jesus—the great Rock
   Foundation,
Whereon our feet were set with sovereign
   grace;
Not life, nor death, with all their agitation,
Can thence remove us, if we see his face.

3 We would see Jesus—other lights are pal-
   ing,
Which for long years we have rejoiced
   to see;
The blessings of our pilgrimage are failing,
We would not mourn them, for we go
   to thee.

4 We would see Jesus—this is all we're
   needing,
Strength, joy, and willingness come with
   the sight;
We would see Jesus, dying, risen, pleading,
Then welcome day, and farewell mortal
   night!
G

879   *Trust, strength, calmness.*   S. JOHNSON, *alt.*

SAVIOUR, in thy mysterious presence kneeling,
Fain would our souls feel all thy kindling
   love;
For we are weak, and need some deep revealing
Of trust, and strength, and calmness from
   above.

2 Lord, we have wandered forth through
   doubt and sorrow,
And thou hast made each step an onward one;
And we will ever trust each unknown morrow,—
Thou wilt sustain us till its work is done.

3 In the heart's depths a peace serene and
   holy
Abides, and when pain seems to have its
   will,
Or we despair,—oh, may that peace rise
   slowly,
Stronger than agony, and we be still!

4 Now, Saviour, now, in thy dear presence
   kneeling,
Our spirits yearn to feel thy kindling love;
Now make us strong, we need thy deep revealing
Of trust, and strength, and calmness from
   above.

880 7s, 6s, 8s.   "Calvary."   C. WESLEY.

LAMB of God, whose dying love
  We now recall to mind,
Send the answer from above,
  And let us mercy find:
Think on us who think on thee,
  And every struggling soul release;
Oh, remember Calvary,
  And bid us go in peace!

2 By thine agonizing pain,
  And bloody sweat, we pray,
By thy dying love to man,
  Take all our sins away:
Burst our bonds, and set us free;
  From all iniquity release;
Oh, remember Calvary,
  And bid us go in peace!

3 Let thy blood, by faith applied,
  The sinner's pardon seal;
Speak us freely justified,
  And all our sickness heal:
By thy passion on the tree,
  Let all our griefs and troubles cease;
Oh, remember Calvary,
  And bid us go in peace!

881 P. M.   Cant. 5: 1.   T. HASTINGS.

FORGET thyself! Christ bade thee come
  To think upon his love,
Which could reverse the sinner's doom,
  And write his name above;
Bid the returning rebel live,
And freely all his sins forgive.

2 Forget thyself! and think what pain,
  What agony he bore,
To wash away each guilty stain,
  To bless thee evermore:
To fit thee for his high abode,
The temple of the living God.

3 Forget thyself! but let thy soul
  With memories o'erflow,
Rejoice in his supreme control,
  And seek his will to know:
With thankful heart approach the feast,
And thou wilt be a welcome guest.

882 C. M.   Long-suffering.   A. STEELE.

DEAR Saviour, when my thoughts recall
  The wonders of thy grace,
Low at thy feet ashamed, I fall,
  And hide this wretched face.

2 Shall love like thine be thus repaid?
  Ah, vile, ungrateful heart!

By earth's low cares so oft betrayed,
  From Jesus to depart.

3 But he for his own mercy's sake,
  My wandering soul restores;
He bids the mourning heart partake
  The pardon it implores.

4 Oh, while I breathe to thee, my Lord,
  The deep repentant sigh,
Confirm the kind, forgiving word,
  With pity in thine eye.

5 Then shall the mourner at thy feet
  Rejoice to seek thy face;
And, grateful, own how kind, how sweet,
  Thy condescending grace.

883 7s, 6 l.   "In remembrance."   T. HASTINGS.

SAVIOUR of our ruined race,
Fountain of redeeming grace,
Let us now thy fullness see,
While we here converse with thee;
Hearken to our ardent prayer,—
Let us all thy blessing share.

2 While we thus, with glad accord,
Meet around thy table, Lord,
Bid us feast with joy divine,
On the appointed bread and wine:
Emblems may they truly prove,
Of our Saviour's bleeding love.

3 Weak, unworthy, sinful, vile,
Yet we seek thy heavenly smile:
Canst thou all our sins forgive?
Dost thou bid us look and live?
Lord, we wonder and adore!
Oh, for grace to love thee more!

884 C. M.   "Planted in Christ."   S. F. SMITH.

PLANTED in Christ, the living vine,
  This day, with one accord,
Ourselves, with humble faith and joy,
  We yield to thee, O Lord!

2 Joined in one body may we be:
  One inward life partake;
One be our heart, one heavenly hope
  In every bosom wake.

3 In prayer, in effort, tears, and toils,
  One wisdom be our guide;
Taught by one Spirit from above,
  In thee may we abide.

4 Then, when among the saints in light
  Our joyful spirits shine,
Shall anthems of immortal praise,
  O Lamb of God, be thine!

885 7s, 6s, D. *Ancient Hymn.* RAY PALMER, tr.

O BREAD, to pilgrims given,
  O Food, that angels eat,
O manna, sent from heaven,
  For heaven-born natures meet!
Give us, for thee long pining,
  To eat till richly filled;
Till, earth's delights resigning,
  Our every wish is stilled.

2 O Water, life-bestowing,
  From out the Saviour's heart!
A fountain purely flowing,
  A fount of love thou art;
Oh, let us, freely tasting,
  Our burning thirst assuage!
Thy sweetness, never wasting,
  Avails from age to age.

3 Jesus! this feast receiving,
  We thee unseen adore;
Thy faithful word believing,
  We take, and doubt no more;
Give us, thou true and loving!
  On earth to live in thee;
Then, death the vail removing,
  Thy glorious face to see.

886 7s, 6s, D. *Hope at the Cross.* ANON.

WHEN human hopes all wither,
  And friends no aid supply,
Then whither, Lord, ah! whither
  Can turn my straining eye?
'Mid storms of grief still rougher,
  'Midst darker, deadlier shade,
That cross where thou didst suffer,
  On Calvary was displayed.

2 On that my gaze I fasten,
  My refuge that I make;
Though sorely thou mayst chasten,
  Thou never canst forsake:
Thou, on that cross didst languish,
  Ere glory crowned thy head!
And I, through death and anguish,
  Must be to glory led.

887 L. M. *Crucifying Afresh.* C. F. ALEXANDER.

O JESUS! bruised and wounded more
  Than bursted grape, or bread of wheat,
The Life of life within our souls,
  The Cup of our salvation sweet;—
  G

2 We come to show thy dying hour,
  Thy streaming vein, thy broken flesh;
And still the blood is warm to save,
  And still the fragrant wounds are fresh.

3 O Heart! that, with a double tide
  Of blood and water, maketh pure;
O Flesh! once offered on the cross,
  The gift that makes our pardon sure;—

4 Let never more our sinful souls
  The anguish of thy cross renew;
Nor forge again the cruel nails,
  That pierced thy victim body through.

888 L. M. *Consecration.* J. MONTGOMERY.

JESUS! our best belovéd Friend,
  On thy redeeming name we call;
Jesus! in love to us descend,
  Pardon and sanctify us all.

2 Our souls and bodies we resign,
  To fear and follow thy commands;
Oh, take our hearts, our hearts are thine,
  Accept the service of our hands.

3 Firm, faithful, watching unto prayer,
  Our Master's voice will we obey,
Toil in the vineyard here, and bear
  The heat and burden of the day.

4 Yet, Lord, for us a resting-place,
  In heaven, at thy right hand prepare;
And till we see thee face to face,
  Be all our conversation there.

889 L. M. *"Our Lord is Crucified."* F. W. FABER.

OH, come, and mourn with me awhile;
  Oh, come ye to the Saviour's side;
Oh, come, together let us mourn;
  Jesus, our Lord, is crucified.

2 Have we no tears to shed for him,
  While soldiers scoff and Jews deride?
Ah, look how patiently he hangs;
  Jesus, our Lord, is crucified.

3 Come, let us stand beneath the cross;
  So may the blood from out his side
Fall gently on us drop by drop;
  Jesus, our Lord, is crucified.

4 A broken heart, a fount of tears
  Ask, and they will not be denied;
Lord Jesus, may we love and weep,
  Since thou for us art crucified.

CHURCH:—MISSIONS AND GROWTH.

MISSIONARY HYMN. 7s, 6. D. LOWELL MASON.

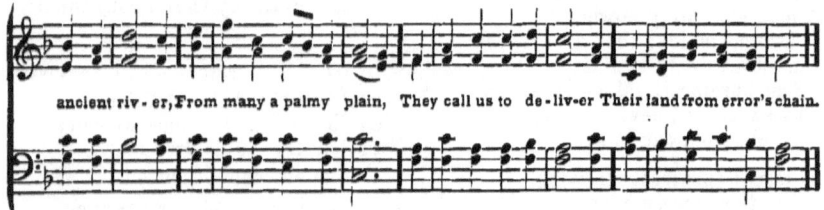

890 "*Come over, and help us.*" R. HEBER.

From Greenland's icy mountains,
From India's coral strand,
Where Afric's sunny fountains
Roll down their golden sand,—
From many an ancient river,
From many a palmy plain,
They call us to deliver
Their land from error's chain.

2 What though the spicy breezes
Blow soft o'er Ceylon's isle;
Though every prospect pleases,
And only man is vile;
In vain with lavish kindness
The gifts of God are strown;
The heathen, in his blindness,
Bows down to wood and stone!

3 Shall we, whose souls are lighted
With wisdom from on high,—
Shall we, to men benighted,
The lamp of life deny?
Salvation, oh, salvation!
The joyful sound proclaim,
Till earth's remotest nation
Has learned Messiah's name.

4 Waft, waft, ye winds, his story,
And you, ye waters, roll,
Till, like a sea of glory,
It spreads from pole to pole;
G

Till o'er our ransomed nature
The Lamb for sinners slain,
Redeemer, King, Creator,
In bliss returns to reign!

891 *The day of Jubilee.* B. GOUGH.

How BEAUTEOUS on the mountains,
The feet of him that brings,
Like streams from living fountains,
Good tidings of good things;
That publisheth salvation,
And jubilee release,
To every tribe and nation,
God's reign of joy and peace!

2 Lift up thy voice, O watchman!
And shout, from Zion's towers,
Thy hallelujah chorus,—
"The victory is ours!"
The Lord shall build up Zion
In glory and renown,
And Jesus, Judah's lion,
Shall wear his rightful crown.

3 Break forth in hymns of gladness;
O waste Jerusalem!
Let songs, instead of sadness,
Thy jubilee proclaim;
The Lord, in strength victorious,
Upon thy foes hath trod;
Behold, O earth! the glorious
Salvation of our God!

MISSIONS AND GROWTH.

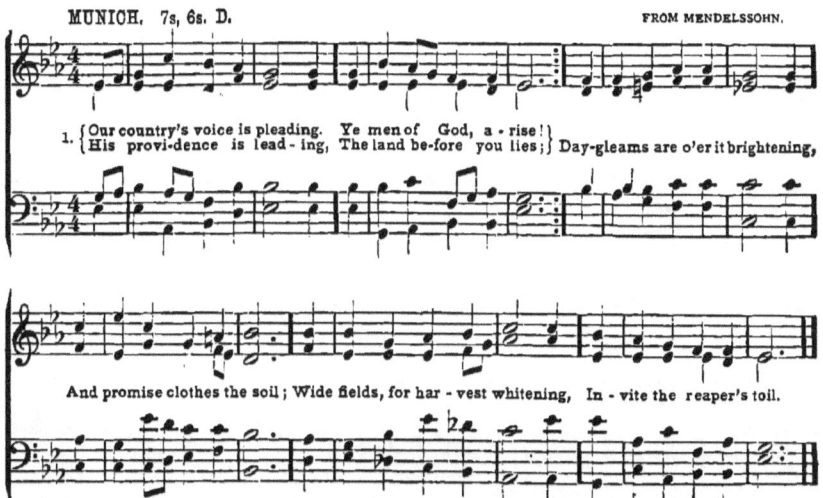

MUNICH. 7s, 6s. D.   FROM MENDELSSOHN.

1. Our country's voice is pleading. Ye men of God, a-rise! His providence is lead-ing, The land be-fore you lies; Day-gleams are o'er it brightening, And promise clothes the soil; Wide fields, for har-vest whitening, In-vite the reaper's toil.

892   *Home Missions.*   M. F. ANDERSON.

Our country's voice is pleading.
  Ye men of God, arise!
His providence is leading,
  The land before you lies;
Day-gleams are o'er it brightening,
  And promise clothes the soil;
Wide fields, for harvest whitening,
  Invite the reaper's toil.

2 Go, where the waves are breaking
  On California's shore,
Christ's precious gospel taking,
  More rich than golden ore;
On Alleghany's mountains,
  Through all the western vale,
Beside Missouri's fountains,
  Rehearse the wondrous tale.

3 The love of Christ unfolding,
  Speed on from east to west,
Till all, his cross beholding,
  In him are fully blest.
Great Author of salvation,
  Haste, haste the glorious day,
When we, a ransomed nation,
  Thy sceptre shall obey.

893   *Christian Union.*   J. BORTHWICK.

And is the time approaching,
  By prophets long foretold,
    G

When all shall dwell together,
  One shepherd and one fold?
Shall every idol perish,
  To moles and bats be thrown,
And every prayer be offered
  To God in Christ alone?

2 Shall Jew and Gentile, meeting
  From many a distant shore,
Around one altar kneeling,
  One common Lord adore?
Shall all that now divides us
  Remove and pass away,
Like shadows of the morning
  Before the blaze of day?

3 Shall all that now unites us
  More sweet and lasting prove,
A closer bond of union,
  In a blest land of love?
Shall war be learned no longer,
  Shall strife and tumult cease,
All earth his blessed kingdom,
  The Lord and Prince of Peace?

4 O long-expected dawning,
  Come with thy cheering ray!
When shall the morning brighten,
  The shadows flee away?
O sweet anticipation!
  It cheers the watchers on,
To pray, and hope, and labor,
  Till the dark night be gone.

334   CHURCH:—MISSIONS AND GROWTH.

WEBB. 7s, 6s. D.   G. J. WEBB.

1. Hail to the Lord's anointed, Great David's greater Son! Hail, in the time ap-pointed, His reign on earth begun! He comes to break oppres-sion, To set the captive free,
D. S.—To take a-way transgression,
And rule in eq-ui-ty.

894   *Psalm 72.*   J. MONTGOMERY.

HAIL to the Lord's anointed,
  Great David's greater Son!
Hail, in the time appointed,
  His reign on earth begun!
He comes to break oppression,
  To set the captive free,
To take away transgression,
  And rule in equity.

2 He comes, with succor speedy,
  To those who suffer wrong;
To help the poor and needy,
  And bid the weak be strong;
To give them songs for sighing,
  Their darkness turn to light,
Whose souls, condemned and dying,
  Were precious in his sight.

3 He shall come down like showers
  Upon the fruitful earth,
And love, and joy, like flowers,
  Spring in his path to birth:
Before him, on the mountains,
  Shall peace the herald go,
And righteousness in fountains
  From hill to valley flow.

4 Arabia's desert-ranger
  To him shall bow the knee;
The Ethiopian stranger
  His glory come to see:
G

With offerings of devotion,
  Ships from the isles shall meet,
To pour the wealth of ocean
  In tribute at his feet.

5 Kings shall fall down before him,
  And gold and incense bring:
All nations shall adore him;
  His praise all people sing;
For he shall have dominion
  O'er river, sea, and shore,
Far as the eagle's pinion
  Or dove's light wing can soar.

6 For him shall prayer unceasing
  And daily vows ascend;
His kingdom still increasing,
  A kingdom without end.
The heavenly dew shall nourish
  A seed in weakness sown,
Whose fruit shall spread and flourish,
  And shake like Lebanon.

7 O'er every foe victorious,
  He on his throne shall rest;
From age to age more glorious,
  All-blessing and all-blessed.
The tide of time shall never
  His covenant remove;
His name shall stand for ever;
  His great, best name of Love!

895 7s, 6s. *The morning light.* S. F. SMITH.

The morning light is breaking;
   The darkness disappears!
The sons of earth are waking
   To penitential tears;
Each breeze that sweeps the ocean
   Brings tidings from afar,
Of nations in commotion,
   Prepared for Zion's war.

2 See heathen nations bending
   Before the God we love,
And thousand hearts ascending
   In gratitude above;
While sinners, now confessing,
   The gospel call obey,
And seek the Saviour's blessing—
   A nation in a day.

3 Blest river of salvation!
   Pursue thine onward way;
Flow thou to every nation,
   Nor in thy richness stay:
Stay not till all the lowly
   Triumphant reach their home:
Stay not till all the holy
   Proclaim—"The Lord is come!"

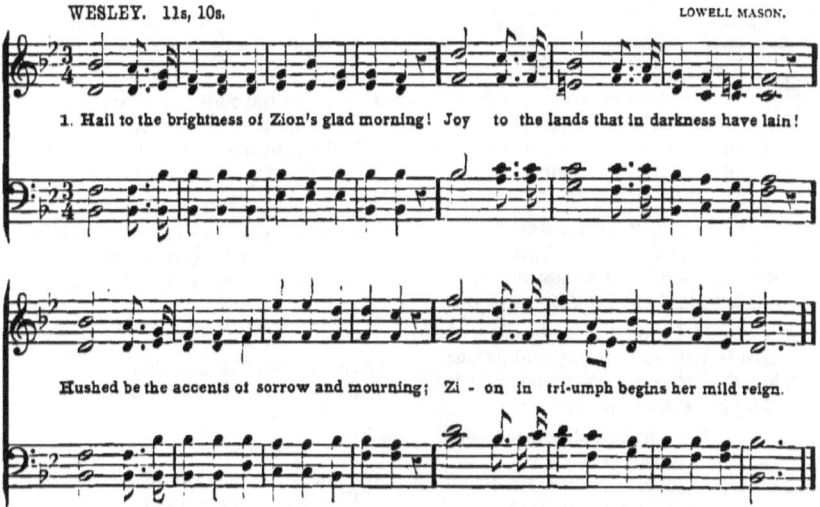

WESLEY. 11s, 10s. LOWELL MASON.

1. Hail to the brightness of Zion's glad morning! Joy to the lands that in darkness have lain!
Hushed be the accents of sorrow and mourning; Zi-on in tri-umph begins her mild reign.

896 *The Promise.* T. HASTINGS.

Hail to the brightness of Zion's glad
   morning!
Joy to the lands that in darkness have lain!
Hushed be the accents of sorrow and
   mourning;
Zion in triumph begins her mild reign.

2 Hail to the brightness of Zion's glad
   morning,
Long by the prophets of Israel foretold;
Hail to the millions from bondage returning;
Gentile and Jew the blest vision behold.

3 Lo! in the desert rich flowers are springing,
Streams ever copious are gliding along;
Loud from the mountain-tops echoes are
   ringing,
Wastes rise in verdure, and mingle in
   song.

4 See, from all lands—from the isles of the
   ocean,
Praise to Jehovah ascending on high;
Fallen are the engines of war and commotion,
Shouts of salvation are rending the sky.

CHURCH:—MISSIONS AND GROWTH.

RATHBUN. 8s, 7s.   I. CONKEY.

1. Sav-iour, vis-it thy plant-a-tion! Grant us, Lord, a gra-cious rain: All will come to des-o-la-tion, Un-less thou re-turn a-gain.

897 *Revival Implored.* J. NEWTON.

Saviour, visit thy plantation!
Grant us, Lord, a gracious rain:
All will come to desolation,
Unless thou return again.

2 Keep no longer at a distance,
Shine upon us from on high,
Lest, for want of thine assistance,
Every plant should droop and die.

3 Once, O Lord, thy garden flourished;
Every part looked gay and green;
Then thy word our spirits nourished:
Happy seasons we have seen.

4 But a drought has since succeeded,
And a sad decline we see:
Lord, thy help is greatly needed:
Help can only come from thee.

5 Let our mutual love be fervent:
Make us prevalent in prayer;
Let each one esteemed thy servant
Shun the world's bewitching snare.

6 Break the tempter's fatal power,
Turn the stony heart to flesh,
And begin from this good hour
To revive thy work afresh.

898 *"Westward."* ANON.

Hark! the sound of angel-voices,
Over Bethlehem's star-lit plain;
Hark! the heavenly host rejoices,
Jesus comes on earth to reign.
G

2 See celestial radiance beaming,
Lighting up the midnight sky;
'Tis the promised day-star gleaming,
'Tis the day-spring from on high.

3 Westward, all along the ages,
Trace its pathway clear and bright;
Star of hope to Eastern sages,
Radiant now with gospel light.

4 Angels from the realms of glory,
Peace on earth delight to sing;
Christian, tell the wondrous story,
Go proclaim the Saviour King!

899 *Home Missions.* ANON.

Where the woodman's axe is ringing,
Where the hunter roams alone,
Where the prairie-flowers are springing,
Make the great Redeemer known.

2 While, from California's mountains,
Pure and sweet the anthem swells;
Oregon's dark wilds and fountains
Hail the sound of Sabbath-bells.

3 Like an armed host with banners,
Terrible in war array,
Zion comes with glad hosannas,
To prepare her Monarch's way.

4 Unto him all power is given,
All the world his sway shall own,
And on earth, as now in heaven,
Shall his will be done alone.

MISSIONS AND GROWTH.

ZION. 8s, 7s, 4s. — THOS. HASTINGS.

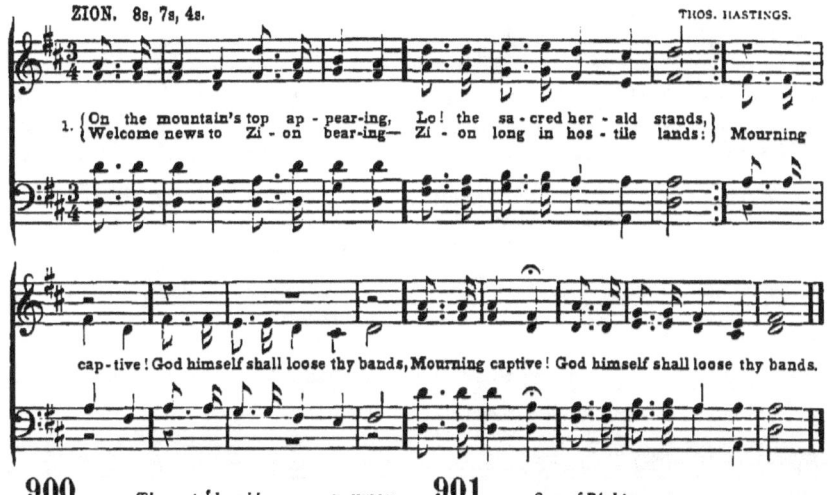

900 *The gospel herald.* T. KELLY.

On the mountain's top appearing,
 Lo! the sacred herald stands,
Welcome news to Zion bearing—
 Zion long in hostile lands:
  Mourning captive!
 God himself shall loose thy bands.

2 Has thy night been long and mournful?
 Have thy friends unfaithful proved?
Have thy foes been proud and scornful?
 By thy sighs and tears unmoved?
  Cease thy mourning;
 Zion still is well beloved.

3 God, thy God, will now restore thee;
 He himself appears thy Friend;
All thy foes shall flee before thee;
 Here their boasts and triumphs end:
  Great deliverance
 Zion's King will surely send.

901 *Sun of Righteousness.* W. WILLIAMS.

O'er the gloomy hills of darkness,
 Cheered by no celestial ray,
Sun of righteousness! arising,
 Bring the bright, the glorious day;
  Send the gospel
 To the earth's remotest bound.

2 Kingdoms wide that sit in darkness,—
 Grant them, Lord! the glorious light:
And, from eastern coast to western,
 May the morning chase the night;
  And redemption,
 Freely purchased, win the day.

3 Fly abroad, thou mighty gospel!
 Win and conquer, never cease;
May thy lasting, wide dominions
 Multiply and still increase;
  Sway thy sceptre,
 Saviour! all the world around.

HAMDEN. 8s, 7s, 4s. — LOWELL MASON.

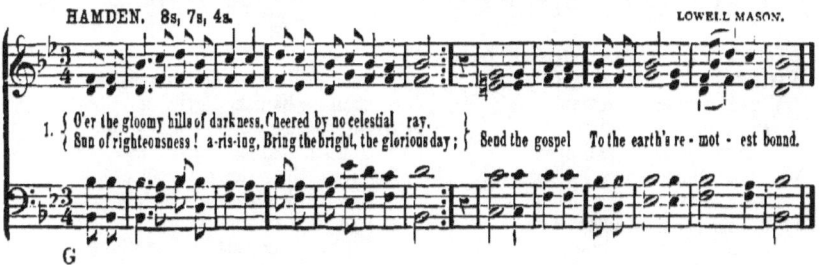

CHURCH:—MISSIONS AND GROWTH.

PERRY. 7s. D.   J. P. HOLBROOK, arr.

1. Hark! the song of Ju-bi-lee, Loud as might-y thunders roar, Or the full-ness of the sea, When it breaks up-on the shore! Hal-le-lu-jah! for the Lord God om-nip-o-tent shall reign! Hal-le-lu-jah! let the word Ech-o round the earth and main.

902   *"The Lord God reigneth."* J. MONTGOMERY.

Hark! the song of jubilee,
  Loud as mighty thunders roar,
Or the fullness of the sea,
  When it breaks upon the shore!
Hallelujah! for the Lord
  God omnipotent shall reign!
Hallelujah! let the word
  Echo round the earth and main.

2 Hallelujah! hark, the sound,
  From the depths unto the skies,
Wakes above, beneath, around,
  All creation's harmonies!
See Jehovah's banners furled!
  Sheathed his sword! he speaks—'tis done!
And the kingdoms of this world
  Are the kingdoms of his Son!

3 He shall reign from pole to pole,
  With illimitable sway;
He shall reign, when like a scroll
  Yonder heavens have passed away.
Then the end: beneath his rod
  Man's last enemy shall fall:
Hallelujah! Christ in God,
  God in Christ, is all in all!

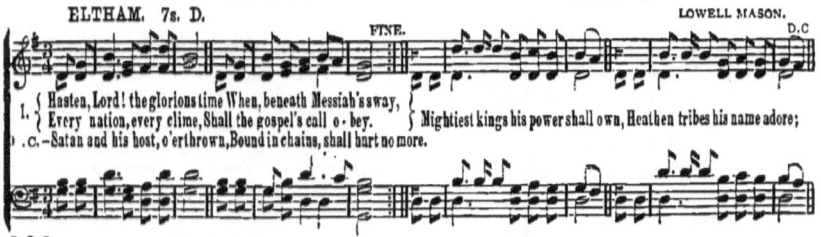

ELTHAM. 7s. D.   LOWELL MASON.

1. { Hasten, Lord! the glorious time When, beneath Messiah's sway, }
   { Every nation, every clime, Shall the gospel's call o-bey. } Mightiest kings his power shall own, Heathen tribes his name adore;
.C.—Satan and his host, o'erthrown, Bound in chains, shall hurt no more.

903   *The World's Conversion.* H. AUBER.

Hasten, Lord! the glorious time
  When, beneath Messiah's sway,
Every nation, every clime,
  Shall the gospel's call obey.
Mightiest kings his power shall own,
  Heathen tribes his name adore;
Satan and his host, o'erthrown,
  Bound in chains, shall hurt no more.

2 Then shall wars and tumults cease,
  Then be banished grief and pain;
Righteousness and joy and peace
  Undisturbed shall ever reign.
Bless we, then, our gracious Lord;
  Ever praise his glorious name;
All his mighty acts record;
  All his wondrous love proclaim.

G

MISSIONS AND GROWTH.

904 *Awake, arm of the Lord.* W. SHRUBSOLE.
ARM of the Lord! awake, awake:
Put on thy strength, the nations shake;
And let the world, adoring, see
Triumphs of mercy, wrought by thee.

2 Say to the heathen, from thy throne,
"I am Jehovah—God alone!"
Thy voice their idols shall confound,
And cast their altars to the ground.

3 No more let human blood be spilt,
Vain sacrifice for human guilt;
But to each conscience be applied
The blood that flowed from Jesus' side.

4 Almighty God! thy grace proclaim,
In every clime, of every name,
Till adverse powers before thee fall,
And crown the Saviour—Lord of all.

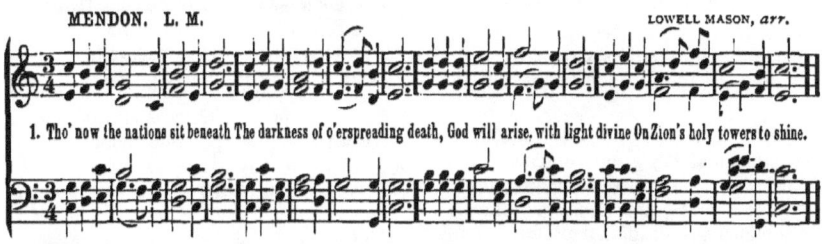

905 *"O Light of Zion."* L. BACON.
THOUGH now the nations sit beneath
The darkness of o'erspreading death,
God will arise, with light divine
On Zion's holy towers to shine.

2 That light shall shine on distant lands,
And wandering tribes, in joyful bands,
Shall come thy glory, Lord, to see,
And in thy courts to worship thee.

3 O light of Zion, now arise!
Let the glad morning bless our eyes!
Ye nations, catch the kindling ray,
And hail the splendor of the day.

906 *Zion's Glory.* W. SHRUBSOLE.
ZION! awake, thy strength renew;
Put on thy robes of beauteous hue;
And let the admiring world behold
The King's fair daughter clothed in gold.

2 Church of our God! arise and shine,
Bright with the beams of truth divine;
Then shall thy radiance stream afar,
Wide as the heathen nations are.

3 Gentiles and kings thy light shall view,
And shall admire and love thee too;—
They come, like clouds across the sky,
As doves that to their windows fly.

23

CHURCH:—MISSIONS AND GROWTH.

GROSTETTE. L. M.   H. W. GREATOREX.

1. Soon may the last glad song a-rise Through all the mill-ions of the skies— That song of tri-umph which re-cords That all the earth is now the Lord's!

907   *The last song.*   MRS. VOKE.

Soon may the last glad song arise
Through all the millions of the skies—
That song of triumph which records
That all the earth is now the Lord's!

2 Let thrones and powers and kingdoms be
Obedient, mighty God, to thee!
And, over land and stream and main,
Wave thou the sceptre of thy reign!

3 Oh, let that glorious anthem swell,
Let host to host the triumph tell,
That not one rebel heart remains,
But over all the Saviour reigns!

908   *Missionary Convocation.*   W. B. COLLYER.

Assembled at thy great command,
Before thy face, dread King, we stand;
The voice that marshaled every star,
Has called thy people from afar.

2 We meet, through distant lands to spread
The truth for which the martyrs bled;
Along the line, to either pole,
The thunder of thy praise to roll.

3 Our prayers assist, accept our praise,
Our hopes revive, our courage raise;
Our counsels aid, to each impart
The single eye, the faithful heart.

4 Forth with thy chosen heralds come,
Recall the wandering spirits home;
From Zion's mount send forth the sound,
To spread the spacious earth around.

909   *Christ's coming.*   W. H. BATHURST.

Jesus! thy church, with longing eyes,
For thine expected coming waits;
When will the promised light arise,
And glory beam from Zion's gates?

2 Ev'n now, when tempests round us fall,
And wintry clouds o'ercast the sky,
Thy words with pleasure we recall,
And deem that our redemption's nigh.

3 Oh, come and reign o'er every land;
Let Satan from his throne be hurled;
All nations bow to thy command,
And grace revive a dying world.

4 Teach us, in watchfulness and prayer,
To wait for the appointed hour;
And fit us, by thy grace, to share
The triumphs of thy conquering power.

910   *"Ascend thy throne."*   B. BEDDOME.

Ascend thy throne, almighty King,
And spread thy glories all abroad;
Let thine own arm salvation bring,
And be thou known the gracious God.

2 Let millions bow before thy seat,
Let humble mourners seek thy face,
Bring daring rebels to thy feet,
Subdued by thy victorious grace.

3 Oh, let the kingdoms of the world
Become the kingdoms of the Lord!
Let saints and angels praise thy name.
Be thou through heaven and earth adored.

CHURCH:—MISSIONS AND GROWTH.

911   *Psalm 72.*   I. WATTS.

Jesus shall reign where'er the sun
Does his successive journeys run;
His kingdom stretch from shore to shore,
Till moons shall wax and wane no more.

2 For him shall endless prayer be made,
And endless praises crown his head;
His name, like sweet perfume, shall rise
With every morning-sacrifice.

3 People and realms of every tongue
Dwell on his love, with sweetest song;
And infant voices shall proclaim
Their early blessings on his name.

4 Blessings abound where'er he reigns;
The prisoner leaps to lose his chains;
The weary find eternal rest,
And all the sons of want are blest.

5 Let every creature rise and bring
Peculiar honors to our King;
Angels descend with songs again,
And earth repeat the loud Amen!

912   *Conversion of the World.*   MRS. VOKE.

Sovereign of worlds! display thy power;
Be this thy Zion's favored hour;
Bid the bright morning Star arise,
And point the nations to the skies.

2 Set up thy throne where Satan reigns,—
On Afric's shore, on India's plains,
On wilds and continents unknown,—
And make the nations all thine own.

3 Speak! and the world shall hear thy voice;
Speak! and the desert shall rejoice;
Scatter the gloom of heathen night,
And bid all nations hail the light.

913   *"Sun of Righteousness."*   P. DODDRIDGE, alt.

O Sun of righteousness, arise,
 With gentle beams on Zion shine;
Dispel the darkness from our eyes,
 And souls awake to life divine.

2 On all around, let grace descend,
 Like heavenly dew, or copious showers:
That we may call our God our friend;
 That we may hail salvation ours.

CHURCH:—MISSIONS AND GROWTH.

914 *Phillipians* 2: 10, 11. C. WESLEY.

O THOU whom we adore!
  To bless our earth again,
Assume thine own almighty power,
  And o'er the nations reign.

2 The world's Desire and Hope,
  All power to thee is given;
Now set the last great empire up,
  Eternal Lord of heaven!

3 A gracious Saviour, thou
  Wilt all thy creatures bless;
And every knee to thee shall bow,
  And every tongue confess.

4 According to thy word,
  Now be thy grace revealed;
And with the knowledge of the Lord,
  Let all the earth be filled.

915 *"Thy kingdom come!"* J. JOHNS.

COME, kingdom of our God,
  Sweet reign of light and love!
Shed peace and hope and joy abroad,
  And wisdom from above.

2 Over our spirits first
  Extend thy healing reign;
There raise and quench the sacred thirst,
  That never pains again.

3 Come, kingdom of our God!
  And make the broad earth thine;
Stretch o'er her lands and isles the rod
  That flowers with grace divine.

4 Soon may all tribes be blest
  With fruit from life's glad tree;
And in its shade like brothers rest,
  Sons of one family.

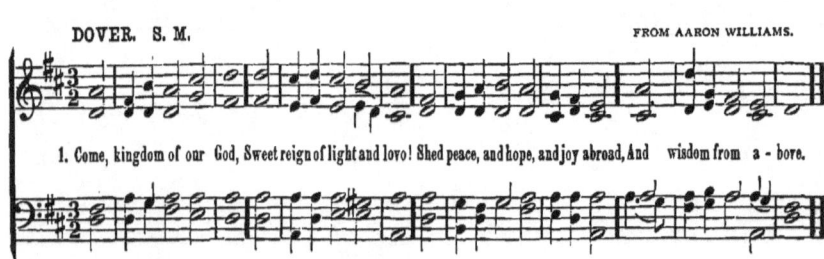

MISSIONS AND GROWTH.

ST. BRIDE. S. M.   S. HOWARD.

1. Come, Lord, and tar-ry not! Bring the long-looked-for day! Oh, why these years of wait-ing here, These a-ges of de-lay?

916   *"Come, Lord Jesus."*   H. BONAR.

Come, Lord, and tarry not!
  Bring the long-looked-for day;
Oh, why these years of waiting here,
  These ages of delay?

2 Come, for thy saints still wait;
  Daily ascends their sigh;
The Spirit and the Bride say, Come!
  Dost thou not hear the cry?

3 Come, for creation groans,
  Impatient of thy stay,
Worn out with these long years of ill,
  These ages of delay.

4 Come, and make all things new,
  Build up this ruined earth,
Restore our faded paradise,—
  Creation's second birth.

5 Come, and begin thy reign
  Of everlasting peace;
Come, take the kingdom to thyself,
  Great King of Righteousness!

917   *Declension.—*   C. W. BETHUNE.

Oh, for the happy hour
  When God will hear our cry,
And send, with a reviving power,
  His Spirit from on high.

2 We meet, we sing, we pray,
  We listen to the word,
In vain;—we see no cheering ray,
  No cheering voice is heard.

3 While many crowd thy house,
  How few, around thy board,
Meet to recount their solemn vows,
  And bless thee as their Lord!

4 Thou, thou alone canst give
  Thy gospel sure success;
Canst bid the dying sinner live
  Anew in holiness.

5 Come, then, with power divine,
  Spirit of life and love!
Then shall this people all be thine,
  This church like that above.

918   *"Revive thy work."*   P. H. BROWN, *al'.*

O Lord, thy work revive,
  In Zion's gloomy hour,
And make her dying graces live
  By thy restoring power.

2 Awake thy chosen few
  To fervent earnest prayer;
Again may they their vows renew,
  Thy blessèd presence share.

3 Thy Spirit then will speak
  Through lips of feeble clay,
And hearts of adamant will break,
  And rebels will obey.

4 Lord, lend thy gracious ear;
  Oh, listen to our cry;
Oh, come and bring salvation here:
  Our hopes on thee rely.

CHURCH:—MISSIONS AND GROWTH.

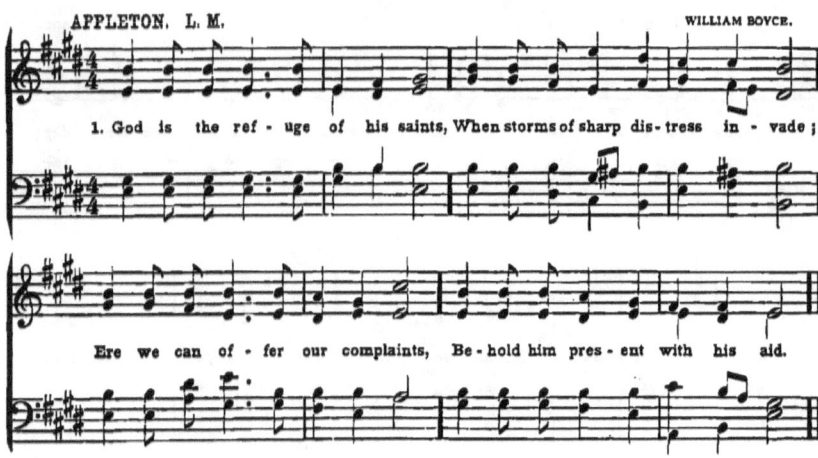

919   *Psalm 46.*   L. WATTS.
GOD is the refuge of his saints,
  When storms of sharp distress invade;
Ere we can offer our complaints,
  Behold him present with his aid.

2 Let mountains from their seats be hurled
  Down to the deep, and buried there,
Convulsions shake the solid world—
  Our faith shall never yield to fear.

3 Loud may the troubled ocean roar—
  In sacred peace our souls abide;
While every nation, every shore,
  Trembles, and dreads the swelling tide.

4 There is a stream, whose gentle flow
  Supplies the city of our God;
Life, love, and joy, still gliding through,
  And watering our divine abode.

5 That sacred stream, thy holy word,
  Our grief allays, our fear controls;
Sweet peace thy promises afford,
  And give new strength to fainting souls.

6 Zion enjoys her Monarch's love,
  Secure against a threatening hour;
Nor can her firm foundation move,
  Built on his truth, and armed with power.

920   *Psalm 72.*   I. WATTS.
GREAT God! whose universal sway
  The known and unknown worlds obey;
Now give the kingdom to thy Son;
  Extend his power, exalt his throne.

2 As rain on meadows newly mown,
  So shall he send his influence down;
His grace, on fainting souls, distills
  Like heavenly dew on thirsty hills.

3 The heathen lands, that lie beneath
  The shades of overspreading death,
Revive at his first dawning light,
  And deserts blossom at the sight.

4 The saints shall flourish in his days,
  Dressed in the robes of joy and praise;
Peace, like a river, from his throne,
  Shall flow to nations yet unknown.

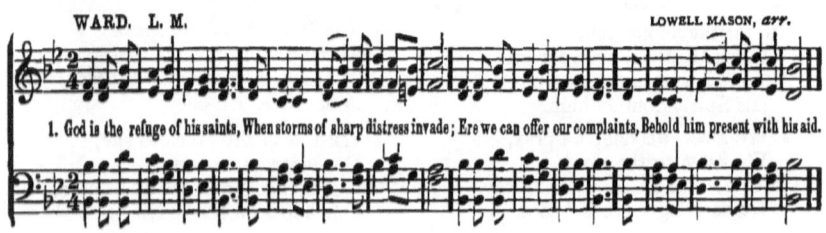

MISSIONS AND GROWTH.

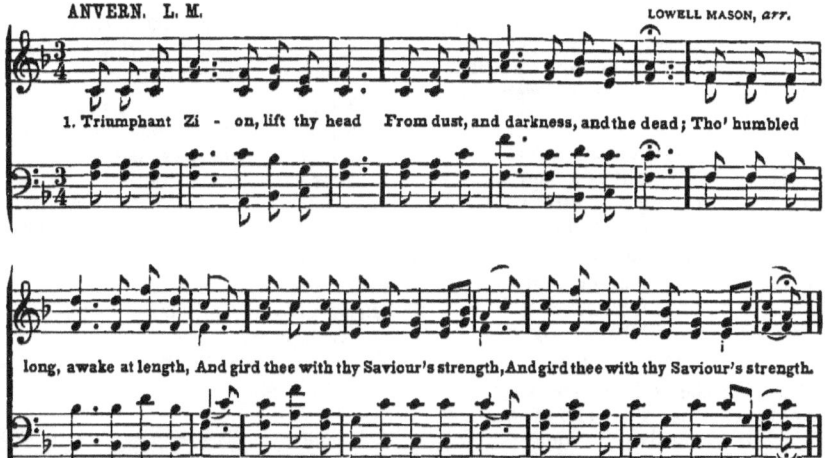

ANVERN. L. M. — LOWELL MASON, arr.

1. Triumphant Zi-on, lift thy head From dust, and darkness, and the dead; Tho' humbled long, awake at length, And gird thee with thy Saviour's strength, And gird thee with thy Saviour's strength.

921   *"Triumphant Zion."*   P. DODDRIDGE.

TRIUMPHANT Zion, lift thy head
  From dust, and darkness, and the dead;
Though humbled long, awake at length,
  And gird thee with thy Saviour's strength.

2 Put all thy beauteous garments on,
  And let thy various charms be known:
The world thy glories shall confess,
  Decked in the robes of righteousness.

3 No more shall foes unclean invade,
  And fill thy hallowed walls with dread;
No more shall hell's insulting host
  Their victory and thy sorrows boast.

4 God, from on high, thy groans will hear;
  His hand thy ruins shall repair;
Nor will thy watchful Monarch cease
  To guard thee in eternal peace.

922   *Ancient Israel.*   J. JOYCE.

WHY on the bending willows hung,
  Israel! still sleeps thy tuneful string?—
Still mute remains thy sullen tongue,
  And Zion's song denies to sing?

2 Awake! thy sweetest raptures raise;
  Let harp and voice unite their strains:
Thy promised King his sceptre sways:
  Jesus, thine own Messiah, reigns!

3 No taunting foes the song require;
  No strangers mock thy captive chain;
But friends provoke the silent lyre,
  And brethren ask the holy strain.

4 Nor fear thy Salem's hills to wrong,
  If other lands thy triumphs share:
A heavenly city claims thy song;
  A brighter Salem rises there.

5 By foreign streams no longer roam;
  Nor, weeping, think of Jordan's flood:
In every clime behold a home,
  In every temple see thy God.

923   *Home Missions.*   W. C. BRYANT

LOOK from thy sphere of endless day,
  O God of mercy and of might!
In pity look on those who stray,
  Benighted in this land of light.

2 In peopled vale, in lonely glen,
  In crowded mart, by stream or sea,
How many of the sons of men
  Hear not the message sent from thee!

3 Send forth thy heralds, Lord, to call
  The thoughtless young, the hardened old,
A scattered, homeless flock, till all
  Be gathered to thy peaceful fold.

4 Send them thy mighty word to speak,
  Till faith shall dawn, and doubt depart,
To awe the bold, to stay the weak,
  And bind and heal the broken heart.

5 Then all these wastes, a dreary scene,
  That makes us sadden as we gaze,
Shall grow with living waters green,
  And lift to heaven the voice of praise.

924 L. M.   *Psalm 87.*   I. WATTS.
God, in his earthly temple, lays
Foundations for his heavenly praise ;
He likes the tents of Jacob well ;
But still in Zion loves to dwell.

2 His mercy visits every house
That pay their night and morning vows,
But makes a more delightful stay
Where churches meet to praise and pray.

3 What glories were described of old !
What wonders are of Zion told !
Thou city of our God below !
Thy fame shall Tyre and Egypt know.

4 Egypt and Tyre, and Greek and Jew,
Shall there begin their lives anew ;
Angels and men shall join to sing
The hill where living waters spring.

5 When God makes up his last account
Of natives in his holy mount,
'T will be an honor to appear,
As one new-born, or nourished there.

925 L. M.   *Psalm 80.*   I. WATTS.
Great Shepherd of thine Israel !
Who didst between the cherubs dwell,
And lead the tribes, thy chosen sheep,
Safe through the desert and the deep ; —

2 Thy Church is in the desert now ;
Shine from on high and guide us through ;
Turn us to thee, thy love restore ;
We shall be saved, and sigh no more.

3 Hast thou not planted, with thy hand,
A lovely vine in this our land ?
Did not thy power defend it round,
And heavenly dews enrich the ground ?

4 Return, almighty God ! return,
Nor let thy bleeding vineyard mourn :
Turn us to thee, thy love restore ;
We shall be saved, and sigh no more.

926 8s, 7s, 6 l.   *"Alleluia."*   ANON.
Hallelujah ! song of gladness,
 Song of everlasting joy ;
Hallelujah ! song the sweetest
 That can angel-hosts employ ;
Hymning in God's holy presence
 Their high praise eternally.

2 Hallelujah ! church victorious,
 Thou mayst lift this joyful strain :
Hallelujah ! songs of triumph

Well befit the ransomed train :
We our song must raise with sadness,
 While in exile we remain.

3 Hallelujah ! strains of gladness
 Suit not souls with anguish torn ;
Hallelujah ! notes of sadness
 Best befit our state forlorn :
For, in this dark world of sorrow,
 We, with tears, our sin must mourn.

4 But our earnest supplication,
 Holy God, we raise to thee ;
Bring us to thy blissful presence,
 Make us all thy joys to see ;
Then we 'll sing our Hallelujah,—
 Sing to all eternity.

927 7s, 6s, D.   *Psalm 14.*   H. F. LYTE.
Oh, that the Lord's salvation
 Were out of Zion come,
To heal his ancient nation,
 To lead his outcasts home !
How long the holy city
 Shall heathen feet profane ?
Return, O Lord, in pity,
 Rebuild her walls again.

2 Let fall thy rod of terror,
 Thy saving grace impart ;
Roll back the vail of error,
 Release the fettered heart ;
Let Israel, home returning,
 Their lost Messiah see ;
Give oil of joy for mourning,
 And bind thy Church to thee.

928 7s, 6s, D.   *The Gospel Banner.*   T. HASTINGS.
Now be the gospel banner,
 In every land unfurled ;
And be the shout,—" Hosanna ! "
 Re-echoed through the world ;
Till every isle and nation,
 Till every tribe and tongue,
Receive the great salvation,
 And join the happy throng.

2 Yes,—thou shalt reign for ever,
 O Jesus, King of kings !
Thy light, thy love, thy favor,
 Each ransomed captive sings :
The isles for thee are waiting,
 The deserts learn thy praise,
The hills and valleys greeting,
 The song responsive raise.

MISSIONS AND GROWTH.

929 7s, D.   *Gospel Increase.*   C. WESLEY.

See! how great a flame aspires,
 Kindled by a spark of grace!
Jesus' love the nations fires,—
 Sets the kingdoms on a blaze;
Fire to bring on earth he came;
 Kindled in some hearts it is;
Oh, that all might catch the flame,
 All partake the glorious bliss!

2 When he first the work begun,
 Small and feeble was his day:
Now the word doth swiftly run;
 Now it wins its widening way:
More and more it spreads and grows,
 Ever mighty to prevail;
Sin's strongholds it now o'erthrows,—
 Shakes the trembling gates of hell.

3 Sons of God! your Saviour praise;
 He the door hath opened wide;
He hath given the word of grace;
 Jesus' word is glorified;
Jesus, mighty to redeem—
 He alone the work hath wrought;
Worthy is the work of him,—
 Him who spake a world from naught.

930 C. M.   *Psalm 102.*   I. WATTS.

Let Zion and her sons rejoice—
 Behold the promised hour!
Her God hath heard her mourning voice,
 And comes to exalt his power.

2 Her dust and ruins that remain
 Are precious in our eyes;
Those ruins shall be built again,
 And all that dust shall rise.

3 The Lord will raise Jerusalem,
 And stand in glory there;
Nations shall bow before his name,
 And kings attend with fear.

4 He sits a sovereign on his throne,
 With pity in his eyes;
He hears the dying prisoners' groan,
 And sees their sighs arise.

5 He frees the souls condemned to death;
 Nor, when his saints complain,
Shall it be said that praying breath
 Was ever spent in vain.

931 C. M.   *Isaiah 52: 1, 2.*   J. MONTGOMERY.

Daughter of Zion! from the dust
 Exalt thy fallen head;
Again in thy Redeemer trust,—
 He calls thee from the dead.

2 Awake, awake, put on thy strength,—
 Thy beautiful array;
The day of freedom dawns at length,—
 The Lord's appointed day.

3 Rebuild thy walls, thy bounds enlarge,
 And send thy heralds forth;
Say to the south,—"Give up thy charge,
 And keep not back, O north!"

4 They come! they come! thine exiled bands,
 Where'er they rest or roam,
Have heard thy voice in distant lands,
 And hasten to their home.

5 Thus, though the universe shall burn,
 And God his works destroy,
With songs, the ransomed shall return,
 And everlasting joy.

932 7s, D.   *"Tell us of the Night."*   J. BOWRING.

Watchman! tell us of the night,
 What its signs of promise are;—
Traveler! o'er yon mountain's height,
 See that glory-beaming star!—
Watchman! does its beauteous ray
 Aught of joy or hope foretell?—
Traveler! yes; it brings the day,
 Promised day of Israel:—

2 Watchman! tell us of the night;
 Higher yet that star ascends;—
Traveler! blessedness and light,
 Peace and truth, its course portends;—
Watchman! will its beams alone
 Gild the spot that gave them birth?—
Traveler! ages are its own;
 See, it bursts o'er all the earth!—

3 Watchman! tell us of the night,
 For the morning seems to dawn;—
Traveler! darkness takes its flight,
 Doubt and terror are withdrawn;—
Watchman! let thy wanderings cease;
 Hie thee to thy quiet home!—
Traveler! lo! the Prince of Peace,
 Lo! the Son of God, is come!

THE CHRISTIAN'S DEATH.

FREDERICK. 11s.   GEO. KINGSLEY.

1. I would not alway; I ask not to stay Where storm after storm rises (Omit)...... dark o'er the way: The few lurid mornings that dawn on us here Are enough for life's woes, full enough for its cheer.

933 "*I would not live alway.*" W. A. MUHLENBERG.

I WOULD not live alway: I ask not to stay
Where storm after storm rises dark o'er
   the way;
The few lurid mornings that dawn on us here
Are enough for life's woes, full enough for
   its cheer.

2 I would not live alway, thus fettered by sin—
Temptation without and corruption within:
Ev'n the rapture of pardon is mingled with
   fears,
And the cup of thanksgiving with penitent
   tears.

3 I would not live alway; no, welcome the
   tomb;
Since Jesus hath lain there, I dread not its
   gloom;
There sweet be my rest till he bid me arise
To hail him in triumph descending the skies.

4 Who, who would live alway, away from his
   God,
Away from yon heaven, that blissful abode,
Where the rivers of pleasure flow o'er the
   bright plains,
And the noontide of glory eternally reigns?

5 Where the saints of all ages in harmony
   meet,
Their Saviour and brethren transported to
   greet;
While the anthems of rapture unceasingly
   roll,
And the smile of the Lord is the feast of
   the soul.

934 (*See also* SCOTLAND, *p.* 152.) R. HEBER.

THOU art gone to the grave! but we will
   not deplore thee,
Though sorrows and darkness encompass
   the tomb;
The Saviour hath passed through its portals
   before thee,
And the lamp of his love is thy guide
   through the gloom.

2 Thou art gone to the grave! we no
   longer behold thee,
Nor tread the rough paths of the world by
   thy side;
But the wide arms of mercy are spread to
   enfold thee,
And sinners may hope, for the Sinless hath
   died.

3 Thou art gone to the grave! and, its
   mansion forsaking,
Perchance thy weak spirit in doubt lingered
   long;
But the sunshine of glory beamed bright
   on thy waking,
And the sound thou didst hear was the
   seraphim's song.

4 Thou art gone to the grave! but we
   will not deplore thee,
Since God was thy ransom, thy guardian,
   and guide:
He gave thee, he took thee, and he will restore thee,
And death has no sting, since the Saviour
   hath died.

THE CHRISTIAN'S DEATH.

935 *Death of a little child.* C. WINKWORTH, tr.

TENDER Shepherd, thou hast stilled
  Now thy little lamb's brief weeping:
Ah, how peaceful, pale, and mild
  In its narrow bed 'tis sleeping!
And no sigh of anguish sore
Heaves that little bosom more.

2 In this world of care and pain,
  Lord, thou wouldst no longer leave it;
To the sunny heavenly plain
  Thou dost now with joy receive it;
Clothed in robes of spotless white,
Now it dwells with thee in light.

3 Ah, Lord Jesus, grant that we
  Where it lives may soon be living,
And the lovely pastures see
  That its heavenly food are giving;
Then the gain of death we prove,
Though thou take what most we love.

936 *" Ye shall live also."* F. E. COX, tr.

JESUS lives! no longer now
  Can thy terrors, Death, appall me;
Jesus lives! and well I know,
  From the dead he will recall me;
Better life will then commence—
This shall be my confidence.

2 Jesus lives! to him the throne
  Over all the world is given;
I shall go where he is gone,
  Live and reign with him in heaven:
God is pledged; weak doubtings, hence!
This shall be my confidence!

3 Jesus lives! henceforth is death
  Entrance into life immortal;
Calmly I can yield my breath,
  Fearless tread the frowning portal;
Lord, when faileth flesh and sense,
Thou wilt be my confidence!

THE CHRISTIAN'S DEATH.

ST. ASAPH. C. M. D. J. M. GIORNOVICHI.

1. Behold the western evening light! It melts in deepening gloom: So calmly Christians sink away, Descending to the tomb. The winds breathe low, the withering leaf Scarce whispers from the tree: So gently flows the parting breath, When good men cease to be......

937 *Life's Sunset.* W. B. O. PEABODY.

Behold the western evening light!
 It melts in deepening gloom:
So calmly Christians sink away,
 Descending to the tomb.
The winds breathe low, the withering leaf
 Scarce whispers from the tree:
So gently flows the parting breath,
 When good men cease to be.

2 How beautiful on all the hills
 The crimson light is shed!
'Tis like the peace the Christian gives
 To mourners round his bed.
How mildly on the wandering cloud
 The sunset beam is cast!
'Tis like the memory left behind
 When loved ones breathe their last.

3 And now above the dews of night
 The rising star appears:
So faith springs in the heart of those
 Whose eyes are bathed in tears.
But soon the morning's happier light
 Its glory shall restore,
And eyelids that are sealed in death
 Shall wake to close no more.

938 *"Number our days."* R. HEBER.

Beneath our feet and o'er our head
 Is equal warning given;
Beneath us lie the countless dead,
 Above us is the heaven!
Death rides on every passing breeze,
 And lurks in every flower;
Each season hath its own disease,
 Its peril every hour!

2 Our eyes have seen the rosy light
 Of youth's soft cheek decay;
And fate descend in sudden night
 On manhood's middle day.
Our eyes have seen the steps of age
 Halt feebly to the tomb;
And yet shall earth our hearts engage,
 And dreams of days to come?

3 Then, mortal, turn! thy danger know;
 Where'er thy foot can tread,
The earth rings hollow from below,
 And warns thee of her dead!
Turn, mortal, turn! thy soul apply
 To truths divinely given:
The dead, who underneath thee lie,
 Shall live for hell or heaven!

THE CHRISTIAN'S DEATH.

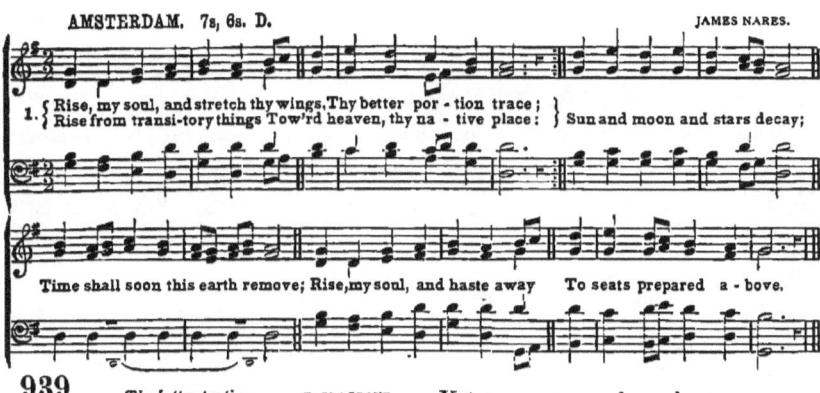

AMSTERDAM. 7s, 6s. D. JAMES NARES.

1. Rise, my soul, and stretch thy wings, Thy better por-tion trace; Rise from transi-tory things Tow'rd heaven, thy na-tive place: Sun and moon and stars decay; Time shall soon this earth remove; Rise, my soul, and haste away To seats prepared a-bove.

939 *The better portion.* R. SEAGRAVE.

Rise, my soul, and stretch thy wings,
  Thy better portion trace;
Rise from transitory things
  Toward heaven, thy native place:
Sun and moon and stars decay;
  Time shall soon this earth remove;
Rise, my soul, and haste away
  To seats prepared above.

2 Rivers to the ocean run,
  Nor stay in all their course;
Fire ascending seeks the sun;
  Both speed them to their source:
So a soul that's born of God,
  Pants to view his glorious face;
Upward tends to his abode,
  To rest in his embrace.

3 Cease, ye pilgrims, cease to mourn,
  Press onward to the prize;
Soon our Saviour will return
  Triumphant in the skies:

Yet a season,—and you know
  Happy entrance will be given,
All our sorrows left below,
  And earth exchanged for heaven.

940 *"Our earthly house."* J. BURTON.

Time is winging us away
  To our eternal home;
Life is but a winter's day—
  A journey to the tomb;
Youth and vigor soon will flee,
  Blooming beauty lose its charms;
All that's mortal soon shall be
  Enclosed in death's cold arms.

2 Time is winging us away
  To our eternal home;
Life is but a winter's day—
  A journey to the tomb;
But the Christian shall enjoy
  Health and beauty, soon, above,
Far beyond the world's annoy,
  Secure in Jesus' love.

GENEVA. 7s, 6s. D. LOWELL MASON.

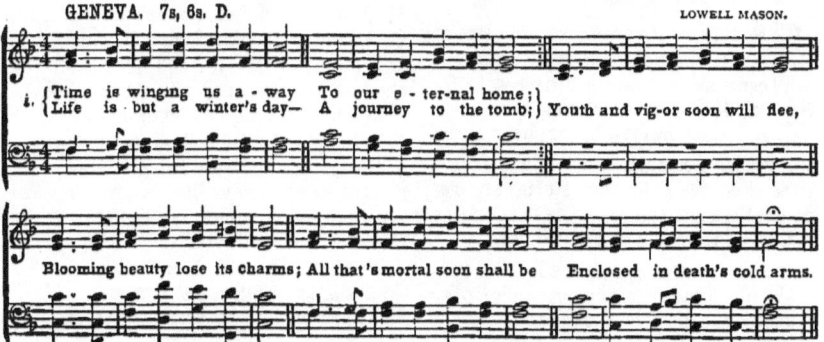

1. Time is winging us a-way To our e-ter-nal home; Life is but a winter's day— A journey to the tomb; Youth and vig-or soon will flee, Blooming beauty lose its charms; All that's mortal soon shall be Enclosed in death's cold arms.

THE CHRISTIAN'S DEATH.

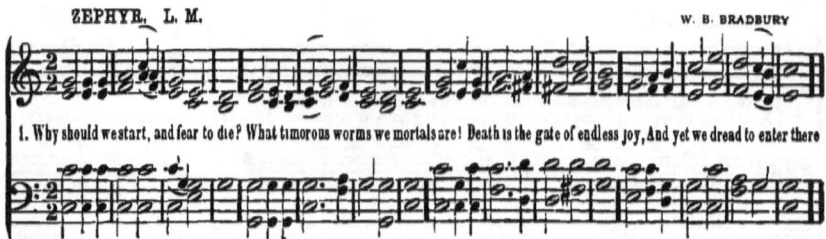

ZEPHYR. L. M. — W. B. BRADBURY

1. Why should we start, and fear to die? What timorous worms we mortals are! Death is the gate of endless joy, And yet we dread to enter there

941 *"His beloved sleep."* I. WATTS.

Why should we start, and fear to die?
What timorous worms we mortals are!
Death is the gate of endless joy,
And yet we dread to enter there.

2 The pains, the groans, the dying strife
Fright our approaching souls away;
We still shrink back again to life,
Fond of our prison and our clay.

3 Oh, if my Lord would come and meet,
My soul should stretch her wings in haste,
Fly fearless through death's iron gate,
Nor feel the terrors as she passed.

4 Jesus can make a dying bed
Feel soft as downy pillows are,
While on his breast I lean my head,
And breathe my life out sweetly there!

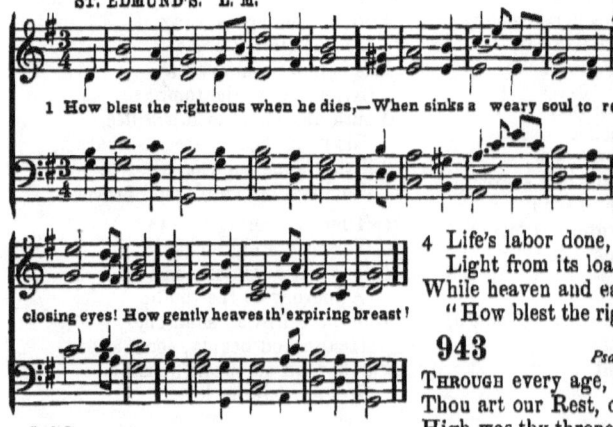

ST. EDMUND'S. L. M. — F. J. HAYDN.

1 How blest the righteous when he dies,—When sinks a weary soul to rest! How mildly beam the closing eyes! How gently heaves th' expiring breast!

942 *Death of the Righteous.* A. L. BARBAULD.

How BLEST the righteous when he dies,—
When sinks a weary soul to rest!
How mildly beam the closing eyes!
How gently heaves the expiring breast!

2 So fades a summer-cloud away;
So sinks the gale when storms are o'er;
So gently shuts the eye of day;
So dies a wave along the shore.

3 A holy quiet reigns around,—
A calm which life nor death destroys;
And naught disturbs that peace profound,
Which his unfettered soul enjoys.

4 Life's labor done, as sinks the clay,
Light from its load the spirit flies;
While heaven and earth combine to say,—
"How blest the righteous when he dies!"

943 *Psalm 90.* I. WATTS.

Through every age, eternal God!
Thou art our Rest, our safe Abode;
High was thy throne, ere heaven was made,
Or earth thy humble footstool laid.

2 Long hadst thou reigned, ere time began,
Or dust was fashioned into man;
And long thy kingdom shall endure,
When earth and time shall be no more.

3 Death, like an overflowing stream,
Sweeps us away; our life's a dream;
An empty tale; a morning flower,
Cut down, and withered in an hour.

4 Teach us, O Lord, how frail is man;
And kindly lengthen out our span,
Till thine own grace, so rich, so free,
Fit us to die and dwell with thee.

THE CHRISTIAN'S DEATH.

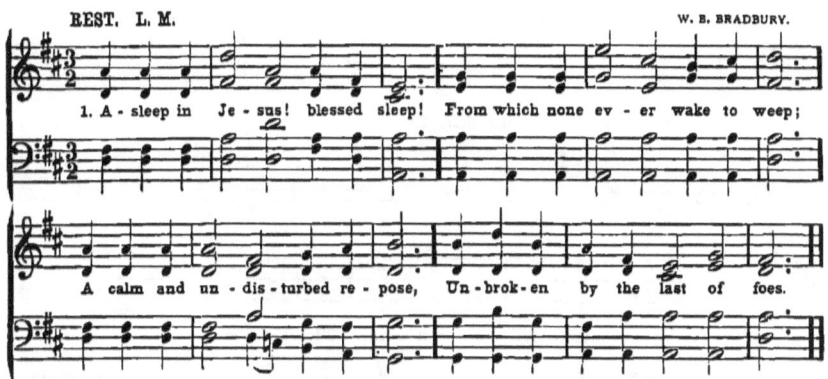

REST. L. M. — W. B. BRADBURY.

1. A-sleep in Je-sus! blessed sleep! From which none ev-er wake to weep;
A calm and un-dis-turbed re-pose, Un-brok-en by the last of foes.

944 *"Asleep in Jesus."* M. MACKAY.

ASLEEP in Jesus! blessèd sleep!
From which none ever wake to weep;
A calm and undisturbed repose,
Unbroken by the last of foes.

2 Asleep in Jesus! oh, how sweet
To be for such a slumber meet!
With holy confidence to sing
That death hath lost its venomed sting!

3 Asleep in Jesus! peaceful rest!
Whose waking is supremely blest;
No fear—no woe, shall dim the hour
That manifests the Saviour's power.

4 Asleep in Jesus! oh, for me
May such a blissful refuge be:
Securely shall my ashes lie,
And wait the summons from on high.

FEDERAL STREET. L. M. — H. K. OLIVER.

1. So fades the love-ly, bloom-ing flower,—Frail, smiling sol-ace of an hour!
So soon our tran-sient com-forts fly, And pleasure on-ly blooms to die.

945 *Death of an Infant.* A. STEELE.

So FADES the lovely, blooming flower,—
Frail smiling solace of an hour!
So soon our transient comforts fly,
And pleasure only blooms to die.

2 Is there no kind, no lenient art,
To heal the anguish of the heart?
Spirit of grace! be ever nigh,
Thy comforts are not made to die.

3 Thy powerful aid supports the soul,
And nature owns thy kind control;
While we peruse the sacred page,
Our fiercest griefs resign their rage.

4 Then gentle patience smiles on pain,
And dying hope revives again;
Hope wipes the tear from sorrow's eye,
And faith points upward to the sky.

THE CHRISTIAN'S DEATH.

OLMUTZ. S. M.   LOWELL MASON, arr.

1. "For-ev-er with the Lord!" So, Je-sus! let it be;
Life from the dead is in that word; 'Tis im-mor-tal-i-ty.

946   "*For ever.*"   J. MONTGOMERY.

"For ever with the Lord!"
  So, Jesus! let it be;
Life from the dead is in that word;
  'Tis immortality.

2 Here, in the body pent,
  Absent from thee I roam:
Yet nightly pitch my moving tent
  A day's march nearer home.

3 My Father's house on high,
  Home of my soul! how near,
At times, to faith's aspiring eye,
  Thy golden gates appear!

4 "For ever with the Lord!"
  Father, if 't is thy will,
The promise of thy gracious word
  Ev'n here to me fulfill.

5 So, when my latest breath
  Shall rend the vail in twain,
By death I shall escape from death,
  And life eternal gain.

6 Knowing as I am known,
  How shall I love that word,
And oft repeat before the throne,
  "For ever with the Lord!"

947   *Resurrection.*   S. F. SMITH.

Oh, for the death of those
  Who slumber in the Lord!
Oh, be like theirs my last repose,
  Like theirs my last reward!

2 Their bodies in the ground,
  In silent hope may lie,
Till the last trumpet's joyful sound
  Shall call them to the sky.

3 Their ransomed spirits soar
  On wings of faith and love,
To meet the Saviour they adore,
  And reign with him above.

4 With us their names shall live
  Through long succeeding years,
Embalmed with all our hearts can give,
  Our praises and our tears.

948   "*I will wait.*"   H. BONAR.

A few more years shall roll,
  A few more seasons come;
And we shall be with those that rest,
  Asleep within the tomb;—

2 A few more storms shall beat
  On this wild rocky shore;
And we shall be where tempests cease,
  And surges swell no more:—

3 A few more struggles here,
  A few more partings o'er,
A few more toils, a few more tears,
  And we shall weep no more.

4 Then, O my Lord, prepare
  My soul for that glad day;
Oh, wash me in thy precious blood,
  And take my sins away!

THE CHRISTIAN'S DEATH.

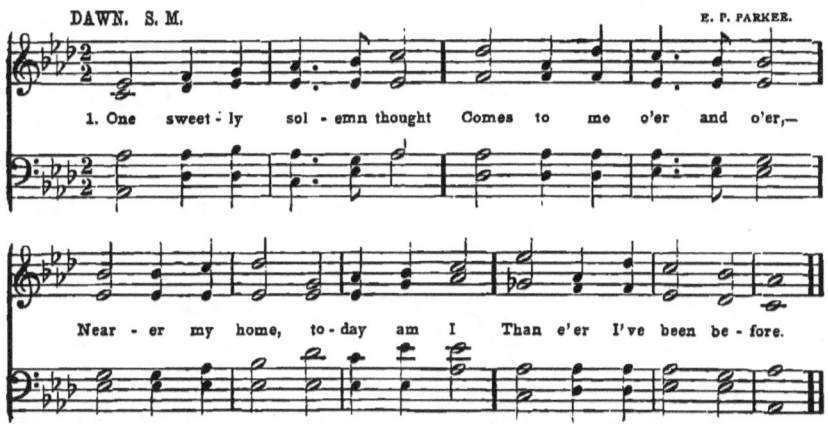

DAWN. S. M. — E. P. PARKER.

949 *"Nearer."* P. CARY.

ONE sweetly solemn thought
Comes to me o'er and o'er,—
Nearer my home, to-day, am I
Than e'er I've been before.

2 Nearer my Father's house,
Where many mansions be;
Nearer to-day the great white throne,
Nearer the crystal sea.

3 Nearer the bound of life,
Where burdens are laid down;
Nearer to leave the heavy cross;
Nearer to gain the crown.

4 But, lying dark between,
Winding down through the night,
There rolls the deep and unknown stream
That leads at last to light.

5 Ev'n now, perchance, my feet
Are slipping on the brink,
And I, to-day, am nearer home,—
Nearer than now I think.

6 Father, perfect my trust!
Strengthen my power of faith!
Nor let me stand, at last, alone
Upon the shore of death.

DUNBAR S. M. — E. W. DUNBAR.

THE CHRISTIAN'S DEATH.

BARBY. C. M. — W. TANSUR.

1. Oh, for an o-ver-com-ing faith, To cheer my dy-ing hours; To tri-umph o'er ap-proach-ing death, And all his fright-ful powers!

950 *"Where is thy sting?"* I. WATTS.

OH, for an overcoming faith,
 To cheer my dying hours;
To triumph o'er approaching death,
 And all his frightful powers!

2 Joyful, with all the strength I have,
 My quivering lip should sing,—
"Where is thy boasted victory, grave;
 And where, O death, thy sting?"

3 Now to the God of victory
 Immortal thanks be paid;—
Who makes us conquerors, while we die,
 Through Christ, our living Head!

951 *"I shall go to him."* H. K. WHITE.

THROUGH sorrow's night, and danger's path,
 Amid the deepening gloom,
We, followers of our suffering Lord,
 Are marching to the tomb.

2 There, when the turmoil is no more,
 And all our powers decay,
Our cold remains, in solitude,
 Shall sleep the years away.

3 Our labors done, securely laid
 In this our last retreat,
Unheeded o'er our silent dust
 The storms of earth shall beat.

4 Yet not thus buried or extinct,
 The vital spark shall lie:
For o'er life's wreck that spark shall rise
 To seek its kindred sky.

5 These ashes, too, this little dust,
 Our Father's care shall keep,
Till the last angel rise and break
 The long and dreary sleep.

6 Then love's soft dew o'er every eye
 Shall shed its mildest rays,
And the long silent voice awake
 With shouts of endless praise.

952 *Resurrection sure.* RAY PALMER.

WHEN downward to the darksome tomb
 I thoughtful turn my eyes,
Frail nature trembles at the gloom,
 And anxious fears arise.

2 Why shrinks my soul?—in death's embrace
 Once Jesus captive slept:
And angels, hovering o'er the place,
 His lowly pillow kept.

3 Thus shall they guard my sleeping dust,
 And, as the Saviour rose,
The grave again shall yield her trust,
 And end my deep repose.

4 My Lord, before to glory gone,
 Shall bid me come away;
And calm and bright shall break the dawn
 Of heaven's eternal day,

5 Then let my faith each fear dispel,
 And gild with light the grave;
To him my loftiest praises swell,
 Who died, from death to save.

THE CHRISTIAN'S DEATH.

CHINA, C. M. — T. SWAN.

953   *"We are confident."*   I. WATTS.

Why do we mourn departing friends,
  Or shake at death's alarms?
'Tis but the voice that Jesus sends,
  To call them to his arms.

2 Are we not tending upward, too,
  As fast as time can move?
Nor would we wish the hours more slow,
  To keep us from our love.

3 Why should we tremble to convey
  Their bodies to the tomb?
There the dear flesh of Jesus lay,
  And scattered all the gloom.

4 The graves of all the saints he blessed,
  And softened every bed;
Where should the dying members rest,
  But with the dying Head?

5 Thence he arose, ascending high,
  And showed our feet the way;
Up to the Lord we, too, shall fly
  At the great rising-day.

6 Then let the last loud trumpet sound,
  And bid our kindred rise;
Awake! ye nations under ground;
  Ye saints! ascend the skies.

ST. AGNES, C. M. — J. B. DYKES.

THE CHRISTIAN'S DEATH.

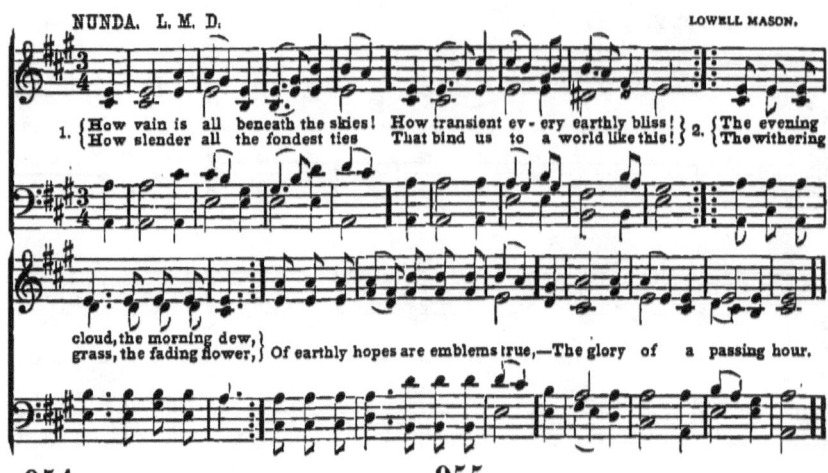

954 *Heaven alone unfading.* D. E. FORD.

How VAIN is all beneath the skies!
How transient every earthly bliss!
How slender all the fondest ties
That bind us to a world like this!

2 The evening-cloud, the morning dew,
The withering grass, the fading flower,
Of earthly hopes are emblems true,—
The glory of a passing hour.

3 But, though earth's fairest blossoms die,
And all beneath the skies is vain,
There is a land whose confines lie
Beyond the reach of care and pain.

4 Then let the hope of joys to come
Dispel our cares and chase our fears:
If God be ours, we're traveling home,
Though passing through a vale of tears.

955 *Psalm 17.* I. WATTS.

WHAT sinners value I resign;
Lord! 'tis enough that thou art mine;
I shall behold thy blissful face,
And stand complete in righteousness.

2 This life's a dream—an empty show;
But the bright world, to which I go,
Hath joys substantial and sincere;
When shall I wake, and find me there?

3 Oh, glorious hour! oh, blest abode!
I shall be near, and like my God;
And flesh and sin no more control
The sacred pleasures of the soul.

4 My flesh shall slumber in the ground,
Till the last trumpet's joyful sound;
Then burst the chains, with sweet surprise,
And in my Saviour's image rise!

THE CHRISTIAN'S DEATH.

MILLINGTON. 8s, 7s, 7s. W. B. BRADBURY.

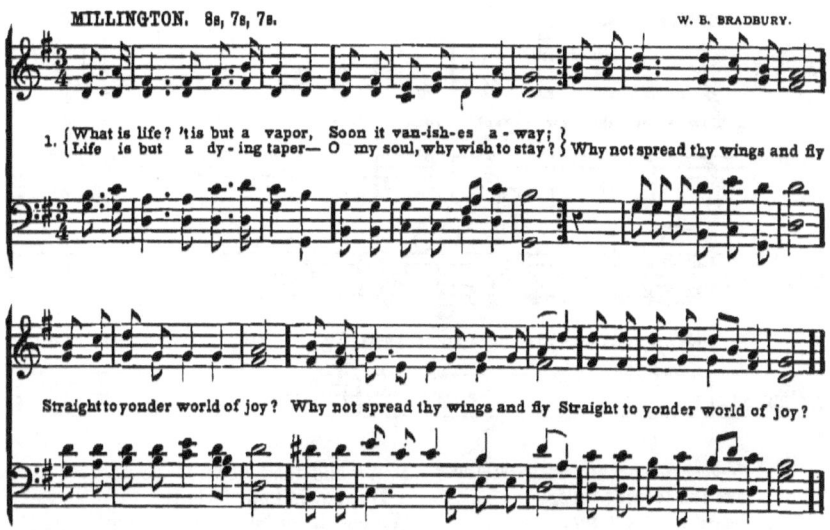

1. What is life? 'tis but a vapor, Soon it van-ish-es a-way;
Life is but a dy-ing taper— O my soul, why wish to stay? Why not spread thy wings and fly Straight to yonder world of joy? Why not spread thy wings and fly Straight to yonder world of joy?

---

956 "*What is your life?*" T. KELLY.

WHAT is life? 't is but a vapor,
 Soon it vanishes away;
Life is but a dying taper—
 O my soul, why wish to stay?
Why not spread thy wings and fly
Straight to yonder world of joy?

2 See that glory, how resplendent!
 Brighter far than fancy paints;
There, in majesty transcendent,
 Jesus reigns—the King of saints.
 Why not spread, etc.

3 Joyful crowds his throne surrounding,
 Sing with rapture of his love;
Through the heavens his praise resounding,
 Filling all the courts above.
 Why not spread, etc.

4 Go, and share his people's glory,
 'Midst the ransomed crowd appear;
Thine a joyful wondrous story,
 One that angels love to hear.
 Why not spread, etc.

---

957 C. P. M. *The Tribunal.* LADY HUNTINGTON.

WHEN thou, my righteous Judge, shalt come
 To take thy ransomed people home,
  Shall I among them stand?
Shall such a worthless worm as I,
Who sometimes am afraid to die,
  Be found at thy right hand?

2 I love to meet thy people now,
Before thy feet with them to bow,
  Though vilest of them all;
But, can I bear the piercing thought,
What if my name should be left out,
  When thou for them shalt call?

3 O Lord, prevent it by thy grace,
Be thou my only hiding-place,
  In this the accepted day;
Thy pardoning voice, oh, let me hear,
To still my unbelieving fear,
  Nor let me fall, I pray.

4 Among thy saints let me be found,
Whene'er the archangel's trump shall sound,
  To see thy smiling face;
Then loudest of the throng I 'll sing,
While heaven's resounding mansions ring
  With shouts of sovereign grace.

THE CHRISTIAN'S DEATH.

WATCHMAN. S. M.   JAMES LEACH.

1. How swift the tor-rent rolls That bears us to the sea,
The tide.... that hur-ries thoughtless souls To.... vast e-ter-ni-ty!

958   *Our fathers; where are they.*   P. DODDRIDGE.

How swift the torrent rolls,
  That bears us to the sea,
The tide that hurries thoughtless souls
  To vast eternity!

2 Our fathers, where are they,
  With all they called their own?
Their joys and griefs, and hopes and cares,
  And wealth and honor gone.

3 God of our fathers, hear,
  Thou everlasting Friend!
While we, as on life's utmost verge,
  Our souls to thee commend.

4 Of all the pious dead
  May we the footsteps trace,
Till with them, in the land of light,
  We dwell before thy face.

959   *"How long, O Lord!"*   H. BONAR.

THE Church has waited long
  Her absent Lord to see;
And still in loneliness she waits,
  A friendless stranger she.

2 How long, O Lord our God,
  Holy and true and good,
Wilt thou not judge thy suffering Church,
  Her sighs and tears and blood?

3 Saint after saint on earth,
  Has lived and loved and died;
And as they left us, one by one,
  We laid them side by side.

4 We laid them down to sleep,
  But not in hope forlorn;
We laid them but to ripen there,
  Till the last glorious morn.

5 We long to hear thy voice,
  To see thee face to face,
To share thy crown and glory then,
  As now we share thy grace.

6 Come, Lord, and wipe away
  The curse, the sin, the stain,
And make this blighted world of ours
  Thine own fair world again.

960   *The Pious Dead.*   R. MANT.

FOR all thy saints, O God,
  Who strove in Christ to live,
Who followed him, obeyed, adored,
  Our grateful hymn receive.

2 For all thy saints, O God,
  Accept our thankful cry,
Who counted Christ their great reward,
  And yearned for him to die.

3 They all, in life and death,
  With him, their Lord, in view,
Learned from thy Holy Spirit's breath
  To suffer and to do.

4 For this thy name we bless,
  And humbly pray that we
May follow them in holiness,
  And live and die in thee.

THE CHRISTIAN'S DEATH.

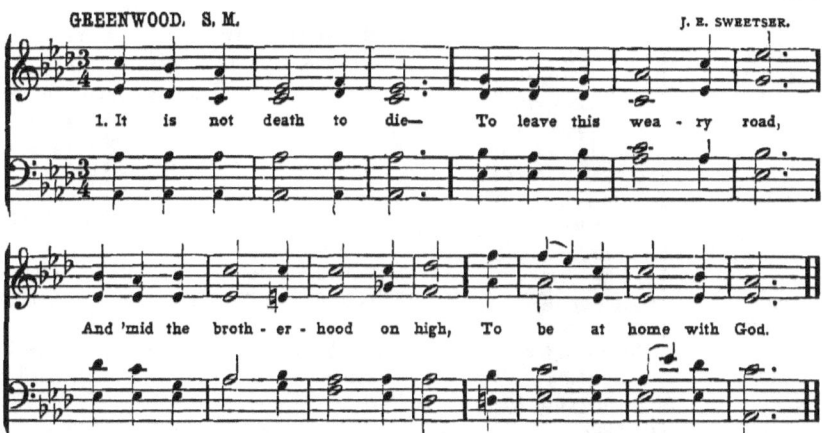

GREENWOOD. S. M. — J. E. SWEETSER.

1. It is not death to die—
To leave this weary road,
And 'mid the brotherhood on high,
To be at home with God.

961 *"Where is thy victory?"* G. W. BETHUNE.

It is not death to die—
To leave this weary road,
And 'mid the brotherhood on high,
To be at home with God.

2 It is not death to close
The eye long dimmed by tears,
And wake, in glorious repose
To spend eternal years.

3 It is not death to bear
The wrench that sets us free
From dungeon chain,—to breathe the air
Of boundless liberty.

4 It is not death to fling
Aside this sinful dust,
And rise, on strong exulting wing,
To live among the just.

5 Jesus, thou Prince of life!
Thy chosen cannot die;
Like thee, they conquer in the strife,
To reign with thee on high.

962 *Death of a Minister.* J. MONTGOMERY.

Servant of God, well done!
Rest from thy loved employ:
The battle fought, the victory won,
Enter thy Master's joy!

2 The voice at midnight came;
He started up to hear;
A mortal arrow pierced his frame;
He fell, but felt no fear.

3 His spirit with a bound
Left its encumbering clay:
His tent, at sunrise, on the ground
A darkened ruin lay.

4 The pains of death are past,
Labor and sorrow cease,
And, life's long warfare closed at last,
His soul is found in peace.

5 Soldier of Christ, well done!
Praise be thy new employ;
And, while eternal ages run,
Rest in thy Saviour's joy.

963 *"With thy might."* H. BONAR.

Make haste, O man, to live,
For thou so soon must die;
Time hurries past thee like the breeze;
How swift its moments fly!

2 To breathe, and wake, and sleep,
To smile, to sigh, to grieve,
To move in idleness through earth—
This, this is not to live.

3 Make haste, O man, to do
Whatever must be done;
Thou hast no time to lose in sloth,
Thy day will soon be gone.

4 Up, then, with speed, and work;
Fling ease and self away—
This is no time for thee to sleep—
Up, watch, and work, and pray!

THE CHRISTIAN'S DEATH.

964 C. M. D.   *Psalm 90.*   I. WATTS.

OUR God, our help in ages past,
  Our hope for years to come;
Our shelter from the stormy blast,
  And our eternal home:—
Under the shadow of thy throne
  Thy saints have dwelt secure;
Sufficient is thine arm alone,
  And our defence is sure.

2 Before the hills in order stood,
  Or earth received her frame,
From everlasting thou art God,
  To endless years the same.
A thousand ages, in thy sight,
  Are like an evening gone;
Short as the watch that ends the night,
  Before the rising sun.

3 Time, like an ever-rolling stream,
  Bears all its sons away;
They fly, forgotten, as a dream
  Dies at the opening day.
Our God, our help in ages past,
  Our hope for years to come,
Be thou our guard while troubles last,
  And our eternal home.

965 P. M.   *Death is Transition.*   R. P. DUNN, *tr.*

No, no, it is not dying
  To go unto our God;
This gloomy earth forsaking,
  Our journey homeward taking,
    Along the starry road.

2 No, no, it is not dying
  Heaven's citizen to be;
A crown immortal wearing,
And rest unbroken sharing,
    From care and conflict free.

3 No, no, it is not dying
  To wear a heavenly crown;
Among God's people dwelling,
The glorious triumph swelling,
    Of him whose sway we own.

4 Oh, no! this is not dying,
  Thou Saviour of mankind!
There, streams of love are flowing,
No hindrance ever knowing;
    Here, only drops we find.

966 L. M.   *Burial of Believers.*   I. WATTS.

UNVAIL thy bosom, faithful tomb!
  Take this new treasure to thy trust,
And give these sacred relics room
  To seek a slumber in the dust.

2 Nor pain, nor grief, nor anxious fear,
  Invade thy bounds;—no mortal woes
Can reach the peaceful sleeper here,
  While angels watch the soft repose.

3 So Jesus slept; God's dying Son
  Passed thro' the grave and blessed the bed!
Rest here, blest saint! till, from his throne,
  The morning break, and pierce the shade.

4 Break from his throne, illustrious morn!
  Attend, O earth! his sovereign word;
Restore thy trust;—a glorious form
  Shall then arise to meet the Lord.

967 Irr. M.   *The Soul Departing.*   A. POPE.

VITAL spark of heavenly flame!
Quit, oh, quit this mortal frame;
Trembling, hoping, lingering, flying—
Oh, the pain!—the bliss of dying!
Cease, fond nature, cease thy strife,
And let me languish into life!

2 Hark! they whisper; angels say,
" Sister spirit, come away;"
What is this absorbs me quite?—
Steals my senses, shuts my sight,
Drowns my spirits, draws my breath?—
Tell me, my soul, can this be death?

3 The world recedes—it disappears!
Heaven opens on my eyes!—my ears
With sounds seraphic ring!
Lend, lend your wings! I mount! I fly!
"O Grave! where is thy victory?
O Death! where is thy sting?"

968 L. M.   *John 17: 24.*   C. ELLIOTT.

LET me be with thee where thou art,
  My Saviour, my eternal Rest;
Then only will this longing heart
  Be fully and for ever blest.

2 Let me be with thee where thou art,
  Thine unvailed glory to behold;
Then only will this wandering heart
  Cease to be false to thee and cold.

3 Let me be with thee where thou art,
  Where none can die, where none remove;
There neither death nor life will part
  Me from thy presence and thy love.

THE CHRISTIAN'S DEATH.

969 C. M. *Job* 3: 17-20. R. BLAIR.
How still and peaceful is the grave!
 Where, life's vain tumults past,
The appointed house, by heaven's decree,
 Receives us all at last.

2 The wicked there from troubling cease;
 Their passions rage no more;
And there the weary pilgrim rests
 From all the toils he bore.

3 There servants, masters, small and
 Partake the same repose; [great,
And there, in peace, the ashes mix
 Of those who once were foes.

4 All, leveled by the hand of death,
 Lie sleeping in the tomb,
Till God in judgment calls them forth
 To meet their final doom.

970 C. M. *To die is gain.* W. H. BATHURST.
Why should our tears in sorrow flow,
 When God recalls his own;
And bids them leave a world of woe
 For an immortal crown?

2 Is not ev'n death a gain to those
 Whose life to God was given?
Gladly to earth their eyes they close,
 To open them in heaven.

3 Their toils are past, their work is done,
 And they are fully blest:
They fought the fight, the victory won,
 And entered into rest.

4 Then let our sorrows cease to flow,—
 God has recalled his own;
And let our hearts in every woe,
 Still say,—"Thy will be done!"

971 P. M. *The Cemetery.* J. MONTGOMERY.
This place is holy ground!
 World, with its cares, away!
A holy, solemn stillness, round
 This lifeless, mouldering clay;
Nor pain, nor grief, nor anxious fear,
Can reach the peaceful sleeper here.

2 Behold the bed of death,
 The pale and mortal clay!
Heard ye the sob of parting breath?
 Marked ye the eye's last ray?
No! life so sweetly ceased to be,
It lapsed in immortality.

3 Bury the dead, and weep
 In stillness o'er the loss!
Bury the dead! in Christ they sleep
 Who bore on earth his cross;
And from the grave their dust shall rise,
In his own image to the skies.

972 10s. *Death at Prime.* J. MONTGOMERY.
Go to the grave in all thy glorious prime!
 In full activity of zeal and power;
A Christian cannot die before his time;
 The Lord's appointment is the servant's hour.

2 Go to the grave; at noon from labor
  cease; [done;
Rest on thy sheaves, thy harvest-task is
Come from the heat of battle, and in
  peace, [won.
Soldier! go home; with thee the fight is

3 Go to the grave, for there thy Saviour
  lay
In death's embraces, ere he rose on high;
And all the ransomed, by that narrow
  way,
Pass to eternal life beyond the sky.

4 Go to the grave? no, take thy seat
  above!
Be thy pure spirit present with the Lord,
Where thou for faith and hope hast perfect love,
And open vision for the written Word.

973 L. M. *Be Pitiful, O God.* C. F. ALEXANDER.
O Son of God, in glory crowned,
 The Judge ordained of quick and dead!
O Son of man, so pitying found
 For all the tears thy people shed!

2 Be with us in this darkened place,—
 This weary, restless, dangerous night;
And teach, oh, teach us by thy grace,
 To struggle onward into light!

3 And since, in God's recording book,
 Our sins are written, every one,—
The crime, the wrath, the wandering look,
 The good we knew, and left undone;—

4 Lord, ere the last dread trump be
  heard,
And ere before thy face we stand,
Look thou on each accusing word,
 And blot it with thy bleeding hand.

THE GENERAL JUDGMENT.

TAMWORTH. 8s, 7s, 4s. — C. LOCKHART.

1. See th' eternal Judge descending! View him seated on his throne!
Now, poor sinner, now lamenting, Stand and hear thine awful doom;
Trumpets call thee, Trumpets call thee, Stand and hear thine awful doom.

974 *"They shall look on him."* ANON.

SEE the eternal Judge descending!
View him seated on his throne!
Now, poor sinner, now lamenting,
Stand and hear thine awful doom;
Trumpets call thee,
Stand and hear thine awful doom!

2 Hear the cries he now is venting,
Filled with dread of fiercer pain;
While in anguish thus lamenting
That he ne'er was born again—
Greatly mourning
That he ne'er was born again.

3 "Yonder sits my slighted Saviour,
With the marks of dying love;
Oh, that I had sought his favor
When I felt his Spirit move—
Golden moments,
When I felt his Spirit move!"

975 *"Day of wonders."* J. NEWTON.

DAY of judgment! day of wonders!
Hark!—the trumpet's awful sound,
Louder than a thousand thunders,
Shakes the vast creation round:
How the summons
Will the sinner's heart confound!

2 See the Judge, our nature wearing,
Clothed in majesty divine!
You, who long for his appearing,
Then shall say, "This God is mine!"
Gracious Saviour!
Own me in that day for thine.

3 At his call, the dead awaken,
Rise to life from earth and sea;
All the powers of nature, shaken
By his looks, prepare to flee:
Careless sinner!
What will then become of thee?

BREST. 8s, 7s, 4s. — LOWELL MASON.

1. Day of judgment! day of wonders! Hark!—the trumpet's awful sound, Louder than a
thousand thunders, Shakes the vast creation round: How the summons Will the sinner's heart confound!

THE GENERAL JUDGMENT.

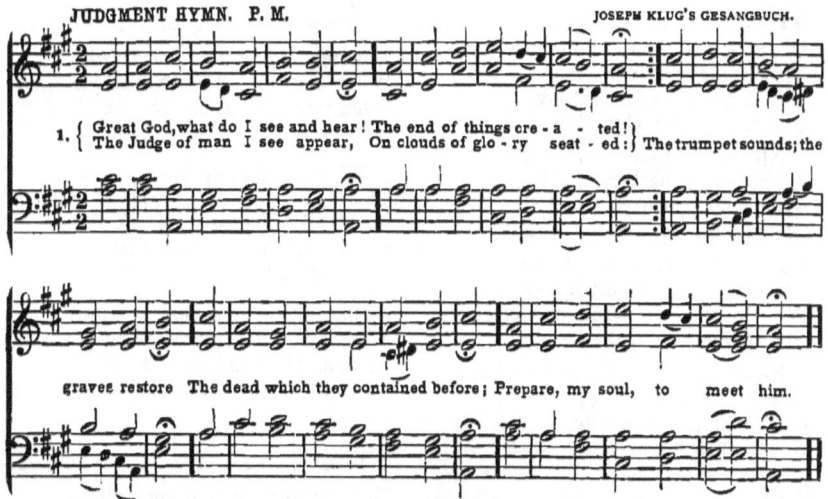

976 *Prepare to meet God.* W. B. COLLYER, *tr.*

GREAT God, what do I see and hear!
 The end of things created!
The Judge of man I see appear,
 On clouds of glory seated:
The trumpet sounds; the graves restore
The dead which they contained before;
 Prepare, my soul, to meet him.

2 The dead in Christ shall first arise,
 At the last trumpet's sounding—
Caught up to meet him in the skies,
 With joy their Lord surrounding;
No gloomy fears their souls dismay,
His presence sheds eternal day
 On those prepared to meet him.

3 But sinners, filled with guilty fears,
 Behold his wrath prevailing;
For they shall rise, and find their tears
 And sighs are unavailing:
The day of grace is past and gone;
Trembling they stand before the throne,
 All unprepared to meet him.

4 Great God! what do I see and hear!
 The end of things created!
The Judge of man I see appear,
 On clouds of glory seated:
Beneath his cross I view the day
When heaven and earth shall pass away,
 And thus prepare to meet him.

977 *"Into thine hand."* E. A. BOWRING, *tr.*

WHEN my last hour is close at hand,
 My last sad journey taken,
Do thou, Lord Jesus! by me stand;
 Let me not be forsaken:
O Lord! my spirit I resign
Into thy loving hands divine;
 'Tis safe within thy keeping.

2 Countless as sands upon the shore,
 My sins may then appall me;
Yet, though my conscience vex me sore,
 Despair shall not enthrall me;
For as I draw my latest breath,
I'll think, Lord Christ! upon thy death,
 And there find consolation.

3 I shall not in the grave remain,
 Since thou death's bonds hast severed:
By hope with thee to rise again,
 From fear of death delivered,
I'll come to thee, where'er thou art,—
Live with thee, from thee never part;
 Therefore I die in rapture.

4 And so to Jesus Christ I'll go,
 My longing arms extending;
So fall asleep, in slumber deep,
 Slumber that knows no ending;
Till Jesus Christ, God's only Son,
Opens the gates of bliss, leads on
 To heaven, to life eternal.

THE GENERAL JUDGMENT.

978 7s.   *All over and gone.*   H. ALFORD.

EARTH is past away and gone,
All her glories, every one,
All her pomp is broken down;
God is reigning, God alone!

2 All her high ones lowly lie,
All her mirth hath passéd by,
All her merry-hearted sigh;
God is reigning, God on high!

3 No more sorrow, no more night;
Perfect joy and purest light!
With his spotless saints and bright,
God is reigning in the height!

4 Blessing, praise and glory bring;
Offer every holy thing;
Everlasting praises sing;
God is reigning, God our King!

979 S. M.   *The Last Day.*   B. BEDDOME.

BEHOLD, the day is come;
The righteous Judge is near;
And sinners, trembling at their doom,
Shall soon their sentence hear.

2 How awful is the sight!
How loud the thunders roar!
The sun forbears to give his light,
And stars are seen no more.

3 The whole creation groans;
But saints arise and sing:
They are the ransomed of the Lord,
And he their God and King.

980 S. M.   *Now is the time.*   P. DODDRIDGE.

AND will the Judge descend,
And must the dead arise,
And not a single soul escape
His all-discerning eyes?

2 How will my heart endure
The terrors of that day,
When earth and heaven before his face
Astonished shrink away?

3 But, ere the trumpet shakes
The mansions of the dead,
Hark, from the gospel's cheering sound
What joyful tidings spread!

4 Ye sinners! seek his grace
Whose wrath ye cannot bear;
Fly to the shelter of his cross,
And find salvation there.

981 L. M.   *"The Day of the Lord."*   W. SCOTT.

THE day of wrath! that dreadful day,
When heaven and earth shall pass away!
What power shall be the sinner's stay?
How shall he meet that dreadful day?—

2 When, shriveling like a parchéd scroll,
The flaming heavens together roll,
And louder yet, and yet more dread,
Swells the high trump that wakes the dead!

3 Oh, on that day, that wrathful day,
When man to judgment wakes from clay,
Be thou, O Christ, the sinner's stay,
Though heaven and earth shall pass away.

982 8s, 7s, 4.   *"The Mighty God."*   W. GOODE.

Lo! the mighty God appearing—
From on high Jehovah speaks!
Eastern lands the summons hearing,
O'er the west his thunder breaks:
    Earth beholds him:
Universal nature shakes.

2 Zion, all its light unfolding,
God in glory shall display:
Lo! he comes,—nor silence holding,
Fire and clouds prepare his way:
    Tempests round him
Hasten on the dreadful day.

3 To the heavens his voice ascending,
To the earth beneath he cries—
"Souls immortal now descending,
Let the sleeping dust arise!
    Rise to judgment;
Let my throne adorn the skies.

4 "Gather first my saints around me,
Those who to my covenant stood;
Those who humbly sought and found me,
Through the dying Saviour's blood:
    Blest Redeemer!
Choicest sacrifice to God!"

5 Now the heavens on high adore him,
And his righteousness declare:
Sinners perish from before him,
But his saints his mercies share:
    Just his judgment!
God, himself the Judge, is there.

983 7s. 3 l.   *"Dies Iræ."*   H. ALFORD.

Day of anger! that dread day
Shall the sign in heaven display,
And the earth in ashes lay!

2 Oh, what trembling shall appear,
When his coming shall be near,
Who shall all things strictly clear!

3 When the trumpet shall command,
Through the tombs of every land,
All before the throne to stand!

4 What shall I before him say?
How shall I be safe that day—
When the righteous scarcely may?

5 King of awful majesty,
Saving sinners graciously,—
Fount of mercy! save thou me:

6 Leave me not, my Saviour! one,
For whose soul thy course was run!
Lest I be that day undone!

7 Though unworthy is my prayer,
Make my soul thy mercy's care,
And from death eternal spare!

8 When thy voice in wrath shall say,
Cursèd one, depart away!
Call me with thy blest, I pray!

984 L. M.   *The Lord Coming.*   R. HEBER.

The Lord shall come! the earth shall quake!
The mountains to their centre shake;
And, withering from the vault of night,
The stars withdraw their feeble light.

2 The Lord shall come! but not the same
As once in lowly form he came,—
A silent Lamb before his foes,
A weary man, and full of woes.

3 The Lord shall come! a dreadful form,
With wreath of flame, and robe of storm,
On cherub-wings, and wings of wind,
Anointed Judge of human kind!

4 While sinners in despair shall call,
" Rocks, hide us! mountains, on us fall!"
The saints, ascending from the tomb,
Shall sing for joy, "The Lord is come!"

985 L. M. 7 l.   *Isa.* 57 : 15.   C. WINKWORTH, *tr.*

Eternity! eternity!
How long art thou, eternity!
And yet to thee time hastes away,
Like as the war horse to the fray,
Or swift as couriers homeward go,
Or ships to port, or shafts from bow;
Ponder, O man, eternity!

2 Eternity! eternity!
How long art thou, eternity!
As long as God is God, so long
Endure the pains of hell and wrong,
So long the joys of heaven remain;
Oh, lasting joy! oh, lasting pain!
Ponder, O man, eternity!

3 Eternity! eternity!
How long art thou, eternity!
O man, full oft thy thoughts should dwell
Upon the pains of sin and hell,
And on the glories of the pure,
That do beyond all time endure;
Ponder, O man, eternity!

986 8s, 7s, 4s.   *"Lo! he comes!"*   C. WESLEY.

Lo! he comes with clouds descending,
  Once for favored sinners slain!
Thousand thousand saints attending,
  Swell the triumph of his train!
    Hallelujah!
  Jesus comes, and comes to reign.

2 Every eye shall now behold him,
  Robed in dreadful majesty!
Those who set at naught and sold him,
  Pierced and nailed him to the tree,
    Deeply wailing,
  Shall the true Messiah see!

3 Lo! the last long separation,
  As the cleaving crowds divide,
And one dread adjudication
  Sends each soul to either side!
    Lord of mercy!
  How shall I that day abide?

4 Yea, Amen! let all adore thee,
  High on thine eternal throne!
Saviour, take the power and glory;
  Make thy righteous sentence known!
    Men and angels
  Kneel and bow to thee alone!

THE GENERAL JUDGMENT.

987 *"That awful day."* I. WATTS.

THAT awful day will surely come,
The appointed hour makes haste,
When I must stand before my Judge,
And pass the solemn test.

2 Thou lovely Chief of all my joys,
Thou Sovereign of my heart!
How could I bear to hear thy voice
Pronounce the sound, "Depart!"

3 Jesus, I throw my arms around,
And hang upon thy breast;

Without one gracious smile from thee,
My spirit cannot rest.

4 Oh, tell me that my worthless name
Is graven on thy hands!
Show me some promise in thy book,
Where my salvation stands.

5 Give me one kind, assuring word,
To sink my fears again;
And cheerfully my soul shall wait
Her threescore years and ten.

988 *The Test.* J. ADDISON.

WHEN, rising from the bed of death,
O'erwhelmed with guilt and fear,
I see my Maker face to face,
Oh, how shall I appear?

2 If yet while pardon may be found
And mercy may be sought,

My heart with inward horror shrinks,
And trembles at the thought;—

2 When thou, O Lord! shalt stand disclosed
In majesty severe,
And sit in judgment on my soul,
Oh, how shall I appear?

THE REST OF HEAVEN.

TAPPAN. C. M.   GEO. KINGSLEY.

1. On Jordan's rug-ged banks I stand, And cast a wish-ful eye To Canaan's fair and happy land, To Canaan's fair and happy land, Where my pos-ses-sions lie.

989   *"Let me go over!"*   S. STENNETT.

On Jordan's rugged banks I stand,
And cast a wishful eye
To Canaan's fair and happy land,
Where my possessions lie.

2 Oh, the transporting, rapturous scene,
That rises to my sight!
Sweet fields arrayed in living green,
And rivers of delight!

3 O'er all those wide extended plains
Shines one eternal day;
There God, the Son, for ever reigns,
And scatters night away.

4 No chilling winds, or poisonous breath,
Can reach that healthful shore;
Sickness and sorrow, pain and death,
Are felt and feared no more.

5 When shall I reach that happy place,
And be for ever blest?
When shall I see my Father's face,
And in his bosom rest?

6 Filled with delight, my raptured soul
Can here no longer stay;
Though Jordan's waves around me roll,
Fearless I'd launch away.

990   *Jesus exalted.*   I. WATTS.

Behold the glories of the Lamb,
Amid his Father's throne;
Prepare new honors for his name,
And songs before unknown.

2 Let elders worship at his feet,
The church adore around,
With vials full of odors sweet,
And harps of sweeter sound.

3 Now to the Lamb that once was slain,
Be endless blessings paid!
Salvation, glory, joy remain
For ever on thy head!

4 Thou hast redeemed our souls with blood,
Hast set the prisoners free;
Hast made us kings and priests to God,
And we shall reign with thee.

991   *"A building of God."*   I. WATTS.

There is a house not made with hands,
Eternal, and on high:
And here my spirit waiting stands,
Till God shall bid it fly.

2 Shortly this prison of my clay
Must be dissolved and fall;
Then, O my soul, with joy obey
Thy heavenly Father's call.

3 We walk by faith of joys to come;
Faith lives upon his word;
But while the body is our home,
We're absent from the Lord.

4 'Tis pleasant to believe thy grace,
But we had rather see;
We would be absent from the flesh,
And present, Lord, with thee.

THE REST OF HEAVEN.

BEYOND. Chant. — W. A. TARBUTTON.

992   *"Lord, tarry not."*   H. BONAR.

BEYOND the smiling and the weeping, |
   I shall be soon; ||
Beyond the waking and the sleeping, |
Beyond the sowing and the reaping, |
   I shall be soon.

REF.—Love, rest and home! Sweet home!
   Lord, tarry not, but come.

2 Beyond the blooming and the fading, |
   I shall be soon; ||
Beyond the shining and the shading, |
Beyond the hoping and the dreading, |
   I shall be soon. ||—REF.

3 Beyond the rising and the setting, |
   I shall be soon; ||
Beyond the calming and the fretting, |
Beyond remembering and forgetting |
   I shall be soon. ||—REF.

4 Beyond the parting and the meeting, |
   I shall be soon; |
Beyond the farewell and the greeting, |
Beyond the pulse's fever beating, |
   I shall be soon. ||—REF.

5 Beyond the frost-chain and the fever, |
   I shall be soon; ||
Beyond the rock-waste and the river, |
Beyond the ever and the never, |
   I shall be soon. ||—REF.

OAK. 6s, 4s. — LOWELL MASON.

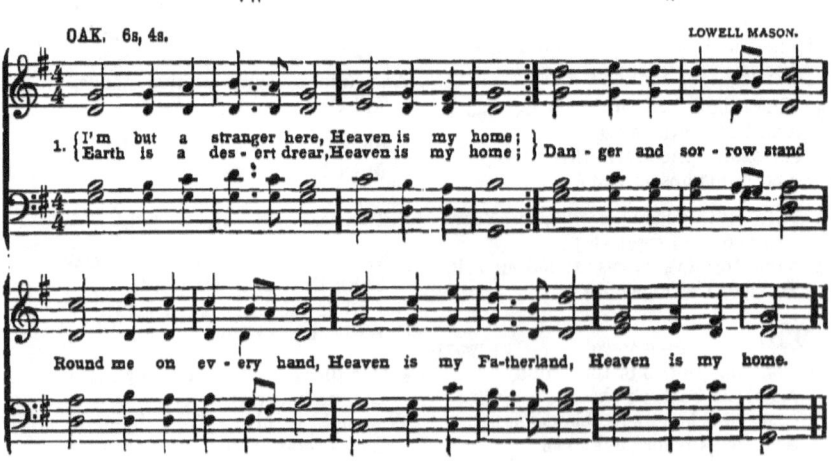

HEAVEN. 371

PARADISE. P. M.   J. BARNBY.

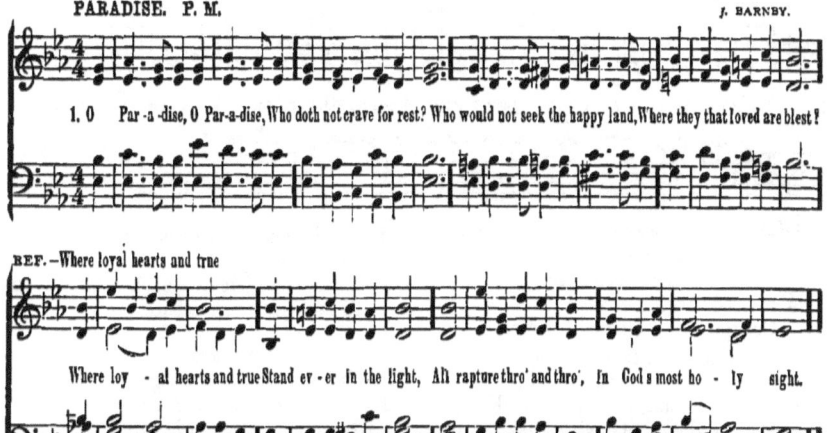

993   "O Paradise."   F. W. FABER.

O PARADISE, O Paradise,
  Who doth not crave for rest?
Who would not seek the happy land
  Where they that loved are blest?
    Where loyal hearts and true
      Stand ever in the light,
All rapture through and through,
  In God's most holy sight.

2 O Paradise, O Paradise,
  The world is growing old;
Who would not be at rest and free
  Where love is never cold?
    Where loyal hearts and true, etc.

3 O Paradise, O Paradise,
  I greatly long to see
The special place my dearest Lord
  In love prepares for me;
    Where loyal hearts and true, etc.

4 Lord Jesus, King of Paradise,
  Oh, keep me in thy love,
And guide me to that happy land
  Of perfect rest above;
    Where loyal hearts and true,
      Stand ever in the light,
All rapture through and through,
  In God's most holy sight.

---

994   6s, 4s. "Heaven is home."   T. R. TAYLOR.

I'M but a stranger here,—
  Heaven is my home;
Earth is a desert drear,—
  Heaven is my home;
Danger and sorrow stand
Round me on every hand,
Heaven is my Fatherland,
  Heaven is my home.

2 What though the tempests rage?
  Heaven is my home;
Short is my pilgrimage,
  Heaven is my home;
And time's wild, wintry blast,
Soon will be overpast,
I shall reach home at last,—
  Heaven is my home.

3 Therefore I murmur not,—
  Heaven is my home;
Whate'er my earthly lot,
  Heaven is my home;
And I shall surely stand
There, at my Lord's right hand;
Heaven is my Fatherland,
  Heaven is my home.

25

THE REST OF HEAVEN.

VIGIL. S. M. — ST. ALBAN'S TUNE BOOK.

1. I have a home a-bove, From sin and sorrow free; A mansion which e-ter-nal love Designed and formed for me.

995   *"A place for you."*   H. BENNETT.

1 I HAVE a home above,
  From sin and sorrow free;
A mansion which eternal love
  Designed and formed for me.

2 My Father's gracious hand
  Has built this sweet abode;
From everlasting it was planned—
  My dwelling-place with God.

3 My Saviour's precious blood
  Has made my title sure;
He passed thro' death's dark raging flood
  To make my rest secure.

4 The Comforter has come,
  The earnest has been given;
He leads me onward to the home
  Reserved for me in heaven.

HAVERHILL. S. M.   LOWELL MASON.

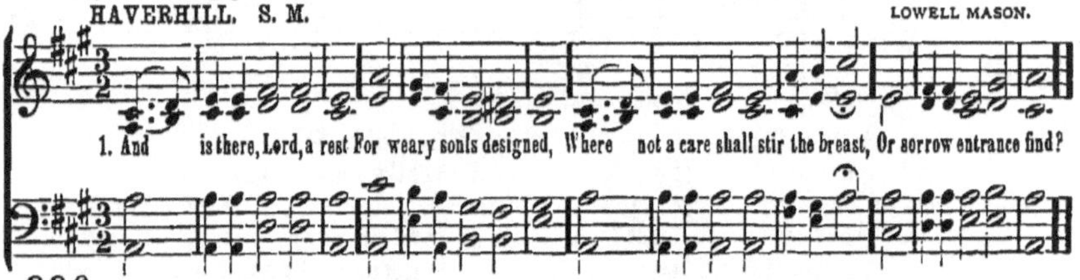

1. And is there, Lord, a rest For weary souls designed, Where not a care shall stir the breast, Or sorrow entrance find?

996   *"A rest."*   RAY PALMER.

1 AND is there, Lord, a rest
  For weary souls designed,
Where not a care shall stir the breast,
  Or sorrow entrance find?

2 Is there a blissful home,
  Where kindred minds shall meet,
And live, and love, nor ever roam
  From that serene retreat?

3 For ever blessèd they,
  Whose joyful feet shall stand,
While endless ages waste away,
  Amid that glorious land!

4 My soul would thither tend,
  While toilsome years are given;
Then let me, gracious God, ascend
  To sweet repose in heaven!

VARINA. C. M. D.   G. F. ROOT, arr.

1. { There is a land of pure delight, Where saints immortal reign; In-finite day excludes the night, And pleasures banish pain, } There ever-lasting spring abides, And never-withering flowers: Death, like a narrow sea, divides This heavenly land from ours.

HEAVEN.

997   *"Go over this Jordan."*   I. WATTS.

THERE is a land of pure delight,
  Where saints immortal reign;
Infinite day excludes the night,
  And pleasures banish pain.
There everlasting spring abides,
  And never-withering flowers;
Death, like a narrow sea, divides
  This heavenly land from ours.

2 Sweet fields beyond the swelling flood
  Stand dressed in living green;
So to the Jews old Canaan stood,
  While Jordan rolled between.
But timorous mortals start and shrink
  To cross this narrow sea;
And linger, shivering on the brink,
  And fear to launch away.

3 Oh, could we make our doubts remove,
  These gloomy doubts that rise,
And see the Canaan that we love
  With unclouded eyes:—
Could we but climb where Moses stood,
  And view the landscape o'er,
Not Jordan's stream, nor death's cold flood,
  Should fright us from the shore.

998   *"Hold fast."*   C. F. ALEXANDER.

THE roseate hues of early dawn,
  The brightness of the day,
The crimson of the sunset sky,
  How fast they fade away!
Oh, for the pearly gates of heaven!
  Oh, for the golden floor!
Oh, for the Sun of Righteousness,
  That setteth nevermore!

2 The highest hopes we cherish here,
  How soon they tire and faint!
How many a spot defiles the robe
  That wraps an earthly saint!
Oh, for a heart that never sins!
  Oh, for a soul washed white!
Oh, for a voice to praise our King,
  Nor weary day or night!

3 Here faith is ours, and heavenly hope,
  And grace to lead us higher;
But there are perfectness and peace,
  Beyond our best desire.
Oh, by thy love and anguish, Lord,
  And by thy life laid down,
Grant that we fall not from thy grace,
  Nor fail to reach our crown!

THE REST OF HEAVEN.

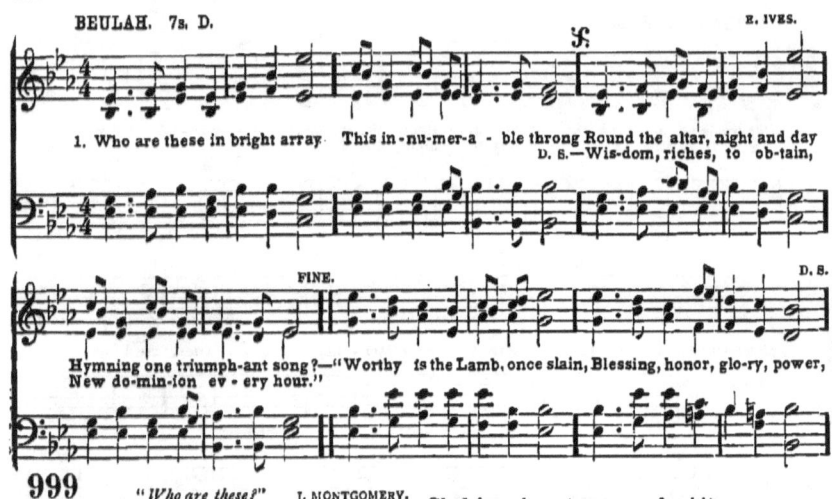

999
"Who are these?" J. MONTGOMERY.

Who are these in bright array,
 This innumerable throng
Round the altar, night and day
 Hymning one triumphant song?—
"Worthy is the Lamb, once slain,
 Blessing, honor, glory, power,
Wisdom, riches, to obtain,
 New dominion every hour."

2 These through fiery trials trod;
 These from great afflictions came:
Now, before the throne of God,
 Sealed with his almighty name,
Clad in raiment pure and white,
 Victor-palms in every hand,
Through their dear Redeemer's might,
 More than conquerors they stand.

3 Hunger, thirst, disease unknown,
 On immortal fruits they feed;
Them the Lamb, amid the throne,
 Shall to living fountains lead:
Joy and gladness banish sighs—
 Perfect love dispel all fears—
And for ever from their eyes
 God shall wipe away the tears.

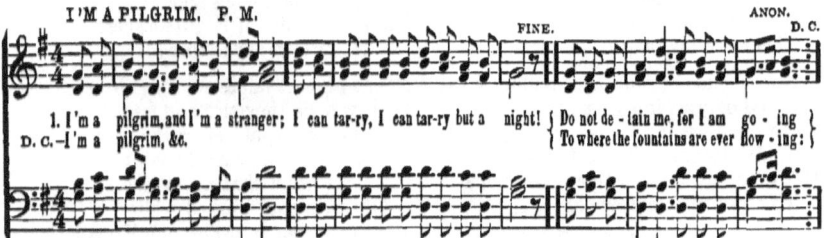

1000
Pilgrimage. M. S. B. DANA.

I'm a pilgrim, and I'm a stranger;
 I can tarry, I can tarry but a night!
Do not detain me, for I am going
 To where the fountains are ever flowing:
  I'm a pilgrim, etc.

2 There the glory is ever shining!
 Oh, my longing heart, my longing heart is there!

Here in this country so dark and dreary,
 I long have wandered forlorn and weary:
  I'm a pilgrim, etc.

3 There's the city to which I journey;
 My Redeemer, my Redeemer, is its light!
There is no sorrow, nor any sighing,
 Nor any tears there, nor any dying!
  I'm a pilgrim, etc.

HEAVEN.

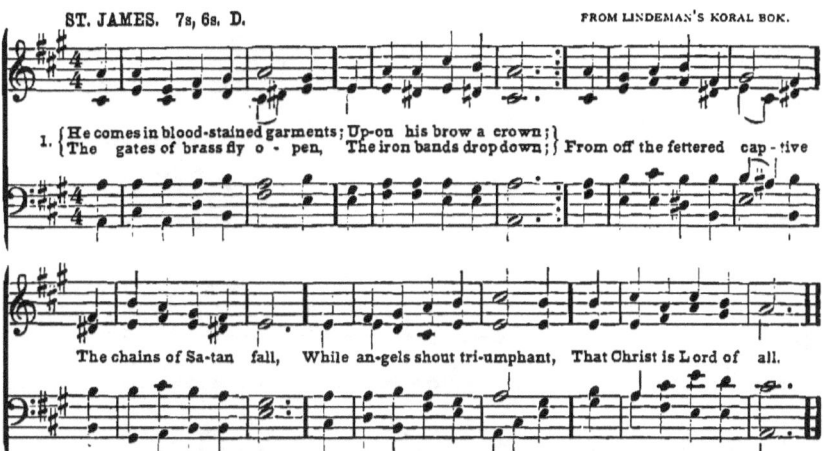

1001 *"Mighty to save."* C. L. BANCROFT.

He comes in blood-stained garments;
  Upon his brow a crown;
The gates of brass fly open,
  The iron bands drop down;
From off the fettered captive
  The chains of Satan fall,
While angels shout triumphant,
  That Christ is Lord of all.

2 Oh, Christ, his love is mighty!
  Long-suffering is his grace;
And glorious is the splendor
  That beameth from his face.
Our hearts up-leap in gladness
  When we behold that love,
As we go singing onward
  To dwell with him above.

1002 *Never separated.* R. MASSIE, *tr.*

I know no life divided,
  O Lord of life, from thee;
In thee is life provided
  For all mankind and me:
I know no death, O Jesus,
  Because I live in thee;
Thy death it is that frees us
  From death eternally.

2 I fear no tribulation,
  Since, whatsoe'er it be,
It makes no separation
  Between my Lord and me.

If thou, my God and Teacher,
  Vouchsafe to be my own,
Though poor, I shall be richer
  Than monarch on his throne.

3 If, while on earth I wander,
  My heart is right and blest,
Ah, what shall I be yonder,
  In perfect peace and rest?
Oh, blessed thought! in dying
  We go to meet the Lord,
Where there shall be no sighing,
  A kingdom our reward.

1003 *Heaven begun below.* R. MASSIE, *tr.*

I build on this foundation,—
  That Jesus and his blood
Alone are my salvation,
  The true eternal good.
To mine his Spirit speaketh
  Sweet words of soothing power,
How God to him that seeketh
  For rest, hath rest in store.

2 My merry heart is springing,
  And knows not how to pine:
'Tis full of joy and singing,
  And radiancy divine.
The sun whose smiles so cheer me
  Is Jesus Christ alone:
To have him always near me
  Is heaven itself begun.

THE REST OF HEAVEN.

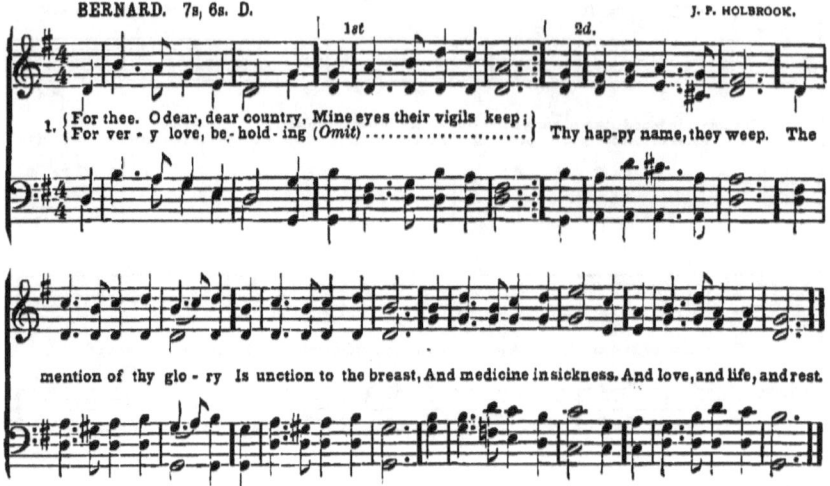

1004 *Paradise of joy.* J. M. NEALE, tr.

For thee, O dear, dear Country,
　Mine eyes their vigils keep;
For very love, beholding
　Thy happy name, they weep
The mention of thy glory
　Is unction to the breast,
And medicine in sickness,
　And love, and life, and rest

2 With jasper glow thy bulwarks,
　Thy streets with emeralds blaze;
The sardius and the topaz
　Unite in thee their rays;
Thine ageless walls are bonded
　With amethyst unpriced;
The saints build up its fabric,
　The corner-stone is Christ

3 Thou hast no shore, fair ocean;
　Thou hast no time, bright day:
Dear fountain of refreshment
　To pilgrims far away:
Upon the Rock of ages
　They raise thy holy tower;
Thine is the victor's laurel,
　And thine the golden dower.

4 Oh, sweet and blessèd Country,
　The home of God's elect!
Oh, sweet and blessèd Country,
　That eager hearts expect!
Jesus, in mercy bring us
　To that dear land of rest;
Who art, with God the Father,
　And Spirit, ever blest.

1005 *"Follow in his steps."* J. M. NEALE, tr

O HAPPY band of pilgrims,
　If onward ye will tread,
With Jesus as your Fellow,
　To Jesus as your Head.
The cross that Jesus carried,
　He carried as your due:
The crown that Jesus weareth,
　He weareth it for you

2 The faith by which ye see him,
　The hope in which ye yearn,
The love that through all trouble
　To him alone will turn:
What are they but forerunners
　To lead you to his sight?
What are they save the effluence
　Of uncreated light?

3 The trials that beset you,
　The sorrows ye endure,
The manifold temptations
　That death alone can cure:
What are they, but his jewels
　Of right celestial worth?
What are they but the ladder,
　Set up to heaven on earth?

HEAVEN.

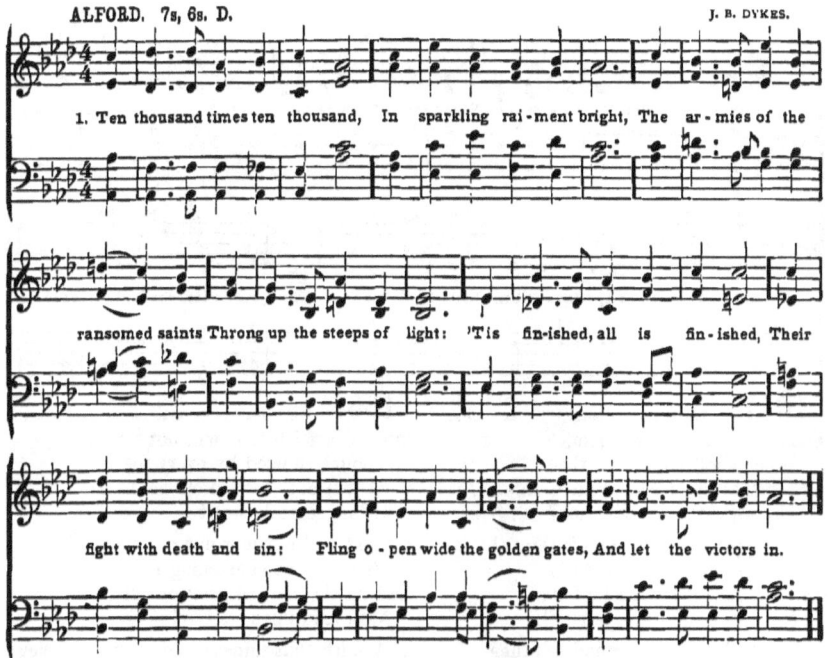

1006 *The armies of God.* H. ALFORD.

TEN thousand times ten thousand,
  In sparkling raiment bright,
The armies of the ransomed saints
  Throng up the steeps of light:
'Tis finished, all is finished,
  Their fight with death and sin:
Fling open wide the golden gates,
  And let the victors in.

2 What rush of hallelujahs
  Fills all the earth and sky!
What ringing of a thousand harps
  Bespeaks the triumph nigh!

Oh, day, for which creation
  And all its tribes were made!
Oh, joy, for all its former woes
  A thousand fold repaid!

3 Oh, then what raptured greetings
  On Canaan's happy shore,
What knitting severed friendships up,
  Where partings are no more!
Then eyes with joy shall sparkle,
  That brimmed with tears of late,
Orphans no longer fatherless,
  Nor widows desolate.

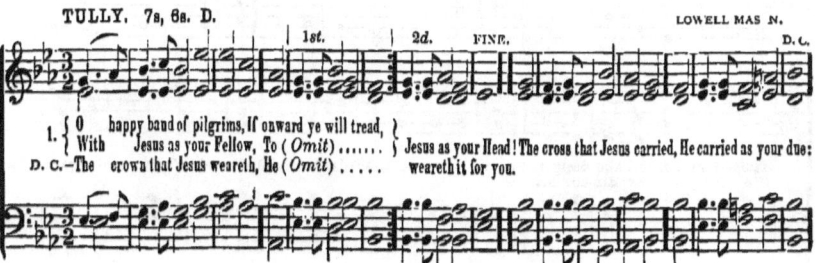

THE REST OF HEAVEN.

1007 *The New Jerusalem.* D. DICKSON.

O MOTHER dear, Jerusalem,
When shall I come to thee?
When shall my sorrows have an end?
Thy joys when shall I see?

2 O happy harbor of God's saints!
O sweet and pleasant soil!
In thee no sorrow can be found,
Nor grief, nor care, nor toil.

3 No dimly cloud o'ershadows thee,
Nor gloom, nor darksome night;
But every soul shines as the sun,
For God himself gives light.

4 Thy walls are made of precious stone,
Thy bulwarks diamond-square,
Thy gates are all of orient pearl—
O God! if I were there!

1008 *Faith and the Future.* W. H. BATHURST.

OH, for a faith that will not shrink
Though pressed by every foe,
That will not tremble on the brink
Of any earthly woe!—

2 That will not murmur nor complain
Beneath the chastening rod,
But, in the hour of grief or pain,
Will lean upon its God;—

3 A faith that shines more bright and clear
When tempests rage without;
That, when in danger, knows no fear,
In darkness, feels no doubt;—

4 Lord, give us such a faith as this,
And then, whate'er may come,
We'll taste, ev'n here, the hallowed bliss
Of an eternal home.

THE REST OF HEAVEN. 379

JOYFUL SOUND. C. M. D. E. L. WHITE.

1. Je-ru-sa-lem! my hap-py home! Name ev-er dear to me!
When shall my la-bors have an end, (Omit) .... } In
D.C.—Where con-gre-ga-tions ne'er break up, (Omit) .... And
joy, and peace, in thee? Oh, when, thou cit-y of my God, Shall I thy courts as-cend,
Sab-baths have no end.

1009 *The New Jerusalem.* ANON.

JERUSALEM! my happy home!
  Name ever dear to me!
When shall my labors have an end,
  In joy, and peace, in thee!
Oh, when, thou city of my God,
  Shall I thy courts ascend,
Where congregations ne'er break up,
  And Sabbaths have no end?

2 There happier bowers than Eden's bloom,
  Nor sin nor sorrow know:
Blest seats! thro' rude and stormy scenes,
  I onward press to you.

Why should I shrink at pain and woe!
  Or feel, at death, dismay?
I've Canaan's goodly land in view,
  And realms of endless day.

3 Apostles, martyrs, prophets there,
  Around my Saviour stand;
And soon my friends in Christ below,
  Will join the glorious band.
Jerusalem! my happy home!
  My soul still pants for thee;
Then shall my labors have an end,
  When I thy joys shall see.

1010 P. M. *"Jordan's Strand."* D. NELSON.

My days are gliding swiftly by,
  And I, a pilgrim stranger,
Would not detain them as they fly,
  Those hours of toil and danger.
    For, oh, we stand on Jordan's strand,
      Our friends are passing over;
    And just before, the Shining Shore
      We may almost discover!

2 We'll gird our loins, my brethren dear,
  Our heavenly home discerning;
Our absent Lord has left us word,
  Let every lamp be burning.—REF.

3 Should coming days be cold and dark,
  We need not cease our singing;
That perfect rest naught can molest,
  Where golden harps are ringing.—REF.

4 Let sorrow's rudest tempest blow,
  Each cord on earth to sever;
Our King says, Come, and there's our home
  For ever, oh, for ever!
    For, oh, we stand on Jordan's strand,
      Our friends are passing over;
    And just before, the Shining Shore
      We may almost discover!

THE REST OF HEAVEN.

NAUMANN. C. M.

1. There is an hour of hallowed peace, For those with cares oppressed, When sighs and sorrowing shall cease, When sighs and sorrowing shall cease, And all be hushed to rest:—

1011   "Sow in tears."   W. B. TAPPAN.

THERE is an hour of hallowed peace,
For those with cares oppressed,
When sighs and sorrowing shall cease,
And all be hushed to rest:—

2 'Tis then the soul is freed from fears
And doubts, which here annoy;
Then they, who oft have sown in tears,
Shall reap again in joy.

3 There is a home of sweet repose,
Where storms assail no more;
The stream of endless pleasure flows,
On that celestial shore.

4 There, purity with love appears,
And bliss without alloy;
There, they, who oft have sown in tears,
Shall reap again in joy.

COVENTRY. C. M.   ENGLISH MELODY.

1. Oh, could our thoughts and wishes fly, Above these gloomy shades, To those bright worlds, beyond the sky, Which sorrow ne'er invades!—

1012   "Things not seen."   A. STEELE.

OH, could our thoughts and wishes fly,
Above these gloomy shades,
To those bright worlds, beyond the sky,
Which sorrow ne'er invades!—

2 There, joys, unseen by mortal eyes
Or reason's feeble ray,
In ever-blooming prospect rise,
Unconscious of decay.

3 Lord! send a beam of light divine,
To guide our upward aim;
With one reviving touch of thine,
Our languid hearts inflame.

4 Oh, then, on faith's sublimest wing,
Our ardent hope shall rise
To those bright scenes, where pleasures spring
Immortal in the skies.

HEAVEN.

1013 "*No more death.*" W. B. TAPPAN.

THERE is an hour of peaceful rest,
  To mourning wanderers given;
There is a joy for souls distressed,
  A balm for every wounded breast:
    'Tis found above—in heaven.

2 There is a home for weary souls,
  By sin and sorrow driven,—
When tossed on life's tempestuous shoals,
Where storms arise, and ocean rolls,
    And all is drear—but heaven

3 There faith lifts up her cheerful eye
  To brighter prospects given;
And views the tempest passing by,
The evening shadows quickly fly,
    And all serene—in heaven

4 There fragrant flowers immortal bloom,
  And joys supreme are given;
There rays divine disperse the gloom;
Beyond the confines of the tomb
    Appears the dawn of heaven!

1014 "*Christ is coming.*" J. R. MACDUFF.

CHRIST is coming! let creation
  Bid her groans and travail cease:
Let the glorious proclamation
  Hope restore and faith increase;
    Christ is coming!
  Come, thou blessed Prince of peace!

2 Earth can now but tell the story
  Of thy bitter cross and pain;
She shall yet behold thy glory
  When thou comest back to reign;
    Christ is coming!
  Let each heart repeat the strain.

3 Long thy exiles have been pining,
  Far from rest, and home, and thee:
But, in heavenly vesture shining,
  Soon they shall thy glory see;
    Christ is coming!
  Haste the joyous jubilee.

4 With that "blessed hope" before us,
  Let no harp remain unstrung;
Let the mighty advent chorus
  Onward roll from tongue to tongue;
    Christ is coming!
  Come, Lord Jesus, quickly come.

THE REST OF HEAVEN.

VESPER. 8s, 7s. E. P. PARKER, arr.

1. This is not my place of rest-ing,— Mine's a cit-y yet to come; On-ward to it I am hast-ing— On to my e-ter-nal home.

1015 *Not our Rest.* H. BONAR.

This is not my place of resting,—
  Mine's a city yet to come;
Onward to it I am hasting—
  On to my eternal home.

2 In it all is light and glory;
  O'er it shines a nightless day:
Every trace of sin's sad story,
  All the curse, hath passed away.

3 There the Lamb, our Shepherd, leads us
  By the streams of life along,—
On the freshest pastures feeds us,
  Turns our sighing into song.

4 Soon we pass this desert dreary,
  Soon we bid farewell to pain;
Never more are sad or weary,
  Never, never sin again!

1016 *"The sea of glass."* C. WORDSWORTH.

Hark! the sound of holy voices,
  Chanting at the crystal sea,
Hallelujah, hallelujah,
  Hallelujah, Lord, to thee!

2 Multitudes, which none can number,
  Like the stars in glory stand,
Clothed in white apparel, holding
  Palms of victory in their hands.

3 They have come from tribulation,
  And have washed their robes in blood,
Washed them in the blood of Jesus;
  Tried they were and firm they stood.

4 Mocked, imprisoned, stoned, tormented,
  Sawn asunder, slain with sword,
They have conquered death and Satan
  By the might of Christ the Lord.

5 Love and peace they taste for ever,
  And all truth and knowledge see
In the Beatific Vision
  Of the blessèd Trinity.

1017 *The City.* S. BARING-GOULD.

Daily, daily sing the praises
  Of the City God hath made;
In the beauteous fields of Eden
  Its foundation-stones are laid.

2 In the midst of that dear City
  Christ is reigning on his seat,
And the angels swing their censers
  In a ring about his feet.

3 From the throne a river issues,
  Clear as crystal, passing bright,
And it traverses the City
  Like a sudden beam of light.

4 There the wind is sweetly fragrant,
  And is laden with the song
Of the seraphs, and the elders,
  And the great redeemèd throng.

5 Oh, I would my ears were open
  Here to catch that happy strain!
Oh, I would my eyes some vision
  Of that Eden could attain!

HEAVEN.

1018 *"The King in his beauty."* C. WINKWORTH, tr.

TIME, thou speedest on but slowly,
 Hours, how tardy is your pace!
Ere with Him, the high and holy,
 I hold converse face to face.
Here is naught but care and mourning;
 Comes a joy, it will not stay;
Fairly shines the sun at dawning,
 Night will soon o'ercloud the day.

2 Onward then! not long I wander
 Ere my Saviour comes for me,
And with him abiding yonder,
 All his glory I shall see.
Oh, the music and the singing
 Of the host redeemed by love!
Oh, the hallelujahs ringing
 Through the halls of light above!

1019 *The Consummation.* J. CONDER.

JESUS, blesséd Mediator!
 Thou the airy path hast trod;
Thou the Judge, the Consummator!
 Shepherd of the fold of God!
Can I trust a fellow-being?
 Can I trust an angel's care?
O thou merciful All-seeing!
 Beam around my spirit there.

2 Blesséd fold! no foe can enter,
 And no friend departeth thence;
Jesus is their sun, their centre,
 And their shield—Omnipotence!
Blesséd, for the Lamb shall feed them,
 All their tears shall wipe away,
To the living fountains lead them,
 Till fruition's perfect day.

3 Lo! it comes, that day of wonder!
 Louder chorals shake the skies:
Hadés' gates are burst asunder;
 See! the new-clothed myriads rise!
Thought! repress thy weak endeavor;
 Here must reason prostrate fall;
Oh, the ineffable Forever!
 And the eternal All in All!

HEAVEN.

MIRIAM. 7s & 6s. D.   J. F. HOLBROOK.

1. Je-ru-sa-lem, the glo-rious! The glo-ry of th'e-lect,— O dear and future vis-ion
D. S.—To thee my thoughts are kindled,
That ea-ger hearts ex-pect! Ev'n now by faith I see thee, Ev'n here thy walls discern;
And strive, and pant, and yearn!

1020   *"A City."*   J. M. NEALE, tr.

JERUSALEM, the glorious!
  The glory of the elect,—
O dear and future vision
  That eager hearts expect!
Ev'n now by faith I see thee,
  Ev'n here thy walls discern;
To thee my thoughts are kindled,
  And strive, and pant, and yearn!

2 The Cross is all thy splendor,
  The Crucified, thy praise;
His laud and benediction
  Thy ransomed people raise;—
Jerusalem! exulting
  On that securest shore,
I hope thee, wish thee, sing thee,
  And love thee evermore!

3 O sweet and blessèd Country!
  Shall I e'er see thy face?
O sweet and blessèd Country!
  Shall I e'er win thy grace?
Exult, O dust and ashes!
  The Lord shall be thy part;
His only, his for ever,
  Thou shalt be, and thou art!

1021   *"Lamps trimmed."*   J. BORTHWICK, tr.

REJOICE, rejoice, believers!
  And let your lights appear!
The shades of eve are thickening,
  And darker night is near;
The Bridegroom is advancing;
  Each hour he draws more nigh;
Up! watch and pray, nor slumber;
  At midnight comes the cry.

2 See that your lamps are burning,
  Your vessels filled with oil;
Wait calmly your deliverance
  From earthly pain and toil.
The watchers on the mountains
  Proclaim the Bridegroom near,
Go, meet him, as he cometh,
  With hallelujahs clear.

3 The saints, who here in patience
  Their cross and sufferings bore,
With him shall reign for ever,
  When sorrow is no more:
Around the throne of glory
  The Lamb shall they behold,
Adoring cast before him
  Their diadems of gold.

4 Our hope and expectation,
  O Jesus, now appear!
Arise, thou Sun so looked-for,
  O'er this benighted sphere!
With hearts and hands uplifted,
  We plead, O Lord, to see
The day of our redemption,
  And ever be with thee.

HEAVEN.

1022 *The New Jerusalem.* J. M. NEALE, tr.

JERUSALEM, the golden,
With milk and honey blest!
Beneath thy contemplation
Sink heart and voice oppressed:
I know not, oh, I know not,
What social joys are there,
What radiancy of glory,
What light beyond compare.

2 They stand, those halls of Zion,
All jubilant with song,
And bright with many an angel,
And all the martyr throng;
The Prince is ever in them,
The daylight is serene;
The pastures of the blessèd
Are decked in glorious sheen.

3 There is the throne of David;
And there, from care released,
The song of them that triumph,
The shout of them that feast:
And they who, with their Leader,
Have conquered in the fight
For ever and for ever
Are clad in robes of white.

1023 *"Short toil."* J. M. NEALE, tr.

BRIEF life is here our portion;
Brief sorrow, short-lived care;
The life, that knows no ending,
The tearless life, is there:
Oh, happy retribution!
Short toil, eternal rest;
For mortals, and for sinners,
A mansion with the blest!

2 And there is David's fountain,
And life in fullest glow;
And there the light is golden,
And milk and honey flow;
The light, that hath no evening,
The health, that hath no sore,
The life, that hath no ending,
But lasteth evermore.

3 There Jesus shall embrace us,
There Jesus be embraced,—
That spirit's food and sunshine;
Whence earthly love is chased:
Yes! God my King and Portion,
In fullness of his grace,
We then shall see for ever,
And worship face to face.

THE REST OF HEAVEN.

1024   "*The Lamb's Wife.*"   E. DENNY.

Bride of the Lamb, awake, awake!
  Why sleep for sorrow now?
The hope of glory, Christ, is thine,
  A child of glory thou.
Thy spirit, through the lonely night,
  From earthly joy apart,
Hath sighed for one that's far away,—
  The Bridegroom of thy heart.

2 But see! the night is waning fast,
  The breaking morn is near;
And Jesus comes, with voice of love,
  Thy drooping heart to cheer.
Then weep no more; 'tis all thine own,
  His crown, his joy divine;
And, sweeter far than all beside,
  He, he himself is thine!

1025   "*Behold, I come quickly.*"   B. H. KENNEDY.

Soon will the heavenly Bridegroom come;
  Ye wedding-guests, draw near,
And slumber not in sin, when he,
  The Son of God, is here!
Come, let us haste to meet our Lord,
  And hail him with delight;
Who saved us by his precious blood,
  And sorrows infinite!

2 Beside him all the patriarchs old,
  And holy prophets stand;
The glorious apostolic choir,
  And noble martyr band.

As brethren dear they welcome us,
  And lead us to the throne,
Where angels bow their vailéd heads,
  Before the Three in One;—

3 Where we, with all the saints of God,
  A white-robed multitude,
Shall praise the ascended Lord, who deigns
  To bear our flesh and blood!
Our lot shall be for aye to share
  His reign of peace above:
And drink, with unexhausted joy,
  The river of his love.

1026   "*Come, Lord Jesus.*"   E. DENNY.

Hope of our hearts, O Lord, appear,
  Thou glorious Star of day!
Shine forth, and chase the dreary night,
  With all our tears, away.
No resting-place we seek on earth,
  No loveliness we see;
Our eye is on the royal crown,
  Prepared for us—and thee!

2 But, dearest Lord, however bright,
  That crown of joy above,
What is it to the brighter hope
  Of dwelling in thy love?
What to the joy, the deeper joy,
  Unmingled, pure, and free,
Of union with our living Head,
  Of fellowship with thee?

HEAVEN.

NORTHFIELD. C. M.   J. INGALLS.

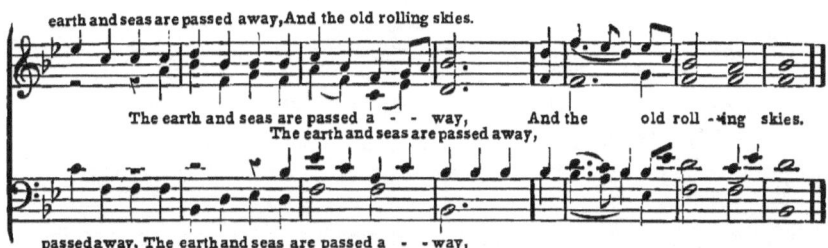

1027   *"Your descending King."*   I. WATTS.
Lo! what a glorious sight appears,
To our believing eyes!
The earth and seas are passed away,
And the old rolling skies.

2 From the third heaven where God resides—
That holy, happy place,—
The New Jerusalem comes down,
Adorned with shining grace.

3 Attending angels shout for joy,
And the bright armies sing,—
"Mortals! behold the sacred seat
Of your descending King:—

4 "The God of glory, down to men,
Removes his blest abode;
Men, the dear objects of his grace,
And he their loving God:—

5 "His own soft hand shall wipe the tears
From every weeping eye;
And pains, and groans, and griefs, and fears,
And death itself shall die!"

6 How long, dear Saviour! oh, how long
Shall this bright hour delay?
Fly swifter round, ye wheels of time!
And bring the welcome day.

1028   *Messiah's Reign.*   M. BRUCE.
BEHOLD, the mountain of the Lord
In latter days shall rise
On mountain tops, above the hills,
And draw the wondering eyes.

2 The beam that shines from Zion's hill
Shall lighten every land:
The King who reigns in Salem's towers
Shall all the world command.

3 No strife shall vex Messiah's reign,
Or mar the peaceful years;
To ploughshares men shall beat their swords,
To pruning-hooks their spears.

1029   *"Come, blessed Lord?"*   E. DENNY.
LIGHT of the lonely pilgrim's heart!
Star of the coming day!
Arise, and with thy morning beams
Chase all our griefs away.

2 Come, blesséd Lord! let every shore
And answering island sing
The praises of thy royal name,
And own thee as their King.

3 Jesus! thy fair creation groans,—
The air, the earth, the sea,—
In unison with all our hearts,
And calls aloud for thee.

4 Thine was the cross, with all its fruits
Of grace and peace divine;
Be thine the crown of glory now,
The palm of victory thine.

THE REST OF HEAVEN.

IMMORTALITY. 7s, 6s. D.   WM. F. SHERWIN.

1. There is a land immortal, The beautiful of lands; Beside its ancient portal A silent sentry stands; He only can undo it, And open wide the door; And mortals who pass through it Are mortal nevermore.

1030 "*They seek a country.*"   T. MACKELLAR.

THERE is a land immortal,
  The beautiful of lands;
Beside its ancient portal
  A silent sentry stands;
He only can undo it,
  And open wide the door;
And mortals who pass through it,
  Are mortal nevermore.

2 Though dark and drear the passage
  That leadeth to the gate,
Yet grace attends the message,
  To souls that watch and wait:
And at the time appointed
  A messenger comes down,
And guides the Lord's anointed
  From cross to glory's crown.

3 Their sighs are lost in singing,
  They're blessèd in their tears;
Their journey heavenward winging,
  They leave on earth their fears:
Death like an angel seemeth;
  "We welcome thee," they cry;
Their face with glory beameth—
  'Tis life for them to die!

1031   *The New Paradise.*   T. DAVIS.

O PARADISE eternal!
  What bliss to enter thee,
And, once within thy portals,
  Secure for ever be!
In thee no sin nor sorrow,
  No pain nor death, is known;
But pure glad life, enduring
  As heaven's benignant throne.

2 There all around shall love us,
  And we return their love;
One band of happy spirits,
  One family above:
There God shall be our portion,
  And we his jewels be;
And gracing his bright mansions,
  His smile reflect and see.

3 So songs shall rise for ever,
  While all creation fair,
Still more and more revealèd,
  Shall wake fresh praises there:
O Paradise eternal!
  What joys in thee are known!
O God of mercy! guide us,
  Till all be felt our own.

HEAVEN.

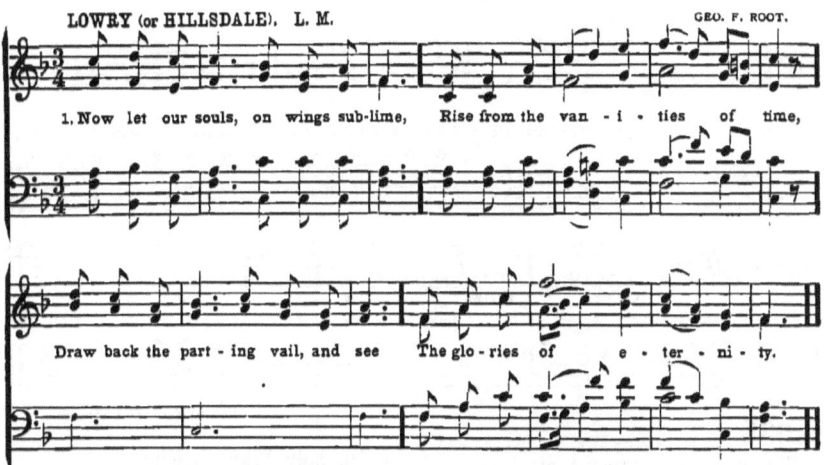

LOWRY (or HILLSDALE). L. M.   GEO. F. ROOT.

1. Now let our souls, on wings sublime, Rise from the vanities of time, Draw back the parting vail, and see The glories of eternity.

1032   *"Eye hath not seen."*   T. GIBBONS.

Now LET our souls, on wings sublime,
Rise from the vanities of time,
Draw back the parting vail, and see
The glories of eternity.

2 Born by a new celestial birth,
Why should we grovel here on earth?
Why grasp at transitory toys,
So near to heaven's eternal joys?

3 Should aught beguile us on the road,
When we are walking back to God?
For strangers into life we come,
And dying is but going home.

4 To dwell with God—to feel his love,
Is the full heaven enjoyed above;
And the sweet expectation now
Is the young dawn of heaven below.

1033   *"A Rest."*   RAY PALMER.

LORD, thou wilt bring the joyful day!
Beyond earth's weariness and pains,
Thou hast a mansion far away,
Where for thine own a rest remains.

2 No sun there climbs the morning sky,
There never falls the shade of night;
God and the Lamb, for ever nigh,
O'er all shed everlasting light.

3 The bow of mercy spans the throne,
Emblem of love and goodness there;
While notes to mortals all unknown,
Float on the calm celestial air.

4 Around that throne bright legions stand,
Redeemed by blood from sin and hell;
And shining forms, an angel band,
The mighty chorus join to swell.

5 O Jesus, bring us to that rest,
Where all the ransomed shall be found,
In thine eternal fullness blest,
While ages roll their cycles round!

1034   *"Many mansions."*   RAY PALMER.

THY Father's house! thine own bright home!
And thou hast there a place for me!
Though yet an exile here I roam,
That distant home by faith I see.

2 I see its domes resplendent glow,
Where beams of God's own glory fall;
And trees of life immortal grow,
Whose fruits o'erhang the sapphire wall

3 I know that thou, who on the tree
Didst deign our mortal guilt to bear,
Wilt bring thine own to dwell with thee,
And waitest to receive me there!

4 Thy love will there array my soul
In thine own robe of spotless hue;
And I shall gaze, while ages roll,
On thee, with raptures ever new!

5 Oh, welcome day! when thou my feet
Shalt bring the shining threshold o'er;
A Father's warm embrace to meet,
And dwell at home for evermore!

THE REST OF HEAVEN.

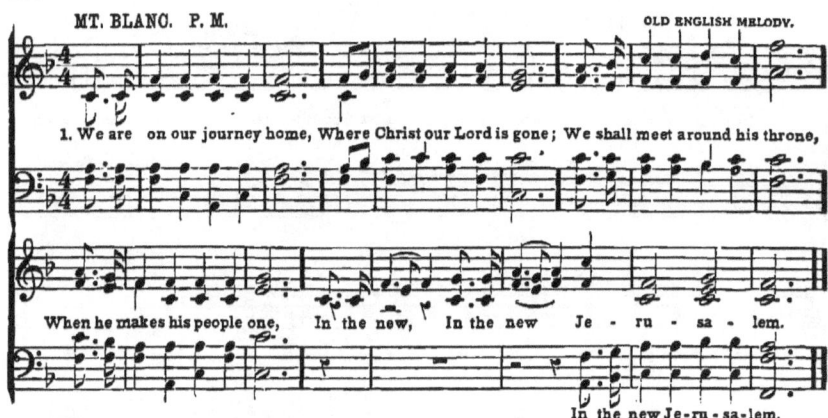

1035 *"The Holy City."* C. BEECHER.

WE are on our journey home,
Where Christ our Lord is gone;
We shall meet around his throne,
When he makes his people one,
In the new Jerusalem.

2 We can see that distant home,
Though clouds rise dark between;
Faith views the radiant dome,
And a lustre flashes keen
From the new Jerusalem.

3 Oh, holy, heavenly home!
Oh, rest eternal there!
When shall the exiles come,
Where they cease from earthly care,
In the new Jerusalem!

4 Our hearts are breaking now
Those mansions fair to see;
O Lord, thy heavens bow,
And raise us up with thee,
To the new Jerusalem.

HEAVEN.

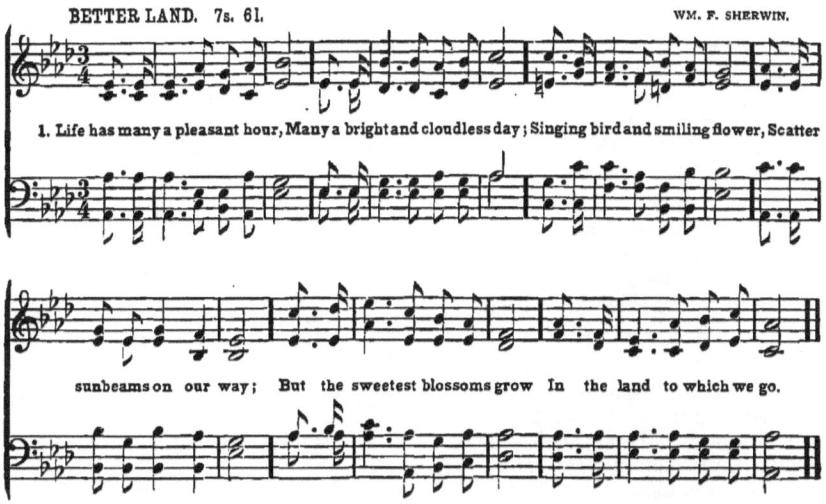

BETTER LAND. 7s. 6l. WM. F. SHERWIN.

1. Life has many a pleasant hour, Many a bright and cloudless day; Singing bird and smiling flower, Scatter sunbeams on our way; But the sweetest blossoms grow In the land to which we go.

1036 *The better land.* F. C. VAN ALSTYNE.

LIFE has many a pleasant hour,
  Many a bright and cloudless day;
Singing bird and smiling flower,
  Scatter sunbeams on our way;
    But the sweetest blossoms grow
    In the land to which we go.

2 Earth has many a cool retreat,
  Many a spot to memory dear;
Oft we find our weary feet
  Lingering by some fountain clear;
    Yet the purest waters flow
    In the land to which we go.

3 Like a cloud that floats away,
  Like the early morning dew,
Here the fairest things decay;
  There, are pleasures ever new.
    Only joy the heart will know
    In the land to which we go.

4 'Tis the Christian's promised land;
  There is everlasting day;
There a Saviour's loving hand
  Wipes the mourner's tears away;
    Oh! the rapture we shall know
    In the land to which we go.

1037 P. M. *Immanuel's Land.* A. R. COUSIN.

THE sands of time are sinking,
  The dawn of heaven breaks,
The summer morn I've sighed for,
  The fair sweet morn awakes:
Dark, dark hath been the midnight,
  But day-spring is at hand,
And glory, glory dwelleth
  In Immanuel's land.

2 Oh, Christ, he is the fountain,
  The deep sweet well of love;
The streams of earth I've tasted,
  More deep I'll drink above.
There to an ocean fullness
  His mercy doth expand,
And glory, glory dwelleth
  In Immanuel's land.

3 The bride eyes not her garment,
  But her dear bridegroom's face;
I will not gaze at glory,
  But on my King of Grace—
Not at the crown he gifteth,
  But on his piercéd hand;—
The Lamb is all the glory
  Of Immanuel's land.

THE REST OF HEAVEN.

1038 C. P. M. *Celestial Praise.* C. WINKWORTH, tr.

Thy mighty working, mighty God!
Wakes all my powers; I look abroad,
And can no longer rest;
I, too, must sing when all things sing,
And from my heart the praises ring
The Highest loveth best.

2 If thou, in thy great love to us,
Wilt scatter joy and beauty thus
O'er this poor earth of ours;
What nobler glories shall be given
Hereafter in thy shining heaven,
Set round with golden towers!

3 What thrilling joy when on our sight
Christ's garden beams in cloudless light
Where all the air is sweet,
Still laden with the unwearied hymn
From all the thousand seraphim
Who God's high praise repeat!

4 Oh, were I there! oh, that I now
Before thy throne, my God, could bow,
And bear my heavenly palm!
Then, like the angels, would I raise
My voice, and sing thine endless praise
In many a sweet-toned psalm.

1039 L. M. *"The Lamb is the Light."* A. STEELE.

Oh, for a sweet, inspiring ray,
To animate our feeble strains,
From the bright realms of endless day—
The blissful realms where Jesus reigns!

2 There, low before his glorious throne,
Adoring saints and angels fall;
And, with delightful worship, own
His smile their bliss, their heaven,
  their all.

3 Immortal glories crown his head,
While tuneful hallelujahs rise,
And love and joy, and triumph spread
Through all the assemblies of the skies.

4 He smiles,—and seraphs tune their
  songs
To boundless rapture, while they gaze;
Ten thousand thousand joyful tongues
Resound his everlasting praise.

5 There all the followers of the Lamb
Shall join at last the heavenly choir:
Oh, may the joy-inspiring theme
Awake our faith and warm desire!

1040 S. M. D. *"No night there."* F. M. KNOLLIS.

There is no night in heaven;
  In that blest world above
Work never can bring weariness,
  For work itself is love.
There is no grief in heaven;
  For life is one glad day,
And tears are of those former things
  Which all have passed away.

2 There is no want in heaven;
  The Lamb of God supplies
Life's tree of twelve-fold fruitage still,
  Life's spring which never dries.
There is no sin in heaven;
  Behold that blessèd throng!
All holy is their spotless robe,
  All holy is their song.

3 There is no death in heaven;
  For they who gain that shore
Have won their immortality,
  And they can die no more.
There is no death in heaven;
  But when the Christian dies,
The angels wait his parted soul,
  And waft it to the skies!

1041 C. M. *The New Song.* I. WATTS.

Earth has engrossed my love too long;
  'T is time I lift mine eyes
Upward, dear Father, to thy throne,
  And to my native skies.

2 There the blest Man, my Saviour, sits;
  The God, how bright he shines!
And scatters infinite delights
  On all the happy minds.

3 Seraphs with elevated strains
  Circle the throne around;
And move, and charm the starry plains
  With an immortal sound.

4 Jesus, the Lord, their harps employs;
  Jesus, my love, they sing;
Jesus, the life of both our joys,
  Sounds sweet from every string.

5 Now let me dwell on earth no more,
  But mount in haste above,
To bless the God that I adore,
  And sing the Man I love.

1042 7s, 6s, D. "A Holy City." ANON.

There is a holy city,
  A happy world above,
Beyond the starry regions,
  Built by the God of love;
An everlasting temple—
  And saints arrayed in white,
There serve their great Redeemer,
  And dwell with him in light.

2 The meanest child of glory
  Outshines the radiant sun;
But who can speak the splendor
  Of that eternal throne
Where Jesus sits exalted,
  In god-like majesty?
The elders fall before him,
  The angels bend the knee.

3 The hosts of saints around him
  Proclaim his work of grace;
The patriarchs and prophets,
  And all the godly race,
Who speak of fiery trials
  And tortures on their way—
They came from tribulation
  To everlasting day.

4 And what shall be my journey,
  How long my stay below,
Or what shall be my trials,
  Are not for me to know;
In every day of trouble,
  I'll raise my thoughts on high;
I'll think of the bright temple,
  And crowns above the sky.

1043 6s, D. *The Rest remaineth.* H. W. BAKER.

There is a blessèd home
  Beyond this land of woe,
Where trials never come,
  Nor tears of sorrow flow;
Where faith is lost in sight,
  And patient hope is crowned,
And everlasting light
  Its glory throws around.

2 There is a land of peace,
  Good angels know it well;
Glad songs that never cease
  Within its portals swell;
Around its glorious throne
  Ten thousand saints adore
Christ, with the Father One,
  And Spirit, ever more.

3 Look up, ye saints of God,
  Nor fear to tread below
The path your Saviour trod
  Of daily toil and woe;
Wait but a little while
  In uncomplaining love,
His own most gracious smile
  Shall welcome you above.

J. M. NEALE, *tr.*

1044 8s, 7s, 6 l. "*The Lamb's Wife.*"

Blessed Salem, long expected,
  Vision bright of peace and dear!
Who, of living stones erected,
  Moulded in the heavenly sphere,
And, by angel-guards protected,
  Dost in bridal-pomp appear.

2 From the heaven of heavens descend-
  All prepared to meet thy Head, [ing,
In thy robes of light attending,
  Thou art to his presence led;
Golden glories, richly blending,
  Round thy streets and walls are shed.

3 Bright with pearls thy gates are beam-
  Wide unfolded they remain: [ing,
Thither come, through grace redeeming,
  All who wear Christ's lowly chain:
And, his last award esteeming,
  Gladly share his cup of pain.

1045 P. M. "*The Golden Shore.*" ANON.

Lo, the seal of death is breaking;
  Those who slept its sleep are waking,
    Heaven opes its portals fair!
Hark! the harps of God are ringing,
Hark! the seraph's hymn is flinging
    Music on immortal air.

2 There, no more at eve declining,
Suns without a cloud are shining
    O'er the land of life and love;
There the founts of life are flowing,
Flowers unknown to time are blowing,
    In that radiant scene above.

3 There no sigh of memory swelleth;
There no tear of misery welleth;
    Hearts will bleed or break no more;
Past is all the cold world's scorning,
Gone the night and broke the morning
    Over all the golden shore!

1046 *Song for Harvest.* H. ALFORD.

COME, ye thankful people, come,
Raise the song of Harvest Home!
All is safely gathered in,
Ere the winter storms begin:
God our Maker doth provide
For our wants to be supplied:
Come to God's own temple, come,
Raise the song of Harvest Home!

2 We ourselves are God's own field,
Fruit unto his praise to yield:
Wheat and tares together sown,
Unto joy or sorrow grown:
First the blade, and then the ear,
Then the full corn shall appear:
Grant, O Harvest-Lord, that we
Wholesome grain and pure may be!

3 For the Lord our God shall come,
And shall take his harvest home:
From his field shall in that day
All offences purge away:
Give his angels charge at last
In the fire the tares to cast:
But the fruitful ears to store
In his garner evermore.

4 Then, thou Church Triumphant, come,
Raise the song of Harvest Home!
All are safely gathered in,
Free from sorrow, free from sin:
There, for ever purified,
In God's garner to abide:
Come, ten thousand angels, come,
Raise the glorious Harvest Home!

1047 *The close of the year.* RAY PALMER.

THOU who roll'st the year around,
Crowned with mercies large and free,
Rich thy gifts to us abound,
Warm our praise shall rise to thee.
Kindly to our worship bow,
While our grateful thanks we tell,
That, sustained by thee, we now
Bid the parting year—farewell!

2 All its numbered days are sped,
All its busy scenes are o'er,
All its joys for ever fled,
All its sorrows felt no more.
Mingled with the eternal past,
Its remembrance shall decay;
Yet to be revived at last
At the solemn judgment-day.

3 All our follies, Lord, forgive!
Cleanse us from each guilty stain;
Let thy grace within us live,
That we spend not years in vain.
Then, when life's last eve shall come,
Happy spirits, may we fly
To our everlasting home,
To our Father's house on high!

1048 New Year. J. NEWTON.

WHILE, with ceaseless course, the sun
  Hasted through the former year,
Many souls their race have run,
  Nevermore to meet us here:
Fixed in an eternal state,
  They have done with all below;
We a little longer wait,—
  But how little none can know.

2 As the wingéd arrow flies
  Speedily the mark to find;
As the lightning from the skies
  Darts, and leaves no trace behind,
Swiftly thus our fleeting days
  Bear us down life's rapid stream;
Upward, Lord, our spirits raise,
  All below is but a dream.

3 Thanks for mercies past receive;
  Pardon of our sins renew;
Teach us henceforth how to live,
  With eternity in view:
Bless thy word to young and old;
  Fill us with a Saviour's love;
And, when life's short tale is told,
  May we dwell with thee above!

1049 Independence Day. N. STRONG.

SWELL the anthem, raise the song;
Praises to our God belong;
Saints and angels join to sing
Praises to the heavenly King.

Blessings from his liberal hand
Flow around this happy land:
Kept by him, no foes annoy;
Peace and freedom we enjoy.

2 Here, beneath a virtuous sway
May we cheerfully obey;
Never feel oppression's rod,
Ever own and worship God.
Hark! the voice of nature sings
Praises to the King of kings;
Let us join the choral song,
And the grateful notes prolong.

1050 Thanksgiving. A. L. BARBAULD.

PRAISE to God, immortal praise,
For the love that crowns our days!
Bounteous Source of every joy,
Let thy praise our tongues employ.
For the blessings of the field,
For the stores the gardens yield;
For the fruits in full supply,
Ripened 'neath the summer sky;—

2 All that spring with bounteous hand
Scatters o'er the smiling land;
All that liberal autumn pours
From her rich, o'erflowing stores;
These to thee, my God, we owe,
Source whence all our blessings flow:
And for these my soul shall raise
Grateful vows and solemn praise.

MISCELLANEOUS.

GLASGOW. C. M.   G. F. ROOT.

1. Lord! while for all man-kind we pray, Of ev-ery clime and coast,
Oh, hear us for our na-tive land, The land we love the most.

1051   *National.*   J. R. WREFORD.

LORD! while for all mankind we pray,
  Of every clime and coast,
Oh, hear us for our native land,
  The land we love the most.

2 Oh, guard our shores from every foe,
  With peace our borders bless,
With prosperous times our cities crown,
  Our fields with plenteousness.

3 Unite us in the sacred love
  Of knowledge, truth, and thee:
And let our hills and valleys shout
  The songs of liberty.

4 Here may religion, pure and mild,
  Smile on our Sabbath hours;
And piety and virtue bless
  The home of us and ours.

5 Lord of the nations, thus to thee
  Our country we commend;
Be thou her refuge and her trust,
  Her everlasting friend.

1052   *The Traveler's Hymn.*   J. ADDISON.

How ARE thy servants blest, O Lord!
  How sure is their defence!
Eternal wisdom is their guide,
  Their help, Omnipotence.

2 In foreign realms, and lands remote,
  Supported by thy care,
Through burning climes they pass unhurt,
  And breathe in tainted air.

3 When by the dreadful tempest borne
  High on the broken wave,
They know thou art not slow to hear,
  Nor impotent to save.

4 The storm is laid, the winds retire,
  Obedient to thy will;
The sea, that roars at thy command,
  At thy command is still.

5 In midst of dangers, fears, and deaths,
  Thy goodness we'll adore;
We'll praise thee for thy mercies past,
  And humbly hope for more.

6 Our life, while thou preserv'st that life,
  Thy sacrifice shall be;
And death, when death shall be our lot,
  Shall join our souls to thee.

1053   *Prayer for Seamen.*   F. H. BROWN.

WE come, O Lord, before thy throne,
  And, with united plea,
We meet and pray for those who roam
  Far off upon the sea.

2 Oh, may the Holy Spirit bow
  The sailor's heart to thee,
Till tears of deep repentance flow,
  Like rain-drops in the sea!

3 Then may a Saviour's dying love
  Pour peace into his breast,
And waft him to the port above
  Of everlasting rest.

MISCELLANEOUS. 397

1054   *New Year.*   W. GASKELL.

Our Father! through the coming year
We know not what shall be;
But we would leave without a fear
Its ordering all to thee.

2 It may be we shall toil in vain
For what the world holds fair;
And all the good we thought to gain
Deceive and prove but care.

3 It may be it shall darkly blend
Our love with anxious fears,
And snatch away the valued friend,
The tried of many years.

4 It may be it shall bring us days
And nights of lingering pain;
And bid us take a farewell gaze
Of these loved haunts of men.

5 But calmly, Lord, on thee we rest;
No fears our trust shall move;
Thou knowest what for each is best,
And thou art Perfect Love.

1055   *Close of the Year.*   I. WATTS.

Thee we adore, eternal Name!
And humbly own to thee
How feeble is our mortal frame,
What dying worms are we!

2 The year rolls round, and steals away
The breath that first it gave;
Whate'er we do, where'er we be,
We're traveling to the grave.

3 Great God! on what a slender thread
Hang everlasting things!
The eternal state of all the dead
Upon life's feeble strings!

4 Infinite joy, or endless woe,
Attends on every breath;
And yet, how unconcerned we go
Upon the brink of death!

5 Waken, O Lord, our drowsy sense
To walk this dangerous road!
And if our souls are hurried hence,
May they be found with God.

1056   *Close of the Year.*   P. DODDRIDGE.

Awake, ye saints! and raise your eyes,
And raise your voices high:
Awake, and praise the sovereign love,
That shows salvation nigh.

2 Swift on the wings of time it flies,
Each moment brings it near:
Then welcome each declining day,
Welcome each closing year.

3 Not many years their rounds shall run,
Nor many mornings rise,
Ere all its glories stand revealed,
To our admiring eyes.

4 Ye wheels of nature! speed your course;
Ye mortal powers! decay;
Fast as ye bring the night of death,
Ye bring eternal day.

MISCELLANEOUS.

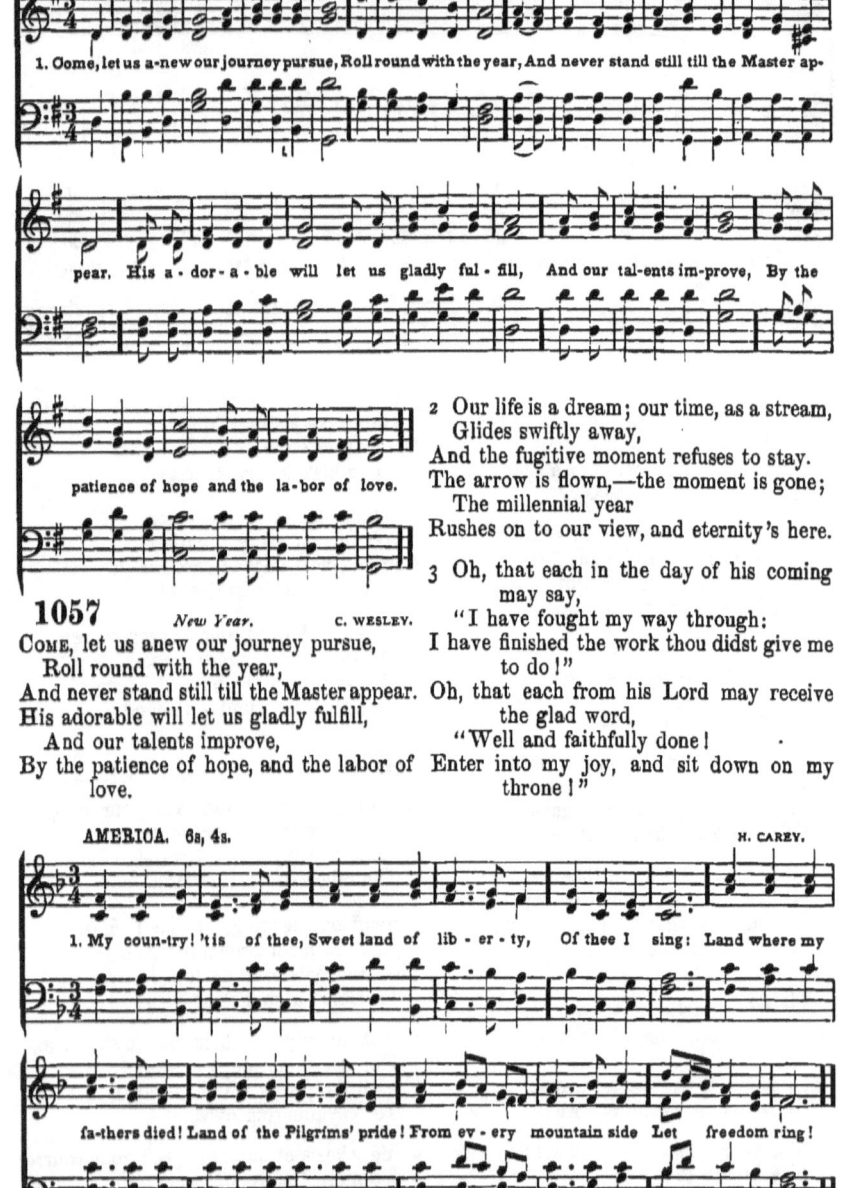

1057 *New Year.*   C. WESLEY.

Come, let us anew our journey pursue,
Roll round with the year,
And never stand still till the Master appear.
His adorable will let us gladly fulfill,
And our talents improve,
By the patience of hope, and the labor of love.

2 Our life is a dream; our time, as a stream,
Glides swiftly away,
And the fugitive moment refuses to stay.
The arrow is flown,—the moment is gone;
The millennial year
Rushes on to our view, and eternity's here.

3 Oh, that each in the day of his coming may say,
"I have fought my way through:
I have finished the work thou didst give me to do!"
Oh, that each from his Lord may receive the glad word,
"Well and faithfully done!
Enter into my joy, and sit down on my throne!"

MISCELLANEOUS.

ST. SYLVESTER. 8s, 7s.   J. B. DYKES.

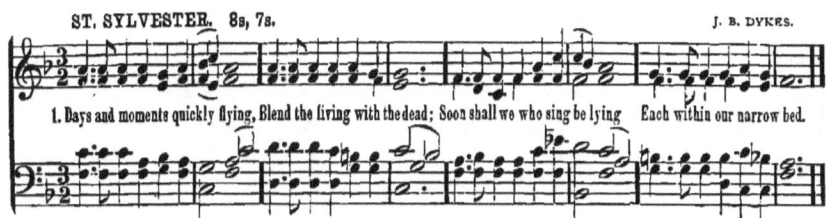

1. Days and moments quickly flying, Blend the living with the dead; Soon shall we who sing be lying Each within our narrow bed.

1058 *Last Day of the year.* E. CASWALL.

Days and moments quickly flying
  Blend the living with the dead;
Soon shall we who sing be lying,
  Each within our narrow bed.

2 Soon our souls to God who gave them
  Will have sped their rapid flight;
Able now by grace to save them,
  Oh, that while we can we might!

3 Jesus, infinite Redeemer,
  Maker of this mighty frame;
Teach, oh, teach us to remember
  What we are, and whence we came:—

4 Whence we came, and whither wending;
  Soon we must through darkness go,
To inherit bliss unending,
  Or eternity of woe.

After fourth verse.

As the tree falls, so must it lie; As the man lives, so will he die; As the man dies, such must he be, All through the days of e - ter - ni - ty. A - men.

1059 6s, 4s. *National Song.* S. F. SMITH.

My country! 'tis of thee,
Sweet land of liberty,
  Of thee I sing;
Land where my fathers died!
Land of the Pilgrims' pride!
From every mountain side
  Let freedom ring!

2 My native country, thee—
Land of the noble, free—
  Thy name I love;
I love thy rocks and rills,
Thy woods and templed hills;
My heart with rapture thrills
  Like that above.

3 Let music swell the breeze,
And ring from all the trees
  Sweet freedom's song:
Let mortal tongues awake;
Let all that breathe partake;
Let rocks their silence break,—
  The sound prolong.

4 Our fathers' God! to thee,
Author of liberty,
  To thee we sing:
Long may our land be bright
With freedom's holy light;
Protect us by thy might,
  Great God, our King!

DUKE STREET. L. M. — J. HATTON.

1. O God, beneath thy guiding hand, Our exiled fathers crossed the sea, And when they trod the wintry strand, With prayer and psalm they worshiped thee.

1060 *Forefathers' Day.* L. BACON.

O God, beneath thy guiding hand,
Our exiled fathers crossed the sea,
And when they trod the wintry strand,
With prayer and psalm they worshiped thee.

2 Thou heardst, well pleased, the song, the prayer—
Thy blessing came; and still its power
Shall onward through all ages bear
The memory of that holy hour.

3 What change! through pathless wilds no more
The fierce and naked savage roams:
Sweet praise, along the cultured shore,
Breaks from ten thousand happy homes.

4 Laws, freedom, truth, and faith in God
Came with those exiles o'er the waves,
And where their pilgrim feet have trod,
The God they trusted guards their graves.

5 And here thy name, O God of love,
Their children's children shall adore,
Till these eternal hills remove,
And spring adorns the earth no more.

1061 *The New Year.* P. DODDRIDGE.

Great God! we sing that mighty hand
By which supported still we stand;
The opening year thy mercy shows;
Let mercy crown it till it close.

2 By day, by night, at home, abroad,
Still we are guarded by our God;
By his incessant bounty fed,
By his unerring counsel led.

3 With grateful hearts the past we own;
The future, all to us unknown,
We to thy guardian care commit,
And peaceful leave before thy feet.

4 In scenes exalted or depressed,
Be thou our joy, and thou our rest;
Thy goodness all our hopes shall raise,
Adored through all our changing days.

5 When death shall interrupt our songs,
And seal in silence mortal tongues,
Our Helper, God, in whom we trust,
In better worlds our souls shall boast.

1062 *The New Year.* P. DODDRIDGE.

Our Helper, God! we bless thy name,
Whose love forever is the same;
The tokens of thy gracious care
Open, and crown, and close the year.

2 Amid ten thousand snares we stand,
Supported by thy guardian hand;
And see, when we review our ways,
Ten thousand monuments of praise.

3 Thus far thine arm has led us on;
Thus far we make thy mercy known;
And while we tread this desert land,
New mercies shall new songs demand.

4 Our grateful souls, on Jordan's shore,
Shall raise one sacred pillar more;
Then bear in thy bright courts above,
Inscriptions of immortal love.

PILOT. 7s. 6l. J. E. GOULD.

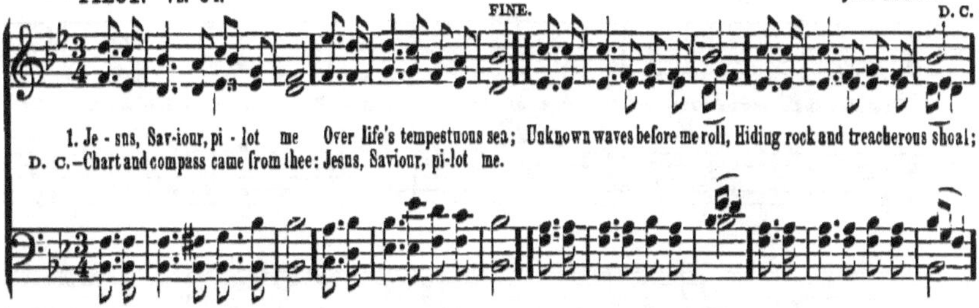
FINE.
D. C.
1. Je - sus, Sav-iour, pi - lot me Over life's tempestuous sea; Unknown waves before me roll, Hiding rock and treacherous shoal;
D. C.—Chart and compass came from thee: Jesus, Saviour, pi-lot me.

1063 *Life's Sea.* E. HOPPER.

JESUS, Saviour, pilot me,
Over life's tempestuous sea;
Unknown waves before me roll,
Hiding rock and treacherous shoal;
Chart and compass came from thee:
Jesus, Saviour, pilot me.

2 As a mother stills her child,
Thou canst hush the ocean wild;
Boisterous waves obey thy will
When thou say'st to them "Be still!"
Wondrous Sovereign of the sea,
Jesus, Saviour, pilot me.

3 When at last I near the shore,
And the fearful breakers roar
'Twixt me and the peaceful rest,
Then, while leaning on thy breast,
May I hear thee say to me,
"Fear not, I will pilot thee!"

1064 SANCTUS. Irr. OLD ENGLISH.

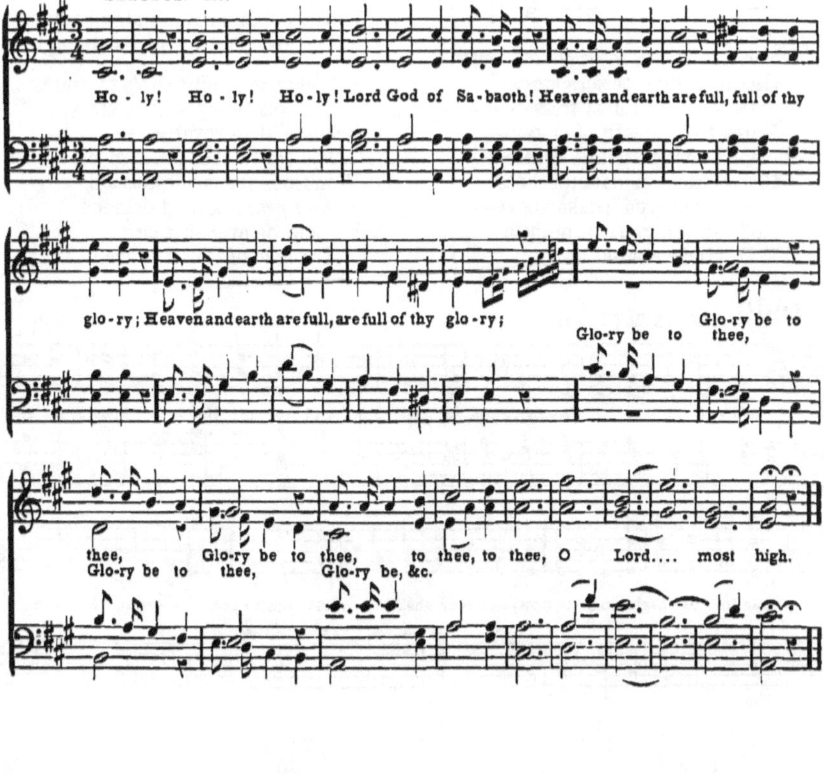
Ho - ly! Ho - ly! Ho - ly! Lord God of Sa - baoth! Heaven and earth are full, full of thy
glo - ry; Heaven and earth are full, are full of thy glo - ry; Glo-ry be to
Glo-ry be to thee,
thee, Glo-ry be to thee, to thee, to thee, O Lord.... most high.
Glo-ry be to thee, Glo-ry be, &c.

MISCELLANEOUS.

GOD'S LOVE. 7s, 6s. D.
WM. F SHERWIN.

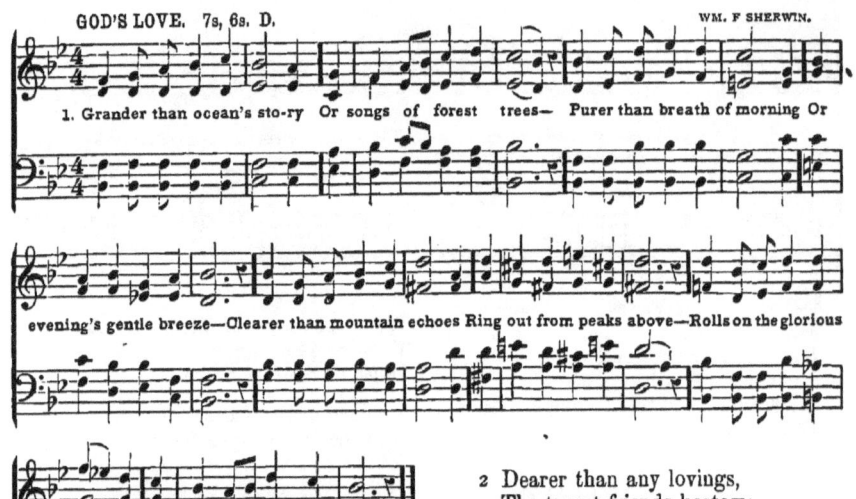

1. Grander than ocean's sto-ry Or songs of forest trees— Purer than breath of morning Or evening's gentle breeze—Clearer than mountain echoes Ring out from peaks above—Rolls on the glorious anthem Of God's e-ter-nal love.

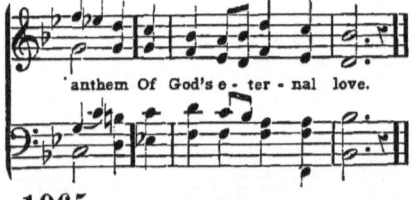

1065 *Giving of thanks.* W. F. SHERWIN.

GRANDER than ocean's story,
 Or songs of forest trees—
Purer than breath of morning,
 Or evening's gentle breeze—
Clearer than mountain echoes
 Ring out from peaks above—
Rolls on the glorious anthem
 Of God's eternal love.

2 Dearer than any lovings,
 The truest friends bestow;
Stronger than all the yearnings,
 A mother's heart can know;
Deeper than earth's foundations,
 And far above all thought;
Broader than heaven's high arches—
 The love that Christ has brought.

3 Richer than all earth's treasure,
 The wealth my soul receives;
Brighter than royal jewels,
 The crown that Jesus gives;
Wondrous the condescension,
 And grace beyond degree!
I would be ever singing
 The love of Christ to me.

1066 GLORIA PATRI. Irr.
GREATOREX COLL.

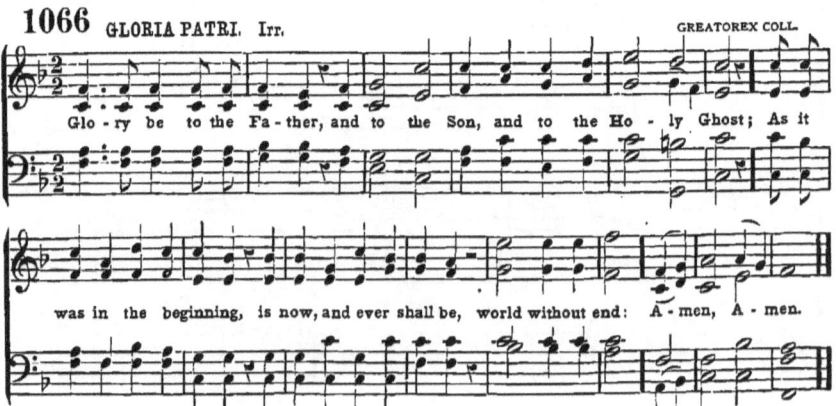

Glo-ry be to the Fa-ther, and to the Son, and to the Ho-ly Ghost; As it was in the beginning, is now, and ever shall be, world without end: A-men, A-men.

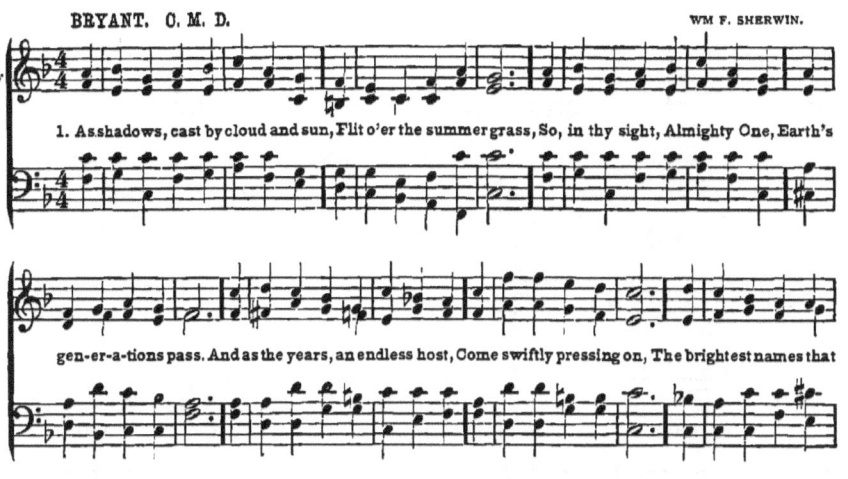

1067 Anniversary. W. C. BRYANT.

As shadows cast by cloud and sun,
  Flit o'er the summer grass,
So, in thy sight, Almighty One,
  Earth's generations pass.
And as the years, an endless host,
  Come swiftly pressing on,
The brightest names that earth can boast
  Just glisten and are gone.

2 Yet doth the star of Bethlehem shed
  A lustre pure and sweet;
And still it leads, as once it led,
  To the Messiah's feet.
O Father, may that holy star
  Grow every year more bright,
And send its glorious beams afar
  To fill the world with light.

1068 The Seasons. I. WATTS.

With songs and honors sounding loud
  Address the Lord on high;
Over the heavens he spread his cloud,
  And waters vail the sky.

His steady counsels change the face
  Of the declining year;
He bids the sun cut short his race,
  And wintry days appear.

2 He sends his word and melts the snow,
  The fields no longer mourn;
He calls the warmer gales to blow,
  And bids the spring return.
The changing wind, the flying cloud,
  Obey his mighty word;
With songs and honors sounding loud
  Praise ye the sovereign Lord.

1069 God's Mercies. H. F. LYTE.

The mercies of my God and King
  My tongue shall still pursue:
Oh, happy they, who, while they sing
  Those mercies, share them too!
As bright and lasting as the sun,
  As lofty as the sky,
From age to age, thy word shall run,
  And chance and change defy.

2 The covenant of the King of kings
  Shall stand for ever sure;
Beneath the shadow of thy wings
  Thy saints repose secure.
In earth below, in heaven above,
  Who, who is Lord like thee?
Oh, spread the gospel of thy love,
  Till all thy glories see!

MISCELLANEOUS.

MORNING PRAISE. 10s.
E. J. HOPKINS.

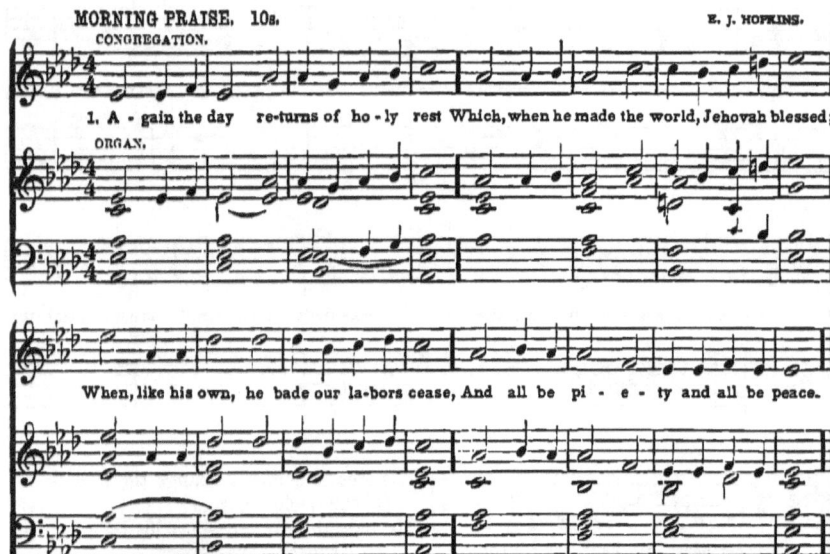

1. A - gain the day re-turns of ho - ly rest Which, when he made the world, Jehovah blessed; When, like his own, he bade our la-bors cease, And all be pi - e - ty and all be peace.

1070 *The Lord's Day.* WM. MASON.

AGAIN the day returns of holy rest
Which, when he made the world, Jehovah blessed;
When, like his own, he bade our labors cease,
And all be piety and all be peace.

2 Let us devote this consecrated day
To learn his will, and all we learn obey;
So shall he hear when fervently we raise
Our supplications and our songs of praise.

3 Father in heaven! in whom our hopes confide,
Whose power defends us and whose precepts guide,
In life our Guardian and in death our Friend,
Glory supreme be thine till time shall end.

DOMINUS REGIT ME.
LOWELL MASON.

A - men.

1071 *Psalm 23.*

1 THE Lord is my Shepherd; I | shall not | want; || he maketh me to lie down in green pastures; he leadeth me beside the | still— | waters.

2 He restoreth my soul; he leadeth me in the paths of righteousness for his | name's— | sake. || Yea, though I walk through the valley of the shadow of death, I will fear no evil: for thou art with me; thy rod and thy | staff they | comfort me.

3 Thou preparest a table before me, in the presence of mine enemies; thou anointest my head with oil; my | cup · · runneth | over. || Surely goodness and mercy shall follow me all the days of my life; and I will dwell in the house of the | Lord for- | ever. || A- | men.
G

EVENING PRAISE. P. M.
WM. F. SHERWIN.

1072 *"Day is dying."* M. A. LATHBURY.

Day is dying in the West;
Heaven is touching earth with rest:
Wait and worship while the night
Sets her evening lamps alight
  Through all the sky.
Holy, holy, holy, Lord God of Hosts!
Heaven and earth are full of thee!
Heaven and earth are praising thee,
  O Lord most high!

2 Lord of life, beneath the dome
Of the Universe, thy home,
Gather us who seek thy face
To the fold of thy embrace,
  For thou art nigh.
Holy, holy, holy, Lord God of Hosts!
Heaven and earth are full of thee!
Heaven and earth are praising thee,
  O Lord most high!

DE PROFUNDIS.
ANON.

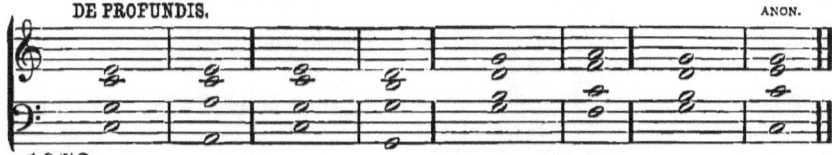

1073 *Palm 130.*

1 Out of the | depths || Have I cried unto thee, O | Lord ! ||
2 Lord, hear my | voice: || Let thine ears be attentive to the voice of my suppli- | cations. ||
3 If thou, Lord, shouldst mark in- | iquities, || O Lord! who shall | stand? ||
4 But there is forgiveness with | thee, || That thou mayest be | feared. ||
5 I wait for the Lord, my soul doth | wait, || And in his word do I | hope. ||
6 My soul waiteth for the Lord more than they that watch for the | morning: || I say, more than they that watch for the | morning. ||
7 Let Israel hope in the | Lord; || For with the Lord there is mercy, and with him is plenteous re- | demption. ||
8 And he shall redeem | Israel || From all his in- | iquities. ||

TE DEUM LAUDAMUS.

ANON.

A - men.

1074
The Ancient "Te Deum."

1 WE praise thee, | O— | God; || we acknowledge | thee to | be the | Lord. ||
All the earth doth | worship | thee, || the Father | ever- | last- — | ing. ||

2 To thee all angels | cry a- | loud, || the heavens, and | all the | powers there- | in.
To thee cherubim and seraphim, con- | tinually · · do | cry, || Holy, holy, holy, Lord | God of | Saba- | oth; ||

3 Heaven and earth are full of the majesty | of thy | glory. || The glorious company of the apostles praise thee. The goodly fellowship of the | prophets | praise — | thee. ||
The noble army of martyrs | praise— | thee. || The holy church throughout all the | world · · doth ac- | knowledge | thee, ||

4 The Father, of an | infi- · · nite | majesty; || thine adorable, | true and | only | Son; ||
Also the Holy | Ghost, the | Comforter. || Thou art the King of glory, O Christ, thou art the everlasting | Son · · of the | Fa- — | ther. ||

5 When thou tookest upon thee to de- | liver | man, || thou didst humble thyself to be | born — | of a | virgin. ||
When thou hadst overcome the | sharpness · · of | death, || thou didst open the kingdom of | heaven · · to | all be- | lievers. ||

6 Thou sittest at the right hand of God, in the | glory · · of the | Father. || We believe that thou shalt | come to | be our | judge.
We therefore pray thee, | help thy | servants, || whom thou hast redeemed | with thy | precious | blood. ||

7 Make them to be numbered | with thy | saints, || in | glory | ever- | lasting. ||
O Lord, save thy people, and | bless thine | heritage; || govern them and | lift them | up for- | ever. ||

8 Day by day we | magni- · · fy | thee; || and we worship thy name ever, | world with- | out — | end. ||
Vouchsafe, O Lord, to keep us this | day with-out | sin; || O Lord, have mercy upon us, have | mer-cy up- | on — | us. ||

9 O Lord, let thy mercy | be up- | on us, || as our | trust — | is in | thee. ||
O Lord, in | thee · · have I | trusted; || let me | never | be con- | founded. || A- | men. ||

1075 GLORIA IN EXCELSIS. PART I. ANON.

1 GLORY be to | God on | high, || and on earth | peace, good- | will· ·towards | men.
2 We praise thee, we bless thee, we | worship | thee, || we glorify thee, we give thanks to | thee for | thy great | glory.

PART II.

3 O Lord God, | heavenly | King, || God the | Father | Al· — | mighty!
4 O Lord, the only begotten Son, | Jesus | Christ; || O Lord God, Lamb of | God, Son | of the | Father,

PART III.

5 That takest away the | sins· ·of the | world, || have mercy | upon | us.
6 Thou that takest away the | sins· ·of the | world, || have mercy | upon | us.
7 Thou that takest away the | sins· ·of the | world, || re- | ceive our | prayer.
8 Thou that sittest at the right hand of | God the | Father, || have mercy | upon | us.

RETURN TO PART I.

9 For thou | only· · art | holy: || thou | only | art the | Lord:
10 Thou only, O Christ, with the | Holy | Ghost, || art most high in the | glory. . of | God the | Father. || A- | men.

1076 RESPONSE TO THE DECALOGUE.

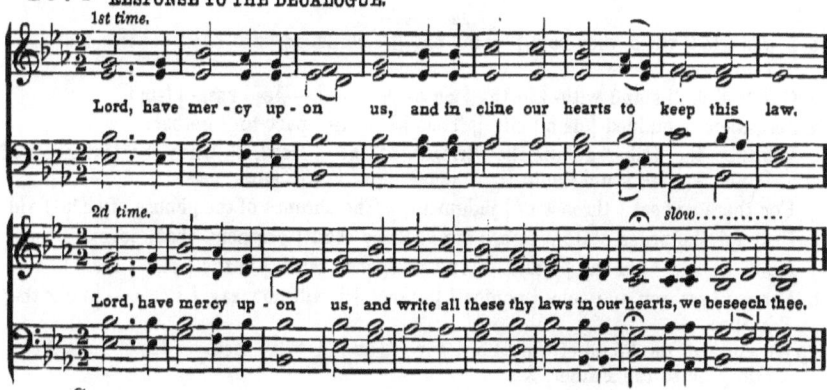

G

CHANTS AND OCCASIONAL PIECES.

VENITE, EXULTEMUS DOMINO. WILLIAM BOYCE.

1077
Psalm 95.

1 Oh, come, let us sing un-| to the | Lord; || Let us heartily rejoice in the | strength of | our sal-| vation.
2 Let us come before his presence | with thanks-| giving; || And show ourselves | glad in | him with | psalms.
3 For the Lord is a | great— | God; || And a great | King a-| bove all | gods.
4 In his hands are all the corners | of the | earth; || and the strength of the | hills is | his— | also.
5 The sea is his | and he | made it; || And his hands pre- | pared | the dry | land.
6 Oh, come, let us worship | and fall | down; || And kneel be- | fore the | Lord our | Maker.
7 For he is the | Lord our | God; || And we are the people of his pasture, and the | sheep of | his— | hand.
8 Oh, worship the Lord in the | beauty·· of | holiness; || Let the whole | earth··stand in | awe of | him.
*9 For he cometh, for he cometh to | judge the | earth; || And with righteousness to judge the world, and the | people | with his | truth.
10 Glory be to the Father, and | to the | Son, || And | to the | Holy | Ghost;
11 As it was in the beginning, is now, and | ever··shall | be, || World without | end. A- | men, A- | men.

1078
Psalm 122.

1 I was glad when they said | unto | me, || Let us go into the | house— | of the | Lord.
2 Our feet shall stand with- | in thy | gates, || O— | —Je- | rusa- | lem!
3 Jerusalem is builded | as a | city || That | is com- | pact to- | gether:
4 Whither the tribes go up, the | tribes··of the | Lord, || Unto the testimony of Israel, to give thanks unto the | name— | of the | Lord.
5 For there are set | thrones of | judgment, || The thrones of the | house of | Da- | vid.
6 Pray for the peace of Je- | rusa- | lem: | They shall | prosper··that | love— | thee.
7 Peace be with- | in thy | walls, || And prosperity with- | in thy | pala | ces.
8 For my brethren and com- | panions' | sakes, || I will now say, | Peace— | be with- | in thee.
*9 Because of the house of the | Lord our | God || I will | seek— | thy— | good.
Glory be to the Father, &c.

G

MISERERE MEI, DEUS.
THOMAS TALLIS.

1079
Psalm 51.

1 Have mercy upon me, O God, according to thy | loving- | kindness: || According unto the multitude of thy tender mercies | blot out | my trans- | gressions.
2 Wash me thoroughly from | mine in- | iquity, || And | cleanse me | from my | sin.
3 For I acknowledge | my trans- | gressions: | And my | sin is | ever·· be- | fore me.
4 Hide thy face | from my | sins, || And blot out | all — | mine in- | iquities.
5 Create in me a clean | heart, O | God; || And renew a right | spirit·· with- | in — | me.
6 Cast me not away | from thy | presence; || And take not thy | Holy | Spirit | from me.
7 Restore unto me the joy of | thy sal- | vation; || And uphold me | with thy | free— | Spirit.
8 Then will I teach trans- | gressors·· thy | ways; || And sinners shall be con- | verted | unto | thee.
9 Deliver me from blood-guiltiness, O God, thou God of | my sal- | vation: || And my tongue shall sing aloud | of thy | righteous- | ness.
10 O Lord, open | thou my | lips: || And my mouth shall | shew forth | thy — | praise.
11 For thou desirest not sacrifice; | else·· would I | give it: || Thou delightest | not in burnt— | offering.
12 The sacrifices of God are a | broken | spirit: || A broken and contrite heart, O God, | thou wilt | not de- | spise.

DEUS MISEREATUR.
RICHARD FARRANT.

1080
Psalm 67.

1 God be merciful unto | us, and | bless us; || And show us the light of his countenance, and be | merci·· ful | unto | us.
2 That thy way may be known | up·· on | earth; || Thy saving | health a- | mong all | nations.
3 Let the people praise thee, | O— | God. || Yea, let | all the·· people | praise— | thee.
4 Oh, let the nations rejoice | and be | glad; || For thou shalt judge the people righteously, and govern the | na·· tions | upon | earth.
5 Let the people praise thee, | O— | God; || Yea, let | all the·· people | praise— | thee.
6 Then shall the earth bring | forth her | increase; || And God, even our own | God shall | give us·· his | blessing.
7 God shall | bless— | us; || And all the ends of the | world shall | fear— | him.
8 Glory be to the Father, and | to the | Son, || And | to the | Holy | Ghost; ||
9 As it was in the beginning, is now, and | ever | shall be, || World | without | end. A- | men.

G

CHANTS AND OCCASIONAL PIECES.

A LITTLE WHILE. 11s, 10s.   F. L. BENJAMIN.

1. Oh, for the peace which floweth like a riv-er, Making life's desert places bloom and smile! Oh, for the faith to grasp heav'n's bright "forever," A-mid the shadows of earth's "little while."

1081   *"A little while."*   J. CREWDSON.

OH, for the peace which floweth like a river,
Making life's desert places bloom and smile!
Oh, for the faith to grasp heaven's bright "forever,"
Amid the shadows of earth's "little while!"

2 A little while for patient vigil-keeping,
To face the storm, to battle with the strong;
A little while to sow the seed with weeping,
Then bind the sheaves and sing the harvest song!

3 A little while to keep the oil from failing,
A little while faith's flickering lamp to trim;
And then, the Bridegroom's coming footsteps hailing,
To haste to meet him with the bridal hymn!

4 And he who is himself the gift and giver,—
The future glory and the present smile,—
With the bright promise of the glad "for ever"
Will light the shadows of the "little while!"

1082 RESPONSE AFTER DECALOGUE.

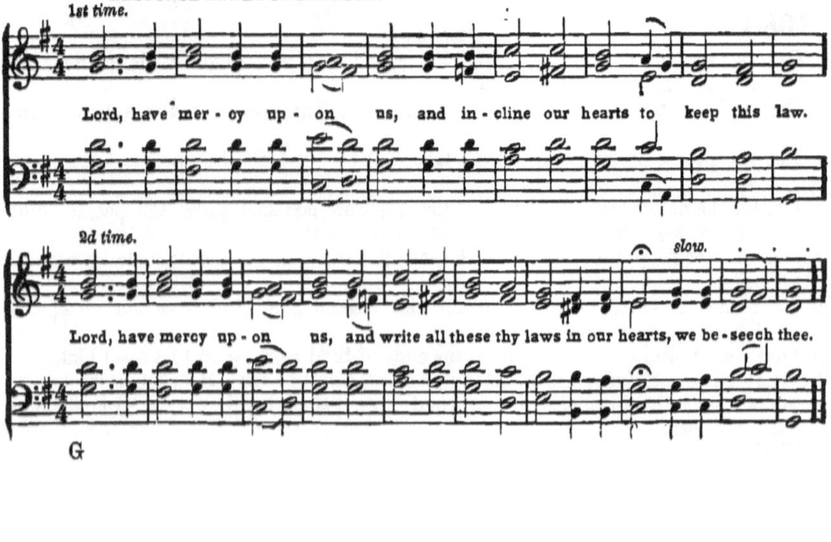

1st time. Lord, have mer-cy up-on us, and in-cline our hearts to keep this law.

2d time. *slow.* Lord, have mercy up-on us, and write all these thy laws in our hearts, we be-seech thee.

G

CHANTS AND OCCASIONAL PIECES. 411

1083 *"Abide in me."* W. F. SHERWIN.

Why is thy faith, O child of God, so small?
Why doth thy heart shrink back at duty's call?
Art thou obeying this—"Abide in me,"
And doth the Master's word abide in thee?

2 Oh, blest assurance from our risen Lord!
Oh, precious comfort breathing from the Word!
How great the promise! could there greater be?
"Ask what thou wilt, it shall be done for thee!"

3 "Ask what thou wilt," but, oh, remember this,—
We ask and have not, for we ask amiss
When, weak in faith, we only half believe
That what we ask we really shall receive.

4 Increase our faith, and clear our vision, Lord;
Help us to take thee at thy simple word,
No more with cold distrust to bring thee grief;
Lord, we believe! help thou our unbelief.

1084 RESPONSE AFTER DECALOGUE.

G

FUNERAL. THOS. TALLIS.

1085
Selections.

1 BLESSED are the dead, who die in the | Lord from | henceforth; || Yea, saith the Spirit, that they may rest from their labors, | and their | works do | follow them.

2 Our days on earth are as a shadow, and there is | none a- | biding; || We are but of yesterday; there is but a | step ·· between | us and | death;

3 Man's days are as grass: as a flower of the field, | so he | flourisheth; || He appeareth for a little time, then | van-ish-| eth a- | way.

4 Watch! for ye know not what hour your | Lord doth | come; || Be ye also ready; for in such an hour as ye think not, the | Son of | Man— | cometh.

5 It is the Lord; let him do what | seemeth ·· him | good; || The Lord gave, and the Lord hath taken away, and | blessed ·· be the | name ·· of the | Lord.

6 Blesséd are the dead, who die in the | Lord from | henceforth; || Yea, saith the Spirit, that they may rest from their labors, | and their | works do | follow them.

OUTTING. 6s, 4s. WM. F. SHERWIN.

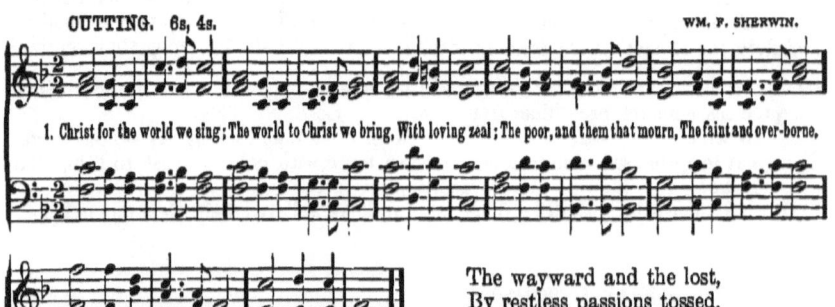

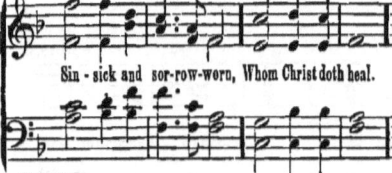

1086
Christ for the World. S. WOLCOTT.

CHRIST for the world we sing;
The world to Christ we bring,
  With loving zeal;
The poor, and them that mourn,
The faint and overborne,
Sin-sick and sorrow-worn,
  Whom Christ doth heal.

2 Christ for the world we sing;
The world to Christ we bring,
  With fervent prayer;
G

The wayward and the lost,
By restless passions tossed,
Redeemed, at countless cost,
  From dark despair.

3 Christ for the world we sing;
The world to Christ we bring,
  With one accord;
With us the work to share,
With us reproach to dare,
With us the cross to bear,
  For Christ our Lord.

4 Christ for the world we sing;
The world to Christ we bring,
  With joyful song;
The new-born souls, whose days,
Reclaimed from error's ways,
Inspired with hope and praise,
  To Christ belong.

DOXOLOGIES.

1 L. M.
Praise God, from whom all blessings flow!
Praise him, all creatures here below!
Praise him above, ye heavenly host!
Praise Father, Son, and Holy Ghost!

2 L. M. 6 l.
To God the Father, God the Son,
And God the Spirit, three in one,
Be honor, praise, and glory given,
By all on earth, and all in heaven.
As was through ages heretofore,
Is now, and shall be evermore.

3 L. M. D.
Eternal Father, throned above,
Thou fountain of redeeming love!
Eternal Word! who left thy throne
For man's rebellion to atone;
Eternal Spirit, who dost give
That grace whereby our spirits live:
Thou God of our salvation, be
Eternal praises paid to thee!

4 C. M.
To Father, Son, and Holy Ghost,
  One God whom we adore,
Be glory as it was, is now,
  And shall be evermore.

5 C. M.
Let God the Father, and the Son,
  And Spirit, be adored,
Where there are works to make him known,
  Or saints to love the Lord.

6 C. M. D.
The God of mercy be adored,
  Who calls our souls from death,
Who saves by his redeeming word
  And new-creating breath;
To praise the Father and the Son
  And Spirit all-divine,—
The one in three, and three in one—
  Let saints and angels join.
  G

7 S. M.
Ye angels round the throne,
  And saints that dwell below,
Worship the Father, praise the Son,
  And bless the Spirit, too.

8 S. M.
The Father and the Son
  And Spirit we adore;
We praise, we bless, we worship thee,
  Both now and evermore!

9 H. M.
To God the Father's throne
  Your highest honors raise;
  Glory to God the Son;
  To God, the Spirit, praise;
With all our powers, Eternal King,
Thy name we sing, while faith adores.

10 7s.
Sing we to our God above
Praise eternal as his love;
Praise him, all ye heavenly host—
Father, Son, and Holy Ghost.

11 7s, 6 l.
Praise the name of God most high,
Praise him, all below the sky,
Praise him, all ye heavenly host,
Father, Son, and Holy Ghost;
As through countless ages past,
Evermore his praise shall last.

12 7s, D.
Praise our glorious King and Lord,
Angels waiting on his word,
Saints that walk with him in white,
Pilgrims walking in his light:
Glory to the Eternal One,
Glory to his only Son,
Glory to the Spirit be
Now, and through eternity.

13   C. P. M.

To Father, Son, and Holy Ghost,
Be praise amid the heavenly host,
   And in the church below;
From whom all creatures draw their
     breath,
By whom redemption blessed the earth,
   From whom all comforts flow.

14   8s, 7s.

Praise the Father, earth and heaven,
   Praise the Son, the Spirit praise;
As it was, and is, be given
   Glory through eternal days.

15.   8s, 7s. 6 l.

Praise and honor to the Father,
   Praise and honor to the Son,
Praise and honor to the Spirit,
   Ever Three and ever One;
One in might and one in glory,
   While eternal ages run.

16   8s, 7s. D.

Praise the God of all creation;
   Praise the Father's boundless love :
Praise the Lamb, our expiation,
   Priest and King enthroned above :
Praise the Fountain of salvation,
   Him by whom our spirits live :
Undivided adoration
   To the one Jehovah give.

17   8s, 7s, 4s.

Glory be to God the Father,
   Glory be to God the Son,
Glory be to God the Spirit,
   Glory to the Three in One;
     Hallelujah!
God, the Lord is God alone.

18   8s, 7s, 4s.

Great Jehovah! we adore thee,
   God the Father, God the Son,
God the Spirit, joined in glory
   On the same eternal throne;
     Endless praises
To Jehovah, Three in One.
  G

19   10s.

To Father, Son, and Spirit, ever blest,
Eternal praise and worship be addressed;
From age to age, ye saints, his name
   adore,
And spread his fame, till time shall be
   no more

20   6s, D.

To Father and to Son,
   And, Holy Ghost! to thee,
Eternal Three in One!
   Eternal glory be;
As hath been, and is now,
   And shall be evermore :
Before thy throne we bow,
   And thee, our God, adore.

21   7s, 6s.

To thee be praise for ever,
   Thou glorious King of kings!
Thy wondrous love and favor
   Each ransomed spirit sings :
We 'll celebrate thy glory
   With all thy saints above,
And shout the joyful story
   Of thy redeeming love.

22   7s, 6s.

Father, Son, and Holy Ghost,
   One God, whom we adore,
Join we with the heavenly host
   To praise thee evermore :
Live, by heaven and earth adored,
   Three in One, and One in Three,
Holy, holy, holy Lord,
   All glory be to thee!

23   11s, or 5s, 6s.

O Father Almighty, to thee be addressed,
With Christ and the Spirit, one God ever
   blest,
All glory and worship, from earth and
   from heaven,
As was, and is now, and shall ever be
   given.

24   6s, 4s.

To God—the Father, Son,
   And Spirit—Three in One,
     All praise be given!
Crown him in every song;
To him your hearts belong;
Let all his praise prolong—
     On earth, in heaven.

INDEX OF TUNES.

It is to be understood that most of the Music included in this Collection is introduced "by permission," either purchased or given. It must, therefore, not be used in any other, without the consent of the authors or of those who hold the copyright of the Tunes.

	PAGE.
A LITTLE WHILE..11s, 10s......	410
Admah .... L. M. 6l......	4
Adrian .... S. M........	319
Aletta .... 7s.......192,	321
Alexander........... S. M.......	213
Alford .... 7s, 6s. D.....	377
All Saints .... L. M........	130
All the Days....... P. M........	201
All to Christ....... P. M........	156
America .... 6s, 4s.......	398
Amsterdam ......7s, 6s, D......	351
An Open Door....P. M.........	171
And Can It Be....L. M. 6l.....	265
Antioch........... C. M.........	88
Anvern .... L. M......20,	345
Apollos .... S. M. D......	286
Appleton.......... L. M.........	344
Arcadia .... C. M.........	207
Ariel .... C. P. M......	211
Arlington .... C. M........	151
Armenia.......... C. M........	234
Arundel........... C. M........	147
Ashwell........... L. M........	163
Assurance....... 10s...........	411
Athens .... C. M. D......	155
Augustus .... C. M.........	308
Aurelia.......... 7s, 6s, D.....	178
Austria .... 8s, 7s, D.....	201
Autumn......... 8s, 7s, D......	121
Avison .... 11s, 10s......	95
Avon............. C. M....106,	174
Azmon........... C. M......126,	303
BADEA .... S. M..........	276
Balerma........... C. M........	161
Barber .... S. M.........	37
Barby .... C. M........	356
Bartimeus ...... 8s, 7s.........	228
Bavaria .... 8s, 7s, D......	305
Bayley .... 8s, 7s, D......	220
Beauteous Day... P. M........	299
Bedan .... S. M........	297
Beethoven........ L. M........	282
Belief .... C. M........	308
Belmont .... C. M........	313
Bemerton .... C. M........	11
Beminster .... 7s............	247
Benevento...... 7s, D......193,	395
Benjamin........ S. M. D......	122
Bennington ..... L. M. D......	131
Bera .... L. M.........	162
Bernard .... 7s, 6s, D......	376
Bethany.......... 6s, 4s........	186
Betterland .... 7s, 6l........	391
Beulah .... 7s, D.........	374
Beyond .... Chant........	370
Blake .... L. M.........	180
Bloomfield Ch....L. M........	260
Blumenthal .... 7s, D.........	84
Boardman .... C. M........	137
Bond............. C. M........	290
Boylston .... S. M.........	311
Braden .... S. M.........	46
Bradford .... C. M.........	125
Brattle St. .... C. M. D.....	70
Bread of Life..... 6s, 4s........	57

	PAGE.
Bremen........... C. P. M......	217
Brest .... 8s, 7s, 4s.....	364
Bridgman .... C. M........	262
Brown .... C. M........	262
Brownell .... L. M. 6l.....	5
Bryant........... C. M. D......	403
Byefield .... C. M........	27
CADDO .... C. M........	174
Calvary .... 8s, 7s, 4s......	120
Cambridge ...... C. M.........	206
Cana .... 11s...........	218
Canaan .... C. M. D......	386
Capello .... L. M.........	61
Carlisle .... S. M.........	230
Carthage .... 8s, 7s........	114
Caskey .... 7s, 6s, D......	214
Chapel .... 7s.............	2
Chenies .... 7s, 6s, D......	66
Chester .... C. M.........	136
Chesterfield .... C. M.........	189
Chimes .... C. M........	65
China .... C. M.........	357
Christmas ...... C. M.....90,	208
Church .... C. M.........	13
Cincinnati...... C. M.........	125
Clapton .... S. M.........	211
Colchester ...... C. M........	27
Come, ye Dis....11s, 10s......	167
Comfort .... 7s, D.........	274
Communion .... C. M........	106
Communion (No.2)C. M......	309
Cooling .... C. M.........	191
Corinth .... C. M.........	253
Coronation ..... C. M.........	127
Coventry .... C. M.........	380
Cowper .... C. M.........	150
Crawford .... L. M.........	98
Creation .... L. M. D......	69
Cutting .... 6s, 4s........	412
DALLAS .... 7s............	24
Dalston .... S. P. M......	1
Darley........... L. M........	306
Dawn .... S. M.........	355
Dedham .... C. M........	323
De Fleury....... 8s, D.........	244
Dennis .... S. M....211,	276
Dependence .... P. M.........	177
Detroit .... S. M........	160
Devizes .... C. M.........	65
Dialemata ...... S. M. D......	123
Dijon .... 7s..........3,	24
Dix .... 7s, 6l........	25
Dorman .... S. M.........	181
Dormance...... 8s, 7s.....280,	324
Dort .... 6s, 4s........	124
Dover .... S. M.........	342
Downs .... C. M........	76
Doxology....... L. M.........	56
Duke Street..... L. M....257,	400
Dunbar .... S. M.........	355
Dundee .... C. M........	77
Dwight .... L. M.........	237
Dykes .... 7s, 6l........	327
EASTER HY..... 7s............	116

	PAGE.
Easton........... L. M........	314
Eckhardtsheim...C. M.......	263
Ein'Feste Burg...P. M.......	82
Eisenach .... L. M........	341
Elizabethtown...C. M.......	63
Ellaconibe...... 7s, 6s, D.....	85
Ellesdie .... 8s, 7s, D......	200
El Paran........ L. M.........	21
Eltham .... 7s, D.........	333
Elvet .... C. M.........	137
Emmelar .... 6s, 5s........	54
Erpan .... L. M.........	181
Essex .... 8s, 7s.........	200
Evan............ C. M.....191,	313
Even Me........ P. M.........	171
Evening......... S. M........	47
Evening Hy.... L. M.........	44
Evening Praise..P. M........	405
Eventide .... 10s...........	48
Every Day...... P. M.........	221
Ewing .... 7s, 6s, D......	385
Exhortation.... C. M........	183
Expostulation...11s.........	165
FABEN .... 8s, 7s, D......	80
Farland........ 8s, 7s, 4s.....	120
Fatherland ..... P. M.........	216
Federal St...... L. M....232,	353
Ferguson .... S. M........	207
Flemming ..... 8s, 6s........	279
Forest .... L. M........	72
Fountain .... C. M........	150
Frederick....... 11s..........	348
Fulton .... 7s........140,	247
GALILEE .... L. M.........	93
Ganges .... C. P. M......	145
Gaylord .... 8s, 7s, D.....	177
Geer .... C. M........	235
Geneva .... C. M.........	71
Geneva .... 7s, 6s, D......	351
Gerhardt ...... 7s, 6s, D......	111
Germany .... L. M.........	99
Gilead .... L. M.........	34
Glasgow .... C. M.....154,	396
Gloria Patri.... Irr...........	402
Glory .... S. M........	15
God's Love.... 7s, 6s, D......	402
Golden Hill.... S. M.........	318
Good Cheer.... S. M........	254
Gorton.......... S. M.........	144
Goshen .... 11s.......219,	242
Grace .... 8s, 7s, 4s.....	166
Grace Church...L. M.......	236
Gratitude....... L. M........	256
Greenport ...... C. M. D.....	264
Greenville...... 8s, 7s, 4s.....	53
Greenwood .... S. M.....231,	361
Grigg .... C. M........	101
Grostette .... L. M........	340
Guidance ..... 8s, 7s, D......	383
Guide .... 7s, 6l........	250
HADDAM ...... H. M........	237
Halle .... 7s, 6l........	8
Hamburg ..... L. M......105,	307

G

INDEX OF TUNES.

Tune	Meter	Page
Hamden	8s, 7s, 4s	337
Hamlin	7s, D	40
Handy	L. M. 6l	271
Happy Day	L. M	307
Hark	P. M	89
Harmony Grove	L. M	93
Harwell	8s, 7s, D	119
Haslam	L. M	105
Haven	C. M	62
Haverhill	S. M	372
Haydn	S. M	136
Heavenly Fold	C. M. D	312
Heber	C. M	239
Hebron	L. M	45
He Leadeth Me	L. M. D	283
Helena	C. M	101
Hendon	7s	2
Heuley	10s	328
Henry	C. M	36
Herald Angels	7s, D	94
Hermon	C. M	190
Herold	7s	25
Holley	7s	49
Hollingside	7s, D	194
Holy Cross	C. M	239
Horton	7s	164
Hosanna	L. M	237
Houghton	10s, 11s	224
Howard	C. M	308
Hummel	C. M	147
Huntington	C. M	203
Hursley	L. M, 44	236
Hymn	C. M	17
Hymn of Joy	8s, 7s, D	108
I Am Coming	P. M	157
I'm a Pilgrim	P. M	374
I Need Thee	P. M	185
Immortality	7s, 6s, D	388
Ingham	L. M	102
Inverness	S. M	304
Invitation	C. M	103
Iola	C. M	64
Iowa	S. M	149
Italian Hy	6s, 4s	85
Jazer	C. M	91
Jerusalem	C. M. D	71
Jesus, My All	6s, 4s	172
Jewett	6s, D	278
Jordan	C. M. D	373
Joyful Sound	C. M. D	379
Judgment Hy	P. M	365
Karl	7s	246
Knox	C. M	62
Laban	S. M	210
La Mira	C. M	234
Lanesboro'	S. M	11
Langton	S. M	29
Laodicea	P. M	178
Last Beam	P. M	51
Laud	L. M	77
Lead Me On	P. M	224
Leighton	S. M, 212, 296	
Lenox	H. M	154
Leoni	6s, 8s, 4s	38
Life	8s, 7s, 7s	170
Linwood	L. M	30
Lisbon	S. M	15
Lischer	H. M	6
Long	L. M	339
Long Home	7s, 8s, 7s	349
Louvan	L. M	73
Love Divine	8s, 7s, D	220
Loving Kindness	L. M	152
Lowry	L. M, 21, 389	
Luther	S. M, 266, 342	
Luton	C. M	315
Lutzen	C. M	74
Lux Benigna	10s, 4s	281
Lyons	10s, 11s	39
Lyte	6s, 4s	233
Madison	8s, D	245
Magill	11s	243
Mainzer	L. M	68
Maitland	C. M	209
Manoah	C. M, 79, 107	
Marlow	C. M	10
Martyn	7s, D, 164, 195	
Mear	C. M	10
Meinhold	7s, 8s, 7s	349
Melcombe	L. M	19
Melody	C. M	238
Memorial	L. M. 6l	229
Mendebras	7s, 6s, D	9
Mendon	L. M	339
Mercy	7s, 140, 275	
Meribah	C. P. M, 145, 358	
Merton	C. M	36
Messiah	7s, D	204
Middleton	8s, 7s, D	289
Migdol	L. M	19
Miles Lane	C. M	127
Millennium	H. M	6
Millington	8s, 7s, 7s, 118	359
Milwaukie	8s, 7s	281
Miriam	7s, 6s, D, 67, 384	
Mission Song	8s, 7s, D	298
Missionary Ch	L. M, 202, 341	
Missionary Hy	7s, 6s, D	332
Monkland	7s	320
Monson	C. M	146
More Love	6s, 4s	186
Morning Praise	10s	404
Mornington	S. M	138
Mozart	7s	117
Mt. Auburn	C. M	232
Mt. Blanc	P. M	390
My Life Flows	P. M	225
Munich	7s, 6s, D	333
Naomi	C. M	253
Nauford	P. M	316
Naumann	P. M	380
Near the Cross	P. M	176
Nettleton	8s, 7s, D	316
Newbold	C. M	91
Newcourt	L. P. M	35
New Haven	6s, 4s	141
New Year's Hy	11s, 5s	398
New-York Tune	C. M	397
Nicaea	P. M	38
Nightfall	11s, 5s	50
Noel	C. M	75
None but Jesus	P. M	166
Northfield	C. M	387
Nunda	L. M. D	358
Nun Danket	P. M	83
Nuremburg	7s, 6l	184
Oak	6s, 4s	370
Oaksville	C. M	12
Oberlin	P. M	31
Old Hundred	L. M	32
Old, Old Story	7s, 6s, D	158
Oliphant	8s, 7s, 4s	52
Olive's Brow	L. M	104
Olivet	6s, 4s, 233, 304	
Olmutz	S. M, 213, 354	
Olney	S. M	139
One More Day	P. M	54
Onido	7s, D	41
Ontario	S. M	254
Ortonville	C. M	102
Overberg	L. M	45
Owen	S. M, 160, 310	
Oxford	C. M	322
Packington	S. M	16
Palestine	L. M. 6l	270
Palestrina	C. M	223
Paradise	P. M	371
Park St	L. M	203
Pass. Chorale	7s, 6s, D	110
Pass Me Not	8s, 5s	170
Patnah	7s, 6s, D	111
Paulina	11s	308
Pax Dei	10s	48
Pearl St	8s, 7s	325
Peniel	C. M	238
Penitence	7s, 6s, 8s	176
Perry	7s, D	338
Peterboro'	C. M	13
Pilot	7s, 6l	401
Pleyel's Hy	7s, 205, 321	
Portuguese Hy	L. M	128
Portuguese Hy	11s	218
Prayer	S. M	149
Prince	L. M	135
Promise	8s, 7s, D	115
Rakem	L. M. 6l	4
Rathbun	8s, 7s, 114, 336	
Raynolds	11s, 10s	329
Reden	6s, 4s	187
Redhead	7s, 6l	173
Refuge	7s, D	195
Regent Square	8s, 7s	88
Remsen	C. M	302
Renovation	S. M	210
Repentance	L. M	148
Repose	7s, 6l	251
Rest	L. M	353
Retreat	L. M	28
Return	C. M	161
Rhine	C. M	378
Rialto	S. M	222
Righini	6s, 4s	124
Rock of Ages	7s, 6l	326
Rockingham	L. M	99
Rogers	C. M	209
Rolland	L. M	18
Romberg	C. M	272
Rose Hill	L. M	292
Rosefield	7s, 6l	250
Rothwell	L. M	129
Rutherford	P. M	390
Sabbath	7s, 6l	7
Samson	L. M	130
Sanctus	Irr	401
Savannah	10s	8
Scotland	12s	152
Scudamore	7s	117
Seasons	L. M	163
Segur	8s, 7s, 4s	52
Selvin	S. M	277
Serenity	C. M	189
Sessions	L. M	317
Seymour	7s	49
Shawmut	S. M	144
Shepherd	8s, 7s	324
Shining Shore	P. M	378
Shirland	S. M	23
Sicily	8s, 7s	325
Siloam	C. M, 273, 303	
Silver St	S. M	37
Simpson	C. M	151
Solid Rock	L. M. D, 92, 265	
Solitude	L. M	104
Solitude	7s	194
Solney	8s, 7s	301
Something for Je	6s, 4s	187
Southport	C. M, 26, 235	
Spanish Hy	7s, 6l, 156, 240	
Spohr	L. M	260
Stabat Mater	P. M	109
St. Agnes	C. M	357
St. Alban	L. M	92
St. Alban's	6s, 5s, D	198
St. Ann's	C. M, 74, 291	
St. Asaph	C. M. D	350
St. Bride	S. M	343
St. Chad	8s, 7s, D	81
St. Edmund's	L. M	352
St. George	7s, D	394
St. Gertrude	6s, 5s, D	199
St. Hilda	7s, 6s, D	179
St. James	7s, 6s, D	375
St. Joseph	8s, 7s, 7s	103
St. Martin's	C. M	291
St. Matthias	L. M. 6l	55
St. Sylvester	8s, 7s	399
St. Thomas	S. M	14
State St	S. M	16
Stephanos	P. M	222
Stephens	C. M	136
Still Water	11s, 10s	240
Stillingfleet	S. M	103
Stockwell	8s, 7s, 53, 301	
Stoughton	8s, 7s, D	288
Stowell	L. M	28
Sweet Hour	L. M. D	30
Tamworth	8s, 7s, 4s	364
Tappan	C. M	369
Tell the Story	7s, 6s, D	159

G

METRICAL INDEX.

	PAGE		PAGE		PAGE
Tema......L. M.	316	Victory......8s, 7s, 4s	381	Wilberforce......7s, 6l	172
Tharaw......7s, 6l	184	Vienna......7s	204	Willington......L. M.	61
Thatcher......S. M.	267	Vigil......S. M.	372	Willoughby......C. P. M.	216
The Lord's Pray..Chant	55	Viola......7s, 6l	251	Wilmot......8s, 7s	229
The Ninetyand N..P. M.	153			Wilson......8s, 7s	289
Theodora......7s	205	WALES......8s, 4s	198	Wimborne......L. M.......134, 202
Thy Will......Chant	279	Ward......L. M.	344	Wirth......C. M.	206
Topaz......P. M.	223	Ware......L. M......33, 293		Wood......S. M.	311
Trett......C. M.	100	Warner......L. M.	175	Woodland......C. M.	381
Triste......8s, 7s. D	280	Warrington......L. M.	261	Woodstock......C. M.	28
Truro......L. M.	72	Warsaw......H. M.	287	Woodworth......L. M......175, 282
Trusting......7s	192	Warwick......C. M.	17	Work Song......P. M.	297
Tully......7s, 6s, D	377	Watchman......S. M.	360	Worship......8s, 7s, 4s	314
UXBRIDGE......L. M.	60	Webb......7s, 6s, D..215, 334			
VALENTIA......C. M.	255	Weber......7s	3	YARMOUTH......7s, 6s, D	215
Varina......C. M. D....78, 372		Wells......L. M.	148	Yoakley......L. M. 6l	5
Vernon......8s, D	244	Welton......L. M.	315	York......C. M.	64
Verona......C. M.	315	Wesley......11s, 10s	335		
Vesper......8s, 7s	382	Westminster......8s, 7s	300	ZEPHYR......L. M.......135, 352
Vesper Hy......8s, 7s, D	81	What a Friend..8s, 7s, D	221	Zerah......C. M.	90
		Whitefield......S, M.	139	Zion......8s, 7s, 4s	337

METRICAL INDEX.

L. M.

	PAGE		PAGE		PAGE		PAGE
All Saints	130	Old Hundred	32	He Leadeth Me	283	Devizes	65
Anvern	20, 345	Olive's Brow	104	Nunda	358	Downs	76
Appleton	344	Overberg	45	Solid Rock	92	Dundee	77
Ashwell	163	Park Street	203	Sweet Hour	30	Eckhardtsheim	263
Beethoven	282	Portuguese Hy	128			Elizabethtown	63
Bera	162	Prince	135			Elvet	137
Blake	180	Repentance	148	### L. P. M.		Evan	191, 313
Bloomfield Ch	260	Rest	353	Newcourt	35	Exhortation	188
Capello	61	Retreat	28			Fonntain	150
Crawford	98	Rockingham	99			Geer	235
Darley	306	Rolland	18	### C. M.		Geneva	71
Dorman	181	Rose Hill	292	Antioch	88	Glasgow	184, 396
Doxology	56	Rothwell	129	Arcadia	207	Grigg	101
Duke St	257, 400	Samson	130	Arlington	151	Haven	62
Dwight	237	Seasons	163	Armenia	234	Heber	239
Easton	314	Sessions	317	Arundel	147	Helena	101
Eisenach	341	Solitude	104	Augustus	368	Henry	36
El Paran	21	Spohr	260	Avon	106, 174	Hermon	190
Ernan	181	St. Alban	92	Azmon	126, 303	Holy Cross	239
Evening Hy	44	Stowell	28	Balerma	161	Howard	368
Federal St	232, 353	Truro	72	Barby	356	Hummel	147
Forest	72	Uxbridge	60	Belief	308	Huntington	263
Galilee	93	Ward	344	Belmont	313	Hymn	17
Germany	99	Ware	33, 293	Bemerton	11	Invitation	103
Gilead	34	Warner	175	Boardman	137	Iola	64
Grace Church	236	Warrington	261	Bond	290	Jazer	91
Gratitude	256	Wells	148	Bradford	125	Knox	62
Grostette	340	Welton	315	Bridgman	282	La Mira	234
Hamburg	105, 307	Willington	61	Brown	262	Lanesboro'	11
Happy Day	307	Woodworth	175, 282	Byefield	27	Land	77
Harmony Grove	93	Zephyr	135, 352	Caddo	174	Lutzen	74
Haslam	105			Cambridge	206	Maitland	209
Hebron	45	### L. M., 6 lines.		Chester	136	Manoah	79, 107
Hosanna	237	Admah	4	Chesterfield	189	Marlow	10
Hursley	44, 236	And Can It Be	265	Chimes	65	Mear	10
Ingham	162	Brownell	5	China	357	Melody	238
Linwood	30	Handy	271	Christmas	90, 208	Merton	36
Long	339	Memorial	229	Church	13	Miles Lane	127
Louvan	73	Palestine	270	Cincinnati	125	Monson	146
Loving-Kindness	152	Rakem	4	Colchester	27	Mt. Auburn	252
Lowry	21, 389	Solid Rock	265	Communion	106	Naomi	253
Luton	315	St. Matthias	55	Communion (No. 2)	309	Naumann	380
Mainzer	68	Yoakley	5	Cooling	191	Newbold	91
Melcombe	19			Corinth	253	New-York Tune	397
Mendon	339	### L. M. D.		Coronation	127	Noel	75
Migdol	19	Bennington	131	Coventry	380	Northfield	387
Missionary Ch	202, 341	Creation	69	Cowper	150	Oaksville	12
Oberlin	31			Dedham	323	Ortonville	102
G						Oxford	322

METRICAL INDEX.

	PAGE.
Palestrina	223
Peniel	238
Peterboro'	13
Ramsen	302
Return	161
Rhine	378
Rogers	209
Romberg	272
Serenity	189
Siloam	273, 303
Simpson	151
Southport	26, 235
St. Agnes	357
St. Ann's	74, 291
St. Martin's	291
Stephens	136
Tappan	369
Trent	100
Valentia	255
Verona	315
Warwick	17
Wirth	206
Woodland	381
Woodstock	26
York	64
Zerah	90

C. M. 5 lines.

Lanesboro'	11
Tappan	369
Woodland	381

C. M. D.

Athens	155
Brattle St.	70
Bryant	403
Canaan	386
Greenport	204
Heavenly Fold	312
Jerusalem	71
Jordan	373
Joyful Sound	379
St. Asaph	350
Varina	73, 372

C. P. M.

Ariel	241
Bremen	217
Ganges	145
Meribah	145, 358
Willoughby	216

S. M.

Adrian	319
Alexander	213
Badea	276
Barber	37
Bedan	297
Boylston	311
Braden	46
Carlisle	230
Clapton	211
Dawn	355
Dennis	211, 276
Detroit	160
Dover	342
Dunbar	355
Evening	47
Ferguson	267
Glory	15
Golden Hill	318
Good Cheer	254
Gorton	144
Greenwood	231, 361
Haverhill	372
Haydn	138
Inverness	304
Iowa	149
Laban	210
Langton	29
Leighton	212, 296
Lisbon	15
Luther	206, 342
Mornington	138
Olmutz	213, 354
Olney	139
Ontario	254
Owen	160, 310
Packington	16
Prayer	149

	PAGE.
Renovation	210
Rialto	222
Selvin	277
Shawmut	144
Shirland	29
Silver Street	37
St. Bride	343
St. Thomas	14
State Street	16
Stillingfleet	230
Thatcher	207
Vigil	372
Watchman	360
Whitefield	159
Wood	311

S. M. D.

Apollos	286
Benjamin	122
Diademata	123

S. P. M.

Dalston	1

H. M.

Haddam	287
Lenox	154
Lischer	6
Millennium	6
Warsaw	287

6s & 4s.

America	398
Bethany	186
Bread of Life	57
Cutting	412
Dort	124
Italian Hymn	85
Jesus, My All	172
Lyte	233
More Love	186
New Haven	141
Oak	370
Olivet	233, 304
Reden	187
Righini	124
Something for	187

6s & 5s.

St. Alban's	198
St. Gertrude	199

6s. D.

Jowett	278

7s.

Aletta	192, 321
Beminster	247
Chapel	2
Dallas	24
Dijon	3, 24
Easter Hymn	116
Fulton	140, 247
Hendon	2
Herold	25
Holley	49
Horton	164
Karl	246
Mercy	140, 275
Monkland	350
Mozart	117
Pleyel's Hymn	205, 321
Scudamore	117
Seymour	49
Solitude	194
Theodora	205
Trusting	192
Vienna	204
Weber	3

7s. 6 lines.

Betterland	391
Dix	25
Dykes	327
Guide	250
Halle	8

	PAGE.
Nuremburg	184
Pilot	401
Repose	251
Rock of Ages	326
Rosefield	250
Sabbath	7
Spanish Hymn	156, 240
Tharaw	184
Viola	251
Wilberforce	172

7s. Double.

Benevento	193, 395
Beulah	374
Blumenthal	84
Comfort	274
Eltham	338
Hamlin	40
Hollingside	194
Martyn	164, 195
Messiah	204
Onido	248
Perry	338
Refuge	195
St. George	394

7s & 6s.

Amsterdam	351
Geneva	351

7s & 6s.

Alford	377
Aurelia	178
Bernard	376
Caskey	214
Chenius	66
Ewing	385
Gerhardt	111
God's Love	402
Immortality	388
Mendebras	9
Miriam	67, 384
Missionary Hymn	332
Munich	333
Old, Old Story	158
Passion Chorale	110
Patmah	111
St. Hilda	179
St. James	375
Tell the Story	159
Tully	377
Webb	215, 334
Yarmouth	215

8s & 4s.

Wales	198

8s & 5s.

Pass Me Not	170

8s & 6s.

Flemming	279

8s & 7s.

Bartimeus	228
Carthage	114
Dorrnance	280, 324
Essex	200
Milwaukie	281
Pearl Street	325
Ratlibun	114, 336
Regent Square	88
Shepherd	324
Sicily	325
Solney	301
St. Sylvester	399
Stockwell	53, 301
Vesper	382
Westminster	300
Wilmot	229
Wilson	289

8s & 7s, D.

Austria	201
Autumn	121
Bavaria	305
Bayley	220

	PAGE.
Ellesdie	200
Faben	437
Gaylord	177
Greenville	53
Guidance	382
Harwell	119
Hymn of Joy	108
Love Divine	220
Middleton	289
Mission Song	298
Nettleton	316
Promise	115
St. Chad	81
Stoughton	288
Triste	280
Vesper Hymn	81
What a Friend	221

8s, 7s & 4s.

Brest	364
Calvary	120
Farland	120
Grace	166
Greenville	53
Hamden	337
Oliphant	52
Segur	52
Tamworth	364
Victory	381
Worship	314
Zion	337

8s, 7s & 7s.

Life	170
Millington	118, 359
St. Joseph	103

7s, 8s & 7s.

Long Home	349
Meinhold	349

7s, 6s & 8s.

Penitence	176

6s, 8s & 4s.

Leoni	38

10s.

Assurance	411
Eventide	48
Henley	328
Morning Praise	404
Pax Dei	48
Savannah	8

10s & 4s.

Lux Benigna	281

10s & 11s.

Houghton	224
Lyons	39

11s.

Cana	218
Expostulation	105
Frederick	348
Goshen	219, 242
Magill	243
Paulina	308
Portuguese Hymn	218

11s & 5s.

New Year's Hymn	398
Nightfall	50

11s & 10s.

A Little While	410
Avison	95
Come, ye Dis	167
Raynolds	329
Still Water	240
Wesley	335

12s.

Scotland	152
Frederick	348

INDEX OF AUTHORS.

The dates of decease are given in most instances; sometimes the date of birth. When neither of these is known, the date of publication is added in parentheses.

ADAMS, Mrs. Sarah Flower, d. 1849. *Hymn* 485.
ADDISON, Joseph, d. 1719. *Hymns* 8, 183, 187, 988, 1052.
ALEXANDER, Mrs. Cecil Frances, b. 1823. *Hymns* 324, 887, 973, 998.
ALEXANDER, Rev. James Waddell, D.D., d. 1859. *Hymns* 285, 290.
ALFORD, Rev. Henry, D.D., d. 1871. *Hymns* 979, 983, 1006, 1046.
ALLEN, Rev. James, d. 1804. *Hymns* 298, 869.
ALLEN, Rev. Jonathan, (1801). *Hymn* 433.
ANDERSON, Mrs. Maria Frances, b. 1819. *Hymn* 892.
ANSTICE, Joseph, d. 1836. *Hymn* 561.
AUBER, Miss Harriet, d. 1862. *Hymns* 54, 373, 791, 903.
AVELING, Rev. Thomas W., b. 1815. *Hymn* 786.

BACON, Rev. Leonard, D.D., b. 1802. *Hymns* 66, 905, 1053, 1060.
BAILEY, Mrs. Urania Locke, (1870). *Hymn* 447.
BAKER, Rev. and Sir Henry Williams, d. 1877. *Hymns* 216, 228, 820, 1043.
BAKEWELL, Rev. John, d. 1819. *Hymns* 282, 302.
BALDWIN, Rev. Thomas, D.D., d. 1825. *Hymn* 807.
BANCROFT, Mrs. Charitie Lees, b. 1841. *Hymn* 1001.
BARBAULD, Mrs. Anna Letitia, d. 1825. *Hymns* 53, 426, 674, 797, 942, 1050.
BARING-GOULD, Rev. Sabine, b. 1834. *Hymns* 141, 518, 1017.
BARTON, Bernard, d. 1849. *Hymn* 655.
BATHURST, Rev. William Hiley, b. 1796. *Hymns* 909, 970, 1008.
BAXTER, Rev. Richard, d. 1691. *Hymn* 537.
BEDDOME, Rev. Benjamin, d. 1795. *Hymns* 68, 160, 182, 352, 363, 416, 680, 712, 765, 818, 819, 825, 910, 979.
BEECHER, Rev. Charles, D.D., b. 1819. *Hymn* 1035.
BENNETT, Henry, (1851). *Hymn* 995.
BETHUNE, Rev. George W., D.D., d. 1862. *Hymns* 814, 917, 981.
BICKERSTETH, Rev. Edward Henry, b. 1825. *Hymns* 176, 873.
BLACKLOCK, Rev. Thomas, D.D., d. 1791. *Hymn* 220.
BLAIR, Rev. Robert, d. 1746. *Hymn* 969.
BLEW, Rev. William John, (1819). *Hymn* 122.
BONAR, Rev. Horatius, D.D., b. 1808. *Hymns* 220, 246, 276, 286, 396, 463, 502, 567, 633, 647, 651, 727, 748, 758, 790, 822, 916, 948, 959, 963, 992, 1015.
BORTHWICK, Miss Jane, b. 1825. *Hymns* 422, 449, 726, 893, 1021.
BOWDLER, Rev. John, d. 1815. *Hymns* 481, 583.
BOWRING, Sir John, LL.D., d. 1872. *Hymns* 132, 163, 225, 257, 300, 673, 730, 932.
BRIDGES, Matthew, d. 1852. *Hymns* 320, 322.
BROWN, Mrs. Phoebe Hinsdale, d. 1861. *Hymns* 18, 65, 915.
BROWNE, Rev. Simon, d. 1732. *Hymns* 354, 511.
BRUCE, Michael, d. 1767. *Hymns* 75, 1023.
BRYANT, William Cullen, d. 1878. *Hymns* 735, 760, 923, 1067.
BURDER, Rev. George, d. 1832. *Hymns* 50, 199.
BURDSALL, Richard, d. 1824. *Hymn* 402.
BURGESS, Rev. George, D.D., d. 1866. *Hymn* 546.
BURNHAM, Rev. Richard, d. 1810. *Hymn* 859.
BURNS, Rev. James Drummond, d. 1864. *Hymns* 120, 283.
BURTON, John, d. 1822. *Hymns* 379, 940.

CAMPBELL, Robert, d. 1868. *Hymn* 831.
CAMPBELL, Thomas, d. 1844. *Hymn* 242.
CARLYLE, Rev. Joseph Dacre, d. 1804. *Hymn* 22.
CAREY, ———. *Hymn* 572.
CARY, Miss Phoebe, d. 1871. *Hymn* 949.

CASWALL, Rev. Edward, d. 1878. *Hymns* 351, 614, 637, 1058.
CAWOOD, Rev. John, d. 1852. *Hymn* 234.
CENNICK, Rev. John, d. 1755. *Hymns* 334, 532.
CHANDLER, Rev. John, d. 1876. *Hymns* 40, 751.
CLEPHANE, Elizabeth C., (1870). *Hymn* 403.
CLEVELAND, Benjamin, (1790). *Hymn* 497.
CODNER, Elizabeth, (1860). *Hymn* 448.
COLES, Abram, M.D., (1875). *Hymn* 523.
COLESWORTHY, D. C., (1857). *Hymn* 153.
COLLYER, Rev. William Bengo, D.D., d. 1854. *Hymns* 442, 731, 908, 976.
CONDER, Josiah, d. 1855. *Hymns* 175, 178, 227, 261, 451, 852, 1019.
COOPER, John, (1808). *Hymn* 179.
COTTERILL, Rev. Thomas, d. 1823. *Hymns* 85, 360.
COUSIN, Mrs. Anne Ross, (1857). *Hymns* 587, 1037.
COWPER, William, d. 1800. *Hymns* 52, 74, 77, 173, 200, 398, 493, 555, 626, 659, 720, 754, 856.
COX, Frances Elizabeth, (1841). *Hymns* 827, 936.
COXE, Rev. Arthur Cleveland, D.D., b. 1818. *Hymns* 258, 757.
CREWDSON, Mrs. Jane Fox, d. 1863. *Hymns* 709, 1081.
CROSWELL, Rev. William, d. 1851. *Hymn* 795.
CUTTING, Rev. Sewall S., D.D., (1876). *Hymn* 462.

DANA, Mrs. Mary S. B., b. 1810. *Hymn* 1000.
DAVIES, Rev. Samuel, d. 1761. *Hymn* 812.
DAVIS, Rev. Thomas, (1864). *Hymn* 1031.
DECK, James George, (1837). *Hymns* 289, 601, 637, 721.
DE FLEURY, Maria, (1791). *Hymn* 625.
DENNY, Sir Edward, b. 1796. *Hymns* 263, 264, 272, 865, 1024, 1026, 1029.
DEXTER, Rev. Henry Martyn, D.D., b. 1821. *Hymn* 803.
DICKSON, Rev. David, d. 1662. *Hymn* 1007.
DIX, William Chatterton, b. 1837. *Hymn* 63.
DOANE, Rev. George Washington, D.D., d. 1859. *Hymns* 129, 265.
DOBELL, John, d. 1840. *Hymn* 418.
DODDRIDGE, Rev. Philip, D.D., d. 1751. *Hymns* 34, 44, 71, 118, 150, 184, 228, 253, 349, 353, 423, 506, 539, 542, 549, 603, 612, 668, 684, 685, 690, 761, 767, 794, 798, 799, 813, 830, 843, 913, 921, 958, 980, 1056, 1061, 1062.
DRYDEN John, d. 1700. *Hymn* 377.
DUFFIELD, Rev. George, D.D., b. 1818. *Hymns* 557, 617.
DUNN, Rev. Robinson P., D.D., d. 1867. *Hymns* 504, 965.
DWIGHT, Rev. Timothy, D.D., d. 1817. *Hymns* 12, 35.
DYER, Rev. Sidney, b. 1814. *Hymn* 783.

EDMESTON, James, d. 1867. *Hymns* 135, 139, 149, 526, 590, 713, 722, 776.
ELLERTON, Rev. John, b. 1826. *Hymn* 128.
ELLIOTT, Miss Charlotte, d. 1871. *Hymns* 457, 508, 715, 728, 738, 968.
ELVEN, Rev. Cornelius, b. 1797. *Hymn* 456.
ENFIELD, Rev. William, D.D., d. 1797. *Hymn* 262.
EVANS, Rev. Jonathan, d. 1809. *Hymn* 315.

FABER, Rev. Frederick William, D.D., d. 1863. *Hymns* 142, 214, 235, 269, 480, 538, 648, 654, 889, 993.
FANCH, Rev. James, (1794). *Hymn* 321.
FAWCETT, Rev. John, D.D., d. 1817. *Hymns* 104, 165, 203, 823.
FELLOWS, John, (1773). *Hymn* 801.
FITCH, Rev. Eleazar T., D.D., d. 1871. *Hymn* 124.
FORD, Rev. David Everard, (1828). *Hymn* 954.
FRANCIS, Rev. Benjamin, d. 1799. *Hymn* 624.
FRY, Mrs. Caroline (Wilson), d. 1846. *Hymn* 622.
FORNEY, Lydia A., (1881). *Hymn* 834.
GATES, Mrs. Ellen H., (1868). *Hymn* 785.

INDEX OF AUTHORS.

GIBBONS, Rev. Thomas, D.D., *d.* 1785. *Hymn* 1032.
GILL, Rev. Thomas Hornblower, *b.* 1819. *Hymns* 592, 646.
GILMORE, Rev. J. H., *b.* 1834. *Hymn* 737.
GOODE, Rev. William, *d.* 1816. *Hymns* 317, 514, 982.
GOUGH, Benjamin, *b.* 1805. *Hymn* 691.
GRANT, Sir Robert, *d.* 1838. *Hymns* 98, 161, 222, 501, 708.
GRIGG, Rev. Joseph, *d.* 1768. *Hymns* 421, 597.
GURNEY, Rev. John Hampden, *d.* 1862. *Hymn* 266.
GUYON, Mme. Jeanne M. B. de la M., *d.* 1717. *Hymn* 742.

HALL, Mrs. E. M., (1870). *Hymn* 410.
HAMMOND, Rev. William, *d.* 1783. *Hymns* 2, 32, 371, 443.
HANAFORD, Mrs. J. H., (1852). *Hymn* 792.
HANKEY, Miss Katharine, (1665). *Hymns* 413, 414.
HART, Rev. Joseph, *d.* 1768. *Hymns* 117, 126, 361, 432.
HARTSOUGH, Rev. L., (1872). *Hymn* 411.
HASTINGS, Thomas, *d.* 1872. *Hymns* 15, 419, 423, 440, 472, 503, 536, 615, 667, 698, 724, 733, 739, 793, 881, 883, 896, 928.
HAVERGAL, Miss Frances Ridley, (1872). *Hymn* 618.
HAWEIS, Rev. Thomas, M.D., *d.* 1820. *Hymns* 412, 455, 639.
HAWKS, Mrs. Annie Sherwood, *b.* 1835. *Hymn* 484.
HAYWARD, —— (1806). *Hymn* 10.
HEATH, Rev. George, *b.* 1781. *Hymn* 547.
HEBER, Rev. Reginald, D.D., *d.* 1826. *Hymns* 96, 250, 716, 800, 890, 934, 938, 984.
HEDGE, Rev. Frederick H., D.D., *b.* 1805. *Hymns* 215, 287.
HEGINBOTHAM, Rev. Ottiwell, *d.* 1768. *Hymns* 162, 632.
HEMANS, Mrs. Felicia Dorothea, *d.* 1835. *Hymn* 291.
HERRICK, Rev. Robert, *d.* 1674. *Hymn* 718.
HILL, Rev. Rowland, *d.* 1833. *Hymns* 719, 768.
HILLHOUSE, Augustus L., *d.* 1859. *Hymn* 477.
HINSDALE, Mrs. Grace W., (1865). *Hymn* 528.
HOLMES, Oliver Wendell, M.D., *b.* 1809. *Hymns* 191, 609.
HOPKINS, Rev. Josiah, *d.* 1862. *Hymn* 427.
HOW, Rev. William Walsham, *b.* 1823. *Hymns* 174, 464, 780.
HUMPHREYS, Rev. Joseph, *b.* 1720. *Hymn* 640.
HUNTINGTON, Selina, Countess of, *d.* 1791. *Hymns* 133, 957.
HURN, Rev. William, *d.* 1829. *Hymn* 239.
HUTTON, James, *d.* 1795. *Hymn* 46.
HYDE, Mrs. Ann Beadley, *d.* 1872. *Hymn* 417.

JERVIS, Rev. Thomas, *d.* 1793. *Hymn* 33.
JOHNS, Rev. Henry D., (1865). *Hymn* 915.
JOHNSON, Rev. Samuel, *b.* 1822. *Hymns* 788, 879.
JONES, Rev. Edmund, *d.* 1765. *Hymn* 420.
JOYCE, Rev. James, *d.* 1850. *Hymn* 922.
JUDSON, Rev. Adoniram, *d.* 1850. *Hymns* 809, 810.

KEBLE, Rev. John, *d.* 1866. *Hymns* 112, 201, 370, 652, 662.
KEITH, George, (1787). *Hymn* 563.
KELLY, Rev. Thomas, *d.* 1855. *Hymns* 6, 56, 57, 137, 306, 309, 310, 311, 312, 314, 318, 328, 544, 551, 630, 835, 900, 956.
KEN, Rev. Thomas, D.D., *d.* 1711. *Hymns* 48, 80, 113.
KENT, John, *d.* 1843. *Hymn* 692.
KETHE, Rev. William, (1561). *Hymn* 79.
KEY, Francis Scott, *d.* 1843. *Hymn* 212.
KNOLLIS, Rev. Francis Minden, (1860). *Hymn* 1040.
KNOX, ——. *Hymn* 429.

LANGE, Rev. Ernest, *d.* 1727. *Hymn* 641.
LATHBURY, Miss Mary A., (1877). *Hymns* 145, 1072.
LAURENTI, Laurentius, *d.* 1722. *Hymn* 218.
LEE, Richard, (1794). *Hymn* 283.
LELAND, Rev. John, (1799). *Hymn* 123.
LLOYD, William Freeman, *d.* 1853. *Hymns* 584, 740.
LOWRY, Rev. Robert, D.D., (1868). *Hymn* 430.
LUTHER, Rev. Martin, D.D., *d.* 1546. *Hymn* 243.
LYTE, Rev. Henry Francis, *d.* 1847. *Hymns* 24, 49, 94, 127, 473, 520, 521, 552, 683, 927, 1069.

MACKAY, Mrs. Margaret, (1832). *Hymn* 944.
MACDUFF, Rev. John Robert, D.D., (1853). *Hymn* 1014.
MACKELLAR, Thomas, *b.* 1812. *Hymn* 1030.
MADAN, Rev. Martin, *d.* 1790. *Hymn* 533.
MANT, Rev. Richard, D.D., *d.* 1848. *Hymns* 211, 213, 872, 960.
MARCH, Rev. Daniel, D.D., *b.* 1816. *Hymn* 734.

MARRIOTT, Rev. John, *d.* 1825. *Hymn* 369.
MARSHMAN, Rev. Joshua, *d.* 1837. *Hymn* 834.
MASON, William, *d.* 1791. *Hymn* 1070.
MASSIE, Richard, (1859). *Hymns* 1002, 1003.
MAUDE, Mrs. Mary F., (1848). *Hymn* 854.
McCHEYNE, Rev. Robert Murray, *d.* 1843. *Hymns* 619, 670.
McCOMB, ——. *Hymn* 453.
McDONALD, Rev. William, (1870). *Hymn* 498.
MEDLEY, Rev. Samuel, *d.* 1799. *Hymns* 254, 393, 399, 404, 470, 616.
MERRICK, Rev. James, *d.* 1769. *Hymns* 4, 507.
MILLARD, Rev. James Elwin, D.D., (1848). *Hymn* 101.
MILTON, John, *d.* 1674. *Hymn* 99.
MITCHELL, Rev. William, (1831). *Hymn* 267.
MONTGOMERY, James, *d.* 1854. *Hymns* 3, 23, 67, 100, 107, 130, 146, 156, 221, 259, 336, 365, 340, 381, 439, 445, 522, 564, 580, 582, 710, 763, 766, 774, 779, 782, 841, 855, 857, 862, 888, 894, 902, 931, 946, 962, 971, 972, 999.
MOORE, Thomas, *d.* 1852. *Hymn* 431.
MORRIS, George P., (1858). *Hymn* 495.
MORRISON, Rev. John, D.D., *d.* 1798. *Hymn* 237.
MOTE, Rev. Edward, *b.* 1797. *Hymn* 688.
MOULTRIE, ——. *Hymn* 653.
MUHLENBERG, Rev. William Augustus, D.D., *d.* 1877. *Hymns* 247, 806, 847, 933.

NASON, Rev. Elias, (1857). *Hymn* 586.
NEALE, Rev. John Mason, D.D., *d.* 1866. *Hymns* 119, 340, 569, 1004, 1005, 1020, 1022, 1023.
NEEDHAM, Rev. John, (1768). *Hymns* 210, 535.
NELSON, Rev. David, M.D., *d.* 1844. *Hymn* 1010.
NETTLETON, Rev. Asahel, D.D., *d.* 1844. *Hymn* 650.
NEVIN, Rev. Edwin H., D.D., *b.* 1814. *Hymns* 588, 643.
NEWMAN, Rev. John Henry, D.D., *b.* 1801. *Hymn* 734.
NEWTON, Rev. John, *d.* 1807. *Hymns* 13, 61, 62, 70, 72, 76, 108, 115, 138, 155, 279, 400, 482, 496, 499, 515, 574, 576, 585, 611, 613, 623, 628, 638, 642, 658, 705, 753, 897, 975, 1048.
NEWCOMER, M. S., (1881). *Hymns* 830, 832.
NOEL, Hon. and Rev. Gerard Thomas, *d.* 1851. *Hymns* 713, 864.

OCCOM, Rev. Samson, *d.* 1792. *Hymn* 383.
OLIVERS, Rev. Thomas, *d.* 1799. *Hymn* 95.
ONDERDONK, Rev. Henry Ustick, D.D., *d.* 1868. *Hymns* 441, 802.

PALMER, Rev. Ray, D.D., *b.* 1808. *Hymns* 17, 193, 261, 294, 330, 332, 368, 460, 465, 598, 600, 604, 606, 608, 621, 828, 885, 952, 996, 1033, 1034, 1047.
PARK, Rev. Roswell, D.D., *d.* 1869. *Hymn* 866.
PEABODY, Rev. William B. O., D.D., *d.* 1847. *Hymn* 937.
PERRONET, Rev. Edward, *d.* 1792. *Hymn* 329.
PETERS, Mrs. Mary Bowly, *d.* 1856. *Hymn* 519.
PHELPS, Rev. Sylvanus Dryden, D.D., (1862). *Hymn* 488.
PIERPONT, Rev. John, *d.* 1866. *Hymn* 154.
PIERSON, Rev. Arthur T., D.D., (1873). *Hymn* 219.
PIRRIE, Rev. Alexander, *d.* 1804. *Hymn* 327.
POPE, Alexander, *d.* 1744. *Hymn* 967.
POTTER, Rev. Thomas J., (1867). *Hymn* 517.
PRENTISS, Mrs. Elizabeth P., *d.* 1878. *Hymn* 486.

RAFFLES, Rev. Thomas, D.D., *d.* 1863. *Hymns* 55, 686.
RANKIN, Rev. J. E., (1855). *Hymn* 478.
RANDOLPH, Anson D. F., (1865). *Hymn* 483.
RAWSON, George, *b.* 1837. *Hymns* 374, 877.
REED, Rev. Andrew, D.D., *d.* 1862. *Hymns* 256, 366, 702, 743.
RIPPON, Rev. John, D.D., *d.* 1836. *Hymn* 376.
ROBINSON, Rev. Charles S., D.D., (1862). *Hymn* 487.
ROBINSON, George, (1842). *Hymn* 752.
ROBINSON, Rev. Robert, *d.* 1790. *Hymns* 316, 876.
ROSCOE, Rev. J. ——. *Hymn* 736.
ROWE, Rev. John, *d.* 1832. *Hymn* 870.
RYLAND, Rev. John, *d.* 1825. *Hymn* 816.

SANDYS, George, *d.* 1644. *Hymn* 103.
SCOTT, Elizabeth, (1764). *Hymn* 190.
SCOTT, Rev. Thomas, *d.* 1776. *Hymn* 297.
SCOTT, Sir Walter, *d.* 1832. *Hymn* 981.
SEAGRAVE, Rev. Robert, *b.* 1693. *Hymn* 939.
SEARS, Rev. Edmund Hamilton, D.D., *d.* 1876. *Hymns* 240, 248.
SHEPHERD, Thomas, *d.* 1739. *Hymn* 543.
SHERWIN, William F., (1872). *Hymns* 461, 1065, 1083.
SHIRLEY, Rev. Walter, *d.* 1786. *Hymns* 136, 704.
SHRUBSOLE, Rev. William, *d.* 1797. *Hymns* 9, 904, 906.
SIGOURNEY, Mrs. Lydia H. H., *d.* 1865. *Hymns* 362, 706.

G

INDEX OF SCRIPTURE TEXTS. 421

SLINN, Sarah, (1779). *Hymn* 251.
SMITH, Mrs. Caroline Sprague, (1855). *Hymn* 747.
SMITH, Rev. Samuel F., D.D., *b.* 1808. *Hymns* 5, 599, 815, 684, 895, 947, 1059.
SMYTHE, Rev. Edwin, (1793). *Hymn* 148.
STEELE, Miss Anne, *d.* 1778. *Hymns* 7, 37, 51, 114, 125, 164, 172, 192, 198, 252, 270, 296, 333, 355, 385, 409, 454, 466, 494, 510, 527, 578, 605, 649, 703, 759, 762, 831, 882, 945, 1012, 1039.
STENNETT, Rev. Joseph, D.D., *d.* 1713. *Hymn* 47.
STENNETT, Rev. Samuel, D.D., *d.* 1795. *Hymns* 28, 59, 268, 274, 344, 471, 676, 989.
STERNHOLD, Thomas, *d.* 1549. *Hymn* 231.
STEWART, ———, (1803). *Hymn* 356.
STOCKER, John, (1776). *Hymn* 367.
STONE, Rev. Samuel J., (1866). *Hymn* 771.
STOWELL, Rev. Hugh, *d.* 1865. *Hymn* 69.
STRONG, Rev. Nathan, D.D., *d.* 1816. *Hymn* 1049.
STRYKER, Rev. Peter, D.D., (1869). *Hymn* 346.
SWAIN, Rev. Joseph, *d.* 1796. *Hymns* 530, 545, 829.

TAPPAN, Rev. William Bingham, *d.* 1849. *Hymns* 273, 1011, 1013.
TATE, Nahum, *d.* 1715. *Hymns* 203, 238, 671.
TAYLOR, Miss Emily, (1864). *Hymn* 60.
TAYLOR, Rev. Thomas R., *d.* 1835. *Hymn* 994.
THOMPSON, Rev. John, *d.* 1818. *Hymn* 207.
THRUPP, Miss Dorothy Ann, *d.* 1847. *Hymn* 804.
THRUPP, Rev. Joseph F., (1860). *Hymn* 282.
TOKE, Mrs. Emma, *b.* 1812. *Hymn* 319.
TOPLADY, Rev. Augustus M., *d.* 1778. *Hymns* 372, 452, 553, 711, 723, 874.
TURNER, Rev. Daniel, *d.* 1798. *Hymn* 656.

VAN ALSTYNE, Mrs. Fanny Crosby, (1869). *Hymns* 446, 450, 459, 568, 1036.
VOKE, Mrs. ———, (1806). *Hymns* 775, 907, 912.

WALFORD, Rev. William W., (1849). *Hymn* 73.
WARDLAW, Rev. Ralph, D.D., *d.* 1853. *Hymn* 629.

WARING, Miss Anna Letitia, (1850). *Hymn* 556.
WARNER, Miss Anna B., ———. *Hymn* 140.
WATERBURY, Rev. Jared B., D.D., *d.* 1876. *Hymn* 444.
WATTS, Rev. Isaac, D.D., *d.* 1748. *Hymns* 1, 11, 19, 20, 21, 25, 26, 29, 30, 31, 36, 38, 39, 41, 42, 43, 45, 58, 78, 81, 82, 83, 84, 86, 87, 88, 89, 90, 91, 92, 93, 109, 116, 121, 151, 158, 159, 166, 167, 168, 169, 170, 171, 186, 188, 189, 195, 196, 197, 200, 202, 204, 206, 208, 230, 233, 236, 244, 260, 275, 277, 278, 280, 295, 325, 326, 331, 335, 337, 338, 341, 342, 345, 347, 348, 350, 357, 359, 382, 386, 387, 388, 389, 390, 391, 392, 395, 401, 407, 434, 435, 436, 437, 438, 468, 469, 474, 509, 513, 524, 525, 529, 540, 541, 550, 571, 593, 595, 596, 610, 636, 657, 661, 663, 664, 665, 669, 677, 679, 681, 682, 693, 695, 696, 699, 701, 725, 741, 749, 770, 772, 777, 811, 827, 833, 836, 839, 845, 861, 911, 919, 920, 924, 925, 930, 941, 943, 950, 953, 955, 964, 987, 990, 991, 997, 1027, 1041, 1055, 1068.
WESLEY, Rev. Charles, *d.* 1788. *Hymns* 14, 27, 97, 102, 106, 111, 147, 223, 245, 299, 303, 305, 307, 323, 339, 378, 384, 397, 405, 406, 425, 458, 467, 476, 479, 489, 490, 504, 507, 508, 516, 558, 566, 578, 589, 644, 666, 672, 689, 694, 750, 755, 756, 824, 826, 846, 849, 850, 863, 875, 880, 914, 929, 986, 1057.
WESLEY, Rev. John, *d.* 1791. *Hymns* 110, 288, 554, 591, 607, 700.
WHITE, Henry Kirke, *d.* 1806. *Hymns* 194, 241, 951.
WHITTIER, John G., *b.* 1808. *Hymns* 271, 729.
WILLIAMS, Miss Helen Maria, *d.* 1827. *Hymn* 185.
WILLIAMS, Rev. William, *d.* 1791. *Hymns* 134, 401.
WILLIS, Nathaniel P., *d.* 1867. *Hymn* 764.
WINKWORTH, Miss Catharine, *b.* 1829. *Hymns* 131, 217, 308, 500, 594, 691, 935, 1018.
WOLFE, Rev. Aaron R., *b.* 1821. *Hymns* 675, 745, 842, 844.
WOLCOTT, Rev. Samuel, D.D., (1869). *Hymn* 1086.
WOODBURY, Isaac B., *d.* 1858. *Hymn* 577.
WORDSWORTH, Rev. Christopher, D.D., *b.* 1807. *Hymns* 16, 313, 526, 1016.
WREFORD, Rev. John R., D.D., (1837). *Hymns* 645, 1051.
WINEBRENNER, John, *d.* 1860. *Hymn* 833.
YOUNG, ———, *Hymn* 232.
ZINZENDORF, Count Nicholas Ludwig, *d.* 1760. *Hymn* 502.

INDEX OF SCRIPTURE TEXTS.

GENESIS.
CH.VER.	HYMN.
1:1 ...78, 93, 99, 183	
1:2 ...369, 351, 377	
1:3 ...369, 147, 99	
1:16 ...99, 205, 196	
1:26 ...608, 221, 605	
2:3 ...16, 94, 122	
3:8 ...200, 188, 202	
3:19 ...951, 943, 963	
5:24 ...493, 487, 556	
6:3 ...428, 355, 974	
7:1 ...841, 508, 505	
16:13 ...188, 200, 202	
17:7 ...527, 684, 563	
18:25 ...182, 193, 195	
19:17 ...402, 428, 424	
22:14 ...574, 555, 576	
28:16 ...485, 64, 56	
28:20 ...734, 804, 737	
32:26 ...2, 77, 62, 70

EXODUS.
3:14....95, 180, 78
13:21....134, 753, 755
16:15....134, 753, 755
25:17-22...69, 74, 450
28:29....349, 333, 327

LEVITICUS.
16:21...382, 280, 408
19:2 ...652, 489, 650

G

NUMBERS.
CH.VER.	HYMN.
21:8, 9...257, 470, 288	
23:10...942, 947, 678	
23:19...189, 161, 208	

DEUTERONOMY.
3:25...997, 980, 1010
12:9 ...1015, 939, 1036
30:19...361, 384, 423
31:6 ...563, 555, 574
32:11...709, 187, 525
32:49...989, 997, 1010
33:25...706, 455, 584
33:27...531, 529, 747

JOSHUA.
1:8 .....27, 65, 168
1:11...941, 952, 969
23:14...189, 208, 553

JUDGES.
8:4 ...565, 768, 734

RUTH.
1:16...837, 857, 640

1ST SAMUEL.
1:13......660, 67, 77
3:18...182, 722, 727
7:12...518, 705, 576
20:3 ...176, 943, 1010

2ND SAMUEL.
CH.VER.	HYMN.
12:23...935, 951, 945	
22:31...163, 167, 173	
23:4 ...555, 735, 111	

1ST KINGS.
8:57.1060, 1059, 772
18:21...424, 422, 428

2ND KINGS.
7:3 ...420, 423, 428

1ST CHRONICLES.
29:15...956, 954, 963

2ND CHRONICLES.
30:18...860, 854, 877

EZRA.
9:6 ...877, 447, 470

NEHEMIAH.
4:6 ...779, 804, 783

ESTHER.
4:16...420, 423, 428

JOB.
CH.VER.	HYMN.
1:21...709, 622, 712	
3:17...969, 620, 961	
7:16...933, 941, 953	
9:33...283, 382, 405	
11:7 ...180, 190, 192	
13:15...713, 705, 643	
19:25...323, 333, 304	
22:21...429, 27, 648	
23:10...556, 720, 722	
26:14...194, 206, 88	
35:10...575, 107, 31	
37:21...713, 709, 622	

PSALMS.
3:8 ...401, 696, 895
3:3 ...36, 40, 46, 48
14:2 ...385, 388, 300
14:7 ...927, 401, 696
15:1 ...394, 7, 9, 22
16:8 ...258, 260, 266
17:15...955, 526, 304
18:10...231, 88, 98
19:1 ..158, 175, 183
21:1 ...595, 564, 636
23:2 ...578, 8, 4, 602
23:5 ...831, 834, 634
24:10...339, 312, 311
25:15...550, 620, 346
27:8 ...91, 27, 2, 12
29:3 ...88, 98, 194

CH.VER.	HYMN.
30:7 ...482, 496, 502	
31:5 ...552, 703, 726	
31:15..740, 712, 727	
32:7 ...686, 683, 871	
32:8 ...600, 487, 737	
34:6 ...671, 185, 732	
35:7 ...408, 553, 186	
36:9 ...84, 111, 191	
37:25...563, 933, 747	
39:12.1000, 728, 958	
41:1 ...797, 785, 807	
42:1 ...473, 21, 29	
43:3 ...12, 158, 145	
45:1 ...331, 341, 345	
46:1 ...919, 215, 560	
47:5 ...307, 347, 311	
48:1 ...78, 770, 772	
50:15..522, 563, 671	
51:2 ...468, 417, 453	
51:10..868, 385, 458	
53:2 ...385, 348, 394	
55:22..719, 705, 732	
56:3 ...536, 643, 554	
56:12..857, 854, 833	
60:4 ...551, 517, 753	
61:2 ...699, 522, 545	
63:1 ...29, 21, 473	
65:1 ...92, 49, 3, 93	
66:16..818, 187, 185	
66:18...22, 664, 650	
71:5 ...348, 187, 185	

INDEX OF SCRIPTURE TEXTS.

CH.VER.	HYMN.
72 : 8	..894, 911, 920
73 : 24..743, 184, 634
73 : 25..503, 222, 466
77 : 20..580, 775, 573
80 : 19..925, 918, 897
84 : 1 ..26, 11, 38, 304
84 : 11...39, 753, 655
85 : 9 ..696, 401, 407
87 : 3 ..924, 753, 655
89 : 1 ..1068, 187, 657
90 : 1 ..964, 176, 943
91 : 1 ..522, 698, 536
92 : 1 ..43, 54, 50, 103
95 : 1 ...93, 1077, 31
98 : 1 ..236, 270, 246
100 : 1 ......78, 79, 104
102 : 13.930, 236, 1014
103 : 13...41, 669, 725
107 : 15.100, 1052, 1033
112 : 6 ..678, 943, 960
116 : 7 ..186, 594, 527
117 : 1 ....82, 86, 90
118 : 24...19, 6, 13, 16
119 : 9 ..170, 179, 165
119 : 71..167, 168, 109
119 : 105.166, 171, 164
119 : 151.191, 485, 567
125 : 2 ..571, 547, 576
126 : 6 ..793, 1011, 546
127 : 1 ..791, 805, 522
130 : 1 .1073, 613, 493
131 : 1 ..642, 672, 685
132 : 8 ......777, 33, 97
135 : 1 .....42, 104, 97
136 : 1 ..435, 99, 1069
137 : 3 ..35, 1, 20, 753
138 : 2 ..235, 163, 167
139 : 1 ..188, 202, 200
139 : 17..207, 187, 195
139 : 23..485, 306, 650
145 : 18...89, 197, 213

PROVERBS.
| 4 : 18...078, 937, 722 |
| 8 : 17...810, 812, 815 |
| 11 : 30..784, 804, 762 |
| 18 : 24..585, 594, 568 |
| 23 : 26...868, 400, 458 |

ECCLESIASTES.
| 9 : 10...963, 442, 428 |
| 11 : 1 ...792, 782, 783 |
| 11 : 6 ..782, 779, 781 |
| 11 : 9 ...988, 974, 973 |
| 12 : 1 ...810, 812, 815 |

CANTICLES.
| 1 : 7, 8..615, 556, 565 |
| 2 : 16...575, 595, 587 |
| 4 : 16...897, 755, 368 |
| 5 : 1 ...850, 861, 866 |

ISAIAH.
| 1 : 18...411, 407, 415 |
| 2 : 2 .1028, 1049, 1051 |
| 6 : 3 ...96, 221, 1064 |
| 7 : 14...244, 245, 628 |
| 9 : 6 ...237, 246, 243 |
| 21 : 11...932, 895, 905 |
| 26 : 3 ..694, 840, 097 |
| 28 : 16...751, 771, 753 |
| 32 : 17..697, 688, 1003 |
| 33 : 17.1024, 1018, 1037 |
| 35 : 10..542, 544, 1036 |
| 40 : 11..564, 556, 532 |
| 40 : 31..525, 790, 568 |
| 43 : 2 ...563, 554, 537 |
| 45 : 22...470, 382, 482 |
| 49 : 14...759, 754, 897 |
| 52 : 7 ..891, 749, 900 |
| 53 : 4-7..276, 280, 285 |
| 54 : 8 ...735, 745, 705 |
| 55 : 1 ...398, 402, 445 |
| 57 : 20...426, 423, 430 |
| 60 : 1, 2..921, 542, 906 |
| 60 18..754, 905, 1028 |

CH.VER.	HYMN.
61 : 10...407, 469, 607
63 : 1 ...310, 280, 277
63 : 3 ...853, 263, 286

JEREMIAH.
| 2 : 2 ..854, 1024, 345 |
| 3 : 4 ..134, 411, 631 |
| 8 : 20...428, 422, 974 |
| 17 : 0 ..385, 390, 868 |
| 23 : 6 ..688, 607, 390 |

LAMENTATIONS.
| 1 : 4 ..897, 907, 357 |
| 3 : 26...522, 537, 553 |

EZEKIEL.
| 11 : 19...868, 458, 385 |
| 33 : 11...427, 419, 425 |
| 36 : 37...67, 77, 64, 71 |

DANIEL.
| 12 : 2 ...938, 988, 053 |
| 12 : 3 ..762, 804, 502 |

HOSEA.
| 11 : 8 ..500, 836, 471 |
| 13 : 9 ..382, 386, 390 |
| 14 : 1 ...419, 427, 411 |

JOEL.
| 2 : 1 ...975, 976, 983 |
| 3 : 14...384, 424, 392 |

AMOS.
| 3 : 3 ...419, 429, 426 |
| 4 : 12...976, 429, 963 |

JONAH.
| 2 : 9 ...401, 696, 522 |
| 3 : 10...500, 836, 471 |

MICAH.
| 2 : 10.1015, 1036, 904 |
| 6 : 6 ...382, 386, 396 |

NAHUM.
| 1 : 3 ...073, 468, 202 |
| 1 : 13...591, 749, 900 |

HABAKKUK.
| 2 : 4 .1003, 1002, 661 |
| 3 : 2 ...918, 897, 357 |
| 3 : 17...535, 661, 522 |

ZEPHANIAH.
| 3 : 17...754, 836, 553 |

HAGGAI.
| 2 : 7 ...756, 914, 787 |

ZECHARIAH.
| 1 : 5 ...953, 947, 960 |
| 4 : 6 ...353, 380, 735 |
| 4 : 10..796, 662, 802 |
| 9 : 9 ...10..283, 288, 974 |
| 12 : 10..283, 288, 974 |
| 13 : 1 ...398, 402, 445 |
| 13 : 7 ...395, 437, 335 |
| 14 : 7 ...707, 937, 942 |

MALACHI.
| 3 : 2 ...988, 973, 271 |
| 3 : 6 ...531, 522, 176 |
| 4 : 2 ......14, 158, 913 |

MATTHEW.
| 1 : 21...613, 601, 246 |
| 2 : 0 ...241, 1067, 63 |
| 4 : 1 ...292, 260, 590 |
| 5 : 3 ...491, 729, 642 |
| 5 : 4 ...735, 718, 709 |
| 5 : 5 ...646, 649, 645 |
| 5 : 6 ...390, 411, 392 |
| 5 : 7 ...264, 266, 800 |

CH.VER.	HYMN.
5 : 8 ...652, 650, 693
5 : 9 ...823, 825, 264
5 : 10...838, 548, 509
5 : 16...664, 640, 670
6 : 9 ...143, 146, 691
6 : 10...894, 915, 916
6 : 10...710, 730, 738
6 : 11...555, 561, 567
6 : 12...264, 268, 800
6 : 13...143, 530, 548
7 : 7 ...70, 76, 72, 567
7 : 14...392, 389, 381
7 : 24...688, 1003, 840
9 : 36...750, 798, 784
10 : 32...541, 597, 856
10 : 42...806, 795, 801
11 : 25...101, 631, 642
11 : 28...426, 431, 411
13 : 17...749, 891, 413
14 : 27...715, 620, 563
16 : 18..757, 771, 688
16 : 24...803, 520, 392
17 : 8 ...586, 620, 617
18 : 3 ...642, 631, 480
18 : 11...239, 270, 403
18 : 20......59, 74, 71
19 : 14..809, 812, 815
21 : 22.......70, 61, 76
24 : 44...938, 963, 976
25 : 13.1025, 1024, 1021
25 : 34..986, 1019, 1018
25 : 40...780, 801, 806
25 : 41..987, 983, 1058
26 : 41..530, 547, 557
26 : 75...438, 447, 430
27 : 30...283, 285, 279
28 : 6 ...305, 319, 339
28 : 20...523, 588, 563

MARK.
| 6 : 34...259, 264, 794 |
| 7 : 50...715, 620, 543 |
| 8 : 34...803, 520, 802 |
| 8 : 38...549, 587, 614 |
| 9 : 24...375, 300, 645 |
| 10 : 14...812, 809, 815 |
| 13 : 37...547, 530, 557 |

LUKE.
| 1 : 73......14, 111, 755 |
| 2 : 13...234, 235, 238 |
| 9 : 23...803, 520, 392 |
| 9 : 25...541, 597, 856 |
| 10 : 2 ...750, 798, 784 |
| 10 : 21...101, 631, 642 |
| 10 : 39...785, 702, 631 |
| 10 : 42...303, 423, 484 |
| 11 : 13...379, 368, 357 |
| 12 : 32...759, 754, 758 |
| 13 : 6 ...181, 197, 500 |
| 15 : 7 ...403, 321, 427 |
| 15 : 18...412, 419, 424 |
| 18 : 1 ......70, 62, 77 |
| 18 : 13...456, 446, 468 |
| 18 : 16...809, 812, 815 |
| 19 : 10...239, 270, 403 |
| 19 : 41...416, 264, 794 |
| 22 : 44...273, 276, 291 |
| 23 : 34...258, 264, 260 |
| 23 : 42...398, 405, 432 |
| 24 : 29...127, 621, 112 |

JOHN.
| 1 : 1 ...174, 244, 218 |
| 1 : 29...281, 382, 457 |
| 3 : 3 ...383, 385, 391 |
| 3 : 14...287, 283, 260 |
| 3 : 16...438, 257, 270 |
| 4 : 35...784, 798, 750 |
| 4 : 37...802, 794, 792 |
| 5 : 39...164, 172, 174 |
| 6 : 20...715, 620, 563 |
| 6 : 35...849, 145, 608 |
| 6 : 38...526, 548, 530 |
| 9 : 4 ...804, 783, 779 |
| 9 : 25...400, 630, 413 |
| 10 : 11...556, 564, 545 |
| 11 : 25...526, 977, 936 |

CH.VER.	HYMN.
11 : 35...272, 264, 708
12 : 21...378, 596, 604
12 : 32..297, 290, 248
13 : 7 ...722, 723, 195
13 : 34...832, 824, 641
14 : 2 .1034, 1023, 995
14 : 6 ...205, 334, 502
14 : 16...339, 362, 355
14 : 26...352, 371, 364
14 : 27...694, 840, 683
15 : 4 ...112, 127, 621
15 : 5 ...617, 547, 529
15 : 13...585, 260, 277
19 : 2 ...328, 282, 290
19 : 25...285, 853, 281
19 : 30...274, 286, 315
19 : 34...539, 871, 889
21 : 15...814, 815, 817
21 : 17...536, 867, 603

ACTS.
| 1 : 11.916, 1027, 1014 |
| 2 : 1 ...370, 368, 355 |
| 2 : 39...803, 812, 816 |
| 4 : 12...382, 597, 430 |
| 7 : 59...077, 982, 968 |
| 14 : 22.999, 1016, 1005 |
| 16 : 9 ...785, 795, 804 |
| 16 : 31...390, 270, 462 |
| 17 : 11...158, 164, 170 |
| 24 : 25...428, 422, 424 |
| 26 : 28...392, 409, 430 |

ROMANS.
| 1 : 16...549, 597, 846 |
| 1 : 17.1003, 1002, 661 |
| 2 : 4 ...181, 212, 422 |
| 3 : 19...388, 386, 390 |
| 5 : 1 ...840, 386, 390 |
| 5 : 8 ...585, 290, 409 |
| 6 : 11...387, 275, 278 |
| 7 : 24...079, 688, 528 |
| 8 : 14...693, 685, 676 |
| 8 : 15...520, 693, 644 |
| 8 : 31...683, 680, 079 |
| 8 : 33...079, 528, 639 |
| 9 : 20...182, 193, 209 |
| 10 : 4 ...382, 386, 390 |
| 10 : 20...453, 818, 178 |
| 11 : 33...180, 190, 193 |
| 12 : 1 ...498, 675, 520 |
| 12 : 2 ...489, 260, 479 |
| 12 : 5 ...822, 827, 829 |
| 12 : 15...740, 794, 807 |
| 13 : 11...049, 946, 953 |
| 14 : 10...976, 957, 973 |

1ST CORINTHIANS.
| 2 : 9 .1022, 993, 1012 |
| 3 : 11.1003, 688, 840 |
| 3 : 20-23.080, 670, 594 |
| 5 : 7 ...531, 282, 287 |
| 9 : 26...525, 539, 548 |
| 11 : 24...845, 864, 806 |
| 12 : 27...826, 827, 829 |
| 13 : 1 ...641, 822, 663 |
| 13 : 12...206, 195, 193 |
| 15 : 10...030, 670, 640 |
| 15 : 55...95C, 961, 907 |

2ND CORINTHIANS.
| 1 : 4 ...718, 716, 737 |
| 1 : 22...359, 355, 372 |
| 4 : 14...526, 938, 904 |
| 4 : 17...735, 722, 622 |
| 4 : 18...854, 939, 956 |
| 5 : 1 .1034, 1011, 991 |
| 5 : 7 ...651, 658, 656 |
| 5 : 8 ...991, 961, 946 |
| 5 : 17...391, 407, 449 |
| 6 : 2 ...418, 406, 424 |
| 7 : 5 ...842, 494, 527 |
| 9 : 15...270, 400, 414 |
| 12 : 10...529, 520, 622 |
| 13 : 14...138, 121, 115 |

GALATIANS.
CH.VER.	HYMN.
2 : 20...630, 276, 285
3 : 28...822, 821, 827
4 : 6 ...693, 685, 520
4 : 15...499, 493, 496
5 : 1 ...524, 528, 557
5 : 6 ...386, 430, 388
6 : 9 ...546, 565, 782
6 : 14...300, 294, 275

EPHESIANS.
| 2 : 8 ...386, 301, 400 |
| 3 : 15...820, 822, 826 |
| 4 : 5 ...752, 771, 826 |
| 4 : 30...358, 424, 428 |
| 5 : 8 ...655, 640, 661 |
| 5 : 19...31, 575, 107 |
| 6 : 13...524, 548, 579 |

PHILIPPIANS.
| 1 : 21...570, 933, 537 |
| 1 : 29...520, 569, 537 |
| 2 : 5-8...270, 342, 794 |
| 2 : 12...073, 305, 691 |
| 3 : 14...544, 558, 573 |
| 3 : 20...889, 939, 1002 |
| 4 : 4 ...653, 594, 654 |
| 4 : 7 ...683, 694, 840 |
| 4 : 11...659, 742, 642 |
| 4 : 13...529, 559, 876 |

COLOSSIANS.
| 2 : 9 ...342, 316, 244 |
| 2 : 10...675, 539, 528 |
| 3 : 1-3...939, 479, 544 |

1ST THESSALONIANS.
| 4 : 14...044, 953, 966 |
| 5 : 16...653, 594, 654 |
| 5 : 18.1046, 1065, 1060 |
| 5 : 23...650, 411, 581 |

2D THESSALONIANS.
| 2 : 8 ...910, 903, 909 |
| 3 : 13...546, 565, 782 |

1ST TIMOTHY.
| 1 : 15...270, 438, 453 |
| 2 : 5 ...283, 327, 405 |
| 2 : 8 ......64, 74, 567 |
| 6 : 12...540, 518, 582 |

2ND TIMOTHY.
| 1 : 9 ...178, 193, 670 |
| 1 : 12...528, 840, 688 |
| 2 : 3 ...540, 548, 569 |
| 2 : 19...563, 545, 567 |
| 3 : 16...159, 174, 163 |

TITUS.
| 2 : 11.664, 1014, 1019 |
| 3 : 5 ...391, 396, 385 |

HEBREWS.
| 1 : 3 ...369, 335, 342 |
| 1 : 14...738, 235, 248 |
| 2 : 3 ...386, 402, 428 |
| 2 : 10...524, 242, 500 |
| 2 : 18...75, 260, 501 |
| 3 : 15...418, 424, 424 |
| 4 : 9 ...996, 1013, 1015 |
| 4 : 12...167, 170, 174 |
| 4 : 15...75, 260, 501 |
| 5 : 8 ...260, 264, 280 |
| 6 : 19...688, 528, 936 |
| 7 : 22...405, 691, 684 |
| 7 : 25...337, 327, 313 |
| 9 : 5 ...69, 74, 77, 450 |
| 10 : 12...301, 302, 312 |
| 11 : 1 ...656, 658, 661 |
| 11 : 6 ...648, 691, 645 |
| 11 : 13.1032, 1000, 994 |
| 11 : 16.1036, 989, 1004 |
| 12 : 1 ...535, 539, 960 |

G

FIRST LINES OF STANZAS.

CH.VER.	HYMN.	CH.VER.	HYMN.	2ND PETER.		CH.VER.	HYMN.	CH.VER.	HYMN.
12 : 2 ...600, 620, 590		4 : 14...956, 954, 963		CH.VER.	HYMN.	3 : 1 ...178, 693, 676		7 : 13...999, 1005, 1006	
12 : 6 ...703, 720, 732		5 : 8 .664, 1029, 1014		1 : 21...150, 164, 173		3 : 2 ...304, 693, 684		7 : 17.1011, 1015, 1019	
12 : 11...709, 722, 735		5 : 20...804, 800, 784		3 : 9 ...189, 208, 563		4 : 8 ...199, 214, 212		11 : 15...902, 894, 911	
12 : 18...821, 820, 687				3 : 10...976, 975, 983		4 : 19...178, 631, 453		14 : 3 ...414, 336, 625	
13 : 5 ...563, 552, 523		1ST PETER.		3 : 11...988, 973, 980		5 : 4 ...527, 556, 682		14 : 13...942, 947, 961	
13 : 13...520, 284, 541		1 : 8 ...604, 596, 626		3 : 13...983, 997, 1014				19 : 6 .1006, 1016, 1018	
13 : 14.939, 1017, 1022		1 : 19...282, 382, 281		3 : 15...181, 212, 648		REVELATION.		19 : 12...320, 314, 328	
		2 : 7 ...613, 591, 601		3 : 18...486, 790, 650		1 : 5, 6..329, 338, 330		21 : 2 .1027, 1022, 1044	
JAMES.		2 : 21...264, 590, 200				3 : 8 ...447, 841, 334		21 : 4 .1031, 1034, 1040	
1 : 2, 3..709, 622, 745		3 : 7 ....77, 68, 496		1ST JOHN.		3 : 11...524, 535, 547		21 : 25.1037, 1033, 1022	
1 : 5 ...462, 461, 732		4 : 14...838, 284, 543		1 : 3 ...687, 556, 568		3 : 20...421, 464, 446		22 : 4 ...304, 990, 1023	
1 : 17...187, 185, 657		4 : 18...988, 976, 973		1 : 7 ...874, 498, 398		4 : 8 ...221, 96, 1064		22 : 16...246, 241, 238	
2 : 17...806, 865, 789		5 : 4 ..524, 532, 1037		2 : 1 ...303, 333, 859		5 : 9 ...329, 338, 330		22 : 17...412, 425, 439	
4 : 6 ...729, 491, 646		5 : 7 ...719, 549, 561		2 ; 17...545, 936, 940		5 : 12...802, 336, 325		22 : 20...756, 601, 916	

FIRST LINES OF STANZAS

EXCEPT THE FIRST.

	HYMN.		HYMN.		HYMN.		HYMN.
A brighter faith....	356	All our follies, Lord,	1047	And though this wo	215	As with joyful......	63
A broken heart, a...	889	All riches are his...	338	And though thy wis	710	Ashamed of Jesus.	597
A cloud of witnesses	539	All that spring with	1050	And thus that dark.	838	Assume my conscieu	359
A faith that shines..	1008	All things hasten...	531	And to his green....	565	"Ask what thou wil	1083
A Father's chasten.	739	All this for us.......	243	And was his mortal.	291	At cost of all........	691
A Father's hand we	724	All thy works, O....	213	And we believe thy.	780	At his call, tho dead	975
A few more storms.	948	All to the great......	761	And what is life....	536	At his right hand...	345
A few more struggle	948	All—wise, almighty,	710	And what shall be.	1042	At home, by word a	779
A glory gilds the...	173	Almighty God! thy	904	And when before th	410	At last I own.......	467
A gracious Saviour.	914	Almighty God! thy	423	And when my chee	355	At the blest mercy-	488
A guilty, weak and.	390	Almighty God! to..	230	And when my Savio	816	Attending angels sh	1027
A hand almighty...	683	Almighty Lord, the	161	And when my taste	737	Awake, awake, put	931
A heart in every....	489	Almighty Son.......	179	And when our days	123	Awake, lift up......	48
A heart resigned....	489	Am I a stranger....	168	And when redeemed	450	Awake thy chosen..	918
A holy quiet reigns.	942	Amazing knowledge	188	And when these fall	862	Awake! thy sweet.	923
A hope so much.....	693	Amen, Lord Jesus..	560	And when these lips	814	Awhile from thy....	292
A little child, thou..	243	Amid ten thousand.	1062	And when thine awf	686		
A little flock!—so...	756	Amidst a thousand.	233	And when to heaven	9	Bane and blessing...	300
A little while for ...	1081	Among thy saints...	957	And when wo early	123	Baptize the nations,	380
A little while to.....	1081	Among the saints...	825	And when we taste	506	Baptized by John...	807
A pilgrim through..	710	Among the saints th	186	And while at thy...	292	Be Christ our patter	262
A pilgrimage my....	570	Author and Guardia	52	And why should I..	615	Be darkness at thy.	380
A second look he....	279	And as now I.......	853	And will this glorio	109	Be earth, with all...	509
A song of praise....	528	And as we rise, with	810	Angels and men in	190	Be near to bless.....	112
A spirit still pre.....	846	And blest is he......	538	Angels! assist our..	434	Be near when I.....	290
A thousand seraphs	342	And, bursting throu	583	Angels from the....	898	Be of good cheer....	560
A voice from the....	615	And duly shall ap..	782	Angels, sing on!....	235	Be our strength in..	789
A whispered word..	796	And ever on thine..	324	Apostles, martyrs,..	1000	Be this my joy......	193
Abide with me from	112	And every virtue...	373	Archangels leave th	244	Be this world the...	783
Above me and be...	177	And, gracious Lord,	475	Arabia's desert-rau	894	Be thou my pattern	260
According to thy....	914	And he who is him.	1081	Are darkness and...	182	Be thou my shield..	515
Adoring angels tune	252	And here thy name,	1060	Are not thy mercies	106	Be with us in this...	973
Ah! bring a wretch	470	And is not mercy...	877	Are there no foes...	540	Bear—bear the......	256
Ah, grace! into.....	674	And lest the shadow	407	Are we not tending	953	Bear witness I am..	650
Ah, Lord Jesus, gra	935	And Lord, when I..	408	Arm me with jealou	397	Before his ever-wat	759
Ah, Lord, our shas..	288	And may I hope....	638	Around that throne	1043	Before me place, in	381
Ah, when shall my.	615	And may tho holy..	115	Around thy throne	125	Before our Father's	823
Alas! I knew not...	279	And now above the	937	Art nigh, and yet...	427	Before the hills in..	961
All-bounteous Lord.	198	And now Christ is..	427	Art thou not mine..	527	Before thy throno..	33
"All glory bo to.....	238	And now my spirit..	729	As a little child.....	62	Behold his patience,	199
All hail! atoning...	411	And, oh, from that..	722	As a mother stills h	1063	Behold the ark of...	847
All hallowed be.....	40	And, oh, when I....	708	As by the light.....	638	Behold the bed of...	971
All her high ones...	978	And palms shall....	543	As in the heavens...	678	Behold the innumer	827
All his creatures....	99	And right is right...	538	As, 'mid tho ever...	678	Behold ! on flying...	337
All honor to his.....	34	And shall my guilty	454	As our steps are....	137	Believing we rejoice	382
All its numbered da	1047	And since, in God's.	973	As the benighted...	513	Beloved self must...	389
All, leveled by the.	969	And so to Jesus Chr	977	As the seed by.....	792	Below he washed...	327
All my capacious...	612	And soon, too soon,	800	As the winged arro	1048	Beneath his watchf	549
All my soul, by.....	294	And sweet, on earth	606	As they offered.....	63	Beside him all the..	1025
All nature sings thy	102	And then, nevermor	626	As rain on weakness		Beyond my light....	35
All needful grace...	39	And then was heard	322	As thou for us didst	825	Beyond the bloomin	992
All our days direct.	517	And there is David's	1023	As true as God's....	560	Beyond the bounds	558

G

424 FIRST LINES OF STANZAS.

HYMN.		HYMN.		HYMN.		HYMN.
Beyond the frost-ch	992	By day, by night,...	1061	Could I joy with....	409	Far, far away, like.	235
Beyond the parting	992	By faith in thee......	821	Could my heart so..	400	Far from us drive...	351
Beyond the rising..	992	By foreign streams.	922	Could we be cast....	650	Father and Saviour!	132
Beyond this vale...	381	By the thorn-road...	748	Countless as sands..	977	Father and Son......	495
Bid me stand on....	573	By thee, through life	639	Creatures no more..	638	Father, fill our heart	152
Bind thy people.....	786	By thine agonizing.	880	Crown him the Lord	320	Father, fix my soul.	672
Bless, O my soul....	41	By thine hour of....	501	Crown him, ye mart	320	Father, forgive the.	736
Bless thou the truth	145	By thine own eterna	756	Crown the Saviour,.	314	Father in heaven! in	1070
Bless ye the Lord...	42	By thy deep expirin	501	Crowns and thrones	518	Father in heaven, oh	133
Blessed and holy....	369	By thy hands the...	733			Father, let me taste	220
Blessed fold! no foe	1019	By thy helpless.....	501	Dark and cheerless.	14	Father, make me pu	868
Blessed fountain, fu	630	By thy most severe.	476	Day and night they.	309	Father, perfect my.	940
Blessed Saviour, th	617			Day by day, with ...	852	Father! source of all	104
Blessing, praise and	978	Call me away from..	509	Days of trial, days..	584	Fear hath no dwelli	430
Blessings abound...	911	Call to mind that....	476	Deal gently, Lord,..	571	Fear not, brethren;	532
Blessings for ever..	338	Calm in the hour....	647	Dear Comforter! ote	480	"Fear not, I am.....	563
Blest are the men...	92	Calm in the sufferan	647	Dear dying Lamb...	308	"Fear not" said he,.	238
Blest are the saints	38	Calmer yet and	581	Dear Lord and Mast	592	Feast after feast.....	876
Blest are the souls	38	Calmly the day	66	Dear Lord, and shall	357	Feeble, trembling,..	747
Blest be the Lord...	19	"Can a woman's ten	856	Dear Lord! if indeed	623	Feed me, Saviour,..	853
Blest hour! for whe	55	Can aught, beneath.	385	Dear Lord! while we	296	Fettered, burdened,	483
Blest hour! when..	55	Careful without care	816	Dear Saviour, let ...	37	Fettered by this....	483
Blest hour! when...	55	Cast thy bread upon	792	Dear Saviour! when	675	Fight on, my soul...	547
Blest is the man....	553	Cast thy guilty......	452	Dear Shepherd, if...	578	Fill each breast with	148
Blest Jesus, come a	497	Cease, ye pilgrims..	939	Dearer than any.....	1065	Fill us with thy.....	153
Blest river of salva	895	Celestial choirs, fro	240	Death, like an over-	943	Filled by thee my...	634
Blest Saviour, intro	539	Chance and change.	225	Death may our souls	843	Filled with delight..	989
Blest Saviour! what	58	Cheer up! cheer up!	744	Decay then, teneme	257	Finding, following..	560
Blind unbelief is....	200	Cheered by a signal	685	Deep in unfathomab	209	Finish then thy.....	566
Bonds and stripes..	284	Cheerful they walk.	38	Deeper, deeper grow	747	Firm as his throne..	541
Born by a new......	1032	Cheerful we tread..	661	"Deny thyself and .	392	Firm, faithful, watc	888
Born, thy people to	756	"Chief of ten thousa	56	Dependent on thy...	800	Firmly trusting in..	620
Bowed down beneat	515	Choose thou for me.	727	Descend, celestial D	10	Flow to restore, but	163
Break forth in hym	891	Christ, by highest..	245	Despairing madness	259	Fly abroad, thou.....	901
Break from his thro	966	"Christ is born, the	234	Did I meet no trials.	720	Foes without and....	293
Break off your tears	205	Christ leads me thro	537	Did the Lord a......	624	For all thy saints,..	906
Break the tempter's	897	Christ, our Paschal.	851	Did the solid earth..	99	For all we love,.....	142
Breathe, breathe on	621	Christ, the Lord is..	343	Did we in our	215	For ever blessed the	996
Breathe, oh, breathe	586	Church of our God!.	906	Direct, control,......	48	For ever firm thy...	84
Bright garlands of	542	Clothe thou with en	765	Divine Instructor,..	172	For ever on thy.....	264
Bright heralds of...	477	Clothed with our....	327	Do more than pardo	142	For God has marked	735
Bright is their glory	820	Cold mountains and	260	Does not my heart..	166	For her my tears....	75
Bright with pearls .	1044	Cold on his cradle...	250	Dost thou not dwell	350	For him I count.....	611
Bring before us all	865	Cold our services....	130	Doth sickness fill...	526	For him shall end...	911
Burdened with sin's	408	Como, all the faithfu	368	Down from the shi.	434	For him shall prayer	894
Buried in sorrow...	401	Come, all who love..	807	Down through the...	254	For life, without.....	29
Bury the dead, and	971	Come, and begin.....	916			For lo! the days.....	248
But a drought has	897	Come, and make all.	916	Each following min	833	For love like this ...	162
But ah! too soon....	164	Come as a messenge	763	Each gift but helps.	646	For nights of anxiet	622
But all the notes....	831	Come as a shepherd.	763	Earth can now but.	1014	For not like kingdo	757
But all through the	403	Come as a teacher...	763	Earth has a joy.....	477	For nothing good ha	410
But all was merciful	437	Come, blessed Lord!	1029	Earth has many a...	1036	For ten thousand...	104
But, bowed in lowlin	729	Come, fill our hearts	45	"Eat, O my friends.	842	For the blessings...	15
But calmly, Lord...	1054	"Come, for all else...	508	E'er since, by faith.	398	For the grandeur...	316
But Christ the heav	382	Come, for creation..	916	Egypt and Tyre, and	924	For the Lord our Go	1046
But, dearest Lord...	1026	Come, for thy saints	916	Elect from every....	771	For the love of.....	214
But drops of grief...	277	Come, freely come, .	704	Enlightened by thy.	350	For thee, my God...	473
But, ere the trumpet	980	Come, gracious Lord	510	Enough, if thou at..	820	For thee our all to..	779
But fixed for ever...	161	Come, holy Comforte	223	Enter, incarnate....	322	For this I should...	622
But God shall raise	395	Come, Holy Ghost..	858	Enter with all thy..	777	For this thy name .	960
But he for his.......	882	Come, Holy Spirit,..	361	Enthroned amid.....	229	For thou hast placed	705
But I amid your....	477	Come, Holy Spirit,..	357	Ere long that happy	470	For thou, within....	74
But, lying dark be..	949	Come, join the angel	255	Ere sin was born ...	244	For thy rich, thy....	316
But lo, he leaves....	244	Come, kingdom of o	915	Eternal are thy mer	82	For thy sorrows we.	869
But no such sac.....	471	Come, in sorrow and	445	Eternal Father! the	226	For voice and silenc	660
But none of the.....	403	Come, in this accept	147	Eternal life thy	466	For why? the Lord.	79
But of all the.......	530	Come, let us stand..	880	Eternal Spirit!	179	Forbid it, Lord!.....	275
But oh, when gloom	605	Come, light serene!.	368	Eternal truth and...	834	Forgive me, Lord,..	113
But our earnest.....	926	Come, Lord, and wip	959	Eternal wisdom.....	436	Forgive thou us, as.	472
But saints are lovely	87	Come, Lord Jesus!..	827	Eternity with all....	204	Forgive us, for our.	472
But see: the night is	1024	Come, Lord! thy lov	37	Even death, which .	258	Forgive us, O thou.	472
But should the surg	723	Come, Lord, when...	537	"Ev'n down to old...	563	Forth with thy chos	1008
But sinners, filled wi	976	Come, sacred Spirit,	685	Ev'n now, above....	736	Fountain of o'erflow	629
But the chief Sheph	758	Come, self-existent.	218	Ev'n now, by faith,.	826	Frail children of	08
But there's a voice.	390	Come, tenderest Fri	368	Ev'n now, perchanc	949	From angel hosts...	330
But thine illustrious	386	Come, then, with all	390	Ev'n now, when tem	909	From a busy scenes ..	56
But thou hast built.	513	Come, then, with po	917	Ev'n the hour that.	225	"From dark tempta.	146
But thy compassions	725	Come, thou incarnat	223	Ever be thou our Gu	803	From day to day....	25
But thy soft hand...	414	Come, thou Spirit of	641	Ever let thy grace..	868	From heaven he cam	257
But to thy house....	36	Come to the bright..	439	Ever thus in God's .	211	From marble domes	53
But, though earth's	954	Come to the house...	60	Every eye shall now	986	From morn till noon	207
But warm, sweet,...	271	"Come, wanderers.	439	Every mournful sin	147	From sorrow, toil, ..	823
But we have no.....	285	Come, worship at hi	93	Exalt our low desire	368	From strength to...	570
But weaker yet that	193	Comfort me; I am...	718	Extol the Lamb of..	406	From the dark grav	14
But what to those..	614	Comfort those who..	2			From the heaven of.	1044
But when he came..	370	Complete in thee.....	675	Fain would I mount	18	From the highest...	316
But, when we view.	196	Conscious of the....	287	Faith in Christ will.	430	From the provisions	84
But while I thus....	383	Constant to my.....	4	Faith is our only....	742	From the sword, at.	62
But who can speak.	89	Convert and send...	750	Faithful may I en...	570	From the third heav	1027
But will he prove...	421	Convince us of our..	361	Far, far above thy..	554	From the throne a...	1017

G

FIRST LINES OF STANZAS.   425

	HYMN.
From thee, the over	525
From thy dear hand,	841
From thy house who	8
From thy works our	103
From vanity turn...	171
Fruitless years with	460
Full of kindness....	213
"Gather first my sal	982
Gentiles and kings..	906
Gethsemane can....	267
Gethsemane car I..	862
Gird him with all...	768
Gird on thy sword..	341
Give glory to his....	231
Give glory to the....	118
"Give me a calm,...	649
Give me a faithful..	488
Give me a will......	507
Give me, O Lord....	28
Give me one kind...	987
Give me to read.....	76
Give tongues of fire.	380
Giver of the heavenl	502
Glorified apostles...	101
"Glory to God!" th	240
Glory to God, who..	239
Glory to thee, who..	48
Go, and share his...	956
Go then, earthly fam	520
Go, where the waves	892
God, from on high,.	921
God in Israel sows..	720
God is our strength.	156
God is our sun,......	39
God of our fathers..	958
God pities all.......	71
God reigns on high;	197
God ruleth on high.	97
God, thine own God,	331
God, thy God, will..	900
God whom we serve	534
God will not always	725
God will support....	673
Goodness and mercy	602
Good-will to men;...	239
Grace all the work..	690
Grace first contrive	690
Grace led my roving	690
Grace!—'tis a sweet	83
Grace will complete	233
Grant one poor sinne	812
Grant that all may..	2
Grant these request	76
Grant to little.......	141
Grant us thy peace..	128
Grant us thy truth..	191
Great Advocate, al.	333
Great are thy con...	358
Great Comforter!...	351
Great God! from in.	204
Great God! I do.....	192
Great God, let all...	25
Great God, mine eye	159
Great God! on what	1055
Great God, we hail..	24
Great God! what do.	976
Great is his love,....	513
Great is our Lord...	87
Green pastures are.	556
Great Shepherd of..	74
Great Shepherd of...	108
Great Sun of right..	158
Great words are the	582
Hail, by all thy.....	102
Hail, great Immanu	58
"Hail, Prince of Lif	321
Hail, sacred feast...	830
Hail! the heaven-bo	245
Hallelujah! church.	926
Hallelujah!—earth.	774
Hallelujah! hark,...	902
Hallelujah! strains.	926
Happy the man who	86
Happy the man who	90
Hark! from the mid	242
Hark! hark!—the.	256
Hark! how the wor	450
Hark! the cherubic	254

	HYMN.
Hark! the wonderin	297
Hark! they whisper	967
Hark, those bursts.	314
Hark! what a sweet.	255
Has thy night been.	900
Hast thou a lamb...	603
Hast thou a rival...	632
Hast thou imparted	356
Hast thou not given	701
Hast thou not plant	925
Haste, prepare the..	287
Haste thee on from.	521
Hasten, mortals!...	234
Hath he marks to...	569
Have I long in......	448
Have we no tears...	889
Have we trials and.	567
Have you no words?	77
He bows his gracious	70
He breaks the power	490
He by his blood.....	808
He came in tongues.	373
He came, sweet influ	373
He comes, from thic	253
He comes, the broke	253
He comes, the priso	253
"He comes to cheer	242
He comes, with succ	894
He crowns thy life..	669
He dies; and in.....	335
He ever lives above.	405
He feeds in pasture.	683
He fills the poor...	669
He formed the deeps	93
He formed the stars	87
He freely redeemed	624
He frees the souls..	930
He gave to the light	105
He has pardons.....	440
He hung its starry..	764
He in the thickest..	182
He knew them all...	291
He knows what wan	839
He leads me to......	595
He left his Father's.	689
He left his starry...	344
He lives! he lives!..	679
He loves his saints.	86
He loves his saints.	90
He prospers day by.	691
Ho raiseth the fallen	565
He rules the world..	236
He sat serene upon.	231
He saw me plunged.	268
He saw me ruined..	404
He sends his word..	1068
He sent his Son.....	435
He shall come down	894
He shall reign from.	902
He sits a sovereign.	930
He smiles,—and sera	1039
He spreads his kind.	797
He sunk beneath...	280
He sustains thee by	719
He that drinks shall	445
He the mighty king.	246
He to the lowly.....	652
He wept that we....	416
He whispers in my..	594
He who bore all....	308
He who has helped.	705
He who me......	531
He who slumbered..	308
He wills that I......	323
He with earthly....	225
Head of thy church	752
Hear and save me..	451
Hear the cries he no	973
Hear us, as thus....	786
Hearer of prayer!..	495
Heaven and earth..	107
Heaven and earth.	719
Heaven unfolds.....	297
Heavenly Father!..	152
Heavenly Fount, thy	805
Hell and thy sins...	524
Help me to watch...	397
Help us, through go	266
Hence, ye vain cares	7
Her dust and ruins.	493

	HYMN.
Here at that cross..	812
Here be thy praise..	769
Here, beneath a virt	1049
Here faith is ours, a	998
Here faith reveals..	160
Here fix, my roving	71
Here have we seen.	844
Here I give my all..	498
Here I'll raise mine.	837
Here I would for....	855
Here, in the body...	946
Here Jesus bids my.	162
Here let him hold...	777
Here let the Son....	777
Here let thy holy...	769
Here my poor heart.	721
Here may religion..	1051
Here may thine hon	789
Here may we gain..	751
Here may we prove.	74
Here, mighty God..	777
Here, O my soul....	527
Here on the mercy.	28
Here reach thy boun	12
Here see the Bread.	431
Here sinners, of an.	160
Here, the fair tree..	172
Here, the Redeemer	172
Here the whole Deit	196
Here to thee a......	774
Here we come thy..	13
Here we feel our...	869
Here would I feed..	676
Here's love and grief	295
Higher yet, and.....	581
Him in whom they..	106
His body broken in.	838
His comforts bear..	744
His cross dispels...	651
His dying crimson..	275
His example while..	870
His fearful drops...	838
His goodness stands	549
His grace will to....	553
His hand divine.....	542
His honor is engag.	681
His love in time....	576
His love, what mort	296
His mercy visits ev	924
His name shall be...	237
His oath, his covena	688
His own soft hand..	1027
His person fixes....	611
His power increasin	237
His providence info	195
His purposes will...	209
His righteousness is	696
His sacred name....	269
His sovereign powe	73
His spirit in me.....	691
His spirit with a...	992
His terrors keep the	109
His truth for ever..	86
His very word of...	208
His voice sublime..	194
His voice we hear..	690
His will he makes..	676
His wondrous work	669
His word of promise	611
His work my hoary.	663
Hither come! for...	426
Hither, then, your.	533
Ho! all ye hungry..	436
Ho, ye needy; come	432
Hold thou thy cross	127
Holy Ghost, no more	644
Holy Ghost! with..	366
Holy, holy, holy,...	221
Holy, holy, holy!...	96
Holy Spirit! all.....	366
Honor immortal mu	338
Hosanna in the.....	19
Hosanna to tho.....	19
Hosanna to the Lam	809
Hosanna to the Wo.	121
How awful is the...	979
How beautiful on all	487
How blest thy saint	49
How can a soul.....	403

	HYMN.
How can my soul...	646
How decent, and ho	770
How doth thy word	188
How dreadful was..	395
How far from this..	561
How gentle was the	724
How glorious was..	395
How God hath built	594
How happy all thy.	186
How happy are our.	749
How happy are the.	543
How kind are thy..	197
How large his boun	71
How long, dear Sav	1027
How long, O Lord..	959
How many hearts..	854
How much is mercy	186
How oft my mourn.	591
How oft they look..	677
How rich the grace!	444
How should our son	37
How sweet the tear	66
How sweet, thro' lo	66
How sweet to look.	66
How will my heart.	980
How will my lips...	348
Howl, winds of nigh	194
Hunger, thirst, dise	999
Hymns of glory.....	851
I am lowest of......	447
I am not worthy...	877
I bless thee for.....	709
"I can but perish..	420
I can do all things..	529
I change—he chang	822
I charge my though	665
"I delivered thee...	656
I fare with Christ..	570
I fear no tribulation	1002
I felt his love.......	346
I find him lifting...	323
I glory in infirmity.	529
I have long with sto	500
I hear thy voice,...	877
I heard the law.....	383
I heard the voice...	633
I know that thou...	1034
I know this cleansin	281
I lay my body.......	116
I lay my wants.....	463
I lift my eyes;......	575
I long to be.........	463
I love by faith......	65
I love her gates....	20
I love in solitude...	65
I love thy church...	35
I love to meet......	957
I love to think.....	65
I need the influence	166
I need the shelterin	461
I need thee every...	484
I need thy presence	127
I need thy Spirit...	461
I praise the God...	651
I praise thee for...	709
I rest upon tho.....	801
I saw his face.......	346
I see its domes resp	1034
I see thee not.......	604
I shall not in the...	977
I sigh to think.....	473
I sing the goodness.	205
I smite upon my....	456
I take thy hand....	745
I thank thee for....	709
I want a godly.....	846
I want a sober......	846
I was not ever......	734
I welcome all thy...	684
I would for ever....	811
I would not breathe	668
I would not murmu	721
I would not walk...	592
I would trust in....	732
I yield my powers..	857
I'd sing the charact	618
I'd sing the preciou	616
If burning beams of	685
If aught should tem	708

G

FIRST LINES OF STANZAS.

First Line	Hymn
If but my fainting..	738
If earthly parents..	379
If e'er I go astray..	595
If he is mine........	680
If I ask him........	569
If I find him........	569
If I still hold......	569
If in my Father's...	693
If joy shall at......	266
If life be long......	537
If love to God......	663
If my immortal.....	527
If, o'er my sins.....	202
If our love were....	214
If pain and sickness	703
If Satan tempt our.	590
If so poor a worm...	875
If tears of sorrow...	471
If the sorrows of....	584
If the way be.......	562
If thou, in thy great	1038
If thou shouldst ca	738
If thou shouldst tak	712
If vapors, with mali	695
If, winged with bea	202
If, while on earth...	1002
If yet while pardon.	988
If you are too.......	785
If you cannot cross.	784
If you cannot in....	785
If you have not.....	785
"I'll go to Jesus....	420
I'll praise him while	90
I'll read the historio	160
I'll sing thy truth..	233
Immortal glories....	1039
In all our Maker's..	229
In answering what.	92
In darkest shades...	610
In darkest skies....	536
In each event of....	185
In every dark.......	333
In every new dis....	772
In every pang that.	75
In foreign realms...	1052
In gentler language	88
In heaven, and cart	182
In heaven the.......	254
In him, who all.....	559
In holy contemplati	555
In holy duties.......	47
In humble faith, be.	767
In Israel stood his..	347
In it all is light......	1015
In life, in death.....	491
In life, thy promisos	526
In midst of dangers	1052
In my darkness and	293
In our joys and.....	867
In our sickness.....	64
In our stead him....	778
In patient hope.....	281
In peopled vale, in..	023
In prayer, in effort.	884
In prayer, my soul.	496
In richos, in pleasur	427
In scenes exalted or	1061
In self-forgetting lo	844
In spite of all.......	595
In the heart's depth	879
In the hour of pain.	608
In the last hour.....	202
In the midst of.....	564
In the midst of that	1017
In the promises I...	408
In the way a thous.	530
In the wilderness...	100
In the world will...	732
In thee I place......	552
In thee we trust....	606
In thine own ap....	2
In this world of.....	935
In thy dear cross....	332
In thy fair book.....	195
In thy trial, and....	866
In us, for us.........	374
In vain I task.......	729
In vain we tune....	357
In wakeful hours...	29
In want, our plentif	599
G	

First Line	Hymn
In us "Abba, Fatho	374
In Zion God is......	772
Incarnate Lord.....	292
Increase my faith...	494
Increase our faith,.	1083
Infinite joy, or endle	1055
Is not even death a.	970
Is there thy name....	603
Is there a blissful..	996
Is there a heart......	409
Is there diadem, as.	569
Is there no kind....	945
Israel's strength an	756
It can bring with...	555
It gives the bur.....	68
"It is finished!" oh.	315
It is that heaven....	714
It makes the wound	613
It may be it shall...	1054
It may bo we shall.	1054
It passed not, thong	201
It shows the preciou	656
It sweetly cheers...	165
It tells me of a......	508
It was my guide....	241
Its joys can now....	638
I've seen thy glory.	21
Jehovah!—Father..	179
Jehovah, the Lord,.	619
"Jesus!"—all earth	330
Jesus can make a...	941
Jesus for me hath..	721
Jesus, give the wear	141
Jesus! guardian of.	719
Jesus! hear our.....	155
Jesus! how glorious	388
Jesus, I hang upon	323
Jesus, I throw my..	987
Jesus! in thy name.	102
Jesus, infinite Rede	1058
Jesus is gone up....	311
Jesus is worthy to..	325
Jesus lives! hencefo	936
Jesus lives! to him.	936
Jesus, Lord and.....	517
Jesus, Master, I am.	618
Jesus, may thy......	285
Jesus, my God!—I..	511
Jesus, my Lord, my	164
Jesus! my Shepherd	613
Jesus only, when....	586
Jesus our Comforter	589
Jesus our God.......	347
Jesus, our great Hig	406
Jesus, our life and..	821
Jesus, our Light!...	840
Jesus, our living....	71
Jesus, our only joy..	614
Jesus, still lead on..	562
Jesus, the Lord, ap..	335
Jesus, the Lord, thei	1041
Jesus, the Lord, will	70
Jesus—the name tha	490
Jesus, the Saviour..	299
Jesus, thee our......	317
Jesus! this feast re	885
Jesus, thou Prince..	961
Jesus! thy fair crea	1029
Jesus, thy name our	606
Jesus, to whom I...	694
Jesus, with thy pres	634
Jesus, whose dwelli	276
Join, all ye ransome	298
Joined in one body..	884
Joined in one spirit.	666
Joy of the comforte	431
Joy to the earth.....	236
Joyful are we.......	306
Joyful crowds his..	959
Joyful, with all.....	950
Joyfully on earth ad	104
Judge not the Lord.	209
Just such as I.......	590
Justice and truth...	341
Keen was the trial..	820
Keep no longer at...	897
Kept peaceful in....	266
Kindle our senses...	351

First Line	Hymn
Kindled his relentin	500
King of awful majes	983
King of glory!......	312
Kings shall fall dow	894
Kingdoms wide that	901
Know that the Lord	79
Knowing as I am...	946
Laboring and heavy	478
Lamb of God! to...	872
Laws, freedom, truth	1060
Lead me, and then..	722
Lead us to God......	354
Lead us to holiness..	354
Leave me not, my...	451
Leave me not, my Sa	983
Leave us not beneat	481
Less of the flesh.....	748
Less wayward let...	748
Let all our powers..	845
Let all that dwell...	325
Let all that own....	375
Let cares like a.....	682
Let earth and all....	18
Let earth and heave	817
Let elders worship..	990
Let endless honors..	345
Let everlasting than	173
Let every act of.....	833
Let every creature..	911
Let every kindred..	329
Let every step, let..	572
Let evil thoughts...	131
Let faith each meek.	22
Let fall thy rod of...	927
Let grace our.......	240
Let good or ill.......	552
Let goodness and...	564
Let him that heareth	441
Let Jew and Gentile	388
Let love, in one.....	829
Let me at thy throne	446
Let me hear thy....	747
Let me in thy......	372
Let me love thee....	568
Let me never from..	367
Let millions bow....	910
Let mountains from	919
Let music swell the.	1059
Let never more our.	887
Let not conscience..	432
Let not thy justice..	471
Let our mutual love	697
Let peace within....	24
Let pious thoughts..	131
Let sinful sweets be	839
Let sorrow's rudest.	1010
Let strangers walk.	770
Let the living here..	774
"Let the sweet hope	649
Let the whole earth.	41
Let the world despis	520
"Let them approach	802
Let these earthly...	130
Let this my every..	27
Let those refuse.....	31
Let thrones and pow	907
Let thronging multi	765
Let us be simple....	269
Let us devote this...	1070
Let us from all......	858
Let us obey, we.....	490
Let us learn the.....	234
Let thy blood, by...	880
Let thy good Spirit.	355
Life and peace to....	367
Life, death, and hell	195
Life, like a fountain.	84
Life's brightest joys	267
Life's labor done....	942
Life's poor distinc..	23
Lift up our hearts..	324
Lift up thy counten	111
Lift up thy voice....	891
Lift us up from.....	313
Light and peace at..	731
Light, in thy light..	111
Like a cloud that....	1036
Like a mighty......	518
Like an armed host.	899

First Line	Hymn
Like arrows went...	370
Like him, through..	795
Like some bright dre	604
Like the dew thy....	374
Like the sun's re....	449
Like them may we..	832
Listen to the wondro	234
Lion of Judah.......	322
Little then myself..	482
Lives again our.....	305
Lo! glad I come....	334
Lo, God is here!.....	110
Lo! he rises, mighty	343
Lo! his triumphal..	339
Lo! in the desert...	896
Lo, it comes, that...	1019
Lo, Jehovah, we....	317
Lo! Jesus, who in...	441
Lo! the last long....	986
Lo, the scene of.....	793
Lo! such the child..	800
Lonely I no longer..	857
Lonely seems the va	747
Long as we live.....	326
Long hadst thou....	943
Long my heart has..	498
Long thy exiles have	1014
Look! how we grove	357
Look up, ye saints..	1043
Loose all your bars..	339
Lord! can a feeble..	389
Lord Christ, we hum	79
Lord, decide the	499
Lord, draw reluctan	418
Lord, ere the last dre	973
Lord, from thine in.	760
Lord, give us such..	1008
Lord God of hosts!..	110
Lord God of truth...	381
Lord! how long shal	514
Lord! I am guilty...	859
Lord, I believe; but	645
Lord, I believe thy..	607
Lord! I come to.....	61
Lord, I desire with..	497
Lord, I my vows....	48
Lord, I shall share..	43
Lord, I would claspd.	737
Lord! if thine arm..	534
Lord, in thy grace...	126
Lord! it is my......	856
Lord Jesus, King of	993
Lord, keep us safe..	123
Lord, lend thy gra...	918
Lord! let not all....	392
Lord, may I ever....	535
Lord, may that grac	820
Lord may the tromb	919
Lord, my God! thine	514
Lord! my longings..	504
Lord, now indeed I..	410
Lord of all life	191
Lord of glory, God..	872
Lord of heaven!.....	222
Lord of life, beneath	1072
Lord of the nations.	1051
Lord, on our souls...	49
Lord, on thee our ...	2
Lord! send a beam.	1012
Lord! send the gra..	256
Lord, should my pat	261
Lord, submissive....	532
Lord, teach our hear	33
Lord, this bosom's..	212
Lord, thou hast here	463
Lord, thy glory.....	211
Lord, 'tis not ours..	764
Lord, turn to thee..	550
Lord, we have wand	879
Lord! we thy presen	652
Loud hallelujahs ...	85
Loud hallelujahs ...	744
Love and grief our..	869
Love and peace they	1016
Love in loving......	631
Love is the golden..	829
Love to God and....	870
Love's redeeming...	305
Low at thy feet.....	466
Low before thee, Lo	481

426

FIRST LINES OF STANZAS.

First Line	HYMN.
Make me to walk	171
Make my stubborn	478
Make us eternal tru	377
Man may trouble an	520
Many days have	62
March on in your	542
Martyrs, in a noble	101
May erring minds	760
May every heart cou	637
May faith grow firm	760
May grace, each idle	40
May I remember	710
May peace attend	1
May the blood of	868
May they that Jesus	761
May thy gospel's	13
May thy rich grace	600
May we thy bountie	780
Mean are all offering	795
Mean the joys of	504
Mercy and truth on	696
'Mid keen reproach	262
Might I enjoy the	39
Mighty to redeem	717
Mighty Victor, reig	310
"Mine is the uncham	856
Mine the God whom	857
Mine will the profit	363
Mocked, imprisoned	1016
More glorious still	163
More of myself gran	650
More of thy presenc	76
Mortals, your homag	247
Mortals with joy	244
Mountains shall sin	775
Mourn for the lost	781
Mourn for the ruine	781
Mourning souls, dry	533
Much of my time	116
Multitudes which	1016
Must I be carried	540
My cheerful hope	51
My conqueror and	592
My days unclouded	114
My faith would lay	382
My Father's graciou	995
My Father's house	946
My feet shall never	701
My feet shall travel	348
My flesh shall shun	955
My flesh would rest	38
My God, how ex	84
My God, how wonde	648
My God, I cry	387
My God! I would	195
My God is reconcile	405
My God, my Father!	703
My God, thy name	721
My gracious Master	490
My great Protector	51
My guilt appeared	387
My heart dissolves	281
My heart for gladne	594
My heart grows war	58
My heart shall tri	43
My hopes of heaven	387
My Jesus, as thou	726
My journey soon wi	570
My knowledge of	537
My life with him	651
My lips with shame	468
My Lord, before to	952
My love is oft-times	822
My merry heart is	1003
My mistakes his	447
My native country	1059
My pathway is not	722
My praise can only	877
My Saviour, and my	849
My Saviour's precio	995
My soul! ask what	72
My soul at rest	528
My soul he doth	602
My soul its every	528
My soul lies humbl	474
My soul looks back	382
My soul obeys the	390
My soul rejoices	173
My soul shall pray	29
My soul would leave	610

First Line	HYMN.
My soul would thith	986
My table thou hast	602
My terrors all vau	619
My thirsty, fainting	29
My thoughts, before	188
My thoughts lie ope	200
My tongue repeats	1
My trust is fixed	513
My willing soul	30
Naught have I of	691
Near the Cross!	459
Nearer my Father's	949
Nearer the bound	949
Needful art thou my	393
Needful is thy most	393
Ne'er think the vict	547
Never bowed a	294
Never, from thy pas	806
New graces ever	16
Night unto night	25
No act falls fruitless	796
No bliss I'll seek	742
No burning heats	701
No chilling winds	989
No condemnation	689
No dimly cloud o'er	1007
No earthly father	648
No! facing all its	263
No force of earth	582
No — I must main	62
No; I must my	628
No longer would	491
No more a lily	758
No more fatigue	44
No more let human	904
No more let sin	230
No more shall foes	917
No more sorrow, no	978
No mortal can	268
No room for doubt	842
No rude alarms	44
No strife shall vex	1028
No sun there climbs	1033
No taunting foes the	922
No treasures so en	168
No; thou art precio	632
No! thy dear name	759
None but Christ: hi	587
None in vain did	153
Nor alms, nor deeds	456
Nor death nor hell	661
Nor doth it yet	693
Nor earth, nor all	593
Nor fear thy Salem's	922
Nor let the good	735
Nor let these blessi	376
Nor pain, nor grief,	966
Nor shall fail from	213
Nor shall the glowin	674
Nor shall thy spread	158
Nor time, nor din	327
Nor voice can sing	614
Nor will our days	149
Nor would I drop	712
Not all that men	679
Not all the harps	593
Not for ever by	789
Not in the name	824
Not in vain	287
Not life itself	21
Not many rich nor	758
Not many years the	1056
Not so your eyes	423
Not softest strains	632
Not the fair palaces	28
Not the labor of	874
Not walls nor hills	571
Not what I feel	396
Nothing in my	874
Nothing more can	147
Now behold him	311
Now bless, thou God	801
Now for the love	469
Now he bids us	308
Now in the Father's	332
Now in thy holy	12
Now let me dwell	1041
Now let our souls be	850
Now, Lord, before	126

First Line	HYMN.
Now may the King	10
Now redemption	283
Now, Saviour, now	863
Now, Saviour, now	879
Now shall my head	91
Now the full glories	196
Now the heavens on	982
Now the heralds	433
Now, though he reig	280
Now thy quickening	371
Now to the God	930
Now to the Lamb th	990
Now to our eyes	364
Now to the God	45
Now to you my	857
Now truth and honor	696
Now, when the even	496
Now we will bless	724
Now we may bow	326
Now we, blest Savio	818
Now, ye mourners	731
O, bid this trifling	46
O, bless the Lord	609
O, blessed hope with	838
O, blessed work	140
O, blest assurance fr	1083
O, blest is he	538
O, by the pangs	615
O, cease, my wander	847
O, change these wre	385
O, Christ, he is the	1037
O, Christ, his love is	1001
O! Christ of God	281
O, come and reign	909
O, could we make	997
O, enter thou his	79
O! Father! thou	226
O, fill my soul	492
O, for a lowly	489
O, for grace our	585
O, for the living	156
O, for thine own	511
O, for this love	434
O, for those humble	492
O, give to every	228
O, give us hearts	264
O, glorious day, whe	828
O, glorious hour	955
O God, let people	224
O God! my inmost	384
O God, our King	39
O gracious God! in	494
O, grant that nothin	700
O, grant us grace	160
O, guard our shores	1051
O, guide our doubtfu	819
O, happy bond, that	813
O, happy, happy	654
O, happy harbor of	828
O, happy hour, whe	345
O, happy souls	11
O, hasten, Lord	6
O Heart! that with	887
O, holy, heavenly ho	1035
O, holy, holy, holy	203
O Hope of every	614
O, how I hate	278
O, how long-sufferin	132
O, I would my ears	1017
O, if my Lord	941
O, if the souls	358
O, if this glimpse	848
O, in thy light	258
O Jesus, bring us	1033
O Jesus, ever with	598
O Jesus, light of	637
O Jesus, our Saviour	814
O Jesus, thou art	464
O, keep me in	494
O, keep my soul	550
O, learn to scorn	538
O, let a holy	833
O, let me think	261
O, let me wing	714
O, let my hand	69
O, let my soul	113
O, let that glorious	899
O, let the dead	607

First Line	HYMN.
O, let the kingdoms	910
O, let them spread	750
O, let thy Spirit	507
O, let thy table	830
O light of Zion	905
O, long-expected	44
O long-expected daw	893
O Lord! amid this	512
O Lord and Master	271
O Lord! in ways	767
O Lord, increase	621
O Lord! our guilt	92
O Lord, prevent	957
O, lovely attitude!	421
O Love! how cheeri	700
O, magnify the Lord	671
O, make but trial	671
O, make thy church	174
O, may I bear	196
O, may I, Lord	713
O, may I, no	790
O, may I reach	83
O, may our sympa	794
O, may our willing	409
O, may that faith	534
O, may the Holy	1053
O, may the sweet	296
O, may these heaven	172
O, may these though	188
O, may this bountee	217
O, may thy counsels	167
O, may thy love	474
O, may thy quick	824
O, may thy Spirit	36
O, may we all	199
O, may we ever	666
O, may we ne'er	327
O, melt this frozen	363
O, might I hear	208
O my Saviour! Shie	623
O, never let my	51
O, no! this is not	965
O, no; till life its	834
O, not in circling	277
O, not my own	599
O, on that day, that	981
O, precious cross!	543
O Saviour, I am	462
O Saviour, I believe	462
O Saviour, then, in	743
O, send thy light	12
O, send thy Spirit	171
O, shall not warmer	864
O, shine on this	454
O, shouldst thou	465
O Source of uncreat	377
O Spirit of the	358
O, spread thy cover	798
O, sweet and blessed	1004
O, sweet and blessed	1020
O, teach us, Lord	687
O, tell me, Lord	680
O, tell me the	615
O, tell of his might	98
O, tell me that my	987
O, that all may	672
O, that each in the	1057
O, that our thoughts	47
O, that with yonder	329
O, the height of	453
O, the rich depths	270
O, the transporting	989
O, then arise and	444
O, then blessed Jesu	621
O, then, on faith's	1012
O, then what raptur	1006
O, then with hymns	751
O, this stubborn	502
O thou, by whom	67
O thou eternal Ru	776
O thou great God!	506
O thou who art	523
O thou who canst	176
O thou, whose infau	800
O, to grace how	837
O voice of mercy	508
O, wash my soul	403
O, watch, and fight	547
O water, life-bestow	885
O, weak to know a	553

G

FIRST LINES OF STANZAS.

	HYMN.		HYMN.		HYMN.		HYMN.
O, welcome day! wh	1034	Our lives through...	204	Saints on earth, lift.	297	So strange, so boun	437
O, were I there! oh,	1038	Our midnight is.....	191	Salvation!—let the.	401	So, though our path	653
O, what a pure......	801	Our prayers assist..	908	Salvation to God,...	97	So, through the oce	678
O, what trembling..	983	Our quickened souls	391	Save us, in thy......	755	So, when my latest.	946
O, when shall that..	122	Our restless spirits.	598	Saviour, breathe for	135	So when thou again	301
O, when will the....	625	Our sacrifice is one.	752	Saviour! hasten.....	312	So, whene'er the....	136
O, while I breathe..	582	Our sins, our guilt,.	687	Saviour! I long to..	437	Soar we now where.	305
O, who like thee.....	258	Our sorrows and....	287	Saviour! may our ..	5	Soft descend the....	793
O, wondrous knowle	200	Our souls and bodies	888	Saviour, Prince, en.	458	Soldier of Christ....	962
O, wondrous love...	515	Our souls — on thee.	465	Saviour, shine and..	482	Sometimes 'mid sce	737
O ye angels, hoverin	433	Our sun is sinking..	119	Saviour! to me, in..	492	Sons of God! your..	929
O, ye beneath	248	Our vows, our praye	798	Say—live for ever,..	205	Soon as the evening	183
O, yet a shelter.....	442	Our years are like ..	176	Say, shall we yield..	250	Soon as the morn...	639
O Zion, learn to.....	750	Over our spirits first	915	Say to the heathen.	904	Soon as the morn...	406
" O Zion I lift thy...	242			Scenes will vary, ...	531	Soon, for me, the....	129
Obedient to thy.....	6	Paschal Lamb, by...	282	Seal my forgiveness	114	Soon may all tribes.	915
Obedient to thy.....	863	Partakers of the	666	Search for us the ...	374	Soon shall close thy.	521
O'er all the sons	331	Pass me not, O......	448	Seasons and months	184	Soon shall my eyes.	289
O'er all the strait...	165	Patriarchs erst and.	778	Season of rest!......	149	Soon shall our dou..	555
O'er all those wide.	980	Peace be within	20	Send forth thy her..	923	Soon shall our doubt	723
O'er every foe victor	894	Peace from the boso	797	Send them thy migh	923	Soon our souls to...	1058
O'er the blue depths	240	Peace is on the......	5	Seraphs with elevat	1041	Soon shall we hear..	32
Of all good art	154	" Peace on earth, go	234	Set up thy throne...	912	" Soon the days of..	412
Of all the pious.....	958	Peace that glorious.	286	See celestial radianc	898	Soon thou wilt come	601
Of his deliverance I	671	Peace to our brethre	124	See, dearest Lord,..	437	Soon we pass this...	1015
Oft have our fathers	772	People and realms..	911	See — flowers of.....	34	Sorrow and fear are	894
Oft I walk beneath.	670	" Perhaps he will ...	420	See, from all lands..	896	Sow thy seed, be....	793
Oft the nights of....	670	" Permit them to....	799	See, from his head,..	275	Speak! and the worl	912
Often to Marah's ...	487	Pity and save my...	467	See heathen nations	895	Speak thou, and fro	353
Old friends, old scen	662	Pity the nations	861	See, Lord, before th	454	Speak thy pardonin	366
On all around, let...	013	Plenteous grace wit	505	See — Salem's gold..	34	Spirit of grace !	24
On cherub and on...	231	Praise and honor....	670	See that glory, how.	956	Spirit of our God ...	135
On earth we want ..	596	Praise be to thee....	131	See that your lamps	1021	Spirit of purity.....	373
On me thy promised	111	Praise God, from wh	115	See, the feast of.....	873	Spirit of truth and.	369
On me thy providen	198	Praise my soul, the.	212	See, the heaven	307	"Spread for thee, th	412
On mightier wing ..	163	Praise shall employ	86	See the Judge, our.	975	"Sprinkled now wit	412
On that my gaze....	886	Praise to God, the..	104	See! the streams of.	753	Stand then in his...	579
On thee alone........	42	Praise ye the God,.	42	See where it shines.	83	Stand up, and bless.	156
On thee we fling....	609	Pray thou, Christian	788	Seek we, then, the..	791	Stand up! stand up.	557
On us the vast	511	Prayer is the burden	67	Shall all that now...	803	Still at thy mercy...	450
On wheels of light ..	242	Prayer is the Christ	67	Shall God invite	423	Still for us he.......	307
On wings of love....	794	Prayer is the con....	67	Shall Jew and Genti	893	Still in ceaseless son	869
Once a sinner, near.	62	Prayer is the simp..	67	Shall love like thine	882	Still let the barren.	181
Once again beside ..	617	Prayer makes the fa	77	Shall persecution or	679	Still let the spirit...	579
Once did the skies..	243	Precious banquet;..	866	Shall they hosannas	394	Still looking to Jesu	620
Once earthly joy....	486	Precious is the......	440	Shall we thy life....	267	Still on thy holy....	126
Once, O Lord, thy...	897	Precious is thy......	157	Shall we, whose sou	890	Still onward urge...	559
Once on the raging.	241	Present we know....	824	Shine thou within..	125	Still the Spirit	5
Once the world's lie	460	Prince of Life! to...	872	Should aught beguil	1032	Still through the....	248
One army of the....	826	"Prostrate I'll lie...	420	Should coming days	1010	Still we wait for....	755
One blessed fellow..	828	Publish, spread to a	106	Should earth agains	682	Stripped of each car	694
One day, amid	30	Put all thy beauteo.	921	Should I distribute.	663	Strong in the Lord..	579
One more day's wor	140			Should my tears for.	871	Strong were thy foe	773
One privilege my...	91	Quick as their thoug	677	Should sudden veng	468	Subdue the power ..	360
One trial more must	706	Quicker yet and.....	581	Should swift death.	130	Such blessings from	798
One with thyself,...	264			Should thy people ..	306	Such, Father, give..	697
One word from thee	577	Raised on devotion's	229	Shortly this prison.	991	Such was our Lord;	263
Only, O Lord, in	662	Rebel, ye waves, an	194	Shout, ye little flock	532	Such was the pity..	436
Onward then! not to	1018	Rebuild thy walls,..	931	Show me what I....	61	Such was thy truth	260
Onward, then, ye ...	518	Rehearse his praise.	547	Show us some token	108	Sun, moon, and star	158
Onward we go, for..	235	Reign, Prince of life	330	Simple, teachable an	672	Son of our life	191
Open the hearts of..	378	Rejoice in hope and.	653	Sin and sorrow......	15	Supported by his ...	365
Open thou the cryst	134	Rejoice when care a	653	Since all that I	576	Sure as thy truth...	35
Order my footsteps.	171	Rejoice in glorious.	200	Since Christ and we	843	Sure I must fight ..	540
Other knowledge I..	479	Rejoice, ye that love	105	Since from his	268	Sure, never, till.....	279
Other lords have lon	618	Religion bears our..	604	Since in thy love...	375	Sure, such infinite .	283
Other refuge have I	505	Remember thee, an	862	Since thou hast been	29	Sweet—at the dawn	54
Our blessed Lord ...	424	Remember thee—th	864	Since thou, the ever	684	Sweet fields beyond	997
Our contrite spirits.	877	Remember thy pure	850	Since, with pure and	522	Sweet hour of praye	73
" Our daily bread...	146	Renew my will from	738	Sing of his dying....	32	Sweet, in the confi..	711
Our daily course....	40	Rent the temple cur	778	Sing the Son's amaz	50	Sweet is the cross..	415
Our days are as.....	725	Renounce thy works	77	Sing we then eter...	50	Sweet is the day....	43
Our days are numbe	742	Repeated crimes aw	333	Sing we, too, the....	50	Sweet is thy speech	341
Our eyes have seen.	833	Restraining prayer.	77	Sinners, believe the	438	Sweet on this day...	54
Our faith adores ...	836	Return, almighty G	925	Sinners, see your ..	343	Sweet the day of....	103
Our father's God! to	1050	Return, O holy Dove	493	Sinners, whose love.	329	Sweet the place, ex.	50
Our fathers where..	953	Return, O wanderer,	419	Slain to redeem.....	336	Sweet to look inwar	711
Our Fellow-sufferer.	75	Revive our drooping	361	So at last, when.....	313	Swift as an eagle ...	525
Our glad hosannas .	253	Richer than all eart	1065	So, blessed Spirit,..	815	Swift on the wings.	1056
Our God in pity.....	424	Rise, Saviour! help.	496	So fades a summer..	942	Swift through the..	254
Our grateful souls,.	1062	Rise, touched with..	421	So, gracious Saviour	340	Swift to its close....	127
Our hearts are break	1035	Riven the rock for..	487	So it shall be.......	718		
Our hearts be pure..	340	Rivers to the ocean.	939	So Jesus looked.....	794		
Our hearts, by dyin	606	Rock of ages, I'm...	584	So Jesus slept; God'	966	Take courage, then,	470
Our heavenly Fathe	843	Round each habitat	753	So let thy grace.....	200	Take my soul and...	875
Our heavenly Fathe	379			So long thy power..	734	Take the things of..	371
Our hope and expect	1021	Sad to his toil.......	546	So now, and till we..	803	Take me all thy.....	631
Our labors done,...	951	Safe the dreary.....	4	So pure, so soul.....	175	Teach me to live....	72
Our life is a dream..	1057	Saint after saint.....	959	So shall my walk ...	403	Teach me to live....	113
Our life while thou.	1032	Saints below with...	107	So songs shall rise..	1031	Teach us, in every..	723

G

FIRST LINES OF STANZAS. 429

First line	Hymn	First line	Hymn	First line	Hymn	First line	Hymn
Teach us, in watch..	909	The hosts of saints.	1042	Their streaming tea	674	There rest shall foll	544
Teach us, O Lord...	943	The humble supplis	68	Their toils are past.	970	There safe thou shal	847
Tell him,—it was...	443	The joy of all........	328	Then all these waste	923	There servants, mas	969
Tell him of that.....	443	The King himself...	30	Their daily wants hi	676	There shall each rap	32
Tell how he cometh;	247	The kingdom that I	727	Then entering the.	758	There shall I bathe.	682
Tell me the same ...	413	The least and feeble	683	Then felt my soul...	387	There shall I offer..	91
Tell me the story...	413	The light of love....	269	Then gentle patienc	945	There shall I wear.	524
Tell of his wondrous	208	The light of smiles..	735	Then if thou thy....	155	There shall no doub	736
Ten thousand thous	187	The lofty hills and..	545	Then I hope like....	630	There the blest Man	1041
Thanks for mercies.	1048	The Lord builds up.	87	Then in a nobler....	308	There the glory is ev	1000
Thanks we give, and	136	"The Lord is risen...	318	Then let me take ...	608	There the glorious..	307
That awful word,...	252	The Lord, our glory.	151	Then let my faith...	952	There the great Mon	26
That blood which flo	848	The Lord proclaims	88	Then let my soul....	524	There the Lamb, our	1015
That heavenly influe	376	The Lord sits sovere	88	Then let the hope...	954	There the wind is...	1017
That light shall.....	905	The Lord will give..	231	Then let the last....	953	There, there, on eagl	69
That, long as life....	819	The Lord will raise.	930	Then let the name..	342	There—there unsha	656
That love this rest..	745	The love of Christ..	892	Then let the visits..	506	There, when the tur	951
That peace which flo	697	The love the Father	828	Then let our songs..	31	There will the gra...	59
That peace which su	697	The Master, whom	775	Then let our sorrow	970	There's not a plant...	205
That power we trace	180	The meanest child..	1042	Then let us adore...	97	There's the city to ..	1000
That rich atoning...	72	The men of grace...	31	Then let us earnest.	70	Therefore I murmur	994
That sacred stream.	919	The mighty God,...	525	Then let us joyful...	544	These ashes, too, thi	951
That tender heart...	263	The more I strove..	334	Then let us open....	94	These speak of these	227
That thus the wilder	779	The more I triumph	646	Then linger not in..	442	These temples of....	772
That truth gives....	745	The mountains in...	764	Then love's soft dew	951	These through fiery	999
That where thou art	324	The mountains melt	150	Then may a Saviour	1053	They all, in life.....	960
That will not murm	1008	The names of all....	349	Then, mortal, turn!	938	They are justified by	640
That word above all	215	The opening heaven	610	Then, my soul, in...	64	They are lights upo	640
The almighty Form	270	The order of thy....	770	Then needful still ..	303	They come! they co	931
The answering hills	240	The pains of death..	962	Then, O my Lord ...	948	They go from streng	11
The apostles' glorio	203	The pains, the groan	941	Then place them in.	132	They have come fro	1016
The apostle's join...	85	The patient soul, th	665	Then shall I end....	537	They saw himon ...	321
The battle soon.....	548	The peaceful gates.	326	Then shall I love ...	166	They scorn to seek.	677
The beam that shin	1028	The pity of the......	725	Then shall I see.....	43	They stand, those...	1022
The beams of noon..	202	The prisoner here ..	160	Then shall my latest	486	They watch for soul	761
The best obedience.	469	The purchase of thy	844	Then shall my soul..	164	Thine all-surroundi.	200
The best relief that.	169	The rising God forsa	295	Then shall new lust	118	Thine armor is......	548
The birds, without .	574	The rising tempest.	442	Then shall our heart	37	Thine image, Lord .	72
The bounties of thy	595	The rolling sun	158	Then shall the mour	882	Thine inward teach	352
The bow of mercy...	1033	The Sabbath to our	94	Then shall wars and	903	Thine the Name to..	306
The bride eyes not..	1037	The saints on earth	827	Then shone almight	252	"Thine, then, for ev	146
The calm retreat....	52	The saints shall flow	920	Then, should the ear	189	Thine was the cross	1029
The captive to relea	780	The saints, who her	1021	Then, then shall I...	620	Thine would I live,.	812
The church from he	174	The Saviour bids th	667	Then, thou Church.	1046	Think of thy sorrow	471
The clouds may go..	822	The Saviour smiles!	477	Then though thou...	713	Think what Spirit..	521
The clouds which...	108	The shadow of	29	Then to draw near..	741	This be my joy......	841
The Comforter has c	995	The shining firmam	762	Then, to thy courts.	46	This glorious hope...	823
The consecrated cro	543	The Son of God.....	416	Then, when among	884	This heavenly calm	47
The covenant of the	1069	The soul by faith ...	694	Then, when on earth	738	This holy bread and	845
The cross is all thy.	1020	"The soul that on..	563	Then, when our wor	706	This hope supports.	551
The crowd of cares.	654	The sovereign will..	301	Then, when the glo.	782	This is the field.....	167
The cup of blessing.	863	The Spirit, like some	391	Then will he own...	541	This is the hidden...	702
The dawn on distant	570	The Spirit wrought.	407	Then will I say,.....	695	This is the judge...	167
The day glides swee	677	The storm is laid ...	1052	Then will I teach...	474	This is the way.....	334
The day is gone.....	142	The sun set in.......	291	Then will I tell,....	334	This lamp, through.	165
The dead in Christ..	976	The sun that lights.	564	Then, with my wak.	485	This life's a dream—	955
The dearest Idol ...	493	The sure provisions.	636	Then with our spirit	360	This only can my ...	703
The deepest reveren	210	The threatenings of	386	Thence he arose, as.	953	This pilgrim-path ..	572
The dew of heaven..	201	The time, how lovel	149	There all around sh.	1031	This precious truth.	199
The dying thief.....	398	The trials that beset	1005	There all the follow	1039	This spotless robe..	607
The earth shall soon	400	The trivial round, th	662	There, low before...	1039	This spring with liv	820
The evening-cloud..	954	The unbelieving wo	337	There faith lifts up.	1013	This was compassio	280
The ever-blessed...	276	The vaulted heavens	545	There for me the....	500	Those joys which ea	835
The eye that rolled.	259	The voice at mid....	962	There fragrant flowe	1013	Those mighty orbs..	196
The faith by which.	1005	The watchmen join.	749	There happier bowe	1009	Thou alone, my.....	504
The Father is in	226	The want of sight...	661	There, if thy spirit..	52	Thou art a God	36
The Father owned..	817	The way the holy...	334	There, in worship...	57	Thou art gone up...	319
The fearful soul tha	392	The weakness I	592	Tucre is a dark	715	Thou art gone up ...	321
The feeling heart,...	108	The whole creation.	325	There is a day.......	735	Thou art gone, whe.	301
The fires that rushe	370	The whole creation	979	There is a death	381	Thou art my ever...	348
The flowery spring.	184	The wicked there f	969	There is a gulf......	715	Thou art my refuge	475
The gladness of....	833	The wilderness affor	658	There is a home for.	1013	Thou art our holy..	803
The glorious sky....	201	The wings of every.	89	There is a home of..	1011	Thou art the earnes	359
The God of Abraha	95	The works and won.	159	There is a laud of...	1043	Thou art the Life...	265
"The God of glory,..	1027	The works of God...	201	There is a place.....	69	Thou art the sea....	503
The God we worship	770	Tho world can never	381	There is a scene.....	69	Thou art the Truth.	265
The grace of Christ.	121	The world recedes...	967	There is a stream ...	919	Thou art the Way...	265
The graves of all...	953	The world shut out.	702	There is no death in.	1040	Thou, blessed Son of	601
The hand, that gave	173	The world's Desire.	914	There is no want in.	1040	Thou callest me.....	27
The healing of......	271	The wounded consci	656	There is the throne.	1022	Thou canst fit me...	503
The heathen lands..	920	The year is with ...	49	There is welcome...	214	Thou canst not toil.	782
The heaven where I	646	The year rolls round	1055	There Jesus shall...	1023	Thou cowest in the.	243
"The heavenly babe	238	Thee may our tongu	637	There, joys, unseen.	1012	Thou didst create ..	332
The highest hopes..	991	Thee will I love,....	591	There, like streams.	754	Thou givest me the.	699
The highest place...	328	Thee, with the tribe	580	There let the way ..	485	Thou hast helped ...	62
The hill of Zion	31	Their bodies in the..	947	There, mighty God..	26	Thou hast no shore	1004
The holy church....	85	Their harmony shall	150	There no sigh of	1045	Thou hast prepared.	840
The holy church....	203	Their joy shall bear.	151	There, no more at...	1045	Thou hast promised	804
The hopes that holy	101	Their ransomed.....	947	Thereon thee I	293	Thou hast raised....	313
The hosts of God....	671	Their sighs are lost.	1030	There, purity with.	1011	Thou hast redeemed	960

G

FIRST LINES OF STANZAS.

First Line	Hymn	First Line	Hymn	First Line	Hymn	First Line	Hymn
Thou heard'st, well	1060	Thus when the night	116	To comfort and to bl	780	Walk in the light!	655
Thou holy God!	210	Thus while his death	279	To-day, a pardoning	417	Was it for crimes	277
Thou knowest, Lord	475	Thus will the church	825	To-day attend his	93	Water can cleanse	808
Thou knowest that I	603	Thus would I live	702	To-day he rose	19	Water with heaven	378
Thou lovely Chief of	987	Thy body, broken	862	To-day on weary	16	We are his people	78
Thou now ascended	75	Thy bountiful care	98	To dwell with God—	1032	We are sinful	374
Thou, O Christ ! art	505	Thy chosen temple	24	To each the soul	674	We are watching	787
Thou, our only Life	449	Thy church is in the	925	To ever fragrant	578	We ask not, Father,	697
Thou, our Saviour,	717	Thy counsels, Lord	741	To faint, to grievo	261	We bless thy Son	219
Thou, Saviour, art	608	Thy cross, thy lone	882	To Father, Son, and	830	We bring them, Lor	790
"Thou shalt see my	856	Thy foes might hate	264	To gentle offices of	707	We can see that dist	1035
Thou spread'st the	657	Thy footsteps we fol	814	To God I cried	233	We come to show	887
Thou the Spring of	446	Thy glory o'er crea	164	To God, the Father	845	We expect a bright	519
Thou, thou alone	917	Thy goodness, like	219	To God, the only	124	We follow thee, our	551
Thou ! who didst co	368	Thy grace, O God	394	To God the Son	230	We have no refuge	131
Thou, who dost fill	362	Thy grace still dwel	612	To God the Spirit's	230	We have not reache	119
Thou, who hast give	201	Thy hand sets fast	49	To the heavens his	982	We hear thy voice,	227
Thou, who houseles	426	Thy hands, dear Jes	187	To heaven, tho	208	We join to sing	17
Thou, who sinless	129	Thy Holy Spirit	375	To him, enthroned	336	We laid them down	959
Thou, who wast so	718	"Thy kingdom come	146	To him I owe	268	We lay our garment	123
Thou, who with "st	302	Thy love, oh, how	621	To Jesus, our atonfu	337	We'll crowd thy gat	78
Thou, whose all-per	129	Thy love will there	1034	To Jordan's stream	807	We'll gird our loins	1010
Thou, whose inspiri	362	Thy mercy-seat is	605	To-morrow's sun	424	We long to hear	959
Thou wilt ! thou dos	572	Thy name my in	460	To mine illumined	352	We love thy name	810
Thou wondrous Adv	859	Thy nature gracious	489	To serve the present	307	We mark her goodly	757
Though cast down	733	Thy noblest wonder	159	To songs of praise	54	We meet at thy	59
Though clouds may	505	Thy precepts make	170	To spread the rays	262	We meet the grace	824
Though coming wea	411	Thy presence makes	850	To the desert or	510	We meet, through	908
Though dark and dr	1030	Thy power and glory	350	To the great One	223	We meet, we sing	917
Though dark be my	576	Thy powerful aid su	945	To thee all angels	208	We, O Lord ! with	301
Though dead, they	535	Thy promise is my	515	To thee, and theo	593	We ourselves are G	1046
Though destruction	139	Thy saints, lu all	540	To thee I tell	605	We see thy hand	132
Though earth and	282	Thy servant, —me	491	To thee ten thous	326	We seek the couse	817
Though faith and ho	728	Thy Spirit shall	843	To thee, the Lamb	830	We share our mutu	823
Though high above	156	Thy Sprit's power!	178	To thee we still	843	We sink beneath	810
Though I lavish all	641	Thy Spirit then will	918	To them tho cross	328	We soon shall see	551
Though in a bare	8	Thy sweet yoke I'd	478	To them the privileg	676	We still like them	94
Though in a foreign	553	Thy teachings make	364	"To thy pardoning	303	We tasto thee, O	595
Though like a wand	485	Thy throne eternal	204	To us remains nor	639	We told him all	724
Though long tho we	609	Thy throne, O God	354	To us the light	354	We trust not in our	819
Though Lord of all,	276	Thy throne, O God !	341	To watch and pray,	766	We walk by faith	991
Though numerous	404	Thy truth unchange	598	To win thee from	762	We would no longer	925
Though oft I seem	728	Thy walls are made	1007	"To you in David's	238	Weak is the effort	613
Though raised to a	349	Thy way is in	580	Toil, trial, sufferings	3	Weak, unworthy	883
Though Sinai's curs	635	Thy word is ever	170	Too faint our autho	125	Weakened by the	483
Though snares and	558	Thy word is richer	175	Too soon we rise;	686	Weary sinner, keep	452
Though the night be	139	Thy work alone	396	Tossed on time's ruf	577	Welcome, all by sin	533
Though to-day we're	733	Thy works with sov	89	Trials make the pro	720	Were half the breath	77
Though unseen now	865	Till, crowned with	814	Trials must and will	720	Were I in heaven,	741
Though unworthy is	963	Till, having all	579	True, 'tis a strait	525	Were I inspired to	663
Though vine nor fig	555	Till, of the prize	551	Truly blessed is	860	Were the whole real	275
Though we are guilt	117	Till then I would	613	Trust thee as the	643	Well might tho heav	409
Though with a scorn	771	Till then—nor is	597	Trust thy blood to	643	Well might the sun	277
Though we pass thr	519	Time, like an ever-	964	Trusting only in	446	Well—the delightful	61
Thrice happy man !	695	'Tis a broad land	109	Tune your harps	315	Well when they see	692
Thrice holy Fount.	377	'Tis but in part	206	'Twas for my sins	278	Westward, all along	598
Through all eternity	187	'Tis by thy death	380	'Twas grace that tau	460	What can I say	467
Through all his wor	109	'Tis conflict here bel	1044	'Twas ho who clean	337	What change! throu	1060
Through all the win	506	'Tis done, tho great	813	'Twas his own	395	What glories were	924
Through changes br	124	'Tis everlasting pea	622	'Twas sovereign me	178	What I am, as one	630
Through duties and	816	'Tis finished all	276	'Twas the same love	861	What I hope to	630
Through each perpl	798	'Tis gloom and dark	544	'Twas thro' the Lam	535	What if the spring	741
Through every peri	187	'Tis God's all-anima	539			What is my being	668
Through floods and	816	'Tis he forgives thy	669	Unnumbered comfo	187	What language shall	290
Through him the	271	'Tis he, my soul !	41	Unnumbered myria	232	What peaceful hour	493
Through many thing	400	'Tis he supports	25	Unite us in the	1051	What rush of halle	1006
Through nature's w	228	'Tis he that works	365	Until the trump of	838	What shall I before	983
Through paths of lo	254	'Tis he that works	673	Unto him all power	899	What thanks I owe	52
Through tho long ni	141	'Tis he who saveth	651	Unto us a child	246	What things shall	523
Through the water.	573	'Tis here whence'er	164	Unshaken as eternal	757	What thou, my Lord	290
Through the valley.	564	'Tis Jesus calls me	411	Unworthy, as I am	578	What thou shalt to	642
Through this chang	568	'Tis like the sun	170	Up, then, with speed	903	What though in lone	738
Through this vain	435	'Tis mercy—mercy	511	Up to her courts	20	What though in sol	183
Through waves, and	554	'Tis not that murmu	754	Up to the hills	36	What though my joy	575
Thus do his willing	818	'Tis only in thee	289	Upon the crystal	543	What, though parte	307
Thus far thine arm	1062	'Tis pleasant to bell	991			What though tempt	608
Thus God descended	815	'Tis sin, alas ! with	510	Vain, sinful man	53	What though the sp	890
Thus may I rejoice	631	'Tis the Christian's	1036	Vain the stone, tho	305	What though the te	904
Thus may we abide	138	'Tis the Saviour	310	Vain were all our	791	What though the wo	728
Thus might I hide	277	'Tis the soul	1011	Vainer still the	791	What though thou	554
Thus—oh, thus an	629	'Tis thine the passio	385	Vainly we offer	250	What thrilling joy	1038
Thus shall the wond	92	'Tis thine to cleanse	361	Victor o'er death	322	Whate'er events be	552
Thus shall they gua	952	'Tis thine to soothe	360	V'dest of the fall	875	Whate'er thy provid	703
Thus shall we best	664	'Tis thy grace alone	306	Vine of heaven ! thy	852	Whate'er thy sacred	703
Thus spake the sera	238	'Tis to my Saviour	668	Visit, then, this soul	14	When all I am	702
Thus till my last	21	'Tis well when Jesus	682			When at last I near	1063
Thus, till my last	497	'Tis well when joys	692	Waft, waft, ye winds	890	When at Marah	573
Thus, through the	931	To a pleasant land	100	Wait, then, my soul !	142	When black the thre	715
Thus we remember.	850	To breathe, and wak	963	Waiting will not	430	When by the dreadf	1052
Thus, when life's toil	65	To chase the shades	385	Waken, O Lord, our	1055	When darkness see	686

G

INDEX OF SUBJECTS.

Entry	Hymn	Entry	Hymn	Entry	Hymn	Entry	Hymn
When death shall in	1061	When the trumpet.	983	While thy glorious..	3	Without thee but...	821
When death these..	604	When the victory...	573	While thy word is..	3	Work on, despair no	706
When doubts distur	193	When the weary...	873	While to thee our...	3	Working will not...	430
When drooping plea	609	When the wildernes	573	While we seek sup.	13	Worship, honor, po.	302
When each can feel.	829	When the woes of...	300	While we thus, with	883	Worthy is he that...	338
When each day's sc	9	When thou didst ...	332	While with a meltin	278	"Worthy the Lamb	23
When ends life's....	600	When thou, O Lord!	988	While with broken.	294	"Worthy the Lamb	325
When fear her chilli	746	"When through tier	563	While yet in anguish	864	Would not my heart	603
When first before hi	705	"When through the	563	Whither, ah! whithe	466		
When, free from env	829	When thy voice in .	983	Who best can drink	790	Ye aged, hither......	60
When free grace aw	619	When to the cross..	882	Who by the closest.	180	Ye are traveling....	532
When from my dyin	410	When trials sore....	455	Who is this that.....	313	Ye chosen seed of...	329
When from the dust	607	When trouble, like a	404	Who made this brea	480	Ye fearful saints.....	209
When gladness wing	185	When troubles rise.	91	Who shall adjudge.	679	Ye mortals, mark its	118
When God inclines.	68	When unto thee I...	601	Who suffer with our	558	Ye nations, bend....	194
When God makes up	924	When we asunder..	823	Who, who would liv	933	Ye, no more your...	754
When he came the..	628	When we disclose...	22	Whose breast expan	797	Ye pilgrims! on.....	32
When first the work	929	When we in dark...	553	Whose space is all..	660	Ye saints! who stan	625
When he lived on...	585	When we pass o'er.	304	Why restless, why .	473	Ye saw of old........	477
When I faint with ..	4	When we seek relief	562	Why should my pass	509	Ye sinners! seek his	980
When I stand on....	573	When we tell the ...	805	Why should this an	549	Ye souls that are...	402
When I touch the...	629	Whence we came, an	1058	Why should we tre	455	Ye wheels of nature	1056
When I tread the...	134	Where all things sh	122	Why shrinks my so	952	Ye who see the	533
When I walk throu.	636	Whene'er to call	355	Why that blood his	310	Ye who, tossed on..	426
When in distress to.	216	Where is the blessed	493	"Why was I made	861	Ye young, before...	60
When, in ecstacy...	855	When prophet's wor	798	Wide as the world..	78	Yea, Amen! let all..	986
When in flowery pat	670	Where should our fe	358	Wide it unvails ce..	656	Yea, though I walk.	602
When, in the slipper	187	Where the cross, Go	790	Wilt thou not cease	417	Yea—when this fies.	400
When in the solemn	455	Where the Paschal.	851	Wisdom and zeal, a	766	Yes,—and I must...	469
When in the sultry.	8	Where the saints of.	933	With a childlike...	631	Yes, God is love;—	746
When life sinks a pac	574	Where we, preserve	122	With boldness, tier	75	Yes! I believe; and	645
When my dim reaso	193	Where we, with all.	1025	With bounding step	250	Yes, keep me calm.	647
When mystery clou	746	Where'er I look, my	632	With grateful heart	1061	Yes, my Redeemer.	278
When nature sinks.	168	Where'er I turn my	198	With high and heav	850	Yes!—thou art prec	612
When no eye its.....	285	Wherever he may ..	556	With him sweet con	658	Yes,—thou shalt rei	928
When on Calvary...	855	Which of all our ...	585	With his rich gifts.	26	Yes, whosoever will	441
When on my aching	455	While all our hearts,	861	With humble faith.	550	Yet doth the star of.	1067
When once it enters	170	While anoints shout.	347	With jasper glow th	1004	Yet doth the world.	288
When once thou visi	637	While, from Californ	899	With joy shall we...	402	Yet, Father, thou ar	722
When our earthly ..	64	While he affords ...	595	With joy the chorus	254	Yet, gracious God..	605
When our eyes grow	716	While he is absent..	839	With joy thy people	770	Yet I may love......	648
When round our hea	523	While I am a.......	61	With joy we bring..	802	Yet I mourn my....	499
When shall I reach.	989	While I draw this...	871	With joy we in his..	818	Yet, Lord, for us....	838
When shall the sovo	550	While I draw this ..	874	With joy we tell ...	647	Yet, Lord, to thy...	125
When should not th	653	While in thy house.	33	With longing eyes..	197	Yet not thus buried	951
When, shriveling lik	981	While life's dark ..	600	With my burden....	61	Yet ours the grateful	607
When soft the dews	112	While looking to Jes	620	With pitying eyes..	434	Yet save a tremblin	468
When sorrowing o'o	708	While many crowd..	917	With prayer and....	548	Yet sinners saved...	232
When storms of fierc	686	While our days on..	57	With sacred awe....	210	Yet there is One....	342
When that happy er	628	While our silent ste	731	With that "blessed	1014	Yet this my soul....	172
When that illustriou	540	While place we seek	659	With thee conversin	27	Yet though I have..	604
When the heart is ..	716	While resounds the.	249	With thee, in thee..	120	Yet whilst around .	831
When the morning .	627	While sinners in des	984	With thee when da.	120	Yet why, dear Lord,	181
When tho morning.	141	While the souls of..	784	With thee when day	120	Yet would I lift.....	190
When the must help	794	While they around.	298	With us in the......	588	"Yonder sits my sli	974
When the pangs of..	272	While this thorny..	130	With us their names	947	Yonder throne for..	309
When the secret	718	While this we do...	850	With us when the..	588		
When the star-beam	627	While through this.	842	With us when we...	588	Zion, all its light....	982
When the storms of.	293	While through this	364	Within thy circling.	188	Zion enjoys her Mon	919
When the sun of....	300	While thus we mou	860	Within thy presence	699	Zion—thrice happy.	1

INDEX OF SUBJECTS.

THE FIGURES REFER TO THE HYMNS.

Abba, Father.......693, 685, 529, 644	To Judgment,......974-988, 319, 337	Ashamed of Jesus......541, 597, 284
Abide with me.127, 119, 120, 112,	To Kingdom...See *Millennium*.	Asleep in Jesus......944, 947, 977, 951
1083, 621, 702	Advocate................See *Christ*.	Assurance:
Absence from God...222, 408, 946, 408	Afflictions........704-748, 622, 431, 499	Expressed......528, 822, 689, 594, 688
Accepted Time.....418, 406, 424, 427	Aged..................See *Old Age*.	Prayed for........362, 359, 367, 499
Access to God...394-415. See *Prayer*.	Almost Christian...392, 430, 420, 469	Urged........553, 525, 576, 533, 558
Activity..........779-797, 963, 517-576	Alms...................797, 780, 792	Atonement:
Adoption....676, 685, 691, 693, 703, 648	Angels......788, 822, 235, 248, 139, 141	Necessary......381-397, 871, 587
Advent of Christ:	Ark of God..................847, 508	Completed........393, 398-415, 696
At Birth.............234-256, 60	Ascension.............See *Christ*.	Autumn...........1050, 1046, 184, 222

G

INDEX OF SUBJECTS.

Backsliding..............458, 481-516
Baptism.......................607-822
Benevolence..............See *Alms*.
Bible......................158-175
Brotherly love..823-829, 674, 663, 641
Burial......See *Death* and *Heaven*.
 A Child..........935, 951, 945, 733
 A Pastor........902, 934, 947, 972

Calmness.........649, 647, 665, 642
Calvary........855, 276, 285, 889, 887
Cares....549, 537, 594, 654, 555, 561, 574
Charity..............663, 794, 641
Cheerfulness...306, 594, 575, 639,
                                654, 1003
Children.........170, 798-806
Childlike spirit....642, 631, 480, 685
Christ:
 Advent at Birth........63, 234-256
 Advocate.....303, 323, 333, 327,
                859, 405, 326, 689
 Ascension.........301, 307, 313, 319
 Captain of Salvation..524, 518,
                           557, 560
 Character of......257-272, 341, 350
 Corner-stone...........751, 771, 753
 Crucifixion................274-290
 Desire of Nations.....909, 787,
                       756, 914, 1029, 1026
 Divinity..252, 342, 316, 218, 251, 244
 Example.........257-272, 590, 672
 Friend......613, 594, 585, 628, 859
 Hiding-place.......656, 683, 289, 871
 Humanity....75, 246, 243, 590,
                         718, 257-272
 Immanuel....251, 628, 244, 606, 245
 King.......328, 301, 311, 320, 330, 341
 Lamb......281, 289, 396, 382, 325, 338
 Life, incidents of......664, 257-272
 Lord, our Righteousness..688,
                     607, 382, 407, 411, 390
 Love......270, 280, 290, 437, 344, 421
 Mediator.....283, 386, 327, 382, 405
 Priest......327, 349, 333, 303, 75, 337
 Prince of Glory.......275, 313, 339
 Prince of Peace......336, 245, 253
 Prophet.......257, 633, 262, 613
 Refuge ...605, 466, 686, 215, 505, 522
 Resurrection of............301-349
 Rock of Ages....871, 874, 753, 176
 Saviour ..253, 236, 270, 303, 317, 390
 Shepherd.....4, 8, 556, 564, 595,
                          602, 634, 799
 Sufferings of................273-299
 Sun of Righteousness.14, 111,
                       158, 627, 913
 Way, Truth, and Life....265,
                            334, 502
 Wisdom......174, 413, 696, 390, 386
 Word..............218, 244, 252
Christians:
 Afflictions....................704-748
 Conflicts......................481-516
 Disciplines....................704-748
 Duties.........................779-797
 Encouragements..............516-584
 Fellowship............786, 823-829
 Graces.........................640-674
 Love for Christ..........585-639
 Privileges....................675-703
Church:
 Afflicted........759, 897, 916, 925
 Beloved of God......759, 35, 924
 Institutions of............749-778
 Missions of.................890-932
 Ordinances of..............807-889
 Revival of......897, 917, 918, 925
 Triumph of........757, 773, 9,1
 Unity of........693, 771, 825, 828
 Uniting with......See *Baptism*.
 Work of......................779-797
Close of Worship............112-157
Comforter........See *Holy Spirit*.
Communion with God.See *Prayer*.
Communion of Saints..See *Union*.
Completeness in Christ..... 675,
                             559, 528
Confession........See *Repentance*.
Confidence......405, 525, 840, 556,
                            688, 576

Conflict with Sin...........481-516
Conformity to Christ...257-271,
                   489, 570, 672, 664
Conscience.....387, 423, 382, 162, 279
Consecration:
 Of Possessions....780, 875, 792, 488
 Of Self....275, 888, 868, 875, 186,
                              498, 449-480
Consistency....664, 497, 482, 512,
                              559, 655, 541
Consolations........See *Afflictions*.
Constancy..519, 536, 541, 556, 565, 568
Contentment...594, 659, 578, 742, 642
Conversion......See *Regeneration*.
Conviction..................See *Law*.
Corner-stone...........751, 771, 753
Courage................789, 517-584
Covenant...527, 691, 684, 563, 681, 688
Creation.............78, 93, 99, 183, 198
Cross:
 Bearing ..543, 540, 529, 263, 266,
                              520, 284
 Glorying in...300, 264, 533, 275,
                          415, 520, 281
 Salvation by..415, 382, 275, 283,
                        270, 277, 286, 386
Crucifixion of Christ........274-290

Death.....................933-973
Decrees....178, 182, 189, 193, 195, 208
Dedication:
 Of a Church......See *Sanctuary*.
 Of one's self...See *Consecration*.
Delay............428, 418, 422, 424
Dependence:
 On Providence....177, 185, 187,
                      192, 209, 563, 213, 217
 On Grace.....382, 219, 408, 630,
                     461, 484, 365, 396
Depravity..................381-396, 462
Despondency See *Encouragements*.
Devotion................See *Prayer*.
Diligence...............See *Activity*.
Doubt............See *Encouragements*.
Doxologies.........80-82, *pp*. 412, 413

Earnestness........See *Activity*.
Earnest of the Spirit....350, 372,
                             355, 359
Election................See *Decrees*.
Encouragements............517-584
Energy..................See *Activity*.
Eternity........940, 743, 958, 985, 946
Evening......113, 123, 139, 141, 1072
Example:
 Of Christ.....257-272, 672, 627, 590
 Of Christians........640, 664, 264, 646
Faint-heartedness..524, 530, 554, 565
Faith...See *Confidence* and *Trust*.
 Gift of God..365, 645, 654, 650,
                    630, 643, 821, 373, 356
 Instrument in Justification:
    639, 430, 382, 651, 691, 688, 871
 Power of..656, 661, 658, 682, 600,
                    534, 688, 629, 527, 563
 Prayer for..645, 660, 605, 507,
                   562, 356, 1008, 820
Faithfulness of God.......See *God*.
Fall of Man........See *Lost State*.
Family..798, 802, 804, 141, 65, 71,
                     114, 120, 123, 139
Father, God our............See *God*.
Fearfulness........524, 530, 554, 565
Fellowship.....805, 823-829, 640, 674
Fidelity..796, 541, 664, 482, 559,
                            512, 497, 655
Forbearance:
 Divine....181, 186, 197, 212, 500,
                       422, 428, 464, 214
 Christian.....258, 264, 800, 647, 796
Forgiveness:
 Of Sin......See *Atonement* and
    Repentance.
 Of Injuries........264, 266, 647
Formality....357, 22, 33, 229, 641, 663
Friend, Christ our..613, 594, 585,
                                 828, 859
Friends in Heaven...See *Heaven*.
Funeral....See *Burial* and *Death*.

Future Punishment....976, 987,
              984, 981, 743, 974, 983, 985
Gentleness.262, 264, 643, 646, 664, 672
Gethsemane..........273, 276, 291
Glory of God................See *God*.
Glorying in the Cross...See *Cross*.
God:
 Attributes...................176-233
 Being.........163, 196, 201, 207, 176
 Benevolence......217, 184, 162, 196
 Compassion...212, 213, 41, 669, 566
 Condescension....280, 270, 209, 75
 Creator......78, 93, 99, 183, 198, 175
 Eternity.......943, 964, 176, 204, 213
 Faithfulness..90, 189, 208, 215,
                     187, 531, 563, 519, 523, 525
 Father....703, 685, 691, 693, 109,
                              203, 326, 207
 Forbearance..181, 186, 197, 212,
                      500, 422, 428, 464, 214, 648
 Glory......14, 98, 39, 84, 191, 196,
                              211, 228, 1074
 Goodness........84, 100, 217, 228
 Grace...41, 83, 92, 186, 196, 212,
                              214, 233, 690
 Holiness.......96, 203, 210, 211, 221
 Infinity..87, 89, 98, 180, 190, 193,
                              204, 206
 Jehovah.......78, 95, 109, 180, 207
 Justice......84, 92, 109, 182, 386, 395
 Love......178, 197, 199, 212, 225, 232
 Majesty......78, 85, 96, 101, 195, 129
 Mercy.......214, 224, 232, 270, 1069
 Mystery......182, 190, 193, 206, 209
 Omnipotence...88, 98, 194, 207,
                              208, 205, 215
 Omnipresence.....177, 64, 191,
                         200, 205, 227, 609
 Omniscience..177, 188, 200, 202,
                              397, 405
 Patience......181, 197, 212, 214,
                              500, 422, 464
 Pity.........71, 75, 224, 669, 566,
                              725, 409, 434
 Providence....84, 190, 192, 195,
                         206, 209, 555, 643
 Sovereignty ..178, 182, 189, 193,
                              195, 209
 Supremacy....82, 85, 78, 93, 96,
                         101, 203, 231, 1064
 Trinity........96, 179, 220, 223,
                              225, 230
 Truth......90, 150, 161, 189, 208,
                         523, 563, 574, 576
 Unchangeableness..86, 90, 522,
                    531, 545, 556, 178, 204, 719
 Unsearchableness..89, 180, 182,
                         190, 193, 195, 206, 209
 Wisdom......87, 193, 205, 225,
                         180, 204, 556, 710
Gospel.................See *Atonement*.
Grace........400, 432, 669, 690, 619,
                              533, 388
Graces, Christian........729, 344,
                              640-674
Gratitude....41, 657, 185-187, 669,
                    671, 648, 622, 709, 212, 217
Grave.............952, 966, 969, 971
Grieving the Spirit......See *Holy
 Spirit*.
Growth in Grace ...486, 790, 575,
                    690, 581, 650, 646, 654, 830, 553, 260
Guidance, Divine..134, 573, 734,
                    737, 135, 542, 487, 698, 556
Happiness....575, 594, 639, 654, 1003
Harvest.........1046, 1050, 184, 224
Hearing the Word..180, 145, 174,
                    136, 117, 124, 126, 142, 151
Heart:
 Change of......385, 388, 357, 350,
                         353, 489, 485, 502
 Deceitfulness of..387, 391, 410,
                         447, 458, 483, 489, 502
 Searching of..495, 366, 437, 340,
                         499, 502, 507, 650
 Surrender of..390, 480, 837, 868,
                    405, 411, 450, 458, 469, 474
Heaven:
 Christ there.....1020, 1039, 989,
                    1002, 1017, 1037, 1041

G

INDEX OF SUBJECTS. 433

Friends there..826, 1033, 1006, 1010, 1043, 953, 970
Home there.....995, 1034, 1043, 992, 994, 1015, 1031, 946
Rest there..990, 993, 1023, 1015, 944, 969, 939
Hell......See *Future Punishment.*
Heirship with Christ....676, 680, 687, 532, 640, 693
Hiding-place............See *Christ.*
Holiness:
 Of Christians.....652, 459, 650, 693
 Of God ....See *God.*
Holy Scriptures........See *Bible.*
Holy Spirit 350-380
 Divine........366, 369, 374, 377, 425
 Grieved.........358, 424, 425, 428
 Striving......355, 362, 365, 416, 425
 Witnessing......350, 372, 355, 359
Home......See *Family* or *Heaven.*
Home Missions.....892, 899, 913, 923, 898
Hope:
 Under Afflictions.....529, 544, 565, 723, 584, 707, 711, 719, 745, 737
 Under Conviction....382, 390, 401, 405, 411, 453, 533, 527, 693
 Under Despondency..519, 523, 521, 516, 537, 554, 558, 570
 In Death.....526, 301, 304, 324, 933, 936, 952, 955, 961
Humility ..729, 491, 642, 646, 665, 672

Immanuel..............See *Christ.*
Immortality ..526, 946, 304, 977, 936
Importunity ..62, 70, 76, 446, 451, 461
Imputation.....382, 386, 390, 396, 567, 407, 410, 688, 691, 1003
Incarnation 239, 244, 252, 270, 419
Ingratitude....495, 464, 421, 423, 425
Inspiration..159, 165, 173, 174, 352
Installation........See *Ministry.*
Intercession ...327, 349, 333, 303, 75, 332
Invitations ....— 416-445

Jehovah...............See *God.*
Jews........891, 900, 922, 927, 930
Jerusalem, The new..1027, 1035, 1004, 1007, 1009, 1017 1022, 1029, 1044
Joining the Church.....807-822, 834, 837, 854, 857, 863, 875, 888
Joy.....306, 653, 594, 610, 654, 682, 639
Judgment Day............973-988
Justice ....See *God.*
Justification...See *Atonement* and *Faith.*

Kindness......See *Brotherly Love.*
Kingdom of Christ....See *Millennium.*
Prayed for..915, 777, 903, 907, 1029, 756, 312
Progress of..757, 749, 754, 895, 902, 911, 329

Labor............See *Activity.*
Lamb of God............See *Christ.*
Law of God:
 And Gospel...167, 382, 386, 390, 396
 Conviction under.....383, 387, 410, 415, 446, 457, 468, 453
Liberality............780, 784, 792
Life:
 Brevity of.....940, 938, 943, 948, 954, 956, 958, 963
 Object of..939, 956, 381, 397, 423, 438, 957, 958
 Solemnity of..397, 949, 958, 963, 973, 987, 384
 Uncertainty of....938, 949, 418, 428, 956, 442, 783
Likeness to Christ...See *Conformity.*
Little Things...706, 662, 606, 765, 802
Longing:
 For God..648, 21, 29, 38, 461, 485, 493, 466, 460, 497
 For Christ....449, 508, 462, 484, 487, 505, 504, 572, 600

For Heaven..1051, 939, 949, 955, 968, 989, 993, 1004
Long-suffering...See *Forbearance.*
Lord's Day...........See *Sabbath.*
Lord's Prayer..............143, 146
Lord's Supper...............830-889
Lord, our Righteousness......See *Christ.*
Lost State of Man...........381-397
Love:
 Of God.................See *God.*
 Of Christ..............See *Christ.*
 Of Holy Spirit........358, 362, 368
 For God........178, 187, 222, 663, 591
 For the Saviour...........585-639
 For Saints.........523-829, 640, 674
 For Souls........397, 416, 414, 765
 For the Church......1, 35, 753, 827
 Loving-kindness 404, 553
Lukewarmness ...See *Formality.*

Majesty of God ....See *God.*
Man...............See *Lost State.*
Marriage 874
Martyrs....960, 569, 534, 548, 799, 1016
Mediator...............See *Christ.*
Mediatorial Reign..See *Kingdom.*
Meditation.....58, 52, 57, 65, 55, 509
Meekness...642, 646, 649, 665, 480, 264
Mercifulness .....See *Forgiveness.*
Mercy..................See *God.*
Mercy-Seat.........69, 74, 77, 51, 450
Millennium..767, 893, 756, 778, 902, 915, 916, 1024-1029, 1019, 932
Ministry...............See *Pastor.*
Commission 749, 761, 762, 771
Convocation 766, 762, 908, 786
Installation 763, 691, 761, 770
Prayer for 750, 765, 767, 768
Miracles..............229, 271, 807
Missions.....690-932, 779-807, 1086
Missionaries......891, 906, 776, 838
Morning 1070, 14, 25, 36, 40, 48
Mortality ......See *Life* and *Death.*
Mysteries of Providence...182, 190, 193, 195, 722, 727, 206, 209
National 1059, 1049, 1051, 1060, 772
Nature, the Material Universe:
 Beauties of......34, 49, 98, 99, 222
 God seen in....158, 102, 205, 177, 183, 198, 201, 227
Nearness:
 To God 572, 485, 609, 191, 493
 To Heaven.....949, 989, 1032, 1010
Needful, One Thing....393, 423, 461, 484
New Song, The 32, 23, 414, 336
New Year......1048, 1054, 1057, 1062
Night................See *Evening.*

Old Age........563, 933, 948, 1010, 747
Old, old Story..........413, 414, 270
Omnipotence............See *God.*
Omnipresence ....See *God.*
Omniscience ....See *God.*
Opening of Service.............1-11
Ordinances................807-889
Ordination............See *Ministry.*
Orphans........694, 780, 794, 1006
Pardons............See *Forgiveness.*
Parting............823, 666, 155, 126
Pastor.................See *Ministry.*
Prayed for.............768, 765, 379
Sought 767, 796, 750
Welcomed 763, 749, 891
Death of................See *Burial.*
Patience......258, 261, 264, 266, 739
Peace:
 Christian....111, 683, 694, 697, 822
 National......1049, 1051, 1028, 903
Peacemakers ..529, 824, 258, 264, 266
Penitence.........See *Repentance.*
Pentecost......368, 370.....See *Holy Spirit.*
Perseverance ..679, 882, 658, 691, 521, 524, 528, 533, 570, 607, 651
Pilgrims 1066
Pilgrim-Spirit..31, 573, 1000, 994, 532, 542, 544, 551, 570

Pity of God ....See *God.*
Pleasures 479, 392, 389, 381, 422, 955
Poor..............750, 785, 794-797, 807
Praise..............78-111, 176-233
Prayer................61-77, 660, 567
Preaching ....See *Ministry.*
Predestination.........See *Election.*
Pride...............See *Humility.*
Procrastination..........See *Delay.*
Prodigal Son 460, 419, 447, 470
Profession .....See *Lord's Supper.*
Progress ....See *Growth in Grace.*
Promises...189, 563, 519, 150, 203, 523
Providence...............See *God.*
Purity..........581..See *Holiness.*
Punishment...See *Future Punishment.*

Race, Christian.....525, 539, 558, 544
Receiving Christ..See *Repentance.*
Redemption ....See *Atonement.*
Refuge................See *Christ.*
Regeneration:
 Necessary 383, 385, 391, 394
 Prayed for 863, 450, 453, 489
 Wrought by God......383, 385, 391
Renunciation :
 Of the World......See *Pleasures.*
 Of Self.........See *Consecration.*
Repentance 446-516
Resignation 703-748
Rest..See *Meditation* and *Heaven.*
Resurrection :
 Of Christ............See *Christ.*
 Of Believers..526, 936, 947, 952, 955, 966, 977, 991, 1008
Retirement ....See *Meditation.*
Return to God......460, 447, 454, 457
Revival 750, 754, 916, 897, 917, 357, 361, 379, 375
Riches 939, 954, 780, 785, 607, 381
Righteousness, Robe of....407, 405, 469, 607, 689, 382
Rock of Ages.......871, 874, 753, 176

Sabbath 1-60
Sabbath-School ......See *Children.*
Sacraments 807-889
Sailors 1053, 1052, 1063, 207
Salvation ....See *Atonement.*
Sanctification......See *Growth in Grace*, and *Assurance.*
Sanctuary :
 Corner-Stone 751, 753, 757, 771
 Dedication 752, 764, 760, 769
 Love for......1, 35, 753, 827
Satan 734, 518, 736, 547, 77
Saviour................See *Christ.*
Science....See *Nature* and *Bible.*
Scriptures.............See *Bible.*
Seamen.................See *Sailors.*
Self-deception..........See *Heart.*
Self-dedication..See *Consecration.*
Self-denial ..802, 803, 799, 389, 392, 662
Self-examination......495, 366, 377, 430, 499, 502, 507, 650
Self-renunciation...See *Consecration.*
Self-righteousness..396, 382, 383, 688
Sensibility...........See *Weeping.*
Shepherd...............See *Christ.*
Sickness 711, 713, 727, 736, 622
Sin :
 Indwelling..........See *Conflict.*
 Original ....See *Lost State.*
 Conviction of.....See *Law* and *Hope.*
Sincerity 664, 665, 650, 641, 672
Soldier, Christian..518, 524, 540, 547
Soul of Man.........See *Immortality.*
Souls, Love for..........See *Love*
Sovereignty ....See *God.*
Spirit..........See *Holy Spirit.*
Spring 1068, 100, 184, 198, 222
Star of Bethlehem..241, 1067, 63, 250
Steadfastness.....529, 545, 556, 563, 571
Storm 194, 88, 231, 98
Strength, as Days..584, 706, 455, 529
Submission 704-748

G

Summer 222, 184, 1068, 100, 198
Sun of Righteousness..See *Christ*.
Sympathy.....See *Brotherly Love*.
Te Deum............1074, 203, 85, 101
Temperance 781, 800, 664, 443
Temptation ....See *Conflict*.
Thanksgiving ..1046, 1050, 1065, 1069
Time......................See *Life*.
To-day 418, 428, 384, 949, 424
To-morrow 418, 428, 424, 442
Trials.......720, 709, 728, 735, 742, 563
Trinity....................See *God*.
Trust:
  In Christ....726, 643, 688, 1003, 640
  In Providence...209, 1083, 705,
        719, 555, 531, 522, 561, 574

Unbelief.....See *Faith* or *Conflict*.
Union of Saints:
  To Christ....680, 637, 689, 1002, 843
  To each other.....823-829, 666, 674
  In Heaven and on Earth..826,
        821, 758, 771, 752, 1010
Vows, Christian........812, 513, 819
Waiting..............See *Patience*.
Wandering.......See *Backsliding*.
War..................1028..See *Peace*.
Warfare, Christian....See *Soldier*.
Warnings..........See *Invitations*.
Washing of Saints' Feet....830-842
Watchfulness.......530, 547, 557, 579
Way of Salvation..See *Atonement*.

Wealth ....See *Riches*.
Weeping........793, 416, 430, 546,
                      447, 1011
Winds, God in the 194, 89, 1068
Winter......................184, 1068
Wisdom ....See *God*.
Witness ....See *Holy Spirit*.
Word of God............See *Bible*.
Worldliness.........See *Pleasures*.
Wrath ...See *Future Punishment*.

Year, Opening and Closing ....
   1061, 1062, 1047, 1058, 1043, 1057,
                      1054-1056
Zeal ....See *Activity*.
Zion................See *Church*.

INDEX OF FIRST LINES OF HYMNS.

HYMN.
A broken heart, my God, my King................ 474
A charge to keep I have....................... 397
A few more years shall roll.................... 948
A mighty fortress is our God................... 215
A mother may forgetful be..................... 739
A parting hymn we sing....................... 844
A pilgrim through this lonely world........... 263
Abba, Father, hear thy child.................. 644
Abide with me! Fast falls the eventide........ 127
According to thy gracious word................ 862
Acquaint thyself quickly, O sinner............ 429
Again our earthly cares we leave.............. 106
Again returns the day of holy rest............1070
Alas! and did my Saviour bleed................ 277
Alas! what hourly dangers rise................ 404
All hail the power of Jesus' name............. 220
All people that on earth do dwell............. 79
All praise to thee, eternal Lord.............. 243
Along my earthly way.......................... 722
Along the mountain track of life.............. 572
Always with us, always with us................ 585
Am I a soldier of the cross................... 540
Amazing grace! how sweet the sound............ 460
And can it be that I should gain.............. 680
And canst thou, sinner! slight................ 417
And dost thou say, "Ask what thou wilt?"..... 76
And is the time approaching................... 833
And is there, Lord, a rest.................... 996
And will the Judge descend 980
Angels rejoiced and sweetly sung.............. 239
Angels! roll the rock away.................... 297
Another six days' work is done................ 47
Approach, my soul! the mercy seat............. 515
Arise, my soul, arise......................... 405
Arise, O King of grace, arise................. 777
Arise, ye saints, arise....................... 551
Arm of the Lord ! awake, awake................ 904
Art thou weary, art thou languid 560
As oft with worn and weary feet............... 590
As pants the hart for cooling streams 473
As shadows, cast by cloud and sun.............1067
As when in silence vernal showers 376

HYMN.
As with gladness men of old................... 63
Ascend thy throne, almighty King.............. 910
Asleep in Jesus! blessed sleep 941
Assembling at thy great command............... 908
At evening time let there be light............ 707
At the Lamb's high feast we sing.............. 851
Awake, and sing the song 32
Awake, awake the sacred song.................. 252
Awake, my heart, arise, my tongue 407
Awake, my soul, and with the sun 48
Awake, my soul, stretch every nerve 539
Awake, my soul, to joyful lays................ 404
Awake, our souls! away, our fears............. 525
Awake, ye saints! and raise your eyes.........1056
Awaked by Sinai's awful sound................. 383
Away from earth my spirit turns............... 608
Awhile in spirit, Lord to thee................ 292
Be merciful to me, O God 475
Be still, my heart! these anxious cares 705
Be tranquil, O my soul........................ 739
Before Jehovah's awful throne................. 78
Before the heavens were spread abroad......... 244
Begin, my tongue, some heavenly theme 208
Begone, unbelief, my Saviour is near 576
Behold a Stranger at the door 421
Behold the day is come 079
Behold the glories of the Lamb 990
Behold, the mountain of the Lord..............1028
Behold the throne of grace.................... 72
Behold the western evening light.............. 937
Behold what wondrous grace.................... 693
Behold, where, in a mortal form............... 262
Beneath our feet and o'er our head............ 938
Beyond, beyond the boundless sea 227
Beyond the smiling and the weeping............ 992
Beyond the starry skies....................... 321
Bless, O my soul, the living God.............. 41
Blessed are the sons of God................... 640
Blessèd are the dead who die in...............1085
Blessèd Comforter, come down.................. 972
Blessèd Fountain, full of grace............... 630
Blessèd Salem, long expected..................1044

G

INDEX OF FIRST LINES OF HYMNS.

	HYMN.		HYMN.
Blesséd Saviour! thee I love	617	Come, O Creator Spirit blest	351
Blest are the pure in heart	652	Come, O my soul, in sacred lays	229
Blest are the souls that hear and know	151	Come on, my partners in distress	558
Blest be the dear uniting love	666	Come, sacred Spirit, from above	353
Blest be the tie that binds	823	Come, said Jesus' sacred voice	426
Blest Comforter divine	362	Come, sound his praise abroad	93
Blest feast of love divine	848	Come, Spirit, Source of light	364
Blest hour! when mortal man retires	55	Come, thou almighty King	223
Blest is the man whose softening heart	797	Come, thou Desire of all thy saints	37
Blest Jesus! when my soaring thoughts	632	Come, thou Fount of every blessing	876
Blest Trinity! from mortal sight	226	Come, thou long-expected Jesus	756
Blow ye the trumpet, blow	406	Come to Calvary's holy mountain	445
Bread of heaven! on thee we feed	852	Come to the house of prayer	60
Break thou the bread of life	145	Come to the land of peace	439
Brethren, while we sojourn here	530	Come, trembling sinner, in whose breast	420
Bride of the Lamb, awake, awake	1024	Come, ye that love the Lord	842
Brief life is here our portion	1023	Come, ye disconsolate, where'er ye languish	431
Bright King of glory, dreadful God	342	Come, ye sinners, poor and wretched	432
Brightest and best of the sons of	250	Come, ye thankful people, come	1046
Brightly gleams our banner	517	Come, ye that know and fear the Lord	199
Broad is the road that leads to death	392	Complete in thee! no work of mine	675
Buried beneath the yielding wave	818	Creator Spirit, by whose aid	377
Buried in baptism with our Lord	808	Cross, reproach, and tribulation	234
By Christ redeemed, in Christ restored	877	Crown him with many crowns	320
By cool Siloam's shady rill	800	Crown his head with endless blessing	317
By faith in Christ I walk with God	658		
		Daily, daily sing the praises	1017
Call Jehovah thy salvation	522	Daughter of Zion! awake from thy	773
Calm me, my God, and keep me calm	647	Daughter of Zion! from the dust	931
Calm on the listening ear of night	240	Day is dying in the west	1072
Can sinners hope for heaven	394	Day of anger! that dread day	983
Cast thy bread upon the waters	792	Day of judgment! day of wonders	975
Cast thy burden on the Lord	719	Days and moments quickly flying	1058
Cease, ye mourners, cease to languish	731	Dear Father, to thy mercy-seat	51
Chief of sinners though I be	453	Dear Lord and Master mine	592
Children of God, who, faint and slow	583	Dear Refuge of my weary soul	605
Children of the heavenly King	532	Dear Saviour! we are thine	843
Chosen not for good in me	670	Dear Saviour, when my thoughts recall	882
Christ, above all glory seated	301	Deem not that they are blest alone	735
Christ for the world we sing	1086	Delay not, delay not, O sinner, draw near	428
Christ is coming! let creation	1014	Depth of mercy! can there be	500
Christ is our corner-stone	751	Did Christ o'er sinners weep	416
Christ, of all my hopes the ground	629	Dismiss us with thy blessing, Lord	117
Christ, the Lord is risen again	308	Do not I love thee, O my Lord	603
Christ, the Lord, is risen to-day, Our	343	Drooping souls, no longer mourn	440
Christ, the Lord, is risen to-day, Sons	305		
Christ, whose glory fills the skies	14	Early, my God, without delay	21
Christian, the morn breaks sweetly	577	Earth has engrossed my love too long	1041
Church of the ever-living God	758	Earth has nothing sweet or fair	627
Come, blesséd Spirit! Source of light	352	Earth is passed away and gone	978
Come, every pious heart	344	Earth's transitory things decay	678
Come, gracious Lord, descend and dwell	45	Eternal Source of every joy	184
Come, gracious Spirit, heavenly Dove	354	Eternal Spirit, God of truth	360
Come, happy souls, adore the Lamb	807	Eternal Spirit, we confess	350
Come, happy souls, approach your God	437	Eternal Sun of righteousness	111
Come, Holy Ghost! in love	368	Eternity! Eternity!	985
Come, Holy Ghost, my soul inspire	650	Everlasting arms of love	531
Come, Holy Ghost! our hearts inspire	373		
Come, Holy Spirit! calm my mind	356	Fading, still fading, the last beam is	133
Come, Holy Spirit, come, Let	361	Faith adds new charms to earthly bliss	656
Come, Holy Spirit, come, With	363	Far as thy name is known	770
Come, Holy Spirit, Dove divine	810	Far from my thoughts, vain world, begone	58
Come, Holy Spirit, heavenly Dove	357	Far from the world, O Lord, I flee	52
Come, Jesus, Redeemer, abide thou with me	621	Father, hear the blood of Jesus	303
Come join, ye saints, with heart and voice	559	Father, hear the prayer we offer	789
Come, kingdom of our God	915	Father! how wide thy glory shines	196
Come, let us anew our journey pursue	1057	Father of heaven, whose love profound	179
Come, let us join our cheerful songs	325	Father of mercies, bow thine ear	765
Come, let us join our songs of praise	327	Father of mercies! in thy word	172
Come, let us lift our joyful eyes	326	Father of mercies! send thy grace	794
Come, let us sing the song of songs	336	Father, Son, and Holy Ghost	875
Come, Lord, and tarry not	916	Father! whate'er of earthly bliss	649
Come, my soul, thy suit prepare	61		

29 G

INDEX OF FIRST LINES OF HYMNS.

	HYMN.
Fear not, O little flock, the foe	560
Fight the good fight! lay hold	582
Firm as the earth thy gospel stands	681
For a season called to part	155
For all thy saints, O God	960
For ever here my rest	849
For ever here my rest shall be	836
"For ever with the Lord!"	946
For me to live is Christ	570
For thee, O dear, dear Country	1004
For the mercies of the day	130
For what shall I praise thee, my God and my...	622
Forget thyself! Christ bade thee come	881
Forgive us, Lord! to thee we cry	472
Fountain of grace, rich, full, and free	526
From all that dwell below the skies	82
From deep distress and troubled thoughts	513
From every stormy wind that blows	69
From Greenland's icy mountains	890
From the cross the blood is falling	286
From the cross uplifted high	412
From the recesses of a lowly spirit	132
From the table now retiring	870
From thee, begetting sure conviction	523
Full of trembling expectation	476
Gently, Lord, oh, gently lead us	698
Give to our God immortal praise	435
Give to the Lord, ye sons of fame	88
Give to the winds thy fears	554
Glorious things of thee are spoken	753
Glory be to God on high, and on	1075
Glory be to God on high,—God	102
Glory be to the Father, and to the	1066
Glory, glory to our King	311
Glory to God on high	298
Glory to God! whose witness-train	534
Glory to thee, my God, this night	113
Go to the grave in all thy glorious	972
God Almighty and all-seeing	154
God be merciful unto us, and make	1080
God calling yet! shall I not hear	422
God eternal, Lord of all	101
God, in his earthly temple, lays	924
God, in the gospel of his Son	160
God is love; his mercy brightens	225
God is the refuge of his saints	919
God moves in a mysterious way	209
God, my King, thy might confessing	213
God, my Supporter, and my Hope	741
God of my life, to thee belong	181
God of our salvation, hear us	137
God's glory is a wondrous thing	538
God with us! oh, glorious name	251
Grace! 'tis a charming sound	690
Gracious Spirit, Love divine	307
Grander than ocean's story	1065
Great God! attend, while Zion sings	39
Great God! how infinite art thou	204
Great God, now condescend	801
Great God! this sacred day of thine	7
Great God! to thee my evening song	114
Great God! we sing that mighty hand	1061
Great God, what do I see and hear	976
Great God, when I approach thy throne	408
Great God! whose universal sway	920
Great is the Lord our God	772
Great Shepherd of thine Israel	25
Guide me, O thou great Jehovah	134
Had I the tongues of Greeks and Jews	663
Hail, happy day! thou day of holy rest	18
Hail the day that sees him rise	307
Hail the night, all hail the morn	249

	HYMN.
Hail! thou God of grace and glory	786
Hail, thou once despiséd Jesus	282
Hail to the brightness of Zion's glad	896
Hail to the Lord's anointed	894
Hail, tranquil hour of closing day	66
Hallelujah! song of gladness	926
Hark! hark, my soul; angelic songs	235
Hark! hark! the notes of joy	256
Hark! my soul! it is the Lord	856
Hark! ten thousand harps and voices	312
Hark, the glad sound! the Saviour comes	253
Hark! the herald angels sing	245
Hark! the song of jubilee	902
Hark! the sound of angel-voices	898
Hark! the sound of holy voices	1016
Hark! the voice of Jesus calling	784
Hark! the voice of love and mercy	315
Hark! what mean those holy voices	234
Haste, traveler, haste! the night comes	442
Hasten, Lord! the glorious time	903
Have mercy upon me, O God, according	1073
He comes in blood-stained garments	1001
He dies!—the Friend of sinners dies	295
He has come! the Christ of God	246
He knelt, the Saviour knelt and prayed	291
He leadeth me! oh, blesséd thought	737
He lives! the great Redeemer lives	333
He that goeth forth with weeping	793
He that hath made his refuge God	695
Hear what God, the Lord, hath spoken	754
Heirs of unending life	673
Here I can firmly rest	691
High in the heavens, eternal God	84
Holy and reverend is the name	210
Holy Father, hear my cry	220
Holy Father, thou hast taught me	732
Holy Ghost, the infinite	374
Holy Ghost! with light divine	366
Holy, holy, holy, Lord	221
Holy, holy, holy, Lord God almighty	96
Holy, holy, holy, Lord God of Sabaoth	1064
Holy Spirit! gently come	371
Hope of our hearts, O Lord, appear	1026
How are thy servants blest, O Lord	1052
How beauteous are their feet	749
How beauteous on the mountains	891
How beauteous were the marks divine	258
How blest are those, how truly wise	762
How blest the righteous when he dies	942
How blest the sacred tie that binds	674
How charming is the place	28
How condescending and how kind	280
How did my heart rejoice to hear	20
How firm a foundation, ye saints of	563
How gentle God's commands	549
How helpless guilty nature lies	385
How pleasant, how divinely fair	38
How pleased and blest was I	1
How precious is the book divine	165
How sad our state by nature is	390
How shall I follow him I serve	261
How shall the young secure their hearts	170
How still and peaceful is the grave	960
How sweet and awful is the place	861
How sweet, how heavenly is the sight	820
How sweetly flowed the gospel sound	257
How sweet the name of Jesus sounds	613
How sweet to leave the world awhile	56
How swift the torrent rolls	958
How tedious and tasteless the hours	623
How tender is thy hand	724
How vain is all beneath the skies	954
I am coming to the cross	498
I ask not now for gold to gild	720

G

INDEX OF FIRST LINES OF HYMNS. 437

	HYMN.
I bless the Christ of God	651
I bless thee, Lord, for sorrows sent	745
I build on this foundation	1003
I cannot always trace the way	746
I did thee wrong, my God	748
I have a home above	995
I hear the Saviour say	410
I hear the words of love	822
I hear thy welcome voice	411
I heard a voice, the sweetest voice	346
I heard the voice of Jesus say	633
I know no life divided	1002
I know that my Redeemer lives	323
I lay my sins on Jesus	463
I love the sons of grace	831
I love thy kingdom, Lord	35
I love to steal awhile away	65
I love to tell the story	414
I'll praise my Maker with my breath	90
I'll speak the honors of my King	341
I'm a pilgrim, and I'm a stranger	1000
I'm but a stranger here	994
I'm not ashamed to own my Lord	839
I need thee every hour	484
I need thee, O my God	461
I once was a stranger to grace and to God	619
I saw One hanging on a tree	270
I saw the cross of Jesus	415
I sing the almighty power of God	205
I stand on Zion's mount	545
I was glad when they said unto me	1078
I would not live alway; I ask not to	933
If God is mine, then present things	680
If human kindness meets return	864
If I would be a child of God	834
If life in sorrow must be spent	742
If on our daily course our mind	62
If, through unruffled seas	723
If you cannot on the ocean	785
In all my Lord's appointed ways	816
In all my vast concerns with thee	200
In every trying hour	744
In heavenly love abiding	556
In Jesus' name once more we meet	835
In the cross of Christ I glory	300
In the dark and cloudy day	718
In thy name, O Lord, assembling	57
In time of fear, when trouble's near	536
In time of tribulation	580
In vain we seek for peace with God	386
Infinite Love! what precious stores	444
Is there ambition in my heart	665
It came upon the midnight clear	248
It is not death to die	961
It is thy hand, my God	721
Jehovah God! Thy gracious power	207
Jehovah reigns; his throne is high	109
Jerusalem! my happy home!	1009
Jerusalem, the glorious	1020
Jerusalem, the golden	1022
Jesus, all redeeming Lord	837
Jesus,—and didst thou leave the sky	409
Jesus! and shall it ever be	597
Jesus, at whose supreme command	863
Jesus, blessèd Mediator	1019
Jesus calls us, o'er the tumult	867
Jesus comes, his conflict over	309
Jesus demands this heart of mine	510
Jesus, engrave it on my heart	393
Jesus, hail, enthroned in glory	302
Jesus! I love thy charming name	612
Jesus, I my cross have taken	520
Jesus invites his saints	845

	HYMN.
Jesus, Jesus! visit me	504
Jesus, keep me near the cross	459
Jesus, Lamb of God, for me	294
Jesus, let thy pitying eye	458
Jesus lives! no longer now	936
Jesus! lover of my soul	505
Jesus, Master! hear me now	853
Jesus, Master, whose I am	618
Jesus, merciful and mild	503
Jesus, my All, to heaven is gone	841
Jesus, my Strength, my Hope	846
Jesus only, when the morning	586
Jesus! our best belovéd Friend	883
Jesus, Saviour, pilot me	1063
Jesus shall reign where'er the sun	911
Jesus spreads his banner o'er us	866
Jesus, still lead on	562
Jesus, Sun of righteousness	449
Jesus, the sinner's Friend, to thee	467
Jesus, the very thought of thee	614
Jesus, these eyes have never seen	604
Jesus, thou art the sinner's Friend	859
Jesus, thou Joy of loving hearts	593
Jesus, thou source of calm repose	589
Jesus, thy Blood and Righteousness	607
Jesus, thy boundless love to me	700
Jesus! thy church, with longing eyes	909
Jesus, thy love shall we forget	267
Jesus, thy name I love	601
Jesus, we look to thee	824
Jesus, we thus obey	850
Jesus wept! those tears are over	272
Jesus, where'er thy people meet	74
Jesus, while our hearts are bleeding	733
Jesus, who knows full well	70
Jesus, who on his glorious throne	611
Jesus, whom angel hosts adore	276
Joy to the world,—the Lord is come	236
Joyful be the hours to-day	306
Just as I am, without one plea	457
Keep silence, all created things	195
Keep us, Lord, oh, keep us ever	157
Know, my soul! thy full salvation	838
Laboring and heavy-laden	478
Laden with guilt, and full of fears	167
Lamb of God, whose dying love	880
Lead, kindly Light! amid the encircling	734
Lead us, heavenly Father, lead us	135
Let every mortal ear attend	436
Let me be with thee where thou art	968
Let me but hear my Saviour say	529
Let party names no more	825
Let saints below in concert sing	826
Let us with a joyful mind	99
Let worldly minds the world pursue	638
Let Zion and her sons rejoice	930
Life has many a pleasant hour	1036
Light of life, seraphic Fire	147
Light of the lonely pilgrim's heart	1020
Light of those whose dreary dwelling	755
Like Noah's weary dove	847
Like sheep we went astray	395
Like the eagle, upward, onward	790
Lo, God is here!—let us adore	110
Lo! he comes with clouds descending	986
Lo! on a narrow neck of land	384
Lo! the mighty God appearing	982
Lo, the seal of death is breaking	1045
Lo! what a glorious sight appears	1027
Look from thy sphere of endless day	923
Look, ye saints, the sight is glorious	314
Lord, as to thy dear cross we flee	266

G

INDEX OF FIRST LINES OF HYMNS.

	HYMN.
Lord, at this closing hour	124
Lord, at thy feet we sinners lie	511
Lord, at thy mercy-seat	450
Lord, before thy throne we bend	481
Lord, bid thy light arise	375
Lord, dismiss us with thy blessing; Bid	148
Lord, dismiss us with thy blessing; Fill	136
Lord God of Hosts, by all adored	85
Lord, have mercy upon us, and incline	1076, 1062
Lord, how mysterious are thy ways	192
Lord, how secure and blest are they	677
Lord, how secure my conscience was	387
Lord, I am thine, entirely thine	812
Lord, I believe; thy power I own	645
Lord! I cannot let thee go	62
Lord! I have made thy word my choice	169
Lord, I hear of showers of blessing	448
Lord, if thou thy grace impart	672
Lord! in the morning thou shalt hear	36
Lord, it belongs not to my care	537
Lord Jesus, are we one with thee	687
Lord, lead the way the Saviour went	795
Lord, my weak thought in vain would climb	193
Lord of all being; throned afar	191
Lord of earth! thy forming hand	222
Lord of Hosts! to thee we raise	774
Lord of mercy, just and kind	514
Lord of the harvest! hear	750
Lord of the worlds above	11
Lord! thou hast searched and seen me through	188
Lord, thou on earth didst love thine own	828
Lord, thou wilt bring the joyful day	1033
Lord, thy glory fills the heaven	211
Lord, we come before thee now	2
Lord! when I all things would possess	646
Lord, when my raptured thought surveys	198
Lord! when we bend before thy throne	22
Lord! where shall guilty souls retire	202
Lord! while for all mankind we pray	1051
Lord, with glowing heart I'd praise thee	212
Love divine, all love excelling	566
Majestic sweetness sits enthroned	268
Make haste, O man, to live	963
May the grace of Christ our Saviour	138
Meekly in Jordan's holy stream	815
Mighty God! while angels bless thee	316
Mine eyes and my desire	550
More love to thee, O Christ	466
Mortals, awake, with angels join	254
Mourn for the thousands slain	781
Must Jesus bear the cross alone	543
My country! 't is of thee	1059
My days are gliding swiftly by	1010
My dear Redeemer and my Lord	260
My faith looks up to thee	600
My Father, God! how sweet the sound	685
My God, how endless is thy love	657
My God, how wonderful thou art	648
My God, my Father!—blissful name	703
My God, my Father, while I stray	738
My God, my King, thy various praise	89
My God, my life, my love	593
My God! permit me not to be	509
My God! permit my tongue	29
My God, the covenant of thy love	684
My God! the spring of all my joys	610
My gracious Lord, I own thy right	668
My gracious Redeemer I love	624
My hope is built on nothing less	688
My Jesus, as thou wilt	726
My life flows on in endless song	575
My opening eyes with rapture see	46

	HYMN.
My Saviour! my almighty Friend	348
My Saviour, whom absent I love	626
My Shepherd will supply my need	696
My soul, be on thy guard	547
My soul complete in Jesus stands	528
My soul, how lovely is the place	26
My soul lies cleaving to the dust	166
My soul, repeat his praise	725
My soul, weigh not thy life	548
My spirit on thy care	552
"My times are in thy hand:"	740
My times of sorrow and of joy	712
Near the cross was Mary weeping	285
Nearer, my God, to thee	485
No more, my God! I boast no more	469
No, no, it is not dying	965
None but Christ: his merit hides me	587
Not all the blood of beasts	382
Not all the nobles of the earth	676
Not all the outward forms on earth	391
Not to condemn the sons of men	438
Not to the terrors of the Lord	827
Not what these hands have done	396
Not with our mortal eyes	596
Now be my heart inspired to sing	331
Now be the gospel banner	928
Now begin the heavenly theme	533
Now, from labor and from care	15
Now God be with us, for the night is closing	131
Now is the accepted time	418
Now let my soul, eternal King	162
Now let our cheerful eyes survey	349
Now let our souls, on wings sublime	1032
Now let our voices join	34
Now thank we all our God	217
Now the day is over	141
Now to the Lord a noble song	83
Now to the Lord, who makes us know	337
Now to the power of God supreme	335
Now to thy sacred house	12
O, bless the Lord, my soul	669
O, blessèd God, to thee I raise	660
O, bow thine ear, Eternal One	769
O Bread, to pilgrims given	885
O Christ! our King, Creator, Lord	332
O Christ, the Lord of heaven! to thee	330
O Christ! with each returning morn	40
O, come, and mourn with me awhile	889
O, come, let us sing unto the Lord	1077
O, could I find from day to day	497
O, could I speak the matchless worth	616
O, could our thoughts and wishes fly	1012
O day of rest and gladness	16
O, do not let the word depart	424
O eyes that are weary, and hearts that	620
O, for a closer walk with God	493
O, for a faith that will not shrink	1008
O, for a heart to praise my God	489
O, for a shout of joy	232
O, for a shout of sacred joy	347
O, for a strong, a lasting faith	189
O, for a sweet, inspiring ray	1039
O, for a thousand tongues to sing	490
O, for an overcoming faith	950
O, for that tenderness of heart	492
O, for the death of those	947
O, for the happy hour	917
O, for the peace which floweth like a	1081
O, gift of gifts! oh, grace of faith	654
O God, beneath thy guiding hand	1060
O God of Bethel, by whose hand	798

G

INDEX OF FIRST LINES OF HYMNS.

	HYMN.
O God, the Rock of Ages	176
O God, to us show mercy	224
O God! we praise thee, and confess	203
O happy band of pilgrims	1005
O, happy day, that fixed my choice	813
O Holy Ghost, the Comforter	358
O holy Saviour! Friend unseen	728
O, how I love thy holy law	168
O, if my soul were formed for woe	278
O Jesus, bruised and wounded more	887
O Jesus! King most wonderful	637
O Jesus, sweet the tears I shed	281
O Jesus, thou art standing	464
O Jesus, we adore thee	288
O, join ye the anthems of triumph that	105
O Lamb of God! still keep me	289
O Lord, how full of sweet content	659
O Lord! how happy should we be	561
O Lord, thy pitying eye surveys	767
O Lord, thy work revive	918
O Love divine! that stooped to share	609
O mother dear, Jerusalem	1007
O, not my own these verdant hills	599
O, not to fill the mouth of fame	491
O Paradise eternal!	1031
O Paradise, O Paradise	993
O sacred Head, now wounded	290
O Saviour, I am blind!	462
O Saviour, who didst come	821
O, see how Jesus trusts himself	269
O Son of God, in glory crowned	973
O Spirit of the living God	380
O Sun of Righteousness, arise	913
O, sweetly breathe the lyres above	606
O, tell me, thou Life and Delight	615
O, that I could for ever dwell	702
O, that the Lord would guide my ways	171
O, that the Lord's salvation	927
O, the sweet wonders of that cross	811
O, this soul, how dark and blind	502
O thou essential Word	218
O thou, from whom all goodness flows	455
O thou God who hearest prayer	451
O thou Lamb of God, descending	830
O thou that hearest prayer	379
O thou who in Jordan didst bow thy meek head	814
O thou whom we adore	914
O thou, whose bounty fills my cup	709
O thou, whose mercy guides my way	713
O thou, whose own vast temple stands	760
O thou, whose tender mercy hears	454
O, turn, great Ruler of the skies	507
O, turn ye, oh, turn ye, for why will ye	427
O, what amazing words of grace	399
O, what if we are Christ's	820
O, where are kings and empires now	757
O, where shall rest be found	381
O word of God incarnate	174
O, worship the King, all-glorious above	98
O'er the gloomy hills of darkness	901
On Jordan's rugged banks I stand	989
On mountains and in valleys	177
On the mountain's top appearing	900
Once I thought my mountain strong	482
Once more, before we part	126
Once more, my soul, the rising day	25
One more day's work for Jesus	140
One prayer I have — all prayers in one	710
One sole baptismal sign	752
One sweetly solemn thought	949
One there is, above all others	840
Onward, Christian soldiers	515
Onward, Christian, though the region	788
Our blest Redeemer, ere he breathed	373

	HYMN.
Our country's voice is pleading	892
Our Father, who art in heaven	143
Our Father! through the coming year	1054
Our God, our Help in ages past	964
Our heavenly Father calls	71
Our heavenly Father, hear	146
Our helper, God! we bless thy name	1062
Our Lord is risen from the dead	339
Our Saviour bowed beneath the wave	809
Out of the depths have I cried unto	1073
Pass me not, O gentle Saviour	446
Peace, troubled soul, whose plaintive moan	704
People of the living God	857
"Perfect in love!" Lord, can it be	512
Planted in Christ, the living vine	884
Plunged in a gulf of dark despair	434
Pour out thy Spirit from on high	766
Praise God, from whom all blessings	80, 144
Praise, Lord, for thee in Zion waits	49
Praise the Lord, who reigns above	106
Praise to God, immortal praise	1050
Praise to thee, thou great Creator	104
Praise ye the Lord; exalt his name	42
Praise ye the Lord; my heart shall join	86
Praise ye the Lord! 'tis good to raise	87
Praise waits in Zion, Lord! for thee	92
Prayer is the breath of God in man	68
Prayer is the soul's sincere desire	67
Prepare us, Lord, to view thy cross	860
Prostrate, dear Jesus, at thy feet	471
Purer yet, and purer	581
Quiet, Lord, my froward heart	642
Rejoice in God alway	653
Rejoice, rejoice, believers	1021
Rejoice! the Lord is king	299
Rejoice to-day with one accord	216
Return, my roving heart, return	506
Return, O wanderer, to thy home	419
Rise, glorious Conqueror, rise	322
Rise, my soul, and stretch thy wings	939
Rise, O my soul, pursue the path	535
Rock of Ages, cleft for me	871, 874
Roll on, thou mighty ocean	776
Safely through another week	13
Salvation is for ever nigh	696
Salvation!—oh, the joyful sound	401
Saviour, again to thy dear name we raise	128
Saviour, breathe an evening blessing	139
Saviour, happy would I be	643
Saviour, I follow on	487
Saviour, in thy mysterious presence	879
Saviour King, in hallowed union	805
Saviour, like a shepherd lead us	804
Saviour, more than life to me	568
Saviour of our ruined race	883
Saviour! teach me day by day	631
Saviour, thy dying love	488
Saviour, visit thy plantation	897
Saviour, when in dust to thee	501
Saviour! who thy flock art feeding	806
Scorn not the slightest word or deed	796
Searcher of hearts! from mine erase	495
See a poor sinner, dearest Lord	470
See! how great a flame aspires	929
See Israel's gentle Shepherd stand	799
See, the Conqueror mounts in triumph	313
See the eternal Judge descending	974
Servant of God, well done	962
Shepherd of tender youth	803
Shepherd! with thy tenderest love	634

G

	HYMN.
Shout the glad tidings, exultingly sing	247
Show pity, Lord! O Lord, forgive	468
Since Jesus is my Friend	594
Sing, all ye ransomed of the Lord	542
Sing to the Lord, our Might	94
Sing we the song of those who stand	23
Sinners, turn, why will ye die	425
Sinners, will you scorn the message	433
So fades the lovely, blooming flower	945
So let our lips and lives express	664
Softly fades the twilight ray	5
Softly now the light of day	129
Soldiers of Christ, arise	579
Sometimes a light surprises	555
Son of God, to thee I cry	872
Songs of praise the angels sang	107
Soon may the last glad song arise	907
Soon will the heavenly Bridegroom come	1025
Soul, then know thy full salvation	521
Sovereign of worlds! display thy power	912
Sow in the morn thy seed	782
Speak to me, Lord, thyself reveal	27
Stand up and bless the Lord	156
Stand up, my soul, shake off thy fears	524
Stand up!—Stand up for Jesus	557
Still, still with thee, my God	120
Strait is the way, the door is strait	389
Sun of my soul! thou Saviour dear	112
Sure the blest Comforter is nigh	355
Surely Christ thy griefs hath borne	452
Sweet hour of prayer! sweet hour of prayer	73
Sweet is the light of Sabbath eve	149
Sweet is the memory of thy grace	197
Sweet is the work, my God, my King	43
Sweet is the work, O Lord	54
Sweet Saviour, bless us ere we go	142
Sweet the moments, rich in blessing	869
Sweet the time, exceeding sweet	50
Sweet was the time when first I felt	496
Sweeter sounds than music knows	628
Swell the anthem, raise the song	1049
Take me, O my Father, take me!	460
Take my heart, O Father, take it	868
Tarry with me, O my Saviour	747
Tell me the old, old story	413
Ten thousand times ten thousand	1006
Tender Shepherd, thou hast stilled	935
Thank and praise Jehovah's name	100
That awful day will surely come	987
The church has waited long	959
The church of God believes it right	833
The church's one foundation	771
The day is past and gone, Great God	122
The day is past and gone, The evening	123
The day, O Lord, is spent	119
The day of praise is done	125
The day of rest once more comes round	6
The day of resurrection	340
The day of wrath! that dreadful day	981
The God of Abraham praise	95
The golden gates are lifted up	324
The harvest dawn is near	546
The head that once was crowned with thorns	328
The heavens declare his glory	175
The heavens declare thy glory, Lord	156
The King of saints,—how fair his face	345
The Lord descended from above	231
The Lord is my Shepherd, I shall not	1071
The Lord is my Shepherd, no want	564
"The Lord is risen indeed"	318
The Lord my pasture shall prepare	8
The Lord my Shepherd is	595
The Lord of glory is my light	91

	HYMN.
The Lord, our God, is full of might	194
The Lord shall come! the earth shall	984
The Lord's my Shepherd, I'll not want	602
The mercies of my God and King	1069
The mistakes of my life are many	447
The morning light is breaking	695
The peace which God alone reveals	115
The people of the Lord	544
The perfect world, by Adam trod	764
The promises I sing	150
The roseate hues of early dawn	998
The sands of time are sinking	1037
The Saviour bids thee watch and pray	667
The Saviour kindly calls	802
The Saviour! oh, what endless charms	270
The spacious firmament on high	183
The Spirit breathes upon the word	173
The Spirit, in our hearts	441
The starry firmament on high	161
The swift declining day	118
The voice of free grace cries, Escape	402
Thee we adore, eternal Name	1055
Thee will I love, my Strength, my Tower	591
There is a blessed home	1043
There is a book that all may read	201
There is a fountain filled with blood	398
There is a holy city	1042
There is a house not made with hands	901
There is a land immortal	1080
There is a land of pure delight	997
There is a safe and secret place	683
There is an hour of hallowed peace	1011
There is an hour of peaceful rest	1013
There is an hour when I must part	743
There is no night in heaven	1040
There were ninety and nine that safely	403
There's a wideness in God's mercy	214
They who seek the throne of grace	64
Thine earthly Sabbaths, Lord, we love	44
Thine for ever! God of love	854
Thine holy day 's returning	17
This is not my place of resting	1015
This is the day the Lord hath made	19
This place is holy ground	971
Thou art gone to the gravel but we will	934
Thou art gone up on high	319
Thou art my hiding-place, O Lord	686
Thou art the way; to Thee alone	265
Thou, from whom we never part	152
Thou lovely Source of true delight	164
Thou, O Lord, in tender love	516
Thou only Sovereign of my heart	466
Thou very present Aid	694
Thou who art enthroned above	103
Thou who didst on Calvary bleed	293
Thou who roll'st the year around	1047
Thou! whose almighty word	369
Though faint, yet pursuing, we go	565
Though I speak with angel tongues	641
Though now the nations sit beneath	905
Though sorrows rise and dangers roll	635
Though troubles assail, and dangers	574
Through all the changing scenes of life	671
Through every age, eternal God	943
Through sorrow's night, and danger's	951
Through the love of God our Saviour	519
Thus far the Lord has led me on	116
Thy Father's house! thine own bright	1034
Thy home is with the humble, Lord	480
Thy mighty working, mighty God	1039
Thy way, not mine, O Lord	727
Thy way, O Lord, is in the sea	206
Thy will be done! I will not fear	736
Thy will be done! in devious way	730

G

INDEX OF FIRST LINES OF HYMNS.

First Line	HYMN
"Till he come:" oh, let the words	873
Time is winging us away	940
Time, thou speedest on but slowly	1018
'Tis a point I long to know	499
'Tis by the faith of joys to come	661
"'Tis finished!"—so the Saviour cried	274
'Tis God the Father we adore	817
'Tis God the Spirit leads	365
'Tis midnight; and on Olive's brow	273
'Tis my happiness below	720
'Tis not a cause of small import	761
'Tis not that I did choose thee	178
To God the Father, God the Son	81
To God the only wise	121
To our Redeemer's glorious name	296
To thee, my God and Saviour	639
To thee, O God, we raise	219
To thy pastures fair and large	4
To thy temple we repair	3
To us a Child of hope is born	237
Together with these symbols, Lord	858
Traveling to the better land	573
Trembling before thine awful throne	477
Triumphant, Lord, thy goodness reigns	228
Triumphant Zion, lift thy head	921
'Twas by an order from the Lord	159
'Twas the day when God's Anointed	287
Unshaken as the sacred hill	571
Unvail thy bosom, faithful tomb	966
Upon the gospel's sacred page	163
Upward I lift mine eyes	701
Vain are the hopes the sons of men	388
Vain, delusive world, adieu	470
Vainly through night's weary hours	791
Vital spark of heavenly flame	967
Wait, my soul, upon the Lord	584
Wait, O my soul! thy Maker's will	182
Wake, O my soul, and hail the morn	235
Wake! the welcome day appeareth	778
Walk in the light! so shalt thou know	655
Watchman! tell us of the night	932
We are on our journey home	1035
We are watching, we are waiting	787
We bid thee welcome in the name	763
We bless thee for thy peace, O God	697
We come, O God, before thy throne	1053
We give immortal praise	230
We give thee but thine own	780
We may not climb the heavenly steeps	304
We praise thee, O God; we acknowledge	1074
We shall see Him, in our nature	304
We stand in deep repentance	465
We would see Jesus—for the shadows	878
Weary, Lord, of struggling here	483
Weeping will not save me	430
Welcome, delightful morn	10
Welcome, sweet day of rest	30
What a Friend we have in Jesus	567
What cheering words are these	692
What equal honors shall we bring	338
What finite power, with ceaseless toil	190
What grace, O Lord, and beauty shone	264
What is life? 'tis but a vapor	956
What shall I render to my God	186
What sinners value I resign	955
What various hindrances we meet	77
When adverse winds and waves arise	706
When all thy mercies, O my God	187
When along life's thorny road	717
When, as returns this solemn day	53
When downward to the darksome tomb	952
When gathering clouds around I view	708
When God, of old, came down from heaven	370
When human hopes all wither	886
When I can read my title clear	682
When I survey the wondrous cross	275
When I view my Saviour bleeding	283
When Jordan hushed his waters still	242
When languor and disease invade	711
When, like a stranger on our sphere	259
When, marshaled on the nightly plain	241
When musing sorrow weeps the past	714
When my last hour is close at hand	977
When on Sinai's top I see	855
When, overwhelmed with grief	699
When our heads are bowed with woe	716
When, rising from the bed of death	988
When sins and fears, prevailing, rise	527
When streaming from the eastern skies	9
When thou, my righteous Judge, shalt come	957
When waves of trouble round me swell	715
Where high the heavenly temple stands	75
Where the woodman's axe is ringing	899
Where two or three, with sweet accord	59
While darkness reigns o'er Olive's brow	832
While in sweet communion feeding	865
While my Redeemer's near	578
While shepherds watched their flocks	238
While thee I seek, protecting Power	185
While we lowly bow before thee	153
While, with ceaseless course, the sun	1043
Who are these in bright array	999
Who is this that comes from Edom	310
Who shall the Lord's elect condemn	679
Why do wo mourn departing friends	953
Why is thy faith, O child of God	1083
Why on the bending willows hung	922
Why should our tears in sorrow flow	970
Why should the children of a King	359
Why should we start, and fear to die	941
Why will ye waste on trifling cares	423
With all my powers of heart and tongue	233
With broken heart and contrite sigh	456
With deepest reverence at thy throne	180
With heavenly power, O Lord, defend	768
With joy we hail the sacred day	24
With joy we lift our eyes	33
With songs and honors sounding loud	1068
With tearful eyes I look around	508
Witness, ye men and angels, now	819
Work, for the night is coming	783
Work while it is to-day	779
Would you win a soul to God	443
Ye angels! who stand round the throne	625
Yo messengers of Christ	775
Ye servants of God, your Master proclaim	97
Your harps, ye trembling saints	553
Zion! awake, thy strength renew	906

G

www.ingramcontent.com/pod-product-compliance
Lightning Source LLC
Chambersburg PA
CBHW022144300426
44115CB00006B/344